ISRAEL IN EXILE

Society of Biblical Literature

Studies in Biblical Literature

General Acquisitions Editors

Dennis T. Olson,
Old Testament/Hebrew Bible

Sharon H. Ringe,
New Testament

Number 3

ISRAEL IN EXILE
The History and Literature of the Sixth Century B.C.E.

ISRAEL IN EXILE

The History and Literature of the Sixth Century B.C.E.

by
Rainer Albertz

translated by
David Green

Society of Biblical Literature
Atlanta

ISRAEL IN EXILE
The History and Literature of the Sixth Century B.C.E.

Copyright © 2003 by the Society of Biblical Literature

Original title: *Die Exilszeit*, by Rainer Albertz, copyright © 2001 by Verlag W. Kohlhammer GmbH, Stuttgart. English translation from the original German with the approval of the publisher.

All rights reserved. No part of this work may be reproduced or transmitted in any form or by any means, electronic or mechanical, including photocopying and recording, or by means of any information storage or retrieval system, except as may be expressly permitted by the 1976 Copyright Act or in writing from the publisher. Requests for permission should be addressed in writing to the Rights and Permissions Office, Society of Biblical Literature, 825 Houston Mill Road, Atlanta, GA 30329 USA.

Library of Congress Cataloging-in-Publication Data

Albertz, Rainer, 1943–
    [Exilszeit. English]
    Israel in exile : the history and literature of the sixth century B.C.E. / by Rainer Albertz ; translated by David Green.
        p. cm. — (Studies in biblical literature ; 3)
    Includes bibliographical references and indexes.
    ISBN 1-58983-055-5 (pbk. : alk. paper)
    1. Jews—History—Babylonian captivity, 598–515 B.C. 2. Bible. O.T.—Criticism, interpretation, etc. 3. Bible. O.T.—History of Biblical events. I. Title. II. Series: Studies in biblical literature (Society of Biblical Literature) ; 3.
    DS121.65 .A6213 2003
296'.09'013—dc22   2003018254

11 10 09 08 07 06 05 04 03   5 4 3 2 1

Printed in the United States of America on acid-free, recycled paper conforming to ANSI/NISO Z39.48-1992 (R1997) and ISO 9706:1994 standards for paper permanence.

Contents

Foreword ix
Preface to the English Edition xi
Abbreviations xv
Chronological Table xxi
Map of the Ancient Near East xxii

Introduction 1

I. The Biblical Picture of the Exilic Era 3
I.1. The Exile As a Historical Lacuna 3
I.2. Conceptions of the Exile 4
    I.2.1.   The Exile As a Lost Opportunity (Jeremiah 39–43) 4
    I.2.2.   The Exile As the (Temporary) End of History (2 Kings) 8
    I.2.3.   The Exile As a Sabbath for the Land (2 Chronicles) 12
    I.2.4.   Narrative Additions 15
    I.2.4.1.   The Stories of Daniel (Daniel 1–6) 16
    I.2.4.2.   The Stories of Susanna and Bel and the Dragon 22
    I.2.4.3.   The Story of the Three Youths (1 Esdras 3:1–5:6) 28
    I.2.4.4.   Tobit 29
    I.2.4.5.   Judith 34
    I.2.5.   Integration of the Exile into Apocalyptic
              Conceptions of History 38

II. The History of the Exilic Era 45
II.1. The Neo-Babylonian Empire 45
    II.1.1.   Sources 46
    II.1.2.   The Rise of the Neo-Babylonian Empire 47
    II.1.3.   The Golden Age of Nebuchadnezzar 52
    II.1.4.   Destabilization, Restoration, and End 60

II.2. Israel in the Exilic Period 70
    II.2.1.   Sources 72
    II.2.2.   Principles of Historical Reconstruction 74
    II.2.2.1. Number of Deportations 74
    II.2.2.2. Dates of the Deportations 76

II.2.2.3.	Numbers Deported 81
II.2.3.	Judah in the Exilic Period 90
II.2.4.	The Egyptian Golah 96
II.2.5.	The Babylonian Golah 98

II.3. The Thwarted Restoration 112
    II.3.1.   The Persian Empire from Cyrus to Darius I 113
    II.3.2.   Return and Rebuilding of the Temple 119

II.4. Social Displacements and Their Religious Consequences 132

III. The Literature of the Exilic Period 139

III.1. Genres of Exilic Literature 139
    III.1.1.   Communal Lament and City Lament 140
    III.1.2.   Hybrid Genres 160
    III.1.3.   Salvation Oracles 166
    III.1.4.   Oracles against the Nations 179
    III.1.5.   "Sermons" 197

III.2. Exilic Literary Works 203
    III.2.1.   The Book of the Four Prophets (Hosea, Amos,
                Micah, Zephaniah) 204
    III.2.1.1. Micah 211
    III.2.1.2. Zephaniah 216
    III.2.1.3. Amos 224
    III.2.1.4. Hosea 230

    III.2.2.   The Book of Habakkuk 237

    III.2.3.   The Exilic Patriarchal History 246
    III.2.3.1. The First Edition of the Exilic Patriarchal History 257
    III.2.3.2. The Second Edition of the Exilic Patriarchal History 264

    III.2.4.   The Deuteronomistic History 271

    III.2.5.   The Book of Jeremiah 302
    III.2.5.1. The Deuteronomistic Books of Jeremiah 312
    III.2.5.2. The First Deuteronomistic Book of Jeremiah 327
    III.2.5.3. The Second Deuteronomistic Book of Jeremiah 332
    III.2.5.4. The Third Deuteronomistic Book of Jeremiah 339

    III.2.6.   The Book of Ezekiel 345

    III.2.7.   The Book of Deutero-Isaiah 376
    III.2.7.1. The First Edition of the Book of Deutero-Isaiah:
               Reconstruction 393
    III.2.7.2. The First Edition of the Book of Deutero-Isaiah:
               Place and Date 399

    III.2.7.3. The First Edition of the Book of Deutero-Isaiah:
                   Interpretation 404
    III.2.7.4. Appendix: Fourth Servant Song (Isa 52:13–53:12)..........425
    III.2.7.5. The Second Edition of the Book of Deutero-Isaiah........427

IV.   Theological Contribution 435

IV.1. Theological Appropriation of a Calamitous History......................436
IV.2. Theological Interpretation of History 439
IV.3. Foiling Imperial Theology 441
IV.4. God's Glory and Separation of Powers 443

Primary Sources Index...447
General Index 457

FOREWORD

Like all volumes in the Biblische Enzyklopädie series, this book comprises four major sections:

The first section attempts to sketch the "biblical picture of the exilic era," even though the Bible contains only sporadic information about this period. First we examine why the exilic period represents a yawning gap in the historical tradition of the Bible. Then we describe how this gap was slowly filled in the narrative tradition of late books (often apocryphal) such as Daniel, Bel and the Dragon, 1 Esdras, Tobit, and Judith, until this "historical vacuum" found a central role in the apocalyptic conception of history.

There follows in the second section a reconstruction of the "history of the exilic period," to the extent that the fragmentary biblical and extra-biblical sources and archaeological evidence permit. We attempt to present the history of the various Jewish groups in Babylonia, Judah, and Egypt, relating it organically to the history of the Neo-Babylonian Empire (627–539 B.C.E.) and the early Persian Empire (539–520). We also test a new kind of historiography, which examines the role of mentality in political history and avoids the distortions occasioned by partisanship—privileging Israel, say, or even the Babylonian golah. Here I draw on insights gained by *Sonderforschungsbereich* 493, which has been meeting at Münster since the beginning of 2000: here Protestant and Catholic biblical scholars and church historians have been working side by side with scholars in such fields as ancient Near Eastern studies, Egyptology, ancient history, and philology to study the "functions of religion in the ancient societies of the Near East." The historical section concludes with a short description of the social and religious changes experienced by Israel during the exilic period.

The primary focus of this volume appears in the third section, which examines the "literature of the exilic period." Approximately half the material in the Hebrew Bible came into being or was substantially shaped during this era. First we examine the major literary genres of exilic literature, then discuss in detail the documents that can be assigned to this period with reasonable assurance. This discussion includes their literary reconstruction and form, their theological and political substance, and their sociohistorical context.

This approach may appear to be a risky undertaking at present, when the origin and date of many of the textual units discussed are vigorously debated. I therefore examine the relevant scholarly literature in some detail; in dialogue with it, I attempt to incorporate and cautiously to expand on both earlier hypotheses (Deuteronomistic History, Ezekiel) and more recent theories (exilic patriarchal history, Book of the Four Prophets). For example, I distinguish two editions of the exilic Patriarchal History (analogous to J and E), three Deuteronomistic books of Jeremiah, and two editions of Deutero-Isaiah. Thus I hope that the readers of this book will feel that they have not only received solid and comprehensive information about the texts in question but also have gained new insights that will stimulate them to study the exilic documents for themselves.

In the fourth section, which is intended to identify "theological contributions," I limit myself to a brief outline of a few themes of the exilic discourse that seem to me to have immediate significance for the present. Should readers feel inclined to think further about the problems addressed, I would be happy to hear from them (albertz@uni-muenster.de).

This book strives to present the thought of Old Testament scholars concerning one of the most fascinating eras of Israel's history. It attempts deliberately to provide more ready access to this often difficult material, not only for students but also for colleagues in other disciplines and all those interested in theology. Study of the Hebrew Bible has become so complex and discordant that it must take care to remain comprehensible outside its own scholarly domain and be recognized as theologically relevant. Therefore, this book seeks to focus on certain problems, uncover the very real scholarly consensus concerning many texts, and formulate hypotheses that are as simple as possible.

I wish to express my thanks to the students at the universities of Siegen and Münster whose ideas have contributed to writing of this book in recent years. I am particularly grateful to my assistants during this period, Dr. Suzanne Otto, Ingo Zocher, Dr. Thilo Rudnig, Christian Fabritz, Bettina Lorenz, and Jakob Wöhrle, who have been tireless in assembling the bibliographical resources on the many topics covered and in many cases have composed research summaries. Jakob Wöhrle, Marcus Held, and Dr. Thomas Podella were of great help in the proofreading. I am likewise grateful to my editor, Professor Walter Dietrich, for his suggestions and corrections. Not least, I am grateful to my secretary, Mrs. Gertrudis Sieg, for her diligent work. Marcus Held and Jakob Wöhrle compiled the indexes of the German edition.

Altenberge, July 28, 2001   Rainer Albertz

PREFACE TO THE ENGLISH EDITION

Two years after the publication of the original German edition, the support of the Society of Biblical Literature has made it possible to publish the English edition of this book. I am pleased and grateful that this has come about.

While the German edition represents one volume in a Biblische Enzyklopädie intended to cover in twelve volumes the entire span of biblical history, from the earliest history of Israel to the beginnings of the church, the English edition is an independent monograph that would be the first comprehensive presentation of the exilic period since Peter Ackroyd's classic *Exile and Restoration,* published in 1968.

English-speaking readers may wonder about the relationship of the present book to Ackroyd's magisterial presentation, which is still of major importance. They will find many similarities. Like *Exile and Restoration,* this book treats the major literature of the period in detail (Jeremiah, the Deuteronomistic History, Ezekiel, Deutero-Isaiah). I agree totally with Ackroyd's assessment that the exilic period was a highly creative phase in the history of Israelite literature. However, whereas Ackroyd focused his attention on the development of theological ideas in these documents, I place more emphasis on the literary themes of form, composition, origin, and redaction as well.

Readers may note the absence of a few texts discussed in *Exile and Restoration.* Their absence is due in part to changes in scholarship. In the opinion of many scholars, only the beginning stages (at best) of the Priestly Document and Holiness Code date from the exilic period; in their present form, they did not come into being until the postexilic period (fifth century B.C.E.). Instead, I discuss a series of "books" whose clear exilic imprint has been recognized only in recent studies: the "exilic Patriarchal History," the "Four Prophets book" (Hosea, Amos, Micah, Zephaniah), and the book of Habakkuk. I also discuss certain smaller groups of texts, such as psalms of lament, the book of Lamentations, salvation oracles, foreign nation oracles, and "sermons."

In part, however, the different choice of texts reflects a different thematic emphasis. Ackroyd's study has two clear thematic foci: "exile" and "restoration." He was interested primarily in the new beginning in Judah and treated the catastrophe of the exile as its prehistory. Therefore, he discusses Haggai and Zechariah in detail. I also treat the exilic period down to the rebuilding of the temple (520 B.C.E.) and even attempt to offer a new historical reconstruction of the new beginning, which I have titled the "Thwarted Restoration." However, my book views these developments only in prospect: discussion of Haggai and Zechariah is reserved for the next volume of the Biblische Enzyklopädie.

Apart from the obvious fact that my book discusses the more recent literature that has appeared during the thirty-five years since *Exile and Restoration* was published, the remaining differences fall primarily into two categories.

1. In accordance with the design of the Biblische Enzyklopädie, which begins each volume with a detailed presentation of the biblical perspective on the period before going on to historical and literary reconstruction, the present book also covers the reflexes of the exilic period in the late biblical (Daniel) and apocryphal books (Bel and the Dragon, 1 Esdras, Tobit, Judith) deliberately excluded by Ackroyd. Their inclusion makes it possible to trace the influence of the exile within the Bible, an influence that extends beyond the intertestamental literature into the New Testament.

2. The present book places substantially more emphasis on historical reconstruction of the exilic period (598/587–520 B.C.E.). There has been little to change Ackroyd's description of the "dark years of exile,"[1] since the Bible says virtually nothing of the period. However, some new Babylonian sources have appeared in the interim (for example, the Moussaïeff collection), and archaeological discoveries in Palestine have multiplied, so that we can reconstruct the series of deportations as well as the situation and development of the scattered Judean groups much better than thirty years ago, although much must remain extremely hypothetical. While Ackroyd, making a virtue of necessity, traced only very loose associations between historical and political developments, on the one hand, and literary and theological developments, on the other, I undertake to illuminate as accurately as possible the political and sociohistorical background of the exilic documents and their theological conceptions. The result is interpretations anchored more concretely in history.

---

[1] *Exile and Restoration*, 13.

Whether this new attempt at a comprehensive presentation of the exilic period contributes to a better understanding of the significance of this important era in Israel's history, only the reader can decide. I would be happy if the English edition would also contribute to strengthening the exchange between German-speaking and English-speaking Old Testament scholarship.

Finally, I wish to express my thanks to the Society of Biblical Literature and especially its editorial director, Rex D. Matthews, for their ready willingness to publish my book in America. I am also grateful to David Green for his careful and judicious translation.

Münster, November 2, 2002   Rainer Albertz

ABBREVIATIONS

*	Indicates biblical passages with intrusive sections
Θ	Theodotion
AASF.B	Annales Academiae Scientiarum Fennicae, series B
ÄAT	Ägypten und Altes Testament
AB	Anchor Bible
ADPV	Abhandlungen des Deutschen Palästina-Vereins
AfO	*Archiv für Orientforschung*
AfOB	Archiv für Orientforschung: Beiheft
Ag. Ap.	Josephus, *Against Apion*
ALASP	Abhandlungen zur Literatur Alt-Syrien-Palästinas und Mespotamien
ANEP	*The Ancient Near East in Pictures Relating to the Old Testament.* Edited by J. B. Pritchard. Princeton: Princeton University Press, 1954.
ANET	*Ancient Near Eastern Texts Relating to the Old Testament.* Edited by J. B. Pritchard. 3d ed. Princeton: Princeton University Press, 1969.
ANRW	*Aufstieg und Niedergang der römischen Welt: Geschichte und Kultur Roms im Spiegel der neueren Forschung.* Edited by H. Temporini and W. Haase. Berlin: de Gruyter, 1972–.
Ant.	Josephus, *Antiquities*
AOAT	Alter Orient und Altes Testament
Aram.	Aramaic
ATANT	Abhandlungen zur Theologie des Alten und Neuen Testaments
ATD	Das Alte Testament Deutsch
ATDA	Das Alte Testament Deutsch. Apokryphen
Babyl.	Babylonian
BASOR	*Bulletin of the American Schools of Oriental Research*
BBB	Bonner Biblische Beiträge
BBET	Beiträge zur biblischen Exegese und Theologie

BEATAJ	Beiträge zur Erforschung des Alten Testaments und des antiken Judentums
BETL	Bibliotheca ephemeridum theologicarum lovaniensium
Bib	*Biblica*
BibLit	Bible and Literature
BibSem	The Biblical Seminar
Bijdr	*Bijdragen: Tijdschrift voor filosofie en theologie*
BM	British Museum
BN	*Biblische Notizen*
BK	Biblischer Kommentar
BThSt	Biblisch-theologische Studien
BWANT	Beiträge zur Wissenschaft vom Alten und Neuen Testament
BZ	*Biblische Zeitschrift*
BZAW	Beihefte zur Zeitschrift für die Alttestamentliche Wissenschaft
CAH	Cambridge Ancient History
CHJ	*Cambridge History of Judaism*. Edited by W. D. Davies and Louis Finkelstein. Cambridge: Cambridge University Press, 1984–.
cj.	conjecture
CThM.A	Calwer theologische Monographien. Reihe A: Bibelwissenschaft
Dept.	Department
DJD	Discoveries in the Judaean Desert
DtIE^{1}/^{2}	First/second edition of the book of Deutero-Isaiah
Dtr	Deuteronomist (author of DtrH), Deuteronomistic
DtrH	Deuteronomistic History
DtrN	Nomistic redaction of the Deuteronomistic History
DtrP	Prophetic redaction of the Deuteronomistic History
EdF	Erträge der Forschung
EHS.T	Europäische Hochschulschriften. Reihe 23, Theologie
EP	Elephantine Papyrus
ETL	*Ephemerides theologicae lovanienses*
EvT	*Evangelische Theologie*
FAT	Forschungen zum Alten Testament
FB	Forschung zur Bibel
FPR	Four Prophets redactor(s)
FRLANT	Forschungen zur Religion und Literatur des Alten und Neuen Testaments
GAT	Grundrisse zum Alten Testament
Geog.	Strabo, *Geography*
GM	Göttinger Miszellen

HAT	Handbuch zum Alten Testament
HCOT	Historical Commentary on the Old Testament
HDR	Harvard Dissertations in Religion
HerBS	Herders biblische Studien
Hist.	*History / Histories*
HK	Handkommentar zum Alten Testament
HR	Habakkuk redactor
HSM	Harvard Semitic Monographs
HThK.AT	Herders theologischer Kommentar zum Alten Testament
ICC	International Critical Commentary
IEJ	*Israel Exploration Journal*
Inaug.-Diss.	Inaugural dissertation
Int	*Interpretation*
JAOS	*Journal of the American Oriental Society*
JBL	*Journal of Biblical Literature*
JEA	*Journal of Egyptian Archaeology*
JerD	Deuteronomistic book of Jeremiah
JNSL	*Journal of Northwest Semitic Languages*
JQR	*Jewish Quarterly Review*
JSHRZ	Jüdische Schriften aus hellenistisch-römischer Zeit
JSJSup	Supplements to the Journal for the Study of Judaism
JSOT	*Journal for the Study of the Old Testament*
JSOTSup	Journal for the Study of the Old Testament Supplement Series
JTS	*Journal of Theological Studies*
KAI	*Kanaanäische und aramäische Inschriften.* H. Donner and W. Röllig. 2d ed. Wiesbaden: Harrassowitz, 1966–69.
KAT	Kommentar zum Alten Testament
KHC	Kurzer Hand-Commentar zum Alten Testament
KST	Kohlhammer Studienbücher Theologie
LCL	Loeb Classical Library
LXX	Septuagint
Mes	*Mesopotamia* (Turin)
MT	Masoretic Text
NBL	*Neues Bibel-Lexikon*
NCB	New Century Bible
NEAEHL	*The New Encyclopedia of Archaeological Excavations in the Holy Land.* Edited by E. Stern. 4 vols. Jerusalem: Israel Exploration Society; New York: Simon & Schuster, 1993.
NedTT	*Nederlands theologisch tijdschrift*
NEB	Neue Echter Bibel
NS	new series
NSK.AT	Neuer Stuttgarter Kommentar. Altes Testament

NStB	Neukirchener Studienbücher
OBO	Orbis biblicus et orientalis
ÖBS	Österreichische biblische Studien
obv.	obverse
OLA	Orientalia lovaniensia analecta
OTL	Old Testament Library
OTS	Old Testament Studies
OtSt	*Oudtestamentische Studiën*
Pap.	Papyrus
PD	Late Deuteronomistic Pentateuch Redaction
PH	Patriarchal History (exilic edition)
pl.	plate(s)
PP	Priestly Pentateuch Redaction
PTA	Papyrologische Texte und Abhandlungen
RA	*Revue d'assyriologie et de archéologie orientale*
RB	*Revue biblique*
RE^1	redactor of E^1
rev.	reverse
RGG^2	*Die Religion in Geschichte und Gegenwart.* Edited by H. Gunkel et al. 5 vols. 2d ed. Tübingen: Mohr Siebeck, 1927–32.
RPH^1	redactor of the first exilic edition of PH
RPH^2	redactor of the second exilic edition of PH
SAA	State Archives of Assyria
SAHG	*Sumerische und akkadische Hymnen und Gebete.* Edited and translated by A. Falkenstein and W. von Soden. Zurich: Artemis-Verlag, 1953.
SANE	Sources from the Ancient Near East
SBAB	Stuttgarter biblische Aufsatzbände
SBB	Stuttgarter biblische Beiträge
SBLDS	Society of Biblical Literature Dissertation Series
SBLEJL	Society of Biblical Literature Early Judaism and Its Literature
SBS	Stuttgarter Bibelstudien
SGKAO	Schriften zur Geschichte und Kultur des Alten Orients
SHANE	Studies in the History of the Ancient Near East
SKAB	Schriften der Katholischen Akademie in Bayern
SMHVL	Scripta minora (Lund, Sweden)
SO.S	Symbolae Osloenses. Fasciculus suppletionis
STL	Studia theological Lundensia
SUNT	Studien zum Umwelt des Neuen Testaments
TB	Theologische Bücherei
TCS	Texts from Cuneiform Sources

TGI	*Textbuch zur Geschichte Israels.* Edited by K. Galling. 2d ed. Tübingen: Mohr Siebeck, 1968.
ThW	Theologische Wissenschaft
TLZ	*Theologische Literaturzeitung*
TRE	*Theologische Realenzyklopädie.* Edited by G. Krause and G. Müller. Berlin: de Gruyter, 1977–.
TRu	*Theologische Rundschau*
TSTS	Toronto Semitic Texts and Studies
TThSt	Trierer theologische Studien
TTZ	*Trierer theologische Zeitschrift*
TUAT	*Texte aus der Umwelt des Alten Testaments.* Edited by Otto Kaiser. Gütersloh: Mohn, 1984–.
ThW	Theologische Wissenschaft
UET	*Ur Excavation Texts*
UNHAII	Uitgaven van het Nederlands Historisch-Archeologisch Instituut te Istanbul
VF	*Verkündigung und Forschung*
VT	*Vetus Testamentum*
VTSup	Supplements to Vetus Testamentum
WMANT	Wissenschaftliche Monographien zum Alten und Neuen Testament
WuD	*Wort und Dienst*
YNER	Yale Near Eastern Researches
ZA	*Zeitschrift für Assyriologie*
ZAW	*Zeitschrift für die alttestamentliche Wissenschaft*
ZBK.AT	Zürcher Bibelkommentare. AT
ZDMG	*Zeitschrift der deutschen morgenländischen Gesellschaft*
ZThK	*Zeitschrift für Theologie und Kirche*

Chronological Table

Almost every survey, including volumes in the Biblische Enzyklopädie series, employs a different chronology of the ancient Near East. The following table summarizes the chronology on which this book is based.

Judah/Babylonian Golah	Babylonia/Persia	Egypt
death of Josiah (609)	Nabopolassar (626–605)	Neco (610–595)
Jehoiakim (609–598/588)	battle of Carchemish (605)	
	Nebuchadnezzar (605–562)	
Jehoiachin (598/7)		
first deportation (3/16/597)		
Zedekiah (598/7)		Psamtik II (595–589)
anti-Babylonian conspiracy (594)		
beginning of the siege of Jerusalem (winter 589/8)		Apries (Hophra) (589–568)
pause in siege (early summer 588)		
conquest of Jerusalem, 2d deportation (July/August 587)		
Gedaliah (587–582?)	siege of Tyre (585–572)	
third deportation (582)		
	Egyptian intervention (568/7)	Amasis (571–526)
Release of Jehoiachin (562)	Amēl-Marduk (562–560)	
	Neriglissar (560–556)	
	Lābâši-Marduk (556)	
	Nabonidus (556–539)	
	Cyrus takes Babylon (539)	
	Cyrus II (558–530)	
	Cambyses (530–522)	
	Persian conquest of Egypt (525)	
	Gaumata's revolt (March 522)	
	Darius's usurpation (9/29/522)	
	revolts in Babylon, October 522, August 521	
negotiations between Darius and the golah (521)		
return under Zerubbabel and Joshua (520)		
rebuilding of temple (520–515)		

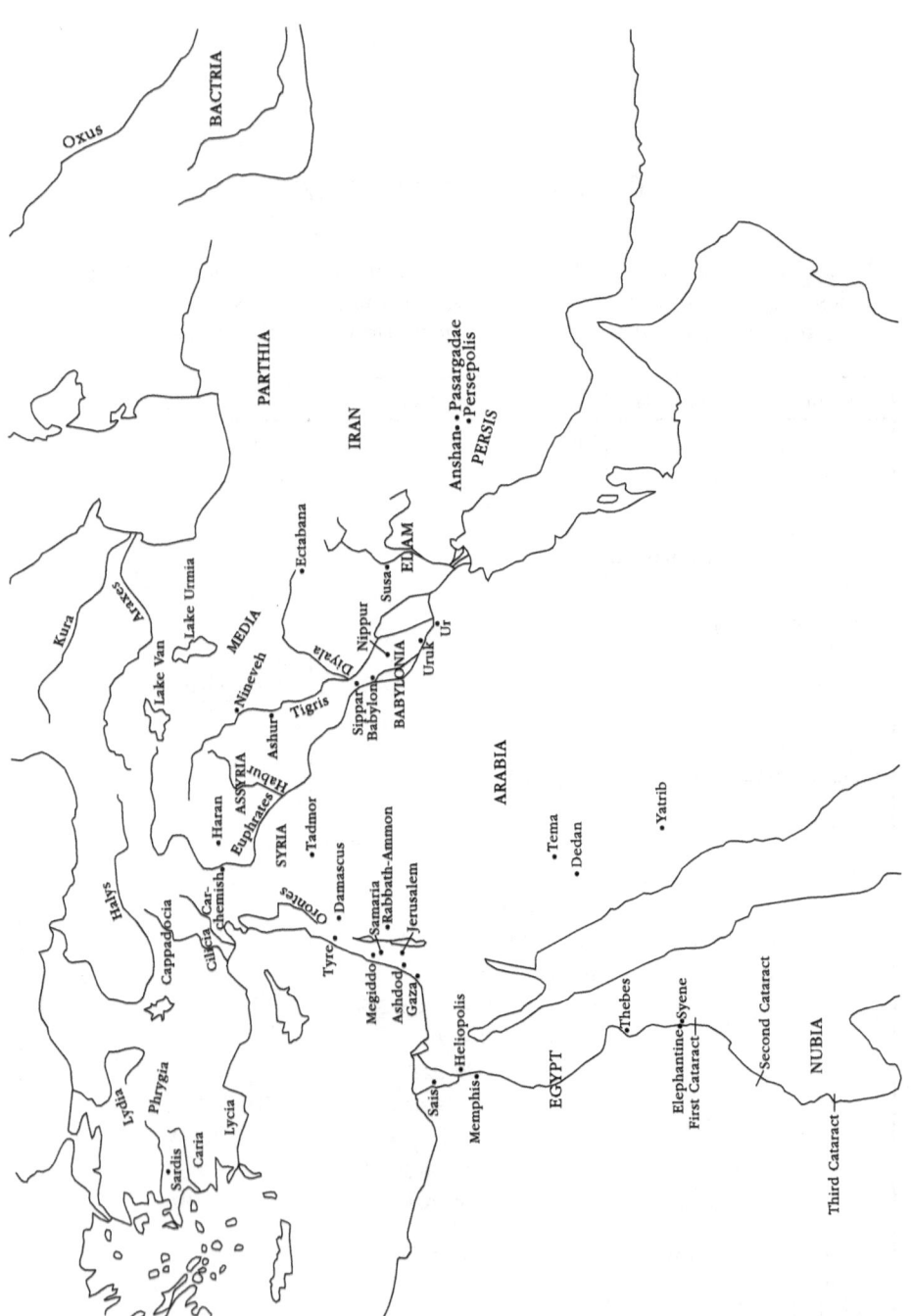

INTRODUCTION

Albertz, Rainer. *A History of Israelite Religion in the Old Testament Period* (trans. J. Bowden; 2 vols.; OTL; Louisville: Westminster John Knox, 1994). **Diebner,** Bernd. "Exil, Babylonisches," *NBL* 1:625–31. **Mosis,** Rudolf. "Das Babylonische Exil Israels in der Sicht christlicher Exegese," in *Exil, Diaspora, Rückkehr: Zum theologischen Gespräch zwischen Juden und Christen* (ed. R. Mosis; SKAB 81; Düsseldorf: Patmos, 1978), 55–77.

Of all the eras in Israel's history, the exilic period represents the most profound caesura and the most radical change. Its significance for subsequent history can hardly be overstated. Here the religion of Israel underwent its most severe crisis, but here too was laid the foundation for its most sweeping renewal.[1] Here began the dispersal of Israel among the nations and thus also its often painful Diaspora existence, lasting to the present. Here, too, the religion of Israel opened itself for the first time to the nations, a development that made possible the subsequent appearance of Christianity.[2]

The profound changes that took place during the exilic period, only hinted at here, have justifiably led to the conventional division of the history of ancient Israel into preexilic, exilic, and postexilic periods, even though Christians must remember that for Judaism the "exilic period" extends down to the present, even after the establishment of the modern state of Israel.[3] On this same basis, the preexilic history of Israel may be distinguished from the history of early Judaism, beginning with the exile, if this distinction is not allowed to deny—with a subliminal hint of anti-Semitism—the ethnic and religious continuity of the two.

---

[1] Albertz, *History*, 1:369ff.
[2] Mosis, "Das Babylonische Exil," 59ff.
[3] As pointed out by Diebner, "Exil," 629–30.

It is one of the great miracles of human history that the exile, the loss of Israel's national and territorial integrity, did not spell the end of Israel's history; this history continued on, sustained by Israel's relationship with God and constantly focused on the land from which portions of it have been, in part, expelled.

Clear as this caesura is, especially in its aftereffects, it is difficult to delimit the exilic period historically. For the northern kingdom of Israel, the exilic period began in 732 and 722 B.C.E. with its conquest by the Assyrians. But the people deported from the northern kingdom have left almost no trace in subsequent tradition; plainly they were largely assimilated or else linked up with the Judean exiles. Their history, therefore, is lost. The southern kingdom of Judah suffered substantial deportations by the Assyrians in 701 but remained in existence until the punitive expeditions of the Neo-Babylonians in 598/597 and 587/586.[4] Thus it is usual to have the exilic period begin with the destruction of Jerusalem and the final elimination of Judah as a state in 587/586 B.C.E., even though there was already a golah (group of exiles) in Babylonia in 598/597, and Gedaliah's attempted reform and a further deportation in 582 still lay in the future (Jer 52:30). Usually, in agreement with the Chronicler's History, the end of the exilic period is identified with the conquest of Babylon by the Persian king Cyrus in 539 B.C.E. (2 Chr 36:33; Ezra 1:1). But because substantial numbers probably did not return from the Babylonian exile until shortly before 520, and only the start of work on the temple in 520 marks a clear new beginning, it is desirable to set the lower boundary there. There is also support for this definition within the biblical tradition, since Zech 1:12 and 7:15 state that the seventy years of exile (cf. Jer 15:11–12; 29:10) lasted until the prophet's day (587–517).

This volume, which deals with the exilic era, will therefore cover the period from 587/586 to 520 B.C.E., with references back to 598/597 as necessary to treat the history of the Babylonian golah.

---

[4] On the problem of dating, see pp. 76–81 below.

I. THE BIBLICAL PICTURE OF THE EXILIC ERA

Ackroyd, Peter. *Exile and Restoration: A Study of Hebrew Thought of the Sixth Century B.C.* (London: SCM, 1968), 232–47. **Albertz**, Rainer. *A History of Israelite Religion in the Old Testament Period* (trans. J. Bowden; 2 vols.; OTL; Louisville: Westminster John Knox, 1994), 369–436, 534–97.

Scholars have paid little attention to the biblical picture of the exilic period. The following observations are exploratory.

I.1. THE EXILE AS A HISTORICAL LACUNA

Flavius Josephus, *Jewish Antiquities*, Books 9–11: *Josephus with an English Translation* (ed. H. St. J. Thackeray et al.; LCL; Cambridge: Harvard University Press, 1966), vol. 6 (ed. Ralph Marcus).

It is a striking fact, not sufficiently noted, that the Bible does not contain a continuous account of the exilic period. Only the margins are recorded—how the exile came about (2 Kgs 24–25; Jer 39; 2 Chr 36) and how it ended (Ezra 1ff.)—together with a few isolated events such as the fall of Gedaliah and its consequences (Jer 40:1–43:7; 2 Kgs 25:22–26) at the very beginning of the exilic period and the pardon of Jehoiachin by Evil-Merodach (Amēl-Marduk) in 562, the thirty-seventh year of his exile in 597 B.C.E. The book of Daniel adds a couple of dramatic episodes that Daniel and his friends are said to have experienced as Jews at the court of Nebuchadnezzar and his "son" Belshazzar (Dan 1–5). But these, too, do not form a continuous historical narrative; they do not write the history of the Babylonian golah.

The exilic period thus represents a huge lacuna in the historical narrative of the Hebrew Bible. It stands as a murky, gaping hole in the history of Yahweh and his people, illuminated only briefly by isolated beams of light. How difficult it is to deal with this lacuna in a continuous account of Israel's history is already evident in the Jewish historian Josephus, who feels compelled in his *Antiquities* to supplement the biblical account with material from extrabiblical sources such as Berossus (*Ant.* 10.186–281).

In the New Testament, the Babylonian exile still constitutes an epochal event in the history of God and his people, culminating in Jesus Christ (Matt 1:11–12, 17); it is the archetypal judgment of God upon Israel (Acts 7:43), which now threatens Jerusalem once more (Luke 21:23–24).

I.2. CONCEPTIONS OF THE EXILE

Why did the history of the exile come to be left a blank within the Bible? To answer this question, we might first posit purely external political factors: the dissolution of the state, the loss of the archives, the lack of scribes to continue the historical record; or social explanations: the chaos of war and the hardships of exile, which so exhausted the resources of the survivors that they had no time or energy left to worry about trivial matters such as documentation for the future; or even psychological causes: survivors so depressed and discouraged that they saw no point in recording for posterity the afflictions they had been forced to undergo. All these considerations may have played a role in the startling interruption of Israel's historical tradition in the exilic period. As we shall see later, however, the exilic period witnessed an almost frenzied literary production in all other genres; therefore, additional factors must have contributed to this lack of interest in the history of the period. The differing perspectives of the biblical books suggest that, besides the factors cited, certain theological assessments of the exilic period turned it into a historical "black hole" hardly worth recounting and ultimately defying description.

I.2.1. The Exile As a Lost Opportunity (Jeremiah 39–43)

Hardmeier, Christoph. *Prophetie im Streit vor dem Untergang Judas: Erzählkommunikative Studien zur Entstehungssituation der Jesaja- und Jeremiaerzählungen in II Reg 18–20 und Jer 37–40* (BZAW 187; Berlin: de Gruyter, 1990). **Pohlmann,** Karl-Friedrich. *Studien zum Jeremiabuch: Ein Beitrag zur Frage nach der Entstehung des Jeremiabuches* (FRLANT 118; Göttingen: Vandenhoeck & Ruprecht, 1978). **Stipp,** Hermann-Josef. *Jeremia im Parteienstreit: Studien zur Textentwicklung von Jer 16, 36-43 und 45 als Beitrag zur Geschichte Jeremias, seines Buches und judäischer Parteien im 6. Jahrhundert* (BBB 82; Frankfurt am Main: Hain, 1992). **Wanke,** Gunther. *Untersuchungen zur sogenannten Baruchschrift* (BZAW 122; Berlin: de Gruyter, 1971).

Jeremiah 39–43 contains an account of events surrounding the Babylonian conquest of Jerusalem; despite the shock occasioned by the catastrophe, this account narrates what took place from a remarkably positive perspective (in comparison to 2 Kgs 24–25) and with great attention to detail.[1]

After the Babylonians took Jerusalem (Jer 38:28b)—the siege of the city having lasted three years, from the ninth through the eleventh year of Zedekiah, until a breach was made in the city wall (39:1–2)—several Babylonian officers, each mentioned by name, entered the city to decide its fate (39:3). Their entry caused Zedekiah to flee Jerusalem, but the Babylonians captured him in the plains of Jericho and brought him to King Nebuchadnezzar at Riblah, where he was punished cruelly. His sons were slaughtered before his eyes, and his own eyes were put out; later he was taken to Babylon in fetters (39:4–7). In the course of their depredations, the Babylonians burned the palace and the "houses"[2] of the people, broke down the city wall, and deported the rest of the people as well as those who had deserted to them (39:8–9).

To this point, the account largely parallels 2 Kgs 25:1–11;[3] now, however, the emphasis shifts. While 2 Kgs 25:13–17 focuses on the sack of the destroyed temple, Jer 39:8—unlike 2 Kgs 29:9—hardly mentions its destruction. Instead, Jer 39:10 singles out a social measure carried out by the Babylonians: on the day Jerusalem was destroyed, Nebuzaradan gave vineyards and fields to the poor people left behind, who had nothing. In other words, he allotted them the property confiscated from the deportees. This extraordinary act is noted only very briefly in 2 Kgs 25:12.

Even more astonishing, though, is the next measure carried out by the Babylonians, as recorded in Jer 39:11–14 and 40:1–6. Nebuzaradan, a high Babylonian officer, set the prophet Jeremiah free from the imprisonment imposed on him as punishment for his continual appeals to surrender to the Babylonians (Jer 37:9–10; 38:2, 17–18). The details of how this took place are not entirely clear from the text. One version has Jeremiah set free from the court of the guard and handed over directly to Gedaliah, whom the Babylonians had appointed governor (39:13–14). According to another, Nebuchadnezzar himself gave

---

[1] See the observations of Hardmeier, *Prophetie*, 174ff., which are independent of his particular literary-historical hypothesis.

[2] The MT has the singular, but cf. Jer 52:13 and 2 Kgs 25:9.

[3] Earlier scholars tended to view Jer 39:4–10 as a secondary interpolation from 2 Kgs 25:2–12, but Hardmeier has shown (*Prophetie*, 185–223) that the text is an integral part of the Jeremiah narrative, which is quite distinct from the version in 2 Kgs 25, although both probably derive from a common source.

the order to treat Jeremiah well (39:11–12). Jeremiah had already been marked for deportation (40:1b) but was sought out and released from his fetters by Nebuzaradan, who gave Jeremiah the choice of coming with him to the Babylonian court or remaining in Judah as a free man (40:2–5). Jeremiah chose the latter; he stayed with his defeated people and went to Gedaliah (40:6).

The astonishing aspect of this account is that the conquest of Jerusalem meant not simply destruction, annihilation, death, and deportation but for a portion of the population improved circumstances and for certain individuals even liberation.

This differentiated perspective is developed extensively in the narrative of Gedaliah's governorship and its tragic end (Jer 40:7–43:7), with even greater emphasis on the positive element: when the scattered troops and their officers heard that the Babylonians had appointed Gedaliah governor, they came to him at his residence in Mizpah (40:7–8). The Judeans who had fled to neighboring countries returned and gathered about him (40:11–12). Gedaliah urged them to serve the Babylonians loyally for the common good and asked their support for his role as intermediary. He allowed them to continue living in the occupied towns left behind by the deportees and asked them to devote their energies to harvesting the fields, vineyards, and olive groves (40:9). A fresh start in the land seemed possible; when 40:12 stresses the abundance of the harvest, God appears to have blessed this course of action. In short: for at least some of the Judeans under the governorship of Gedaliah, the exilic period offered a new opportunity for salvation and prosperity, albeit in return for recognizing Babylonian sovereignty.

In this theological assessment, Jer 40:7–12 diverges totally from the perspective of Kings. The account in 2 Kgs 25:22–26 briefly mentions the governorship of Gedaliah but passes over in silence all the positive consequences it made possible. Here Gedaliah's governorship is only a milestone on the road to ruin.

It is true that Jer 40:13ff. recounts in detail how this opportunity for salvation was lost, naming those responsible. Despite the warnings of one of the officers, Johanan ben Kareah, Gedaliah refused to believe that Ishmael ben Nethaniah was seeking to take his life, goaded on by the king of the Ammonites. He was not prepared to use force to defend his reforms (40:13–16). Thus Ishmael, who belonged to a collateral line of the royal family, was able to carry out his murderous plan unhindered. He used the occasion of a meal with Gedaliah to kill the governor along with all his court, Judeans and Babylonians (41:1–3). Without hesitation, he also slaughtered almost all of a group of pilgrims from Shechem, Shiloh, and Samaria who had witnessed the assassination, then tried to go over to the Ammonites with the remaining Judeans from Mizpah in order to escape

Babylonian retribution (41:4–10). Thus the governorship of Gedaliah was brought down after a relatively short time[4] by the impatience of a fanatical monarchist who refused to accept rule by a non-Davidic ruler who was also a Babylonian collaborator.

Too late the officer Johanan ben Kareah heard of the disaster Ishmael had brought about. He and his forces came upon Ishmael at Gibeon; the Judeans whom Ishmael had carried away captive returned, but Ishmael himself escaped to the Ammonites (41:11–15). Even Johanan, however, saw little prospect for life in Judah after Gedaliah's murder; fearing Babylonian retribution, he conceived the plan of emigrating to Egypt with a group of Judeans (41:16–18). In their uncertainty, the group asked Jeremiah for divine guidance and promised to obey the voice of God, whatever the decision might be (42:1–6). However, when Jeremiah promised God's help and support against the Babylonians only if they stayed in Judah (42:7–12), forcefully threatening God's judgment if they emigrated to Egypt (42:13–22), they refused to listen. Smelling a political trap, they accused Jeremiah, incited by his friend Baruch, of seeking to deliver them into the hands of the Babylonians (43:1-4). Terrified of being deported to Babylon, all who had formerly gathered around Gedaliah set off for Egypt, taking Jeremiah and Baruch with them (43:5–7).

Their emigration spelled the total failure of the promising experiment that would have allowed a substantial number of Judeans, explicitly loyal to the Babylonians, to live politically secure lives in war-ravaged Judah. The reader can still sense the sadness with which this tragic failure is recounted in all its detail. The author clearly had a great personal stake in the governorship of Gedaliah.

Thus we owe the most detailed biblical account of the exilic period—albeit only of a brief episode at its beginning—primarily to the existence of groups who viewed the exile not simply as a terrible catastrophe but also as a God-given chance for a new beginning. Only when the Israelites could see a future-oriented intervention of God in political history were they encouraged to write this history to preserve it for posterity. But this was not the case during long stretches of the exilic period. At the point where the chance of salvation was lost, the historical narrative of the book of Jeremiah breaks off.[5]

---

[4] After two months, according to the MT of Jer 41:1, but the year is not given. On the historical question, see pp. 94–95 below.

[5] What follows in Jer 43:8ff. is just a tradition of the word of the Lord during Jeremiah's time in Egypt.

I.2.2 The Exile As the (Temporary) End of History (2 Kings)

Noth, Martin. *The Deuteronomistic History* (trans. J. Doull et al.; JSOTSup 15; Sheffield: University of Sheffield, Dept. of Biblical Studies, 1981). **Pohlmann,** Karl-Friedrich. "Erwägungen zum Schlusskapitel des deuteronomistischen Geschichtswerks," in *Textgemäss: Festschrift für Ernst Würthwein* (ed. A. H. J. Gunneweg and Otto Kaiser; Göttingen: Vandenhoeck & Ruprecht, 1979), 94–109. **Würthwein,** Ernst. *1. Kön 17–2. Kön 25,* vol. 2 of *Die Bücher der Könige.* (ATD 11/2; Göttingen: Vandenhoeck & Ruprecht, 1984). **Zenger,** Erich. "Die deuteronomistische Interpretation der Rehabilitierung Jojachins," *BZ* NS 12 (1968): 16–30.

Unlike the book of Jeremiah, the books of Kings assess the exile absolutely negatively. It is simply a catastrophe, indeed the ultimate catastrophe—or, put theologically, the judgment of Yahweh upon his disobedient people. Yet more: by presenting the trajectory of Israel's history as leading to the exile, this account characterizes the exile as a conclusion, an end to this history.[6] This trajectory begins its precipitous descent in the history of the northern kingdom, with the "sin of Jeroboam," the worship of the golden calf at Bethel (1 Kgs 12:28–30), which provoked Yahweh's devastating decision to root up Israel out of its good land and scatter it beyond the Euphrates (1 Kgs 14:15–16). This decision was realized in the conquests of the invading Assyrians and the deportations of 732 (2 Kgs 15:29) and 722 (2 Kgs 17:21–22): "So Israel was exiled from its own land to Assyria until this day" (17:23).

The history of the southern kingdom is initially smoother, with minor ups and downs. Here the irreversible descent toward the end does not begin until the reign of Manasseh (2 Kgs 21). It was his monstrous sins that provoked Yahweh's decision to destroy Jerusalem as totally as he had destroyed Sodom[7] and to cast off Judah, the remnant of his heritage, and to give it into the hand of its enemies (21:13–15). Thus the road to ruin was marked out. Its inevitability is clear from the tragic irony of Josiah: even the cultic reform of this faithful king, which eliminated all the abominable foreign cults introduced by Manasseh, could only delay, not avert, the realization of Yahweh's terrible decision (2 Kgs 22:15–29; 23:26–27). The wrath of Yahweh provoked by Manasseh was so fierce (23:26) that it finally brought about the incomprehensible rebellion of

---

[6] Noth, *Deuteronomistic History,* 98. Noth's insight remains true regardless of how one assesses the character and purpose of the Deuteronomistic History; see pp. 279–82 below.

[7] Note the use of the verb הפך "turn upside down," characteristic of the destruction of Sodom (Gen 19:21, 25, 29; Amos 4:11; Lam 4:6; cf. Deut 29:22 [23]; Jer 49:18; etc.).

Jehoiachim and Zedekiah against Nebuchadnezzar (2 Kgs 24:3–4, 20), provoking in retribution the Babylonian invasions of 598/597 and 587/586. Thus the southern kingdom finally met the same fate as the northern kingdom: "So Judah went into exile out of its land" (25:21).

How radically the books of Kings present the exile as the end of Israel's history is also shown by the losses Israel suffered in the deportations. Worst of all, as the summary conclusions in 2 Kgs 17:23 and 25:21 show, it lost its land. This loss hit both the northern and the southern kingdoms. In the overall historical tradition of Genesis through Kings, the land is not simply a given; together with the Torah, it is the most significant gift of Yahweh to Israel. He had already promised it to the patriarchs (Gen 12:7; 13:14–17; 28:13–14; Deut 1:8; Josh 1:6; etc.) and pledged it as homeland to the Israelites he brought out of Egypt under Moses' leadership (Exod 3:7–8). Finally, at Yahweh's command, Joshua occupied and settled it. From the perspective of this biblical account, the deportation of the Israelites from the land to which God had brought them meant the termination of Israel's history.

The southern kingdom suffered additional bitter losses: the loss of Jerusalem and the Jerusalem temple, which Yahweh had chosen for himself (1 Kgs 8:16, 44, 48; 11:32, 36; 14:21; 2 Kgs 21:7; 23:27), and the loss of the Davidic monarchy, which Yahweh had promised would endure forever (2 Sam 7:14–16; 1 Kgs 2:4; 8:16, 25; 9:5; 11:12–13; 15:4; 2 Kgs 8:19). Thus Yahweh's saving gifts, given to Israel during its existence as a state, were revoked; the history of Israel as a state and a cultic community was terminated.

This concern to describe the end of history also explains the account of the final years of Judah until the exile in 2 Kgs 24–25. Terrified by Nebuchadnezzar's advance on Palestine, Jehoiakim voluntarily became a Babylonian vassal but—for no apparent reason—rebelled just three years later (24:1). Therefore—according to the Hebrew text—he was punished by Yahweh, who sent marauding bands to destroy Judah (24:2). Thus the land was already devastated. The punitive expedition of Nebuchadnezzar that followed cut the Davidic monarchy to the quick: after a reign of three months, Jehoiakim's son Jehoiachin gave himself up along with his mother and his court in order to forestall the threatened storming of the city. But he found mercy only to the extent that he was not slain but deported to Babylon in the eighth year of Nebuchadnezzar (597) (24:10–12, 15). Thus Judah lost its legitimate king. As further punishment, Nebuchadnezzar destroyed the golden vessels in the temple (24:13) and deported ten thousand officers and warriors together with all the artisans and smiths (24:14); he also took an additional seven thousand warriors and one thousand artisans and smiths, possibly from the surrounding countryside (24:16).

This description of the first deportation shows clearly that the text focuses on how the monarchy was shattered, the temple plundered, and the people deported from the land. This account suggests that only the poorest people of the land were left (24:14b). But this impression does not square with subsequent details, which presuppose the presence of influential groups (cf. 25:18ff.), not to mention with what we know from the narratives in the book of Jeremiah.

The description of the second deportation from Judah is structured similarly. Zedekiah, the vassal king appointed by Nebuchadnezzar, rebels, again for no apparent reason (24:20), and Nebuchadnezzar sends another punitive expedition against Jerusalem. The siege begins in the ninth year of Zedekiah and lasts until the eleventh year (25:1–3),[8] which 25:8 identifies with the nineteenth year of Nebuchadnezzar (586). When a breach is made in the wall of the starving city, Zedekiah tries to flee with the soldiers but is captured by the Babylonians in the plains of Jericho and harshly punished by Nebuchadnezzar: his sons are slaughtered before his eyes, and he is then blinded and taken to Babylon in fetters (25:4–7). This account, similar to Jer 39, is intended to conjure up a vivid picture of the wretched end of the Davidic monarchy.

According to 2 Kgs 25:8ff., the city was not actually destroyed until a month after it was taken, primarily on the orders of Nebuzaradan, a high official, whom Jer 39:13ff. describes as having set Jeremiah free. He burned the temple, the palace, and all the (great) houses of Jerusalem (25:10) and then deported the rest of the population and the artisans.[9] He left behind only the poorest people of the land to be vinedressers and tillers of the soil (25:12). Thus the temple was destroyed, Jerusalem laid waste and totally depopulated. The account does not totally deny that some people remained behind in the land, but they play almost no role in the narrative, since they represent the dregs of society. The text totally ignores the fact that these people represent an attempted reform on the part of the Babylonians (as shown by Jer 39:10), intended to give the devastated land another chance. It does not square with the sense of total ruin that the books of Kings seek to convey.

The text goes on to recount in detail how all the remaining bronze, silver, and gold vessels of the temple were plundered and in part destroyed by the Babylonians (2 Kgs 25:13–16). When 25:17 describes in all their glory the bronze pillars that once graced the entrance to the temple, grief over the loss of the temple is palpable once more.

---

8 The Hebrew text of 2 Kgs 25:3–4 is corrupt but can be reconstructed on the basis of Jer 39:2ff. and 52:6–7.

9 Reading ההמון with Jer 52:15 instead of האמון.

The story closes with a detailed account of how the high cultic, political, and military functionaries were condemned and slain by Nebuchadnezzar at Riblah, just like Zedekiah (2 Kgs 25:18–21a). The high priest and the second priest of the Jerusalem temple were also executed. The text does not mention that these were probably the people responsible for the rebellion. Its only concern is to show how the Babylonian policy of merciless conquest robbed Judah of its elite as well as its king.

The summary in 25:21b reads: "So Judah went into exile out of its land." In other words, the exile spelled the end of everything. It marked the loss of everything that had made Israel and Judah what they were: the land, the capital, the temple, the monarchy. Through his absolute judgment, Yahweh had brought Israel and Judah to naught.

This sweeping verdict, totally negative, stands in marked contrast to Jer 39–43: Judah—without any exception or qualification—went into exile, as though the land had been almost totally depopulated. We know from Jer 40–43 that this was patently not the case: a substantial group had rallied around Gedaliah. Quite clearly, the vision of total deportation reflects a different theological assessment. If the exile was Yahweh's absolute judgment on his rebellious people, it had to involve virtually the entire nation. From this theological perspective, therefore, all of "Judah"—apart from the insignificant poor—had to go into exile, even if the number known to have been deported[10] does not really support this conclusion.

It is clear that the attempted new beginning under Gedaliah, which plays such a large role in the book of Jeremiah, does not chime with this totally negative view of the exile. For the authors of the books of Kings, no one worth speaking of could have been left in the land; the notion of a fresh opportunity presented by the deportation of the large landowners was inconceivable. Thus 2 Kgs 25:22–26 reduces the story of Gedaliah to a brief episode, described as though doomed to failure from the start. Interest focuses primarily on the end of this episode, the emigration of yet another group, bound for Egypt, once again depopulating the land. Now Judah had truly come to an end.

In this theological conception, there could be no further history of Israel without land, temple, and king; in the account of the books of Kings, therefore, the history of Israel ceases with the exile. The exile is God's absolute judgment, the annulment of all that once constituted Israel; it could be mourned but not described. Yahweh had removed Israel and Judah out of his sight (2 Kgs 17:23; 23:27; 24:20); there was no sense to be made of any subsequent history.

---

[10] At most eighteen thousand in 597; no numbers are given for 586.

Nevertheless, 2 Kings does not conclude in total darkness. In 25:27–30, it reports how Nebuchadnezzar's son Evil-Merodach, in the year of his accession (562), released the exiled King Jehoiachin from prison, thirty-seven years after his deportation, and gave him a place of honor among the vassal kings at his court. The text does not explain what this totally isolated event during the exile might mean; the situation was still too confused. But in the darkness of the exile it was remembered and recorded, because it hinted that Yahweh might still have plans for the royal house of David, that the end of Israel's history at the exile was not absolute but only temporary.

I.2.3. The Exile As a Sabbath for the Land (2 Chronicles)

Becker, Joachim. *1 Chronik* (NEB 18; Würzburg: Echter Verlag, 1986). **Becker.** *2 Chronik* (NEB 20; Würzburg: Echter Verlag, 1988). **Begg,** Christopher. "Babylon and Judah in Chronicles," *ETL* 64 (1988): 142–52. **De Vries,** Simon J. "The Land's Sabbath in 2 Chronicles 36:21," *Proceedings, Eastern Great Lakes and Midwest Biblical Societies* 6 (1986): 96–103. **Rudolph,** Wilhelm. *Chronikbücher* (HAT 1/21; Tübingen: Mohr Siebeck, 1955). **Willi,** Thomas. *Juda, Jehud, Israel: Studien zum Selbstverständnis des Judentums in persischer Zeit* (FAT 12; Tübingen: Mohr Siebeck, 1995). **Williamson,** H. G. M. *1 and 2 Chronicles* (NCB; London: Marshall, Morgan & Scott, 1982).

Whereas the books of Kings present the exile as a black hole of undetermined duration, the books of Chronicles view it as a well-defined historical period on which one can look back. It lasts until "the establishment of the kingdom of Persia" (2 Chr 36:20). In this account, King Cyrus of Persia decreed in the first year of his reign that the survivors of the exile be permitted to return and rebuild the temple (Ezra 1:1–3; cf. 2 Chr 36:22–23). Today we generally date the end of the exile in the year 539, accepting the Chronicler's conception.

But the historical account of Chronicles, Ezra, and Nehemiah, the earliest narrative to look back upon the exilic period, does not fill out the era with a chain of events. It is still a historical lacuna, covered in two verses:

> 2 Chr 36:20 He [Nebuchadnezzar] took into exile in Babylon those who had escaped from the sword,
> and they became servants to him and to his sons
> until the establishment of the kingdom of Persia,
> 21 to fulfill the word of Yahweh by the mouth of Jeremiah,
> until the land had made up for its Sabbaths.
> All the days that it lay desolate it kept Sabbath,
> to fulfill seventy years.

Except for the statement that the exiles became the servants or slaves of Nebuchadnezzar and his sons, the Chronicler does not find any concrete historical information concerning the period of the exile worth reporting. Instead, he embeds his meager account of the exilic period in a complex of theological interpretations. First, the exile was the fulfillment of a prophecy spoken by Jeremiah; second, it served as a Sabbath rest for the land; third, it had to last for seventy years.

That the exile realized the message of judgment spoken by the prophets was also the theological perspective of the books of Kings (2 Kgs 21:10; 24:2), but the books of Chronicles amplify this view: the account in 2 Chr 36 specifically refers to Jeremiah (36:12, 21), whom 2 Kgs 24–25 curiously does not mention. It shows that the prophetic message of judgment continued to be proclaimed until the last phase of Judah's history but failed to evoke repentance (36:12–13, 15–16). In this account, the exile ceases entirely to be the ineluctable disaster described in the books of Kings. Finally, the account in 2 Chr 36 makes clear that it was ultimately the peoples' mockery and disregard of the prophets that brought about the exile (36:12–13, 16). The exile was therefore the personal fault of the last preexilic generation, who ignored the word of God proclaimed by the prophets. It was Yahweh who set in motion the fulfillment of his word by dispatching Nebuchadnezzar against Judah (36:17–21).

This strongly theological perspective of Chronicles continues in the interpretation of the exile as a belated Sabbath rest for the land. This notion, only touched on here, is developed at greater length in Lev 26:34–35, 43. It presupposes the law of the Sabbatical Year in Lev 25:1–7, which decrees that every seven years the entire land must lie fallow to observe a Sabbath for Yahweh free of agricultural exploitation (25:2, 4–5). The idea here is that Israel did not observe this law in the preexilic period, when it dwelt in the land; now in the exilic period, with Israel forced out of the land, the failure to observe these Sabbatical Years can be made good. The incorporation of this notion in 2 Chr 36 attempts theologically to impose a limited positive meaning on the gloomy, baffling period of the exile: from God's perspective, the loss and devastation of the land were necessary in order to grant it en bloc the years of rest it had not received.[11]

To this imposed theological meaning, however, the books of Chronicles, Ezra, and Nehemiah link additional ideas about the exile that

---

[11] The Chronicler appears to assume that the monarchy lasted 490 years: the reigns starting with David total 474 years, to which are added the years of Saul's reign, of uncertain duration (cf. 1 Sam 13:1). Thus the seventy years of exile would compensate fully for the seventy missed Sabbatical Years. Cf. Williamson, *1 and 2 Chronicles*, 418.

further strengthen the global theological vision of the books of Kings. First, these years of exile were "days of desolation"; that is, during this period the land lay totally fallow and uninhabited (cf. Lev 26:43). Second, even more totally than in Kings, the entire surviving population of Judah (and Benjamin) was deported (2 Chr 36:20); there is no more mention of anyone left in the land. Third, continuity between preexilic and postexilic Israel could be established only through the Babylonian golah. Only those returning from the Babylonian exile, who had fully experienced God's radical judgment, could claim to be the "true Israel" (Ezra 2:1ff.; 3:1; 5:16); only they had the right to continue the history of Israel that Yahweh had inaugurated when he stirred up Cyrus (2 Chr 36:22; Ezra 1:1; cf. Ezra 4:3–4; 6:16, 19–20). All others belonged to the "nations of the land," from whose pollutions they had to separate themselves if they wished to join the community of the returned exiles (6:21). Not only ethnic but cultic continuity could come only through the Babylonian golah. This notion is expressed in 2 Chr 36:7, 10, 18, where the bringing of the undamaged (!) temple vessels to Babylon is noted repeatedly and emphatically. Ezra 1:7–11; 5:14–15; 6:5 describe in detail their return to the rebuilt temple.[12]

Finally, this theological view of the exile goes hand in hand with its restriction to seventy years. This number comes from the Jeremiah tradition: according to Jer 25:11–12 and 29:10, Jeremiah had proclaimed that Yahweh would allow Babylonian rule to last seventy years, at the end of which he would visit the exiles once more and bring them back to their homeland.[13] In the Chronicler's view, it is ultimately God's word spoken through the prophets that governs history; in this theology of history, therefore, the Babylonian exile must have lasted seventy years: these seventy years are the term established by God. Since the historical exile lasted a much shorter time (forty-eight years, from 587 to 539), ending in the Chronicler's view with Cyrus's victory over Babylon, the account in 2 Chr 37 adds years to its beginning. Nebuchadnezzar had already carried Jehoiakim off to Babylon along with some of temple vessels (36:6–7). When exactly this took place during the eleven years of Jehoiakim's reign is not disclosed.[14] But since his reign began in 609, exactly seventy years

---

[12] There is one minor discrepancy: 2 Chr 36:7 says that Nebuchadnezzar put the vessels in his palace, whereas Ezra 1:7 says that he placed them "in the house of his god."

[13] Cf. the three generations in Jer 27:7, borrowed by Zech 1:12; 7:5; Dan 9:2.

[14] The expression תשובת השנה ("the next spring") in 2 Chr 36:10 may suggest that the Chronicler was thinking of the end of Jehoiakim's reign, but this is not certain, since no date is mentioned for the other events that befell Jehoiakim (36:8). Dan 1:1–2 goes a step further, dating Jehoiakim's exile in the third year of his reign (606 or 605).

before the victory of Cyrus, at least there is a historical period to which the theological notion of seventy years can be assigned.

It is striking that this "first" deportation involves only Jehoiakim; it is an act of immediate personal retribution for his misdeeds—a notion found elsewhere in Chronicles.[15] It is even more noteworthy that the "second" deportation is still limited to Jehoiachin; only some precious vessels from the temple are taken along (2 Chr 36:10). In the view of Chronicles, the exile proper, encompassing the whole population, is the "third" deportation, in 587/586 (36:11–21). On the one hand, this is because the retrospective vision of Chronicles sees the year of Jerusalem's destruction as the critical date for the fall of Judah. But this view also reflects the peculiar concept of retribution in Chronicles in contrast to Kings: the general deportation of the whole population must punish a wrong committed by the whole population. But since God's punishment is always inflicted directly on the guilty, such a wrong could be committed only once, namely, just before the final deportation. It is therefore described in detail (36:12–16).

The author of Chronicles makes every effort to avoid characterizing the exile as a stroke of fate, presenting it instead as God's just and fitting punishment for human misconduct; however, the same author has no interest in finding reasons for the end of the exile. In his view, it is purely Yahweh's own initiative in stirring up the spirit of Cyrus and those wanting to return (2 Chr 36:22–23; cf. Ezra 1:1, 5) that sets the history of Israel back on track after seventy years of Sabbath rest.

I.2.4. Narrative Additions

The gaping hole that the exilic period tears in the historical tradition of the Hebrew Bible has been filled in some measure by edifying stories such as those found in the books of Daniel (1–6), Susanna (Dan 13), Bel and the Dragon (Dan 14), 1 Esd 3:1–5:6 (the Story of the Three Youths), Tobit, and Judith.[16] Critical examination shows that these narratives are secondary; except for 1 Esdras, no attempt is made to integrate them into Israel's historical tradition.[17] That they are also relatively late

---

15 Cf. the deportation and repentance of Manasseh in 2 Chr 33:11–13.

16 Baruch and the Letter of Jeremiah are also set in the exilic period, but they comprise didactic discourses and prayers rather than narratives.

17 Even attempts to provide a historical setting are only sporadic and sometimes clearly secondary; cf. Dan 1, a Hebrew introduction to the Aramaic book of Daniel; the additions to Dan 3 in 3:24–91 of the Septuagint and Theodotion; Tob 14; etc.

compositions is clear from the failure of many of them to enter the Hebrew canon, to be recognized as authoritative by all Jewish parties. The majority found an undisputed place only in the Greek Bible and hence belong, by Luther's definition, to the Apocrypha. But these stories set in the exilic period do provide yet another biblical picture of that era.

I.2.4.1. The Stories of Daniel (Daniel 1–6)

Albertz, Rainer. *Der Gott des Daniel: Untersuchungen zu Dan 4–6 in der Septuagintafassung sowie zur Komposition und Theologie des aramäischen Danielbuches* (SBS 131; Stuttgart: Katholisches Bibelwerk, 1988). **Koch,** Klaus, Till Niewisch, and Jürgen Tubach. *Das Buch Daniel* (EdF 144; Darmstadt: Wissenschaftliche Buchgesellschaft, 1980). **Kratz**, Reinhard Gregor. *Translatio imperii: Untersuchungen zu den aramäischen Danielerzählungen und ihrem theologiegeschichtlichen Umfeld* (WMANT 63; Neukirchen-Vluyn: Neukirchener Verlag, 1991). **Lebram,** Jürgen-Christian. *Das Buch Daniel* (ZBK.AT 21; Zurich: Theologischer Verlag, 1984).

The text of the Daniel stories presents substantial problems. Daniel 1:1–2:4a is in Hebrew, 2:4b–6:29 (28) in Aramaic. It is likely that 2:1–4a represents a Hebrew translation of an Aramaic text; it is disputed whether this is true of chapter 1 as well or whether this chapter, in whole or in part, represents a secondary introduction to the Aramaic book of Daniel (Dan 2–7*). In Dan 3, the versions of the Septuagint and Theodotion have preserved even more the character of a separate narrative, including in 3:24–91 substantial additions to the Aramaic text. The stories of Daniel in chapters 4–6 of the Septuagint differ so extensively in text and intention that they cannot be considered translations of the Aramaic text. In my opinion, the Septuagint text is an independent narrative complex in Greek based on separate earlier Hebrew-Aramaic stories; this complex is traditiohistorically prior to the Aramaic book of Daniel.[18] Here I nevertheless follow the Hebrew-Aramaic version in the Masoretic Text, since that version ultimately was accepted as canonical. I must point out, however, that the "biblical picture of the era" of the exile presented by the MT in the book of Daniel looks very different from that presented by the Septuagint.[19] The complex questions surrounding the literary development cannot be discussed here.[20] To enable a better understanding of

---

[18] Albertz, *Gott,* 147–56.
[19] See the comments on p. 27 below.
[20] For details, see Koch, *Buch Daniel,* 55–76.

the discussion that follows, I will state here that I consider the Aramaic book of Daniel (Dan 2–7), apart from a few minor revisions, to be a single literary unit: that is, the Aramaic Daniel stories were set from the outset in an apocalyptic framework (Dan 2 and 7).[21] It is only for reasons of clarity that this framework is treated separately in I.2.5 below.

According to Dan 1:1–5, Daniel came to Babylon with the deportation under Jehoiakim postulated in 2 Chr 36:6 and dated here more precisely in the third year of Jehoiakim's reign (606/605). He belonged to a group of young Judean noblemen whom Nebuchadnezzar had chosen to be educated at his court. Although Daniel and his three friends were given Babylonian or Persian names by the outside world (1:6), Daniel preserved their Jewish identity by courageously finding a way to observe the dietary laws even at court. To eliminate the danger of being defiled by the food of the royal court, he asked to have their rations reduced to water and vegetables (1:17–20). Since the youths thrived in spite of this diet, their Babylonian tutor allowed them this peculiar Jewish lifestyle. Thanks to God's help, after three years of training (1:5, 18) the four stood out by virtue of their intelligence, wisdom, and knowledge of every aspect of literature; Daniel was also versed in visions and dreams (1:17). They impressed even Nebuchadnezzar with their understanding and were taken into the king's service (1:17–20).

In Dan 2, Daniel immediately[22] has a chance to demonstrate his unique wisdom. When Nebuchadnezzar has a dream and demands arbitrarily that his Babylonian soothsayers not only interpret it but divine its content, Daniel comes forward voluntarily and tells the king the dream and its interpretation (2:24–45). The wise and insightful "man from among the exiles from Judah" (2:25), with the help of his God, puts to shame all the machinery of the vaunted Babylonian mantic arts and saves his colleagues from the cruel punishment threatened by Nebuchadnezzar. The Babylonian potentate, still furious, is so amazed at the Jewish dream interpreter Daniel that he almost worships him (2:46), pays homage to his God (2:47), and rewards him richly: Daniel is promoted to ruler over the whole province of Babylon and chief prefect over all its wise men, and his friends also receive high posts in the Babylonian provincial administration (2:48–49).

---

[21] For a discussion of the evidence, see Lebram, *Buch Daniel*, 20–21; Albertz, *Gott*, 157–93.

[22] The date in the second year of Nebuchadnezzar (Dan 2:1) conflicts with the three years of training in 1:5, 18. It is often emended to the "twelfth" year, the reading of Pap. 967. But the date may also be evidence that the Aramaic Daniel stories were originally independent of the Hebrew introductory chapter.

In Dan 3, however, the bright picture of life in the golah darkens ominously. In his megalomania, Nebuchadnezzar orders an enormous statue to be set up, before which all subjects of his empire must fall and worship on command (3:1–7). Daniel's friends, although they are high Babylonian officials, refuse to do public homage; thereupon "the Jews" are denounced (3:8, 12). In their hearing before the king, they steadfastly and confidently defend their monotheistic faith (3:17–18), despite all temptations and threats. But when Nebuchadnezzar in his rage has the three friends thrown in chains into a blazing furnace, he is forced to the terrible realization that the power of the Jewish God is greater than his own: God sends an angel to his faithful worshipers in the furnace to deliver them from Nebuchadnezzar's totalitarian demands (3:24–27). Thus the Babylonian king is forced to acknowledge the superior power of the Jewish God (3:28–29) and to rehabilitate Daniel's friends (3:30).

In the next story (Dan 3:31–4:34 [4:1–37]), the Babylonian king is forced to experience in his own body the sovereign power of God.[23] In a letter to all his subjects he reports how this came to pass (3:31–33 [4:1–3]). Once more Nebuchadnezzar had a dream, once more his Babylonian soothsayers could not interpret it, once more, as "chief of the magicians," Daniel had to demonstrate his extraordinary abilities (4:1–6 [4–9]). Just as the great world tree the king saw in his dream was cut down at God's command, so the Babylonian world ruler would be brought down and regain his kingdom only when he recognized God's sovereignty (4:7–23 [10–27]). And it came to pass as Daniel had prophesied: as Nebuchadnezzar was gazing upon his magnificent metropolis of Babylon and reveling in his power, he was bereft of his kingdom by God and degraded to the state of an animal (4:25–30 [28–33]). For seven years he had to vegetate among the animals, cut off from human society, until his human reason returned and he praised the supreme sovereignty of God (4:31–32 [34–35]). Only then were his majesty and splendor restored. So Nebuchadnezzar was forced to learn personally and bear witness that the Babylonian Empire could endure only by acknowledging the universal sovereignty of the Jewish God.

The story that follows (Dan 5) constitutes the antitype to Dan 4, explaining why the Babylonian Empire perished. King Belshazzar, whom the book of Daniel calls the son of Nebuchadnezzar (5:2, 11), gives a great feast. Intoxicated by wine, he scornfully desecrates the vessels from the Jerusalem temple that Nebuchadnezzar had carried off to Babylon (cf. 1:2)

---

23 The LXX dates this event in the eighteenth year of Nebuchadnezzar, which was seen alongside the nineteenth as the date when Jerusalem was taken (cf. Jer 52:29; Jdt 2:1); see pp. 79–81 below.

and praises the dead gods of the Babylonians (5:1–4; cf. 23–24). Thereupon a mysterious hand writes an incomprehensible inscription on the wall, causing Belshazzar to panic. The Babylonian soothsayers, summoned in haste and offered extravagant rewards, are unable once again to interpret the divine revelation. The queen mother introduces Daniel, "one of the exiles of Judah" (5:13), as a famous interpreter of dreams during the reign of Nebuchadnezzar; again, he alone can provide the interpretation. Proudly he rejects the gifts offered by the king and fearlessly accuses him of exalting himself above the God of heaven and refusing to honor God's sovereignty, even though the fate of his father should have taught him better. Therefore God has written his condemnation on the wall: his kingdom will be brought to an end and divided between the Medes and the Persians (5:17–24). Again the prophecy of Daniel—whom the king makes co-regent—is fulfilled immediately: Belshazzar is slain, and Darius the Mede takes over the kingdom (5:30–6:1 [5:30–31]).

The last story of Daniel (Dan 6) takes place under Darius. Like Dan 3, it makes clear at a stroke the calumnies and dangers to which Jews in exile could be exposed. The aging Darius, whom the book of Daniel calls king of the Medes, reorganizes his kingdom, making Daniel one of his three presidents and intending, on account of Daniel's great abilities, to appoint him over the whole kingdom (6:1–4 [5:31–6:3]). This favoritism provokes the intense resistance of the Median satraps. With the presidents, they cook up a plan to bring down the otherwise blameless Daniel by capitalizing on his Jewish faith. They urge the king to issue an edict, to be in force for thirty days, forbidding on pain of death any prayer not addressed to the king (6:5–10 [4–9]). Daniel, unimpressed, holds to his Jewish faith and continues to address his daily prayers to his God, praying toward Jerusalem (6:11–12 [10–11]). Naturally he is reported by his opponents. King Darius, entrapped by the rigid legal system of his state, is compelled to have the man who refused to acknowledge the totalitarian claims of the Mede thrown into a den of lions (6:13–19 [12–18]). But once again God sends an angel and delivers Daniel on account of his unshakable faith and demonstrated innocence (6:22–24 [21–23]). Moved by Daniel's faithful witness and the saving power of his God, Darius commands the whole slanderous bureaucracy to be thrown into the den of lions and acknowledges the sovereignty of Daniel's God (6:25–28 [24–27]). Thus Daniel continued to live and prosper under Darius and Cyrus (6:29 [28]).

This colorful collection of miracle stories about Daniel conveys a sharply ambivalent picture of the exilic period.[24] On the one hand (and

---

24 Contra Kratz, *Translatio*, 200, according to whom the Daniel stories are intended to represent the exile as a "salvific state established by God's governance of the world and the

this is a totally new element not found in the established historical tradition) it offered the exiles fantastic opportunities for advancement at the very heart of the victorious empire. Individuals "from among the Jewish exiles" such as Daniel and his friends, it is claimed, could rise to the highest offices, sacred and secular, of the Babylonian and Median court (Dan 1; 2; 6:1–4 [5:30–6:3]).[25] In this success they could proudly see a sign of the help of their God in the golah and the superiority of their monotheistic religion. On the other hand, the exiles were profoundly threatened in the environment of pagan religions. Precisely because of their monotheistic faith, they repeatedly found themselves in conflict with the religiously exaggerated claims of the foreign state even when they served it loyally (Dan 3; 6). They were exposed repeatedly to the envy and calumny of their host nations. The opportunities that the golah offered could turn suddenly into jeopardy and mortal danger.

In this conflict, despite all the necessary political loyalty toward the foreign power and all the inescapable assimilation into the pagan culture of the environment, the Daniel stories plead for a primary loyalty to the exiles' own God and faithful observance of the Jewish way of life. As one who observes the Jewish dietary laws punctiliously even at the royal court of Babylon (Dan 1:8–17) and recites the prescribed prayers three times a day facing toward Jerusalem (6:11 [10]), Daniel is a model for all faithful Jews in the Diaspora. As those who choose to suffer death for their faith in the only God rather than pay homage to other power, Daniel and his friends are impressive witnesses on behalf of steadfastness and readiness to suffer, which were repeatedly demanded of Jews in the Diaspora. Finally, the Daniel stories take up the challenge of a fundamental theological problem that the exile presented to all who believed in Yahweh and may well have been especially difficult in the Diaspora: What was the relationship between the sovereign omnipotence of Yahweh and the claims to omnipotence of the empires to which Israel was now subject (Dan 4–5; 6:26–28 [25–27])?

Almost nothing in the miraculous tales of the exilic period recounted in the book of Daniel is verifiable historically. According to Kings, there was no deportation under Jehoiakim (Dan 1:1–2); it probably is an outgrowth of a theological postulate of the Chronicler (2 Chr 36:6). Even the

---

empire." Kratz arrives at this uniformly positive view of the exile, which seems quite strange in light of the dramatic conflicts in Dan 3–6, by postulating a harmonious interweaving of divine and human sovereignty, which the stories present as a relationship of competition and conflict.

[25] That this claim—at least for the Persian period—was not made up out of whole cloth is shown by the example of Nehemiah and Ezra.

figure of Daniel, depicted now as an extraordinary interpreter of dreams (Dan 2; 4; 5), now as an outstanding official (Dan 6), is legendary. Despite his alleged fame, he is not mentioned in any Babylonian or Persian sources. What we have here is an Israelite borrowing of the legendary king Dan'ilu, mentioned in the texts from Ugarit. He appears in Ezek 14:13, 19–20 alongside Noah and Job as a man of exemplary righteousness and in Ezek 28:3 as a mantic sage.[26] The transmogrification of Nebuchadnezzar into an animal in Dan 4 turns out to be a legendary elaboration of the mysterious sojourn of Nabonidus in the desert;[27] the description of Nebuchadnezzar as a potentate alternating between hubris and obsequiousness is more like the discordant pictures of this last Babylonian king in contemporary documents.[28] Belshazzar was not the son of Nebuchadnezzar, as stated in Dan 5:2, 18, but the son and co-regent of Nabonidus in Babylon.[29] And the book of Daniel passes over in silence the three kings who reigned, albeit briefly, between Nebuchadnezzar and Nabonidus.[30]

It is even more difficult to explain a Median king Darius as heir to the Babylonian Empire, particularly since other biblical texts correctly associate its conquest with the Persian king Cyrus (Isa 45:1–7; 2 Chr 36; Ezra 1), and the reorganization of the empire described in Dan 6:1–4 (5:30–6:3) clearly recalls the Persian king Darius I,[31] who reigned after Cyrus and

---

[26] The foreign provenance of Daniel is shown indirectly by the fact that he—like Job—has no recognizable Israelite ancestors.

[27] See the Prayer of Nabonidus in the Qumran texts (4Q242), which recalls Dan 4. Between 550 and 540 B.C.E. Nabonidus dwelt in the Arabian oasis of Tema, where he led campaigns against the Arabs.

[28] Cf. the discrepancy between Nabonidus's description of himself as a model of religious devotion in his inscriptions (e.g., the Haran inscription [Wolfgang Röllig, "Erwägungen zu den neuen Stelen Nabonids," ZA 56 (1964): 218–60]) and the picture of him in the Persian anti-Nabonidus propaganda, which attacks him as a hubristic violator of the cult.

[29] During Nabonidus's sojourn in Tema, he was represented in Babylon by his son, Bel-šarra-uṣur.

[30] Amēl-Marduk (562–560; cf. 2 Kgs 25:27), Neriglissar (557–556), and Lābâši-Marduk (556). Nabonidus (556–539) was a usurper but was on the fringes of Nebuchadnezzar's family (see pp. 68–69 below).

[31] Klaus Koch, "Dareios, der Meder," in *The Word of the Lord Shall Go Forth: Festschrift in Honor of David Noel Freedman* (ed. C. L. Myers and M. P. O'Connor; Winona Lake, Ind.: Eisenbrauns, 1983), 287–99. Koch proposes (288–89) identifying the Darius of Dan 6 with Ugbaru, the governor of Babylon appointed by Cyrus. But it is not clear how Ugbaru came to be called Darius or how he could have become monarch of the whole empire. On Darius's reform of the imperial government, see Herodotus., *Hist.* 3.89; according to Herodotus, however, Darius established only twenty satrapies. The Persian king Darius I also appears in the Story of the Three Youths in 1 Esd 3, which presupposes in 3:2 an organization of the empire similar to that in Dan 6:2 (1).

Cambyses (522–486). His identification as the Median king who reigned before Cyrus is a product of the speculative theological history of the book of Daniel, which is based on a sequence of four world empires (Babylonian, Median, Persian, and Greek; Dan 2:31–45; 7:1–14).[32]

Thus the Daniel stories convey only blurred memories of the historical circumstances of the exilic period.[33] It is impossible to use them to reconstruct a history of the exile, not least because they say almost nothing of the fate of the Babylonian golah except for Daniel and his friends.[34] Probably, however, they do reflect typical experiences of the exilic community, especially Diaspora Jews in the centuries following the deportations. The opportunities and dangers that the Diaspora presented to Israel, the protective strategies demanded by the Diaspora, the problems of faith that it posed, became focused in these stories on the period of the Babylonian exile. In the book of Daniel, the Babylonian exile became the prototype for Israel's life in the Diaspora.[35]

I.2.4.2. The Stories of Susanna and Bel and the Dragon

Engel, Helmut. *Die Susanna-Erzählung* (OBO 61; Fribourg: Universitätsverlag, 1985). **Geissen,** Angelo. *Der Septuaginta-Text des Buches Daniel Kap. 5–12, zusammen mit Susanna, Bel et Draco sowie Ester Kap. 1,1a–2,15 nach dem Kölner Teil des Papyrus 967* (PTA 5/3; Bonn: Habelt, 1968). **Haag,** Ernst. *Daniel* (NEB 30; Würzburg: Echter Verlag, 1993). **Koch,** Klaus. *Deuterokanonische Zusätze zum Danielbuch* (2 vols.; AOAT 38/1–2; Neukirchen-Vluyn: Neukirchener Verlag, 1987). **Kottsieper,** Ingo. "Zusätze zu Esther und Daniel," in Odil Hannes Steck, Reinhard G. Kratz, and Ingo Kottsieper, *Das Buch Baruch, der Brief des Jeremia, Zusätze zu Ester und Daniel* (ATDA 5; Göttingen: Vandenhoeck & Ruprecht, 1998). **Moore,** Carey A. *Daniel, Esther and Jeremiah: The Additions* (AB 44; New York: Doubleday, 1977). **Plöger,** Otto. *Zusätze zu Daniel* (JSHRZ 1/1; Gütersloh: Mohn,

---

32 See pp. 42–43 below.

33 Their dating is disputed (Koch, *Buch Daniel*, 65; Albertz, *Gott*, 165ff.). In my opinion, the earliest possible date for the precursors of these stories is the late Persian period (end of the fifth to the middle of the fourth century B.C.E.). The Greek narrative complex can date at the earliest from the first half of the third century. The Aramaic book of Daniel probably dates from the end of the third century, the present Hebrew-Aramaic book from the Maccabean period (167 B.C.E.).

34 Only Dan 3:97 in the text of Theodotion connects the high office Daniel received from Nebuchadnezzar with the golah, probably in an attempt to forge a link with the story of Susanna.

35 This is probably why the introductory chapter Dan 1 emphasizes that Daniel's life spanned the entire period of the exile until "the first year of King Cyrus" (1:21), even though he would have been very old then. According to 10:1, he was still alive in the third year of Cyrus.

1973). **Schüppenhaus,** Joachim. "Das Verhältnis von LXX- und Theodotion-Texte in den apokryphen Zusätzen zum Danielbuch," *ZAW* 83 (1971): 49–72. **Steussy,** Marti J. *Gardens in Babylon: Narrative Faith in the Greek Legends of Daniel* (SBLDS 141; Atlanta: Scholars Press, 1993).

In the Greek and Latin Bible, there are two additional stories in which Daniel plays a role: Susanna and Bel and the Dragon. Their differing order in the various manuscripts[36] shows that they represent distinct traditions concerning Daniel, which could not be integrated into the canonical book of Daniel. Both appear in two different text types, of which the Septuagint (LXX) may be considered earlier than Theodotion (Θ).[37]

Of the two apocryphal stories of Daniel, only Bel and the Dragon makes any contribution to the biblical picture of the exilic period. Although Daniel appears in Susanna (LXX), this story lacks any Babylonian background or Diaspora milieu. In it Daniel is the outstanding representative of the younger generation, which in its wisdom and faithfulness to the Torah challenges the corrupt older generation (cf. the narrative setting in Dan 13:5–6, 62). As such Daniel thoughtfully and courageously exposes the false charges brought by two elders who lust after the beautiful Susanna. When she refuses their advances, they accuse her of adultery so that she will be condemned to death. The location of this conflict within the Jewish community is vague (13:28: "the synagogue of the city"). Daniel's accusation that one of the elders has perverted his Jewish heritage as though he came from Sidon (13:56) suggests Palestine. The notion of a superior court of elders to which legal cases of other cities may be referred (13:6) really fits only Jerusalem.

Only 13:5, which mentions Babylon, establishes a loose connection with the Babylonian Daniel tradition; the words "from Babylon," however, are a secondary insertion into the key text of the story ("the wickedness came forth from the elders"); the syntax shows that the

---

[36] In the main Greek tradition (Θ), Susanna precedes and Bel and the Dragon follows the canonical book of Daniel. The Vulgate places Susanna, followed by Bel and the Dragon, at the end of the book of Daniel. The Vulgate's designation of the former as Dan 13 and the latter as Dan 14 is followed here. The original order of the LXX is now illustrated by Pap. 967: Daniel, Bel and the Dragon, Susanna; it shows that Susanna is the latest addition to the book of Daniel.

[37] Already demonstrated by Schüppenhaus ("Verhältnis," 49–69). The attempt by Koch (*Deuterokanonische Zusätze*, 200–202) to prove that the Θ text of Bel and the Dragon is earlier on the grounds of its similarity to the Aramaic Josippon-Jerahmeel text is not convincing, since this medieval manuscript does not represent any ancient textual tradition; cf. Kottsieper, "Zusätze," 220.

words are a gloss.³⁸ It is unclear whether they are an allusion to Zech 5:6, 8 or Jer 29:23, meant as a sideswipe at the Babylonian golah, or simply a careless connection, since the story says nothing more of any Babylonian origin or influence with regard to the two wicked elders. In the earlier Septuagint recension, the historical background may well have been the conflict between the young Maccabean elite and the Jerusalem establishment, influenced by Hellenism, that wracked Judah in the second century B.C.E.³⁹ The later Θ recension, harmonizing with the other Daniel stories, shifted the setting to Babylon (13:1–4), though without reflecting any particular features of Diaspora life.⁴⁰

By contrast, the double narrative of Bel and the Dragon, apparently unknown to the canonical Daniel tradition,⁴¹ takes us deep into the Babylonian milieu. Here, unlike Dan 1, Daniel is introduced as a priest (Dan 14:2) and confidant of an unnamed Babylonian king. The king disputes Daniel's claim that there is nothing divine about either Bel (i.e., the chief god Marduk), whose idol the Babylonians worship assiduously (14:3–22), or the mythological dragon they revere (14:23–42) and that the only true deity is Yahweh, the Creator of the world (14:5).

The king is of the opinion that the huge amounts of food provided for the idol demonstrate Bel's divinity; Daniel convincingly exposes the whole cultic production as a pious fraud (Dan 14:7, 19). It was not Bel who devoured the enormous quantities of sacrificial offerings, as the overseers of the temple credulously claimed (14:8) and the king naively believed when he saw that the offering tables in the carefully sealed temple had been cleared (14:18). As the footprints in the ashes secretly scattered by Daniel proved, it was the priests themselves and all the members of their families who had entered the temple through secret

---

38 Note the repeated preposition ἐκ. The gloss also interrupts the original poetic structure of the framework 13:5b, 6, and 62. See Kottsieper, "Zusätze," 304.

39 Verse 1 does not yet associate the narrative with the Daniel tradition but with the Habakkuk tradition, probably because of the interpolated Habakkuk episode in vv. 33–39, originally a separate element. Verses 31–32 introduce the lions' den, describing it in detail as a place where enemies of the state are punished, whereas Dan 6 assumes that it is familiar. Despite the similarity of motifs, Bel and the Dragon differs markedly from Dan 6 in detail and terminology. What the latter mentions briefly, the former describes at some length. Instead of being called a Judean, as in Dan 1:3, 6, Daniel is a priest of Levitical descent. The idol of Bel recalls the statue made by Nebuchadnezzar in Dan 3, but the command to worship it is still specifically cultic.

40 Kottsieper, "Zusätze," 289–90.

41 The original beginning of the Septuagint version is no longer extant; even Pap. 967 begins with 14:5, after a lacuna. The Hexaplaric Recension replaced the missing text with the beginning of the Θ narrative. It may be reconstructed roughly as follows: "[There were once two elders of the kind] concerning whom the ruler said..." (Kottsieper, "Zusätze," 300).

doors (14:19–21). Thus enlightened by Daniel, the king, who had extolled Bel (14:18), puts an end to the Bel cult: he expels the deceitful priests from the temple of Bel, which he hands over to Daniel. Daniel destroys the statue of Bel and its temple (14:22). Thus the king of Babylon himself finally recognizes that the Babylonian idol cult is worthless.

In a second act, this religious confrontation is ratcheted up. This time the story involves a dragon whose divinity seems to be beyond question because it is alive, because it eats and drinks. Thus the king commands Daniel to worship the dragon properly, as do all Babylonians (14:23–24). Daniel, however, asks the king's permission to prove that he can destroy this seemingly divine being without any weapon. Permission is granted. Daniel cleverly bakes loaves of a deadly mixture,[42] which causes the greedy beast to burst (14:26–27). Can such a creature, which can be slain by a human stratagem, be worthy of worship (14:27)?

This drastic deconstruction now provokes the indignant resistance of the populace. They conspire against Daniel and accuse the king, converted to the side of the Jews by Daniel, of being responsible for the destruction of their most sacred objects (14:28). For reasons of state, he declares his willingness to sacrifice Daniel (14:30), and so the outraged mob throw Daniel into a den of lions, where those considered enemies of the state were consigned to an appalling death (14:31–32).

Daniel is in the lions' den for six days; on the seventh day he is saved from starvation by the prophet Habakkuk, transported to Babylon by an angel of Yahweh (14:33–37). Then Daniel realizes that Yahweh did not desert him in his direst need, into which his courageous witness on behalf of Yahweh in the golah had brought him (14:38). God's protective love for the faithful confessor now also delivers Daniel from the lions' den, thus definitively ending the religious contest: the king, coming to the lions' den to mourn for Daniel, is astonished to find him alive; he praises the greatness of Yahweh and recognizes him as God alone (14:41). Daniel is pulled from the den in the king's presence, and those who had sought his destruction are thrown in instead (14:42).

Unlike the canonical Daniel stories, the double narrative of Bel and the Dragon—the conclusion of which recalls Dan 6—conceives of the exile not as the place where Yahweh's sovereignty over the secular powers of the world is demonstrated but as the site of bitter confrontation between monotheistic Judaism, an aniconic religion, and Babylonian

---

42 Kottsieper ("Zusätze," 165–66) argues convincingly that the original mixture comprised nails, fat, and barley, not pitch, fat, and hair, a misunderstanding of certain Aramaic terms in the Greek textual tradition.

religion. In Dan 5:4, 13 it is accepted that the Babylonian gods are not alive. Here, however, Babylonian religion with its imposing statue of Marduk, its vast cult, and its impressive mythology is still taken seriously as an aggressive challenge to the Jewish faith. Behind it stood an influential priesthood and a militant body of adherents whom even the king felt compelled to take seriously. It took the wise and courageous intervention of a young Jewish man to unmask the magnificent Babylonian cult of Marduk as a pious fraud and the impressive symbolic world of its mythology as worthless.[43]

Scholars long dismissed the picture of Babylonian religion drawn by Bel and the Dragon as the product of much later fantasy.[44] Recently, however, Kottsieper has shown that the story of the dragon in particular displays detailed knowledge of Babylonian religious traditions.[45] The dragon (Babyl. *ušumgallu*) represented the invincible power of gods and kings; it is also the theriomorphic symbol of the god Marduk (see the so-called Ishtar Gate of Babylon). In the Babylonian tradition of the primeval sages (*apkallu*), a certain Lu-Nanna was said to have driven an *ušumgallu* from a temple. The designation of Daniel as a priest in Dan 14:2 is probably best explained as an allusion to this tradition: as a loanword in Aramaic, probably the original language of the story, *apkallu* had acquired this specialized meaning. Furthermore, many aspects of Daniel's slaying of the dragon recall the victory of the god Marduk over the chaos monster Tiamat, celebrated at every New Year festival in *Enuma Elish*, the Babylonian creation epic. When the author of the dragon story cast his Jewish hero in the role of a primeval sage or even the god Marduk, the intent was to defeat Babylonian religion with its own weapons. The Babylonians themselves claimed that divine beings could be defeated, whether by gods or by sages; this claim was now paraded before their eyes in the figure of Daniel, who had succeeded in slaying the beast that symbolized the invincible power of their primary god. Thus the story of the dragon still bears witness to a living religious confrontation, presupposing detailed knowledge of the position under attack.

---

[43] The enlightened tone of the stories of Bel and the Dragon recalls the polemic of Deutero-Isaiah against idols (Isa 40:19–20; 41:6–7; 42:17; 44:9–20; 45:16–17, 20b; 46:5–8; cf. Jer 10:1–16; Hab 2:18–19), which may be a product of the same Babylonian or early Persian period.

[44] See Moore, *Daniel*, 124, 128, 142. The argument that there was no serpent cult in Babylonia plays a central role in this view, but the story does not say anything about cultic worship of the dragon. The individual stories are commonly dated in the third century, the double narrative in the second half of the second century. See Moore, *Daniel*, 128; Steussy, *Gardens*, 183–86.

[45] "Zusätze," 251–52.

Clearly the dragon story was once an independent narrative. Whether it should be dated close to the exilic period, as Kottsieper suspects,[46] may be left an open question. In my opinion, the picture of a Jew operating as royal confidant presupposes Persian circumstances (cf. Nehemiah). This is clearly true—as even Kottsieper admits—for the parallel story, which is already removed from the Babylonian milieu[47] and probably presupposes and reflects theologically on the punitive campaign of Xerxes, the Persian king, against the cult of Marduk following the defeat of a Babylonian revolt in 482. In the course of this campaign, the statue of Marduk was destroyed or carried off.[48] If the double narrative of Bel and the Dragon dates from the middle of the fifth century, it is struggling with a new religious challenge: after Cyrus's conquest of Babylon in 539, the Persian kings, whose political favor the Jews enjoyed and with whom they felt religious ties, could become devout adherents and promoters of Babylonian religion, which the Jews profoundly despised if only account of its pervasive worship of images and crude mythology.[49] In a legendary setting, it expresses the not-unreasonable hope that the change in Persian religious policy would enable the Diaspora Jews, through their sagacity and courageous witness and with the support of Yahweh, to bring the Persian kings to an aniconic cult and acceptance of the monotheistic Jewish faith. But this change retrospectively made the Babylonian exile—probably for the first time—the setting for a religious contest imposed by God upon Israel, living in exile in the very center of a world empire espousing an alien religion.

The collection of Daniel stories in Dan 4–6, for which the Septuagint text differs from the canonical book of Daniel, accepted this view of the exile and sometime in the middle of the third century developed out of it a true missionary theology. Through Yahweh's intervention and the courageous witness of Daniel, the ruler of the world was converted

---

46 He has in mind the period between 539 and 482 ("Zusätze," 252–54), more precisely the end of the sixth or the beginning of the fifth century.

47 It is true that Bel ("Lord") had been an important epithet of Marduk since the end of the second millennium, and probably there was a famous statue of Marduk in Babylon that was lavishly provided with offerings. But the Babylonian cult involved multiple offerings of food rather than a single offering, and the Bel story makes no mention at all of the beer that was so important in Mesopotamia (see *TUAT* 2/2:212ff.). In addition, the leftovers from the cultic meal went to the royal table, so that the king must have known that the food offerings were not totally consumed (Kottsieper, "Zusätze," 275–80). The presence of royal overseers in Babylonian temples, however, is an accurate feature.

48 See Strabo, *Geog.* 16.1.1. Herodotus (*Hist.* 1.183) speaks of two statues of Marduk; he reports that Xerxes destroyed one and that the priest of Marduk protecting it was killed.

49 See the similar discussion of the polemic against idols in Deutero-Isaiah by Reinhard Gregor Kratz, *Kyros im Deuterojesaja-Buch* (FAT 1; Tübingen: Mohr Siebeck, 1991), 200.

totally to the faith of Yahweh; thus Judaism was elevated to the official religion of the entire empire (Dan 4:33A–37B; 6:26–28 LXX). From the optimistic perspective of early Hellenistic Diaspora Judaism, Israel's exile became a great opportunity for world mission.

I.2.4.3. The Story of the Three Youths (1 Esdras 3:1–5:6)

Pohlmann, Karl-Friedrich. *3. Esra-Buch* (JSHRZ 1/5; Gütersloh: Mohn, 1980).
Pohlmann. *Studien zum dritten Esra* (Göttingen: Vandenhoeck & Ruprecht, 1970).

The apocryphal book of 1 Esdras is preserved only in the Septuagint (Esdra a) and the Vulgate (3 Ezra); it presents in a different sequence the historical tradition extending from 2 Chr 36 through Ezra 10 (plus Neh 7:72–8:13a). It includes a separate tradition similar in many ways to the Daniel stories: the so-called Story of the Three Youths (3:1–5:6).[50]

The story is set at a festal banquet given by the Persian king Darius for his court and dignitaries. At this banquet, three young men ("pages") belonging to the king's bodyguard engage in a gallant contest to determine which will be judged the wisest and be allowed to occupy the place of honor beside the king. They agree on the subject: What is the strongest thing on earth? The first writes "wine," the second "the king," and the third "women and truth." Then each defends his choice in a sophisticated speech before the company. Naturally the victor is the third, with his initially amusing but then thoughtful answer (4:13–40). Surprisingly, this youth turns out to be Zerubbabel (4:13). When Darius asks him what reward he wishes, he seizes the opportunity to ask the king to fulfill the vow he made at his enthronement: to rebuild Jerusalem and the temple, destroyed by the Edomites (4:43–46).[51] Impressed by this wise youth, Darius showers favors on Zerubbabel and the Babylonian golah. He issues orders throughout his kingdom decreeing privileges for the Jews: safe conduct for those returning under Zerubbabel's leadership, building material for the fortification of the city, money for the rebuilding and support of the temple, provisions for the priests and exemption from taxes for all, land and wages for those guarding the city, and the return of the surrounding territory, including the southern settlements taken by the Edomites. Finally, the decree includes the return of the temple vessels,

---

50 Pohlmann, *Studien*, 35–52; Pohlmann, *3. Esra-Buch*, 380–83, 397–403.
51 The charge against the Edomites in 4:45 is surprising, since 2 Kgs 25:8–9 says that the Babylonians burned the temple. But Obad 11 suggests that the Edomites took part at least indirectly in the conquest of Jerusalem.

already promised by Cyrus (4:47–57). As soon as Zerubbabel leaves the palace to tell the exiles the good news, he prays toward Jerusalem, thanking his God for the wisdom that God has granted him; the Babylonian golah joins in praising God and celebrates a seven-day festival (4:58–63). Then they set out to return, as described in Ezra 2 (1 Esd 5:1ff.).

The purpose of the Story of the Three Youths is to explain how the return of the exiles under Zerubbabel came about and how the Jews came to enjoy the many privileges granted by the Persians. It does this in the form of a typical court narrative, large portions of which do not reflect a Jewish milieu; only the identification of the third youth with Zerubbabel (1 Esd 4:13; 5:6) and the nature of the reward for his victory in the wisdom contest connect with the history of Israel at the end of the exilic period. To the miracle that Israel's history did not end with the exile, thanks to God's intervention (Ezra 1:1ff. = 1 Esd 2:1ff.), it adds a human explanation: it was a Diaspora Jew at the Persian court who through his surpassing wisdom—with God's help—seized the opportune moment to pave the way for the release of his people from their Babylonian captivity (4:62). Unlike the Daniel stories, this account sees no problem in the service of Jews at the court of a foreign power. Such service, the story claims optimistically, can only benefit Israel.

There is much in the view of 1 Esdras that reflects the historical end of the exile more accurately than the account in the canonical book of Ezra: above all, the date of the crucial moment marking the return and the rebuilding of the temple—not under Cyrus (539) but only in the second year of King Darius (520; 1 Esd 5:6).[52] On the whole, however, the Story of the Three Youths is every bit as legendary as the Daniel stories, as is clear simply from the still recognizable Jewish reworking of the narrative material. The list of the privileges granted by Darius links the rebuilding of the temple under Zerubbabel (520) with the fortification of Jerusalem under Nehemiah (ca. 445), historically separated by more than seventy years. Some of the privileges turn out to be nothing more than wishful thinking, such as general exemption from taxes and the return of the settlements lost to the Edomites.[53] Nevertheless, viewed at some distance the Story of the Three Youths recounts accurately—albeit from a clearly pro-Persian perspective—the unexpected support the Jews received from the Persians and the benefits Israel gained by cooperating with them.

---

[52] See pp. 120ff. below.

[53] Neh 5:4 speaks of the oppressive burden of Persian taxes. According to Ezra 7:24, at the end of the fifth century only the temple personnel were granted exemption from taxes by the Persians. Defeat of the Idumeans had to wait for John Hyrcanus (127 B.C.E.).

I.2.4.4. Tobit

Deselaers, Paul. *Das Buch Tobit: Studien zur seiner Entstehung, Komposition und Theologie* (OBO 43; Fribourg: Universitätsverlag, 1982). **Engel,** Helmut. "Auf zuverlässigen Wegen und in Gerechtigkeit: Religiöses Ethos in der Diaspora nach dem Buch Tobit," in *Biblische Theologie und gesellschaftlicher Wandel: Festschrift für Norbert Lohfink* (ed. B. Braulik, W. Gross, and S. McEvenue; Freiburg: Herder, 1993), 83–100. **García Martínez,** Florentino, and Eibert J. C. Tigchelaar. *The Dead Sea Scrolls Study Edition* (2 vols.; Leiden: Brill, 1997–98). **Gross,** Heinrich. *Tobit, Judit* (NEB 19; Würzburg: Echter Verlag, 1987). **Moore,** Carey A. *Tobit: A New Translation with Introduction and Commentary* (AB 40A; New York: Doubleday, 1996). **Rabenau,** Merten. *Studien zum Buch Tobit* (BZAW 220; Berlin: de Gruyter, 1994).

The book of Tobit likewise appears only in the Greek and Latin Bibles.[54] Unlike the Story of the Three Youths but like the Daniel stories, it views the exilic situation with profound ambivalence. It also includes non-Israelite material having nothing to do with the exile: a tale of how a young man assisted by higher powers delivers a young woman from a ravening demon, a theme that appears in other settings.[55] This fabulous material is transformed into a symbol of the mortal danger to Jewish families in the exile and their deliverance. The perspective that shapes the narrative background of the exile, however, clearly differs from the Story of the Three Youths and the Daniel stories: it is not the perspective of the court and high politics, influenced by noted Jewish individuals, but rather the perspective of the "normal"—albeit devout—Jewish family that suffers the fate of exile and, in an alien land, must wrestle with God for survival.

The book of Tobit actually deals with the Assyrian exile (732 or 722 B.C.E.), but it links directly with the Babylonian exile, which Tobit foretells at the end of his life (Tob 14:4). The book even has its young hero experience the division of the kingdom in 922 (1:4ff.), far outside the limits of his already-long lifespan of 112 years, making it clear immediately that its purpose is not an authentic account of a single individual and his fate: the figure of Tobit embodies and exemplifies the fate of Israel.

---

[54] The text appears in a shorter recension (G1) in Codex Alexandrinus and Codex Vaticanus; Codex Sinaiticus and the Old Latin Bible preserve a longer recension (G2). The Aramaic and Hebrew fragments from Qumran (García Martínez and Tigchelaar, *Dead Sea Scrolls*, 383–99 [4Q196–4Q200]) suggest that G2 is closer to the original text. I follow the text reconstructed by Rabenau (*Studien*, 226–49), dealing only with the text in its final form and disregarding possible earlier stages.

[55] Deselaers, *Buch Tobit*, 280ff.

Throughout the entire introductory section (Tob 1:3–3:6), Tobit personally recounts his harsh fate in exile. Living in the north of Israel, despite his great devotion he was caught up in the deportation of Israel by the Assyrians and taken to Nineveh (1:2–3). Only in exile was he able to establish a small family: he married a Jewish woman from his tribe and fathered an only son, whom he named Tobias (1:9). In the alien land, unlike the other exiles and the rest of his family, he resisted the cultural pressure to assimilate and refused to have table fellowship with the Gentiles. This fidelity to his ancestral tradition already set him well on the way to social isolation.

Despite being a religious outsider, through God's merciful providence he was able to become purveyor to the court of Shalmaneser, the Assyrian king, and to achieve substantial prosperity through trade with Media (Tob 1:13–14). Soon, however, he lost a portion of his wealth: under Sennacherib the highways into Media became unsafe, and he lost access to a large sum of money he had deposited there with a business partner (1:14–15). Nevertheless, he labored tirelessly on behalf of his impoverished and persecuted fellow Jews, giving alms generously and devoutly burying the slain whose corpses had been thrown over the walls of Nineveh and left to rot (1:16–17).

Precisely because of Tobit's solidarity with his people, his fall was precipitous. Sennacherib, angered at his unsuccessful siege of Jerusalem, launched a pogrom among the Jews of Nineveh; an informer told the king that Tobit was burying the victims, and all his property was confiscated. Only flight enabled him to escape with his life (Tob 1:18–20). Now he did not even have his family to protect him.

When Esarhaddon became king, at the intercession of Tobit's "nephew" Ahiqar[56] he was allowed to return to his family (Tob 1:21–2:1). But a dinner during the Festival of Weeks, to which Tobit sought to invite the poor among his fellow exiles, ended in sorrow and misery. Again a Jew had been murdered on a public street; again Tobit out of solidarity undertook to bury him and secretly mourned him through the night. Exhausted by his efforts, he fell asleep outdoors; sparrow droppings fell into his eyes and blinded him. No physician could help him (2:2–10). Despite Tobit's great piety and devotion, under the murderous conditions of the exile he had become an impoverished, socially isolated, and chronically sick man whose family could barely keep their heads above water through the charity of Ahiqar and the occasional work his wife was able to find (2:10–14). When his relationship with his wife

---

[56] Ahiqar was a famous sage who had his ups and downs as counselor at the Assyrian court (*TUAT* 3/2:320ff.); the book of Tobit turns him into a devout Jew (cf. Tob 14:10).

seemed on the point of collapsing, Tobit was *in extremis*. He prayed to God to release him by death from the overwhelming misery he had been forced to undergo (3:1–6).

To this point, the image of the exile sketched by the book of Tobit is primarily gloomy. Even under the conditions of exile in a foreign land, Jews have an occasional opportunity to achieve prosperity (Tobit) and influence (Ahiqar), but this good fortune is short-lived, always under the threat of changed imperial policies over which ordinary Jewish families have no influence. Quite the contrary: they are defenseless against attacks by the local populace and arbitrary acts of those in power. They are killed like criminals in the public street, and no one cares.

The picture of the Jewish exiles is also depressing. Most have assimilated to the civilization of their alien environment, either out of fear or indifference. They have so lost their sense of solidarity that they no longer feel obliged to carry out even the most fundamental familial obligations such as burying fellow Jews or caring for impoverished family members. There are few like Tobit who battle against this desolidarization among the families in exile and work for the good of the golah outside the boundaries of their own extended family, in the spirit of brotherhood inculcated by the Torah. When even such individuals are forsaken by God and fall into misery, living as a Jew in the Diaspora appears totally pointless. Under the harsh conditions of the exile, Tobit is *in extremis* not only physically and materially but also religiously. His conscientious Jewish way of life, walking in truth, righteousness, and mercy (Tob 1:3), has brought about his ruin, as his wife bitterly points out to him (2:14).[57]

At its great historical distance from the exile,[58] the book of Tobit certainly does not paint an authentic picture of life in the Assyrian golah, especially since the Bible contains no other relevant sources. It may, however, provide a heavily stylized outline of Jewish experiences during centuries of the Diaspora.

The book of Tobit uses the family of Raguel to illustrate a further problem of life in exile that weakens clan solidarity and threatens the survival of the Jewish families: the isolation of geographical dispersal.

---

[57] Rabenau (*Studien*, 116ff.) is too one-sided in emphasizing the surprisingly "positive attitude" of his reconstructed core narrative toward the Assyrian state. But even if he should be right in contending that revisions have darkened the picture of life in the exile, his core narrative still presupposes the murder and defilement of Diaspora Jews (2:3) and culminates in Tobit's lament and wish to die (3:6).

[58] The book was composed between the third and second century B.C.E. (Rabenau, *Studien*, 175–90).

Although a member of the same clan as Tobit, Raguel dwells with his wife and only daughter Sarah far from Nineveh, in the Median city of Ecbatana. Raguel is wealthy, but his family's survival is threatened because in the alien land his daughter is plagued by a demon that has already killed seven men in her bridal chamber. Sarah faces the threat of childless disgrace, her family the threat of perishing in social isolation.

The narrator arranges to have Sarah lament to God her pointless life as a Jewish woman simultaneously with Tobit's lament. Since there seems to be no other member of her clan for whom she should keep herself as wife, she prays to die in her disgrace (Tob 3:11–15).

To understand the book of Tobit, it is important to realize that both Sarah and Tobit in their individual affliction reflect the fate of all Israel in exile. In her hopeless situation, Sarah sees herself trapped "in the land of [her] exile" (Tob 3:15); in his hopeless situation, Tobit feels that along with all Israel he has been given over "to plunder, exile, and death" (3:4). In this view, the judgment of exile that God has inflicted on Israel is continued individually in the ruin of devout Jewish men and women in the Diaspora, which they experience as separation from God. To put it another way: in their despair, Sarah and Tobit represent Israel amid the constant afflictions of life in exile.

It is all the more important that the actual narrative corpus of Tobit (3:4–12:22) can recount the almost fairy-tale deliverance of these two exilic families, both threatened with disintegration. God hears the laments of Tobit and Sarah (3:16–17) and sends his angel Raphael. Secretly accompanying Tobit, Raphael reunites the two related families and provides a cure for both Sarah and Tobit. Guided by Raphael, Tobit, despite his mortal danger, finds the courage in family solidarity to marry Sarah, simultaneously saving Raguel's family from extinction and his own family from poverty. Finally, Tobit's blindness is healed, and Sarah finds heartfelt welcome with her parents-in-law. Beyond these two exilic families, all this is intended as a miraculous sign that God will one day deliver all Israel from the affliction of exile. This is the subject of the book's conclusion, Tobit's hymn of thanksgiving (13) and last words (14).

It is noteworthy that the book of Tobit vastly expands the temporal horizon of the exile. It encompasses not just the Assyrian exile, which Tobit actually experiences, but also the Babylonian exile, which he foresees clairvoyantly (Tob 14:4). But even the return and the rebuilding of the temple in 520 does not bring the exile to an end—in contrast to the conception of the Chronicler's History and the Story of the Three Youths (14:5). In the view of Tobit, the exile will not end "until the period when the times of fulfillment shall come," when all the Jews of the Diaspora shall return and rebuild Jerusalem as a splendid cosmopolis to which all the nations shall come and be converted to Yahweh (13:11; 14:5–7).[59]

In this view, the exile includes the entire present and future history of Israel until the great eschatological day of salvation, promised by the prophets (Tob 14:5). It becomes the most inclusive category for interpreting the course of Israel's history until the eschaton. The miraculous deliverance of Tobit and Sarah when their lives are threatened in the Diaspora serves as a symbol of hope that God will fulfill the great eschatological promises that put an end to all affliction.

At the end of the book, Tobit's son Tobias, still in Media, learns that the hated city of Nineveh where his father suffered exile and humiliation has been destroyed (612 B.C.E.) and sees its inhabitants being taken into exile in Media (Tob 14:15). It is clear that God is already at work to reverse the affliction of the exile.

I.2.4.5. Judith

Craven, Toni. *Artistry and Faith in the Book of Judith* (SBLDS 70; Chico, Calif.: Scholars Press, 1983). **Gross,** Heinrich. *Tobit, Judit* (NEB 19; Würzburg: Echter Verlag, 1987). **Moore,** Carey A. *Judith: A New Translation with Introduction and Commentary* (AB 40; New York: Doubleday, 1985). **VanderKam,** James C., ed. *"No One Spoke Ill of Her": Essays on Judith* (SBLEJL 2; Atlanta: Scholars Press, 1992). **Zenger,** Erich. *Das Buch Judit* (JSHRZ 1/6; Gütersloh: Mohn, 1981). **Zenger.** "Der Juditroman als Traditionsmodell des JHWHglaubens," *TTZ* 83 (1974): 65–80.

The apocryphal book of Judith dates roughly from the middle of the second century B.C.E.[60] Its narrative is set in the exilic period, but—like the historical tradition itself—it views the exile from its margins (Jdt 2:9; 4:3, 12; 5:18–19; 8:18–23). We shall discuss it here because, like Tobit, it deals in a fundamental way with the life of Israel in exile.

The book's point of departure is Israel's traumatic experience of deportation and exile (Jdt 2:1ff.): Nebuchadnezzar's campaign against Jerusalem, which ended historically in 587/586 with the conquest of the city, the destruction of the temple, and the deportation the populace. In the story of Judith, however, the stage is broadened enormously and the setting fundamentally exaggerated: the famous Babylonian ruler Nebuchadnezzar is described as the "king of the Assyrians" (Jdt 1:1 and

---

[59] A similar theory of a continuing exile is found in the Animal Apocalypse in *1 En.* 89:57–90:19.

[60] Zenger, *Buch Judit,* 431; his edition of the text in JSHRZ 1/6, 449–522, is followed here.

passim); he has a general with a name that is clearly Persian (Holofernes); and so forth. In other words, he combines in his own person the Near Eastern empires that ruled Israel, thus representing all the world powers that threatened Israel.

The campaign that Nebuchadnezzar launches in the eighteenth year of his reign[61] is therefore not an isolated action meant to punish Jerusalem; it is targeted at the whole world. He wants to "carry out his revenge on the whole earth" (Jdt 2:1) because its inhabitants have refused to join him, the "lord of the whole earth" (1:11–12; 2:5). Like the Aramaic Daniel stories, the story of Judith sees in the onslaught of Nebuchadnezzar the idolatrous self-glorification of imperial power: it puts its faith in weapons (2:5) and sets itself in the place of God by its claim to absolute authority (6:2). In conducting total war it seeks not only to plunder, slay, and take captive the nations (2:8–9) but also to destroy all gods and demolish their shrines (3:8).[62] Thus the threatened exile of Israel becomes an attack on the power and divinity of Yahweh.

The book of Judith tells how Israel was the only nation on earth to resist the enormous self-aggrandizing military machine that Nebuchadnezzar set in motion under the command of Holofernes. The population of Jerusalem, though terrified, occupied the passes in the difficult mountainous terrain of Samaria, where the fortified city of Bethulia played a key role (Jdt 4). When the enraged Holofernes laid hard siege to Bethulia and cut off its water supply, the resistance of its inhabitants appeared to waver. Like Jeremiah during the siege of Jerusalem (Jer 38:2), they pled for unconditional surrender so that at least their lives might be spared (Jdt 7:23–29). With a fiery speech, however, Judith succeeded in strengthening the resolve of her fellow citizens (Jdt 8). Showing the courage to trust in God and using all the means at her disposal as a beautiful and clever woman, she beguiled and slew Holofernes. Thus she was able to defeat the mighty Assyrians and save her people from exile (Jdt 9–12). Her heroic deed showed that Yahweh, "the God of the lowly and helper of the oppressed," in his incomparable power, which does not depend on military might (9:11), is able to rout the self-aggrandizing world power with its full military arsenal (16:3–5).

---

[61] The tradition that the conquest of Jerusalem took place in the eighteenth rather than the nineteenth year of Nebuchadnezzar (as in 2 Kgs 25:8) appears also in Jer 52:28–29 and Dan 4:1 LXX.

[62] This description probably reflects the experience of the Maccabean wars against Antiochus IV Epiphanes. Many details of Nebuchadnezzar's onslaught recall the campaign of the Seleucid general Nicanor in 161 B.C.E. (1 Macc 7; 2 Macc 15). See Zenger, *Buch Judit*, 442–43.

Thus the theologically stylized book of Judith replays the threat of exile that Israel was forced to live through under Nebuchadnezzar and gives it an outcome totally contrary to the actual course of history.[63] In the legendary counterworld that it conjures up, the exile did not take place. It was forestalled by Israel's will to resist and the courageous intervention of a woman who trusted that Yahweh would not stand for the idolatrous attack of the imperialistic world power. The book of Judith is thus a unique protest against the fated life of Israel in exile.

Of course the book cannot deny that Israel had to suffer the experience of exile. It must therefore attempt to limit the significance of the exile for the present and reinterpret it theologically. It does so in three ways.

First, the counterworld created by the book of Judith so telescopes time that the great gulf of the exile almost vanishes. In Jdt 4:3, the reader is surprised to learn that those who stand in terror of Holofernes' advance and undertake defensive measures are the very people who have just returned from exile, reconstituted themselves as a nation, and reconsecrated the defiled temple.[64] The time frame of the narrative has the exile end before it even began. What this strange narrative device means is probably that those who repeatedly face new threats of exile, symbolized by the traumatic events of 587/586, are always identical with those who have been fortunate enough to survive the exile and therefore cannot admit that their work of reconstruction is to be destroyed once more.

Second, the book of Judith reinterprets the place of the exile in the history of Israel. This takes place in the speech of Achior, the leader of the Ammonites, who in the role of pious Gentile explains to Holofernes on the basis of Israel's history where this people gets its power of resistance (Jdt 5:5–21). In this narrative, the exile was not a unique catastrophe interrupting the history of Israel. Israel was forced repeatedly to experience what it meant to live as an alien, whether it was Abraham in Mesopotamia (5:6) or all the people in Egypt (5:10). However, as long as they continued faithfully to worship God, God repeatedly gave to them their homeland in Palestine, where they could settle (5:9, 15–16). The exile was no different. On account of its disobedience, Israel was taken captive, banished to a foreign land, and scattered, but as soon as the exiles returned to Yahweh, they were able to return and possess the

---

[63] The model is provided by the deliverance of Jerusalem from the campaign of Sennacherib in 701, as described in the Isaiah legends in 2 Kgs 18:13–19:37.

[64] The placement of the consecration of the defiled temple before the rebuilding of the temple again establishes a parallel between the events of 520 and the dedication of the temple by Judas Maccabeus in 164 B.C.E.

(uninhabited) land once more (5:18–19). Thus Achior turns the retributive theology of the Deuteronomist and Chronicler on its head, deriving from the exile the positive doctrine that as long as Israel obeys the law of its God it is invincible—that is, it can never again be driven from its land into exile.

Third, the fiery speech of Judith herself, with which she seeks to strengthen her fellow citizens' will to resist, makes a clear theological distinction between the exile of the past and imminent exile. Israel's ancestors, Judith argues, were forced to suffer sword, pillage, and great catastrophe because they had worshiped idols; that exile was a punishment from God that they had to suffer (Jdt 8:18–19). But in the present, she asserts, Israel has overcome idolatry entirely. The present threat of exile therefore cannot be a punishment from God; instead, it is a test (8:21–27) by which Yahweh seeks to determine whether Israel truly trusts in him. Furthermore, capitulation would have incalculable consequences: the Jerusalem temple would be defiled, and Yahweh would call Israel to account for its desecration (8:21). Therefore, Israel could no longer hope for God's mercy, as in the exile past, because Israel would have brought the new exile upon itself through its lack of faith (8:23). Precisely contrary to the pleas of Jeremiah, Judith therefore demands determined resistance to the aggressor, in the hope that Yahweh will not forsake his people who are truly devoted to him (8:20). As a "pious woman" who trusts in God, she is prepared to take an active part in this resistance (8:32–33).

The book of Judith is concerned to correct explicitly Israel's attitude toward its exilic fate. The exile is not—as in the book of Tobit—an inclusive interpretative category for the past, present, and future of Israel. It is not an ineluctable fate to which every devout Jew must submit humbly as God's just punishment in the hope of God's deliverance in the future. As an instantiated reality, the book of Judith restricts the exile totally to Israel's past, long surmounted; in the present it no longer offers any chance for Israel's survival. God is now testing Israel; confronted with the continual threats posed by the powers of the world, Israel must for all time strive to prevent a new exile by stubborn resistance.

This repudiation of the exile,[65] so vehemently espoused by the book of Judith, probably reflects the experience of the Maccabean war of liberation against the Seleucids. In certain groups this experience forged a

---

[65] Cf. the way the praise of ancestors in Sir 49:4–13 passes over the exile in silence: 49:5–6 mention only the destruction of Jerusalem and the temple; the latter is rebuilt by Zerubbabel and Joshua in 49:12. The only mention of deportation refers to the northern kingdom (48:15). Thus the supporters of the conservative restoration at the beginning of the second century clearly did not consider the exile a relevant theme.

new self-awareness, a realization that Israel clearly could hold its own against the superior forces of the great powers. Therefore the book inveighs passionately against the approach of other groups that had come to terms with the Diaspora in which they had made themselves at home. The book of Judith does not, however, celebrate the military revival of Judah under the Maccabees but rather Yahweh's power to save, a power manifested above all in the powerless.

The later legendary stories supplied to fill the lacuna of the exile show clearly how difficult it often was to integrate the exile meaningfully into the history of Yahweh with his people. The exile could be tied only loosely to Israel's history, in part through exemplary stories recounting the fate of individual Jews in exile (Tobit, Sarah), in part through the representation of individual Jews as confidants or opponents of foreign rulers, individuals who could influence the course of world history before which Israel as a whole stood helpless (Daniel, Zerubbabel the "page," Judith).

Quite different views and assessments of the exile were possible. On the one hand, it offered the deported Jews unimaginable opportunities to rise in the world. On the other, it plunged them into terrible dangers. The exile saw not only the defense of the Jewish faith against the temptations of foreign religions and the totalitarian claims of foreign rulers but also an opportunity for mission and a chance to demonstrate God's universal sovereignty. Two views could not be more opposite than those of Tobit and Judith: the former enlarges the exile to become a comprehensive interpretative category; the latter denies the exile as a determinative historical reality and a possibility for life in the future.

I.2.5 INTEGRATION OF THE EXILE INTO
APOCALYPTIC CONCEPTIONS OF HISTORY

Hultgård, Anders. "Das Judentum in der hellenistischen-römischen Zeit und die iranische Religion: Ein religionsgeschichtliches Problem," *ANRW* 2.19.1:512–19. **Koch,** Klaus. *Daniel* (BK 22/1–2; Neukirchen-Vluyn: Neukirchener Verlag, 1986, 1994). **Kratz,** Reinhard Gregor. *Translatio imperii: Untersuchungen zu den aramäischen Danielerzählungen und ihrem theologiegeschichtlichen Umfeld* (WMANT 63; Neukirchen-Vluyn: Neukirchener Verlag, 1991). **Uhlig,** Siegbert. *Das Äthiopische Henochbuch* (JSHRZ 5/6; Gütersloh: Mohn, 1984).

In contrast to this rather free and diverse suppletory material, apocalyptic historical speculation sets the period of the exile firmly within a comprehensive historical schema, making it an integral interpretative category. It does so not in narrative but in the form of a visionary interpretation of history.

The central role the exile could play in the apocalyptic conception of history is strikingly clear in chapter 9 of the Hebrew book of Daniel. In the first year of Darius I (521 B.C.E.), Daniel was searching the scriptures to learn the meaning of the seventy years foretold by Jeremiah as the duration of the Babylonian exile (Dan 9:2; cf. Jer 25:11–12; 29:10). The angel Gabriel instructs him that the number signifies weeks of years (Dan 9:24). But this means that the end of the Babylonian exile, which Daniel had experienced or was just experiencing,[66] represented just a preliminary realization of God's word to Jeremiah. The first seven weeks of years (587–49 = 538) had just passed. Jerusalem would be rebuilt in part (9:25)—characteristically, nothing is said of the rebuilding of the temple—but there still remained a "troubled time," since the sins of Israel and Jerusalem were far from atoned (9:24). Only after a long interim of sixty-two weeks of years would the final seven-year period dawn.[67] At its end, following the murder of a priest, desecration of the temple, and terrible chaos, the word of God to Jeremiah would finally be fulfilled with the annihilation of the desolator and the dawning of eternal salvation (9:26–27).

The instruction from heaven that Daniel receives as he studies the scriptures expands the temporal scale of the exile enormously, from seventy to 490 years. The entire era beginning with the days of Jeremiah, including the period we call postexilic, down to the present day of the author, is understood as a continuous period of exilic affliction. On the one hand, this interpretation provides a theological explanation for the horrors of religious persecution under Antiochus IV: they are the culmination of the sufferings Israel has had to accept throughout its long life in exile. On the other, it provides a comforting assurance that these afflictions must soon come to an end. If God gave Jeremiah the knowledge that the period of the exile was clearly defined, then the history of Israel's sufferings must be drawing near its end—after three and a half years, according to the revealed calculation (cf. Dan 8:14; 12:11–12). Surely there must follow the great dawning of the age of salvation of which Jeremiah and the other prophets had already spoken. In Dan 9,

---

[66] Dan 9:25 telescopes the events of 539 and 520.

[67] The symbolic periodization cannot be harmonized with our chronology. From the end of the exile in 538 to the death of Onias III in 170, to which 9:26 probably alludes, is 368 years, not 434 (62 × 7). For the final week of years, however, there are reference points: the desecration of the temple under Antiochus IV actually took place in 167 after approximately half a week of years.

the apocalyptic revelation of the imminent end of history is nothing other than an interpretation of the exilic period.

Of course, no one can prove that the apocalyptic conception of an eschaton when all prior history would come to an end and an entirely new age of salvation would dawn sprang directly from reflection on the exilic fate of Israel.[68] But the many substantive and structural points of contact between the understanding of the exile as a period of divine judgment, long-lasting but limited by God's faithfulness, and this new conception of history meant that the latter could be supported, interpreted, and even calculated on the basis of the exile. In any case, it is no accident that this darkest period in the history of Israel could not be integrated fully until there was a historical schema based on the termination of a history gone massively awry.

In early apocalyptic literature, we may identify two different ways of incorporating the exile into the apocalyptic schema of history. The first and more traditional—comparable to Dan 9—is found in Ethiopic *Enoch*.

In the Animal Apocalypse (*1 En.* 85–90), the antediluvian figure of Enoch has a vision of all human history, from the universal primal age (85:3–89:9) through the particular history of Israel (89:10–90:19) to the universal end of history (90:20–39). For the preexilic period (85:3–89:56), the presentation by and large follows the historical tradition of the Bible in Genesis–2 Kings. The long period of the exile, however, is treated freely: it extends to the author's day in the period of the Maccabean wars (89:57–90:19) and does not end until the last judgment and the coming of the messianic kingdom (90:20–39). The rebuilding of the temple by the returnees in 520 is mentioned in passing (89:72–73), but—contrary to the view of the Chronicler—it did not signal a turning point, since its cult remained defiled. Not until the messianic kingdom will God, who forsook his sanctuary long before the deportations (89:56), build a new temple and thus do away with the defiled temple (90:28–29).

The central interpretative role played by the exile in the Animal Apocalypse is already clear in the history of the preexilic period: even then the Israelites were exposed for long periods to the afflictions of life in exile, having to live as sheep among wolves. This was the experience of the patriarchs (*1 En.* 89:13ff.) and the Israelites in Egypt (89:21ff.). Israel was forced to defend itself constantly with God's help against overwhelming foes. Only for brief periods was it successful: under Moses (89:21ff.), Saul (89:43ff.), and David (89:48), when it was open to the visions of God (89:28, 41). Finally, however, Israel's blindness and

---

[68] In what is probably the earliest apocalyptic schema of history, *1 En.* 6–11, the concept of an eschaton derives from the story of the flood (cf. Gen 6:13).

estrangement from the temple caused God to forsake his sanctuary and hand Israel over permanently to the wild beasts (89:56).

In the Animal Apocalypse, the account of the ensuing exilic period is almost as long as that of Israel's preexilic history. This is all the more astonishing because the dearth of biblical material for this period means that there are hardly any specifics to record. Only with the beginning of the second century does the account become more detailed once again (1 En. 90:6ff.).

The first book of *Enoch* interprets the exile as God's rejection of Israel and the surrender of Israel to ongoing foreign rule: the emphasis is not on the loss of the land but on the hegemony of foreign rulers. In this schema, only the intercession of Enoch is able to limit the number of foreign rulers ("shepherds") to seventy (1 En. 89:57–59).[69]

Of course, this number is entirely schematic and probably derives once more from the seventy years of exile in Jeremiah's prophecy (25:11–12; 29:10). The text, however, makes some attempt to give the visionary construction of history a certain basis in the actual course of history by dividing the seventy shepherds into twenty-three representing Assyrian and Babylonian rule, twelve Persian, twenty-three Ptolemaic, and twelve Seleucid.[70] This division seeks to uncover a regularity in the history of the exilic period that lends plausibility to the claim that it will end soon.

God commissioned the seventy shepherds to punish Israel. In this respect, 1 *Enoch* understands the exile as God's punishment for Israel's apostasy. But the foreign rulers did not obey God's instructions; instead, they decimated and oppressed Israel far beyond what God had prescribed (1 En. 89:69, 74; 90:2, 4, 8, 11). Therefore, the archangel Michael was commissioned to keep a precise tally of their arbitrary acts throughout the entire period (89:62–63), for which they would be held responsible at the last judgment (90:17, 22, 25). In 1 *Enoch,* therefore, the exile is also a long period of suffering unjustly imposed on Israel by murderous foreign rulers. Despite God's patient delay (89:71, 79), this suffering must one day be avenged in a great judgment on Israel's oppressors. In the view of the book of *Enoch,* this is just what begins to happen in the Maccabean war of liberation.

A different—and less conventional—way of incorporating the exile into an apocalyptic schema of history is found in the Aramaic book of Daniel (Dan 2–7). In contrast to the book of *Enoch,* this account largely

---

[69] On shepherds symbolizing foreign rulers who exercise hegemony over Israel, see Zech 11:4–16.

[70] See 1 *En.* 89:72; 90:1, 5, 17; in 90:1, the number "thirty-seven" in the manuscripts should be emended to "thirty-five."

ignores the preexilic history of Israel. The history that matters and is subject to visionary interpretation does not even begin until the time of the Babylonian exile.

In Nebuchadnezzar's second year (i.e., at the very beginning of his reign; Dan 2:2), the Babylonian king had a dream. He saw a huge statue made of various materials that was broken into pieces by a stone (2:31–35). In Daniel's interpretation of the dream, this statue represents the system of the four ancient Near Eastern kingdoms, a system that would be destroyed and replaced by the kingdom following the end of the fourth (2:36–45). The order and decreasing value of the materials symbolizes the sequence and degradation in quality of these kingdoms. The head of gold is identified explicitly with the Babylonian kingdom of Nebuchadnezzar, who had been given his kingship by God (2:37–38). In the setting of the book of Daniel, the parts of the statue made of silver, bronze, and iron mixed with clay can be identified clearly with the Median, Persian, and Greek Empires. With the latter, political hegemony has brought violence and instability on such a scale that God—without any human help as in the book of *Enoch*—determines to destroy the whole system of earthly empires and replace it with the kingdom of God (2:24, 44–45).

The vision of Daniel that corresponds to the dream of Nebuchadnezzar is dated in the first year of Belshazzar (Dan 7:1); the book of Daniel represents him as the last Babylonian king, who died at an early age (Dan 5). The apocalyptic texts framing the Aramaic book of Daniel are clearly set deliberately at the beginning and end of the Babylonian exile.

In his vision, Daniel sees four great beasts rising from the raging sea, once again representing the four empires of the ancient Near East. The decay of their dominion is represented as increasing bestiality. The Babylonian and Median Empires still had some human features (Dan 7:4–5); the Greek Empire simply behaves like a voracious beast that tramples everything before it (7:7*).[71] Therefore, in Daniel's vision, God will sit in judgment over these kingdoms, destroy them (7:9–12), and in their place establish the kingdom of God. The description of God's kingdom as the investment of a "human being" (son of man) with divine dominion is probably meant to suggest its more humane character in contrast to that of the beasts (7:13–14). In the interpretation given to Daniel by the heavenly council, the community of the faithful, whose sufferings have made them immune to the brutal self-aggrandizement of political power, share in the dominion of God (7:27).

---

71 In 7:7bβ–8, the description of the fourth beast has been expanded secondarily to describe Antiochus IV.

Both the notion of four successive kingdoms or empires and that of four increasingly corrupt ages is probably of Iranian origin; the author of the Aramaic book of Daniel most likely borrowed it from intermediary Greek sources.[72] Originally neither notion had anything to do with the exile, and the association with the exilic period is forced.

The author of the Aramaic book of Daniel took into account the particular history of Israel, which was forced into exile under Babylonian rule, by substituting the Babylonians for the Assyrians at the beginning of the borrowed four-kingdom schema.[73]

The schema of four ages was harder to adapt. Although it comported well with the apocalyptic model of history rushing toward its end, it conflicted markedly with the usual assessment of the exilic period. In what sense, the author of the Aramaic book of Daniel was forced to ask, could the grievous period of the Babylonian exile have been a "golden age," as required by this schema?

The author of the Aramaic book of Daniel sought to find a more positive assessment for the exilic period by relying on Jer 27:6–7 and interpreting the rule of Nebuchadnezzar as have been legitimized explicitly by Yahweh. This more favorable appraisal of Babylonian rule allowed him to integrate the relatively optimistic Daniel legends set at the courts of Babylonia and Persia into his apocalyptic conception of history. Nothing could have been further from his mind, however, than using the borrowed four-ages schema to turn the exile into an age of salvation pure and simple.[74] Instead, he used the Babylonian court to exemplify the profound dangers of political power, which always tends to godless absolutism and totalitarianism. In his view, the Babylonian kingdom could stand only so long as the Babylonian kings submitted to the sovereign kingship of God (Dan 5:18–22). In addition, the Babylonian exile repeatedly demanded of faithful Jews courageous resistance and an intrepid readiness to confess their faith even if their confession led to martyrdom, as illustrated by the stories in Dan 3 and 6. In this sense, he did not look on the Babylonian exile as a "golden age," as in the four-ages schema.[75]

The period of Babylonian and Median rule differed from the later empires in just one way: in this earlier period the kingship of God, toward which the entire history of the world empires was moving (Dan 2:44; 7:12–13), could on occasion be realized symbolically (3:31–33

---

[72] Hultgård, "Judentum," 524–25; Koch, *Daniel*, 126ff.; Kratz, *Translatio*, 198ff.

[73] This change made the schema historically inaccurate, since the Median Empire did indeed succeed the Assyrian Empire, but alongside the Babylonian.

[74] Contra Kratz, *Translatio*, 268–69.

[75] Note also the ambivalent characterization of the Babylonian Empire in Dan 7:4.

[4:1–3]; 4:31–32 [34–35]; 6:27–28 [26–27]). Thus the Babylonian exile, which begins the sequence of world empires, comes to play a positive role—quite unlike its role in 1 Enoch—by pointing toward the awaited age of salvation.

Taking this perspective into account, we can understand how the apocalyptic schemas depicting the decline and fall of the world empires and the irruption of God's kingdom came to be placed at the beginning and end of the Babylonian period. Despite all the bitter afflictions that Israel had to suffer in exile under Babylonian rule, the rise of the Babylonian Empire proved that the God of Israel governed the history of the world powers. The fall of the Babylonian Empire and the new beginning for Israel—however limited—after the Babylonian exile concealed a potential for hope: one day all earthly empires must perish and yield to the sovereign rule of Yahweh.

The incorporation of the exilic period into the apocalyptic conception of history could take diverse forms, now extending the exile to the eschaton and assessing it entirely negatively (Dan 9; 1 Enoch), now limiting it to the period of Babylonian and Median rule and judging it conditionally positive (Dan 2–7). It is still remarkable that the exilic period acquired such an important role. The substantive and structural parallels have been mentioned already. With the exile, Israel had been forced to suffer an abrupt end to its political history; it nevertheless survived. It is probably no accident that in Israel the apocalyptic concept of the end of world history and the beginning of a new age could come to appear so plausible.

II. THE HISTORY OF THE EXILIC ERA

Since the exilic era constitutes a gaping hole in the historical narrative of the Bible, historical reconstruction of this era faces almost insurmountable difficulties. Like the premonarchic period and the late Persian period (fourth century), the exilic period, although set in the bright light of ancient Near Eastern history, remains historically obscure. Since there are very few Israelite sources, the only recourse is to try to cast some light on this darkness from the history of the surrounding empires under whose dominion Israel came in this period.

II.1. THE NEO-BABYLONIAN EMPIRE

Albertz, Rainer. "Die Exilszeit als Ernstfall für eine historische Rekonstruktion ohne biblische Texte: die neubabylonischen Königsinschriften als 'Primärquelle,'" in *Leading Captivity Captive: "The Exile" As History and Ideology* (ed. L. L. Grabbe; JSOTSup 278; Sheffield: Sheffield Academic Press, 1998), 22–39. **Beaulieu,** Paul-Alain. *The Reign of Nabonidus, King of Babylon, 556–539 B.C.* (YNER 10; New Haven: Yale University Press, 1989). **Borger,** Riekele. *Die Inschriften Asarhaddons Königs von Assyrien* (AfOB 9; Graz: Weidner, 1956). **Burstein,** Stanley Mayer. *The Babyloniaca of Berossos* (SANE 1/5; Malibu: Undena, 1978). **Dandamaev,** Muhammad A. "Neo-Babylonian Society and Economy," *CAH*² 3/2:252–75. **Dandamaev.** *Slavery in Babylonia from Nabopolassar to Alexander the Great (626–331 B.C.)* (trans. V. A. Powell; DeKalb: Northern Illinois University Press, 1984). **Edel,** Elmar. "Amasis und Nebukadnezar II.," *GM* 29 (1978): 13–20. **Frame,** Grant. *Babylonia 689–627 B.C.: A Political History* (Istanbul: Nederlands Historisch-Archaeologisch Instituut te Istanbul, 1992). **Gerardi,** Pamela. "Declaring War in Mesopotamia," *AfO* 33 (1986): 30–38. **Grayson,** Albert Kirk. *Assyrian and Babylonian Chronicles* (TCS 5; Locust Valley: Augustin, 1975). **Grayson.** *Babylonian Historical-Literary Texts* (TSTS 3; Toronto: University of Toronto Press, 1975). **Hübner,** Ulrich. *Die Ammoniter: Untersuchungen zur Geschichte, Kultur und Religion eines transjordanischen Volkes im 1. Jahrtausend v.Chr.* (ADPV 16; Wiesbaden: Harrassowitz, 1992). **Hunger,** Hermann, and Stephen A. Kaufman. "A New

Akkadian Prophecy Text," *JAOS* 95 (1975): 371–75. **James,** T. H. G. "Egypt: The Twenty-Fifth and Twenty-Sixth Dynasties," *CAH*² 2/2:677–747. **Joannès,** Francis. "Trois textes de *ṣurru* á l'époque Néo-Babylonienne," *RA* 81 (1987): 147–58. **Katzenstein,** H. Jacob. *The History of Tyre: From the Beginning of the Second Millennium B.C.E. until the Fall of the Neo-Babylonian Empire in 538 B.C.E.* (Jerusalem: Schocken Institute, 1973). **Lambert,** W. G. "Nebuchadnezzar King of Justice," *Iraq* 27 (1965): 1–11. **Leahy,** Anthony. "The Earliest Dated Monument of Amasis and the End of the Reign of Apries," *JEA* 74 (1988): 183–99. **Röllig,** Wolfgang. "Erwägungen zu den neuen Stelen Nabonids," *ZA* 56 (1964): 218–60. **Sack,** Ronald Herbert. "Nebuchadnezzar and Nabonidus in Folklore and History," *Mes* 17 (1982): 67–131. **Sack.** *Neriglissar, King of Babylon* (AOAT 236; Neukirchen-Vluyn: Neukirchener Verlag, 1994). **Schaudig,** Hanspeter. *Die Inschriften Nabonids von Babylon und Kyros des Großen samt den in ihrem Umfeld entstandenen Tendenzschriften: Textausgabe und Grammatik* (AOAT 256; Münster: Ugarit-Verlag, 2001). **Soden,** Wolfram von. "Kyros und Nabonid: Propaganda und Gegenpropaganda," in idem, *Aus Sprache, Geschichte und Religion Babyloniens: Gesammelte Aufsätze* (ed. L. Cagni and H.-P. Müller; Naples: Istituto Universitario Orientale, Dipartimento di Studi Asiatici, 1989), 285–92. **Unger,** Eckhard. *Babylon: Die heilige Stadt nach der Beschreibung der Babylonier* (Berlin: de Gruyter, 1931, repr., 1970). **Von Voigtlander,** Elizabeth Nation. "A Survey of Neo-Babylonian History" (Ph.D. diss., University of Michigan, 1963). **Weidner,** Ernst. "Hochverrat gegen Nebukadnezar II: Ein Grosswürdenträger vor dem Königsgericht," *AfO* 17 (1954/55): 1–9. **Wiseman,** Donald J. "Babylonia 605–539 B.C.," *CAH*² 3/2:229–51. **Wiseman.** *Nebuchadrezzar and Babylon* (SchLBA 1983; Oxford: Oxford University Press, 1985).

The history of the Neo-Babylonian Empire extends from 626 to 539 B.C.E. This span of just eighty-eight years, so momentous for Israel, covers the reigns of six Babylonian kings, varying greatly in length.

626–605 B.C.E.	Nabopolassar	Nabû-apla-uṣur
605–562	Nebuchadnezzar	Nabû-kudurrī-uṣur
562–560	Awīl/Amēl-Marduk	Bible: Evil-merodach
560–556	Neriglissar	Nergal-šarra-uṣur
556	Lâbâši-Marduk	Lā-abâši-Marduk
556–539	Nabonidus	Nabû-na'id

II.1.1. Sources

Compared to the sources for the Neo-Assyrian Empire, the sources for reconstructing the political history of the Neo-Babylonian Empire are significantly scantier and inferior. This is true in part because no official Babylonian archives comparable to the Assyrian archives have been found. In addition, unlike the Assyrian kings, the Babylonian kings generally did not celebrate their military and political triumphs in their inscriptions but instead used such inscriptions almost exclusively to portray themselves as tireless builders and patrons of the temples. What we know of their political and military accomplishments comes almost entirely from the Babylonian chronicles, which were probably drafted in the early Persian period even though they survive only in later Seleucid copies.[1] Unfortunately, these chronicles are fragmentary, with gaps for the years 594–558, 556, 552–550, and 544–540, so that we have little concrete information about the last three-quarters of Nebuchadnezzar's forty-three-year reign, the brief reigns of Amēl-Marduk and Lābâši-Marduk, and the important years of Nabonidus. These gaps are filled only in part by scattered information from Babylonian literary texts[2] and sporadic material from Berossus, Josephus, and other ancient historians.[3] Numerous Neo-Babylonian commercial and legal documents allow us to date the accession of new kings to month and day but otherwise contribute little to political history. Their study as a source for a comprehensive reconstruction of the social history of the Neo-Babylonian Empire is just beginning.[4]

II.1.2. The Rise of the Neo-Babylonian Empire

The rise of the Neo-Babylonian Empire toward the end of the seventh century B.C.E. was anything but a foregone conclusion.[5] Babylonia maintained its preeminence in the intellectual and religious sphere, continuing to feed on the golden ages of Sumer and the Old Babylonian Empire at the end of the third millennium and in the first half of the second millennium. In the first half of the first millennium, however, Babylonia experienced a long period of political decline. The multiplicity of rival population groups long prevented the development of a stable and powerful central government. First there was the urban group of "Akkadians," descendants of the indigenous population or of groups that had arrived during the third and second millennia (Akkadians, Sumerians, Amorites,

---

[1] Grayson, *Chronicles*, 69–114.

[2] Grayson, *Historical-Literary Texts*, 24–37, 79–97; Unger, *Babylon*; Hunger and Kaufman, "New Akkadian Prophecy Text"; the text "Nebuchadnezzar King of Justice" published by Lambert has been ascribed more recently to Nabonidus: see von Soden, "Kyros," 287.

[3] Burstein, *Babyloniaca*, 26–28; Josephus, *Ag. Ap.* 1.128–160; *Ant.* 10.186–281; see Sack, "Nebuchadnezzar."

[4] See the summary in Dandamaev, "Neo-Babylonian Society."

[5] For further discussion, see Frame, *Babylonia*.

Kassites); they lived in the large cities and the famous cultic centers, primarily in the northwest (Babylon, Borsippa, Cuth, Dilbat, Sippar). They dominated the intellectual and economic life of Babylonia but politically promoted the divergent interests of their own cities. The second element comprised tribal groups of Chaldeans (originally Arameans) who had penetrated as far as Babylonia by the end of the second millennium, settling in the southern and western regions (first mentioned in 878). They comprised five rival tribes (e.g., Bīt Amukāni, Bīt Yakīn), which defended their autonomy over against the cities. They represented a major military presence in the land; during the eighth and seventh centuries, they led the resistance to the Assyrian occupation forces. Finally, there were the Arameans living along the eastern border, many of whom were still nomads; they were organized into a large number of tribes (e.g., Gambūlu, Puqūdu) and were almost beyond political control. There were also a great many foreigners: Elamites, Egyptians, Assyrians, and Arabs.

The divergent interests of the rival groups made it substantially easier for the Assyrians to subjugate Babylonia after 730 B.C.E. and incorporate it into the Neo-Assyrian Empire. The Assyrian kings were masters at playing the various interest groups against each other; to support their rule they relied on the urban population, to whose cities they granted generous privileges (*kiddinūtu*). For this very reason, however, the Assyrians found the Babylonians hard to govern, despite their outstanding military and civilian organization. Babylonia remained a hotbed of unrest. The first great series of rebellions followed the death of Sargon II in 705; the Chaldean Marduk-apla-iddin[6] of the tribe Bīt Yakīn repeatedly played a leading role, not hesitating to summon the Elamites as allies against the Assyrians. This episode ended in total disaster, the absolute nadir of Babylonian history. On the ninth of Kislev in 689, Sennacherib took Babylon after a fifteen-month siege, leveled the city including its temples, scattered or deported its population, inundated the area with water from the Euphrates, and destroyed the statue of Marduk. So ruthless an onslaught against the center of Babylonian civilization, which the Assyrians admired, so great a sacrilege against the religion to which many Assyrians themselves adhered is unparalleled in the history of Mesopotamia.[7] It

---

[6] The Merodach-baladan of the Bible, who was also in touch with the rebellious Hezekiah of Judah (2 Kgs 20:12–19).

[7] Cf. Esarhaddon's graphic account in his Babylon inscriptions (Borger, "Inschriften," 12–15); he ascribes the destruction to the wrath of Enlil and Marduk without mentioning the name of Sennacherib. As one of the reasons for destroying Esagila, the temple of Marduk, he cites the use of the temple treasure to pay the Elamites, who supported the revolt of Marduk-apla-iddin.

can be explained only as Sennacherib's response to a personal affront: the revolt had cost the life of his eldest son. He therefore sought relentlessly to eliminate once for all the political resistance of Babylonia by destroying its cultural and religious identity.[8] But the political success of Sennacherib's act of vengeance was brief. Over the longer term, the excesses of his response provoked an anti-Assyrian resistance movement that began to unite the various ethnic groups of Babylonia.[9] Later, when Neo-Babylonian kings traced the fall of the Assyrian Empire to Sennacherib's destruction of Babylon, this nadir of Babylonian history marked for them the decisive turning point that led to a new, undreamt-of political rise.

Sennacherib's inflexible policy of suppressing Babylonia did not achieve lasting consensus even in Assyria. Soon after the violent death of his father, Esarhaddon (681–669) introduced a policy of cautious reconciliation, beginning to rebuild and resettle Babylon, which had been deserted for a decade. He also returned the statue of Marduk—or more likely sent a new statue—to Babylon, although allowing only an assyrianized cult in the rebuilt temple of Esagila. With regard to succession to the throne, he decreed that his son Ashurbanipal should govern the empire and his elder brother Shamash-shuma-ukin function as king of Babylon; even this wise decision did not create lasting peace, even though when Shamash-shuma-ukin came to the throne in 668 he restored the Babylonian form of the Marduk cult. As early as 651–648, a violent new revolt of the Babylonians against Assyria broke out, led by Shamash-shuma-ukin. This revolt was due only apparently to rivalry between two brothers; its real driving force was a broad coalition of Chaldeans, Arameans, and Akkadians who joined forces for the first time on behalf of Babylonian independence. This second great Babylonian revolt also failed, because the Babylonians were still insufficiently united and the military forces that Ashurbanipal raised to defeat it were too powerful. In the year 650, Babylon was again besieged and in 648 reconquered. But this debilitating civil war led to the collapse of the Assyrian Empire, and the experience of fighting together against Assyria forged a new sense of Babylonian identity among the various ethnic groups, without which the growth of the Neo-Babylonian Empire would not have been possible.

---

8 Babylonia, too, suffered substantial losses at the hands of the Assyrians. If we can trust the Babylonian records, Tiglath-pileser III, Sargon II, and Sennacherib deported half a million people from Babylonia, of whom roughly half were Chaldeans (Frame, *Babylonia*, 51).

9 The hatred of Sennacherib was so great that the Babylonian Chronicle passes over his eight-year reign in Babylon as kingless (Grayson, *Assyrian and Babylonian Chronicles*, 81: Chronicle 1, 3.28).

It is therefore not by chance that the rise of the Neo-Babylonian Empire began as a revolt against Assyria. This movement was led by members of an ethnic group that, although originally marginal to Babylonian society, had earned its spurs in earlier revolts: the Chaldeans.

After the death of Ashurbanipal and his Babylonian governor in 630, conditions were ripe. Into the power vacuum occasioned by the usual succession conflicts among the sons of Ashurbanipal ambitiously stepped Nabopolassar (Nabû-apla-uṣur, "May Nabu protect the son"), a Chaldean from the Sea Land. He instigated uprisings in the almost inaccessible delta region of the Euphrates and Tigris and involved the Assyrian occupation forces in costly skirmishes, as many previous revolts had begun. Meanwhile, the new sense of Babylonian identity led the citizens of Babylon, who had just fought a successful campaign of liberation against the occupying Assyrian forces, to offer Nabopolassar the kingship, thus providing him with an important power base that raised morale and provided material support. Nabopolassar himself later described his rise to the kingship by saying that, though he had been an inconsequential "son of a nobody" whom Marduk would not have noticed among the people, Marduk had nevertheless destined him for great things.[10] But "king of Babylon" was still little but a title. It took years of struggle to drive the Assyrian army from Babylonia, years about which we have minimal information. Not until 616 was Nabopolassar able to go over to attacking Assyrian territory. He defeated the Assyrian army at Qablinu on the middle Euphrates but was forced to retreat by the Egyptian troops who had come to the aid of the Assyrians.[11] Whether Nabopolassar would ultimately have been able to win the defensive battle if he had not unexpectedly received help from the Medes is an open question. In any case, it was the Medes who took the cities of Tarbisu and Ashur. Nabopolassar arrived too late to participate but used the opportunity to sign a treaty of nonaggression and mutual assistance with Cyaxares, the Median king, reported by Berossus to have been sealed by a political marriage.[12] Thus the conquest of the Assyrian capital of Nineveh in 612 was a shared victory of the Median-Babylonian coalition.

One may well wonder how the revolt against Assyrian hegemony over Babylon could turn so easily into destruction of the Assyrian power centers. The Assyrians were "brothers," bound to the Babylonians by a long history. In his inscriptions, Nabopolassar ascribes the destruction of

---

10 VAB 4:66–67: Nabopolassar 4, 4.10–12.
11 Grayson, *Assyrian and Babylonian Chronicles*, 91: Chronicle 3.1–11.
12 Burstein, *Babyloniaca*, 26.

Assyria to a command of the gods Marduk and Nabu.[13] In one, he claims more specifically that the harsh yoke of the Assyrians had injured the Babylonians.[14] More revealing is a text containing a stylized declaration of war, probably composed to justify Babylonian participation in the destruction of Nineveh.[15] Here Nabopolassar—though not named in the text—accuses the Assyrian king of having become an enemy of Babylonia, of plundering its wealth, making a spectacle of the temple treasure of Babylon, and taking it off to Nineveh. This language refers to the rigid exploitation policies of the Assyrians, especially the sacrilege of Sennacherib in desecrating Esagila, the temple of Marduk in Babylon. Therefore, Nabopolassar continues, Marduk has chosen him from the Sea Land to rule over lands and their people, "to avenge the land of Akkad" (*ana turri māt URI^KI*).[16] In other words, it was Sennacherib's total destruction of Babylon in 689 that gave Nabopolassar divine legitimation for paying Nineveh back with its own coin. Some sixty years later the basalt stela of Nabonidus, the last Babylonian king, continues to speak of Sennacherib's atrocities, using a similar theological argument to justify the destruction of Assyrian cities and sanctuaries as divinely willed "revenge for Babylon."[17] Here we are clearly dealing with a real "foundation myth" of the Neo-Babylonian Empire.[18] The mighty Assyrian Empire must perish because Sennacherib's total destruction of Babylon and removal of the statue of Marduk had provoked the wrath of the god that now fell upon it. In this theology, Assyria's fall and Babylon's rise at the expense of Assyria were simply divine justice compensating Babylon for the shame it had so long endured.

The total collapse of Assyria nevertheless took several years. After the fall of their central power base, the Assyrians tried to establish a rump state in Haran, in northern Syria. They were actively supported by the Egyptians, who wanted to maintain an Assyrian buffer state separating

---

13 VAB 4:60–61, 66–67: Nabopolassar 1, 1.23–41; 3, 2.1–4.

14 VAB 4:68–69: Nabopolassar 4, 17–18.

15 Gerardi, "Declaring War," 34–37: BM 55467.

16 Gerardi, "Declaring War," 35: obv. 10–12. Cf. the so-called "Nabopolassar Epic" in Grayson, *Babylonian Historical-Literary Texts*, 82–85, which probably demonstrates that the desire to avenge Babylon extended even to the Neo-Babylonian coronation ritual: cf. the unfortunately somewhat damaged line 3.21 [*x* (*x*)] *x gi-mil* KUR URI.KI EN [...], where the parallel BM 55467, obv. 12, suggests reading the damaged signs as *imp. târu* D.

17 VAB 4:270–75: Nabopolassar 8, 1.1'–2.41', esp. 2.11–12': *ātir gimillu bābili*^KI (ANET, 309).

18 Beaulieu, *Reign*, 115. The Neo-Babylonians were only borrowing an expression used earlier by the Assyrian king Esarhaddon—indirectly confirming Sennacherib's unjust treatment of Babylon—for the rebuilding of the city that he initiated in 678 (Borger, *Inschriften*, 18, recension A, lines 47–48).

them from Media and Babylonia; this arrangement would allow them to take over the Assyrian interests in Phoenicia and Palestine. From 612 to 605, the battle wavered back and forth. In the year 610, Median and Babylonian forces destroyed Haran and its temple of Sin.[19] For several years, the crown prince Nebuchadnezzar had shared military leadership and civil rule with his father Nabopolassar; in 605, he finally succeeded in defeating the Egyptian troops decisively at the battle of Carchemish, driving them from the region as far as Hamath. Thus the Neo-Assyrian Empire passed out of existence, and a new constellation of power was established in the Near East. The Babylonians left the heartland of Assyria to the Medes, along with its possessions in northern Syria, including Haran; they themselves laid claim to the western and southwestern territories of the Assyrian Empire in Cilicia, southern Syria, Phoenicia, and Palestine.

II.1.3. THE GOLDEN AGE OF NEBUCHADNEZZAR

In this midst of his campaign, Nebuchadnezzar was surprised by the news of his father's death. In forced marches he returned to Babylon to assert and, if possible, establish his claim to the Babylonian throne. Babylonia did not have a purely dynastic line of succession. As the coronation ritual for Nabopolassar shows, the kingship was bestowed by the nobility (*rubû ša māti*). The king enjoyed a divine commission that the members of the court had only to confirm by acclamation.[20] Consensus was needed among the leaders of the various ethic groups to elect a successor. For the first succession of the Neo-Babylonian Empire, clearly this consensus was achieved without any difficulties. If we can trust Berossus, the leaders of the Chaldean tribes had largely taken control[21] when Nebuchadnezzar arrived in Babylon three weeks after his father's death.

In Nebuchadnezzar II (Nabû-kudurrī-uṣur, "Nabu, protect my offspring"), the Babylonian throne passed to the most energetic of the Neo-Babylonian kings. During his forty-three-year reign (605–562 B.C.E.), he was to lead the new empire to its greatest heights of power and culture. The policies of the empire as a great power still reflected the anti-Assyrian animus that had united the diverse ethnic groups and laid the groundwork for the Babylonian Empire, even though Nebuchadnezzar employed the instrumentalities put in place by the effective Assyrian

---

[19] For more on the following events, see Wiseman, *Nebuchadnezzar*, 12ff.
[20] Grayson, *Babylonian Historical-Literary Texts*, 85: Nabopolassar Epic 3, 3–13, 14–17.
[21] Burstein, *Babyloniaca*, 28.

civil and military administration. It was the goal of his foreign policy to inherit the Neo-Assyrian Empire. Since the road to the east and north was effectively blocked by the Medes, he had to subjugate the former Assyrian possessions to the west and southwest. This goal required the total elimination of Egyptian influence in Palestine, Phoenicia, and Syria, which had been the last ally of Assyria. His domestic goal was to build magnificent cities and temples in the Babylonian heartland by exploiting to the full the economic goods and labor forces of the subject territories. Nebuchadnezzar's breathtaking building program enabled the cities of Babylonia, and especially Babylon, his "first love," to rise in new glory. The nature of his reign is probably best explained by a drive to transform the terrible humiliation of the land under Assyrian rule into his greatest triumph.

All of Nebuchadnezzar's individual actions that we know of serve these two overarching goals. In 605 and then in the following years, he regularly campaigned in Hatti-land (Syria-Phoenicia-Palestine) to demonstrate his ascendancy in this region, which he reinforced by the occasional conquest of cities that were threatening to become Egyptian outposts, such as Ashkelon in 604 and another fortified city, possibly Sidon, in 603. The rulers of most of the lands of the region submitted to Babylonian rule without resistance and voluntarily sent tribute to Nebuchadnezzar, among them Jehoiakim of Judah (2 Kgs 24:1). In 601, a pitched battle with Pharaoh Neco II near the Egyptian border ended indecisively and cost Nebuchadnezzar heavy losses, but this battle clearly defined the two spheres of influence.

When Jehoiakim saw this stalemate, he concluded that, with the Egyptians protecting his rear, he could revoke his vassal treaty with Nebuchadnezzar. This action provoked the latter's fierce retribution. From the Babylonian perspective, it looked as though Egypt could capitalize on the insubordination of tiny Judah to gain a foothold in Palestine, outside its own borders. After rebuilding his forces, in 598/597 Nebuchadnezzar personally led a punitive expedition aimed specifically at Jerusalem. From the Babylonian perspective, it was necessary to secure the former Assyrian territories against any possible Egyptian designs on their southwest flank. This was so important that the Babylonian Chronicle mentions it together with its date as the only event of Nebuchadnezzar's eleventh year.[22] The primary target was Egypt; the tiny rebel state of Judah was of secondary concern but had to be made a terrible example. After the death of his father Jehoiakim, Jehoiachin surrendered to save the city from destruction;

---

22 Grayson, *Assyrian and Babylonian Chronicles:* Chronicle 5, rev. 11–13; cited on p. 78 below.

he was taken hostage as a punishment and replaced with Zedekiah, who promised to represent Babylonian interests in the border zone. This was the crucial outcome from the perspective of foreign policy. The payment of a large tribute served the domestic goal of acquiring resources. The Babylonian Chronicle does not even mention the deportation of part of the population, which had such crucial significance for Judah. In the Babylonian view, it was a secondary measure, increasing security as well as strengthening the economy of the Babylonian heartland.

After securing his southwest flank, Nebuchadnezzar turned in the following years to the northwest and southeast boundaries of his kingdom. In 595 a rebellion broke out in Babylonia.[23] We know nothing of its causes and extent. From the fact that it even happened, we can conclude that, despite the great successes of Nebuchadnezzar's foreign policy and the immense riches he pumped into the Babylonian economy, he was not entirely unopposed by the various groups making up Babylonian society. One critical point may have been his strongly preferential treatment of Babylon. Nebuchadnezzar was able to put down the rebellion after two months. Nevertheless, the fragility of Babylonian rule that it revealed raised hopes for its imminent end among the minor states in Palestine and Phoenicia. In addition, in the same year the energetic Pharaoh Psamtik II (595–589) ascended the throne of Egypt. In the following year,[24] Jer 27–28 reports an anti-Babylonian conspiracy in Jerusalem. Campaigns of Nebuchadnezzar against Hatti-land in 595 and 594 may have been meant to demonstrate to both his western vassals and Psamtik that his readiness for military action continued undiminished.

The text of the Babylonian Chronicle breaks off in the year 594, so we have only scattered bits of information about Nebuchadnezzar's further actions abroad. One important event was another destabilization of the southwest border of the Neo-Babylonian Empire, when Zedekiah, the Judean vassal king, rebelled against his patron Nebuchadnezzar (2 Kgs 24:20; 25:1ff.). He was probably encouraged by Psamtik II, who had brilliantly demonstrated the military might of Egypt in his victory over Nubia in 591. Nebuchadnezzar must have taken this revolt as a personal affront as well as a sign that his policy of isolating Egypt had failed. Zedekiah owed his kingship solely to Nebuchadnezzar, who had chosen him personally. In Nebuchadnezzar's second punitive campaign against Jerusalem, it may be taken as an expression of disdain for his

---

[23] Grayson, *Assyrian and Babylonian Chronicles*, 102: Chronicle 5, rev. 21–22. See also the 594 court document in Weidner, "Hochverrat," 1–5, in which Nebuchadnezzar condemns a certain Baba-aḫu-iddina for high treason.

[24] Reading in Jer 27:1 "In the fourth year of Zedekiah," after the analogy of 28:1.

Judean vassal that he did not participate in person. He oversaw the siege and conquest of Jerusalem from Riblah (2 Kgs 25:6), more than 175 miles away.

From the Babylonian perspective, this second campaign against Jerusalem was also aimed primarily to prevent an Egyptian incursion into Palestine. This is clear from the fact that Nebuchadnezzar broke off his siege of Jerusalem, which had begun on January 1, 588, in early summer to repel the advance of an Egyptian army (Jer 37:5; Josephus, *Ant.* 10.110). The defeat he inflicted on the Egyptians was so severe that from then on Egypt totally gave up trying to take territory in Palestine and Phoenicia.[25] This time, though, Nebuchadnezzar inflicted harsh retribution for the breach of faith. When the wall of the starving city was breached on July 29, 587,[26] the fleeing Zedekiah was pursued and captured by a Babylonian unit, probably on personal orders from Nebuchadnezzar, who condemned him brutally at Riblah. His sons were slain before his eyes, and he himself was blinded and taken to Babylon in fetters (2 Kgs 25:4–7).

It is noteworthy that a month passed between the conquest of the city and its destruction (2 Kgs 25:8). It appears that Nebuchadnezzar hesitated to inflict on Jerusalem the same terrible fate that Sennacherib had inflicted on Babylon about a century before. That the Neo-Babylonian kings did not lightly destroy foreign temples is clear from the shamefaced insistence of Nabonidus that the Medes alone were responsible for destroying the temple of Sin at Haran, whereas Nabopolassar regretted the act.[27] When Nebuchadnezzar nevertheless commanded his officers to set fire to the Jerusalem temple (25:9) and plunder what was left of its furnishings, his action was truly extraordinary, in fact contravening the theological principles of the Neo-Babylonian state. As in the case of Sennacherib, the action may be explained in part as a response to the personal affront felt by the king. That said, we must remember that the Babylonians were quite familiar with Judean partisan conflicts. It is reasonable to suppose that Nebuchadnezzar intended to strike at the theological foundation of the anti-Babylonian party, which even during the siege insisted that Yahweh's presence in Zion would prevent the city from being taken, as it had defended the city against Sennacherib in 701.[28]

---

25 James, "Egypt," 718–19.

26 On this date, see 78–81 below.

27 VAB 4:272–75: Nabonidus 8, 2.14'ff.; see also the improved translation in *ANET*, 309.

28 For a detailed discussion, see Rainer Albertz, *A History of Israelite Religion in the Old Testament Period* (trans. John Bowden; 2 vols.; OTL; Louisville: Westminster John Knox, 1994), 1:236–41.

When Nebuchadnezzar decided to disprove so dramatically the myth of Zion's inviolability, he sought to extinguish once and for all the religious roots of anti-Babylonian machinations in Judah. That he was far from wishing to eradicate Yahwism as such is shown by his appointment of Gedaliah, a prominent member of the faction that had been trying to reform and renew Yahwism since the days of Josiah, as his governor, as well as by his offer of special protection to the prophet Jeremiah, one of its most eloquent supporters during the conquest (Jer 39:1ff.), and even a generous living in Babylon (40:4). But when the Gedaliah experiment failed, Nebuchadnezzar appears to have lost interest in Judean self-government in his southwestern province.

After the conquest of Jerusalem, Nebuchadnezzar's foreign campaigns vanish in obscurity. Jeremiah 52:30 speaks of a third deportation of Judeans in the year 582; in the same year, Josephus (*Ant.* 10.181) records a campaign of Nebuchadnezzar against Coele-Syria, Moab, and Ammon. This evidence might suggest another anti-Babylonian resistance movement. If Josephus did not extrapolate the war against Judah's Transjordanian neighbors from Jeremiah's oracles against the nations (Jer 48; 49:1–6),[29] at least the punitive campaign against Ammon could be associated with the murder of the Judean governor Gedaliah, in which the Ammonite king Baalis was complicit (Jer 40:14; 41:15).[30]

Josephus states that Nebuchadnezzar marched into Egypt, slew and replaced the reigning king, and deported Jews from Egypt to Babylon, but his claim is probably not historical.[31] Amasis's violent usurpation of the pharaonic throne from Apries in the year 571, to which Josephus is probably alluding, was provoked by an internal conflict over the increasing hellenization of Egypt.[32] Contrary to the hopes expressed in the books of Jeremiah and Ezekiel (Jer 43:8–13; 46:13–26; Ezek 29:17–21; 30–32), no Egyptian sources describe an invasion of Egypt by Nebuchadnezzar.[33] The flight of Apries to Babylon, however, allowed Nebuchadnezzar to intervene in Egypt, which had been weakened by the civil war. In the year 568/567, he appeared in the Nile Delta with a fleet to reinstall the deposed Apries as the legitimate pharaoh, by the grace of Nebuchadnezzar. But the action, in which Apries perished,

---

[29] Note the identical sequence Moab–Ammon, which is geographically opposite the direction of an attack from the north. Hübner (*Ammoniter*, 202, 206–7) considers the campaign historical; in his opinion, it sealed the fate of both states. The alternative would be that Nabonidus first subjugated the Transjordanian states in 553.

[30] See pp. 94, 189–90 below.

[31] *Ant.* 10.182.

[32] As stated clearly by Herodotus, *Hist.* 2.161–163.

[33] James, "Egypt," 719.

was a pathetic disaster:[34] in 567 Amasis was at last firmly in the saddle. Thus Josephus probably extrapolated his account of a conquest of Egypt by Nebuchadnezzar from the prophetic oracles cited above.[35]

More credible is Josephus's belief that Nebuchadnezzar besieged Tyre for thirteen years during the reign of its king Ethbaal,[36] for which he cites ancient historians. There is abundant cuneiform evidence that Nebuchadnezzar succeeded in imposing his rule on this harbor city, situated on an island off the Phoenician coast and therefore highly defensible. The king of Tyre, for example, appears in a list of defeated vassals in Nebuchadnezzar's "court and state calendar" from around the year 570.[37] The only question has been the date of this siege, since Josephus's statement that Nebuchadnezzar began the siege "in the seventh year of his reign"[38] cannot be reconciled with the Babylonian Chronicle and other dates. Recently Katzenstein has shown that Josephus is probably referring to the seventh year of Ethbaal, not of Nebuchadnezzar (598/597). According to his reconstruction, the siege of Tyre took place between 585 and 572.[39] Contrary to the prophetic hope expressed in Ezek 26:7–28:18, it ended not with the conquest and destruction of the city but with a political understanding, as we learn from Ezek 29:17–18, dated in the year 572.

The tenacity with which Nebuchadnezzar kept Tyre cut off from its Phoenician hinterland for thirteen years as well as the clemency he showed when it capitulated are explained by his consistent interest in forcing Egypt out of the Syro-Palestinian region of the Neo-Babylonian Empire. Tyre was traditionally the most important port for Egypt's sea trade with Phoenicia and Syria, which Nebuchadnezzar was able to interdict by blockading Tyre. But after their severe defeat on land in 588, the Egyptians themselves began to build a fleet with Greek help, and Nebuchadnezzar faced the threat of Egyptian dominance in the eastern Mediterranean at the expense of Phoenician trade. He was concerned,

---

34 VAB 4:206ff.: Nebuchadnezzar 48; *ANET*, 308. For a reconstruction of events drawing on additional evidence from Egyptian and Greek sources, see Edel, "Amasis," 14–19; Leahy, "Earliest Dated Monument," 188–93.

35 Cf. the highly unlikely deportation of Jews from Egypt that Josephus describes as taking place during this campaign; it derives from the prophecy in Jer 46:26.

36 *Ant.* 10.228; cf. *Ag. Ap.* 1.156.

37 Unger, *Babylon*, 286, 293: No. 26, 5, 23. See also Unger's collection of administrative documents (*ZAW* 44 [1926]: 314–17), which speak of a campaign against Tyre and also indicate that Tyre was firmly under Babylonian control by 570 at the latest. The Wadi Brisa inscriptions from the mountains of Lebanon (VAB 4:150ff.: Nebuchadnezzar 19A/B, partially translated in *TUAT* 1/4:405) may also belong in this context.

38 *Ag. Ap.* 1.159.

39 *History*, 328ff.; cf. the cluster of references to Tyrians in the Nippur region from the thirty-fourth year of Nebuchadnezzar (572 B.C.E.) onward: Joannès, "Trois textes," 148–49.

therefore, to strengthen the commercial position of Phoenicia under the aegis of Babylon so as to profit as much as possible from Phoenician sea trade.

Nebuchadnezzar's entire foreign policy of establishing and securing Babylonian hegemony over large portions of the former Neo-Assyrian Empire directly served his domestic goal of guiding the ancient kingdom of Babylonia, long derelict and divided, to new prosperity, new cultural achievements, and new political unity. If his autobiographical inscriptions are trustworthy, his military campaigns served the sole purpose of diverting to Babylonia the riches of the lands he conquered, which Marduk had placed under his rule, so that he could restore the temple and cities of Marduk to new splendor, to the glory of their gods.[40] This concentration on building projects naturally represents an artificially narrow perspective, due to the circumstance that most of the extant texts belong to the genre of building inscriptions. As some formularies show,[41] Nebuchadnezzar was concerned with much more than siphoning off the wealth and labor of the subject peoples to strengthen the economy of the Babylonian heartland. To an extent previously unknown, his extensive building projects served to demonstrate to his own subjects and to all the world the newly won power and greatness of Babylon.

Unfortunately, the inscriptions are not dated, and so we are not in a position to arrange Nebuchadnezzar's building projects chronologically. For the most part, they must have paralleled his military campaigns. Only the construction of the new palace can be dated with some assurance to the year 570. He built many structures, both sacred and secular, in at least twelve Babylonian cities; his rebuilding and expansion of Babylon as the magnificent capital of the empire deserves special note. Nebuchadnezzar energetically pursued this project, begun by Nabopolassar, obviously in the interests of creating a clear political, cultural, and religious center for the rival cities and ethnic groups of Babylonia, a center that would symbolize the unity and identity of the newly created empire.

Nebuchadnezzar had to give top priority to eliminating for all time the danger of the terrible destruction that Babylon had undergone in 689.

---

40 VAB 4:94–95: Nebuchadnezzar 9, 3.18–22, 50–55; 112–115: Nebuchadnezzar 14, 1.13–31; 124–125: Nebuchadnezzar 15, 2.2–39; 146–149: Nebuchadnezzar 17, 2.12–37; 3.1–24; 152–153: Nebuchadnezzar 19A, 3.24–34; etc. Cf. the reflex in Jer 51:34.

41 In VAB 4:140–41: Nebuchadnezzar 16, 1.4, for example, Nebuchadnezzar calls himself "strengthener of the foundations of the land"; in VAB 4:150–51: Nebuchadnezzar 19A, 2.1–3, he sees his rule as being divinely ordained "to bring peace and prosperity to the people ... and to oversee their provisioning [*zāninussu*]." Thus Nebuchadnezzar sees himself as more than a provider (*zāninu*) for the sanctuaries.

He secured the city against the waters of the Euphrates by means of new outworks, better and higher quay walls, and an ingenious system of canals, so that the city could not be flooded as it was after its conquest by Sennacherib. At the same time, to avert another military destruction of the city, he built strong fortifications north of the city, a double ring of walls with moats, and an additional outer wall to the east. As a further defense of the heartland against attack from the north, he built a defensive wall between the Euphrates and the Tigris north of Sippar, which Xenophon later called the "Median Wall."

Nebuchadnezzar's second goal was to turn Babylon, which still bore the scars of seventh-century destruction, into the supreme cultic metropolis of the land. Besides renovating many temples and chapels of a wide range of Babylonian gods, he restored magnificently the cultic focus of the city, the temple Esagila with its chapels for Marduk, Nabu, and Sarpanitu, which had suffered particularly heavy damage at the hands of Sennacherib. Nebuchadnezzar's most symbolic and most costly undertaking was the completion, after more than five centuries, of Etemenanki, the ziggurat of Marduk, which had lain in ruins since the days of Nebuchadnezzar I (1123–1101). When completed, it was almost three hundred feet square and approximately three hundred feet high. Now Babylon possessed one of the greatest ziggurats of Babylonia, which gave the city an impressive silhouette visible for miles. The magnificent development of the processional highway between the temple quarter and the Ishtar Gate provided a festal ambience for the New Year festival, when the images of Marduk and Nabu were borne along it. All of this development vividly underlined the preeminent role of Marduk. It was Nebuchadnezzar's cultic policies that began to turn the traditional city god of Babylon into an imperial god.

Third, Nebuchadnezzar developed Babylon into the administrative center of the empire. Unlike the earlier Babylonian kings, who had their capitals in several different cities and came to Babylon only for the ceremonies of the New Year festival, he boasted of having chosen this city as his permanent capital.[42] Therefore he attached great importance to his palace complex. He called the great southern palace, completed around 570, the "wonder of humankind" (*tabrāti nīši*) and the "bond of unity of the land" (*markasa māti*);[43] we can see how he wanted to use his magnificent residence to forge a kind of emotional and administrative unity for traditionally decentralized Babylonia. When he also called his palace the "bond of unity of the great nations" (*markas nīši rabāti*) and the place

---

[42] VAB 4:114–15: Nebuchadnezzar 14, 1.44–53; 134–135: Nebuchadnezzar 15, 7.9–33.
[43] VAB 4:114–15: Nebuchadnezzar 14, 2.2; 136–137: Nebuchadnezzar 15, 7.37.

"where the rebellious are subdued,"[44] he was also assigning his residence the function of securing the unity of the empire's subject vassal peoples. Both aspects were illustrated vividly during the dedication of the southern palace, documented in the so-called "court and state calendar" of Nebuchadnezzar: the ceremonies included not only the court officials, the governors of the Babylonian provinces, and the chief priests of the Babylonian cities but also the hostage kings of conquered lands,[45] lands whose tribute and labor contributed significantly to the building of the palace.[46]

Nebuchadnezzar's ambitious building program, by which he hoped to make his "favorite city"[47] Babylon the "crown of all lands and dwelling places,"[48] thus served the purpose of unifying Babylonia and the empire by providing a representative local center. Apparently he was able to achieve this goal throughout most of his forty-three-year reign. But this means of unifying the empire demanded extraordinary resources. It needed continuing demonstrations of military might and could be financed only as long as immense tribute could be extorted from the conquered lands and repeated deportations could fill the immense need for labor. Broad support among the various Babylonian ethnic groups could be assured only as long as they all shared in the economic prosperity and could bask in the glow of the restored greatness and magnificence of Babylonia, without themselves having to bear much of the burden of the monumental royal building program. When resources began to stagnate, the preferential treatment of Babylon, which was intended to unify the land, could evoke resentment on the part of the disadvantaged and reawaken the ancient conflicts between the rival ethnic groups of Babylonia. Thus the costly unification policies of Nebuchadnezzar bore within themselves the seeds of the conflict that was to bring down the Neo-Babylonian Empire a mere generation after his death.

II.1.4. DESTABILIZATION, RESTORATION, AND END

One of the most striking features of the Neo-Babylonian Empire is its descent into total destabilization of central political power immediately after the forty-three-year reign of Nebuchadnezzar. In the brief period

---

[44] VAB 4:94–95: Nebuchadnezzar 9, 3.27–8.30.

[45] Unger, *Babylon*, 284ff.: no. 26, 3.35–5.29.

[46] Unger, 284; Unger, 289: no. 26, 2.21–34. Cf. Jer 51:58 and Hab 2:13, which describe the exhaustion of the peoples laboring to build the walls and gates of Babylon.

[47] VAB 4:114–15: Nebuchadnezzar 14, 2.1: *āl nīš īnēya ša aramma*, literally "city of the raising of my eyes, which I love." Cf. 134–35: Nebuchadnezzar 15, 7.35.

[48] VAB 4:174–75: Nebuchadnezzar 19B, 9.7–8; cf. 140–41: Nebuchadnezzar 15, 9.54–56.

between 562 and 556, no fewer than four rulers ascended the throne. The aging Nebuchadnezzar appears still to have had sufficient authority to settle the succession on his son Amēl-Marduk, Old Babylonian Awīl-Marduk ("man of Marduk"). Just two years later, however, he was replaced by Neriglissar (Nergal-sharezer), probably violently.[49] It is hard to determine what provoked this coup, since the only information we have about Amēl-Marduk's reign concerns a few building projects in Babylon. Berossus reports that he reigned "lawlessly and scandalously" (ἀνόμως καὶ σελγῶς); Nabonidus did not count him among his predecessors and claims in a literary propaganda text that Babylon had given him bad advice.[50] A "prophetic text from Uruk," however, can extol him as ruler of the world.[51] As far as we can see, these divergent but generally negative assessments have nothing to do with religious conflicts; Amēl-Marduk was faithful to the Marduk cult of the capital. If we remember, however, that in the year of his accession, shortly before his first New Year festival, he released the Judean king Jehoiachin from prison to give him a place of honor among the other vassal kings (2 Kgs 25:27–30), it is worth considering whether it might have been a reorientation in foreign policy that drew criticism. His father Nebuchadnezzar's first priority had been to use the constant threat of military force to extort the maximum possible tribute from his vassal lands for the benefit of Babylon without concern for their own development. It appears that Amēl-Marduk may have been interested in achieving a balance that would give the vassal states more independence. Perhaps he even intended to send Jehoiachin back to Judah[52] to rebuild an ordered society in war-ravaged Judah—to the long-range profit of the Babylonians. This theory would be consonant with his refusal to follow the usual practice of demonstrating the might of Babylonia by military campaigns at the very beginning of his reign. Possibly he even allowed Tyrian deportees to return home.[53] But Amēl-Marduk's

---

[49] According to Berossus, cited by Burstein, *Babyloniaca*, 28; cf. Neriglissar's indirect self-justification in VAB 4:214–17: Neriglissar 2, 1, 15–2, 2. A similar background is suggested by an overlap in dates involving Amēl-Marduk and Neriglissar in economic texts from Sippar, recently pointed out by Sack, *Neriglissar*, 25–26.

[50] Grayson, *Babylonian Historical-Literary Texts*, 88–91, obv. 5. Nabonidus appears to accuse him here of a naive piety that rejected the counsel of his family, but to this day the precise meaning of the text is obscure.

[51] Hunger and Kaufman, "New Akkadian Prophecy Text," 372: Warka 22307, rev. 16.

[52] As already suggested by A. T. Olmstead, *History of the Persian Empire* (Chicago: University of Chicago Press, 1948, repr., 1959), 57, 136.

[53] As suggested by Joannès, "Trois textes," 149; cf. Bob Becking, "Jojachin's Amnesty, Salvation for Israel? Notes on 2 Kings 25,27–30," in *Pentateuchal and Deuteronomistic Studies* (ed. C. Breckelmans and J. Lust; BETL; Louvain: Louvain University Press, 1990), 282–92.

balanced policy died aborning; the groups that had grown rich and powerful under Nebuchadnezzar perceived it as a threat to Babylonia's political and economic ascendancy. Therefore, Amēl-Marduk was removed on grounds of incompetence after a reign of just two and a half years.

Neriglissar (Nergal-šarra-uṣur, "May Nergal protect the king"), who seized the Babylonian throne from Amēl-Marduk, belonged to the Aramean tribe of Puqūdu (biblical Pekod). His family had achieved considerable wealth and influence under Nebuchadnezzar: his father was the governor of the Puqūdu district on the east bank of the Tigris;[54] he himself had probably participated in the conquest of Jerusalem as a young officer (Jer 39:3, 13)[55] and had risen to be governor of the district of Sin-magir, north of Babylon. The "state and court calendar" lists him as second among the "great ones of the land of Akkad," immediately after the governor of the Sea Land,[56] from whom the royal family came. It is therefore not surprising that Nebuchadnezzar gave him one of his daughters in marriage. Economic texts show Neriglissar to have been a wealthy businessman with substantial land holdings near Sippar who was on cordial terms with many influential people. Possibly he also held the office of a royal commissioner in the Ebabbar temple of Sippar.

With Neriglissar, a leading member of the wealthy and influential Babylonian oligarchy seized the throne; out of economic self-interest, this group had a stake in continuing the military strategy of the empire and exploiting the provinces for the benefit of Babylonia. The two extant inscriptions of Neriglissar make full use of the imperialistic *topoi* of Nebuchadnezzar, sometimes sounding even more aggressive.[57] In the third year of his reign (557), he had an opportunity to demonstrate his military prowess: when King Appuwašu of Piriddu, a small state in southeast Anatolia, led a raid into Syria, Neriglissar responded with a war of extermination, burning the cities and taking thousands of prisoners.[58] Thus he signaled the interests of the Neo-Babylonian Empire vis-à-vis the Medes in Asia Minor, where it already controlled eastern Cilicia as a former part of the Neo-Assyrian Empire. But Neriglissar died toward the end of April in 556, soon after returning from this campaign, and was therefore unable to pursue his imperialistic policies.

---

54 Unger, *Babylon*, 290–91: no. 26, 4.24.

55 Unfortunately, the text is somewhat corrupt: 39:13 speaks of a נֵרְגַל שַׂר־אֶצֶר רַב־מָג, "*nērgal-śar-ʾeṣer*, the great one of Mag." As part of another personal name, 39:3 preserves the element סַמְגַּר (*samgar*), which may be considered a superior variant of מָג, standing for the title "the great one of Sin-magir."

56 Unger, *Babylon*, 290: no. 26, 4.22.

57 VAB 4:209–19: Neriglissar 1, 1.1–16; 2.28–40; Neriglissar 2, 1.14, 18–2.2.

58 Grayson, *Assyrian and Babylonian Chronicles*, 103–104: Chronicle 6.

Domestically, too, Neriglissar was unable to establish a permanent dynasty. He had just enough authority to install his son Lābâši-Marduk (actually Lā-abâši-Marduk, "May I not be destroyed, O Marduk") as his successor. But after a reign of only three months[59] the latter was killed by a group of conspirators. The "Dynastic Prophecy" states that he had been unable to exercise authority over the land.[60] Nabonidus dismissed him as a young man who had not "learned how to behave" and had, as it were, set himself on the throne against the will of the gods.[61]

The conspirators who removed Lābâši-Marduk were recruited from among like-minded members of the Babylonian oligarchy, the same group that had set Neriglissar on the throne and seized political power to advance their own economic interests. This time, however, a leading role was played by a man who did not belong to the old upper-class Babylonian establishment: Belshazzar (Bel-šarra-uṣur, "Bel protect the king"), the son of Nabonidus, whose family came from Haran in northern Syria and was thus of Aramean stock. His grandmother Adad-guppi, who still bore an Aramaic name (= Hadad-ḫappe, "Hadad has protected"), had probably been carried off to Babylon as a prisoner of war when Nabopolassar and the Medes took Haran in 610. As a mature woman some forty years old, she was able during Nebuchadnezzar's reign to become an attendant lady and acquire political influence.[62] Apparently neither her husband Nabû-balāssa-iqbi nor her son Nabonidus, however, was able to play a major role at court; unlike Neriglissar, they are not mentioned during the reign of Nebuchadnezzar.[63] It was her grandson Belshazzar who was able to enter the higher ranks at court (^{LÚ}rēš šarri).[64] He clearly gained possession of Neriglissar's property confiscated in the coup, becoming a wealthy member of the Babylonian oligarchy and a prominent businessman.[65]

When the conspirators in league with Belshazzar made his father Nabonidus king, they probably thought of his kingship as a temporary

---

59 Beaulieu, *Reign*, 86.
60 Grayson, *Babylonian Historical-Literary Texts*, 32–33: 2.9–10.
61 VAB 4:276–77: Nabonidus 8, 4:34'–41' (*ANET*, 309).
62 Cf. the memorial inscription composed in her name, two copies of which were found at Haran (H1 A/B); translation in *ANET*, 560–62; *TUAT* 2/4:479–85. There is no evidence to support the theory that she was a priestess of Sin; cf. Beaulieu, *Reign*, 74ff.
63 Unless the "Labynetos from Babylon" whom Herodotus (*Hist.* 1.74) says arranged a peace treaty between the Medes and the Lydians is to be identified with Nabonidus, whom he calls by the same name in 1.77 and 1.188. In this case, Nabonidus would have already embarked on a military career under Nebuchadnezzar.
64 Von Voigtlander, "Survey," 166.
65 Beaulieu, *Reign*, 90ff.

expedient. Probably Belshazzar hoped that he would soon inherit the estate of his father, who must have been at least sixty years old at the time. But they were fooling themselves. In Nabonidus (Nabû-na'id, "Praised be Nabu") an energetic monarch ascended the Babylonian throne. He was determined to guide the Neo-Babylonian Empire to new splendor and power after a period of weakness; he also had a vision of setting its unity and identity on a new footing.

Clearly Nabonidus was surprised when he was chosen; in his inscriptions, at any rate, he insists that he had never thought of royal office. As a deeply religious person he wrestled intensely with the question as to why the divine election had settled on him, an outsider of non-Babylonian origin.[66] In the summer of 556, just after he had been recognized as king throughout all Babylonia, he demonstrated his military prowess with a campaign in Cilicia. Following in the footsteps of Neriglissar and Nebuchadnezzar, he presented himself as their "mighty emissary."[67] Other campaigns in Syria and the mountains of Amananus followed in 555 and 554.[68] But the basalt stela that he set up shortly after his first regnal year already exhibits a clear shift in the political and theological goals he was seeking for the Neo-Babylonian Empire. Here Nabonidus still describes himself as ruling under the aegis of the god Marduk and recapitulates once more the anti-Assyrian foundation myth of the Neo-Babylonian Empire, based on Marduk's wrathful response to Sennacherib's destruction of his temple. In Nabonidus's opinion, however, the wrath of the gods had not been totally appeased by the slaying of Sennacherib and the destruction of Assyria. Complete reconciliation with the gods had still not been accomplished even after Nebuchadnezzar and Neriglissar restored the Babylonian temples: the temple of Sin at Haran, the home of Nabonidus's family, still lay in ruins. When the Neo-Babylonian Empire was established in 610, Nabonidus had diplomatically laid the blame for its destruction at the feet of the Medes alone, but Nabopolassar cannot have been entirely blameless, as the removal of its cultic images to Babylon shows. Therefore Nabonidus believed that the primary purpose for which Marduk had chosen him as king was to rebuild the Ehulhul temple at Haran and restore the statues of its gods.[69]

---

66 VAB 4:280–81: Nabonidus 8, 7.37'–56' (*ANET*, 310); cf. the new edition of the stela by Schaudig, *Inschriften*, 514–29.

67 VAB 4:276–77: Nabonidus 8, 5.14'–17' (*ANET*, 309).

68 Grayson, *Assyrian and Babylonian Chronicles*, 105: Chronicle 7, 1–17.

69 Cf. the historico-theological framework of the stela (VAB 4:270ff.: Nabonidus 8, 1.1'–4.33'; 10.1'–31'; *ANET*, 309–11), which leads up directly to Marduk's commission to rebuild the temple in Haran (10.12'ff.).

It does not do justice to Nabonidus's concern to explain it simply as the product of nostalgia for his homeland and the personal religious predilections he shared with his aged mother. Here Nabonidus, undoubtedly sensitive on account of his non-Babylonian roots, hit upon an inconsistency in the theology of the Neo-Babylonian Empire. This theology derived Babylon's right to dominion from the terrible destruction of its own temples, but the same theology did not prevent and even condoned equally brutal destruction of foreign temples to establish this dominion. The religious, military, and economic policies of the empire had always favored the interests of the Babylonian heartland. Nebuchadnezzar and Neriglissar had devoutly restored temples throughout Babylonia, and Nabonidus himself had contributed generously to the temples of the capital. When Nabonidus placed his plan to build a temple in far-off northern Syria on the same level, he called these policies into question, policies that had dominated the history of the Neo-Babylonian Empire since its beginnings—with the possible exception of the brief reign of Amēl-Marduk. For the first time, campaign booty as well as the tribute and forced labor extorted from conquered nations were to be employed in rebuilding a region outside Babylonia. This decision signaled a revision of Nebuchadnezzar's policy of securing the unity of Babylonia and the empire by giving first priority to establishing Babylon as the single dominant local center. Nabonidus promoted a polycentric structure, which gave more power to the peripheral regions of the empire.[70] In the course of Nabonidus's reign, it became increasingly clear that there was to be a new, more inclusive religious identity uniting the empire: the worship of the moon god Sin, who unlike Marduk was not tied to a single city but was indigenous to both the Babylonian south (Ur) and the Aramean north (Haran).

A reading of Nabonidus's "speech from the throne" from this perspective casts light on certain "enigmatic" features of his reign that have long puzzled scholars. Because at the beginning of his reign Haran was still within the sphere of influence of the Median Empire, he could not immediately realize his plan to rebuild Ehulhul.[71] During his first three years, therefore, his domestic policies for the most part continued along the traditional lines of the Babylonian kings. His own goal was visible only in his moderate diminution of Babylon's special

---

[70] Such a reorientation is also suggested by the reappointment of kings in Tyre (Josephus, *Ag. Ap.* 1.158), all of whom probably fall within the period of Nabonidus's reign (Katzenstein, *History*, 324–25).

[71] See the dream revelation in VAB 4:218–21: Nabonidus 1, 1.15–32 (*TUAT* 2/4, 494–95), which Nabonidus later used to justify the delay.

position while he visited other major cultic centers and supported them with booty from his military campaigns and in his promotion of the temple of Sin at Ur by granting it certain privileges and by consecrating his daughter to be the local *ēntu* priestess. In 553, however, the Persian Cyrus rebelled against his Median overlords; the rebellion culminated in Cyrus's victory over Astyages in 550. Now Nabonidus had his chance to rebuild Ehulhul and probably began at once to make preparations for the building project in Haran. Despite his earlier policy of reconciliation, he encountered bitter resistance on the part of almost all the major Babylonian cities and their temples. Judging by Nabonidus's retrospective account on his stela at Haran, the result was a full-scale revolt, which rocked the whole land.[72] The fact that even the city of Ur took part in the revolt shows that the building of the temple at Haran involved more than promotion of the cult of Sin. The Babylonian citizens and priests were united in opposing any redistribution of national economic and human resources to benefit a non-Babylonian region. The fact that Haran had been the last capital of the Assyrian archenemy and that the Sargonids had promoted its cult of Sin may well have aggravated Babylonian resentment.

Unfortunately, the sources are not clear as to whether Nabonidus was able nevertheless to complete the rebuilding of the temple in 553/552.[73] The preponderance of the evidence suggests that construction had to be suspended. Despite this defeat, however, Nabonidus did not give up his policy of decentralization.

Much ink has been spilled over Nabonidus's puzzling ten-year sojourn in Tema, an oasis city in northwestern Arabia. I believe that it must be viewed from this perspective. It cannot be dated precisely because the Nabonidus Chronicle has gaps for the fourth through sixth and eleventh through sixteenth years of his reign; however, the Haran stela associates it directly with the rebellion. It is likely, therefore, that

---

[72] Röllig, "Erwägungen," 219–20, 224: H 2 1.11–20; cf. *ANET*, 562.

[73] Whether Nabonidus built Ehulhul before or after his sojourn in Tema is a matter of scholarly debate, summarized by Beaulieu, *Reign*, 205ff. The "Verse Account of Nabonidus" asserts that it was built before (*ANET*, 313: 2.4'–17'), and the Adad-guppi stela appears to presuppose that it had been built at the time of the queen mother's death (547) (*TUAT* 2/4:482: H 1, 2.13–20). But Nabonidus's own stela, two copies of which were found at Haran (H 2, A/B), dates the construction after his sojourn at Tema (Röllig, "Erwägungen," 223, 226: H 2, 3.17–35; cf. *ANET*, 563). The simplest explanation of the discrepancy between the Haran stela and Nabonidus's account in VAB 4:220–21: Nabonidus 1, 1.34ff. (*TUAT* 2/4:496–96), which dates the building of the temple immediately after Cyrus's victory over Astyages, is that Nabonidus began construction in 553 but had to suspend it because of the revolts throughout the land.

Nabonidus seized the occasion of his western campaign in 553/552, which took him as far as Edom, to establish himself in northern Arabia. First, this move was intended to pacify the rebels: Nabonidus made his son co-regent for the Babylonian heartland. We know that Belshazzar, though loyal to Nabonidus, harbored some reservations about the ultimate consequences of his father's policies. He was more acceptable to the rebellious urban population of Babylonia; as an influential member of the indigenous oligarchy, he provided a smaller target. Second, by firmly incorporating the tribes of northwest Arabia into the Neo-Babylonian Empire, Nabonidus's action aimed at opening up new economic resources for it. By advancing from Tema to Medina, he was able to control the entire Arabian caravan trade with such luxury commodities as incense and gold, divert it, and siphon off some profit. Finally, Nabonidus was able to demonstrate to the self-absorbed Babylonians the feasibility of decentralizing the organization of the empire. He developed the oasis city of Tema into a second royal residence, where he received diplomatic delegations and forged effective communication and transportation links through the Arabian Desert to Babylon, so that he could monitor and influence political developments there at will.

Nabonidus showed that abandoning the policies of the Assyrian and Babylonian kings, focused solely on campaigns of plunder, did not necessarily end in political chaos and economic disaster but offered incalculable advantages for strengthening the empire. The new policy reinforced the empire's internal unity through development of its periphery and created flexible avenues of retreat in the face of external threats. During these ten years, Nabonidus systematically avoided Babylon; as a result, the New Year festival with its procession of gods in honor of Marduk, for which the king's presence was absolutely necessary, could not be celebrated.[74] Given the heavily didactic intent of Nabonidus's inscriptions, its omission served as a punitive public lesson through which he sought to convince the populace of the ancient capital that his policies were correct.

After ten years, Nabonidus had clearly achieved such broad support for his policies, even in the Babylonian heartland, that he believed the time was ripe for him to return to Babylon (543) so as to devote his energies to completing the religio-political portion of his reform. We must remember that most of Nabonidus's years in Tema

---

[74] See the entries in the Babylonian Chronicle: Grayson, *Assyrian and Babylonian Chronicles*, 106–8: Chronicle 7, 2.5–6, 10–11, 19–20, 23–24; also the "Verse Account" (*ANET*, 313: 2.10'–11').

were a very good time for Babylonia: the economy flourished, as economic texts demonstrate; great building projects such as the restoration of the Larsa ziggurat (546) could be completed successfully. Only for the year 545 is a famine recorded; its speedy end was seen as a good omen by Nabonidus and undoubtedly also by broad strata of the population.[75] In addition, the brilliant triumphal march of Cyrus in 547/546, through which he victoriously brought Lydia and with it large portions of Asia Minor under his sway, probably caused many Babylonians to rethink the possibilities of a better way to secure the Neo-Babylonian Empire. From southeast to northwest it was now surrounded by the semicircle of the newly established Persian Empire. How might it be possible to assert Babylonian identity against this empire and mobilize its defenses?

Nabonidus, too, felt a sense of urgency in realizing his plan to lay a new, emotionally deeper religious foundation for the Neo-Babylonian Empire in the worship of the moon god Sin. Immediately upon his return in 543 he resumed the restoration of the temple of Sin in Haran; drawing on all the resources of his kingdom, he brought the project to a rapid conclusion and returned the statues of its gods.[76] Thus the cult of the moon god, which as early as the seventh century had expanded deep into Palestine, was reestablished in its traditional Syrian center. In northern Arabia, too, where the moon god had always played a major role, its cult could once more find its place.

At the same time, Nabonidus embarked on an extensive campaign of religious propaganda to establish Sin as the highest god of the Babylonian pantheon even in the Babylonian heartland. In his building inscriptions of this period, he praises Sin as "king of the gods of heaven and earth"[77] and ascribes to even his earliest temple-building projects, such as the temple of the sun god Shamash and the goddess Anunitu in Sippar, the goal of promoting "the fear of Sin, the lord of the gods and goddesses, in the hearts of his people."[78] The polemic of the "Verse Account"[79] reveals that he even tried to incorporate Esagila, the tradition-

---

[75] Dandamaev, "Neo-Babylonian Society," 265; Beaulieu, *Reign*, 202–3. Probably the Haran inscription (Röllig, "Erwägungen," 220–21, 224: H 2: 1.31–38) and stela fragment H 3 (Röllig, "Erwägungen," 247–48) also refer to the end of the famine; in any case, they depict a period of well-being brought about by Sin. The description to the contrary in the "Verse Account" (*ANET*, 312–13: 1.3ff.) is at least highly exaggerated.

[76] VAB 4:220–23: Nabonidus 1, 1.34–2.25 (*TUAT* 2/4:495–96); Röllig, "Erwägungen," 223, 226: H 2, 3.17–35.

[77] VAB 4:222–23, 224–25: Nabonidus 1, 2.26, 33 (*TUAT* 2/4:496), etc.

[78] VAB 4:242–43: Nabonidus 4, 1.21'–22'.

[79] *ANET*, 314: 5.16'–21'.

laden temple of Marduk in Babylon, into the cult of Sin by virtue of its symbol of the crescent moon. Sin was to replace Marduk, who, though the god of the empire, continued to have local ties as the city god of Babylon. The moon god not only had several cultic centers (Ur, Haran) but also was widely worshiped outside Babylonia. Just as Nabonidus had called on "the people of Akkad and Hatti" to join in building Ehulhul,[80] so now the whole empire was to be united in the worship of Sin. Nabonidus's universalistic conception of the empire is illustrated in the political sphere by his adoption—besides the title "king of Babylon"—of the Assyrian royal titles "king of the world" and "king of the four corners of the earth."[81]

However, despite his extraordinary efforts to reorganize the empire and establish a new theology, Nabonidus failed. His failure was due to the traditional fragmentation of the ethnic groups in Babylonia. The Babylonian oligarchy saw its profits from the empire vanishing, and the cities saw their privileges threatened. Above all, the powerful priesthood of Marduk in Babylon, which had to fear the loss of their primacy, pulled out of the renewal movement inaugurated by Nabonidus and encouraged the people to lampoon the king in the streets.[82] Possibly they and others even secretly called on Cyrus, the Persian king, for help. The remarkably rapid fall of the Neo-Babylonian Empire and the relatively slight resistance it offered the Persians are explicable only on the assumption that influential circles were Persian collaborators.

When the Persian attack was imminent in the summer of 539, the images of the gods in several cities were taken to Babylon for protection. In the fall, the Persians pressed their attack. At the beginning of October, Cyrus defeated the defending Babylonian army at Opis on the Tigris; on the tenth of October, Sippar was taken without a fight, and two days later the advance guard of the Persian army entered Babylon without meeting substantial resistance. It is possible that Belshazzar was slain when the city was taken;[83] Nabonidus, who had fled when Sippar fell, surrendered and was detained in Babylon. He may later have been sent

---

80 Röllig, "Erwägungen," 223, 226: H 2, 3.19; cf. the striking equal treatment of "the people of Akkad and Hatti" in 2.6–8: Shamash gave the Babylonians into the hands of Nabonidus just like the foreigners of Syria and Palestine!

81 For example: VAB 4:218 –19: Nabonidus 1: 1.2: šar kiššati ... šar kibrāti erbetti (TUAT 2/4:494).

82 See the "Verse Account" (ANET, 312–15), even though in its present form it dates from the period after the invasion of Cyrus.

83 Cf. Dan 5:30, contra Xenophon, Cyropaedia 7.5.157, which says that the king of Babylon perished.

into exile.⁸⁴ When Cyrus entered Babylon in triumph on October 29, 539 B.C.E., he had the priests of Marduk hail him as a liberator appointed by Marduk to deliver the inhabitants of the city from the yoke outrageously imposed on them against the will of the gods by Nabonidus, who did not fear Marduk.⁸⁵ Many may have believed this, especially since the priests of Marduk defamed Nabonidus so spitefully that he could easily have been pictured as a madman.⁸⁶ Cyrus capitalized on the popular mood and staked everything on the Babylonian traditionalists. Only later did it become apparent that the policies of the Persian Empire had much in common with the imperfect vision that Nabonidus had attempted to realize.

II.2. ISRAEL IN THE EXILIC PERIOD

Albertz, Rainer. "Wer waren die Deuteronomisten? Das historische Rätsel einer literarischen Hypothese," *EvT* 57 (1997): 319–38. **Albright,** William Foxwell. *The Biblical Period from Abraham to Ezra* (New York: Harper & Row, 1963). **Barstad,** Hans M. *The Myth of the Empty Land: A Study of the History and Archaeology of Judah During the "Exilic" Period* (SO.S 28; Oslo: Scandinavian University Press, 1996). **Becking,** Bob. *The Fall of Samaria: A Historical and Archaeological Study* (SHANE 2; Leiden: Brill, 1992). **Becking.** "Jojachin's Amnesty, Salvation for Israel? Notes on 2 Kings 25,27–30," in *Pentateuchal and Deuteronomistic Studies* (ed. C. Breckelmans and J. Lust; BETL 94; Louvain: Louvain University Press, 1990), 282–92. **Bickerman,** E. J. "The Babylonian Captivity," *CHJ* 1:326–42. **Böhl,** Franz Marius Theodor. "Nebukadnezar en Jojachin," in idem, *Opera minora* (Groningen: Wolters, 1953), 423–29, 525. **Bronner,** Leila Leah. "Sacrificial Cult among the Exiles in Egypt but Not in Babylon," *Dor le Dor* 9 (1980): 61–71. **Broshi,** Magen, and Israel Finkelstein. "The Population of Palestine in Iron Age II," *BASOR* 287 (1992): 47–60. **Donner,** Herbert. *Geschichte des Volkes Israel und seiner Nachbarn in Grundzügen,* vol. 2 (2d ed.; GAT 4/2; Göttingen: Vandenhoeck & Ruprecht, 1995). **Eph'al,** Israel. "On the Political and Social Organization of the Jews in Babylonian Exile," *ZDMG* 5 (1983): 106–12. **Finkelstein,** Israel. "The Archaeology of the Days of Manasseh," in *Scripture and Other Artifacts: Essays on the Bible and Archaeology in Honor of Philip J. King* (ed. M. D. Coogan, J. C. Exum, and L. E. Stager; Louisville: Westminster John Knox, 1994), 169–87. **Gunneweg,** Antonius H. J. *Geschichte Israels: Von den Anfängen bis Bar Kochba und von Theodor Herzl bis zur Gegenwart* (6th ed.; ThW 2; Stuttgart: Kohlhammer, 1989). **Herrmann,** Siegfried. *A History of*

---

⁸⁴ Grayson, *Assyrian and Babylonian Chronicles,* 110: Chronicle 7, 3.14, 16. Nabonidus's exile is mentioned in the "Dynastic Prophecy" (Grayson, *Babylonian Historical-Literary Texts,* 32–33: 2.18–21).

⁸⁵ See the Cyrus Cylinder, lines 17, 25–26 (*TUAT* 1/4:408–409; *ANET,* 315).

⁸⁶ Cf. the image (transferred to Nebuchadnezzar) in Dan 4.

Israel in Old Testament Times (2d ed.; trans. J. Bowden; Philadelphia: Fortress, 1981). **Jamieson-Drake,** David W. *Scribes and Schools in Monarchic Judah: A Socio-Archeological Approach* (JSOTSup 109; Sheffield: Almond, 1991). **Janssen,** Enno. *Juda in der Exilszeit: Ein Beitrag zur Frage der Entstehung des Judentums* (FRLANT 69; Göttingen: Vandenhoeck & Ruprecht, 1956). **Joannès,** Francis, and André Lemaire. "Trois tabelettes cunéiforms à onomastique ouest-sémitique (collection Sh. Moussaïeff)," *Transeu* 17 (1999): 17–34. **Klamroth,** Erich. *Die jüdischen Exulanten in Babylonien* (BWANT 10; Leipzig: Hinrichs, 1912). **Kreissig,** Heinz. *Die sozialökonomische Situation in Juda zur Achämenidenzeit* (SGKAO 7; Berlin: Akademie Verlag, 1973). **Mayer,** Walter. *Politik und Kriegskunst der Assyrer* (ALASP 9; Münster: Ugarit-Verlag, 1995). **Metzger,** Martin. *Grundriss der Geschichte Israels* (7th ed; NStB 2; Neukirchen-Vluyn: Neukirchener Verlag, 1988). **Miller,** James Maxwell, and John Haralson Hayes. *A History of Ancient Israel and Judah* (Philadelphia: Westminster, 1986). **Mitchell,** T. C. "The Babylonian Exile and the Restoration of the Jews in Palestine (586–c.500 BC)," *CAH*^{2} 3:410–60. **Noth,** Martin. *The History of Israel* (trans. S. Godman, rev. by P. R. Ackroyd; 2d ed.; London: Black, 1960). **Oded,** Bustenay. "Judah and the Exile," in *Israelite and Judaean History* (ed. J. H. Hayes and J. M. Miller; London: SCM, 1977), 435–88. **Oded.** *Mass Deportations and Deportees in the Neo-Assyrian Empire* (Wiesbaden: Reichert, 1979). **Oded.** "Observations on the Israelite/Judaean Exiles in Mesopotamia during the Eighth–Sixth Centuries BCE," in *Immigration and Emigration within the Ancient Near East: Festschrift E. Lepiński* (ed. K. van Lerberghe and A. Schoors; OLA 65; Louvain: Peeters, 1995), 205–12. **Oswald,** Wolfgang. *Israel am Gottesberg: Eine Untersuchung zur Literargeschichte der vorderen Sinaiperikope Ex 19–24 und deren historischem Hintergrund* (OBO 159; Fribourg: Universitätsverlag, 1998). **Porten,** Bezalel. "The Jews in Egypt," *CHJ* 1:372–400. **Porten** and Ada Yardeni, *Textbook of Aramaic Documents from Ancient Egypt* (4 vols.; Jerusalem: Hebrew University, Department of the History of the Jewish People, 1986–99). **Smith,** Daniel L. *The Religion of the Landless: The Social Context of the Babylonian Exile* (Bloomington: Meyer-Stone, 1989). **Smith-Christopher,** Daniel L. "Reassessing the Historical and Sociological Impact of the Babylonian Exile (597/587–539 BCE)," in *Exile: Old Testament, Jewish, and Christian Conceptions* (ed. J. M. Scott; JSJSup 56; Leiden: Brill, 1997), 7–36. **Stern,** Ephaim, ed. *The New Encyclopedia of Archaeological Excavations in the Holy Land* (4 vols.; Jerusalem: Israel Exploration Society, 1993). **Stolper,** Matthew W. *Entrepreneurs and Empire: The Murašû Archive, the Murašû Firm and Persian Rule in Babylonia* (UNHAII 54; Leiden: Nederlands Historisch-Archaeologisch Instituut te Istanbul, 1985). **Weidner,** Ernst F. "Jojachin, der König von Juda, in babylonischen Keilschrifttexten," in *Mélanges syriens offerts à Monsieur René Dussaud* (2 vols.; Paris: Geuthner, 1939), 2:923–35. **Weinberg,** Joel. *The Citizen-Temple Community* (JSOTSup 151; Sheffield: JSOT Press, 1992). **Wellhausen,** Julius. *Israelitische und jüdische Geschichte* (9th ed.; Berlin: de Gruyter, 1958). **Wilkie,** John M. "Nabonidus and the Later Jewish Exiles," *JTS* NS 2 (1951): 36–44. **Würthwein,** Ernst. *Die Bücher der Könige* (2 vols.; ATD 11; Göttingen: Vandenhoeck & Ruprecht, 1977–84), vol. 2. **Zadok,** Ran. *The Jews in Babylonia during the Chaldean and Achaemenian Periods according to the Babylonian Sources* (Haifa: University of Haifa, 1979). **Zadok.** "Some Jews in Babylonian Documents," *JQR* 74 (1984): 294–97.

Despite the gaps in the sources, the history of the Neo-Babylonian Empire can be reconstructed more or less continuously and in some detail; however, such a reconstruction of the history of Israel in this era is possible only within very narrow limits. The primary reason is simply the course of history: Judah was a minor state crushed between the great powers of Babylonia and Egypt in their contest for the remains of the Neo-Assyrian Empire. But the second reason is that the historical tradition of the Bible largely leaves the exilic period remarkably blank—probably for theological reasons.[87] Babylonian and Egyptian sources cannot fill this lacuna, because what was left of Israel in this period was too marginal in the eyes of the great powers to merit more than casual mention in passing.

II.2.1. Sources

Although the Hebrew Bible reflects extensively on the theological significance of the exile, it provides scant information about its actual history. The sources for the historical events leading up to the two deportations are relatively good. In 2 Kgs 23:29–25:21,[88] Jer 39, and 2 Chr 36, we have historical narratives that—as we have seen[89]—illuminate these events from a variety of perspectives and with different assessments. Jeremiah 52:28–30 also supplies a short list of the exiles.

For the golah of 597, Jer 27–29 and the book of Ezekiel furnish important information. For the exilic period "proper," after the destruction of Jerusalem in 587/586, the initial years are covered primarily by Jer 40:14–37 (cf. 2 Kgs 25:27–30 par. Jer 52:31–34) and Lam 1–5. From the later period, only the pardon of Jehoiachin by Amēl-Marduk in 562 is mentioned (2 Kgs 25:27–30 par. Jer 52:31–34). Texts such as Ps 137, Ezek 19, and Isa 40 provide some insight into the trying psychological state of the Babylonian golah later in the exilic period. Jeremiah 43:8–44:30 gives some information about the Egyptian golah. The continuous historical narrative in Ezra and Nehemiah does not begin until the year 539, in the Persian period. It enables a reconstruction of the final phase of the exilic era down to the year 520, but it also contains much significant data for the preceding years.

Archaeological excavations in a whole series of Judean cities (Jerusalem, Ramath Rachel, Lachish, Gezer, Tell el-Hesi, Arad, Tel Masos)

---

[87] See pp. 3–4 above.

[88] Jer 52:1–27 represents a parallel tradition to 2 Kgs 24:18–25:21, which diverges only in a few details.

[89] See pp. 5–15 above.

have confirmed the destruction wrought by the Babylonians in 587/586.[90] Some of the evidence, however, has had to be sorted out and corrected subsequently. The destruction of En-Gedi probably did not take place until 582.[91] The destruction of Tell Beit Mirsim and Beth-Shemesh, formerly associated with the Babylonian conquest,[92] has been assigned more recently to the Assyrian conquest in 701.[93] Later studies have cast substantial doubt on the destruction of Beth-Zur;[94] clearly Tell el-Fûl was destroyed only partially and continued to be inhabited.[95] Highly significant is the archaeological evidence that the cities of the Benjaminite north such as Tell en-Naṣbeh, Gibeon, and Bethel escaped destruction and remained continuously inhabited well into the early Persian period.[96]

There are few extrabiblical written sources for the history of the Neo-Babylonian period. The Babylonian Chronicle confirms in essence the events surrounding the first deportation in 598/597.[97] There are also four cuneiform tablets from a royal archive (still not published in full) that German excavations in Babylon discovered in the south palace of Nebuchadnezzar, published initially by Weidner in 1939. Among other things, they record royal rations of oil for "Jehoiachin, the king of Judah" (*ya'ukin šarri ša* ᴷᵁᴿ*yaḫudu*), his five sons, and thirteen other Judeans (five mentioned by name). These tablets cast an interesting spotlight on a small fragment of the Babylonian golah that lived at the court of Nebuchadnezzar.[98] The archive as a whole is reported to contain texts dating from the years 595–570; unfortunately, the date is preserved on only one of the four tablets (28186, Text C). It points to the year 592, before the destruction of Jerusalem.

From the numerous Neo-Babylonian economic texts, Zadok[99] has been able to list a mere handful of individuals whose names indicate that they may be identified as Judeans. There is an interesting legal document from the early Persian period (531) in which the daughter of a

---

[90] *NEAEHL*, 708ff., 1265, 909–10, 505, 633, 82, 989. The destruction of these and other cities of the Negev is more likely the result of Edomite attacks.

[91] *NEAEHL*, 402.

[92] Most recently Oded, "Judah," 475.

[93] See the corrected discussion in *NEAEHL*, 180 and 251–52.

[94] *NEAEHL*, 261: "The scattered evidence of a violent destruction in about 587 BCE, found in 1931, could not be confirmed in 1957."

[95] *NEAEHL*, 447–48.

[96] *NEAEHL*, 1101–2, 513, 194.

[97] Grayson, *Assyrian and Babylonian Chronicles* (II.1), 102: Chronicle 5, rev. 11–13 (*TGI*, 74).

[98] Weidner, "Jojachin," 924–31 (*TGI*, 78–79; *ANET*, 308).

[99] *Jews*, 38–40; "Some Jews," 294ff. Strikingly more numerous are the fifty or so Israelite personal names collected by Becking (*Fall*, 61–93) from Assyrian sources; some of these may also be Judeans deported by Sennacherib in 701.

Judean family in Sippar is threatened with enslavement if she continues to meet her friend without her father's approval.[100] Seven additional Judeans appear in two recently published documents from the years 532 and 498.[101] The archives of the Murashu firm mention many Judeans in the vicinity of Nippur: of the 2,500 or so persons named in these documents, some seventy (about 2.8 percent) can be identified as Jews.[102] But these documents date from the years 455–403, nearly a century later than our period.[103] We must therefore be extremely cautious in using them to draw conclusions about the social situation of the exiles in the sixth century.

The same holds true for the Elephantine texts from Upper Egypt, which provide a detailed insight into the life of a Jewish military colony on this island in the Nile during the second half of the fifth century.[104]

II.2.2. Principles of Historical Reconstruction

Before attempting to reconstruct the history of Israel in the exilic period from these patchy sources, we must clarify a few basic principles, some of which are controversial.

II.2.2.1. Number of Deportations

While 2 Kgs 24–25 reports two Babylonian deportations, 2 Chr 36:6–7 assumes a third deportation, during the reign of Jehoiakim, when Nebuchadnezzar carried off the king and some of the temple vessels. Daniel 1:1 dates this deportation more precisely in the third year of Jehoiakim (606), when Daniel and his friends arrived at the Babylonian court. According to Josephus,[105] this deportation took place in the fifth year of Jehoiakim; three thousand prisoners were carried off, including the young Ezekiel. In addition, Jer 52:30 mentions yet another deportation of 745 Jews by Nebuzaradan in the twenty-third year of Nebuchadnezzar (582).

There is no doubt about the deportation in 582; it is probably best understood as a punitive action carried out by Babylon for the murder of

---

100 Dandamaev, *Slavery* (II.1), 105: Cyrus 307.
101 Joannès and Lemaire, "Trois tablettes," 17–30.
102 Zadok, *Jews*, 49–81.
103 For a general treatment of the Murashu archive, see Stolper, *Entrepreneurs*.
104 Recently republished in Porten and Yardeni, *Textbook*.
105 *Ant.* 10.96ff.

Gedaliah. But a deportation in the time of Jehoiakim, especially prior to the battle of Carchemish in 605, when Nebuchadnezzar first gained the upper hand over Egypt, is historically most unlikely. Berossus does report that Nebuchadnezzar took a great number of prisoners in this battle, including Jews as well as Egyptians, Phoenicians, and Syrians, and on his return "assigned them domiciles in the most appropriate regions of Babylonia."[106] However, this account cannot be reconciled either chronologically or substantially with the statements in 2 Chr 36:6–7, Dan 1:1, and *Ant.* 10.96ff., which differ in detail. According to the Babylonian Chronicle, Nebuchadnezzar did not even come near Judah until the following year.[107] If Berossus is not simply lumping together later deportations from Syria and Palestine and assigning them proleptically to the time of Nebuchadnezzar's crucial victory,[108] the Judeans in question could only have been mercenaries in Pharaoh's army. Klamroth[109] defended the historicity of this early deportation, but recent scholarship has generally rejected it. Since the discovery of the Babylonian Chronicle, it may be considered disproved.

It must be remembered, however, that Judah had once before been forced to suffer a terrible wave of destruction and mass deportation, which is often overlooked: in Sennacherib's account of his punitive campaign against Hezekiah in 701, he boasts of having laid waste forty-six walled cited and many unfortified villages in Judah and of having deported an enormous number of people and animals.[110] Only Jerusalem escaped, by the skin of its teeth. The figure of 200,150 in Sennacherib's account is improbably high; if it is not a propagandistic exaggeration, Mayer may be correct in suggesting that the Assyrians were counting both human beings and animals.[111] But the archaeological evidence, too,

---

106 Burstein, *Babyloniaca* (II.1), 28.

107 The account of this campaign places special emphasis on the conquest of Ashkelon; see Grayson, *Assyrian and Babylonian Chronicles*, 100: Chronicle 5, obv. 15–20.

108 He assumes anachronistically that Nebuchadnezzar had already settled matters with Egypt and the other outlying territories.

109 *Die jüdischen Exulanten*, 10–12.

110 See *TGI*, 68–69; *ANET*, 287–88; also the depiction of the "conquest of Lachish" on the Nineveh relief in *ANEP*, 129–32. The illustration on the cover of the German edition of the present volume comes from this relief.

111 *Politik*, 41–45. Mayer estimates 100,000 human beings, but the archaeological evidence suggests that even this number is too high. According to Finkelstein ("Archaeology," 176), in the eighth century the southern kingdom had a population of only about 120,000 or—if the settlements north and west of Jerusalem are included—140,000. Population estimates based on archaeological surveys are still fraught with uncertainty: even in 1992, Broshi and Finkelstein still estimated the population of the southern kingdom in the eighth century at about 110,000 ("Population," 54).

shows that Judah had to accept substantial destruction and population loss. The cities of Lachish, Tell Beit Mirsim, Beth-Shemesh, Beersheba, Tel Eton, Tel Batash, and the fortress of Arad were destroyed and only partially rebuilt, and then on a smaller scale. Sometimes they were replaced with farmsteads. According to Finkelstein's calculations, the Shephelah, home to more than half the population of the southern kingdom in the late eighth century, had lost 70 percent of its built-up area by the seventh century.[112] We must take this loss into account when we seek to determine the scope of the deportations of 597 and 587/586.

II.2.2.2. Dates of the Deportations

Edwards, Ormond. "The Year of Jerusalem's Destruction: 1 Addaru 597 B.C. Reinterpreted," *ZAW* 104 (1992): 101–6. **Galil,** Gershon. "The Babylonian Calendar and the Chronology of the Last Kings of Judah," *Bib* 72 (1991): 367–78. **Hardmeier,** Christof. *Prophetie im Streit vor dem Untergang Judas* (BZAW 187; Berlin: de Gruyter, 1990), 247–51. **Kutsch,** Ernst. *Die chronologischen Daten des Ezechielbuches* (OBO 62; Fribourg: Universitätsverlag, 1985). **Kutsch.** "Das Jahr der Katastrophe, 587 v.Chr.: Kritische Erwägungen zu neueren chronologischen Versuchen," *Bib* 55 (1974): 520–45. **Malamat,** Abraham. "The Last Kings of Judah and the Fall of Jerusalem: An Historical-Chronological Study," *IEJ* 18 (1968): 137–56. **Malamat.** "The Twilight of Judah: In the Egyptian-Babylonian Maelstron," in *Congress Volume: Edinburgh, 1974* (VTSup 28; Leiden: Brill, 1974): 123–45. **Vogt,** Ernst. "Bemerkungen über das Jahr der Eroberung Jerusalems," *Bib* 56 (1975): 223–320. **Wiseman,** D. J. *Chronicles of Chaldean Kings (626–556 B.C.) in the British Museum* (London: Trustees of the British Museum, 1956, repr., 1974).

Chronology of the Last Years of Judah				
Year	Nb	Jehoiakim	Zedekiah	Comments
609/608		Acc.		Death of Josiah; Neco deposes Jehoahaz, appoints Jehoiakim
608/607	1			Jehoiakim reigned eleven years (2 Kgs 23:36)
607/606	2			

---

[112] "Archaeology," 172–74, 176–77. Of the 276 sites with a built-up area of 250 hectares in the late eighth century, only 38, with an area of 80 hectares, were left in the late seventh century (Finkelstein, "Archaeology," 172–74). If we accept Finkelstein's population density coefficient of 250 per built-up hectare (176), then the Shephelah suffered a loss of 48,000 inhabitants following the 701 invasion. It is reasonable to assume that not all of these were deported; some probably found protection as refugees in other parts of Judah or in Jerusalem.

606/605		3	
605/604	Acc.	4	Battle of Carchemish (Jer 46:1: 4th year of Jehoiakim); death of Nabopolassar
604/603	1	5	Fall of Ashkelon (Bab. Chr.); fasting (Jer 36:9)
603/602	2	6	Jehoiakim becomes a Babylonian vassal (2 Kgs 24:1)
602/601	3	7	
601/600	4	8	Nb attacks Egypt (Bab. Chr.); Jehoiakim's revolt (2 Kgs 24:1, 7)
600/599	5	9	Raids on Judah
599/598	6	10	
598/597	7	11	First deportation (Bab. Chr., Jer 52:28: 7th year; 2 Kgs 24:12: 8th year); three months of Jehoiachin not counted (2 Kgs 24:8)
597/596	8	1 (Acc.?)	Zedekiah appointed by Nb (eleven years: 2 Kgs 24:18)
596/595	9	2 (1)	
595/594	10	3 (2)	Revolt in Babylon; Psamtik II ascends the Egyptian throne
594/593	11	4 (3)	Anti-Babylonian conspiracy in Jerusalem (Jer 28:1)
593/592	12	5 (4)	
592/591	13	6 (5)	
591/590	14	7 (6)	Psamtik II invades Nubia; revolt of Zedekiah (?)
590/589	15	8 (7)	Revolt of Zedekiah (?)
589/588	16	9 (8)	Death of Psamtik II; beginning of siege (2 Kgs 25:1)
588/587	17	10 (9)	Early summer: break in the siege (Ezek 29:1; 31:1); 10th year of Zedekiah = 18th year of Nb (Jer 32:1)
587/586	18	11 (10)	Second deportation, 18th year (Jer 52:29)
586/585	19	(11)	Second deportation (?), 19th year (2 Kgs 25:8; Jer 52:12)

Legend: Acc. = Accession year; Bab. Chr. = Babylonian Chronicle; Nb = Nebuchadnezzar

The date of the first deportation has been fixed unambiguously by the Babylonian Chronicle BM 21946, first published by Wiseman in 1956.[113] Lines 11–14 of the reverse read:

(11) Seventh year: In the month of Kislev [November/December], the king of Akkad mustered his troops and marched to Hatti [Syria/Palestine]. (12) He besieged the city Judah[114] and in the month of Adar [February/March], on the second day, he seized the city. He took the king captive. (13) He appointed there a king after his own heart. He imposed heavy tribute and took [it] to Babylon.
(14) Eighth year: In the month of Tebet [December/January], the king of Akkad marched to Hatti as far as Carchemish....

According to obverse lines 10, 12, and 15, "king of Akkad" refers to the Babylonian king Nebuchadnezzar II. In Assyro-Babylonian practice, the regnal years of kings were counted as beginning with the new year in spring (Nisan). Therefore, the seventh regnal year of Nebuchadnezzar ran from spring 598 to spring 597. Adar is the last month of this regnal year. The capture of Jerusalem on the second day of Adar therefore corresponds approximately to March 16, 597 B.C.E., in our calendar.

This date agrees with the short list in Jer 52:28–30, which dates a deportation of 3,023 Judeans in the seventh year of Nebuchadnezzar. The only inconsistency is that 2 Kgs 24:12 dates the surrender of Jehoiachin during the first deportation in the eighth year of the Babylonian king.

The date of the second deportation, however, is still disputed. The majority of scholars formerly identified it as 587; today an increasing number are inclined to date the second deportation in 586. There are three reasons for that uncertainty. First, the text of the Babylonian Chronicle breaks off in the year 594/593, so that we have no extrabiblical data to verify the date of the second deportation.

Second, the Bible gives contradictory dates. The primary tradition dates the capture of Jerusalem in the nineteenth year of Nebuchadnezzar (2 Kgs 25:8; Jer 52:12); the special tradition in Jer 52:28–30, however, dates

---

[113] This text, also called the "Wiseman Chronicle" (cf. Wiseman, *Chronicles*, 72–73 and pls. V and VXI) appears as "Chronicle 5" in Grayson, *Assyrian and Babylonian Chronicles* (II.1), 99ff. Partial German translations are in *TGI*, 73–74, and *TUAT* 1/4:403–4.

[114] The use of "city Judah" or "city of Judah" (URU *ya-a-ḫu-du*) does not necessarily indicate careless generalization from the perspective of a great power; it may reflect the circumstance that at this time Judah comprised primarily the capital and the surrounding countryside. The same name was also given to a settlement of Judean exiles in Babylon (Joannès and Lemaire, "Trois tablettes," 18 [line 23] and 24–26).

the second deportation in his eighteenth regnal year (52:29).[115] If we are not to postulate yet another deportation (of which we know nothing), we are left with the difference of a year.

Finally, the synchronization of Babylonian and Judean chronologies is fraught with problems. The unanimous witness of the Old Testament places the second deportation in the eleventh regnal year of Zedekiah (2 Kgs 24:18; 25:2; Jer 1:3; 39:2; 52:5). Since Jer 32:1 identifies the tenth year of Zedekiah with the eighteenth year of Nebuchadnezzar, Zedekiah's eleventh year should correspond to Nebuchadnezzar's nineteenth year. If, as the Babylonian Chronicle (obv. lines 12–15) confirms, the year of the famous battle of Carchemish (605/605) from which Nebuchadnezzar emerged victorious while still crown prince is to be counted as his accession year, so that his first regnal year did not begin until Nisan of the year 604/603, then his nineteenth regnal year would in fact fall in the year 586/585. But dating the reigns of the last Judean kings presents problems. According to Jer 46:2, the year of the battle of Carchemish was the fourth year of Jehoiakim;[116] the eleven years of Jehoiakim's reign (2 Kgs 23:36) together with the three months of Jehoiachin's reign (24:8) thus encompass the years from 608/607 to 598/597. But if the second deportation is dated in the year 586/585, the eleven-year reign of Zedekiah would not begin until 596/595. There would then be a gap of a year between the first deportation in 598/597 and the accession of Zedekiah (see table).

Scholars have tried in various ways to close the regnal gap of 597/596. Vogt,[117] for example, theorized that the first deportation, more specifically the capture of Jehoiachin and the appointment of Zedekiah, extended beyond the last month of 598/597 into the following year, the remainder of which would be counted as the accession year of Zedekiah. He believed that his argument was supported by 2 Kgs 24:12 and 2 Chr 36:10; the former dates Jehoiachin's capture in the eighth year of Nebuchadnezzar, the latter "at the turn of the year." But this theory is contradicted by the Babylonian Chronicle, which assigns the removal of Jehoiachin and the appointment of Zedekiah to the seventh year of Nebuchadnezzar; it also raises the problem that an entire year in the Judean royal chronology is not counted at all. If we assume that Judah used a "postdating" enumeration such as that in the Babylonian Chronicle, logic

---

115 Also Dan 4:1 LXX; Jdt 2:1; Josephus, *Ant.* 10.146; *Ag. Ap.*, 1.154.

116 This synchronism is confirmed by Jer 36:9: the fast before Yahweh in Kislev of the fifth year of Jehoiakim is very probably connected with the Palestinian campaign of Nebuchadnezzar in his first regnal year (604/603), during which he captured Ashkelon in the month of Kislev (Chronicle 5, obv. line 18).

117 "Bemerkungen," 224ff.

would require assigning the year when there was a change of regime entirely to the former king, so that the accession year of Zedekiah would still have to be included in the reign of Jehoiachin or Jehoiakim (one year and three months for Jehoiachin, or twelve years for Jehoiakim).[118] But this is not the case.

The solution proposed by Malamat[119] seems more elegant. He attempts to explain the difficulties of synchronizing the regnal years of Nebuchadnezzar with those of the last Judean kings by assuming that the regnal years of the latter still began in the fall (Tishri), in contrast to the Babylonian practice of vernal dating. On this assumption, the eleventh year of Jehoiakim would still extend half a year into the eighth regnal year of Nebuchadnezzar; this would explain the discrepancy in 2 Kgs 24:12, and the accession year of Zedekiah would be correspondingly shorter. But this theory raises problems of synchronicity at other points: for example, the battle of Carchemish, which took place in the summer of 605, would fall in the third year of Jehoiakim rather than the fourth, contrary to Jer 46:2.

Galil[120] has an interesting theory that the seventh regnal year of Nebuchadnezzar, contrary to the Judean calendar, was an intercalary year, lengthened by inclusion of a "leap month" to compensate for the difference between the lunar and solar years. If so, its final month of Adar, in which the Babylonian Chronicle has the first deportation take place, would have coincided with Nisan of the following Judean year. This theory would explain neatly why 2 Kgs 24:12 is a year off from the Babylonian Chronicle, but it does not solve the problem of why the accession year of Zedekiah was not reckoned to his predecessors.

There is thus something to be said for the theory of Kutsch[121] that the capture of Jehoiachin and the appointment of Zedekiah took place in the final month of the seventh regnal year of Nebuchadnezzar, as stated in the Babylonian Chronicle, so that the year 597/596 would already have to be counted as the first regnal year of Zedekiah. In this case the second deportation, in the eleventh year of Zedekiah, would fall in the eighteenth year of Nebuchadnezzar (587), not the nineteenth. Not only is this date supported by Jer 52:29, but the statement in Ezek 33:21 that the exiles

---

118 See esp. Kutsch, "Jahr," 526.

119 "Last Kings," 146ff. (see especially the outline on p. 156); "Twilight," 133ff. (outline on p. 144).

120 "Babylonian Calendar," 373ff. Edwards ("Year") similarly proposes that the beginning of the year shifted in the Babylonian calendar in the years 598/597, making it diverge from the Judean year.

121 "Jahr," 523–34.

of the first deportation received news of the fall of Jerusalem in Babylon "in the twelfth year of our exile" fits well with this interpretation, since, as Kutsch was able to show,[122] with just one exception (Ezek 24:1–2) all the dates in the book of Ezekiel are based on the deportation of Jehoiachin in the year 598/597, counting the initial year. In Ezek 40:1, similarly, the twenty-fifth year of the exile (574/573) counts as the fourteenth year after the fall of Jerusalem.

The erroneous assignment of the first deportation to the eighth year of Nebuchadnezzar (2 Kgs 24:12) and the second to the nineteenth (2 Kgs 25:8; Jer 52:12; cf. Jer 32:1) can be explained relatively easily by a trick of memory that identified the year of his great victory at Carchemish as his first regnal year.

Thus we can reconstruct the following dates for the three deportations:

	The Deportations of Judah	
First Deportation	2 Adar of the 7th year of Nebuchadnezzar	16 March 597
Second Deportation	Wall breached: 9 Tammuz Destruction: 7 or 10[123] Av of the 18th year of Nebuchadnezzar	29 July 587 ca. 25 August 587
Third Deportation	23d year of Nebuchadnezzar	582

II.2.2.3. Numbers Deported

The Chronicler maintains that Nebuchadnezzar took into exile the entire surviving population of Judah and Benjamin (2 Chr 36:20) and that the land lay empty of inhabitants until the return of the exiles (36:21). One of the fundamental principles in reconstructing the history of the exile is the critical insight that this notion is not historically accurate. Barstad (II.2) rightly speaks of the "Myth of the Empty Land."

This insight rests first on a comparison of the Chronicler's claim with the divergent accounts in 2 Kgs 24–25 and Jer 39–43. It is true that we can already observe a totalizing tendency in 2 Kgs 25:21, in the formula "so Judah went into exile out of its land." This tendency feeds on

---

[122] *Die chronologischen Daten*, 38–40, 44. The news of the fall of Jerusalem in July/August 587 thus reached the exiles around January 19, 586—a plausible length of time for news to take in covering a distance of a thousand miles.

[123] Minor difference between Jer 52:12 and 2 Kgs 25:8.

the theological view that God's judgment on Israel must have struck all Israel (cf. 17:23).[124] But the account cannot entirely hide the fact that both deportations left some people behind in Judah, even if only the insignificant "poorest people of the land" (24:14; 25:12).

The narrative tradition in Jer 39–43, with its wealth of detail, clearly stands closer to the events than the account in 2 Kgs 24–25, not to mention 2 Chr 36; it is clear that the account in Kings can be accurate only in broad outline. Undoubtedly the Babylonians preferentially deported members of the upper class; however, besides the poor to whom they gave vineyards and fields (Jer 39:10; 40:10), influential and educated individuals such as Gedaliah, Baruch, Jeremiah, and a large number of officials were left behind in the land or returned to it from their places of refuge (40:7–8, 11–12). We are also told, of course, that most of those mentioned emigrated to Egypt after the murder of Gedaliah (43:5–7), but despite certain generalizing formulas ("all the remnant of Judah"), the text does not claim that the land lost its entire population.

Second, although archaeology shows that several sites were destroyed, the destruction was not as extensive as was once believed. In the Benjaminite north, above all, the urban settlements were undamaged (Gibeon, Tell en-Naṣbeh [Mizpah], Bethel, Tell el-Fûl [Gibeah]). In the hill country of Judah, settlement was reduced to small villages, but this development had already begun with the depredations of Sennacherib.

Third, cuneiform sources show that even the Assyrians, who had developed mass deportations as a standard instrument for exercising their imperial power,[125] never carried off and relocated entire nations. On the whole, Assyrian deportations were selective;[126] as a rule, men were exiled with their families.[127] The Babylonians borrowed this instrument of control from the Assyrians. Unfortunately, the deportations of the Neo-Babylonians are very poorly documented, but we can assume that their practice resembled that of the Assyrians. Nabonidus, for example, mentions the relatively limited number of 2,850 prisoners of war from the land of Hume that he donated to the temples of the capital,[128] though it is likely that they represent only a portion of the total; surely the king had already satisfied his own need for soldiers and laborers.

---

[124] See p. 11 above.

[125] Oded's *Mass Deportations* is fundamental. He counts 157 mass deportations, of which 124 fall in the period from Tiglath-pileser III to Ashurbanipal (pp. 19–20).

[126] Ibid., 47.

[127] Ibid., 23ff.; cf. the standard formula *nišē ṣeḫer rabi zikar u šinniš*, "people, small and great, male and female."

[128] VAB 4:284–85: Nabonidus 8, 9.29'–39' (*ANET*, 311).

Indeed, there is evidence that the Babylonians were even more selective than the Assyrians: they deported only those groups that served the military, economic, and political interests of the empire—above all the military and civilian elite who could have organized and mounted revolts, along with soldiers and artisans who could be used in the army and in governmental building projects. Such selectivity can also be seen in the biblical account (2 Kgs 24:14, 16; 25:11).

Today all scholars assume that the history of exilic Israel is not coextensive with the history of the Babylonian golah; there is also a history of those left behind in the land and those who emigrated to Egypt. The only difference of opinion concerns the relative sizes of the various groups and the role they played in the subsequent course of history. Some scholars view the deportations as very limited in extent; they downplay the great importance attached to the Babylonian golah by a large portion of the biblical tradition. Noth gives a classic statement of this position:

> Certain though it is that very important developments in life and thought took place among those deported to Babylon, which were to influence the whole later history of Israel, nevertheless even the Babylonian group represented a mere outpost, whereas Palestine was and remained the central arena of Israel's history. And the descendants of the old tribes who remained in the land, with the holy place of Jerusalem, constituted not only numerically the great mass but also the real nucleus of Israel.[129]

On the other side, scholars have cited "archaeological evidence" to support the claims of the biblical tradition: assuming extensive destruction in Judah and deportation of substantial numbers, they emphasize the importance of the Babylonian golah for the subsequent life of Israel. Smith, for example, estimating the number of exiles at almost half the population,[130] explicitly challenges Noth's assessment: "The work on Palestine during the Exile, however, does not justify Noth's belief that the exiles were 'merely an outpost.' As will be shown their unique social and religious attitudes became major determinants in the postexilic reconstruction."[131]

---

[129] Noth, *History*, 296. Barstad (*Myth*, 42) presses this argument even further: "However, with the great majority of the population still intact, life in Judah after 586 in all probability before long went on very much in the same way that it had done before the catastrophe." We may agree insofar as Judean society during the exile undoubtedly developed cultural forms that gave rise to important parts of the biblical tradition. In my opinion, however, Barstad underestimates the profound rupture caused by the exile.

[130] *Religion*, 32.

[131] Ibid., 35.

The biblical texts themselves vary widely as to the number of exiles. According to 2 Kgs 24:5–16, in the first deportation (597) Nebuchadnezzar carried away—besides Jehoiachin, his family and officials, and the "elite of the land"[132]—seven thousand members of the landed upper class (אנשי חיל) and one thousand artisans (החרש והמסגר, i.e., builders, carpenters, and smiths), all described in summary as men strong and fit for war (הכל גבורים עשי מלחמה). Verse 14 lumps together Jerusalemites, officials, and members of the landed military elite (גבורי חיל), ten thousand exiles altogether, and also mentions an unspecified number of artisans. Since the two lists are not mutually exclusive, the verses are probably doublets. Because 24:14 with its *wāw* + perfective + x construction interrupts the ductus of the narrative, which is formulated as a series of consecutive imperfectives (24:10–12 [13], 15–17),[133] it is probably a secondary addition, to be interpreted as a variant of 24:15–16. On the other hand, Jer 52:28 gives for the first deportation the substantially smaller figure of 3,023 Jews (יהודים).

For the second deportation, Kings does not record the number of exiles. The text simply speaks inclusively in 2 Kgs 25:11 of the rest of the people who were left in Jerusalem, the deserters, and the rest of the "artisans";[134] Jer 52:29 speaks of 832 persons (נפש). For the third deportation, Jer 52:30 says once more "of the Jews 745 persons" (יהודים נפש). This special tradition summarizes the number of those affected by all three deportations as 4,600.

How are we to assess these conflicting statements? Scholars have varied widely in their use and interpretation of the data. Wellhausen[135] assumed a figure of ten thousand for the first deportation and estimated that a substantial proportion of those left in the city and land were carried off in the second deportation. More recent scholars tend to prefer the substantially smaller numbers in the Jeremiah list[136] or refrain from giving any numbers on account of the conflicting evidence.[137] Still others have tried to harmonize the conflicting figures, for example, by explaining the difference between the seven thousand in 2 Kgs 24:16 and the ten thousand in 2 Kgs 24:14 by adding to those deported from Jerusalem the 3,023

---

132 Reading either the Qere אילי הארץ, literally "rams of the land" (cf. Ezek 17:13), or the Kethib אולי, understood as a loanword from Babylonian (*awīlu*, "human being, free citizens").

133 Similarly Würthwein, *Bücher*, 2:469–73.

134 The text has ההמון, "the multitude"; read האמון with Jer 52:15.

135 *Israelitische und jüdische Geschichte*, 135–36.

136 For example Janssen, *Juda*, 28–39; Metzger, *Grundriss*, 136ff.; Diebner, "Exil" (Introduction), 628.

137 For example Ackroyd, *Exile* (I), 21–24; Gunneweg, *Geschichte*, 123–26.

"Judeans" from the surrounding countryside in Jer 52:28[138] or by identifying the three thousand additional persons in 2 Kgs 24:14 with the "elite of the land" in 24:15 and then adding the eight thousand in 24:16 to the 4,600 in the Jeremiah list, for a grand total of 15,600.[139]

But such attempts to combine the numbers in 2 Kgs 24–25 with those in Jer 52:28–30 are impossible. The 3,023 persons in Jer 52:28 cannot be assigned to a preliminary deportation and the seven or eight thousand to a subsequent main deportation, as Malamat proposes,[140] once it is clear that the two different years (the seventh year in Jer 52:28 and the eighth in 2 Kgs 24:12) do not stand in chronological succession but reflect different systems of dating.[141] Neither can the seven thousand soldiers and one thousand artisans of 2 Kgs 24:16 be categorized as "Jerusalemites," to whom may be added the 3,023 "Judeans" of Jer 52:28, as Herrmann proposes. First, 2 Kgs 24:15 speaks of a deportation from Jerusalem involving only the royal family and the "elite of the land"; second, the term יהודים used in Jer 52:28, 30 refers almost everywhere else to the general population of Judah, not "Judeans of the land"—that would be איש/בני יהודה, "man/sons of Judah."[142] The narrative in Kings and the list in Jeremiah must be kept distinct.[143]

Given this choice, the brief Jeremiah list seems clearly preferable. In contrast to the round numbers of the books of Kings, its precise figures (3,023; 832; 745) give the impression of being more trustworthy, even if

---

138 Herrmann, *History*, 291; similarly Donner, *Geschichte*, 406; Malamat, "Twilight" (II.2.2.2), 133–34.

139 Kreissig, *Sozialökonomische Situation*, 21–24. The latter calculation is possible only because Kreissig, accepting an ancient emendation, has Jer 52:28 refer not to the seventh year but to the seventeenth—that is, a deportation at the beginning of the siege of Jerusalem.

140 "Twilight," 133–34.

141 See p. 81 above.

142 This term makes its first appearance in the eighth century; it denotes "Jews" or "Judeans" in contrast to other peoples (2 Kgs 16:6; 25:25; Jer 31:3) or living in foreign lands (Jer. 40:11–12; 43:9; 44:1). This usage suggests that the term originated as a foreign loanword; this origin is confirmed by Weidner list B (28178) 2.40 (see below). Furthermore, the form ᴸᵁya-a-ḫu-da-a+a suggests that we are dealing with what was originally an Aramaic term (emphatic plural: יְהוּדָיֵא, yəhûdāyēʾ) subsequently borrowed by Hebrew. Later the term could be used as a self-designation without implying dissociation from others (Jer 32:12; 38:19; cf. the singular in 34:9). But these texts refer not to "Judeans of the land" in contrast to residents of the capital but to members of the ethnic community in a situation where the state with its clear boundaries has collapsed. Neither can such a meaning be inferred from the circumstance that the list in 52:29 speaks of a deportation from Jerusalem only; the inhabitants of Jerusalem are also "Judeans" in this sense of the term (cf. Jer. 34:9; 38:19). When the toponym itself occurs, further identification of the people in question is optional.

143 Clearly the redactors of the Septuagint thought so and therefore omitted the Jeremiah list.

their round sum (4,600) does raise some doubts. Its dating of the first and second deportations in the seventh and eighteenth rather than eighth and nineteenth years of Nebuchadnezzar is probably correct and suggests that it is closer to the original events. Finally, the list's consistent use of the regnal years of the Babylonian king to identify dates and its identification (twice) of the exiles as יהודים ("Jews" or "Judeans"), using the same term (^{lú}ya-a-$ḫu$-da-a+a) as the Babylonian ration list published by Weidner,[144] may indicate that it drew on Babylonian sources. If so, we would be dealing with official figures from the Babylonian administration.

There is nevertheless a crucial problem with the numbers in the list: they are simply too small! If we accept the usual assumption that the population of the state of Judah numbered between 150,000 and 250,000,[145] then between 1.8 and 3 percent of the population would have been deported.[146] Even given that the exiles were largely members of the upper class, such a marginal percentage would explain neither how the Babylonian golah could come to play so major a role in the subsequent history of Israel and its religion nor why the exile was perceived as so serious a rupture. So small a group of deportees, comprising some 1,150 families, would not even be capable of surviving the strain of the journey, the disruption of relocation, the demands of military service and forced labor, and dispersal among many towns. Janssen appears to be aware of this problem when he argues that the figure of 4,600 refers only to the men, whose wives and children need to be added in. "The total would then be some three to four times as large,"[147] that is, 13,800 to 18,400—which brings him back to the scale of the numbers reported in Kings. But the context of the numbers in Kings (eight thousand or ten thousand) suggests that the count includes men only.

Such a harmonizing interpretation of the text of the list is probably out of the question. The numbers it assigns to the second and third deportations, as well as their total, expressly use the term נפש, which when used in such enumerations refers to *persons*, without regard to gender.[148]

---

[144] Text B (28128), obv. 2.40; cf. *TGI*, 79.

[145] The higher figure goes back to an estimate made by Albright, *Biblical Period*, 56 and 105 n. 118; the lower comes from Janssen, *Juda*, 28.

[146] Diebner ("Exil" [Introduction], 628) claims 3 to 4 percent, basing his calculations on 2 Kgs 15:19–22 and 2 Sam 24:9. How he arrives at this figure is a mystery to me. But even the higher percentage would be too low.

[147] Janssen, *Juda*, 35.

[148] Cf. Exod 12:4; Num 31:28ff.; Josh 10:28ff.; 11:11; 1 Sam 22:22. Women are specifically included in Num 31:35 and Jer 43:6. If this is not what the text means to say, the variant usage needs to be noted explicitly (cf. Gen. 47:26–27), contra Janssen, *Juda*, 35 n. 8. Assyrian texts use the plural *napištu* in a similar way.

If it is correct to assume that the list derives from Babylonian sources, this interpretation is reinforced: both the Assyrians and the Babylonians included all persons in a single total.[149]

Now Diebner believes that he can support the numbers of the Jeremiah list by pointing out that the 27,280/90 people Sargon claims to have deported from Samaria constituted only 8 to 10 percent of the population of the northern kingdom, which he estimates at 300,000 to 350,000.[150] But this percentage is two to five times as great; furthermore, it increases considerably when one remembers that this deportation affected only the rump state of Samaria, while the parts of the kingdom that had been split off in 732 (Dor, Megiddo, Gilead), which constituted two-thirds of the state, had been subject to previous deportations. If we assume a figure of 102,000 inhabitants, which Broshi and Finkelstein estimate for the Samarian hill country (including Carmel and Gilboa), corresponding roughly to the rump state of Samaria, in the middle of the eighth century on the basis of the Survey of Israel,[151] the deportees represented about 27 percent of the population. This percentage agrees much better with the archaeological evidence of the survey, which indicates that the number of settlements in the northern and southern hill country of Samaria fell by more than half as a result of Assyrian military operations.[152] The population loss of an additional 20 to 30 percent probably includes war casualties and refugees.

Unfortunately, we lack external data and extensive field surveys for sixth-century Judah. It would appear that archaeology is still not in a posi-

---

[149] The terms used—*nišū*, "people"; *napšāti*, "persons"; *ṣābū*, "host"; *šallatu*, "prisoners"; etc.—are quite general and are not specific as to gender or age (Oded, *Mass Deportations*, 2ff., 22, 79ff. Nabonidus speaks of "2,850 [persons] from the troops, booty from the Land of Hume" (VAB 4:284–85: Nabonidus 8, 9.31N–32N).

[150] "Exil" (Introduction), 628. Diebner speaks of 27,289 persons, whereas the Calah prism speaks of 27,280, and the great inscription from the palace at Khorsabad has 27,290 (*TUAT* 1/4:382–83)). For the latest interpretation of the historical background, see Becking, *Fall*, 21ff. The earlier view, based on the tribute of one thousand talents paid by King Menahem in 738, which he raised by exacting fifty shekels (one mina) from each of the wealthy (2 Kgs 15:19–22), surprisingly agrees with more recent calculations based on archaeological surveys (Broshi and Finkelstein, "Population," 287). According to Exod 38:25–26, one talent equals three thousand shekels. That would mean some sixty thousand full citizens. If we assume that the average family size was four and that there were some 100,000 people who were not landowners, we come to the figure given by Diebner.

[151] "Population," 50–51, 54.

[152] In the northern hill country of Samaria, the number of settlements dropped from 238 to 95 between Iron II and Iron III; in the southern hill country, 190 settlements in the Iron II period contrast with 90 in the Persian period (*NEAEHL*, 1311–12, 1313–14). This reduction occurred despite the Assyrians' resettlement of foreign ethic groups (2 Kgs 17:24ff.), now confirmed in part by ceramic evidence.

tion to distinguish with sufficient clarity finds associated with the period of Babylonian rule from those of the seventh century and the Persian period.

Our only recourse, then, is to base our picture of the Babylonian deportations in the southern kingdom on data from the Assyrian deportations in the northern kingdom. If we do so, it is quickly apparent that the figure of 832 deportees given by Jer 52:29 for the second deportation simply cannot be right. The annals of Tiglath-pileser show that 625, 650, or 656 people were deported from totally insignificant towns in Galilee;[153] substantially larger numbers would be expected in the case of the capital. Jerusalem, swollen since the end of the eighth century and during the seventh century by streams of refugees from the north (after 722) and the southwest (after 701), covered an area of between 120 and 150 acres,[154] expanding beyond the southeast hill of the traditional City of David to include the southwest hill, so that in this period it must have had a population of twelve to fifteen thousand.[155] The figure of 832 can only refer to the final contingent deported, people who had held out to the bitter end in the besieged and starving city. Jeremiah 38:19 and 2 Kgs 25:11 speak of deserters who had left the city long before. According to Jer 39:9 and 2 Kgs 25:11, they were also deported; the list in Jer 52:28–30, however, where 52:29 refers exclusively to people deported "from Jerusalem," clearly does not include them. This means that the numbers in the list are probably accurate but by no means include all the groups that the Babylonians assembled for deportation.

I believe, therefore, that it is more realistic to go beyond the Jeremiah list and assume a quota of some 25 percent to be deported from Judah, as in the case of Samaria. An estimate of the population of Judah in the late seventh and early sixth centuries is therefore critical for any calculation. Recent archaeological studies have shown that estimates made in the past are clearly too high. For the eighth century, Albright gave a figure of 250,000 Judeans;[156] assuming the population ratio of the northern to the southern kingdom to be 8 to 5, as reported by David's census in 2 Sam 24:9, Diebner came up with about 220,000.[157] Relying on a census in the year 1922, Janssen estimated the population of Judah in the seventh century at between 150,000 and 170,000.[158] On the basis of earlier excavations and their own field surveys, Broshi and Finkelstein arrived at a

---

[153] Becking, *Fall*, 15–16.
[154] *NEAEHL*, 708.
[155] Finkelstein, "Archaeology," 175.
[156] *Biblical Period*, 56 and 105 n. 118.
[157] "Exil" (Introduction), 628.
[158] *Juda*, 28.

substantially smaller estimate:[159] in their opinion, even in the second half of the eighth century, the period of its densest settlement, Judah had a population of only about 110,000. In 1994, however, Finkelstein himself adjusted this estimate a bit upward, giving a figure of 120,000, not including the areas north and west of Jerusalem.[160] If the population of these areas is added in, we arrive at a figure of about 140,000 for the population of Judah toward the end of the eighth century.

For all further calculations, it is critically important to take into reasonable account the depredations and deportations of Sennacherib in 701, to which earlier studies often paid little or no attention. In 1994, Finkelstein laid the groundwork for an archaeological approach to a realistic assessment by using the ceramic typology of Lachish (strata III and II) to distinguish structures built in the eighth century from those built in the seventh. The result of his field surveys is dramatic: the 1,160 acres of settlement in the eighth century had shrunk to 630 in the seventh. This means that the population of Judah was effectively halved by Sennacherib's campaign and did not recover substantially until near the end of the seventh century.[161] Finkelstein estimates the population of Judah at the end of the seventh century and the beginning of the sixth at just 65,000. It must be noted, however, that Finkelstein did not take into account the areas north and west of Jerusalem: the latter had not yet been studied, and surveys of the former were not yet able to distinguish between the eighth and sevenths centuries. If we cautiously include these areas in the estimates, we arrive at a figure of about eighty thousand for the population of the southern kingdom on the eve of the Babylonian deportations.

It is of no little importance that the geographical distribution of the population clearly shifted at the end of the seventh century. The Shephelah had lost 70 percent of its inhabitants (ca. 48,000); some had been deported, others had fled to the hill country of Judah or to Jerusalem. Almost all Judeans were now living in the hill country; the percentage of the total population living in Jerusalem had risen from 6 percent to more than 20 percent. The limited resources of the hill country forced settlement to expand into the arid regions to the east and south.

On the basis of these archaeological studies—admittedly still subject to some uncertainties—we may make the following calculations: if the population of Judah at the end of the seventh century and the beginning of the

---

159 "Population," 54.
160 "Archaeology," 176.
161 Strangely, Jamieson-Drake (*Scribes*, 61–62) still believed that the population of Judah grew by 40 percent between the eighth and seventh centuries and therefore concluded that the population was reduced during the exilic period by a disastrous 70 percent or more. For a discussion of this negative assessment, see p. 93 below.

sixth was approximately eighty thousand, and if we assume something like the 25 percent deported from Samaria, about twenty thousand individuals were deported from Judah. This would be a substantially greater number than reported by the Jeremiah list (4,600) and more in line with the higher numbers given in 2 Kgs 24, especially if the figures in 24:14 (10,000) and 24:16 (8,000) are added together. If it is true that the Deuteronomistic writers deliberately refrained from giving numbers in describing the deportation of 587 so as to allow their all-inclusive interpretation of the exile as God's final judgment on Israel, it is quite possible that the figure of ten thousand deportees in 24:14, clearly a secondary addition, referred originally to the second deportation and was transferred to the first by these writers. If so, the present account would actually report the total losses due to both deportations. Of course, relating a calculation based on archaeological evidence to the account in 2 Kgs 24 assumes that the latter's figure of eighteen thousand includes at least some women and children.

A major element of uncertainty is estimating how many perished in the war, were executed by the Babylonians, or emigrated to Egypt. If we assume another twenty thousand, then Judah lost approximately half its inhabitants between 600 and 580 and was reduced to a population of some forty thousand. In truth, the exile meant a severe bloodletting for Judah.

Such an estimate yields a highly realistic ratio of about two to one for the number of people remaining in Judah and the number in the Babylonian golah. Given the higher proportion of educated individuals in the golah, the two major population elements of the exilic period were of roughly equal importance.

The proposed numbers are in part speculative, but they chime with the available textual and archaeological data. The large number of exiles makes it easier to understand why the Babylonian exile represents so massive a rupture in the history of Israel, even though life in Judah continued to go on. On the one hand, when the exiles surviving in various locations returned, they were able in part to impose their claim to leadership, displacing those who had stayed behind. On the other hand, those left in Judah were clearly strong enough to resist them. In any case, one cannot minimize the deportations as historical events and at the same time exalt the golah as the decisive factor in the history of Israel and Israel's religion. The calculations we have proposed suggest a realistic middle course between these two extremes.

II.2.3. Judah in the Exilic Period

For the period immediately following the destruction of Jerusalem in 587, we can draw on relatively contemporary sources in Jer 40:7–43:3 and Lam

1–2; 4–5. These sources, however, paint totally opposite pictures of the situation of those left behind. The Jeremiah narrative describes an opportunity for rapid improvement of the survivors' living conditions in cooperation with the Babylonians. The book of Lamentations, especially Lam 5, bewails the sufferings of the populace under the heel of the occupation forces. If the texts are not to be assigned to different historical situations (before and after the murder of Gedaliah?), then we must reckon with the presence of distortions, probably on both sides. The account in 2 Kgs 25:1–26, too, is clearly more negative than the corresponding narrative in Jeremiah.[162] Its description of the events involving Gedaliah (25:22–26) is a secondary source. The account in 2 Chr 36 is so distant from events and so shaped by theological interests that it is worthless as a historical source.

The Babylonians had a clear interest in consolidating as rapidly as possible the situation in war-torn Judah, traumatized by destruction, famine, and depopulation. Their harsh punitive measures were intentionally selective, aimed primarily at the groups and institutions that had supported the revolt against Babylon: the rebellious vassal king Zedekiah (2 Kgs 25:1–7) and the leaders of the nationalist party (25:18–21), as well as officers, soldiers, and workers with a role in the war effort (25:11, 19). Since the two chief priests of Jerusalem (Seraiah and Zephaniah) were among those ruthlessly condemned, the destruction of the Jerusalem temple was probably due to its having been a stronghold and symbol of national revolt.[163]

Contrariwise, the supporters of the pro-Babylonian party, who had been among the opposition under Jehoiakim and Zedekiah, certainly enjoyed the favor of the occupying power. As early as 594, Jeremiah had demonstrated against the policy of revolt against Babylon (Jer 27–28); when the siege began, he constantly urged capitulation. He was released from prison by a Babylonian officer (39:13–14) and even offered a generous living in Babylon, which he nevertheless refused. More important than this gesture, however, was the Babylonians' appointment of the Shaphanide Gedaliah ben Ahikam, a leading member of the opposition, as governor of Judah (40:7). Gedaliah's father had protected the prophet Jeremiah from a mob inspired with nationalistic and religious rage (26:24), and his grandfather had been a major supporter of the Josianic reform (2 Kgs 22). Having largely neutralized the nationalists, the

---

[162] See pp. 5–12 above.
[163] The Babylonians not only used deportation to punish those responsible for the revolt but also clearly selected people they could use for their own purposes, as is shown by the deportation of deserters (2 Kgs 25:11; Jer 39:19–20).

Babylonians thus made a serious attempt with the help of the reform party to rebuild autocephalous structures under Babylonian authority in the shattered land.

For the first time after the collapse of the Josianic reform with the death of Josiah in 609, the reform party had another chance to put their policies into effect. It appears that Gedaliah, who probably held the office of steward under Zedekiah,[164] energetically seized the opportunity. He built his capital at Mizpah, that is, in the Benjaminite territory north of Jerusalem (Jer 40:6, 8), which the archaeological evidence shows was little involved in the military conflicts. The primary goal of his policies was to provide bread and jobs for the remaining population as soon as possible. He had the complete support of the Babylonians, who assigned to the poor the abandoned property of the deported upper and middle classes (39:10). In a similar vein, Gedaliah expressly approved the occupation—by force, if necessary—of the deserted villages by groups of refugees returning to Judah from neighboring lands (40:10).[165] By these actions, Gedaliah restored agricultural production and the food supply of the population with astonishing speed.

Just how extraordinary and controversial Gedaliah's redistribution of property was is shown by the bitter response it evoked among the former property owners deported to Babylon (Ezek 11:14–21; 33:23–29). Their reaction suggests that Gedaliah saw the redistribution from the perspective of the Deuteronomic social reform that the reform party had fought for during the reign of Josiah but that collapsed with his death. Gedaliah and his supporters saw the breakdown of the structures of national government and the deportation of a large percentage of the upper class as a great opportunity to establish in Judah a less-stratified society, based on Deuteronomic brotherhood ethics.[166]

---

[164] A sixth-century seal from Lachish reads: גדליהו אשר על הבית, "Gedalyahu, who (is appointed) over the house." See Miller and Hayes, *History*, 422.

[165] From distant Babylonia, Ezekiel divides those remaining in Judah into three groups (Ezek 33:27): those living in the ruins, those in the open field, and those in "strongholds and caves." He is probably envisioning the situation shortly after 587, as reported to him by the deportees.

[166] It is therefore unlikely that Gedaliah assumed the title of king, as Miller and Hayes (*History*, 421–25) and Oswald (*Israel*, 132–133) believe. There is nothing to indicate that the king's daughters in Jer 41:10 and 43:6 were daughters of Gedaliah, and even if the seal reading ליאזניהו עבד המלך ("Property of Ya'azanyahu, the servant of the king") found at Mizpah, does refer to the Jezaniah named as an officer at Gedaliah's court in Jer 40:8, it can equally well refer to his position under Zedekiah. The seal can be dated epigraphically from the late eighth to the seventh century and is therefore most likely too old. The words ורבי המלך ("and the chief officers of the king") in Jer 41:1 are textually uncertain and do not refer to Gedaliah. They are a gloss that has entered the text in the wrong place, being intended to

Nevertheless, the account in Jer 40:7ff., which very likely emanates from a member of the reform group around Gedaliah, possibly the scribe Baruch who was a friend of Jeremiah,[167] is probably a good bit too pro-Babylonian. The prayer in Lam 5 laments that farmland and homes have been turned over to aliens (5:2), corvée and socage have been imposed (5:5, 8, 13), payment is being demanded for the bare necessities of life (5:4), women are raped (5:11), and the representatives of the people are not respected but shamefully murdered (5:12). This description, too, may be the somewhat one-sided view of a writer with close ties to the party of religious nationalism.

Jamieson-Drake arrives at a very negative assessment of the situation in Judah during the exilic period through a statistical analysis of archaeological evidence. He speaks of a "complete societal collapse"[168] and an "almost complete dissolution"[169] of the regional social system. In his view, the extent of this decline was due not so much to the Babylonians' military action and deportation policies as to the collapse of the centralized administrative control and distribution system in Jerusalem after the removal of the elite who managed it.[170] There followed a sharp drop in productivity; famine and emigration reduced the population drastically. Unfortunately, Jamieson-Drake does not discuss the textual evidence that contradicts such a view. In addition, some of his observations have been called into question by more recent archaeological studies. According to Finkelstein ("Archaeology"), for example, the population had already reached its maximum in the eighth century, not, as Jamieson-Drake believes, in the seventh century, which was marked by a substantial reduction in population brought about by Sennacherib's campaign in 701.[171] It is also highly questionable whether the settled area of Jerusalem in the sixth century can simply be set at zero, as Jamieson-Drake does.[172] This has not been demonstrated archaeologically, and despite all the destruction and the removal of the administrative center to Mizpah, one would not expect the former capital to be totally devoid of inhabitants. The social decline in the sixth century was probably less dramatic than Jamieson-Drake makes it out to be.

---

describe the Chaldeans sitting at Gedaliah's table mentioned in 41:2—they are Babylonian officials of Nebuchadnezzar assigned to the provincial administration.

167 That he must have been a person of some rank is shown by his seal "Berechiah ben Neriyahu": see Nahman Avigad, "Baruch the Scribe and Jerachmeel the King's Son," *IEJ* 28 (1978): 52–56.

168 *Scribes*, 75.
169 Ibid., 146.
170 Ibid., 75–76.
171 See pp. 78–80 above.
172 *Scribes*, 161.

The reality probably lay somewhere in between. The Babylonians were undoubtedly not beneficent. Of course they expropriated land for their own ends, to be cultivated by Judean clients; they imposed taxes and exacted tribute and demanded corvée and socage from the subject population. Of course there were instances of rape and humiliation of the dignitaries of the vanquished, as is typical of all occupying powers. As the inscriptions of Nebuchadnezzar clearly show, the primary aim of Babylonian policy was to promote the architectural splendor and prosperity of the Babylonian heartland as much as possible by exploiting the subject provinces. The situation will have been no different in Judah. The Babylonians supported Gedaliah's reform policies only to the extent that they furthered this imperial purpose by restoring agricultural productivity.

Thus Gedaliah's promising attempts at reform were hampered from the start by the excesses and separate interests of the occupying power. It is therefore quite understandable that this attempt failed after a relatively short time. Although warned in advance, Gedaliah was slain as a despicable Babylonian collaborator by Ishmael, a commander belonging to a collateral line of the royal house, who had been one of Zedekiah's chief officers (Jer 41:1–2). The failure of the attempted reform was due to the impatience of a nationalist who still could not imagine a state without its own king and enjoying a more equitable distribution of property.

Unfortunately, we do not know precisely how long Gedaliah's regime lasted. Jeremiah 41:1 does not mention a year but only the "seventh month." If the year in question was the year of the conquest of Jerusalem, which took place during the fourth and fifth months (Jer 39:4; 2 Kgs 25:8), then Gedaliah had only two months for his social experiment. But so short a period can hardly accommodate all the events recounted in Jer 40. There is thus some reason to associate the deportation of an additional 745 Judeans in the year 582 (Jer 52:30) with the murder of Gedaliah.[173] Since the first two Babylonian deportations from Judah were clearly punitive, the third requires a similarly weighty motive. The murder of the governor appointed by the Babylonians along with the Babylonian officials appointed to assist him would undoubtedly supply such a motive. If we accept this date, then Gedaliah had some four or five years to carry

---

[173] This connection is gaining increasing acceptance; see Oded, "Judah," 424–25; Miller and Hayes, *History*, 425; Mitchell, "Babylonian Exile," 413; Oswald, *Israel*, 134. Possibly Nebuchadnezzar's campaign in Coele-Syria, Moab, and Ammon mentioned by Josephus (*Ant.* 10.181) for the year 582 has at least something to do with the murder, since the murderer Ishmael was supported by Baalis, the Ammonite king (Jer 40:14; 41:15). But the historicity of this campaign is not beyond doubt (see p. 56 above).

out his social reform. When we remember that the murder of Gedaliah was still regularly memorialized in Judah by a public fast in the early postexilic period (Zech 7:5; 8:19), it is clear how deeply embedded his reform project was in the memories of many Judeans and how great the hopes accompanying it were.

The abrupt reaction of the Babylonians makes it likely that the situation in Judah worsened perceptibly after 582.[174] Probably they now appointed a Babylonian governor, but it is also possible that they administered Judah from Samaria. Jeremiah 52:30 says that this third deportation was carried out by Nebuzaradan, the destroyer of Jerusalem; this may mean that he was the Babylonian commissar in Judah and now took direct charge of the administrative machinery. According to Jer 41:16ff., fear of Babylonian reprisals led a substantial group of Gedaliah's followers to emigrate to Egypt, against the advice of Jeremiah. Moreover, it is possible that the complaints about the oppressive Babylonian occupation voiced in Lam 5 refer to the period after 582.

The distrust of Baruch and Jeremiah on the part of the officers formerly loyal to Gedaliah (43:2–3) demonstrates that the reform coalition backing Gedaliah was split by the events of 582, but this coalition probably did not simply dissolve after his death. On the contrary, it is reasonable to assume that the punitive measures of the Babylonians weakened the party of religious nationalism in Judah once more, since deportation focused on its supporters and many of its members preferred to flee or emigrate. For reasons of internal security, the Babylonian provincial administration had an interest in strengthening the remnants of the submissive reform party once more.[175] In any case, the Deuteronomistic book of Jeremiah, a memorial to Baruch and the other members of the reform party (cf. Jer 36; 45), shows that in the second half of the sixth century the sons and grandsons of those who lost most of their power when Gedaliah was murdered still constituted a cohesive group in Judah, even if they were not dominant.

The simple rural populace was less affected by the deportation and emigrations of the year 582. Even though the Babylonian provincial administration became increasingly oppressive, taxes, corvée, and socage hardly differed from what they had been under Judean kings. It is also

---

[174] On the consequences of the murder of Gedaliah for the Babylonian golah, see pp. 103–4 below.

[175] Possibly the early sixth-century seal impression reading "Hananiah ben Gedalyahu" bears witness to the existence of an otherwise unknown son of Gedaliah in Judah; see Nahman Avigad, "Seals and Sealings," *IEJ* 14 (1964): 193; Mitchell, "Babylonian Exile," 410.

reasonable to assume that the food supply soon stabilized once more. There are even hints that it was possible under the Babylonian regime to establish a limited degree of self-government based on elders (Lam 5:14). There were obviously no further confrontations.

Although the Babylonians refrained from settling foreign ethnic groups in Judah, the real threat facing the Judean people came from without. It emerged from the minor states surrounding Judah, who took advantage of the diminished population and the weak Babylonian military presence to invade the territory of Judah from all sides and advance their own political and economic interests.

When this process began is uncertain. By the middle of the sixth century at the latest, the Negev (Amos 1:11–12; Obad 29; Ezek 35:10; 36:5) and possibly also the southern portion of the Judean hill country (cf. Jer 32:44) had been lost to the Edomites, the Shephelah to the expansionistic Phoenicians and Philistines (Obad 19; Ezek 25:15; 26:2), and Gilead to the Ammonites (Jer 49:1). There were also attacks on the civilian population (Lam 5:9) and slave raids by the Phoenicians (Amos 1:9), from which there was no protection since almost all the fortifications and strongholds had been razed. In this period even Jerusalem was an open city; in the early postexilic period, the Samarians were still trying to prevent its refortification (Ezra 4:7–16). Thus it is not surprising that during these years the Samarian Sanballat, the Ammonite Tobiah, and the Arab Geshem should have their say in Jerusalem (Neh 2:10, 19).

The military weakness and uncertain legal status of Judah in the exilic period thus led to the shrinkage and fragmentation of the area of Judean settlement and to constant confrontations with foreigners from the surrounding states. Without any effective means of resistance, the population could only gnash their teeth and learn to live with the political and economic influence of these foreigners. Although they were dwelling in their own land, those who remained in Judah had largely lost their territorial social integrity.

II.2.4. The Egyptian Golah

Concerning the Egyptian golah in the sixth century B.C.E. we have only the scanty information in Jer 43:7–44:30, a heavily Deuteronomistic text interested primarily in theological questions. Not until a century or two later does the Jewish military colony of Elephantine (an island in the Nile near Aswan) emerge into the clear light of history. Its archives (texts dating from 495–399 B.C.E.) admit only tentative conclusions about the earlier period. There is also some information in the *Letter of Aristeas* (third or second century B.C.E.).

After the murder of Gedaliah, a group of Judeans fearing Babylonian retribution decided to emigrate to Egypt. They were following a common trend. During the Twenty-Sixth Dynasty (672–525), with the encouragement of the Egyptian authorities, a great number of foreigners (Greeks, Carites, Syrians, and Phoenicians) entered Egypt, where they made their living primarily as mercenaries and merchants. Thus the band of refugees in the early exilic period had reason to hope for a good chance to survive in Egypt, especially since most of them were soldiers.

According to Jer 43:7–8, the group settled in Tahpanhes (Greek Daphnae), in Lower Egypt; according to Jer 44:1, there were already Judeans living at Migdol, Noph (Memphis),[176] and in the land of Pathros, that is, Upper Egypt. This means that the Egyptian golah was connected only in part with the conquests of Nebuchadnezzar; Judeans had emigrated to Egypt previously for various reasons. The *Letter of Aristeas* (v. 13), for example, reports that Judeans were dispatched as auxiliaries—probably by Zedekiah—during the Nubian campaign of Psamtik II in 591.[177] It is easy to imagine that they remained in Egypt as mercenaries in the Egyptian army, on account of the good living conditions. Other Judean soldiers may already have come to Egypt with the Assyrian army under Sargon in 716 or Ashurbanipal in 667/666 and decided to stay there.

These various groups had not been forcibly relocated; they had emigrated to Egypt or settled there more or less of their own free will. The Egyptian golah, therefore, unlike the Babylonian, could hardly have desired to return to Judah to undo a wrong.[178] On the contrary, what we know of the Judean military colony at Elephantine (admittedly from a much later date) indicates that the people had adapted long before to living permanently in Egypt.

The most important evidence is their construction of their own Yahweh temple at Elephantine, built (on the evidence of EP 30.15–16; 31.12)[179] even before the invasion of Egypt by the Persian king Cambyses in 525. Possibly it was founded as early as the Babylonian period. As the Elephantine letters attest, there could be serious abuse of the resident Jews by the indigenous population: the letter writers complain to the

---

176 Astonishingly, very few Jewish names have appeared in the papyri from Saqqara (Persian period); see J. B. Segal, *Aramaic Texts from North Saqqâra with Some Fragments in Phoenician* (London: Egypt Exploration Society, 1983), 8–9, 66–67, 77–78.

177 Porten ("Jews," 378–79) thinks instead of an emigration under Psamtik I, in the time of King Manasseh.

178 Smith-Christopher ("Reassessing," 27) has pointed out the profound difference between the "chosen 'exile'" of the Egyptian Diaspora and the "forcible relocation" of the Babylonian Diaspora, as well as the significance of this difference for the trauma of the exile.

179 Porten and Yardeni, *Textbook*, 1:68–75: A4.7, lines 13–14; A4.8, line 12.

authorities in Jerusalem, for example, that the priests of the god Chnum had pillaged their temple in the year 410. But such events did not make the Jews of Elephantine feel an urge to return. Because the Egyptian Jews were integrated solidly into Egyptian society, they did not care much about the reforms that Israelite religion underwent in Judah shortly before the exile. Despite Josiah's centralization of the cult, they had no problem with operating another temple of Yahweh outside Jerusalem. At least in their personal devotions, they placed other deities such as the goddess Anat-*yhw* alongside *yhw*,[180] practicing a syncretistic religiosity of preexilic provenance.[181] This integration, coupled with a religiously conservative self-sufficiency, is probably the primary reason why the Egyptian golah had little use for the theological renewal of Yahwism and was therefore judged extremely negatively by the proponents of this renewal (Jer 24:8; 44).

II.2.5. The Babylonian Golah[182]

Unlike those who had emigrated to Egypt, the Babylonian golah had undergone the terrible experience of forcible displacement; unlike those who remained in Judah, they had experienced a humiliating social uprooting. They had lost not only their homeland but also their real property and their generally influential position. The sense of having been uprooted and dispossessed against their wills kept alive their hopes to return and revise the facts of history.

The majority of Judeans, adherents of religious nationalism, had suffered bodily the failure of their anti-Babylonian policies; they must have found it enormously difficult to adapt to the new situation. This is well documented for the group deported with Jehoiachin in the first deportation of 597. When a rebellion broke out in Babylonia in 595 and the Neo-Babylonian Empire showed its first signs of weakness, hopes for a speedy return flared up among the Judean exiles. They eagerly followed the attempts to forge an anti-Babylonian coalition that were going forward in Jerusalem in 591. There the prophet Hananiah proclaimed that Jehoiachin would return within two years, along with the temple vessels and the others who had been carried off to Babylon (Jer 28:2–4). Among

---

180 E.g., EP 44.3: Porten and Yardeni, *Textbook*, 2:B7.3, line 3.

181 Thus the cautious conclusion of Porten, "Jews," 385. Contrary to what one often reads, the syncretism of the Elephantine Jews was well within the limits of preexilic Israelite religious practice.

182 For a discussion of the sources, see pp. 72–74 above.

the exiles, the prophets Ahab and Zedekiah came forward, fanning the flames of similar hopes (29:21–22). In this overheated atmosphere, when Jeremiah, who had demonstrated publicly against the policies of religious nationalism by going about the streets of Jerusalem bearing a yoke on his shoulders (Jer 27), wrote a letter to the "elders among the exiles" in which he called on his people to prepare for a lengthy stay in far-off Babylonia (29:1–7), a storm of indignation broke out among the exiles. A leader of the religious nationalists in Babylonia, Shemaiah, sent an ultimatum to the priest Zephaniah in Jerusalem, demanding that he finally carry out his duty to control Jeremiah (29:24–29). Jeremiah, however, refused to be intimidated and announced condemnation and death for the nationalistic spokesmen in exile (Jer 29:30–32; cf. 29:21–22; Ezek 13:16). In a similar vein, the prophet Ezekiel attacked the nationalistic hopes for deliverance that were rife among the exiles. He castigated Zedekiah's intended revocation of his vassal oath not only as a breach of treaty but also as a transgression of an obligation to Yahweh under sacral law, which Yahweh as guarantor of the treaty would surely punish (17:11–21).

But none of the expected coups got off the ground. Nebuchadnezzar was soon firmly in control again, probably by 594. In putting down the revolt, it is quite possible that he decided to make an example of the Judean exiles, in view of the very specific curse cited in Jer 29:22: "May Yahweh make you like Zedekiah and Ahab, whom the king of Babylon roasted in the fire," said to be in the mouth all the exiles. All in all, however, the exiles appear to have been treated leniently. Tablet C of the archive published by Weidner shows that in the year 592 Jehoiachin and his five sons were still receiving their normal rations of ten and two and a half $qû$[183] of oil, respectively, from the Babylonian palace administration (rev. II, lines 17–18; cf. tablet B, obv. II, lines 38–39). The great quantity given Jehoiachin, twenty times the normal individual ration (half a $qû$), argues that he still enjoyed a position of respect at the Babylonian court, as is further emphasized by his being given the title "king of Judah" (*šarri ša* ᴷᵁᴿ*ya-ḫu-du*[184] or *ya-ku-du*[185]).

Despite this relatively respectful treatment of their political leader, the Babylonian exiles—as we know from the preaching of Ezekiel—could not be dissuaded from following the subsequent fate of Jerusalem with close attention. The exile community was buzzing with all kinds of rumors as to the real goal of Nebuchadnezzar's decisive invasion of Palestine. Many obviously hoped that the great king had his eyes not on

---

[183] Almost twenty quarts.
[184] Tablet B obv. II, lines 38–39; D obv. lines 20–21.
[185] Tablet C rev. II, lines 17–18.

Jerusalem but on Rabbath-Ammon, which had also joined the anti-Babylonian conspiracy in 594 (Ezek 21:23–27 [18–22]). The exiles were worried about their relatives left behind in Jerusalem (24:21) and especially about the temple, which Ezekiel calls "the pride of your power, the delight of your eyes, and your heart's desire" (24:21; cf. 24:25). This language shows how intense were the religious and emotional ties of the golah to this symbol of hope for religious nationalism. As Ezekiel's proleptic symbolic action makes clear, the grief over its destruction must have been profound (24:15–24). Not until hopes for a speedy change of fortunes were shattered in the aftermath of 595 and 589 were a majority of the exiles—influenced in part by the prophecies of Jeremiah and Ezekiel, which were gradually coming to pass—ready to come to terms with their situation and to accept integration into Babylonian society.[186]

This step was made easier by the Babylonians' policy of settling ethnic minorities such as Egyptians, Greeks, and Phoenicians in cohesive groups and allowing them their own organization.[187] Except for Jehoiachin and his small household, the majority of those deported in 597 were settled in Tel-abib by the river Chebar in the vicinity of Nippur (Ezek 1:2; 3:15).[188] As cuneiform texts from the year 498 now show, other Judeans deported from Jerusalem were settled in a place called "the city (of) Judah" (URU ya-a-ḫu-du),[189] which may have been near Sippar. Later other towns were built,[190] probably to accommodate an influx of Judeans from the later deportations of 587 and 582 as well as Israelites and Judeans from the earlier Assyrian deportations of 732, 722, and 701.

The exiles lived in their various towns grouped together either by families (Ezra 2:59) or occupation; despite having no function, the priests and other members of the temple staff constituted independent groups (Ezra 2:36ff.; 8:17). Besides priests and prophets, elders played a leadership role on the model of premonarchic society (Ezek 8:1; 14:1; 20:1). The "elders of the golah" (זִקְנֵי הַגּוֹלָה) to whom Jeremiah addressed his letter may have

---

186 Ezekiel had to contend with the fact that his fellow exiles were more interested in flatteries and material gain than in his prophecies (Ezek 33:31).

187 Cf. the "village of the Tyrians" located in the vicinity of Nippur between 575 and 565 (Joannès, "Trois textes" [II.1], 147ff.).

188 This river is the *nar kabari*, which can probably be identified with the *šaṭṭ en nīl*, which flows eastward from the Euphrates near Babylon, runs through the site of ancient Nippur, and later rejoins the Euphrates.

189 Joannès and Lemaire, "Trois tablettes," 17–27. Since the name is identical with the official term for Jerusalem in the Babylonian Chronicle (see p. 78 above), this "New Jerusalem" was probably established on the official initiative of the government.

190 Tel-melah, Tel-harsha, Cherub-addan, Immer (Ezra 2:59), Casiphia (Ezra 8:17).

constituted a leadership council.[191] Unlike the Assyrian golah, which largely disappeared through assimilation, the Babylonian golah enjoyed better basic conditions for maintaining its identity.

From the fact that three of the town names begin with "Tel," which denotes a site of former habitation, we can conclude that the Babylonian regime settled the Judean exiles in places where they could return the land to cultivation. Probably these were crown lands, assigned to the exiles by the state to farm (cf. 2 Kgs 18:32); in return, they owed the state taxes, corvée and socage, and military service. Despite the metaphor of "Babylonian captivity," it must be stressed that the "exiles" were neither prisoners of war in the modern sense,[192] kept in prison camps, nor slaves in the legal sense, meaning that they could be bought and sold. The overwhelming majority were semifree tenants on state land; tied to their plot of ground, they owed their economic status to the crown, to which they owed service. Their status was comparable to that of the Babylonian *ikkaru*.[193] There is no evidence of oppression on ethnic or religious grounds.

In the early exilic period, the overwhelming majority of Judean exiles appear to have been engaged in state-sponsored agriculture, as Jeremiah's letter to them presupposes (Jer 29:5). Subjectively, those who had been members of the upper class—large landowners, officials, and merchants—probably felt farming to be an almost unbearable social degradation. This feeling was one of the roots of the "trauma of exile" evident in the texts, emphasized by Smith-Christopher in his argument against downplaying the gravity of the exile.[194] The Judean artisans mentioned in the account of the deportation (2 Kgs 24:14, 16; 25:11) were also employed—like other deportees—primarily in the vast state-sponsored building programs of Nebuchadnezzar and Nabonidus. The ration list published by Weidner mentions specialists from a variety of nations at

---

191 Cf. the "council of elders [*puḫur šibuti*] of the Egyptians" (Eph'al, "On the Political and Social Organization of the Jews," 110).

192 This is true also of the 2,850 prisoners of war from Hume in Cilicia whom Nabonidus consecrated to his gods Bel, Nabu, and Nergal, probably meaning that he donated them to the temple Esagila. They were assigned to construction work in the temple precincts (VAB 4:284–85: Nabonidus 8, 10.31'–42'). The legal text Cyr 307 from the early Persian period (531 B.C.E.) threatens to sell a young Judean woman into slavery as a civil penalty; her family must therefore have been free (see pp. 73–74 above).

193 Dandamaev, "Neo-Babylonian Society" (II.1), 266–69. Whether the Judeans constituted cooperative associations (*ḫaṭru*) like some ethnic groups appearing later in the Murashu archives cannot be demonstrated; cf. the stimulating discussion by Bickerman, "Babylonian Captivity," 345–46.

194 "Reassessing," 27ff.

court, including a Judean gardener named Shalamyama (= Shelemyahu).[195] The sources available to date contain no evidence that members of the Babylonian golah, unlike the Assyrian, rose to high administrative or military rank, but they too must have been subject to military service.

It would appear, then, that after some initial difficulties the legal and economic situation of the Babylonian golah was far from oppressive. All signs pointed to increasing legal and economic integration.[196] For the end of the exilic period, the same situation is suggested by the legal text Cyr 307, in which a Judean and a Babylonian family from Sippar have equal rights. The archives of the house of Murashu, an agricultural banking firm, demonstrate that by the second half of the fifth century (455–403 B.C.E.) the Judeans in Babylon had been fully integrated legally and could make their livelihood by normal economic means. Most of them were members of simple occupational groups, engaged in farming, raising livestock, or fishing, but some were able to rise to higher positions in the service of Persian overlords (e.g., as irrigation experts). The knowledge that the Babylonian golah at the end of the exile was in a position to make a sizable financial contribution to Jerusalem (Zech 6:10–11; cf. Ezra 2:69; 8:30) and the fact that only a limited number were prepared to return demonstrate that most of the Babylonian golah had found a way to make a good livelihood during their distant exile.[197]

The tribulations afflicting the Babylonian exiles were primarily political, psychological, and religious. The political problem had to do with the person of Jehoiachin. When he was deported to Babylonia in 587 at the age of eighteen, along with his mother and household, the Judean exiles, most of whom were supporters of religious nationalism, quite naturally recognized him as their leader even in a foreign land. As though he were a reigning king, they reckoned the years from the date of Jehoiachin's exile, which would have been his first regnal year (Ezek 1:2; 33:21; 40:1). As the Weidner tablets show, Nebuchadnezzar unquestionably allowed Jehoiachin to be titled "king of Judah," whether to honor Jehoiachin's surrender of the city without a fight or to put pressure on Zedekiah, the vassal king still reigning in Jerusalem. If need be, Zedekiah could be replaced by Jehoiachin. Be that as it may, the Weidner tablets show that Jehoiachin lived at the Babylonian court with a small retinue, initially

---

[195] A obv., line 3.

[196] Toward the end of the exile (532 B.C.E.) we find a Judean named *abdayahū* (Obadiah) entrusted with the office of tax collector (Joannès and Lemaire, "Trois tablettes," 27–30). From the year 498, the sale of a bull to a Judean by a Babylonian is recorded, indicating full legal equality in the realm of civil law (Joannès and Lemaire, "Trois tablettes," 17–27).

[197] Cf. Josephus, *Ant.* 11.9.

(592) well provided for and respected. By the age of twenty-three he had already fathered five sons;[198] thus he lived with his wife or wives and saw to the continuance of the Davidic line. Therefore the exiles' hope to return and make a new beginning, based on the promises made to David and his descendants (2 Sam 7), could concentrate on Jehoiachin (cf. Jer 28:4).

This bright picture is totally at odds with the statement in 2 Kgs 25:27 that in 562 Evil-merodach released Jehoiachin from prison (בֵּית כֶּלֶא). The evidence of the Weidner tablets has led many to play down this statement by taking the word "prison" more or less metaphorically[199] or by interpreting the context of the Weidner tablets as a kind of hostage situation on the basis of 2 Kgs 25:27–28.[200] But the Babylonian expression *bīt kīli* used as a loanword in 25:27 refers specifically to a prison, and a literal interpretation is strongly suggested by the mention of the prison clothes Jehoiachin put aside after his release (25:29). Not until after this release was Jehoiachin allowed once more to share the table of the other vassal kings and thus regain the status of an honored "hostage." Nebuchadnezzar's "court and state calendar" does not mention Jehoiachin among the vassal kings who took part in the dedication of the new palace in the year 570. The damaged condition of the text means that it cannot be used to support this theory, but at least it does not contradict it.

This means that between 592 and 562 Jehoiachin must have forfeited his honored status at the Babylonian court and been thrown into prison. What was the reason? One possible suggestion is the anti-Babylonian conspiracy of Zedekiah, which led to the second deportation.[201] Jehoiachin would have been forced to serve as a hostage on account of the rebellious policies of his uncle, because as "king of Judah" he was generally responsible for the good conduct of the Judean people. Against this theory is Nebuchadnezzar's appointment of Zedekiah to the throne of the Judean rump state as "king after his own heart," held personally responsible on the basis of his oath of fealty.[202] Because Zedekiah had broken this oath, Nebuchadnezzar punished him personally extremely harshly (2 Kgs 25:6–7). That he also punished Jehoiachin is not out of the question but would contradict the known Babylonian policy of punishing only those who were personally guilty.

---

[198] B obv. II, line 29; C rev. II, line 18.

[199] E.g., Oded, "Observations," 210.

[200] E.g., Böhl, "Nebukadnezar," 427–28; Miller and Hayes, *History*, 432; Dandamaev, "Neo-Babylonian Society" (II.1), 269.

[201] Mitchell, "Babylonian Exile," 418–19.

[202] Chronicle 5, rev., line 13: *šarra ša libbišu*; cf. Grayson, *Assyrian and Babylonian Chronicles* (II.1), 102; Ezek 17:11–22; 2 Kgs 24:17.

It is more likely, therefore, that Jehoiachin was condemned and imprisoned on account of the murder of Gedaliah, which probably took place in 582, the year of the third deportation. Quite apart from whether Jehoiachin had anything to do with this murder, which is unlikely,[203] the murder had been carried out by a relative—however distant—of the royal family, for which Jehoiachin was directly responsible. Furthermore, after the removal of Zedekiah, Jehoiachin was the sole political representative of the Judean people. At least Nebuchadnezzar could hold him personally liable for failing to put a stop to fanatical religious nationalism even within his own family, all the more so since the culprit had escaped by fleeing to Ammon (Jer 41:15).

For whatever reason one chooses to accept, Jehoiachin vanished into a royal prison for some twenty to twenty-five years. His imprisonment must have been a severe shock to the Babylonian golah; the Judeans had lost not only their political representative at court but also their most important symbol of hope. When Jehoiachin disappeared from the public life of the capital, the party of religious nationalism lost its last prop. The chance to return to Judah had vanished for a long period. How oppressive this political dispossession must have been during the first half of the exilic period can be heard in Ps 89, a shattering exilic lament for the king.[204] It is also apparent from the conclusion of the Deuteronomistic History (2 Kgs 25:27–30), which explicitly records the pardon of Jehoiachin as though it were the only event of the exilic period worth reporting.

The psychological problems are evident from Ps 137: the initial wistful homesickness for Jerusalem was threatening to disappear and had to be kept alive by self-imprecations not to forget Jerusalem (137:1–6). There was also a depressing sense of helplessness, of inability to influence the course of political events, which exploded in a violent desire for vengeance on the victorious Babylonians and their opportunistic Edomite allies (137:7–9).

---

[203] According to Jer 40:14, it was Baalis, king of the Ammonites, who incited Ishmael. After the murder, when Ishmael was threatened by a band of Gedaliah's supporters, he took refuge with the Ammonites (41:15). Nevertheless, his role in this Judean conflict, which was primarily internal, remains unclear. It is likely that Ammon was among the anti-Babylonian hardliners, since Nebuchadnezzar's retaliation against it was expected as early as 589 (Ezek 21:25–26). It is therefore no accident that Baalis provided refuge for Judean supporters of religious nationalism. Possibly he expected some personal advantage from a further destabilization of his former ally; see also Hübner, *Ammoniter* (II.1), 204–5. The alternative proposed by Hübner—a desire to exonerate Ishmael—is ruled out by the bias of the text, which is hostile to religious nationalism.

[204] See pp. 144–45 below.

There was also a sense of bitterness toward those left behind. The helpless exiles had to accept the fact that they, members of the former upper class, had been robbed of their property (Ezek 11:15; 33:24) and their claim to leadership. They had been struck by God's judgment with particular ferocity, and those at home had clearly written them off. Indeed, they had to hear in detail from the supporters of the reform party in Jerusalem that it was by no means all the Judeans but just the supporters of religious nationalism—in other words, they and their parents—who were primarily to blame for the terrible catastrophe (Jer 36; 37–40). Many were quite ready to admit their transgressions; they suffered an overwhelming burden of guilt. How great this sense of guilt and loss of self-confidence must have been for many of the exiles is clear from the way that the prophet Ezekiel or his disciples exercised what amounted to a pastoral ministry among them, promising them that their property and positions of leadership would be restored (Ezek 11:16–21) and showing them how personal repentance and return offered a way to escape the burdensome guilt of their parents (Ezek 18).

In addition to political and psychological problems, there were religious problems. The hopes for a speedy return in the years 594/593 had proven deceptive; the last spark of hope had been extinguished by the imprisonment of Jehoiachin in 582. Yahweh appeared simply to have disregarded his people's rights (Isa 40:27), to have turned his back on them (50:1) and forgotten his own city (49:14). The symbols and images of the Babylonian gods were paraded through the streets in magnificent processions, accompanied by the rejoicing of the crowd (46:1–2); they obviously ruled over human society and world history. Yahweh was unwilling or unable (40:12–30) to intervene in history. In their private lives, the exiles could clearly still sense the presence of Yahweh: when a child was born without incident, when a family member recovered from illness or work brought prosperity and happiness. In the domain of political history, however, Yahweh appeared to have been so distant for so long that they had ceased to expect anything of him. The longer the exile lasted, the more they had to accept the conclusion that they must leave their nationalistic hopes behind and try to find happiness in family life and rewarding work.

This constellation of a relatively untroubled legal and economic situation combined with political, psychological, and social problems undoubtedly favored assimilation of the Judean exiles. They faced the temptingly easy possibility of ridding themselves of all their burdensome problems at a stroke by turning their backs on the muddled history of their own people and immersing themselves in the ethnic mosaic of the Babylonian Empire. Undoubtedly, not a few chose this path, just as the majority of the Assyrian golah had done in the past.

But the majority of the Babylonian golah did not assimilate, in part because they had the above-mentioned chance to live together in certain towns and the opportunity to establish their own local political organization. They also capitalized on very specific survival strategies conceived and put in place by the intellectual elite of the Babylonian golah, the elders, priests, and prophets.[205]

The first step was a tightly knit organization based on genealogy. The Judean community of the early postexilic period was organized in kinship groups; everyone who wanted to be a member of the community had to be registered in writing in one of these groups (Ezra 2:3–20, 39–62; Neh 7:5ff.). These kinship groups bear the new title בֵּית אָבוֹת, "fathers' house," replacing the earlier clan (מִשְׁפָּחָה). Since Ezra 2—regardless of whether the numbers in the list are authentic—states that those returning from exile were already organized in these new kinship groups, it is likely that these groups had been introduced in the Babylonian golah during the exilic period.[206] The new term, a pluralized form of בֵּית אָב, "father's house, family," indicates that the group was formed by an amalgamation of families that were related or thought to be related. In other words, the *bêt ʾābôt* were in part artificially constructed clan alliances comprising related families, into which could be integrated individuals who had been separated in consequence of the deportations,[207] families living in the same locality, and even Judeans and Israelites deported by the Assyrians .[208] The genealogical organization into *bêt ʾābôt* gave to the Babylonian golah dwelling in various towns a clearly defined identity and ethnic solidarity, whatever may have been the origin of their individual members. Probably even in the exilic period this kinship system was reinforced by a prohibition against mixed marriages like that described for the postexilic period (Ezra 10; Neh 13:23–27).

A high degree of genealogical continuity throughout the exilic period and after is particularly clear for the two most prominent families. According to 1 Chr 3:17–18, Jehoiachin fathered seven or eight

---

[205] For further details, see Albertz, *History* (Introduction), 1:395–98.

[206] Very clear evidence of their exilic origin is found in Ezek 13:9, where Ezekiel declares to the false prophets in the golah that they will not be "enrolled in the register of the house of Israel" and will therefore be excluded from the return. In any case, the word כְּתָב denotes a written document; the same word is used for "genealogical register" in Ezra 2:62 and Neh 7:64.

[207] Ezek 24:21, for example, assumes that at least some of those deported in 597 had to leave their children behind in Jerusalem—in other words, that families had been broken up by the deportations.

[208] See Weinberg, *Citizen-Temple Community*, 49ff.; also Smith, *Religion*, 115–20.

sons,[209] two or three more than the five mentioned in the Weidner tablets. One of his grandsons was Zerubbabel (3:19), who led the group that returned in 520.[210] Similarly, although Seraiah, the last chief priest of Jerusalem, had been executed by Nebuchadnezzar, his son Jehozadak was deported in 587 (1 Chr 5:41 [6:15]), and the latter's son Joshua joined Zerubbabel in 520 to lead the reconstruction of the temple; in 515, Joshua became its first high priest (Hag 1:1, 12, 14; 2:2, 4; Zech 3:1, 6, 8–9; 6:11; called Jeshua in Ezra 2:2; 3:8). These two leading families demonstrate that, despite the political chaos, continuity on a familial level could survive the crisis of exile uninterrupted.

The other survival strategies were religious and ceremonial in nature. To secure the identity of every individual male belonging to the golah and as a token of his membership in the Judean ethnic group, the ritual circumcision of infants was introduced (Gen 17:12; 21:4; Lev 12:3). Circumcision appears originally to have been an ancient apotropaic rite associated with puberty or preparation for marriage (cf. Exod 4:25; Gen 17:25; 34). Since it was also practiced by other peoples (Jer 9:24–25: Egyptians, Arabs, Edomites, Moabites, Ammonites), it was not inherently suited to be a distinctive mark of the Judean people. But since circumcision was not common in Mesopotamia, in the Babylonian golah it could become a confessional badge by which the father of every family could declare his membership in the community of exiles and his fidelity to the ancestral religion. From the exilic period onward, circumcision became such an accepted hallmark of Jewish faith that it could be required of converts (Jdt 14:10; Esth 8:17 LXX).

Besides circumcision, it was probably during the exilic period that certain foods and methods of preparation became marks of identity. Foreign lands (Amos 7:17) and their food were considered potentially unclean (Hos 9:3; Ezek 4:13). Therefore, it became important for those who had been deported to Babylonia to frame purity regulations governing the choice and preparation of foods and to make these regulations binding on the community. The great importance of the dietary laws as a mechanism of separation for the Babylonian golah in an alien environment is reflected retrospectively in Dan 1:8–16. Even though many of

---

[209] The Hebrew word אַסִּר is interpreted by the Septuagint and Vulgate as an additional proper name (Asir); probably, however, an adjective is intended: הָאַסִּר, "the captive" (Jehoiachin).

[210] In Hag 1:1; 2:23; Ezra 3:2, 8; 5:2; Neh 12:1, Zerubbabel is called the son of Jehoiachin's first son Shealtiel; in 1 Chr 3:19, he is called the son of Jehoiachin's third son Pedaiah. In the latter genealogy, Shealtiel has no children; we may therefore be dealing with a levirate marriage entered into by Pedaiah on behalf of Shealtiel when the latter died childless.

these laws go back to the preexilic period (cf. the consumption of blood in 1 Sam 14:32–34), their systematization and casuistic elaboration (Deut 14; Lev 11) probably arose from the needs of the exilic period. They provided the exilic families with an important badge of identity by means of which they could show in their everyday lives whether or not they counted themselves members of the Judean ethnic community and adhered to its religious traditions.

A third confessional badge, besides circumcision and dietary practices, was the specifically religious observance of Sabbath rest.[211] The traditional forms of familial worship—the offering of firstfruits, sacrificial meals, and sacrificial vows—could not be performed in a foreign land without a shrine of Yahweh. As a substitute, it was probably the theological reformers of the Babylonian golah who enjoined familial observance of the Sabbath every seven days. Before the exile, the Sabbath had probably been a full moon festival, celebrated at the temple alongside the new moon festival to mark the rhythm of the lunar phases (2 Kgs 4:23; Isa 1:13; Hos 2:13 [11]; Lam 2:6). During it—and probably during other festivals as well—trade was prohibited (Amos 8:5). In addition, in the preexilic period there had been a taboo requiring agricultural work to be interrupted every seven days so as not to exploit the last ounce of working animals' strength and to give a time of relaxation to dependent laborers (Exod 23:12; 34:21). But this day of rest was not yet called the Sabbath, and it had no cultic connotations.

The theological reformers of the exilic community probably combined these two institutions by detaching the Sabbath from the temple and the lunar cycle and combining it with the weekly day of rest. The temple festival became the Sabbath day (יום השבת) and the day of rest acquired all the dignity of cultic worship (שבת ליהוה אלהיך, "a Sabbath to Yahweh your God"; cf. Deut 5:12–15 and Exod 20:8–11). Thus the golah gained a regular act of worship that could be observed by families without the temple and far from their homeland. Rest from labor, that is, relinquishing the proceeds of one day's work, replaced the familial offerings that had formerly linked Yahweh with agricultural production. In the bustling Babylonian world, which did not have such festivals independent of the lunar cycle, regular rest from labor on a particular day was also a highly visible external confessional badge of the Judean ethnic group. Internally, it provided a control mechanism identifying deviants who wanted to split from the Judean ethnic group and bringing group pressure to bear on them.

---

[211] See Albertz, *History* (Introduction), 2:408–10.

It is striking that the theological reformers of the exile evolved only ritual and religious survival strategies that did not need a cultic center. Unlike the Egyptian golah, the Babylonian golah—as far as we know—never built a temple in their foreign land.[212] There may have been tendencies in this direction in the Babylonian golah, but Ezekiel and his disciples brusquely rejected them (Ezek 20:30–32). The religious elite remained faithful to the cultic centralization law of the Josianic reform (Deut 12). There could not be, must not be, another temple of Yahweh outside of Jerusalem. Thus they prevented total integration into Babylonian society and nurtured the hope of return. The Babylonian golah expressed their tie to their homeland and the Jerusalem temple by the custom of praying toward Jerusalem (1 Kgs 8:48; Dan 6:11–12 [10–11]).

Probably the Babylonian golah also knew forms of worship that went beyond these familial observances. The most important were probably public lamentations, but when and how they were observed is beyond our ken. It cannot be shown that synagogues and synagogue worship originated in the Babylonian exile; the earliest evidence of them is much later.[213] It is possible, however, that in the exile forms of worship evolved in which the focus was no longer on sacrificial offering but on the word (readings from scripture, confession of faith, prayer) and that these forms represent one of the roots of later synagogue worship. However that may be, it is clear that during the exilic period the family and the kinship alliance became one of the principal agents responsible for the ethnic and religious identity of the golah.

The release of Jehoiachin from prison marks an important turning point in the history of the Babylonian golah. After the long reign of Nebuchadnezzar, the accession of his son Amēl-Marduk in the year 562 appeared to set history in motion once more for the exiles. A shift of Babylonian policy in a direction more favorable to the provinces became apparent. It was no longer out of the question that Jehoiachin might be sent back to Judah as a Babylonian vassal, to rebuilt the land, which still suffered from the ravages of war. As the express mention of this event at the end of the Deuteronomistic History shows (2 Kgs 25:27–30), cautious new hopes for deliverance were abroad among the Babylonian golah,

---

212 Bronner, "Sacrificial Cult," 423–27.

213 The earliest inscriptions mentioning a synagogue (*proseuchē*) are from Hellenistic Egypt and date from the third century B.C.E.; the first building that can be identified as a synagogue was built on the island of Delos in the first century. The earliest synagogues discovered in Palestine date from the first half of the first century C.E. (Gamala, Masada, Herodium); see *NEAEHL*, 1421–27; Lee I. Levine, *The Synagogue in Late Antiquity* (Philadelphia: American Schools of Oriental Research, 1987); Lester L. Grabbe, "Synagogues in Pre-70 Palestine: A Reassessment," *JTS* 39 (1988): 401–10.

especially among the leaders, who were still exponents of religious nationalism.[214] The reappointment of Baalezer as king of Tyre and the return of two of his successors who had been held hostage (Maharbaal, Hiram) a few years later show that such hopes were not entirely baseless.[215] In any case, the possibility that Jehoiachin and his family might return was so real that in the following years the Deuteronomistic redactors of the book of Jeremiah, descendants of the Shaphanide reform party, started a vigorous campaign of counterpropaganda among those left in Jerusalem: let the whole land hear that neither Jehoiachin nor any of his offspring would ever again reign in Judah (Jer 22:29–30); he was still rejected by God, as Jeremiah had prophesied (22:24–28).[216]

But the situation remained confused. After just two and a half years, Amēl-Marduk was slain by Neriglissar, and the Babylonian Empire slid into political destabilization. The leaders of the golah might harbor renewed hope for a return under Babylonian rule when Nabonidus came to the throne in 556, since he reinstituted the policy of accommodating the provinces. In any case, kings were reappointed in Tyre, according to Katzenstein's reconstruction in the years 556, 555, and 552, in each case probably under the aegis of Nabonidus.[217] Wilkie's belief that the situation of the Judean exiles deteriorated significantly under Nabonidus, since they came into conflict with his religious policies,[218] cannot be established on the basis of Deutero-Isaiah; the overall political climate makes this theory highly unlikely. There is even some evidence, albeit uncertain, that Nabonidus had contacts with the Judeans: in the *Prayer of Nabonidus* from Qumran (4Q242), it is a Judean soothsayer (גזר והוא יהודי) at Teman who shows the king, afflicted with leprosy, the way to be healed. Admittedly this text dates from the first century B.C.E., but the prayer is traditio-historically earlier than the fourth chapter of the Aramaic book of Daniel (late third century) and could preserve an accurate memory that this king, who was virtually obsessed with the interpretation of dreams and omens, employed Judean prophets at his court in Tema. There is also evidence that Nabonidus may have used a sizable contingent of Judean exiles to build

---

214 On this background of the Deuteronomistic History, see Albertz, "Wer waren die Deuteronomisten?" 333–34; see also pp. 282–86 below.

215 This is particularly true if Joannès ("Trois texts" [II.1], 149) is correct in his thesis that Amēl-Marduk had already allowed Tyrian deportees to return to their homeland.

216 For a detailed discussion, see Albertz, "Wer waren die Deuteronomisten?" 325ff.

217 Katzenstein, *History* (II.1), 342–43. Katzenstein believes that Baalezer at least was reappointed by Neriglissar as a reward for Tyrian support in his campaign against Cilicia, but his aggressively imperialistic policies make this unlikely.

218 "Nabonidus," 36ff.

and maintain his new residence at Tema, as one element in his policy of decentralization. In any case, it is striking that almost all the sites in northwest Arabia mentioned in the Haran inscription of Nabonidus (Tema, Dadanu, Padakku, Hibra, Yadihu, Yatribu)[219] were centers of Jewish settlement in the seventh century C.E.[220] Even though the historical distance of a thousand years urges caution, it is possible that Nabonidus resettled the first Judeans to this region.

Despite these possible contacts, the Judean exiles derived little recognizable benefit from Nabonidus's policy of conciliation. The king's interest was focused on rebuilding his north Syrian homeland; the massive resistance he met in the Babylonian heartland left him little room for the promotion of other regions. The concomitant disappointment of expectations coupled with the damage Nabonidus's reputation suffered in the internal conflicts beginning in 553 may be one reason why many elements of the golah gave up hoping for any turn for the better under Babylonian aegis (cf. Isa 40:27; 49:14; 50:1).

In this situation, the prophet Deutero-Isaiah and his disciples came forward among the exiles and proclaimed that the Persian king Cyrus, who had revolted against his Median overlords in 553, taken control of the Median Empire with his victory over Astyages in 550, and subjugated the kingdom of Lydia and the Ionian cities with an impressive blitzkrieg in 547/546, would be the liberator sent by Yahweh to deliver his people from their Babylonian exile by conquering Babylon (Isa 41:2; 44:28a; 45:1–7; 46:11). The narrow circle of exilic leaders at court, the descendants of David and Hilkiah, naturally had to continue showing loyalty to Nabonidus and Belshazzar, but a prophetic group probably drawn from the former temple singers, with roots in religious nationalism but having no political responsibilities, campaigned openly for a shift from the Babylonian option to a Persian option. It is reasonable to suppose that this open turnabout within the Babylonian golah was controversial and involved some danger. To the ears of the Babylonian royal house, such a message was high treason. But the Judeans had a stroke of timely good fortune when influential Babylonian groups, led by the priests of Marduk in Babylon, polemicized against their own royal house in opposition to Nabonidus's imperial and religious policies and were openly pro-Persian. When Cyrus did in fact enter Babylon victorious in 539 and had himself hailed as a liberator by the priests of Marduk, at least some of the Babylonian golah were already on the side of the Persians.

---

[219] H2, 1.24–25. See Röllig, "Erwägungen," 220, 224.
[220] Mitchell, "Babylonian Exile," 425.

II.3. THE THWARTED RESTORATION

The years 538–520 B.C.E. still belong to the exilic period as defined earlier.[221] Therefore, the early Persian period from Cyrus to Darius I is included here. This era of Israel's history is often referred to as the restoration.[222] It is crucial to remember, however, that the monarchic state of preexilic Judah was never restored after the exile.

Ackroyd, Peter R. "Problems in the Handling of Biblical and Related Sources in the Achaemenid Period," in *Achaemenid History III: Method and Theory* (ed. A. Kuhrt and H. Sancisi-Weerdenburg; Leiden: Nederlands Instituut voor het Nabije Osten, 1988), 33–54. **Ahn,** Gregor. *Religiöse Herrscherlegitimation im achämenidischen Reich* (Acta Iranica 17; Leiden: Brill, 1992). **Albertz,** Rainer. "The Thwarted Restoration," in *Yahwism after Exile: Perspectives on Israelite Religion in the Persian Era* (ed. R. Albertz and B. Becking; STAR 5; Leiden: Deo, 2002), 1–17. **Alt,** Albrecht. "Die Rolle Samarias bei der Entstehung des Judentums," in idem, *Kleine Schriften zur Geschichte des Volkes Israel* (3d ed.; 3 vols.; Munich: Beck, 1964), 3:316–37. **Avigad,** Nahman. *Bullae and Seals from a Post-Exilic Judean Archive* (Qedem 4; Jerusalem: Institute of Archaeology, the Hebrew University of Jerusalem, 1976). **Berquist,** Jon L. *Judaism in Persia's Shadow: A Social and Historical Approach* (Minneapolis: Fortress, 1995). **Bianchi,** Francesco. "Le role de Zorobabel et la dynastie davidique en Judée du VIe siècle au IIe siècle av. J.-C.," *Transeu* 7 (1994), 153–65. **Briant,** Pierre. *From Cyrus to Alexander: A History of the Persian Empire* (Winona Lake, Ind.: Eisenbrauns, 2002). **Dandamaev,** Muhammad A. *Persien unter den ersten Achämeniden (6. Jahrhundert v.Chr.)* (Beiträge zur Iranistik 8; Wiesbaden: Reichert, 1976). **Dandamaev** and Vladimir G. Lukonin, *The Culture and Social Institutions of Ancient Iran* (trans. P. L. Kohl; Cambridge: Cambridge University Press, 1989). **Eph'al,** Israel. "Syria-Palestine under Achaemenid Rule," *CAH*² 4:139–64. **Galling,** Kurt. *Studien zur Geschichte Israels im persischen Zeitalter* (Tübingen: Mohr Siebeck, 1964). **Grabbe,** Lester L. *The Persian and Greek Periods* (vol. 1 of *Judaism from Cyrus to Hadrian;* Minneapolis: Fortress, 1992). **Gunneweg,** Antonius H. J. *Esra* (KAT 9/1; Gütersloh: Mohn, 1985). **Heltzer,** Michael. "A Recently Published Babylonian Tablet and the Province of Judah after 516 B.C.E.," *Transeu* 5 (1992), 57–61. **Herodotus.** *The Histories* (trans. Robin Waterfield; Oxford: Oxford University Press, 1998). **Hoglund,** Kenneth G. *Achaemenid Imperial Administration in Syria-Palestine and the Missions of Ezra and Nehemiah* (SBLDS 125; Atlanta: Scholars Press, 1992). **Kippenberg,** Hans G. *Religion und Klassenbildung im antiken Judäa: Eine religionssoziologische Studie zum Verhältnis von Tradition und gesellschaftliche Entwicklung* (SUNT 14; Göttingen: Vandenhoeck & Ruprecht, 1978). **Koch,** Heidemarie. *Es kündet Dareios der König: Vom Leben im persischen Grossreich* (Kul-

---

221 See pp. 1–2 above.
222 Ackroyd, *Exile and Restoration* (I); Donner, *Geschichte* (II.2), 437ff.

turgeschichte der antiken Welt 55; Mainz: P. von Zabern, 1992). **Koch.** "Götter und ihre Verehrung im achämenidischen Persien," *ZA* 77 (1987): 239–78. **Kuhrt,** Amelie. "Babylonia from Cyrus to Xerxes," *CAH*² 4:112–38. **Kuhrt.** "The Cyrus Cylinder and Achaemenid Imperial Policy," *JSOT* 25 (1983): 83–97. **Lemaire,** André. "Zorobabel et la Judée à la lumière de l'épigraphie (fin du VIᵉ s. av. J.-C.)," *RB* 103 (1996): 48–57. **Maier,** Franz Georg. "Cyprus and Phoenicia," *CAH*² 4:297–336. **Meyers,** Eric M. "The Persian Period and the Judean Restoration, from Zerubbabel to Nehemiah," in *Ancient Israelite Religion: Essays in Honor of Frank Moore Cross* (ed. P. D. Miller, P. D. Hanson, and S. D. McBride; Philadelphia: Fortress, 1987), 509–21. **Olmstead,** A. T. *History of the Persian Empire* (Chicago: University of Chicago Press, 1948, repr., 1959). **Stern,** Ephraim. *Material Culture of the Land of the Bible in the Persian Period, 538–332 B.C.* (Jerusalem: Israel Exploration Society, 1982). **Stern.** "The Persian Empire and the Political and Social History of Palestine in the Persian Period," *CHJ* 1:70–87. **Tadmor,** Hayim. "Judah," *CAH*² 4:261–92. **Timm,** Stefan. "Die Bedeutung der spätbabylonischen Texte aus Nērab für die Rückkehr der Judäer aus dem Exil," in *Meilenstein: Festgabe für Herbert Donner* (ÄAT 30; Wiesbaden: Harrassowitz, 1995), 276–88. **Weippert,** Helga. *Palästina in vorhellenistischer Zeit* (Handbuch der Archäologie 2/1; Munich: Beck, 1988). **Widengren,** Geo. "The Persian Period," in *Israelite and Judaean History* (ed. J. H. Hayes and J. M. Miller; London: SCM, 1977), 489–503. **Wiesehöfer,** Josef. *Das antike Persien* (Zurich: Artemis & Winkler, 1993). **Wiesehöfer.** *Der Aufstand Gaumātas und die Anfänge Dareios I.* (Habelts Dissertationsdrucke, Reihe alte Geschichte 13; Bonn: Habelt, 1978). **Young,** T. Cuyler, Jr. "The Early History of the Medes and the Persians and the Achaemenid Empire to the Death of Cambyses," *CAH*² 4:1–52.

II.3.1. THE PERSIAN EMPIRE FROM CYRUS TO DARIUS I

The most important sources for the history of the Persian Empire between 538 and 520 are: the Chronicle of Nabonidus (Grayson, *Assyrian and Babylonian Chronicles* [II.1], 104–11), the Verse Account of Nabonidus (*ANET*, 312–25; Schaudig, *Inschriften* [II.1], 563–78), the Cyrus Cylinder,[223] the Behistun inscription of Darius I (*TUAT* 1/4:419–50), and Herodotus, *Histories*, especially 3.61–97.

The Neo-Babylonian Empire fell into the lap of Cyrus (558–530) almost without a fight. On October 29, 539 B.C.E., he entered Babylon and with great propagandistic extravagance had himself hailed as a liberator.

---

[223] The text published in *ANET*, 315–16, and *TGI*, 85–86, has been expanded since 1975 by inclusion of a fragment that was actually known as early as 1920; see *TUAT* 1/4:407–8; Schaudig, *Inschriften* (II.1), 548–56.

From the perspective of his Babylonian allies, not least the powerful priesthood of Marduk, the god Marduk himself, enraged at the conduct of Nabonidus, had called Cyrus to be king of Babylon to free Babylonia from the yoke of Nabonidus and undo his cultic aberrations.[224] The clearly Babylonian authorship of the Cyrus Cylinder casts doubt on whether this view of the matter was shared by Cyrus himself.[225] As far as we can tell, Cyrus kept the Neo-Babylonian administration and also left the existing social structures more or less intact. As governor in Babylon, for example, he initially installed Nabû-aḫḫē-bulliṭ, who had held high office under Nabonidus, and the satrapy of "Babylon and the Territory beyond the River," over which he appointed the Iranian Gobryas in 535, was simply coextensive with the Neo-Babylonian Empire.

In view of this clear evidence of continuity, scholars today often ask whether Persian rule really meant the historical revolution in the politics and religious policies of the great Near Eastern empires that it was long customary to ascribe to it—not least because of its positive assessment in the Bible. Donner still states the traditional view: "The great kings of Persia truly went their own new way in their treatment of the peoples within their empire.... They tried to base their policies on toleration rather than force."[226] Kuhrt, however, denies that there was any religio-political change in the treatment of subject peoples under Cyrus: "The emphasis in the relevant passage of the cylinder is not on any actual restoration of cults but the re-establishment of a normal, i.e. correct, state of affairs."[227]

As is so often the case, the truth probably lies somewhere in between. The lines of the Cyrus Cylinder that are claimed to support the religious and political "toleration" of the Persians (30–34) deal with two distinct measures. First, Cyrus restored to their sanctuaries the statues of the Babylonian gods that Nabonidus—probably for reasons of security—had brought to the capital before the Persian invasion:[228]

> 33 ... and the gods of the land of Sumer and Akkad,
> 34 whom Nabonidus had brought to Babylon to the anger of the lord of the gods,
> at the command of Marduk, the great lord,

---

[224] See the Cyrus Cylinder, lines 1–19, and the Verse Account of Nabonidus, 6.12'–18'.
[225] As pointed out by Galling, *Studien*, 35, and Kuhrt, "Cyrus Cylinder," 88.
[226] *Geschichte* (II.2), 425.
[227] "Cyrus Cylinder," 93.
[228] Chronicle 7, 3.5–12; cf. 3.20–22; Grayson, *Assyrian and Babylonian Chronicles* (II.1), 109–10.

> I resettled unharmed in their chambers,
> a dwelling place to rejoice their hearts.

This passage actually deals simply with the restoration of the "normal" cultic order. Second, Cyrus also restored temples and cities east of the Tigris:

> 30 ... from Nineveh [?], Assyria, and Susa,
> 31 Akkad, Eshnunna, Zaban, Meturnu, and Der, as far as the region of Gutium,
> the cities beyond the Tigris,
> whose dwellings had long lain in ruins—
> 32 the gods who had dwelt in them I brought back to their place
> and established for them an eternal dwelling.
> All their people I gathered
> and brought them back to their dwelling places.

This significant passage does not speak broadly of rebuilding all ruined temples throughout the Persian Empire and a general return of deported groups to their homelands, as many scholars from Dandamaev[229] to Berquist[230] would have us believe;[231] neither, however, is it simply concerned with internal Babylonian problems.[232] The places listed lie in the border region between Babylonia and Persia; in part, as in the case of Nineveh and Assyria, they are sites that had been devastated by the Neo-Babylonians in alliance with Medes and then lay neglected.[233] These lines of the Cyrus Cylinder thus indicate the intent of the Persian regime to rebuild and restore to productivity regions that, like these borderlands, lay between the Persian and Median heartlands and were of strategic importance within the newly conquered empire. Such a policy included the restoration of ruined temples, the return of temple property, and the resettlement of ethnic groups that still identified with their ancient homelands.

If this interpretation is correct, the political goals of Cyrus coincided only in part with those of his Babylonian allies. Cyrus was certainly ready

---

229 *Persien*, 98–99.

230 *Judaism*, 24ff.

231 Dandamaev, *Persien*, 98–99, says that Cyrus "assembled all the people and restored their dwelling places," but the text actually reads *kul-lat nišu-šú-nu*, "all their people," and refers only to the inhabitants of the cities east of the Tigris.

232 Contra Kuhrt, "Cyrus Cylinder," 124.

233 Perhaps it is not by accident that Cyrus mentions on his cylinder (line 42) an earlier inscription of Ashurbanipal that he discovered near the wall of Babylon during construction work.

to support Babylon with its cult of Marduk and to do away with the innovations of Nabonidus. To a not inconsiderable extent, however, Cyrus also set new goals when, to advance Persian interests, he brought back under cultivation the ancestral lands of Assyria, Babylon's archenemy. To the extent that Cyrus was concerned with border regions, his policies were not at all unlike those of Nabonidus. It is simply that, warned by Nabonidus's fall, he did not embark on religio-political experiments. He certainly did not attempt to introduce a new imperial cult, such as the worship of the Iranian god Ahura Mazda; he kept to a conservative policy of restoring local cults so as to reinforce the local identity of the population and increase their loyalty to the Persian crown. Persian control depended as much as possible on the existing local power structures. The Persian policy of religious "toleration" was thus an expression of conservative support for local regions to serve the political interests of the whole. If the interests of the empire were seriously threatened—for example, if local cults became foci of anti-Persian rebellion—the Persian kings did not hesitate to intervene highhandedly in cultic matters, as the removal of a statue of Marduk from Esagila and the destruction of the Acropolis by Xerxes bear witness.

At the outset, the basic principle of Persian imperial policy, respect for the various regions and their idiosyncracies, was at odds with the interests of the Persian nobility. The Medes and the Persians had originally been tribal societies, far inferior to the highly advanced Assyrian and Neo-Babylonian Empires. The emergence of the Achaemenids as a royal house beginning in the eighth century and the meteoric rise of the Persian Empire in the sixth were possible only because the Persian king and the tribal nobility had an understanding that the latter would share directly in the power and riches gained by their military service. The nobles who held positions of leadership in the Persian army claimed a major share of the spoils of war. The same held true for the nobles appointed to the highest administrative position of satrap or governor: their primary interest was in wringing as much wealth as possible from the provinces. At the outset, therefore, the imperial policy of the Persian Empire differed little from that of its predecessors, except that in its case the heartland itself, Persis, suffered like the rest of the provinces.

The interests of the nobles could be satisfied only so long as Cyrus's string of victories remained intact. In 530, when he fell in a bloody battle against the Massagetes on the northeast border of his empire, the nobles' policy of plunder reached its apogee. Cyrus's son Cambyses (530–522) continued the old policy of conquest, vanquishing Egypt with a surprise attack in the year 525, after lengthy preparations. After thirty years of conquest, however, he was finally forced to shift the empire to an overdue phase of consolidation, especially when his Nubian campaign failed in 524. This change brought him into bitter conflict with the Persian tribal nobility, who saw their privileges threatened. In 522, while still in Egypt, Cambyses had himself enthroned as pharaoh of the Twenty-Seventh Dynasty; in the same year, a revolt broke out in Persis, plunging the newly born Persian Empire into its deepest crisis. It was led by the magus Gaumata, who claimed to be Bardiya (Greek: Smerdis), Cambyses' brother, who secretly had been murdered. Cambyses hastened to return but died in Syria on the way back in April of 522.[234] At first Gaumata had the support of the nobles against Cambyses, and he was quickly recognized in the provinces. But no sooner had he ascended the throne (January 7, 522) than—according to Herodotus[235]—he exempted all his subjects from military service and taxes for three years, so as to give them respite after the long years of war. According to the Behistun inscription (1.61ff.), Gaumata expropriated most of the land belonging to the nobility[236] in order to reduce their power and increase that of the crown. This action naturally infuriated the tribal nobility. On the twenty-ninth of September, 522, Gaumata was assassinated by a group of conspirators that included six leading nobles as well as Darius, who belonged to a collateral line of the Achaemenids.

The favor Gaumata must have enjoyed throughout the Persian Empire is demonstrated by the fact that, when he was murdered, not only—as Herodotus reports (*Hist.* 3.67)—did grief encompass all Asia but also, as the Behistun inscription describes in detail, a huge insurgent movement broke out in the central and eastern portions of the empire. Darius, who had emerged from the group of conspirators to seize the Persian throne, needed three full years to put out the fire. It is noteworthy that Babylon, which had greeted Cyrus as a liberator in 539, immediately tried twice to free itself once more from the Persian yoke—so disillusioning must the experience of Persian rule have been! Immediately after the assassination of Gaumata, Nidintu-Bēl, probably a son of the formerly despised Nabonidus, rose up and had himself crowned king of Babylon on the tenth of March, 522, under the name Nebuchadnezzar III. Not until the eighteenth of December was Darius able to defeat the rebel with the aid of elite Persian troops; he was forced to stay in Babylon for six more months before he was able to bring the province totally to heel once more.[237] No sooner had he left Babylon than a new revolt broke out (August 521), led by the Armenian Arakha, who took the Babylonian

---

[234] Herodotus, *Hist.* 3.61–66.
[235] *Hist.* 3.67.
[236] Wiesehöfer, *Das antike Persien*, 99–100.
[237] Behistun inscription 1.83–2.5; 4.12–14; appendix D; *TUAT* 1/4:428–29, 450.

throne as Nebuchadnezzar IV. This time Darius had his commander suppress the rebel. Not until November 27, 521, did Babylon fall into the hands of the Persians for good.[238]

Suppression of the last revolts in the empire extended into the second and third years of Darius (520–519); the last to be defeated were the Elamites and the Scythians.[239] The victory ended with a compromise: Darius reversed the radical innovations of Gaumata, returned the property of the Persian nobles, and restored them to their privileged positions. At the same time, however, he instituted two important reforms intended to put an end to the uncontrolled exploitation of the native and foreign populations and to consolidate the Persian Empire economically and politically: he reformed the administrative and fiscal systems.

According to Herodotus (*Hist.* 3.89), Darius divided the Persian Empire into twenty satrapies and thus created for the first time a clearly organized, hierarchical administrative structure. The Persian nobles, who were usually appointed as satraps and frequently also as the subordinate provincial governors, were thus integrated into the political structure, with well-defined jurisdictions, rights, and responsibilities. As part of this administrative reform, Syria/Palestine, the territory of Transeuphratene, "Beyond the (Euphrates) River" (Aram. *'abar naharā*, Babyl. *ebīr nāri*), was made more independent of Babylon[240] and finally became an independent satrapy, according to Herodotus (3.91–92) the fifth (Babylon being the eighth). From 520 to 502, Tattanu—who appears in Ezra 5:3, 6; 6:6, 13 as Tattenai—held the office of (sub)satrap of Transeuphratene, responsible to the satrap of "Babylon and the Territory beyond the River" (in the year 516 Ushtanu).

Closely connected with Darius's reform of the administrative structure was his reform of the tax system. According to Herodotus (3.90–97), every satrapy had to collect a specified amount in taxes: Babylonia a thousand talents of silver, for example, and Transeuphratene 350. Thus the crown was assured of a set income from taxes, independent of the claims of the nobles. At the same time, the subjects were protected against arbitrary exploitation on the part of the nobles. Herodotus (3.97) is wrong in claiming that Persis was exempt from taxes, since the multitude of cuneiform tablets found in Persepolis attest to a great many payments made by the Persian heartland.[241] Taxes paid in precious metals

---

[238] Behistun inscription 3.76–4.1, 29–30; appendix I; *TUAT* 1/4:441–43, 450.

[239] Behistun inscription 5.1–36; *TUAT* 1/4:448–49.

[240] A newly-discovered text shows that in 486 the two parts of the satrapy were still united; see Heltzer, "Recently Published Tablet," 59.

[241] Koch, *Es kündet*, 64–67.

were sent to the central government from the more distant satrapies. Taxes in kind, of which there were many, largely remained in the provinces, if only because of the cost of transportation. Herodotus is also inaccurate when he writes (3.89): "During the reigns of Cyrus and Cambyses there was no such thing as a fixed amount of taxes [φόρος, lit. 'tribute'], but the various people brought donations [δῶρον]." Payment of tribute is documented under Cyrus,[242] and Gaumata had already issued a decree concerning taxes.[243] What was new in Darius's tax reform was his administrative improvement of the existing system of taxes and tribute by creating an objective basis for determining in advance the amount of taxes to be collected, thus guaranteeing the Persian state a set income and providing his subjects with a degree of legal protection against the state.[244]

Darius's reform of the administration and the tax system was thus intended to safeguard his rule; it emerged directly from the deep crisis of the Persian Empire during the years 522 to 519. The new systems established a legal basis, binding equally on rulers and on subjects, for the government of a great Near Eastern empire. Only through these reforms was it possible fully to realize the political philosophy of the Persians, already discernible in Cyrus: strengthen local regimes and use the resources of the empire to support politically important regions. A polycentric political structure—outwardly symbolized by the four official capitals of Persepolis, Susa, Babylon, and Ecbatana—that left certain rights to the individual regions, anticipated in some ways by Nabonidus, was realized by Darius. It gave the Persian Empire astonishing stability, considering the circumstances of the ancient world.

II.3.2. Return and Rebuilding of the Temple

For the history of Judah between 539 and 515, we have at our disposal the historical narrative in Ezra 1–6 and the prophetic books of Haggai and Zechariah. The seals cited by some scholars are uncertain as to date and interpretation.[245]

---

242 Cyrus Cylinder, lines 28–30; *TUAT* 1/4:409.
243 Behistun inscription 1.17–20; *TUAT* 1/4:424; Herodotus, *Hist.* 3.67.
244 Contra Dandamaev and Lukonin, *Culture,* 188ff.; Kippenberg, *Religion,* 49–52; and Hoglund, *Achaemenid Imperial Administration,* 61–62, Darius's innovation was not the introduction of coinage. First, the gold daric coined by Darius was used only for trade with the Greeks; second, coins do not appear in Palestine until the fourth century B.C.E., and then as a Greek import. No coins minted in Judah itself antedate 360 B.C.E. (Weippert, *Palästina,* 696; cf. Mildenberg's discussion, 719–27).
245 Avigad, *Bullae;* Grabbe, *Judaism,* 68–69.

A first problem is presented by the book of Ezra itself: it cites sources that contradict in part its own view of what took place. According to Ezra 1:7–11, in the first year of Cyrus (538 B.C.E.) Sheshbazzar brought back from Babylon to Jerusalem the exiles together with the temple vessels carried off by Nebuchadnezzar. But the list of those returning to the province of Judah incorporated into Ezra 2 does not even mention Sheshbazzar; here the leaders are Zerubbabel and Jeshua (2:2). In Ezra 3, it is the latter who, after setting up an altar (3:2–3), two years later (536) laid the foundations of the temple (3:8–10). In the Aramaic account of Tattenai's intervention, this had already been done by the governor Sheshbazaar (5:14–16). The postponement of temple building until the second year of King Darius (4:5, 24; the year 520, if the text means Darius I [521–486]) is explained in 4:6, 7–24 on the basis of an Aramaic tradition having to do with complaints about the Jerusalemites associated with the rebuilding of the city wall under Xerxes (486–465) and Artaxerxes (465–424). Finally, while the Hebrew translation of the edict of Cyrus (1:2–4) includes both the rebuilding of the temple and permission for the exiles to return, the Aramaic "memorandum" of this edict (6:3–5) mentions only the rebuilding of the temple and the return of the temple vessels. A second problem has to do with the difference between the historical narrative and the prophetic books. According to Hag 1:1ff., the temple lay in ruins until the middle of the year 520 (1:4); there is no hint that work had begun earlier. Zechariah 4:9 explicitly ascribes the laying of the cornerstone to Zerubbabel, contradicting Ezra 5:14–16.

Probably the author of Ezra identified the figures of Sheshbazzar and Zerubbabel in order to reconcile the contradictions, as did Josephus,[246] and as some modern commentators still do. But the two different Babylonian names rule out this explanation.[247] The name "Sheshbazaar" probably goes back to Babylonian *šamaš-aba-uṣur*, "May Shamash (the sun god) protect the father"; "Zerubbabel" represents Babylonian *zēr-bābili*, "Seed of Babylon." In other words, we are confronted with two divergent traditions concerning the return of the golah and the rebuilding of the temple: one connected with the name Sheshbazzar and associated with the year 538, the other connected with the names Zerubbabel and Jeshua or Joshua and centered on the year 520.[248] How they are to be reconciled is the primary problem that any reconstruction of the closing years of the exilic era must resolve.

---

[246] *Ant.* 11.13–14.
[247] Tadmor, "Judah," 263.
[248] Galling, *Studien*, 127ff.; Grabbe, *Judaism*, 75–79.

According to the view of the book of Ezra, Cyrus's conquest of the Neo-Babylonian Empire marked the end of the exile. In his very first year as king of Babylon (538 B.C.E.; correctly specified in Ezra 5:13, in contrast to the less specific wording of 1:1 and 6:3), Cyrus issued an edict on behalf of the deported Judeans in which he gave his permission for them to return to Jerusalem and there rebuild the temple of Yahweh (1:2–4; cf. 3:7; 4:3; 6:3–5). But the same book has substantial difficulties explaining the delay of eighteen years, until the year 520 (4:1–24). In the view of the books of Haggai and Zechariah, it is the latter year, the second regnal year of Darius (520/521), when the rebuilding of the temple was begun, that marks the decisive turning point that ended the exilic period.

The existence of the now fragmentary Sheshbazzar tradition (Ezra 1:7–11; 5:14–16) suggests that under Cyrus there was already an initial accommodation between the Babylonian golah and the Persian regime. The question is what this accommodation involved and to what extent it was realized.

Of the two versions of Cyrus's edict (Ezra 1:2–4; 6:3–5), the former is clearly fictive.[249] First, it is formulated entirely in the language of the author of the book of Ezra (cf. 1:5–6); second, it is in many ways highly improbable. Cyrus had just had himself hailed as the king chosen by Marduk. Given the marginal status of the Judean community, it is inconceivable that at the same time and in the same place he would describe himself as called to the throne by Yahweh (1:2). It may be pointed out that on a fragmentary cylinder from Ur[250] Cyrus probably describes himself as having been entrusted with rule over the whole earth by the primary local god Sin, but this is in a different locale, and Ur was an important cultic center. Furthermore, the command in 1:4 that the Babylonians should contribute generously to their Jewish neighbors to facilitate their return and make freewill offerings for the Jerusalem temple is pure fantasy.

The Aramaic version, on the contrary, has features of a Persian document and could be in part authentic. Its title דכרונה ("memorandum"; Ezra 6:2) occurs similarly in the document permitting the rebuilding of the temple at Elephantine, dating from the year 407 (EP 32.1: זכרון). Formally, then, we are dealing not with a public edict but with an internal Persian administrative memorandum.[251] Its specific statement that the

---

[249] The judgment of most German scholars: Gunneweg, *Esra*, 40–44; Donner, *Geschichte* (II.2), 439–42. Others such as Miller and Hayes (*History* [II.2], 444ff.) and Tadmor ("Judah," 262) argue that the version of the edict in Ezra 1:2–4 is substantially accurate.

[250] Kuhrt, "Cyrus Cylinder," 89 (*UET* 1:307).

[251] Gunneweg (*Esra*, 107) objects that the designation of the document as a מְגִלָּה, "scroll," argues against its authenticity, since Cyrus's local practice would have been to use

Jerusalem temple is to be a place "where sacrifices are offered" (6:3) is quite understandable, given that the offerings of the official Persian cult were generally unbloody (*lan* offerings);[252] here a local exception is permitted.[253] It is clear that when the Jewish temple at Elephantine was rebuilt the right to offer burnt offerings (EP 30.21, 25) was revoked and the cult was restricted to grain and incense offerings (EP 32.9–10).[254] The absence of a figure for the length of the temple in 6:3 may be due to a gap in the papyrus being cited. The statement that the costs of rebuilding were to be met by the "house of the king," that is, the royal treasury, is not unrealistic in light of the privileges that the Persians granted to other temples within their empire.[255] It is true, however, that this statement presupposes an organized system of taxation in the Persian Empire, which was first created by Darius. It is more likely, therefore, despite the mention of Cyrus in 6:3, that the text concerns a decree issued by Darius in his first regnal year (521).

In contrast to the lapidary style of 6:3–4, 6:5 is more expansive and shifts to the second person, formally out of place in a memorandum. The provision concerning the return of the temple vessels is therefore probably an independent text fragment belonging originally to a different context and possibly going back to Cyrus, since Ezra 1:7–8 describes Cyrus himself as returning the temple vessels, outside the context of the edict. Since 1:8 even preserves the name of a Persian treasurer, Mithredath, there is some evidence that we have here an earlier tradition recording an act of magnanimity on the part of Cyrus, suppressed when Darius's permission to return and rebuild the temple became associated retrospectively with Cyrus.

Cyrus did not reorganize the conquered Neo-Babylonian Empire, and its southwestern provinces were still quite peripheral to the imperial interests; it is thus unlikely that he undertook a broad initiative to repatriate the Judean population of Babylon and initiate the rebuilding of

---

tablets; his claim forgets that the Aramaic script had already come into use in the Assyrian and Neo-Babylonian period alongside cuneiform.

[252] Koch, "Götter," 241–45.

[253] A different solution was found in Elam, where the official Persian grain offerings were probably converted into animals so that the traditional bloody *gušum* sacrifices of the Elamite population could be offered.

[254] See the text in Porten and Yardeni, *Textbook* (II.2), 1:76–77 (A4.9, lines 1 and 9–10), 68–71 (A4.7, lines 21 and 25).

[255] We may note in particular the temple of Apollo at Magnesia, whose personnel were exempted from taxes and corvée labor because of a favorable oracle given by Apollo, probably in the war against Lydia. On the letter of Darius to Gadatas explicitly reconfirming these privileges, a parallel to Ezra 6:3–12, see Briant, *History*, 491–93.

far-off Judah, as the author of the book of Ezra describes. The evidence of the Cyrus Cylinder indicates that in this period his interest was focused on bringing the border land between Persia/Media and Babylonia back under cultivation (lines 30–32). It is more likely that his act of magnanimity was much more modest, being limited to the return of the vessels taken from the Jerusalem temple by Nebuchadnezzar in 597 and 587 and deposited in the temples of Babylon. Such an act chimes well with his propagandistic revision of Nabonidus's religious policies, returning the statues of the gods brought to Babylon by Nabonidus to their traditional homes.[256] Inspecting the temples of Babylon for statues of the gods that did not belong there, he could easily have come upon the furnishings of the Jerusalem temple, only in this case not idols but precious cultic paraphernalia. Their return to Sheshbazzar with instructions to bring them back to Jerusalem (Ezra 1:7–8; 5:14) probably took place in Cyrus's first regnal year. Thus the Judean exiles profited from a general inspection of the cult.

Who was this Sheshbazzar? Many attempts have been made to turn him into a Davidide by identifying him with Shenazzar, the fourth son of Jehoiachin in 1 Chr 3:18.[257] This identification is unlikely, if only on etymological grounds: the name "Shenazzar" goes back to Babylonian *sîn-uṣur*, "May Sin protect," which is clearly distinct from the Babylonian form of "Sheshbazzar," *šamaš-aba-uṣur*, "May Shamash (the sun god) protect the father." In addition, it is noteworthy that the name of Sheshbazzar's father never appears, in contrast to that of Zerubbabel's father (Ezra 3:3, 8; 5:2; Neh 12:1; Hag 1:1, 12, 14; 2:2, 23). The frequent and emphatic mention of Zerubbabel's Davidic lineage but never that of Sheshbazzar practically rules out the latter.[258] Quite the contrary: the report of the elders in Ezra 5:14 speaks somewhat distantly of "a man named Sheshbazzar." The absence of a patronymic makes it likely that Sheshbazzar was not a Judean[259] but, as his name indicates, a Babylonian, either appointed by Cyrus as governor (פחה) of Judah (5:14) or—given the continuity between the Babylonian and the Persian regimes—confirmed by him as the last Babylonian governor of Judah.[260] The choice of a reliable government official for the mission was appropriate, since vessels of great value from the temple treasury were involved.

---

256 Cyrus Cylinder, lines 33–34.
257 See most recently Tadmor, "Judah," 263.
258 The title נשיא יהודה, "prince of Judah," given to Sheshbazzar in Ezra 1:8 merely echoes less precisely the title of governor in 5:14 and cannot support the theory of Davidic lineage.
259 Cf. the absence of a patronymic in the case of the foreigner Job (Job 1:1).
260 As conjectured by Miller and Hayes, *History* (II.1), 446.

It is possible that the return of the cultic vessels was associated with vague plans and financial commitments for rebuilding the Jerusalem temple, so that the vessels could once again be restored to their ancient function. It is likely that Cyrus was already considering a campaign in Egypt, and possibly he was laying the groundwork. But until the time of his death in 530, Cyrus's military activity was restricted to the eastern portions of his empire; any other designs, if seriously considered at all, never got beyond the planning stage. If the report that Sheshbazzar laid the foundation of the temple (Ezra 5:15–16, contrary to Zech 4:9) is more than a later fabrication intended to trace the rebuilding of the Jerusalem temple all the way back to the revered father of the Persian Empire, then the project came to a halt shortly after, whether because the Persian nobles administering the satrapy of Babylon and Transeuphratene were interested in extracting the maximum possible personal profit from the provinces and would not for a moment consider bearing construction costs or because the Judeans left in Jerusalem had no particular interest in rebuilding the temple.[261] It is to be expected that Cyrus's half-hearted interest in a remote province meant that only a few members of the golah were prepared to return to their homeland, much of which still suffered the ravages of war.[262] The interest of the Persian regime in rebuilding the province was still too slight.

This situation did not change until 525, when Cambyses, following the death of his father in 530, embarked on his Egyptian campaign. Now for the first time Syria and Palestine took on strategic importance for the Persian regime. Unfortunately, the sources do not allow us to say precisely when the decisive arrangements were made between the Persian regime and the Judean community in Babylonia. It is possible that the first overtures were made as early as 524, when Cambyses was planning his campaign, and that the process of return began soon thereafter. There is much to say for the theory of Galling[263] that the large group of returnees under the official leadership of Zerubbabel and Joshua (Ezra 2) did not enter Palestine until the spring of 520. In any case, according to Ezra 5:1–2; 6:14; Hag 1–2, it was Zerubbabel and Joshua who took the first step toward rebuilding the temple in the summer of 520. But this means that the rebuilding of the ruined temple and probably also the first great wave of returnees came at the beginning of the reign of

---

[261] Cf. the hostile attitude of the Jeremiah Deuteronomists in Jer 7:1–15; they set the tone in Judah.

[262] Even for the author of the book of Ezra, it took divine intervention in the year 538 to arouse the spirits of the golah and make them decide to return (Ezra 1:5, 11b)

[263] *Studien*, 121.

Darius I.²⁶⁴ At this time Darius was still busy putting down the revolts that had erupted throughout the empire—except in Syria and Palestine—after the murder of Gaumata, in whom so many had placed their hopes; the rebuilding of the Jerusalem temple and the repatriation of the Judean community must therefore be understood as measures undertaken by Darius to secure his throne.

In addition, the only possible parallel to the return of the Babylonian golah comes from the same period, the return of the Nusku-gabbe family from southern Mesopotamia to their home in Syria, which can be reconstructed from the family archives found at Neirab, four miles south of Aleppo.²⁶⁵ This event probably took place during the initial years of Darius's reign, after the Babylonian uprisings in 522/521.

Since Zerubbabel, the leader of the returning group, bore the official title פֶּחָה, "governor" (Hag 1:1, 14; 2:2, 21; cf. Ezra 6:7 [text?]), we are dealing with an action undertaken with the permission and support of the Persian state. Since representatives of the two leading families of the Babylonian golah, the Davidide Zerubbabel and the Hilkiad Joshua, led the return, it is reasonable to assume that the undertaking was preceded by official negotiations between the Judean community and the Persian regime. There was a favorable opportunity for such negotiations in the first half of 521, when Darius, having put down the revolt of Nidintu-Bēl (Nebuchadnezzar III), remained in Babylonia from December 22, 522, to June of 521.²⁶⁶

Eager to consolidate his rule in Babylonia, Darius surely was pleased to have an ethnic group in Babylonia, within his war-torn empire, assure him explicitly of their loyalty; he must have been attracted to the suggestion that rebuilding the province of Judah with their help would secure the southwest flank of the empire, now strategically important because of the conquest of Egypt. Persian investment in such a project appeared worthwhile. The minor damage to the Babylonian economy caused by the emigration of a substantial number of people could be accepted at a time when the Babylonians had to be given a warning about their insubordination. Granting the wishes of the golah would ensure the enduring loyalty of the Judean community throughout the whole empire.

---

264 The apocryphal "Story of the Three Youths" in 1 Esd 3:1–5:6 does not know of any return until the time of Darius; here the rebuilding of the temple and other privileges are traced to a vow Darius is said to have made at his accession (4:43–46). Cyrus had promised only the return of the temple vessels (4:44). Possibly this legendary narrative has preserved an accurate historical reminiscence on these points; see pp. 28–29 above.

265 Timm, "Bedeutung," 282ff.

266 Kuhrt, "Babylonia," 129.

What were these wishes? There are many signs that the leadership of the Babylonian golah was seeking the maximum feasible political reinstatement of Judah and especially restoration of the Davidic monarchy. Many of them were descended from members of the party of religious nationalism. Although they had learned their lesson from the prophets and the Deuteronomistic theologians, they were not prepared simply to write off the beliefs in which their ancestors had placed their trust: the divine election of the Davidic dynasty and the Jerusalem temple. Throughout most of the exile, the Davidide Jehoiachin had naturally been their political representative and the symbol of their hopes. They also held in honor the leading priestly family of the Hilkiads, who once had led the party of religious nationalism. True to their convictions, in the early Persian period the Babylonian golah collected a great amount of silver and gold, eagerly preparing for the coronation of Zerubbabel and Joshua in Judah (Zech 6:9–14).

Quite clearly Darius went a long way to accommodate the Judean community during the negotiations in Babylon. He agreed to repatriate a substantial number of people, a step that would have been impossible without the help of Persian logistics. He also agreed to the rebuilding of the Jerusalem temple and even permitted the bloody sacrifice of animals there, which the Persians did not like, and promised Persian support for the rebuilding.[267] Indeed, he even declared his readiness to endue Zerubbabel, a grandson of Jehoiachin and a Davidide (1 Chr 3:19), with the authority of a Persian governor and put him in charge of the repatriation and the rebuilding of the temple. To this day, I believe that Darius's cooperation has not been sufficiently appreciated. It means that initially Darius was willing to go a long way toward meeting the wishes of the Judean community for a restoration of the Davidic monarchy. The title פחה, which can hardly be reduced to the meaning "commissar for repatriation,"[268] indicates that the Persians were quite ready to make the local dynasty of the Davidides, should they prove themselves able, hereditary governors of Judah or even recognize them as vassal kings.[269] In itself this was nothing unusual: Samaria was under the authority of a dynastic governor, and there were regions in the Persian Empire, such as Cilicia, the Phoenician city states, and Cyprus, where the Persians even accepted

---

[267] Based on the memorandum in Ezra 6:3–4, which our previous discussion ascribes to Darius.

[268] Alt, "Rolle," 336; more recently Donner, Geschichte (II.2), 444.

[269] This is also the view of Stern, "Persian Empire," 82, and Lemaire, "Zorobabel," 54–56. Bianchi ("Role," 156ff.) and others go too far, claiming that Sheshbazzar and Zerubbabel had been vassal kings under Persian suzerainty.

semiautonomous kings.²⁷⁰ But such an arrangement was always a privilege granted for an extraordinary demonstration of loyalty or in recognition of special local circumstances.²⁷¹

In short, a rather far-reaching restoration of the preexilic monarchic status quo was well within the realm of possibility, granted the special initial conditions. It is understandable, therefore, that this promising outlook encouraged a substantial number of the Babylonian Jews to accept the risk of returning to their homeland.

This risk was not insubstantial. On the one hand, it entailed giving up a secure occupation and acceptance of financial loss with the sale of property. On the other, it was clearly an open question whether ancient claims to property ownership would be recognized, given the redistribution of property by the Babylonians and Gedaliah. Legal proceedings involving a difficult body of evidence were in prospect (Zech 5:1–4). Conflicting economic interests and differing political and religious convictions meant that the returnees could not count on being welcomed with open arms and taken in by those who had been left behind, especially since economic conditions in Palestine were poor (Hag 1:6, 9–12; Zech 8:10).

The list in Ezra 2 and Neh 7 sets the number of returnees at 42,360, to which must be added 7,337 male and female slaves (Ezra 2:64–65). The total of some twenty thousand persons deported, calculated above,²⁷² makes this number seem incredibly large, especially since it should probably be multiplied by a factor of three to allow for women and children. Even if we postulate a high birth rate, as is sometimes the case for ethnic minorities, and assume that exiles from earlier deportations joined the Babylonian golah, the number remains unrealistic, since we know from later returns (almost eight thousand more in Ezra 3:1–30) and other sources that the majority of the Judean exiles stayed in Babylonia. It has therefore been suggested repeatedly that this list, as its position in Neh 7 indicates, represents the total membership of the Judean community in the time of Nehemiah, all of whom had meanwhile come to think of themselves as descendants of the returnees.²⁷³ The number of those who

---

270 This possibility, previously ignored, is now seen more frequently: see Bianchi, "Role," 156–57; Lemaire, "Zorobabel," 53–54. Tadmor ("Judah," 263) dismisses it too quickly.

271 Cilicia was granted special status in return for the military assistance it had provided for Cyrus; the Phoenician city states put their fleet at the disposal of the Persians. On Cyprus, the Persians left the traditional monarchies in place; see Maier, "Cyprus," 297ff., 317ff.; Eph'al, "Syria-Palestine," 156–57.

272 See pp. 88–90 above.

273 Weinberg, *Citizen-Temple Community* (II.1), 41 ff.; Gunneweg, *Esra*, 53–66; etc.

returned through the year 520 probably does not exceed ten thousand. The majority of the Judeans stayed in Babylonia because prospects there seemed more attractive.

Returning in the spring of 520, Zerubbabel undertook the rebuilding of the temple without delay, in early August, as the spirit of religious nationalism would expect. He had to overcome substantial resistance. There were fundamental theological objections, on the grounds that the time to rebuild the temple had not yet come (Hag 1:4): Jeremiah and the Deuteronomistic theologians associated with him had spoken of seventy years of judgment, which had not yet passed (587 − 70 = 517). This argument may have been brought forward by those who remained behind: their spokesmen were naturally hostile to the temple as the former hub of religious and nationalistic resistance (Jer 7:1–15). But there was also the pragmatic objection that the returnees had to worry first about getting roofs over their own heads (Hag 1:9). In addition, a failed harvest made the economic situation in Judah desolate (Hag 1:6, 9–12). Nevertheless, thanks to the divine legitimation of his work by the prophets Haggai and Zechariah, Zerubbabel succeeded in dispelling all reservations and arousing great enthusiasm for rebuilding the temple among the majority of the population.

Now the rebuilding of the temple and the prophetic movement supporting it aroused nationalistic hopes that the Persians in this period had to interpret as the threat of a new uprising.[274] While Darius was still busy stamping out the last embers of revolt among the Scythians and Elamites, the prophet Haggai was preaching an imminent cataclysm shaking all the nations of the world, causing their wealth to flow not into the Persian coffers but to the Jerusalem temple, to fill it with splendor (Hag 2:3–9). The prophet Zechariah expected a great political upheaval in 517/516 (Zech 1:8–16; 6:1–8) and saw a vision in which the horns of the nations were struck off (2:1–4 [1:18–21]). Both prophets projected glowing messianic hopes upon Zerubbabel: for Haggai, he was Yahweh's own signet ring, the mandatary of his reign after the overthrow of the nations (Hag 2:20–23). With the gold and silver provided by the golah, Zechariah even planned a coronation of Zerubbabel and the high priest Joshua (Zech 6:9–14), who as Yahweh's "anointed ones" would share his universal rule (4:1–6aα, 10aβ–14). The nationalistic prophets of deliverance, whom Zerubbabel did not silence because he needed them to mobilize all his forces, threatened to upset the accommodation he had achieved with the Persians.

---

[274] This view is close to that advocated already by Olmstead, *History*, 135–42, although many of his conjectures are rather too daring.

The cataclysm never took place. By the end of 519 at the latest, Darius was firmly in control. The Persians, who had an excellent system of postal messengers, considered the situation in Jerusalem so dangerous that they ordered Tattenai, the satrap of Transeuphratene, to go there (Ezra 5:3–17). Tattenai's intervention, which made it necessary to negotiate with Darius once more, resulted in a compromise: Zerubbabel, on whom the dangerously subversive hopes had focused, was removed—an action that forced Zechariah to emend his prophecy.[275] Probably the prophets Haggai and Zechariah were also silenced or gotten rid of, since neither mentions the dedication of the temple in his prophecy. In return, Darius confirmed the promise he had made to the Judean community concerning the temple (6:3–4), explicitly permitted the rebuilding to continue, and—now that his administrative and fiscal reforms were in place—promised generous support for rebuilding the temple and financing the sacrificial cult from the royal revenues of Transeuphratene (6:6–12). In return, as proof of loyalty, he expected regular prayers for him and his sons (6:10; cf. lines 34ff. of the Cyrus Cylinder). This new agreement with the Persian crown allowed the rebuilding to be finished swiftly; the temple was dedicated in 515.

The nationalistic faction, which was ready to renounce allegiance to the Persians in order to pursue the chimera of a totally independent state, had suffered a great fiasco. The dream of restoring the Davidic monarchy had ended. After this disillusioning experience, the Persians—as far as we know—never again ventured to entrust a Davidide with political office.[276]

The visit of Tattenai limited the political damage and allowed cooperation with the Persians to continue confidently on a new basis; this was because, besides the party of religious nationalism, there were other groups in Judah to whom the rebuilding of the temple was more

---

[275] See the textual corruptions in Zech 6:9–14. He made the abortive coronation refer solely to the high priest Joshua (6:11), interpreting him as a stand-in for a future king (3:8b).

[276] Lemaire ("Zorobabel," 56–57), however, following Meyers ("Persian Period," 508), finds Davidides in public office after Zerubbabel. He identifies the owner of the seal יהוד/חננה ("Yehud/Hananah"; Avigad, Bullae, 4–5), whom the province name shows to have had a public function, with Hananiah (חנניה), the second son of Zerubbabel named in 1 Chr 3:19, and identifies the owner of the seal לשלמית אמת אלנתן פח[וא] ("property of Shelomith, the maid of Elnathan the governor"; Avigad, Bullae, 11–13) with the daughter of Zerubbabel named in the same verse, taken as wife or concubine by a non-Davidic governor in order to claim the Davidic heritage. Thus Lemaire reconstructs a gradual elimination of the Davidides from the office of governor, a consequence of the growing prestige of the high priest. As Lemaire himself admits, however, these identifications are uncertain; the redactional corrections in the books of Haggai and Zechariah argue instead for an abrupt termination.

important than the Davidides or who simply did not want a restoration on the model of the preexilic monarchy.

First there was the group of priestly reformers who had also returned from exile. In the preexilic period, the priests had been royal officials subject to the authority of the king; the end of the monarchy made them independent for the first time. The Babylonian temples were always able to maintain a certain autonomy vis-à-vis the palace. Encouraged by this example, during the Babylonian exile the priestly reformers had already espoused the development of a cult administered solely by the priests themselves (Ezek 40–48; later P). It would have been difficult if not impossible to carry out this projected reform under a restored Davidic monarchy, which since time immemorial had seen the close association of temple and palace as the legacy of the Jebusite priest-kings. The role assigned to the future high priest Joshua alongside Zerubbabel in rebuilding the temple (Ezra 5:2; Hag 1:1, 12, 14; 2:4) and the concept of two anointed figures, a royal messiah and a priestly messiah, in the book of Zechariah (Zech 4:11–14; 6:11 cj.) may have been compromises intended to accommodate the desire of some members of the priesthood for independence, a compromise to which the nationalistic laity with their traditional conception of an official state cult (1 Kgs 6–8; 2 Kgs 22–23) could only just accede. Abandonment of the Davidic monarchy naturally made it much easier to establish priestly independence. This realization may have led Joshua and the Hilkiads to abandon their traditional ties to the Davidides and join instead with the priestly reformers in order to guarantee that they would hold the office of high priest in the new temple.[277]

Second, besides the priestly reformers there was a group of lay leaders descended from the reform party backing the Shaphanides, who had remained in Judah during the exile. Their ancestors had already supported a non-Davidide in the person of Shaphan's grandson Gedaliah. They seized the end of the Davidic monarchy as a chance to put through reforms embodying Deuteronomic social legislation, reforms that the religious nationalists had reversed after the death of Josiah. This group, which left the Deuteronomistic book of Jeremiah as a literary monument to themselves and their leaders Jeremiah and Baruch, was absolutely opposed to any Davidic monarchy. Even during the exilic period, probably in response to the pardon of Jehoiachin in 562, the authors of the first

---

[277] The charge against Joshua mentioned in Zech 3:1–7 could well have been associated with this change of allegiance: Joshua will be put in charge of the temple if he keeps the requirements of Yahweh, i.e., the new regulations governing priestly ministry framed by the reformers.

edition of Deuteronomistic Jeremiah had made a point of Jeremiah's prophetic statement that Jehoiachin was a signet ring that Yahweh had discarded and that none of his offspring would ever again sit on the throne of David and rule over Judah (Jer 22:24-30).

It is reasonable to suppose that these lay leaders who had remained in Judah were mistrustful of Zerubbabel's mission. But they had not been able to prevent the rebuilding of the ruined temple, although they—like Jeremiah—castigated mistaken trust in the temple, pleading instead for moral renewal of society as a whole (Jer 7:1-7). Toward the end of 520 or the beginning of 519, Haggai ventured publicly in the name of God to rescind their Jeremianic prophecy concerning the rejection of Jehoiachin (Hag 2:20-23). This action shows that during the upsurge of religious nationalism these lay reformers had no influence.

Now, however, after the religious nationalists had suffered their fiasco, the lay leaders had a chance to devote their energies to realizing their reforming vision of a Judean society without a monarchy. In alliance with the priestly reformers, they were in a position to offer the Persians a more reliable political alternative to Davidic rule, in line with the Persians' own interests. This coalition took the reins in 517. The experiences of the exilic period made its members firmly determined to prevent any restoration of the preexilic state.

The new arrangement with the Persians ushered in a new form of political and religious organization in Judah.[278] At its head stood the Persian governor and the Persian provincial administration. Below them were three Judean organs of self-government: at the head a council of elders and a college of priests, below these a popular assembly. This organization clearly was based on premonarchic Israel, which also had councils of elders and popular assemblies. But this premonarchic model was adapted to the needs of the postexilic community by the formation of a college of priests, coordinate with the council of elders. Also new was the requirement that all members of the community be registered in "fathers' houses" (בֵּית אָבוֹת), new clan alliances established among the exiles. The organizational principle intended to ensure the survival of the Judean minority amid the alien religions of the Diaspora was thus introduced in the province of Judah, where the Judeans constituted the majority but lived side by side with aliens, without clear territorial demarcation. It was also imposed on those had stayed behind, who had to prove their ethnic identity and demonstrate their faithfulness to

---

[278] It is observable by the middle of the fifth century at the latest. For a more detailed description, see Albertz, *History* (Introduction), 2:446-50; Weinberg, *Citizen-Temple Community* (II.1), 49-61.

Yahweh by accepting the stricter badges of religious separation that had evolved among the exiles (Ezra 6:21). Prohibition of mixed marriages was part of the package (Ezra 10; Neh 12:23–28).

Clearly this novel form of organization, a subnation, was highly attractive to the lay and priestly leaders (רָאשֵׁי הָאָבוֹת), since it gave them a measure of self-determination and codetermination that they could never have attained under the Davidic monarchy. In return, they were prepared to be loyal supporters of Persian rule from that time on, without interruption.

This loyal cooperation of the anti-Davidic coalition of priests and laity with the Persians paid off handsomely for the Judeans. Not only was the rebuilding of the temple completed in 515 with Persian support, but the Persians also allowed the walls of Jerusalem to be rebuilt under Nehemiah in 458 and granted Ezra (probably in 398) quite astonishing privileges: generous financing of the temple cult from the royal treasuries, tax exemption for all cultic personnel, and authorization of the Torah as a locally binding code of Jewish law (Ezra 7:20–26). The Persians granted such privileges to very few temples in their empire.[279]

Of course, agreement not to seek a restoration of political autonomy and the loyal cooperation of the Judean organs of self-government with the Persians came at a high price: acceptance of the strict Persian tax policies that Darius had established in 520. It was the poorer strata of the population who bore the burden. It was all too easy for them to be crushed by the rigid imposition of high taxes. They also had to look on as their own leaders mercilessly collected what was necessary to meet the Persian demands and even profited from the loans that the peasantry had to take out to pay these taxes (Neh 5:1–13). The price of the thwarted restoration was thus a chronic impoverishment of the poorer classes, which created a deep division within Judean society, beginning in the middle of the fifth century at the latest.

II.4. SOCIAL DISPLACEMENTS AND THEIR RELIGIOUS CONSEQUENCES

Albertz, Rainer. *A History of Israelite Religion in the Old Testament Period* (trans. J. Bowden; 2 vols.; OTL; Louisville: Westminster John Knox, 1994). **Albertz.**

---

[279] Besides the temple of Apollo in Magnesia, mentioned above, these were the temple of Marduk in Babylon and the temple of Ptah in Memphis. In general the Persians expanded the taxation of temples. On the temple policies of the Achaemenids, see Dandamaev and Lukonin, *Culture,* 360–66.

Persönliche Frömmigkeit und offizielle Religion: Religionsinterner Pluralismus in Israel und Babylon (CThM.A 9; Stuttgart: Calwer, 1978). **Smith,** Daniel L. *The Religion of the Landless: The Social Context of the Babylonian Exile* (Bloomington: Meyer-Stone, 1989).

If we look back on the history of the exilic era, starting from its close, we see that during this period Israel underwent five profound social changes that had far-reaching consequences. We shall only outline them briefly here, since I have described them in more detail elsewhere.[280]

1. The ravages and deportations of 732 and 722 as well as 597 and 587 meant for Israel and Judah the loss of their existence as independent states after only three hundred and five hundred years of history, a loss—interrupted only briefly in the Hasmonean and Herodian period (135 B.C.E.–70 C.E.)—that lasted until the year 1948. This had far-reaching consequences for the subsequent history of Israel and the further development of Israel's religion and early Judaism.

The fall of the Judean monarchy and the destruction of Jerusalem were a severe blow to the official Jerusalemite theology of king and temple, with its massive appeal to Yahweh in support of state power. The guarantee that the Davidic monarchy would endure forever (2 Sam 7) and the central tenet of Zion theology, that the presence of Yahweh on Mount Zion made the city impregnable to external enemies (Pss 46:2–8 [1–7]; 48:4–8 [3–7]; 76:4–6 [3–5]; 2 Kgs 18–20; Mic 3:11), had been refuted by the course of history. With the exile, consequently, the dominant state-centered theology of the monarchy faded into the background, surviving only in more or less major revisions and mutations. Instead, after a lengthy struggle, the message of the prophets of judgment, which in the preexilic period had been an opposition theology rejected by the majority, came decisively to the fore. With its bias toward political and social criticism, it became a widely accepted element of Israelite religion.

Partly a result of this change, after the loss of political and cultic institutions informal groups of theologians became more and more the vehicles of official Yahwism, to some extent continuing the groups supporting prophetic opposition and Deuteronomic reform. They gathered around the heritage of the prophets of judgment—the reforming Shaphanide officials around the prophecy of Jeremiah, the priestly reformers around the priest-prophet Ezekiel. They worked in part within the confines of the ancient power elites such the editors of the

---

[280] Albertz, *History,* 2:369–436.

Deuteronomistic History; at times, however, drawing on prophetic inspiration, they could stand totally outside these circles—such as the Deutero-Isaiah group, which probably consisted of former temple singers.

The result of this deregulation of religious traditions was an almost explosive increase in literary production and a splintering into various "theological schools" that went considerably beyond the divisions of the preexilic period. The more or less extensive separation of the official religious tradition from its political power base and from political responsibility opened the way for vast utopian designs for the future but contained within itself the danger of a loss of contact with reality. Especially impressive are the utopian revisions of royal theology authored by the Deutero-Isaiah group and of temple theology by the disciples of Ezekiel. With deliverance from exile, the former expected an immediate establishment of God's kingship within history, rendering a Davidic monarchy superfluous (Isa 40:9–11; 52:7–10); the promises made to the monarchy were transferred to the nation as a whole and to Jerusalem (55:4–5). For the restoration, the disciples of Ezekiel had a vision of a temple not only totally separate from the palace geographically but also administered solely by the priests (Ezek 43:1–9). The monarchy would be severely limited in power and deprived of most of its sacral functions (46:1–18). In this utopian mutation, the former theology of the state took on the function of criticizing state authority.

In the historical arena, the emancipation of the priesthood from the royal control imposed on it in the preexilic period was one of the most important social developments of the exilic period. The most momentous theological innovation of this period was the discovery of monotheism by the Deutero-Isaiah group (Isa 41:4, 23–24, 27–29; 43:10–13; 44:6, 8; 45:5–6, 14, 18, 21–22; 46:9; cf. 48:12) and the Deuteronomists (Deut 4:35, 39; 2 Sam 7:22; 1 Kgs 8:60). Without the collapse of the Judean state and the theological problem it raised as to whether this event demonstrated Yahweh's impotence vis-à-vis the Babylonian gods, this discovery would not have been made.

2. The loss of the state and the associated deportations and emigrations led to an irreversible disintegration of Israel's territorial integrity. The exile marks the beginning of Israel's life in the Diaspora, which has continued to this day.

The Israel of the exilic period comprised at least three geographically distinct groups: those who stayed behind, the Babylonian golah, and the Egyptian golah. They underwent different courses of historical development and had different political and religious interests, which not rarely brought them into conflict. What bound these geographically distinct groups together was the loose bond of a common ethnic origin and a common religion; at least for the Babylonian golah, the connection with the land from which they had been taken retained a religious and emotional significance (praying in the direction of Jerusalem: 1 Kgs 8:48 and Dan 6:11 [10]; later pilgrimages).

In consequence of this territorial separation, the religion of Israel developed quite differently in the separate centers. The Judeans who emigrated to Egypt persisted conservatively in the Yahwism of preexilic provenance, laced with syncretisms, whereas the religious elites of those who remained behind and the Babylonian golah saw the exile as a chance and a demand for a radical renewal of Yahwism along the lines of the Josianic reform, that is, an opportunity to impose exclusive and aniconic worship of Yahweh.

Despite this common basis in Deuteronomic theology, the interests of the theologians we lump together under the label "Deuteronomists" differed in detail. The Deuteronomistic historians, who worked within the purview of the leaders of the Babylonian golah, supported a religious renewal from above, under the direction of the monarchy and the temple; the Deuteronomistic redactors of the book of Jeremiah preached to those who had stayed behind a renewal from below, through a general conversion of the people, including a new code of social ethics.[281] Since the identity and the survival of the Judeans in Babylonia were more threatened than at home, they were responsible for many innovative religious and ritual safeguards (Sabbath, circumcision, dietary laws). These innovations, coupled with the impressive theological structures created by the priestly reformers and the Deutero-Isaiah group, may have given rise to a self-assurance among the golah that they, rather than those who stayed behind, could rightfully claim the leadership role. In the later postexilic period, the Judean community as a whole thought of themselves as the descendants of the Babylonian golah (Ezra 2:1; 6:19–21; etc.). In the early postexilic period, however, this vision (as we have seen above) could be realized only partially.

3. The loss of centralized political power led to a strengthening of decentralized forms of organization forms based on kinship. In the Israel of the exilic period, the family or familial alliance became the primary social entity. Relics of tribal organization, never totally forgotten, took on new life. The elders once more became a significant force and took on limited functions of local political leadership alongside the priests and prophets. Instead of a restored monarchy, after the exile a subnational polity was introduced, consisting of a council of elders, a college of

---

281 Albertz, "Wer waren die Deuteronomisten?" [II.2.], 325ff.

priests, and a popular assembly. This development is connected directly with the positive experiences the community had with premonarchic forms of organization during the exilic period.

As a result of this societal shift, during this period the family also became more important in the religious sphere. In the preexilic period, family religious observances had long flourished freely alongside the official religion of Yahweh; following the Josianic reform, they were incorporated rather more formally into the latter.[282] In the deepest crisis of Israel's religion, this family piety played a supportive and substitutionary role that contributed substantially to the overcoming of this crisis.

Family piety could play a supportive role because—in contrast to official Yahwism—here the relationship with God was based not on God's saving acts in history but on God's creation of each individual (Ps 22:10–11 [9–10]; 71:5–6; 119:73; 138:8; Job 10:3, 8–12).[283] Because this piety was rooted in creation, the historical catastrophe of the exile was not a mortal blow. On the contrary, while Yahweh seemed inaccessible to Israel as a whole during the exile, the individual survivors were soon able once more to sense Yahweh's presence, protection, and support. As soon as their situation was a bit more stable, the birth of children brought joy; this person or that recovered from a severe illness; the grain grew in the fields; some experienced great occupational success, others little; many, both at home and in the golah, once more found private happiness. These positive religious experiences in the sphere of family piety constituted a treasury on which the exilic congregations could draw in their worship, finding a new basis for confidence and hope that the historical and political catastrophe did not mean that Yahweh had rejected his people (Isa 64:7 [8]; Lam 3; Isa 49:21; Ezek 37:11). The Deutero-Isaiah group also drew on this primordial personal relationship with God when, to built confidence in its prophecy of salvation, it made use of the salvation oracle, the archetypal message of salvation addressed to an individual (Isa 41:8–13, 14–16; 43:1–4, 5–7; 44:1–5; cf. 54:4–6), thus grounding God's relationship with Israel in God's act of creation (43:1; 44:2, 21, 24; 54:5).

In addition, the family also came to play a substitutionary role in preserving and transmitting the official religion of Yahweh: the new observances, created to safeguard Judean identity in the Babylonian golah, either drew on family customs (circumcision, dietary laws) or

---

[282] Albertz, *History*, 1:94–103, 177–80, 186–95.

[283] For a discussion of this whole subject, see Albertz, *Persönliche Frömmigkeit*, 27–96, 179–90.

created new family observances (Sabbath). When the old institutional agencies failed, families became essential upholders of Israelite religion. The image of Judaism as a family-centered religion had its start in the exilic period.

4. The fall of the Judean state put an end to the unquestioned presumption of a national identity. As long as the state existed, Judean identity was simply a given, part of life within the national community. It was incontrovertible, no matter how far an individual might stray from the religious or ethical norms of society. And as long as there was a state, belief in Yahweh was only one identifying mark among others: territorial, political, and ethnic marks played a much more important role in determining who belonged.

With the destruction of the state and the dislocation of large portions of the population, this situation clearly changed. The exiles lived as an ethnic minority, scattered among several settlements, within the context of an alien majority. Those left behind still constituted the majority in some areas but saw themselves increasingly exposed to the pressure of foreign immigrants and traders. For the exiles but also to a lesser extent for those left behind, membership in the Judean community was no longer simply a given; it had to be demonstrated repeatedly by individual decisions. Now confession of religious faith took on critical importance in an entirely new way. The golah especially went the way of assuring identity by introducing religious observances (circumcision, dietary regulations, Sabbath) as confessional badges that enabled the families to demonstrate publicly their membership in the community and to distinguish themselves from the majority society. At the same time, membership in the Judean ethnic community was made verifiable. A family that did not observe these confessional practices excluded itself or could be excluded from the ethnic group. In the exilic period, Israel acquired for the first time characteristics of a religiously constituted community.

In the exilic and early postexilic period, we actually find a hybrid, a group constituted by elements both ethnic and religious. In the newly created kinship associations, בֵּית אָבוֹת ("fathers' house"), the ethnic principle obtained: only someone who could prove that he or his family was of Israelite descent (Ezra 2:59; cf. 2:62–63) could be a member of the Judean community. But the requirement that every family desiring to belong to this community had to go through a registration process (Neh 7:5) meant that the kinship principle ceased to be automatic: in the examination that was part of this process, the religious attitude of the family undoubtedly played an important role in reaching a positive or negative decision (cf. Ezra 6:21). The possibility that serious cases of refusal to observe the confessional requirements or infidelity to the ancestral religion could result in exclusion is demonstrated above all by the priestly legislation of the postexilic period.[284]

5. The loss of state cohesion ultimately made the boundaries of the group more permeable to outside influences. Especially in the golah but also in the homeland, Judean families found themselves in constant confrontation—and not rarely also in friendly contact—with other nationalities.

The result was two very different attitudes toward these foreign neighbors. On the one hand, strict separation from the foreign nations was preached. The oracles against the nations in particular, most of which date from the exilic period, proclaim God's judgment on Israel's hostile, covetous, or self-assured neighbors (Isa 15–20; Jer 46–49; Ezek 25–32; Obadiah; etc.). The boundless might of Babylon with its totalitarian claims to authority would soon be overthrown and suffer Yahweh's vengeance (Isa 13–14; 21; 47; Jer 50–51).

On the other hand, the "survivors of the nations," who like Israel had been victims of imperial Babylon, were invited by the Deutero-Isaiah group to share in the deliverance that Yahweh was about to bring for his people (Isa 45:20–25); thus they occasioned a momentous opening of the national religion of Israel toward universalism. These theologians never denied the special relationship existing between Yahweh and Israel, but they gave Israel a new and positive mission to the Gentile world, transcending all boundaries,[285] and even believed that people belonging to other nations would join Israel (44:5; 55:5). During the exile, Israel took on the features of a group defined at least in part by its religious identity; this development contained within itself the chance for what was later to be a flourishing Jewish mission and the inclusion of Gentiles by Christianity.

The constant alternation between such astonishing universalism and strict particularism in the religion of Israel during the exilic period was a result of this new and ambivalent reality in the societal setting of Israel.

---

284 Cf. the formula נִכְרְתָה הַנֶּפֶשׁ הַהִיא מֵעַמֶּיהָ, "this person shall be cut off from his people" (Gen 17:14; Lev 7:20–21, 27; 19:8; slight variations in Exod 12:15, 19; 31:14; etc.), employed when someone refused to be circumcised (Gen 17:14) or to observe the Sabbath (Exod 31:14).

285 Above all to witness on Yahweh's behalf in the forum of the Gentile world (Isa 43:10–12; 44:8; 55:4). If the Servant of the Lord is identified with Israel, Israel has additional functions: establishing justice (42:1–4), being a light to the nations (42:6; 49:6), and expiating the sins of the nations through its sufferings (52:13–53:12).

III. THE LITERATURE OF THE EXILIC PERIOD

For the Judeans both in Judea and elsewhere, the demise of the Judean state and the deportation and dispersion of a significant portion of its population represented an almost incalculable catastrophe. They faced the substantial day-to-day problems of simple survival under changed circumstances, sometimes very difficult; furthermore, the entire cultural and theological basis on which the identity of Judean society rested was shaken. Before the exile, the official religion of Yahweh had defined itself primarily in historical terms; therefore, the historical catastrophe appeared to have severed its roots. Yahweh had chosen Jerusalem to be his "city of God" and guaranteed its inviolability; now it lay in ruins. The Jerusalem temple, which Yahweh had singled out as the only legitimate site for his cult, was ravaged. The royal house of David, which Yahweh had promised would endure forever, was pathetically powerless. The land, which Yahweh had given to Israel's ancestors after their deliverance from Egypt, was almost totally lost.

The experience of this demoralizing crisis, which appeared to negate all the central elements that Yahweh had ordained for Israel's well-being, could easily have meant the end of Israel's religion. Remarkably, it provoked instead an almost explosive flowering of theological literature during the exilic period. With the nearly total collapse of Israel's political and cultic institutions, a variety of informal groups of theologians of every stripe engaged in large-scale literary activity, processing and interpreting the crisis theologically and thus striving to mitigate it. The literature of the exilic period is extraordinarily rich, even if we cannot date with certainty everything written during these years.

III.1. GENRES OF EXILIC LITERATURE

In most cases, the exilic authors drew on preexilic literary genres; now that institutional constraints were fewer, they could vary these genres more widely. But there are a few genres that came into being or took on special importance in the exilic period.

III.1.1. COMMUNAL LAMENT AND CITY LAMENT

Aejmelaeus, Anneli. "Der Prophet als Kultsänger: Zur Funktion des Psalms Jes 63,7–64,11 in Tritojesaja," *ZAW* 107 (1995): 31–50. **Albertz,** Rainer. *Persönliche Frömmigkeit und offizielle Religion: Religionsinterner Pluralismus in Israel und Babylon* (CThM.A 9; Stuttgart: Calwer, 1978). **Albertz.** *Weltschöpfung und Menschenschöpfung: Untersucht bei Deuterojesaja, Hiob und in den Psalmen* (CThM.A 3; Stuttgart: Calwer, 1974). **Albrektson,** Bertil. *Studies in the Text and Theology of the Book of Lamentations with a Critical Edition of the Peshitta Text* (STL 21; Lund: Gleerup, 1963). **Berges,** Ulrich. *Das Buch Jesaja: Komposition und Endgestalt* (HerBS 16; Freiburg: Herder, 1998). **Boecker,** Hans Jochen. *Klagelieder* (ZBK.AT 21; Zürich: Theologischer Verlag, 1985). **Brandscheidt,** Renate. *Gotteszorn und Menschenleid: Die Gerichtsklage des leidenden Gerechten in Klgl 3* (TThSt 41; Trier: Paulinus, 1983). **Emmendörffer,** Michael. *Der ferne Gott: Eine Untersuchung der alttestamentlichen Volksklagelieder vor dem Hintergrund der mesopotamischen Literatur* (FAT 21; Tübingen: Mohr Siebeck, 1998). **Fischer,** Irmtraud. *Wo ist Jahwe? Das Volksklagelied Jes 63–64:11 als Ausdruck des Ringens um eine gebrochene Beziehung* (SBS 19; Stuttgart: Katholisches Bibelwerk, 1989). **Gunkel,** Hermann. "Klagelieder Jeremiae," *RGG*[2] 3:1049–52. **Gunkel** and Joachim Begrich. *Introduction to Psalms: The Genres of the Religious Lyric of Israel* (trans. J. D. Nogalski; Macon, Ga.: Mercer University Press, 1998). **Gwaltney,** W. C. "The Biblical Book of Lamentations in the Context of Near Eastern Lament Literature," in *Scripture in Context II: More Essays on the Comparative Method* (ed. W. W. Hallo et al.; Winona Lake, Ind.: Eisenbrauns, 1983), 191–211. **Hartberger,** Birgit. *"An den Wassern von Babylon...": Psalm 137 auf dem Hintergrund von Jer 51, der biblischen Edom-Traditionen und babylonischer Originalquellen* (BBB 63; Frankfurt am Main: Hanstein, 1986). **Hossfeld,** Frank-Lothar, and Erich Zenger, *Die Psalmen I: Psalm 1–50* (NEB 29; Würzburg: Echter Verlag, 1993), *Die Psalmen II: Psalm 51–100* (HThK.AT; Freiburg: Herder, 2000). **Jahnow,** Hedwig. *Das hebräische Leichenlied im Rahmen der Völkerdichtung* (BZAW 36; Giessen: Töpelmann, 1923). **Kaiser,** Otto. "Die Klagelieder," in Hans-Peter Müller, Otto Kaiser, and James Alfred Loader, *Das Hohelied, Klagelieder, Das Buch Ester* (4th ed.; ATD 16/2; Göttingen: Vandenhoeck & Ruprecht, 1992). **Kraus,** Hans-Joachim. *Klagelieder* (3d ed.; BK 20; Neukirchen-Vluyn: Verlag des Erziehungsvereins, 1968). **Kühlewein,** Johannes. *Geschichte in den Psalmen* (CThM.A 2; Stuttgart: Calwer, 1973). **McDaniel,** Thomas F. "The Alleged Sumerian Influence upon Lamentations," *VT* 18 (1968): 198–209. **Renkema,** Johan. *Lamentations* (HCOT; Leuven: Peeters, 1998). **Rokay,** Zoltán. "Die Datierung des Psalms 85," *ZThK* 113 (1991): 52–61. **Seybold,** Klaus. *Die Psalmen* (HAT 1/15; Tübingen: Mohr Siebeck, 1996). **Spieckermann,** Hermann. *Heilsgegenwart: Eine Theologie der Psalmen* (FRLANT 148; Göttingen: Vandenhoeck & Ruprecht, 1989). **Steck,** Odil Hannes. "Zu den jüngsten Untersuchungen von Jes 56,1–8; 63:7–66:24," in idem, *Studien zu Tritojesaja* (BZAW 203; Berlin: de Gruyter, 1991), 229–62. **Veijola,** Timo. *Verheissung in* *der Krise: Studien zur Literatur und Theologie der Exilszeit anhand des 89. Psalms* (AASF.B 220; Helsinki: Suomalainen Tiedeakatemia, 1982). **Westermann,** Claus. *Lamentations: Issues and Interpretation* (trans. C. Muenchow; Philadelphia, Fortress, 1994). **Westermann.** *Praise and Lament in the Psalms* (trans. K. R. Crim and R. N. Soulen; Atlanta: John Knox, 1981). **Westermann.** "Vergegenwärtigung der Geschichte in den Psalmen" (1963), in idem, *Forschung am Alten Testament I* (TB 24; Munich: Kaiser, 1964), 306–35.

In the preexilic period, public lamentation (צום "fasting") was a standard form of occasional worship, proclaimed at times of national catastrophe (war, drought); in the exilic period, as one would expect, it became the dominant form of regular public worship. Zechariah 7:2–7 and 8:18–19 show that a public lament was held four times a year throughout the entire exilic period, memorializing the most critical dates in the demise of the state: the beginning of the siege of Jerusalem in the tenth month, the breach in the wall in the fourth, the destruction of the temple and palace in the fifth, and the murder of Gedaliah in the seventh. Since these liturgies were not bound by tradition to a particular holy place but could be observed at such sites as a battlefield, it was possible to continue the observance after the temple was destroyed. In Judah, they probably took place amid the ruins of the Jerusalem sanctuary, to which pilgrims came from the surrounding countryside (Jer 41:5), possibly also bringing grain and incense offerings. There may have been additional sites of cultic assembly at Mizpah and Bethel, which became the foci of political life during the exile. But even in the golah it was possible to perform ritual lamentation, although Gentile territories were traditionally considered cultically unclean (1 Sam 26:19; Jer 5:19; 2 Kgs 5:17; Ps 137:4 [3]). Praying toward Jerusalem associated the dwelling places of the golah with the homeland (1 Kgs 8:46–50). During the exile, therefore, ritual lamentation became the primary locus where the people could carry out the grief work necessitated by their afflictions and learn to deal appropriately with the political catastrophe.

The genre most clearly associated with this *Sitz im Leben* is the communal lament. Naturally it is difficult to date these texts, since they rarely include references to historical events. We must also allow for the possibility that liturgical formulas might be reused and updated on later occasions of disaster. Nevertheless, eight of the ten texts that clearly belong to the genre of communal lament (Pss 44; 60; 74; 79; [80; 83]; 85; 89; Lam 5; Isa 63:7–64:11)[1] most likely date from the exile or attained their final form during that period.

---

[1] Some scholars include Pss 90; 94; 115; 123; 126, but the structure of these texts clearly differs from that of the communal lament. They should be called "congregational prayers."

Psalm 44: Verse 12 (11) speaks of the scattering of the people; "selling the people for a trifle" (44:13 [12]) also refers to deportation. Seybold considers 44:12 (11) an interpolation that has displaced 44:20 (19) from its original place.[2] If so, the psalm might be preexilic. In any case, the striking affirmation in 44:5–9 (4–8), which emphasizes trusting in God instead of weapons, presupposes the similar words of Isaiah at the end of the eighth century (Isa 28:14–19; 30:1–5, 15–17; 31:1–3) and probably also the Assyria redaction of Isaiah in the time of Josiah.[3] The insistence on Israel's innocence in 44:21 (20) and the unbelievably harsh indictment of God in 44:23 (22)—"Because of you we are being killed all day long and accounted as sheep for the slaughter"—still reflect the bitter disillusionment of people who had fallen on evil times even though they had firmly committed themselves to Yahweh.

The original lament could well date from the year 609, when Judah fell victim to the despotism of Neco after the death of Josiah (2 Kgs 23:33–34). In its present form, it points to a time following a deportation. Since the psalm does not mention the destruction of Jerusalem and the temple, the first deportation in 597 is most likely. The expression "you have scattered us" in 44:12 (11) might indicate that the psalm originated among the exiles in Babylon. The intense feelings of religious nationalism that characterized the Babylonian golah in the first years following 597, as evidenced by Jer 28–29 and Ezek 17, would fit quite well with the outraged tone of Ps 44. Verses 16–17 (15–16) probably derive from a later individualizing expansion of the psalm.[4]

Psalm 60: The first-person plural lament in 60:3–6 (1–4) is probably exilic. It introduces a divine war oracle in the form of a victory hymn (60:8–10 [6–8]) and a prayer spoken by the king (60:7 [5], 11–14 [9–12]), referring to conflicts with Judah's neighbors and with Edom. The former may date from the time of Josiah, the latter from the last decades of the Judean monarchy.[5]

Psalm 74: Verses 3 and 4–7 of this psalm clearly presuppose the destruction of a temple; according to the present text of 74:2, this can only be the Jerusalem temple. The psalm describes the depredations of the enemy in vivid and terrifying detail. This language suggests an exilic date: in the Maccabean period, which has also been proposed

---

[2] *Psalmen*, 182.

[3] Hermann Barth, *Die Jesaja-Worte der Josia-Zeit: Israel und Assur als Thema einer produktiven Neuinterpretation der Jesajaüberlieferung* (WMANT 48; Neukirchen-Vluyn: Neukirchener Verlag, 1977).

[4] Hossfeld and Zenger, *Psalmen I*, 227.

[5] Seybold, *Psalmen*, 237–40.

(Duhm, Donner), the temple was desecrated but not destroyed.[6] The phrase מִשְׁכַּן שְׁמֶךָ, "dwelling place of your name," betrays the influence of Deuteronomic theology (cf. Deut 12:11ff., etc.) . Nevertheless, a date shortly after 587, as proposed by Emmendörffer, is unlikely, since the expression לָנֶצַח, "forever," in 74:1, 10, 19, and 23, which Emmendörffer interprets as indicating the definitive nature of the destruction, together with the "perpetual ruins" in 74:3 and the question "how long" in 74:9 and 10, presuppose a lengthy period of suffering. If Ps 74 is dated some time after the destruction of the temple, we may interpret the "meeting places of God in the land" (74:8), a continual source of confusion in light of Josiah's centralization of the cult, as sites of ritual lamentation during the exile (in Jerusalem, Mizpah, and Bethel), replacing the ruined temple. The Babylonian campaign to destroy these sites as well may be explained, for example, as retribution for the murder of Gedaliah in 582. Psalm 74 clearly was composed in Palestine. Verses 18–21 probably represent a timely revision that would be entirely appropriate to the Maccabean period.

Psalm 79: This psalm likewise speaks of the defiling of the temple, as well as the destruction of Jerusalem (79:1) and the devastation of Judah (79:7); it also bewails a terrible bloodbath round about Jerusalem (79:2–3, 10b). All of this is also consonant with the catastrophe of 587, more particularly the years in which the bloody battles were still a vivid memory. Seybold therefore dates the psalm in the early exilic period.[7] Emmendörffer, however, prefers a postexilic date[8]; in this case, the psalm would be a later memorial to the fall of Jerusalem. But so late a date is not supported by the argument that 79:4 echoes Ps 44:14 (13), and 79:6–7 are cited in Jer 10:25. Mockery of the enemy is a commonplace in this period, and Jer 10:17–25 is part of a prophetic lament that antedates the first Deuteronomistic redaction of the book of Jeremiah (ca. 550).

Despite some similarities, however (e.g., "sheep of your pasture": Ps 79:13; 74:1), the language and mental world of Ps 79 are patently simpler than in Ps 74. The pleas for forgiveness of sins (79:8–9) and the developed theology of the divine name (79:6, 9) associate the author with Deuteronomy and the prophets of judgment. Thus Ps 79 might have been composed by a lay theologian close to the later Deuteronomistic redactors of the book of Jeremiah (descendants of Shaphan),

---

6 Spieckermann, *Heilsgegenwart*, 125–26; Seybold, *Psalmen*, 287–88 (originally referring to Bethel?); Emmendörffer, *Der ferne Gott*, 81–82; etc.

7 *Psalmen*, 314.

8 *Der ferne Gott*, 149–50.

while Ps 74 was composed within a circle that included former temple singers or priests. Later topical additions from the postexilic period may appear in 79:1, 2b (third stich: חסידיך, "your faithful"), and 10a (cf. Ps 115:2).

Psalm 85: This psalm already presupposes a change of fortunes at the end of a period of divine wrath (85:2–4 [1–3]) but still prays that salvation will come to those who lament (85:5–8 [4–7]). This salvation is promised in a divine oracle (85:9–14 [8–13]). The psalm thus belongs to the period between the end of Babylonian rule in 539 and the stabilization of the situation in Judah in 520. It breathes the disappointments of this period. There is a connection with the prophecies of Haggai and Zechariah (Zech 8:2–8, 12). Rokay dates the psalm in the year 521.[9]

Psalm 89: This long psalm incorporates extensively the theology of the Jerusalem temple and kingship in verses 2–3 (1–2), 6–19 (5–18), and 4–5 (3–4), 20–38 (19–37). In 89:39–52 (38–51), it laments the end of the Davidic monarchy. Scholars have attempted repeatedly to explain the unique form of Ps 89 by appealing to models of literary accretion. In his detailed stichometric analysis, Veijola distinguishes three major phases in this growth: first came the introductory hymn (89:2–3 [1–2], 6–19 [5–18]); it became the cornerstone of a longer poem with the addition of 89:4–5 (3–4) and 20–46 (19–45). Finally, two symmetric strophes (89:47–49 [46–48] and 50–52 [49–51]) were added.[10] In similar fashion, Seybold distinguishes a royal hymn (89:6–19 [5–18]; from the northern kingdom: Tabor and Hermon in 89:13 [12]), a royal psalm of lament (89:4–5 [3–4], 20–46 [19–45]), 50 [49], 52 [51]), and a framing lament (89:2–3 [1–2], 47–49 [46–48], 51 [50]).[11] Veijola dates the psalm's origin between 550 and 539, seeing influences of the later strata of the Deuteronomistic History, and therefore locates it in Palestine (in the region of Mizpah and Bethel). Seybold dates the royal lament in the early exilic period, the communal lament in the late exilic period. Although the author of Ps 89 does use earlier material, both analyses founder on the observation that 89:2 (1) and 50 (49) clearly constitute a framework for the psalm (89:2 [1]: חסדי יהוה; 89:50 [49]: חסדיך) and therefore cannot belong to different strata.

Emmendörffer considers the psalm a single unit but dates it in the postexilic period.[12] But neither his linguistic arguments nor his observation that the anointed of Yahweh in Ps 89 is no longer a individual but the

---

9 "Datierung," 61.
10 *Verheissung*, 32–46.
11 *Psalmen*, 350.
12 *Der ferne Gott*, 211ff.

people as a collective entity[13] rules out an exilic date, since חסדי יהוה appears in such exilic and early postexilic texts as Isa 55:3; 63:7; Lam 3:22; and Isa 55:3 already transfers the Davidic covenant to the people. Strictly speaking, Ps 89:50–51 (49–50) (the plural in 89:20 [19] is textually uncertain) does not substitute the people for the descendants of David but only claims the promises made to David for the people as well; that they apply primarily to David's descendants is not disputed.[14] On the contrary, the psalm still shows signs of reference to a very specific king, whose fate it laments. Verse 46 (45) says that the days of his youth were cut short and that he was covered with shame; 89:52 (51) laments that the enemy taunted his footsteps. This certainly sounds very specific. Veijola himself notes that 89:46 (45) refers to Jehoiachin, who surrendered in 597 at the age of eighteen but was nevertheless carried off to Babylon as a hostage by Nebuchadnezzar (2 Kgs 24:8–16).[15] The mention of the "footsteps of your anointed" in 89:52 (51) suggests that Jehoiachin must still have been alive at the time of the communal lament. His footprints in history are still visible (Ps 77:20 [19]), but they became the object of Babylonian calumny. Such a lament is immediately understandable when we realize that Jehoiachin probably languished in prison from 582 to 562 in consequence of the murder of Gedaliah.[16] The lengthy lament for the king in Ps 89 thus looks for the release of Jehoiachin, in whom the exiles placed great hopes (2 Kgs 25:27–30). The psalm therefore probably dates from the years before 562; almost certainly it was composed in the Babylonian golah, since it does not mention the temple or Jerusalem. We may think particularly of the leadership cadre in the capital. The echoes of Deuteronomistic theology (89:31–32 [30–31]) do not conflict with this conclusion, since (contrary to Veijola) the loyal Deuteronomists, who were also responsible for Nathan's promise in 2 Sam 7, probably were living in Babylonia.[17]

Lamentations 5: The exilic origin of the only "normal" communal lament in the book of Lamentations is almost universally accepted.[18] The lengthy first-person plural lament in 5:2–5, 8–18 describes all too graphically the suffering of the people of Judah and Jerusalem under the rigors of foreign rule, which our knowledge of Israel's history indicates can only

---

13 Ibid., 230.
14 See also Veijola, *Verheissung*, 135ff.
15 Ibid., 111.
16 See pp. 102–4 above.
17 See pp. 109–10 above and 282–86 below.
18 Brandscheidt, *Gotteszorn*, 227; Boecker, *Klagelieder*, 88; Westermann, *Lamentations*, 219; Emmendörffer, *Der ferne Gott*, 66.

be Babylonian. Therefore the reference to Assyria in 5:6 must allude to the past. Since this foreign rule has clearly lasted for some time (5:20) and there is no mention of destruction and deportation, Lam 5 probably dates from well into the exilic period. The harsh treatment and coercion of the civilian population at the hands of the Babylonian occupation forces may be connected with the murder of Gedaliah in 582. Accepting the judgment of Brandscheidt that Lam 5 represents a crisis of the Deuteronomistic call for repentance, Kaiser dates it around the turn of the fifth/fourth century.[19] However, Brandscheidt's assessment is questionable, Kaiser's conclusion even more so. Unlike the Deuteronomists, the confession of sin in 5:5–6 does not identify idolatry but rather misguided foreign alliances as the primary cause of affliction (cf. Jer 2:18–19, 36–37; 4:30). In other words, Lam 5 demonstrably exhibits prophetic influence but does not clearly exhibit Deuteronomistic influence. This observation suggests a date prior to 560, before Deuteronomistic theology came into full flower. It must have originated in Judah, since 5:21 should be read as referring to a religious return to Yahweh, not a geographical return from exile.

Isaiah 63:7–64:11 (12): This communal lament in the postexilic book of Trito-Isaiah begins atypically with an introductory praise of Yahweh (63:7; but cf. Ps 89), a historical retrospect (63:8–9; but cf. Ps 44), and a reflection on the past (63:10–14). It very likely refers to the catastrophe of 587, since 64:9–10 (10–11) laments the destruction of Yahweh's "holy cities," Zion, and the "holy and beautiful temple." Steck[20] associates the lament with the capture of Jerusalem by Ptolemy I in 302/301 B.C.E., as reported by Josephus,[21] but this theory is historically most unlikely; Isa 63–64 does not mention the sacrilegious acts of which Josephus accuses Ptolemy. Since 64:10 (11) says that the temple "where our ancestors praised you" was devoured by fire and laid to ruin, at least a generation must have passed since the destruction of the temple, but the temple does not appear to have been rebuilt. Fischer therefore dates the text in the period around 560.[22] Aejmelaeus, however, rightly sets the date somewhat later, because the lament contains echoes of Deuteronomistic language and ideas (e.g., Isa 63:19aβ) and also presupposes Deutero-Isaiah (e.g., 63:16bβ). She therefore arrives at a date between 530 and 520.[23]

---

19 "Klagelieder," 191.
20 "Zu jüngsten Untersuchungen," 237.
21 *Ant.* 12.4–5; *Ag. Ap.* 1.205–211.
22 *Wo ist Jahwe*, 256.
23 "Prophet," 49.

THE LITERATURE OF THE EXILIC PERIOD   147

There is still no entirely satisfactory explanation of how to assess the contextual references in the prayer, pointed out by Steck and more recently by Berges[24] (e.g., 63:7 and 62:6, 64:10 [11] and 60:7; also the catchword תִּפְאֶרֶת in 63:12, 14, 15; 64:10 [11] and 60:7, 19; 62:3). Berges concludes that the lament was composed for its present context around the end of the fifth or the beginning of the fourth century. Steck[25] and (citing him without comment) Emmendörffer[26] date the lament in the late Hellenistic period. However, it is by no means certain that literary dependencies are present and which way they run. At least some of the common terminology may be explained by assuming that the lament was composed in a milieu similar to that from which Isa 60–62 also emerged. Furthermore, the lament does not fit totally into the ductus of Trito-Isaiah, although it does have a structural function. Most likely, therefore, we have here an originally independent poem, perhaps slightly reworked in places, that was composed at the close of the exilic period (530–520).

Further evidence that communal psalms of lament were recited in the Babylonian exile is provided by references to them in the prophecy of Deutero-Isaiah—most clearly the explicit quotation in the "imperative poem" Isa 51:9–10, which the prophetic group probably borrowed from the Judean repertory after their return.[27] Thus we arrive at something like the following temporal and geographical distribution of this genre during the exilic period:

Contemporary Events	Date	Palestine	Babylonia
between deportations	597–587		Ps 44
second deportation to murder of Gedaliah	587–582	Ps 79	
murder of Gedaliah to pardon of Jehoiachin	582–562	Ps 74; Lam 5	Ps 89
pardon of Jehoiachin to fall of Babylon	562–539		
fall of Babylon to rebuilding of the temple	539–520	Isa 51:9–10; 63–64; Ps 85	

Since the works of Gunkel[28] and Westermann,[29] there has been general agreement as to the genre's structure:

---

24 *Buch Jesaja*, 485–97.
25 "Zu jüngsten Untersuchungen," 241–42.
26 *Der ferne Gott*, 266.
27 See pp. 391 and 422–23 below.
28 *Introduction*, 82–98.
29 *Praise*, 52–64.

Structure of the Communal Lament	
address	sometimes with introductory petition
lament	God; "we"; the enemy
reference to God's earlier acts (retrospect)	sometimes interspersed with or replaced by hymnic motifs
petition	to be heard, to be delivered, to destroy the enemy, grounds
double wish	for Israel, against the enemy
vow of praise	

The clear differentiation of three subtypes of lament, depending on the subject (God, "we," the enemy) and the distinction between a petition to be heard and a petition for deliverance, goes back to Westermann.[30] Only the third section raises problems. Gunkel posited a strange attraction between the two antithetical genres of communal lament and hymn, while distinguishing carefully between "hymnlike" or "hymnic" narratives (Pss 44:2–4 [1–3]; 74:12–17; 80:9–12 [8–11]) and originally independent hymns (Ps 89:2–3, 6–19 [1–2, 5–18]).[31] These distinctions are often ignored today. Emmendörffer calls Ps 74:12–17 simply a "hymn."[32] Initially, Westermann had called this section a "confession of trust," as in an individual lament. Later he recognized that it constitutes an authentic element of the communal lament, which he then labeled a "reference to God's earlier acts."[33] In contrast to the indictment, this retrospect holds up before God the blatant contradiction between God's actions in the past and in the present. Here the lament clearly differs functionally from the hymn, which is intended to praise God's greatness and mercy. This difference appears in a characteristic syntactic structure found in the retrospect but not the hymn, typically an inverted verbal clause using the declarative perfective tense, preceded by אתה, "You (yourself) . . ." (Pss 80:9–12 [8–11]; 74:13–17; 89:10–13 [9–12]).[34] Besides normal hymns, which praise God in the third person, there are also some that address God in

---

30 *Praise*, 53–54, 173–81.
31 *Introduction*, 94–95.
32 *Der ferne Gott*, 81.
33 "Vergegenwärtigung," 307ff.
34 Cf. the emphatic את־היא beginning the participial questions in Isa 51:9 and the *figura etymologica* at the beginning of the retrospect in Ps 44:2b–5 (1b–4), which uses different means to provide the same emphasis. Only the historical retrospect and reflection on the past in Isa 63:7–10, 11–14 departs totally from this form, using the third person and the consecutive imperfect. Here the focus is no longer on spurring God to act but on encouraging the memory of the community.

the second person (Pss 8; 65; 104); in none of these, however, do we find the emphatic "you." Only in Ps 89:6–19 (5–18) and Lam 5:20 can we recognize hymnic elements incorporated into a communal lament, and even there they are somewhat modified to serve the disputative function of the retrospect by the initial placement of an emphatic אתה (cf. Ps 89:10–13 [9–12]; Lam 5:20).

Even when a "retrospect" with an undertone of praise begins a communal lament (Pss 44:2–4 [1–3]; 89:2–3, 6–38 [1–2, 5–37]), it does not function as a *captatio benevolentiae*, as in the laudatory introductions of Babylonian private prayers;[35] it is a form of protest against God, related to the direct personal relationship between God and Israel.[36]

Nevertheless, the "reference to God's earlier acts" in the communal lament should be distinguished more clearly from the "confession of assurance" in the individual lament than Westermann suggests. Each plays a comparable role in its own genre, but they clearly differ in content and structure. The "confession of assurance" mostly uses a noun clause or a clause with the auxiliary verb היה (e.g., "You, O Lord, are my hope," Ps 71:5; "You became my refuge," 61:4 [3]), because the focus here is not on the individual acts of God but on God's overall significance for the psalmist. The typical verbs expressing confidence may also appear in the first-person singular perfect, with the psalmist as subject (e.g., "Yahweh, my God, in you I take refuge," Ps 7:2 [1]). Here the difference from the retrospect in the communal lament is even greater. Furthermore, the "confession of assurance" normally does not mention the history of Israel.[37] Thus the "retrospect" and "confession" have only minor points of overlap, for example, where a precentor introduces the former (Pss 44:5 [5]; 74:12) or the community expresses its trust in God (Ps 44:5–9 [4–8]). But even here there are clear differences.[38] The "retrospect" and "confession" sections, in my opinion, constitute the most important difference between the genres of "communal lament" and "individual lament."[39] In contrast to the individual, whose relationship with God was simply a given or a consequence of having been created (Ps 22:10–11 [9–10]), the

---

35 Contra Gunkel, *Introduction*, 91.

36 For a general treatment of the subject, see Kühlewein, *Geschichte*.

37 The only exception, Ps 22:(4), 5–6 ([3], 4–5), is due to the reworking of the psalm within the community of the poor; cf. 22:24–27 (23–26). Ps 143:5 is uncertain; Ps 77 is discussed below (p. 161).

38 Cf. the extended historical and factual perspective of the confessions in Ps 44:5 (4) and 74:12. The confession of the community in Ps 44:5–9 (4–8) links affirmation of Yahweh with eschewing false trust in weapons; such a theme does not appear in individual confessions of confidence.

39 Albertz, *Persönliche Frömmigkeit*, 27–49.

relationship of Israel with God was grounded primarily in historical encounters with Yahweh. Of necessity, therefore, it was shattered by the historical catastrophe of the exile.

This difference accounts for one of the most important changes in the communal lament during the exilic period.[40] Psalms 44 and 80 have preexilic cores[41] in which the retrospective survey of God's previous saving acts still cites Yahweh's intervention in history: the history of God's people from the exodus to the Davidic empire in Ps 80:9–12 (8–11) and the triumphant occupation of the land in Ps 44:2–4 (1–3). Three communal laments from the exilic period, however, refer to Yahweh's mighty acts at the mythical dawn of time: his victory of the chaos monster (Yam, Tannin, Leviathan, Rahab), his creation of the world, and his universal sovereignty (Pss 74:12–17; 89:10–13 [9–12]; Isa 51:9–10). This difference cannot be accidental; it follows naturally from the exile, which proved the historical salvation traditions of Israel to be fragile, so that they largely lost their foundational function. The exilic theologians therefore had to find a new basis for appealing to Yahweh to intervene with might on Israel's behalf against the overwhelming enemy. The former cultic personnel found such a basis in the mythological tradition of the Jerusalem temple: Yahweh's mighty primordial acts described in this tradition could not be called into question even by so terrible a historical catastrophe. In the crisis of the exile, mythological symbols such as the battle with chaos and the creation of the world, found also at Ugarit (the Epic of Baal and Yam)[42] and Babylon (*Enuma Elish*),[43] came to replace the historical traditions that had become problematic.[44] It is no accident that only

---

40 Albertz, *Weltschöpfung*, 110–17.

41 Ps 44 is discussed above. Despite the arguments of Emmendörffer (*Der ferne Gott*, 121–47), we agree with Seybold (*Psalmen*, 317–20) and others in maintaining the preexilic date of Ps 80, or at least its core. The primary evidence is 80:18 (17), which presupposes the presence of a king despite the political catastrophe that the psalm bewails. It has often been observed that Ps 80 combines traditions from both the northern kingdom (80:2–3 [1–2]) and the southern (80:12, 18 [11, 17]). Most likely, therefore, the psalm was originally a lament for the fall of the northern kingdom, composed and sung in the southern kingdom with fugitives from the north participating. We may think of the time of Hezekiah or Josiah. The refrain may be exilic (Seybold).

42 See the editions of Walter Dietrich and Oswald Loretz in *TUAT* 3/6:1091–98; and Mark S. Smith, in *Ugaritic Narrative Poetry* (ed. S. B. Parker; SBLWAW 9; Atlanta: Scholars Press, 1977), 81–93.

43 *TUAT* 3/4:565–602.

44 Spieckermann represents the opposite view: the mythological traditions constituted the core of Jerusalem temple and Psalms theology, and "the theme of history was alien to the Psalms" (*Heilsgegenwart*, 15). This position leads his student Emmendörffer to the questionable rejection of a preexilic date for Ps 80, which he dates after Ps 74 (*Der ferne Gott*, 146).

toward the end of the exilic period, when the fall of the Babylonian Empire had proved once more the power of Yahweh as Lord of history, did historical reminiscence take on renewed importance in the communal lament, albeit with the new element of Israel's guilt (Isa 63:7–64:11 [12]).

The real form-critical problem of the exilic period is that the laments associated most clearly and directly with the catastrophe of 587 do not belong to the genre of communal lament but represent a separate form or even a separate genre: the poems in the book of Lamentations, which the Septuagint already associated in part with the prophet Jeremiah (cf. 2 Chr 35:25 and *b. B. Bat.* 15a) but certainly are not from his pen. While Lam 5 does reflect the structure of the communal lament, despite certain peculiarities (the lengthy "we" lament in 5:2–5, 8–18, twenty-two verses corresponding to the number of letters in the Hebrew alphabet), Lam 1, 2, and 4 are totally different.[45] These three texts begin with the plaintive cry אֵיכָה and are written for the most part in the so-called qinah meter (3+2, 4+2 stresses in the accentual system), typical of the dirge.[46] They are artfully constructed acrostics; that is, they comprise twenty-two verses, the first word of each beginning with the corresponding letter of the Hebrew alphabet. The verses in Lam 1 and 2 have three stichs, those in Lam 4 two. The form of Lam 3 is even more elaborate: here each stich in each group of three begins with the same letter. In contrast to the communal lament, different voices are heard: sometimes a precentor, sometimes Zion herself in the figure of a woman. The organization follows poetic principles rather than the objective features of form criticism (subunits of similar length, sometimes parallel, sometimes chiastic; framework; catchwords).[47]

In each of the three laments in Lam 1, 2, and 4, the middle of the alphabet at the tenth or eleventh verse marks a major break. The first section of Lam 1 is a long lament in which the precentor describes Zion's suffering; there follow two laments of Zion, of equal length and exhibiting similar structure, linked by another introduction by the precentor in 1:17. These two laments begin similarly; in the first, however, Zion describes God's punishment, whereas in the second she addresses Yahweh directly

---

[45] Lam 3 is a composite comprising elements of an individual lament and thanksgiving, on the one hand, and a communal lament, on the other; it is discussed on pp. 161–65 below.

[46] Jahnow, *Das hebräische Leichenlied*, 124–62. Cf. 2 Sam 1:19–27; 3:33–34; Jer 9:16–21 (17–22); 38:22; 48:17 and prophetic adaptations such as Isa 14:4–20 and Ezek 26:17–18. Also typical of the dirge is the contrast between then and now: cf. Lam 1:1, 7; 2:1; 4:1–2, 5, 7–8, 10.

[47] Cf. the analyses proposed by Renkema (*Lamentations*, 85, 207, 483), with cantos, subcantos, canticles, and verses. The extreme formalism of these structures is not always persuasive, but they represent a distinct advance vis-à-vis earlier analyses based on content.

with an appeal for mercy (1:20) and an imprecation against faithless lovers (1:22).

Structure of Lamentations 1			
1–11		Lament describing Zion's suffering by the precentor	
	3	1–3	The desolate city
	3	4–6	Vanished glory
	3	7–9	Reasons for Zion's disgrace, ending with a plea by Zion
	2	10–11	Destruction of the necessities of life, ending with a plea by Zion
12–16		First lament of Zion	
	1	12	Introduction: appeal to those who pass by; summary of God's punishment
	3	13–15	Details of God's punishment
	1	16	Zion's reaction
17		Introduction to the lament by the precentor	
18–22		Second lament of Zion	
	1	18	Introduction: summary confession; appeal to the nations
	3	19–21	Plea for mercy, bracketed by lament over faithless lovers
	1	22	Imprecation against lovers

The first section of Lam 2 (2:1–10) is a long accusatory description of the devastation wrought by God on Zion; the precentor emphasizes its incomprehensible brutality. The second section once again comprises two subsections, a lament coupled with an edifying address to the city by the precentor (2:11–17) and a call to lament followed by Zion's lament (2:18–22). In both sections, three-verse units form a frame surrounding two-verse units. Again the climax is Zion's prayer to Yahweh (2:20–22), comprising a plea for mercy, accusations, "we" laments, and a complaint about the enemy.

Structure of Lamentations 2			
1–10		Accusatory description of Yahweh's brutal treatment of Zion by the precentor	
	3	1–3	The merciless wrath of Adonai
	2	4–5	Adonai rages against Zion like an enemy
	2	6–7	Yahweh destroys his sanctuary
	3	8–10	Yahweh deliberately destroys the city's fortifications; the consequences for the inhabitants

11–17		Lament of the precentor and didactic address to the city
3	11–13	Lament of the precentor over the incalculable suffering of Zion
2	14–15	Background: deceptive preaching of the prophets led to the city's fall
2	16–17	Background: the enemy rejoices over the fulfillment of God's word
18–22		Call to lament and Zion's lament
2	18–19	Call to Zion to lament by the precentor
3	19–22	Zion's lament; plea for mercy, accusation, lament over suffering, lament over the enemy

In contrast to Lam 1 and 2, both halves of Lam 4 consist almost entirely of descriptive lament; there is no prayer. The two halves (4:1–11 and 12–22) are distinguished by their subject matter: the first deals with the suffering of particular population groups; the second meditates sorrowfully on the conquest of Jerusalem, why it happened, and how it took place. A substructure has each subunit conclude with a theological verdict exposing the depths of the event (4:6, 11, 16, [20]). As a result, the groups of verses form a chiastic structure. The movement of Lam 4 is also climactic: in 4:17–20, the precentor is included in the "we" lament of the community; in 4:21–22, Edom and Zion are addressed directly: the faithless Edomites are threatened with God's imminent punishment, whereas Zion is promised the end of her punishment.

	Structure of Lamentations 4	
1–11		Descriptive lament over the sufferings of Zion's inhabitants by the precentor
2	1–2	Introductory lament: the precious inhabitants of Zion are valueless
3	3–5	Fate of the small children
+1	6	The unparalleled sin of Jerusalem
4	7–10	Fate of the aristocratic men and women
+1	11	Yahweh's wrathful judgment on Zion
12–20		Lament over the conquest of Jerusalem
4	12–15	Disbelief of the kings of the earth; guilt and expulsion of the prophets
+1	16	Yahweh's judgment on the leaders

3	17–19	"We" lament over the disillusioning conquest of Jerusalem
+1	20	"We" lament over the capture of Yahweh's anointed
21– 22	2	Concluding conflict with Edom: for Zion God's punishment is coming to an end; for Edom it is yet to come

This poetic structure is so original that Westermann is wrong in claiming that Lam 1, 2, and 4 constitute a "distinctive group of communal laments."[48] These texts are definitely not based on "the structure of the communal lament,"[49] elements of which appear only in the scattered prayer sections. In addition, Westermann's view that Lam 1, 2, and 4 were composed orally and only secondarily turned into acrostic poems is untenable, since the alphabetic structure is fundamental to the structure of all three texts (twenty-two verses; primary break in the middle). The stylized acrostic structure makes a written origin virtually certain.

Much more promising is Kraus's attempt to assign Lam 1, 2, and 4 to a genre of "lamentation for a destroyed sanctuary,"[50] parallel to Sumerian laments for destroyed cities and their temples such as the "Lamentation over the Destruction of Ur."[51] Here, however, the text focuses on the city of Jerusalem rather than the temple, so that it would be more accurate to speak of a "lamentation over the fall of a city." These Sumerian laments were probably sung during the rebuilding of the city and temple. Since fifteen centuries separate them from the book of Lamentations, most scholars have disputed their relevance.[52] In the meantime, however, it has been recognized that the Sumerian lamentation over the destruction of a city lived on in the genre of the BALAG lament, still in use in the Seleucid period.[53] Of course, there are substantial differences between these long (300 to 450 lines!) litany-like texts and the book of Lamentations; however, it is entirely possible that, via the golah of 597, people in Jerusalem knew of such prayers mourning the destruction of a city and created something similar, drawing on local traditions.[54] It was natural to use the dirge form to create a lament for a city, because the prophets had long used this genre to give rhetorical expression to their message of judgment

---

[48] *Lamentations*, 98.
[49] Ibid., 22.
[50] *Klagelieder*, 8–13.
[51] *ANET*, 455–63; *SAHG*, 192–213. Since Kraus, a series of additional lamentations over the destruction of cities have come to light, such as the "Lamentation over the Destruction of Sumer and Ur" (*ANET*, 611–19); see the list in Emmendörffer, *Der ferne Gott*, 17–20.
[52] McDaniel, "Alleged Sumerian Influence."
[53] Gwaltney, "Biblical Book of Lamentations"; Emmendörffer, *Der ferne Gott*, 28–38.
[54] Renkema, *Lamentations*, 45.

on Israel, Judah, and Jerusalem (Amos 5:2; Isa 1:21–26; Jer 9:9, 16–21 [10, 17–22]). The extreme catastrophe of Jerusalem's destruction gave rise to a distinct genre: the "political dirge"[55] or, more accurately, the "lament for a fallen city."

Emmendörffer's form-critical reconstruction suffers from a one-sidedness precisely the opposite of Westermann's: he disputes the very existence of the communal lament as a primary form[56] and maintains that "Lam 2 (and Lam 5) constitute the starting point for the communal laments in the Psalter."[57] As reasons, he cites the alleged similarity of Lamentations to the much earlier Mesopotamian laments and the inconsolable tone of Lam 2. In his view, Israel found its way back only gradually to the "lament before Yahweh,"[58] which included once again elements of praise and temple theology.[59] Emmendörffer attempts to minimize the indisputable difference in form between Lam 2, on the one hand, and Lam 5 and the other communal laments, on the other, which contradicts such a course of development, by assuming ad hoc that Lam 5 specifically[60] and the communal lament in general "arose from the lament of the individual."[61] There is no evidence to support this claim.[62] Clearly a form-critical reconstruction that more or less denies the existence of the communal lament as a preexilic genre[63] will not generate any useful results. Instead, form criticism dissolves into a kind of motif criticism with scarcely any guidelines.

How, then, are we to explain the fact that the destruction of Jerusalem produced a second genre alongside the communal lament? For Kaiser, the difference in genre is a major argument for describing Lamentations as noncultic didactic poetry and dating the book in the postexilic period (between the end of the sixth century and the fourth century): "Psalms of the exilic period ... show that for this purpose [i.e., cultic recitation] the genre of communal lament was sufficient."[64] But Kaiser is

---

55 Gunkel, "Klagelieder Jeremiae," 3:1049.
56 *Der ferne Gott*, 10.
57 Ibid., 44.
58 Ibid., 45.
59 Ibid., 63.
60 Ibid., 66.
61 Ibid., 106.
62 The very existence of Lam 3, a text in which elements of individual lament and communal lament or lament for a fallen city stand in deliberate tension, contradicts this theory.
63 Emmendörffer's methodological qualification (290 n. 1) that there may have been communal laments in the preexilic period but that we cannot say anything about them because their existence cannot be demonstrated is purely rhetorical: if taken seriously, it would undermine the theory outlined above.
64 "Klagelieder," 102.

unable to explain how laments of such terror, power, and despair could come into being centuries after the catastrophe.[65] However, if there are good reasons to date Lamentations in the early or middle years of the exilic period,[66] it is impossible to avoid asking why the exilic period found the genre of communal lament inadequate to voice the misery and sorrow of those who stayed behind in Judah.

Here Renkema's analysis appears to make a positive contribution. He describes Lamentations as noncultic poetry in which former temple singers voiced the despairing lamentations and angry questions of their fellow citizens and embodied them in a poetic structure, so as to express their shared grief in the setting of everyday assemblies and thus bring clarity out of psychic chaos.[67] Such an explanation has the advantage of identifying a *Sitz im Leben* clearly distinct from that of the communal lament. It also accounts for the highly developed poetic form as a way of coping with crisis.[68] The acrostic, as it were, furnishes a clearly delimited and structured framework that uses poetic devices to exorcise seemingly unbridled chaos. The use of the dirge form linked the poetry with the bitter reality of the catastrophe, which presumably included constant keening for family members who had died. By using a variety of different voices, it opened dramatic and didactic ways to embody the grief and despair of the citizenry while making it possible to achieve artistic distance. Thus Lam 1, 2, and 4 could well have been chanted or even performed dramatically during evening gatherings of the men of the villages (סוֹד).[69]

Lamentations 2 contrasts statements about Yahweh's incomprehensible destruction of Zion with ideas and concepts associated with the theology of Zion and the monarchy (2:1, cf. Ps 110:1; 2:5, 8–9, cf. Ps 48:12–14 [11–13]; 2:6, cf. Ps 76:2 [1]; 2:15, cf. Ps 48:3).[70] The author probably was a proponent of religious nationalism or at least aimed to express the bitter disillusionment of this party, which had based their policy of rebellion against Babylon squarely on the promise of Zion's inviolability. However,

---

65 Kaiser obviously sensed this difficulty himself; in the fourth edition of his commentary, he assigned at least Lam 2, which the third edition had still dated in the fifth century, to the last third of the sixth. But he still insists on a fifth-century dating of Lam 1 and 4 and a fourth-century dating of Lam 3 and 5.

66 Kraus, Boecker, Brandscheidt, Westermann, Renkema, et al.

67 *Lamentations*, 46–47.

68 This function would be comparable to that of the poetic dialogue in the book of Job; here, too, the formalism of poetry plays a pastoral role in a situation of extreme suffering.

69 I posit the same *Sitz im Leben* for some of the foreign nation oracles and the first edition of Deutero-Isaiah; see pp. 193–94 and 403–4 below.

70 See also Albrektson, *Studies*, 219–30.

he clearly distances himself from the prophets of salvation, whose illusory assurances he blames for the failure to expose Zion's transgression, so that the chance to avert disaster was lost (2:14). The poet also attempts to communicate to the audience the prophetic and Deuteronomic view (cf. Deut 28) that the catastrophe was not a bolt from the blue but the realization of God's word proclaimed long before (2:17). Thus he seeks to encourage his fellow citizens, despite their bitter disillusionment, to hold fast to their faith in Yahweh and to pray for his mercy and favor (2:18–22).

There are no clear echoes of this royal Zion theology in Lam 1. The author's primary aim is to present Zion's suffering and Yahweh's anger as a punishment for Zion's sins (1:5, 8, 9, 14, 18, 20, 22), while expressly acknowledging that Yahweh is in the right (1:18). In this sense, the poem is clearly closer to the message of the prophets, especially Jeremiah, than is Lam 2. The poet is familiar with the Deuteronomic law safeguarding the purity of the cult (Deut 23:2–9: foreigners are excluded) and accuses God of having effectively nullified it (1:10). His thought thus bears the stamp of Josiah's cultic reform. This chimes with his solidly Deuteronomic description of Zion's sin as rebellion against God's command (1:18). However, he does not belong to the reform wing of the Deuteronomistic movement, since he shows no interest in social injustice. When he becomes more specific, he focuses primarily on the failed policy of reliance on political alliances (1:19; cf. 1:2, 8–9), thus distancing himself from the policies of religious nationalism. The author's stance may be described as a mediating position in the late pre-exilic or early exilic spectrum of opinion. Since he does not associate the catastrophe in any way with the worship of foreign gods, as all the Deuteronomistic groups were to do later, the Deuteronomistic milieu proposed by Brandscheidt[71] is premature.

Lamentations 4 again contains elements of royal Zion theology, appearing in references to the dogma of Jerusalem's impregnability (4:12), the disappointed hope for Egyptian help during the break in the siege (4:17), and the shameful captivity of Zedekiah, the last of Yahweh's anointed kings (4:20). However, this is already past history; the author believes beyond question that the monstrous sin of Zion and Yahweh's wrath brought about Zion's fall (4:6, 11). He is concerned to single out Jerusalem's erstwhile priests and prophets of salvation as being primarily to blame (4:13–15). He virtually gloats over their expulsion from the city and interprets their deportation as Yahweh's explicit rejection of them

---

71 *Gotteszorn*, 211.

(4:16a). In his eyes, their guilt consists in the murder of innocent victims, here probably meaning the violent elimination of the prophets of judgment (cf. Jer 26; the language recalls JerD and DtrH: cf. Jer 7:6; 22:3, 7; 2 Kgs 21:16; 24:4). For the Deuteronomistic disciples of the prophets in the exilic period, however, the silencing of the prophets of judgment was the primary reason why the catastrophe was inescapable (Amos 2:12; 7:10–18; Jer 11–20). Thus the author of Lam 4 represents a new theological elite in Palestine: its members cannot deny their origins among the former supporters of religious nationalism, but they stand clearly on the side of the prophets of judgment and distance themselves deliberately from the former temple elite deported to Babylon.

Lamentations 2, with its long reproachful description, still breathes a spirit of disillusionment with Yahweh; it probably dates from the period immediately after the catastrophe. It is entirely possible that in this period following the total collapse of political and cultic institutions there was simply no way to organize public cultic laments. The noncultic way of coping with the crisis thus stepped into the breach, so to speak, in order to bring some clarity in the midst of the general theological chaos. Lam 1 still has a clear memory of deportations (1:3, 5, 6) and the desecration of the temple (1:10–11) but focuses much more on recognition of Jerusalem's own guilt; it should probably be dated a bit later than Lam 2. Lamentations 4, on the other hand, with its promise that Zion's punishment is ended and that there will be no more deportations (4:22), probably dates from the period between 562 and Deutero-Isaiah (ca. 545), when hopes for improvement flourished (cf. Isa. 40:2). If Brandenscheidt[72] is correct that the author of Lam 3 (who also composed Lam 4) planned and put together the book of Lamentations a whole, incorporating the earlier texts Lam 2, 1, and 5, the present book probably dates from the late exilic period. With its concluding communal lament, it presents itself as an introduction or preparation for a liturgical lament. Thus its structure may reflect the function that the lament for the fallen city, the noncultic means of coping publicly with the crisis, accurately identified and performed, primarily in the early exilic period. With all the foundations of Israel's previous relationship with God destroyed, there had to be a basic dialogue between Israel and Yahweh before people could take part in public cultic lamentations. The texts of the book of Lamentations performed this function. In the late exilic period, therefore, they were collected and incorporated into Judean liturgical lamentations memorializing the fall of Jerusalem (cf. Lam 4:17–20). Thus the appearance of a second genre of

---

[72] Ibid., 228–31.

public lament alongside the communal lament was due to the gravity of the theological crisis that the exile brought upon Israel.

In addition to the communal lament, the exiles also sang noncultic songs to overcome suffering and temptation. Psalm 137 is an example. This psalm resists assignment to any genre. A first-person plural description of an experience in Babylon (137:1–4) is followed by an individual self-imprecation should the speaker forget Jerusalem (137:5–6). The conclusion comprises imprecations asking vengeance upon Edom (137:7) and Babylon (137:8–9); the first is addressed to Yahweh, but the second gleefully extols human agents of vengeance. Like Lam 4, then, Ps 137 is not really a prayer. Compared to the poems of Lamentations, however, its poetic structure is much looser; only in part can we recognize the qinah meter (137:4–6; cf. also the plaintive איך, "How...?" in 137:4). Today the psalm is usually dated in the (probably early) exilic[73] or early postexilic[74] period, depending on how the distancing שם in 137:1 and 3 and the perfective verbs are interpreted: Does the psalm already look back on the exilic period as a whole or only on an isolated event? Since the vow not to forget Jerusalem presupposes that the author is not in Jerusalem, only the second possibility makes sense, unless the poet is envisioned as dwelling somewhere in the non-Babylonian Diaspora. The imprecations against Babylon (similar to the foreign nation oracles [Isa 47; Jer 50–51]) presuppose at least the possibility that the Babylonian Empire might fall; that was the situation after the rise of Cyrus in 550. Therefore a date in the late exilic period is most likely. At this late date, the author of Ps 137 addresses a specific temptation facing the Babylonian golah: the conflict between a sorrowful but slowly fading nostalgia for Jerusalem and the urge to find a place in the advanced riverine civilization of Babylonia ("the rivers of Babylon"). Faced with this conflict, the author, a descendant of former temple musicians, pleads to reject assimilation. He tells of a group of Judean musicians in the capital who refused to fraternize with their Babylonian overseers by turning songs of Zion into happy folklore. What is more, he swears fealty to Jerusalem even at the price of his own livelihood as a singer: his old homeland outranks all other sources of joy and fulfillment. In his imprecations, finally, he stands in solidarity with Jerusalem against its enemies, even the great empire from which he himself profits.

Thus we arrive at the following chronological and geographical distribution of cultic and noncultic collective laments in the exilic period:

---

[73] Hartberger, "An den Wassern," 204; Spieckermann, *Heilsgegenwart*, 116–17; Seybold, *Psalmen*, 509.

[74] Emmendörffer, *Der ferne Gott*, 185.

Contemporary Events	Date	Palestine	Babylonia
between deportations	597–587		Ps 44
second deportation to murder of Gedaliah	587–582	Lam 2; 1; Ps 79	
murder of Gedaliah to pardon of Jehoiachin	582–562	Ps 74; Lam 5	Ps 89
pardon of Jehoiachin to fall of Babylon	562–539	Lam 4; book of Lamentations	Ps 137
fall of Babylon to rebuilding of the temple	539–520	Isa 51:9–10; 63–64; Ps 85	

III.1.2. Hybrid Genres

See the bibliography under III.1.1.

The tendency of public and familial life to come closer together after the political catastrophe coupled with the resurgence of organizational forms based on kinship resulted in, among other things, a fusion of collective and individual psalm genres that had previously been totally distinct. This fusion included both motifs and formal elements.

Psalm 77 is an example of a fusion of individual lament and hymn.[75] Normally, the individual lament appeared in the setting of familial prayer. In the preexilic period, it was far removed both geographically and in substance from the official temple cult, in which hymns were sung. The national history of Israel normally played no role in these private devotions. Both observations have changed in Ps 77. Here a psalmist begins his prayer by describing his unceasing lament to God (77:2–3 [1–2]) and then recounts his affliction (77:4–7 [3–6]), as in other individual laments (Pss 22:3 [2]; 42:2–4 [1–3]; etc.). The affliction that he bewails, however, is not the usual threat to life and limb but a theological challenge: meditation on God has plunged him into grief and confusion, especially when he compares God's present treatment of Israel with God's actions of old. In 77:8–11 (7–10), he reproachfully states the theological problem that he cannot deal with: Does God spurn

---

[75] The date of Ps 77 is not entirely certain, but all the evidence supports the traditional date in the exilic period (Seybold, *Psalmen*, 299–300): the frequent appearance of the verb זנח "reject, spurn," (77:8 [7]) in exilic communal laments (Pss 44:10, 24 [9, 23]; 60:3, 12 [1, 10]; 74:1; 89:39 [38]) and the similarity of 77:8–11 (7–10) to Lam 3:22, 31–33 (also with זנח).

forever? Has God's steadfast love ceased forever? Will God never again show mercy? Or has God's nature so changed that the ancient liturgical formula of Exod 34:6, which celebrates God's great goodness, is no longer true?

Psalm 77 shows how deeply the general catastrophe of the exile could affect the personal life of an individual, albeit less as an existential problem than as a theological problem. The longer the depressing exile dragged on and Yahweh's intervention remained invisible in human history, the more urgent, at least for the theologically sophisticated, became the problem of Yahweh's divinity.

The comfort that the author of Ps 77 found in the midst of his doubts is specific to his occupation and indicates that he had been among the former temple personnel. He determines to meditate in God's presence on God's wonders of old (77:12–13 [11–12]). Then he remembers an old hymn celebrating Yahweh's epiphany at the deliverance of the Israelites at the Sea of Reeds (77:14–21 [13–20]). Reciting the hymn that had been part of the magnificent worship of the temple restores God's greatness in the psalmist's eyes. At the same time, the text, which incorporates an ancient epiphanic hymn (77:17–20 [16–19]; note the tricola) and thus enters a mythological realm far transcending the actual events at the Sea of Reeds, teaches him that God's way has always been בַּקֹּדֶשׁ, "in holiness," that is, separate and distinct from secular history (77:14 [13]) and usually unseen (77:20 [19]), and therefore needs to be revealed, even in the present.

An impressive example of the fusion of individual thanksgiving and communal lament appears in Lam 3. Although this text is also an artful acrostic, it differs totally in structure from the other poems of the book of Lamentations; it nevertheless constitutes the compositional center of the whole book.[76] The complex structure of the text, which has repeatedly caused problems for exegetes,[77] may be outlined in tabular form:

---

[76] Cf. the intertextual relationships between Lam 3:32–33 (ינה hipʿil) and 1:5, 12; 3:42 (פשע) and 1:5, 14, 22; 3:43 (לא חמל) and 2:17, 21; 3:43 (הרג) and 2:4, 21 (טבח); 3:47 (שבר) and 2:13; 3:48 and 2:11; 4,10. Lam 3:46 echoes 2:16. On this assessment, see Brandscheidt, *Gotteszorn*, and Renkema, *Lamentations*.

[77] For earlier discussions, see Albertz, *Persönliche Frömmigkeit*, 183–85, with n. 112. For a similar treatment of more recent discussions, see Boecker, *Klagelieder*, 59–60. The analysis of Brandscheidt (*Gotteszorn*, 48) lacks precision. Kaiser ("Klagelieder," 156–57) takes all of vv. 55–66 as petitions; this interpretation is not impossible grammatically, but is somewhat forced. The analysis of Westermann (*Lamentations*, 168–69) is very complex and not convincing: he distinguishes an individual lament (vv. 1–25 + 64–66), a communal lament (vv. 42–52), an individual psalm of praise (vv. 52–58), and two expansions from the hand of the compiler (vv. 26–41 and 59–63).

	Structure of Lamentations 3
1	Self-introduction of the singer as a man under the rod of God's wrath
2–18	Account of affliction (narrative lament)
2–16	"He" charges: God afflicted the speaker like an enemy
17–18	"You" charges and "I" lament: God rejected the author, and his hope vanished
19–24	Confession of trust
19–21	Transition: determination to hope in the face of affliction
22–24	Confession of trust with reflection on its premises: Yahweh's acts of mercy are not exhausted, and so the speaker may hope
25–33	Instruction based on the confession of trust
25–26	Proposition: Yahweh is good to those who hope in him
27–30	Proverb and exposition: patience and humility under the yoke are good
31–33	Grounds for the proposition: Adonai will not reject forever and does not willingly afflict
34–39	Denial of charges against God
34–36	Citation of charges: Adonai does not see oppression and injustice
37–39	Denial: both good and bad come from God, the latter as a punishment for sin
40–47	Communal lament
40–42	Decision to lament: call to repent and confess
43–45	"You" charge: you have wrapped yourself in anger and killed us without pity
46–47	Lament concerning enemies (= 2:16) and "we" lament
48–51	Lament for the fallen city
52–57	Account of affliction (continued)
52–54	Lament over enemies
55–57	Invocation of Yahweh; Yahweh's response and oracle of salvation
58–63	Beginning of deliverance
59b, 63	New petitions
64–66	Petitions against enemies: pursue them in anger and destroy them

The basic framework of the text is a singer's narrative of his former affliction (3:2–18, 52–54), including quotations from his prayers (3:19–24, 55–56), together with an account of God's favorable response (3:57) and the speaker's deliverance (3:58–62). This outline corresponds to the structure of an individual psalm of praise, albeit with an unusually extended narrative lament. Lamentations 3 is related most closely to the type of psalm recited to the participants in a *tôdâ* ceremony, which speaks of God in the third person (Pss 34; 40; 66:16–20). The only element missing is the cohortative call to praise; in its place we find a self-introduction of the speaker. This framework surrounds a collective prayer (3:40–51) comprising a decision to lament (3:40–41; cf. Hos 6:1–3), a confession of sins (3:42), the communal lament itself (3:43–47), and a lament for the fallen city (3:48–51), such as we find in the other sections of Lamentations. That this mixture of individual and collective genres is intentional is shown by the didactic material preceding the prayer section (3:25–39), in which the individual both addresses the community on the basis of his religious experiences (3:25–33) and leads them into what he considers an appropriate prayer (3:34–39).

It had always been possible for an individual to follow thanksgiving with pious advice to the small assembled congregation (Pss 32:8ff.; 34:5ff. [4ff.]; 40:5ff. [4ff.]). A person who had learned directly from God in the course of deliverance from affliction obviously possessed a certain religious authority. A similar process can be seen behind the literary stylization of Lam 3. Here an individual, probably a former temple singer, describes his affliction and God's deliverance in order to share with a larger congregation something that will help them in their crisis of faith. The difference is that here the congregation is assembled for a communal lament—in other words, the familial *tôdâ* ceremony has been moved to the setting of a public fast. A further difference is that the basis for instruction is not the account of deliverance but the confession of trust from the narrative lament. This means that Lam 3 draws on the still-intact personal relationship of trust between the individual and God as a resource for the relationship between God and the people, which is in crisis. Lamentations 3 is an example of how during the exile personal piety steps into the breach for the shattered official religion of Israel.

This effort to draw on personal religious experience to provide new hope and a new orientation for the community as a whole explains all the features that set Lam 3 apart from the normal psalm of thanksgiving. When the precentor omits the traditional call to praise and instead introduces himself as one who has seen affliction under the rod of God's anger (3:1), he is attempting to meet the community in their affliction. When in his long narrative lament (3:2–18)—untypical of a thanksgiving psalm—he pointedly describes God as the author of his affliction, indeed as his enemy (3:10–13; cf. Job 16), his purpose is to establish a parallel between his own fate and that of Zion and the people, as recounted reproachfully in Lam 2. When, facing an apparently hopeless situation (3:18), he styles his confession of trust a deliberate decision (3:21–24), he does so with the edifying purpose of lifting the community from its hopelessness. The inclusion of the lament over enemies at the end of the narrative lament (3:52–54) also serves to strengthen the parallel with the fate of the community. Finally, the account of the precentor's deliverance underlines God's mercy and favor by quoting the oracle of salvation,[78] "Do not fear" (3:57), even though God's saving intervention is still withheld, so that—if the Hebrew text is correct—it is still necessary to ask God to finish the work of salvation (3:59b, 63). Thus the speaker, though personally set free, can express his solidarity with the people as a whole, who are still afflicted. In the concluding petitions against enemies (3:64–66), both the individual and the community can unite once more in their trust in God.

In Lam 3, the singer is struggling with two crises besetting the religion of Yahweh. The first is the depressing belief suggested by the extended agony of the exile, already expressed in Ps 77:8–11 (7–10), that the steadfast love of Yahweh had ceased and his mercies had come to an end (Lam 3:22). The singer counters with his own personal religious experience: in our personal afflictions, we still place hope in God; therefore, the theory that God is no longer able or willing to help must be wrong. He generalizes in his confession of trust: it remains true that God is good to those who hope in God, who still await God's help (3:25). He grounds his thesis in the didactic lesson of 3:31–33: hope is justified because God does not willingly—literally מִלִּבּוֹ ... לֹא, "not from the heart"—afflict anyone (3:33). To reject or afflict is alien to God's nature; it cannot last but must ultimately yield to God's rich mercy (3:31–32). Here we witness how an individual can advance from personal religious experience to statements about the nature of God that can claim validity for the people as a whole, despite their discouragement with the world around them. Nevertheless, hope in God demands even more staying power from the community than from the individual. Therefore the singer urges his fellow citizens to be humble and tenacious; they must refuse to give up so quickly despite many reverses (3:26–30). To support his plea, he appeals to the stern principles that governed the upbringing of children in his day (cf. Sir 30:11–12).

The singer identifies the second crisis affecting the religion of Yahweh with the ignorant charges against God cited in 3:34–36. People were claiming that God simply did not see the oppression and injustice that the

---

[78] See pp. 168–73 below.

Judeans had to suffer at the hands of the occupation forces and their lackeys. Such harsh accusations are both possible and necessary if those who suffer are to speak openly and honestly to God, as in Lam 2; however, as the precentor points out, such accusations harbor a danger that must not be ignored: self-righteous apostasy. He therefore instructs the community that everything comes from God, even suffering, but suffering is to be understood not as proof of God's impotence but as God's punishment for human sin (3:37–39). If the people are to escape the danger of apostasy, he believes, they may level charges against God only if they honestly confess their sins and are seriously prepared to repent (3:40–45). Therefore he introduces such a communal lament of the people, which both incorporates motifs from Lam 1, 2, and 4 and amends them accordingly. It is reasonable to assume that during actual worship a lengthy lament was sung at this point, which the literary stylization of Lam 3 cites in highly abbreviated form. The mixture of genres in Lam 3 therefore bears eloquent witness that liturgical lamentations in the exilic period not only expressed grief but also did the work of theological education.

A somewhat different influence of familial piety on the religion of the larger group may be seen in Isa 63:7–64:11 (12), a late exilic communal lament. Here the communal lament has incorporated and integrated an element from the individual lament. Not by accident, we are dealing once more with a confession of trust.

> Isa 64:7 (8) Yet, O Yahweh, you are our Father;
> we are the clay, and you are our potter;
> we are all the work of your hand.

Here the confession of trust serves to summarize God's former saving intervention in history, which through the catastrophe of the exile and Israel's apostasy (63:10) had lost its immediate power to assure salvation and, therefore, in this communal lament had become a somewhat peripheral acclamatory memorial (63:7–14). The text addresses Yahweh not as Israel's historical deliverer but as the father and Creator of human individuals, as many Israelites had long done in their private prayers.[79] We will leave open the question whether this language indicates that Deutero-Isaiah had already transferred the motif of individual creation to

---

[79] On the theme of personal creation in laments of the individual, see Pss 22:10–11 (9–10); 71:5–6; 119:73; 138:8; Jer 2:27; Job 10:3, 8–12, 18; 33:6; cf. Job 14:15. On addressing God as father, see Jer 2:27; also Deut 32:6b, 18; Jer 3:4–5, 19; Mal 2:10. The primitive conception of God as father, attested in many religions in the context of the creation of human beings (Albertz, *Weltschöpfung*, 55–81), was not "discovered" by the official theology of Israel until the exilic period and is therefore relatively uncommon in the Old Testament.

Israel (cf. Isa 43:1; 44:2, 24; 54:5) or the salvation oracles in Deutero-Isaiah were responding to such borrowing from personal devotion in liturgical lamentations during the exile. In any case, the result was to take the now-fragile tradition of Israel's election and, by interpreting collectively the relationship between God and the individual, establish that tradition on a new creation-centered foundation no longer vulnerable to historical catastrophe. In the light of the apparently inescapable combination of Yahweh's angry rejection and Israel's continuing sin (64:4b–6 [5b–7]), the exilic community appealed in their distress to their divine father and Creator as directly and trustingly as a terrified child seeks refuge with its human parents, certain that those who fathered it, bore it, and lovingly raised it will be moved to look after it.[80]

A similar confession of trust, defiantly exaggerated, appears in Isa 63:16. Here the exilic community insists that Yahweh alone is their father and is therefore totally responsible for them—disallowing the other possibility of an appeal to the patriarchs. Now we know from Ezek 33:24 that those left behind appealed to Abraham to legitimate their claim to the land vis-à-vis the exiles. This confession may indicate that the communal lament in Isa 63–64 originated within the group of returnees, who were dismayed to realize that the traditions of sacred history were being used against them. Their trusting faith in Yahweh as their father was thus at the same time an appeal to a higher authority. Thus the confidence motif from the individual lament acquired a restrictive aspect that had been totally absent in familial piety.

These fusions of individual and collective psalm genres make two things clear. First, the pain of the exile could become a personal crisis of faith, which found solace in recalling the historico-mythological tradition of the temple. Second, the still-intact practice of personal piety could be a source of healing for the relationship between God and the people, deeply scarred by the catastrophe of the exile.

III.1.3. SALVATION ORACLES

Begrich, Joachim. "Das priesterliche Heilsorakel," *ZAW* 52 (1934): 81–92 = his *Gesammelte Studien zum Alten Testament* (TB 21; Munich: Kaiser, 1964), 217–31. **Begrich.** *Studien zu Deuterojesaja* (BWANT 77; Stuttgart: Kohlhammer, 1938; repr.,

---

[80] Isa 64:7 (8) refers not to the arbitrary power but solely to the responsibility of the creator. Fischer (*Wo ist Jahwe*, 196ff.) and Emmendörffer (*Der ferne Gott*, 285) have once again misinterpreted this point because their word studies are not controlled by form-critical analysis.

TB 20; Munich: Kaiser, 1963). **Crüsemann,** Frank. *Studien zur Formgeschichte von Hymnus und Danklied in Israel* (WMANT 32; Neukirchen-Vluyn: Neukirchener Verlag, 1969). **Herrmann,** Siegfried. *Die prophetischen Heilserwartungen: Ursprung und Gestaltwandel* (BWANT 85; Stuttgart: Kohlhammer, 1965). **Kilian,** Rudolf. "Ps 22 und das priesterlich Heilsorakel," *BZ* NS 12 (1968): 172–85. **Merendino,** Rosario Pius. "Literarkritisches, Gattungskritisches und Exegetisches zu Jes 41:8–16," *Bib* 53 (1972): 1–42. **Parpola,** Simo. *Assyrian Prophecies* (SAA 9; Helsinki: Helsinki University Press, 1997). **Schoors,** Anton. *I Am God Your Saviour: A Form-Critical Study of the Main Genres in Is. XL–LV* (VTSup 24; Leiden: Brill, 1973). **Waldow,** Hans Eberhard von. "Anlass und Hintergrund der Verkündigung des Deutero-Jesaja" (Inaug.-Diss., Bonn, 1953). **Weippert,** Manfred. "De herkomst van het heilsorakel voor Israel bij Deutero-Jesaja," *NedTT* 36 (1982): 1–11. **Weippert.** "'Ich bin Jahwe'–'Ich bin Ištar von Arbela': Deuterojesaja im Lichte der neuassyrischen Prophetie," in *Prophetie und Psalmen: Festschrift für Klaus Seybold* (ed. B. Huwyler et al.; AOAT 280; Münster: Ugarit, 2001), 31–59. **Westermann,** Claus. *Prophetic Oracles of Salvation in the Old Testament* (trans. K. Crim; Louisville: Westminster John Knox, 1991). **Westermann.** "Sprache und Struktur der Prophetie Deuterojesajas," in idem, *Forschung am Alten Testament: Gesammelte Studien zum Alten Testament* (2 vols.; TB 24, 55: Munich: Kaiser, 1964–74), 1:92–170 = Westermann and Andreas Richter, *Sprache und Struktur der Prophetie Deuterojesajas, mit einer Literaturübersicht "Hauptlinien der Deuterojesaja-Forschung von 1964–1979"* (CThM.A 11; Stuttgart: Calwer, 1981). **Westermann.** "Der Weg der Verheissung im Alten Testament," in idem, *Forschung am Alten Testament,* 2:230–49. **Westermann.** "Zur Erforschung und zum Verständnis der prophetischen Heilsworte," *ZAW* 98 (1986): 1–13.

It is a sign of the vitality of the relationship between God and Israel that the radiant oracles of salvation originated in the darkest period of Israel's history. Recitation of lamentations, cultic and secular, did not exhaust the repertoire. As time passed, there came to be more and more oracles giving Israel hope for a new future. Of course, there were also preexilic salvation oracles, spoken by cult prophets and priests (1 Sam 1:17; 2 Kgs 19:20, 32–33), but in the tradition that came to be the norm, the preexilic period was dominated at least from the eighth century on by prophecies of judgment and oracles of disaster in a multitude of forms. Prophecy of judgment (somewhat altered) continued for a time in the exilic period,[81] but the typical prophecy of this era is prophecy of salvation—mostly anonymous. The typical prophetic genres are the various forms of the salvation oracle. The tradents of the book of Ezekiel undoubtedly describe the transformation of prophecy too schematically, but factually they are

---

[81] See the discussion of the prophecy of judgment in the Deuteronomistic redaction of the book of Jeremiah on pp. 327ff. below.

absolutely correct: Ezekiel prophesied to the Babylonian golah after 594 as a prophet of judgment; as soon as he learned the news of Jerusalem's fall (Ezek 33:22–23), he began to prophesy salvation for her (Ezek 34–39).

The prophetic oracle of disaster or judgment has been thoroughly studied; it represents a single genre with many variants and applications. The salvation oracle, by contrast, employs a variety of genres. Westermann initially distinguished three: the promise or oracle of salvation; the announcement of salvation (promise in the narrow sense); and the description of salvation.[82] In his more recent publications, however, he has largely omitted the "description of salvation" genre,[83] relying more on content to differentiate the prophetic messages of salvation.[84] However, these later distinctions are at least partially questionable;[85] they resemble the earlier categorization of salvation oracles on the basis of purely thematic features,[86] which Westermann was actually trying to avoid. A new form-critical analysis of salvation oracles is urgently needed.[87]

These remarks already draw attention to a phenomenon of some theological importance: unlike prophetic oracles of disaster, which regularly involve an accusation grounding God's coming judgment in a transgression committed by Israel, salvation oracles of whatever genre normally include no motivation. When a motivation for God's salvific act does appear, it is grounded not in virtuous human behavior but in God's relationship with Israel (Jer 31:9; cf. Hag 2:23) or in Israel's suffering (Jer 30:17).

The genre of the salvation promise or oracle can be clearly defined and delimited. In 1934, Begrich[88] determined that the messages of salvation in

---

[82] "Weg," 231–38; in his study of Deutero-Isaiah ("Sprache," 117–24), he discusses only the first two.

[83] Here he speaks of a "promise" or "description" of blessing as an element of the announcement of salvation but able to take on independent life ("Zur Erforchung," 8–9), or of restoration and blessing within the promises (*Prophetic Oracles*, 113ff., 150ff.)

[84] He distinguishes four groups: (1) oracles of deliverance and restoration; (2) binary proclamation: salvation for Israel, destruction for the enemy; (3) conditional proclamation of deliverance in Deuteronomistic parenesis; and (4) the fate of the godly and the ungodly in theologized wisdom ("Zur Erforschung," 3–9; *Prophetic Oracles*, 5–6 and passim).

[85] The distinction between the first two groups, for example, is artificial. Already in Deutero-Isaiah we find announcements of deliverance both with and without announcements of judgment on Israel's enemies, without any perceptible formal differences. For the oracle of salvation, cf. Isa 41:11–12, 15 with 43:3–4 and 44:3–5; for the proclamation of salvation, cf. Isa 49:17–19 with 49:22–23, 25–26. The distinction appears to derive from theological interests.

[86] For a comprehensive example, see Herrmann, *Die prophetischen Heilserwartungen*.

[87] Westermann is correct in his insight that such an analysis has to include all the prophetic books, since the same or very similar salvation oracles appear in different books (cf. Isa 2:2–4 and Mic 4:1–4). Only in this way is it possible to study the redactional function of the salvation oracles in the various books.

[88] "Der priesterliche Heilsorakel," reprinted 1964.

Isa 41:8–13, 14–16; 43:1–4, 5–7; 44:1–5, as well as 55:4–8 and Jer 30:10–11 (= Jer 46:27, 28), share a structure and motifs that make them a distinct genre, which he called the "priestly salvation oracle." Its primary characteristic is the expression "Do not fear" (Heb. אַל־תִּירָא), which must not be interpreted as an exhortation to be brave but as a word of comfort in the sense of, "There is nothing to be afraid of." Although the texts in question all apply this genre to Jacob/Israel, Begrich was able to show by comparative analysis of the form and its associated motifs that it must have originated as a positive response to an individual lament.[89] As direct evidence for his theory, Begrich cited allusions to salvation oracles in such laments (Ps 35:3 and Lam 3:57), as well as the occasionally sudden change of mood in certain individual laments (Pss 28:1–5 + 6–7; 54:1–7 + 8–9; 56:1–12 + 13–14). This abrupt transition, he maintained, is best explained by hypothesizing an intervening salvation oracle.

The conclusion was unambiguous, despite the somewhat scanty evidence; however, later this clear result was somewhat muddied, when, in addition to the texts just cited, Begrich assigned some twenty additional texts in Deutero-Isaiah to the genre,[90] and Von Waldow proposed interpreting them as a response to a communal lament, thus connecting them directly with the liturgical lamentations of the exilic period.[91] Westermann, however, was able to place Begrich's thesis on a new and more secure foundation by going back to the original group of texts and assigning most of the others in Begrich's later group to a second genre, the "announcement of salvation."[92] Schoors later subjected Westermann's conclusions to detailed analysis, largely confirming them with certain minor differences.[93]

The handful of scholars who have questioned the very existence of the genre[94] can hardly be correct. It is true in general that psychological explanations can account for the change of mood in a lament; furthermore, an abrupt change from lament to praise such as that in Ps 22 is probably due to the redactional process.[95] Nevertheless, the reading of the

---

[89] *Gesammelte Studien*, 225–31; see also the recent list of motifs in Schoors, *I Am God*, 45–46.
[90] *Studien*, 14ff.
[91] "Anlass," 101ff.
[92] "Sprache," 117–24, = *Sprache und Struktur*, 34–41.
[93] *I Am God*, 32–175.
[94] Kilian, "Ps 22"; Merendino, "Literarkritisches."
[95] Much evidence suggests that this lament was recycled by the community of the poor, who expanded it by adding 22:4–6 (3–5) and 24–27 (23–26). Originally the vow of praise in 22:23 (22) belonged only to the lament; now, as a cohortative summons to praise, it introduces the praise section (cf. the thanksgiving elements in 22:26–27 [25–26], with 22:24–25 [23–24] being an imperative hymn).

Hebrew text concluding 22:22 (21) (עֲנִיתָנִי, "you have answered me"), placed immediately between the lament section and the praise section, presupposes (contra Kilian) that an individual lament could be answered by a positive divine response.

This is even clearer in Lam 3:57, which cites the critical assurance of comfort immediately between the long retrospective description of affliction (3:1–24, 52–55) and the report of deliverance:

> Lam 3:55 I called on your name, O Yahweh, from the depths of the pit,
> 56 you heard my plea, "Do not close your ear to my deliverance."
> 57 You came near on the day I called on you and said, "Do not fear."
> 58 You took up "my" cause, Adonai, redeemed my life....

The return of the thanksgiving to petition (3:59b [not LXX!], 62–66) is due to the special character of the lamentation ceremony, which establishes a parallel between the affliction of the individual and that of the people;[96] however, 3:57 still marks the crucial turning point. Merendino's attempt to interpret these verses as an expression of assurance that the petition will be heard[97] seems forced: it is grammatically problematic (perfective tense) and does not take into account the overall staging of the text.[98] Despite the appearance of a few military motifs (41:11–12; 43:4), Merendino's own derivation of the promise of salvation in Deutero-Isaiah from the wars of Yahweh[99] carries little conviction for the whole group of texts, especially since he can cite only a single war oracle (Josh 10:8) that is at all similar in structure.

Furthermore, the existence of positive divine responses to individual laments is well attested among Israel's neighbors—for example, in the Aramaic inscription of King Zakir of Hamath (ca. 800 B.C.E.),[100] several seventh-century Assyrian prophecies for the kings Esarhaddon and Ashurbanipal,[101] and, finally, the Babylonian poem *Ludlul Bēl Nēmeqi* (3.33–37), from the end of the second millennium.[102] In these parallels,

---

[96] See p. 163 above.

[97] "Literarkritisches," 16–19.

[98] To support his rejection of the salvation oracle as a genre, Merendino claims Ps 69:19 (18) (petition!) as a parallel, saying: "Yahweh draws near to the personal sphere of the individual, whom he encounters in the inward realm of the soul" ("Literarkritisches," 17). However, this argument imposes a questionable modern conception on the religiosity of the ancient world.

[99] "Literarkritisches," 28–29.

[100] *KAI* 202A, lines 13–15; cf. *ANET*, 655; *TUAT* 1/6:626–28.

[101] *TUAT* 2/1:56–64; *ANET*, 449–51, 606; and the complete new edition by Parpola (*Assyrian Prophecies*).

[102] W. G. Lambert, *Babylonian Wisdom Literature* (Oxford: Clarendon, 1975), 50–51.

too, we find the assurance of comfort "Do not fear" (Aram. אל תזחל, Babylonian/Assyrian *lā tapallaḥ*). There are many other formal and thematic parallels.[103] It is true, however, that outside of Israel salvation oracles were almost always addressed to the king or the queen mother. This observation led Weippert[104] to conclude that the texts in Deutero-Isaiah derive from the tradition of Israelite and Assyro-Babylonian royal oracles and that their application to the nation should be understood as a kind of "democratization." However, such an explanation is far from persuasive, since the evidence should probably be considered a product of selective preservation. On the one hand, *Ludlul Bēl Nēmeqi* illustrates the possibility of a salvation oracle addressed to an "ordinary citizen" of Babylonia, albeit one of high social rank; on the other, there were also specialized positive oracles in Israel for persons in positions of responsibility, closely related to the salvation oracle. Such oracles are best attested for the prophets (Jer 1:4–10; Isa 49:1–6), but we also find oracles for kings (1 Sam 23:17; 2 Kgs 19:6–7), military commanders (Josh 8:1; 10:8), and other leaders (Hag 2:4–5; cf. Zeph 3:16–17). Consequently, Begrich's traditio-historical derivation and Westermann's structural definition remain the most likely theories.

The ancient Near Eastern parallels frequently mention female prophets and other temple personnel as speakers of salvation oracles, suggesting that Begrich's restriction of this genre to priests was probably premature. He simply based his conclusion on the cultic connotations of the genre. In Israel, too, we should probably envision promises of salvation spoken by cultic prophets or—if we remember that individual lamentations originated in the familial cult—itinerant prophets, "men of God," or other local experts endowed with mantic or magical gifts.

This is the structure of the promise of salvation:

Structure of the Promise of Salvation		
(messenger formula, with expansions)		... who formed you in the womb
salutation (with expansions)		But you, Israel, my servant
assurance of comfort		אַל־תִּירָא, "Do not fear"
motivation	a. nominal	I am with you; I am your God
	b. verbal (perfective)	I have redeemed you, called you by name

---

[103] Weippert, "Ich bin Jahwe."
[104] "Herkomst."

consequences (future)	for the petitioner	You shall seek those who contend with you but not find them
	for the enemies	All who are incensed against you shall be ashamed and disgraced
(purpose)		You shall rejoice in Yahweh

The messenger formula, which is firmly rooted in the prophetic oracle of judgment, is not a necessary element of the promise of salvation. It appears only in Isa 43:1 and 44:1 (divine utterance formula in Jer 30:10, 11; 46:28); it is absent in Isa 41:8, 14; 51:4; Jer 46:27, 28. In the setting of a lamentation ceremony, no legitimation of the liturgist was necessary. The Assyrian evidence, however, shows that, when collections of salvation oracles were preserved in writing, they were supplied with introductory or concluding formulas ("The word of the Ishtar of Arbela to King...," "From the mouth of *Personal Name* from *Place*...," etc.). The adversative וְעַתָּה ("but now": Isa 43:1; 44:1) or וְאַתָּה ("but you," Isa 41:8; Jer 30:10; 46:27) may suggest the original contrast with a preceding lament, since it sometimes serves no contextual function (Jer 30:10). The predication of Yahweh as the addressee's Creator in the introduction (Isa 43:1; 44:2) or body (54:4) of the promise of salvation is clearly a central element, since it has a counterpart in the acknowledgment of the speaker's personal Creator in the individual lament (Pss 22:10–11 [9–10]; 119:73; 139:15; cf. Job 10:8ff.). The expansions of the salutation sometimes borrow from the first-person lament (cf. "you worm Jacob" in Isa 41:14 with "but I am a worm and not human" in Ps 22:7 [6]) or employ a motif typical of petition (cf. "Israel, my servant" in Isa 41:8 with the petitioner's self-designation "your servant" in Ps 27:9, etc.). Verbless motivation clauses in the promise of salvation ("you are my servant," Isa 41:9; "I am your God," Isa 43:3) have parallels in the confession of trust in the individual lament ("for I am your servant," Ps 143:12; "you are my god," Ps 31:14 [13]). Perfective motivations such as "I have helped you" (Isa 41:10) have their counterpart in petitions for deliverance such as "deliver me" (Ps 3:8 [7], etc.) or "be my helper" (Ps 30:11 [10]). By contrast, the motifs of future consequences usually far transcend the narrow horizon of the individual lament; here the transformation of the form when applied to a collective is most obvious. A statement of purpose—God will deliver the addressees so that they may rejoice in God[105]—appears in just a few texts (Isa 41:16; 43:7); it is a kind of parallel to the vow of praise at the end of a lament.

---

[105] Some Assyrian salvation oracles actually contain the imperative *na-i-da-ni*, "praise me" (see K4310 2.33N, 39N; 6.13, 18 in Parpola, *Assyrian Prophecies*, 6, 10; *TUAT* 2/1:58–59).

The promise of salvation clearly originated in the intimate familial cult. The question remains: Why did groups of exilic prophets make use of this particular genre to proclaim their message of salvation to the people? It was actually alien to the formal cultic setting of a public fast or everyday assembly. Probably the borrowing was due once again to Israel's crisis of faith during the exilic period. Yahweh seemed to have forsaken his people, but his active protection and deliverance could still be experienced within the family and in people's personal lives. Lamentations 3:57 shows that even in the exilic period salvation oracles could be spoken to individuals in response to their laments. The exilic prophets of salvation borrowed the comforting language of these oracles, intensely personal and intimate, familiar from the domain of private life, in order to inspire trust in their incredible message that, even after decades of disappointed hopes, Yahweh still intervenes in history on behalf of his people. They took advantage of the perfective nature of the salvation oracle, which is connected with its calming and comforting function: Yahweh's turn to salvation has already taken place; the people need no longer be afraid, no matter how long their actual deliverance might take. When the Deutero-Isaiah group appealed explicitly to creation as the basis of the individual's relationship with God, their purpose was to set the historical relationship between God and Israel on the firmer foundation of the created world, after the model of the communal lament in Isa 63:16 and 64:17 (18).

Compared with the promise of salvation, the form and *Sitz im Leben* of the announcement of salvation are less clearly defined. Westermann assigned the following individual texts in Deutero-Isaiah to this genre: Isa 41:17–20; 42:14–17; 43:16–21; 45:14–17; 49:7–12 (?), as well as the composite texts 49:14–26 and 51:9–52:6, together with additional texts from Isa 54 and 55.[106] He pointed out the difference that this genre is less interested in deliverance than is the promise of salvation; it focuses instead on a new life for Israel. He defined its structure as follows:

Structure of the Announcement of Salvation		
implicit lament		The needy seek water ...
announcement of salvation (first-person singular)		
	God's response	I Yahweh will answer them
	God's intervention	I will open rivers on the bare heights
purpose		That they may see and know

---

106 "Sprache," 120–22.

The reference to the affliction and lamentation of a group led Westermann to define the announcement of salvation as a response to a communal lament. In contrast to the oracle of salvation, he saw it as mediated by a prophet rather than a priest.[107]

Against a few critical voices, Schoors confirmed Westermann's thesis in its essentials, although undertaking a few corrections in the selection and delimitation of texts, defining some more precisely. He assigns thirteen texts in Deutero-Isaiah to this genre: Isa 41:17–29; 42:14–17; 43:16–21; 46:12–13; 49:7–12, 14–26; 51:1–3, 6–8, 9–14, 17–23; 54:7–10, 11–17; 55:1–5.[108] However, Schoors resists exaggerating the difference between the announcement and the promise of salvation, finding clear thematic similarities between the two genres in their future perspective and their intended purpose.[109] Although there are a few perfective clauses in announcements of salvation (49:8; 54:8), the most significant difference between the two genres is that the announcement of salvation usually uses the imperfective to formulate Yahweh's favorable response. Since it sometimes speaks of Israel and Zion in the singular and also may respond to an individual lament (49:7, 14, 21), its *Sitz im Leben* in liturgical lamentation of the community is not so clear; some texts in Deutero-Isaiah are already imitations of the cultic genre.[110]

That a favorable response from God could be communicated, probably by a cult prophet, following a communal lament is shown directly by the laments in Pss 60 and 85 and indirectly by God's refusal to allow the prophets of judgment to intercede in this context (e.g., Hos 6:1–6; Jer 14:7–14; 15:1–4). Psalm 74:9 laments that signs are not seen and that there is no longer any prophet who can say how long the affliction will last. This language implies that communal lamentation normally included a search for omens and prognostic oracles. Westermann's theory that the announcements of salvation in Deutero-Isaiah likewise had this cultic setting might also be supported by Isa 51:9–14, which explicitly cites a communal lament (51:9–10), and Isa 41:17 and 49:8, which use the verb ענה, "answer," to qualify the announcement of salvation explicitly as a response from God. This theory would also explain the striking decline in the use of the messenger formula, which appears in only three of the thirteen texts (43:16; 49:7, 22, 25), since legitimation of the speaker is unnecessary in a cultic context. There is a problem, however: in the two texts from Psalms, the divine response

---

107 Ibid., 120, 123.
108 *I Am God*, 85ff.
109 Ibid., 170ff.
110 Ibid., 175.

clearly exhibits a different structure. In Ps 85:9–14 (8–13), the positive response is not uttered in the first person, as in Deutero-Isaiah; instead, the text speaks of God in the third person and is less an announcement than a description of blessings. In Ps 60:8–10 (6–8), the lament of the people is followed by quotation of a war oracle, a totally different genre. We must therefore take into account the observation that very diverse forms of positive response by God could be communicated in liturgical lamentation. That these included the type represented in Deutero-Isaiah is likely, though not demonstrable. The individual texts, but not the composite texts, probably still resemble the cultic proclamation of salvation relatively closely.

There is a further problem: the rather homogeneous form of the announcements of salvation in Deutero-Isaiah is almost unparalleled in the other prophetic books. When we examine the poetic oracles of salvation in the books that most likely refer to the sufferings of the northern and southern kingdoms during exile, we do find texts that speak of the sufferings and lamentations or Israel or Zion (Jer 30:12–15; 31:15–17, 18–20; Mic 4:9–10, 11–13; cf. Zeph 3:11–13), usually even more explicitly than in Deutero-Isaiah, but here the announcement of salvation is by no means always uttered by God himself (Jer 31:16–17; Mic 4:10, 12–13), and God's kind response is rarely mentioned (implicitly in Jer 31:20). The focus is rather on God's salvific intervention in contrast to the lament; some passages have unmistakable contentious and didactic overtones (Jer 30:12–15; Mic 4:9–10). The texts sometimes recall the poems in Lamentations. There is thus some evidence that these oracles did not originate in the cult but in prophetic preaching and debate in everyday settings. That some prophetic proclamation of salvation was secular rather than cultic is clearly demonstrated by Jer 28:2–3, where the prophet Hananiah publicly proclaims the return of the golah of 597 within two years, provoking a bitter dispute with the prophet Jeremiah. If the material in Lamentations was actually performed during local evening assemblies, as argued above,[111] then Lam 4:21–22 shows that on such noncultic occasions it was also possible to proclaim salvation for Zion and judgment on the surrounding nations.

Noncultic origin is probably even more likely in the case of announcements of salvation with no detectable reference to a lament (Jer 30:3b–6, 18–20; 31:8–9, 10–14; Mic 2:12; 4:6–7; cf. Hag 2:6–9, 21b–23). This is true in any case for Hananiah's announcement of salvation (Jer 28:2–3). The structure of these texts is even simpler. They usually comprise only

---

[111] See p. 156 above.

two sections: an announcement of Yahweh's salvific intervention, in which God usually speaks in the first person, and a description of the consequences of this intervention, in which other persons or things are the subjects of the clauses or Yahweh is spoken of in the third person. In some announcements of salvation, this latter section, the "description of consequences," also contains a lament element (Jer 30:16; 31:17; Zeph 3:12b, 13). This is true even of some announcements of salvation in Deutero-Isaiah (Isa 49:10, 12; 54:14–15, 17; 55:5). In his earlier work on Deutero-Isaiah, Westermann had disregarded this element (see the schema outlined above), because from the perspective of the "description of salvation" genre it appeared to be a hybrid form. In his work on the prophetic oracles of salvation, he recognized that during the exile an announcement of deliverance could constitute an independent oracle of salvation, whereas after the exile there was often added to this announcement a second element having to do with restoration or a description of blessings.[112] However, the distinction between action and state, deliverance and blessing, which is of systematic importance for Westermann's thought, is quite problematic here. God's acts and their consequences are often so intertwined that they simply cannot be separated (cf. Jer 30:18–20) and placed in temporal sequence. Furthermore, the descriptive sections are not limited to the theme of restoration (cf. Mic 4:7). It is much simpler to posit an analogy to the prophetic oracle of judgment, where the announcement of disaster often follows Yahweh's intervention with a description of its terrible consequences.[113] Thus I prefer to treat the "consequences of God's salvific intervention" as a genuine element of the announcement of salvation, employed whenever the effects of the transition to salvation for Israel needed to be described more concretely.

In contrast to the announcement of salvation, which links two points in history, the afflictions of the present and God's salvific intervention in the future, there are oracles of salvation that contrast the afflictions of the present with an extended description of a state of salvation (e.g., Isa 2:1–4; 11:1–10). Westermann called such oracles "descriptions of salvation." It is uncertain, however, whether they constitute a true ancient genre, which Westermann at one time sought to derive from the seer oracle (cf. Num 24:5–6, etc.) and descriptions of blessings like those in some tribal sayings (cf. Gen 49:11).[114] In his later study of prophetic oracles of salvation, he is more inclined to believe that such descriptions

---

112 "Zur Erforschung," 8.
113 See Claus Westermann, *Basic Forms of Prophetic Speech* (trans. H. C. White; Philadelphia: Westminster, 1967), 171ff.
114 "Weg," 236–37.

might represent an independent development of the descriptive elements in the announcement of salvation.[115] There are three sources of this uncertainty: (1) despite their descriptive character, the texts in question do not share a fixed common form; (2) "pure" descriptions of salvation are relatively rare; and (3) with a few exceptions (e.g., Isa 11:1–6) they are relatively late, that is, mostly postexilic (Isa 2:1–4; 60:19–20; 61:5–6; 62:2–5; 65:[17–19a], 19b–25; Hos 2:1–3 [1:10–2:1]; Amos 9:13, [14–15]; Mic 5:6–8; etc.). To the best of our knowledge, no extended descriptions of salvation date from the exilic period, probably because during the exile attention focused on the actual turning point, namely, God's loving intervention to bring salvation.

Only a few exilic texts resemble the later descriptions of salvation. On the one hand, we find brief statements expressing the hope that, despite the devastating circumstances of the present, the situation will return to "normal" in the future. Jeremiah uttered such an oracle amid the chaos just before the final capture of Jerusalem—"Houses and vineyards shall again be bought in this land" (Jer 32:15)—underlining his message with the symbolic purchase of a field. Similar statements marked by the characteristic עוֹד, "again," appear in Zechariah (Zech 1:17; 8:4–5), at the end of the exilic period. The two promises of a new king in Mic 4:8 and 5:1, (2), 3–4a (5:2, [3], 4–5a) are also descriptive in nature, although the emphasis on the places addressed—here Jerusalem[116] and Bethlehem—which recalls the staging of the poems in Lamentations, gives the passages the character of a promise of salvation.

A totally different transformation of an announcement of salvation into a description is the famous vision in Ezek 37:1–11. The passage is actually a promise that Israel will be requickened from the end foretold by Amos (Amos 8:2; cf. Ezek 7); it is formulated as a normal announcement of salvation in Ezek 37:12–14. It includes a reference to a communal lament (37:11b), but the metaphorical language of the lament ("Our bones are dried up, and our hope is lost; we are cut off completely"[117]) taken literally and contrasted with a visionary description of how the prophet, at God's behest, uses magically effective words to bring about a new creation of Israel, turns the announcement of salvation into a miraculous graphic reality. This transformation of an announcement of salvation into

---

115 "Zur Erforschung," 8–9.

116 In parallel with the Ophel ("citadel") of daughter Zion, Migdal-eder ("tower of the flock") must be a locality near Jerusalem; see Rainer Kessler, *Micha* (HThK.AT; Freiburg: Herder, 1999), 199–200.

117 It is not by accident that these motifs, too, are taken from the individual lament; cf. Ps 102:4 (3); Job 14:19; Lam 3:54.

a visionary description of salvation by the school of Ezekiel pursues by other means the goal of the Deutero-Isaiah group: to underline the trustworthiness of the incredible message of salvation.

Finally, there are a few minor genres used or borrowed by exilic prophets to communicate their message of salvation. One is the call to rejoice, with a promise of salvation (Isa 54:1–3; Zeph 3:14–15; Zech 2:14–16 [10–12]; cf. Lam 4:21 and later Isa 12:6 and Zech 9:9–10). This genre, which resembles the promise of salvation, is usually addressed to a female figure; Crüsemann therefore believes that it could well have been a response to the lament of a barren woman (Isa 49:21; 54:1–3).[118] If so, its original setting would most likely have been a fertility ritual.

The genre of "instructions to a herald," originally used in diplomatic communications, was borrowed to lend dramatic force to the spread of the message of salvation (Isa 40:9–10; 48:20–21; Jer 31:7, 10–11).[119] Finally, drawing on the form of the short victory song (Exod 15:21), the Deutero-Isaiah group created the so-called "eschatological hymn of praise" (plural imperative call to praise, perfective implementation with כִּי), which summons all creation to celebrate the coming of salvation as though already realized (Isa 42:10–13; 44:23; 45:8; 48:20–21; 49:13; 52:9–10). These short hymns also serve to spread and affirm the message of salvation.

Since proclamation of salvation during the exile was usually anonymous, it is difficult to date the oracles more precisely. A late reference point is the preaching of the Deutero-Isaiah group, which clearly reached an initial climax between 550 and 539 B.C.E. (Isa 40:12–46:11*) but was not reduced to written form (40:1–52:12*) until the first years of Darius (522–521).[120] An early reference point is Jeremiah's message of salvation to the inhabitants and exiles of the former northern kingdom (Jer 3:12–13, 19–4:2; 31:3b–6, 15–17, 18–20), which can be assigned to the time of Josiah (prior to 609).[121] Also datable are the unhesitant proclamation of salvation by Hananiah (Jer 28:2–4) to the exiles of 597 and the more restrained message of Jeremiah (29:4–7; 594/593).

These example show that proclamations of salvation were concentrated in years or periods marked by the weakness or even collapse of the world powers oppressing Israel and Judah, the Neo-Assyrian or the Neo-Babylonian Empires. This observation suggests that proclamations of salvation were not distributed evenly throughout the exile but probably reached their climax only in the late exilic period (550–520). Laments such

---

[118] *Studien*, 55–65.
[119] Ibid., 50–55.
[120] See pp. 399–400 below for the first edition of the book of Deutero-Isaiah.
[121] Albertz, "Jer 2–6" (III.2.5), 43–48.

as Ps 74:9 indicate that for many years at the beginning and in the middle of the exilic period the liturgical lamentations heard no positive responses from God; hardly a soul ventured to formulate oracles of salvation in the name of Yahweh in the everyday assemblies. When we recall that shortly before the final catastrophe Jeremiah formulated a cautious positive statement (Jer 32:15) leaving Yahweh out of the picture, it is reasonable to assume that in the first half of the exilic period, if oracles of salvation for Israel were uttered at all, they were vague and timid. A good example might be Mic 4:9–10, an oracle that continues to impugn the false hopes for salvation harbored by the religious nationalists who still trusted in Zion and the king, declaring that only after they had been deported to Babylon would Yahweh rescue them there (שָׁם in emphatic position) some time in the future. However, a chronological discrimination of prophecies of salvation during the exile must await more detailed analysis. Probably only the oracle of salvation for an individual in distress (Lam 3:57) and perhaps also the call to rejoice addressed to a barren woman (Isa 54:1–3) continued throughout the exilic period, once the living conditions of families had become more or less settled.

III.1.4. ORACLES AGAINST THE NATIONS

Bartlett, John R. *Edom and the Edomites* (JSOTSup 77; Sheffield: JSOT Press, 1989). **Beentjes,** Pancratius C. "Oracles against the Nations: A Central Issue in the 'Latter Prophets,'" *Bijdr* 50 (1989): 203–9. **Bentzen,** Aage. "The Ritual Background of Amos i 2–ii 16," *OtSt* 8 (1950): 85–99. **Christensen,** Duane L. *Transformations of the War Oracle in Old Testament Prophecy: Studies in the Oracles against Foreign Nations* (HDR 3; Missoula, Mont.: Scholars Press, 1975). **Dicou,** Bert. *Edom, Israel's Brother and Antagonist: The Role of Edom in Biblical Prophecy and Story* (JSOTSup 169; Sheffield: JSOT Press, 1994). **Fechter,** Friedrich. *Bewältigung der Katastrophe: Untersuchungen zu ausgewählten Fremdvölkersprüchen im Ezechielbuch* (BZAW 208; Berlin: de Gruyter, 1992. **Fritz,** Volkmar. "Die Fremdvölkersprüche des Amos," *VT* 37 (1987): 26–38. **Gosse,** Bernard. *Isaïe 13,1–14,23 dans la tradition littéraire du livre d'Isaïe et dans la tradition des oracles contre les nations* (OBO 78; Fribourg: Universitätsverlag, 1988). **Hayes,** John H. "The Oracles against the Nations in the Old Testament: Their Usage and Theological Importance" (Ph.D. diss., Princeton, 1964). **Hayes.** "The Usage of Oracles against Foreign Nations in Ancient Israel," *JBL* 87 (1968): 81–92. **Höffken,** Peter. "Untersuchungen zu den Begründungselementen der Völkerorakel des Alten Testaments" (Inaug.-Diss., Bonn, 1977). **Hoffman,** Yair. "From Oracle to Prophecy: The Growth, Crystallization and Disintegration of a Biblical Gattung," *JNSL* 10 (1982): 75–81. **Huwyler,** Beat. *Jeremia und die Völker: Untersuchungen zu den Völkersprüchen in Jeremia 46–49* (FAT 20; Tübingen: Mohr Siebeck, 1997). **Kegler,** Jürgen. "Das Leid des Nachbarvolkes: Beobachtungen zu den Fremdvölkersprüchen Jeremias," in *Werden und Wirken des Alten Testaments: Festschrift für Claus Westermann* (ed. R. Albertz et al.;

Göttingen: Vandenhoeck & Ruprecht, 1980), 271–87. **Sæbø,** Magne. *Sacharja 9–14: Untersuchungen von Text und Form* (WMANT 34; Neukirchen-Vluyn: Neukirchener Verlag, 1969). **Vieweger,** Dieter. "Zur Herkunft der Völkersprüche im Amosbuch unter besonderer Berücksichtigung des Aramäerspruchs (Am 1,3–5)," in *Altes Testament, Forschung und Wirkung: Festschrift für Henning Graf Reventlow* (ed. P. Mommer and W. Thiel; Frankfurt: Lang, 1994), 103–19. **Wolff,** Hans Walter. *Dodekapropheton 3, Obadja und Jona* (BK 14/3; Neukirchen-Vluyn: Neukirchener Verlag, 1977). **Wolff.** *Joel and Amos* (trans. W. Janzen, S. D. McBride, and C. A. Muenchow; Hermeneia; Philadelphia: Fortress, 1977). **Wolff.** "Obadja, ein Kultprophet als Interpret," *EvT* 37 (1977): 273–84. **Zapff,** Burkard M. *Schriftgelehrte Prophetie: Jes 13 und die Komposition des Jesajabuches: Ein Beitrag zur Erforschung der Redaktionsgeschichte des Jesajabuches* (FB 74; Würzburg: Echter, 1995).

In addition to salvation oracles, another group of texts became important during the exilic period: oracles against the (foreign) nations. This came about simply because the political turmoil caused by the westward invasions of the Assyrians, Babylonians, and Persians brought Israel and Judah into much closer contact with the other nations and powers of the Near East than ever before. After the collapse of the state, their weal or woe was totally dependent on large-scale international politics.

Whether the oracles against the nations constitute a genre in the strict sense is disputed, because they can appear in a wide variety of different forms: relatively short announcements of disaster without motivation (Zeph 2:12; Obad 5–7; Isa 13:17–22; Ezek 26:7–14) or with motivation (Amos 1:3ff.; Ezek 25:1–5; 26:1–5; etc.), which formally resemble the prophetic oracles of judgment against Israel, as well as descriptions of disaster of varying length (Jer 46:3–11, 12–19; 50:21–28; 51:27–33; etc.), which use exhortations to fight or flee, cries of horror, and similar devices to anticipate dramatically the political collapse of the nation in question. We also find artfully constructed laments over the fall of foreign cities (Ezek 26:17–18; 27:1–36; etc.), taunt songs (Ezek 28:11–19; 31:1–18; etc.), accounts of visions (Isa 21:1–10), and a few other minor genres. Earlier scholars were inclined to treat the foreign nation oracles as a single genre that drew on a variety of forms and genres;[122] more recent studies have shown that the foreign nation oracles do not constitute a genre.[123] The only common features these oracles share are thematic: "They are addressed to a nation or the nations in general or at least thematize in some form the present or future fate of those addressed."[124] Despite all

---

[122] See the surveys in Hayes, "Oracles," 1–38; Höffken, "Untersuchungen," 12–36; and Huwyler, *Jeremia,* 1–31.

[123] Fechter, *Bewältigung,* 304; Huwyler, *Jeremia,* 392.

[124] Huwyler, *Jeremia,* 2.

the formal differences, however, the tradents of the prophetic books quite clearly considered the oracles against the nations a well-defined textual group: the overwhelming majority appear together in the prophetic books as collections or composites (Isa 13–23*; Jer 46–51; Ezek 25–32; Joel 4 (3); Amos 1:2–2:16*; Obad; Zeph 2:5–15; Nah 2–3; Zech 9:1–8). The evidence of this distribution can hardly be used as a criterion for defining the oracles themselves, however,[125] unless one is willing to claim that most were written specifically for such composites. Still, this distribution does make it reasonable to treat them as an independent group of prophetic oracles. Whether it is necessary or even possible to subdivide these oracles into more specific genres will become clear only when scholars devote more study to this still-neglected body of texts.

Although there are some characteristic differences between the foreign nation oracles in the various prophetic books—one need only compare the diction of the oracles in Ezekiel with that of the oracles in Jeremiah—there are also, as in the case of the salvation oracles, many intertextual relations between the prophetic books (cf. Jer 48 and Isa 15–16; Jer 49:7–22 and Obad). These oracles were clearly less closely associated with the name of a particular prophet; they were more anonymous and more easily transferable to a new context than the oracles addressed to Israel. Even though it may be proper to follow the broad early studies of the foreign nation oracles as a group[126] with attention to the texts[127] or composites[128] of individual prophetic books, the study of these oracles must not stop there if it is to do justice to the evidence characterizing this tradition.

The origin and possible *Sitz im Leben* of the foreign nation oracles are also uncertain. Bentzen, citing the analogy of the Egyptian execration texts (eighteenth century B.C.E.), sought to derive these oracles, especially those in the book of Amos (Amos 1:3–2:3), from purification rites during the Israelite New Year festival.[129] In Egypt, the king or priest sought to render foreign princes, cities, and regions powerless by shattering vessels or figurines on which their names were written; so the Israelite cult regularly attempted to weaken actual or potential enemies by reciting oracles against them. However, the two groups of texts are not comparable,[130]

---

125 Contra Fechter, *Bewältigung*, 2.
126 Hayes, "Oracles"; Christensen, *Transformations*; Höffken, "Untersuchungen"; Hoffman, "From Oracle"; see also Hoffman's 1973 dissertation (in Hebrew).
127 Huwyler, *Jeremia*.
128 Fechter, *Bewältigung*.
129 "Ritual Background."
130 Wolff, *Joel*, 144–46.

and there is no evidence for a systematic assault on the power of enemies in the Israelite cult. In the collections of foreign nation oracles, the evident attempt to run through as many as possible of Israel's enemies in the sequence of the points of the compass almost always turns out to be inconsistent; it is invariably a product of redaction.[131] This observation argues unambiguously against a cultic origin and for secondary literary editing.

Much more promising is the commonly accepted theory that the foreign nation oracles derive from war oracles uttered by prophets or priests before and during military campaigns.[132] This theory is supported not only by the military diction of many oracles[133] but also by certain formal similarities: a war oracle can be motivated by misconduct on the part of an enemy (1 Kgs 20:28; cf. 1 Sam 15:2–3) and stylized as a prophetic oracle of judgment against the enemy (Isa 7:4–9a). A war oracle uttered in the temple, in which Yahweh himself celebrates his victory over Judah's neighbors, appears in Ps 60:8–10 (6–8). Similar war oracles were common throughout the West Semitic and Mesopotamian region.[134] There is a particularly eloquent example from Mari in which a prophet promising King Zimrilim victory over Babylon addresses the city directly, threatening it with the judgment of the god Dagan.[135] Such instances of direct address to the enemy—often at a substantial geographical distance—are common in Israelite oracles against the nations (Obad 8–15; Isa 47; Jer 49:3–5; Ezek 25:1–5; etc.). This mode of address also reflects the element of the efficacious word, manifest in magical Israelite war oracles (2 Kgs 13:17). Also related is the practice of weakening the enemy through powerful and efficacious curses, common in the ancient Near East and among the pre-Islamic Arabs as well as in Israel (Num 22:6, 11; 23:7; 1 Sam 17:43). There is

---

[131] The inclusion of all Israel's neighbors in Amos 1:3–2:3 is dependent on the additions in 1:9–12; nevertheless, the sequence Aram/Damascus–Philistines–[Tyre–Edom]–Ammon–Moab appears more or less random. The clearest use of the points of the compass as an organizing principle is in Zeph 2:5–15 (west: seacoast; east: Moab/Ammon; south: Cushites; north: Assyria), but the list is incomplete, since it omits Aram and Edom. Furthermore, the major formal differences show that it is a redactional composite comprising very different individual oracles. The arrangement is clearest and most complete in the composite Ezek 25:1–28:24 (Ammon–Moab–Edom–Philistines–Tyre/Sidon), which runs through Israel's neighbors clockwise: east, south, west, north. Here, too, Aram is not mentioned, and the oracles against Moab and the Philistines are clearly secondary additions to complete the composite (Fechter, *Bewältigung*, 26–103, 286–90).

[132] Hayes, "Oracles"; Hayes, "Usage," 81–87; Christensen, *Transformations*, 17ff.; Hoffman, "From Oracle," 80–82.

[133] Sæbø, *Sacharja*, 166.

[134] Hayes, "Oracles," 82ff.

[135] ARM 13:23; cf. Hayes, "Usage," 85.

thus much to be said for deriving the foreign nation oracles from war oracles or war curses. Their original *Sitz im Leben* would then be mantic and magical rituals before and during a military campaign.

When such a derivation is considered, however, it must be emphasized that the biblical foreign nation oracles, beginning in the eighth century, represent an adaptation of the war oracle by prophets of judgment.[136] Their *Sitz im Leben* and function clearly differ: war oracles were connected with actual military conflicts between Israel and an enemy, and therefore the announcement of the enemy's defeat was always associated with a promise of victory for Israel; in oracles against the nations, however, outside the context of military confrontation, the announcement of military and political catastrophe for a foreign nation no longer had anything to do with a victory for Israel. Instead, both Israel and its neighbors were to share a common fate: disaster was threatened upon all (sometimes highly provocatively, as in Amos). One might even describe the preexilic foreign nation oracles of the prophets as war oracles in support of a third party,[137] namely, the Assyrians or Neo-Babylonians overrunning Israel and its neighbors, even though they are usually not mentioned explicitly.

The altered function of the foreign nation oracles is evident also in their form, which is more or less assimilated to the prophetic forms foretelling judgment on Israel (oracle of judgment, announcement of disaster, description of disaster). The only difference is that threats of disaster to Israel's neighbors include a motivation much less frequently and less accusatorily than threats against Israel itself. When such motivations do appear in foreign nation oracles, in contrast to war oracles, they hardly ever mention actual transgressions of a nation against Israel. Usually they describe crimes against humanity, often in the past, which concerned not only Israel (Amos 1:3, 6, 13) but also its neighbors (Amos 2:1) or else such typical political misconduct as hubris (Isa 9:11 [12]; Jer 46:8; 49:16; etc.) and misplaced self-confidence (Jer 48:7; 49:25; etc.) having nothing to do with Israel.[138]

This means: the widespread scholarly opinion that the foreign nation oracles represent an indirect proclamation of salvation for Israel (thus frequently denying their authorship by the classical prophets of judgment) is incorrect as a general rule. It is demonstrably untrue in the case of the oracles against the nations that can be ascribed with some probability to the prophet Jeremiah (Jer 46:3–12, 14–24; 47:2–6; 48*;

---

[136] Clearly stated by Hoffman, "From Oracle," 81; Huwyler, *Jeremia*, 274–76.
[137] As strikingly pointed out by Huwyler, *Jeremia*, 276.
[138] Höffken, "Untersuchungen," 206ff.

49:2–5, 7–11, 14–16, 23–27*, 28–33), as Huwyler has shown. It is likewise untrue of the earliest foreign nation oracles in the books of Amos and Isaiah (Amos 1:3–8, 13–2:3; Isa 14:28–32*; 17*; 18*; 19*; cf. 20:1–6). In fact, it is probably generally untrue of all preexilic prophecy of judgment.

The transition from war oracle to foreign nation oracle can be traced in the book of Isaiah during the Syro-Ephraimite war (734–732 B.C.E.). At the outset, following the tradition of court prophecy, the prophet foretold the defeat of the attacking Syro-Ephraimite coalition (Isa 7:4–8a, 9a). When Ahab rejected this indirect message of salvation, the prophet shifted to a general proclamation of judgment (7:10–14, 16–17), now including Judah. The foreign nation oracles in Isa 17:1–3, 4–6 drew the logical conclusion from this confrontation: the northern kingdom and Damascus would experience God's judgment equally.

The other foreign nation oracles that can be assigned to Isaiah all date from the period of anti-Assyrian uprisings: 727, 713–711, and 705–701 B.C.E. As can be seen from Isa 20:1–6, Isaiah issued a clear warning against an anti-Assyrian coalition under Egyptian leadership. In this context, he included Egypt (18–19*) and the Philistines (14:28–32) in the judgment threatening Jerusalem (22).[139]

In my opinion, the oracular composite Amos 1:3–2:16*, which provocatively treats Israel in the same way as its neighbors, also goes back to a Judean edition of the Amos book in the period of anti-Assyrian uprisings. Amos 1:8 speaks of a "remnant of the Philistines," presupposing at least the Assyrian campaigns against Gaza in 734 and 720. If the list of Philistine cities omits Gath because it had been taken in 711 (cf. Amos 6:2), we would find ourselves in the period of the Hezekiah uprising (705–701). The substance of individual oracles might be earlier and could go back to Amos. As Vieweger has shown, the oracle against Damascus (1:3–5), for example, refers to the weakening of Damascus's power after the campaign of Shalmaneser IV in 773, shortly before the appearance of the prophet (ca. 760).[140] This analysis refutes the major objection raised by Fritz to the authenticity of all the foreign nation oracles in the book of Amos.[141] His thesis that these oracles—apart from the generally recognized additions in 1:9–12 and 2:4–5—all date from the exilic period is contradicted by the distinctly different character of the exilic oracles against the nations.[142]

Finally, Huwyler has argued convincingly that Jeremiah's foreign nation oracles derive from precarious situations demanding critical

---

[139] On this interpretation, see Berges, *Buch Jesaja* (III.1.1), 139–50.
[140] "Zur Herkunft," 113–14.
[141] "Fremvölkersprüche."
[142] See below.

foreign-policy decisions.¹⁴³ The oracle against the Egyptians (46:1–12), for example, may be assigned to the period shortly before the battle of Carchemish (605 B.C.E.), and the oracles against the minor states of Moab (48*), Ammon (49:3–5), and Edom (49:7–11, 14–16) to the period of anti-Babylonian conspiracy in 594, when, according to 27:3, the ambassadors from Edom, Moab, Ammon, Tyre, and Sidon¹⁴⁴ were staying in Jerusalem and Jeremiah was demonstrating publicly against this coalition.

The one-sided preconception of most scholars concerning the oracles against the nations has prevented them from realizing that the use of these oracles to announce implicit salvation for Israel is probably a development of the exilic period, representing a radical shift from their preexilic function. The change came about because, when Judah lost its status as an independent state, it fell victim to the great powers and was left at the mercy of its neighbors; restitution was conceivable only through Yahweh's judgment on the nations. The developed form of this notion appears most clearly in Ezek 35–37, where oracles against Edom (35) directly precede oracles of salvation for Judah and Israel (36–37). God's judgment on the sister nation that occupied the southern portions of Judah during the exile (35:10, 12) was a necessary condition for the resettlement of the "mountains of Israel" by the exiles. A later addition (36:3–5) makes Edom the representative of all the nations that have derided Israel; it is the harbinger of the postexilic eschatological notion that only judgment on the nations can bring Israel's ultimate deliverance (cf. Ezek 38–39; Joel 4 [3]; Zech 14). This idea also stands behind the conception that brings some of the prophetic books to place the foreign nation oracles between the oracles of judgment and the oracles of salvation addressed to Israel (Isa 1–12; 13–27; 40–55; Jer 1–25; 46–51 [LXX]; 30–33; Ezek 1–24; 25–32; 35–37; [38–39]; 40ff.).

A few examples may illustrate how the function of the foreign nation oracles changed during the exilic period. The oracles against Tyre in the book of Ezekiel (Ezek 26:1–28:19) are the first example. Some closely resemble the preexilic oracles against the nations: the great dirge over the proud commercial power on the verge of destruction (27) or the taunt song against the king of Tyre, who thinks himself a god in his wisdom (28:1–10) but will be cast down like the primal man from the mountain of

---

143 *Jeremia*, 304–23.
144 Remnants of an oracle against Tyre and Sidon appear in 46:4 of the oracle against the Philistines (46:1–6); they are more clearly recognizable in the LXX text. The oracle against the Philistines may be dated originally to the time of Nebuchadnezzar's campaign against Ashdod in 604.

God (28:11–19). With a mixture of sympathy and indignation,[145] Ezekiel or his disciples used them to accompany the stubborn resistance with which the Phoenician metropolis on its island off the coast defied the thirteen-year siege of Nebuchadnezzar (probably between 585 and 572).[146] The Ezekiel group in the Babylonian golah believed that Yahweh himself had commissioned Nebuchadnezzar to subjugate the Gentile world; therefore, Tyre had to fall just as Jerusalem had fallen. There were no positive consequences for Israel. Indeed, we must remember that the Ezekiel circle interpreted Nebuchadnezzar's inability to conquer Tyre despite his best efforts to mean that Yahweh would reward the Babylonian king with the conquest of Egypt to compensate for his labors at Tyre (29:17–21); this reward seemed imminent in Nebuchadnezzar's Egyptian campaign of 568/567 B.C.E. This perspective shows that the scope of these oracles against Tyre extends far beyond Israel and its fate. In them the prophetic circle was concerned to interpret the great international goals of the Neo-Babylonian Empire from the theological premise that Yahweh alone governs history. Thus mysterious laws governing the course of history came to light. What this meant for Israel was simply that, despite all evidence to the contrary, Israel's God was still at work in world history.

By means of Ezek 26:1–5, these and similar oracles against Tyre were linked to form a composite of oracles (25:1–28:24) that is totally different in character. The aim of this composite was to show how Yahweh, through his judgment on Israel's neighbors, would deliver the "house of Israel" from their agonizing incursions and odious contempt (28:24; cf. the thematic word שׁאט in 25:6, 15; 28:24, 26). It was therefore only logical to append to the composite, probably at a later date, an oracle of salvation for Israel promising that those returning from the Diaspora would live in safety in Israel (28:25–26). These exilic oracles against the nations point unambiguously to the future salvation of Israel. The dates (after 587) of the individual oracles are hard to determine; the composite as a whole probably dates from the late exilic period.[147]

In this composite, the individual oracles are presented strictly as prophetic oracles of judgment; their motivations refer clearly to the afflictions of exilic Israel. They indict Ammon for gloating over the destruction of the Jerusalem temple, the devastation of the land, and the deportation of

---

[145] Kegler ("Leid") has shown convincingly that the foreign nation oracles are filled not only with scorn and indignation but also with sympathy and even pity for Israel's neighbors.

[146] See pp. 57–58 above.

[147] Fechter (Bewältigung, 295) proposes the early postexilic period following the return, but this was a fairly long period (539–520), and the foreign nation oracles still refer clearly to the afflictions of the exile.

the "house of Israel" (Ezek 25:3); they accuse Moab of declaring that the elect status of Israel has been abrogated (25:8); they charge Edom with unrestrained vengeance and Philistia with unending hostility (25:12, 15). Finally, they accuse Tyre of seeking ruthlessly to exploit Jerusalem's elimination from international trade (26:2). The extent to which these accusations are justified is not entirely clear. That the Judeans were exposed during the exilic period to incursions of their neighbors, especially population pressure from Edom, and to the economic hegemony of the Phoenicians is well attested.[148] As actually stated, however, the charges—especially in the oracles against Ammon and Moab—sound more like expressions of deeply wounded Judean self-esteem. After their devastating military defeat, the Judeans suffered from the loss of their previous equality with their neighbors, the more so because these nations, former allies in an anti-Babylonian coalition, now refused solidarity and exploited Judah's weakness to their own advantage. In the eyes of the exilic prophetic circle, the judgment of Yahweh proclaimed in the oracles against the nations would restore just equality between Israel and its neighbors. Therefore, these oracles end on a surprisingly conciliatory note: the judgment of Yahweh will bring all Israel's neighbors—except Edom— to the knowledge of Yahweh (25:5, 7, 11, 17; 26:6; 29:22, 23, 24), just as Yahweh's judgment on Israel had done and as Yahweh's deliverance of Israel was about to do.

The oracles against Edom are a second example. Not only can they be dated with some accuracy, but they also contain clear references to the *Sitz im Leben* of the oracles against the nations during the exilic period. The oracles of Jeremiah against Edom in Jer 49:7–12 and 14–16, most likely associated with the anti-Babylonian conspiracy of 594 B.C.E.,[149] still bear the marks of preexilic oracles against the nations: Jeremiah accuses the Edomites of having lost their vaunted wisdom (49:7) and of finding security in a fools' paradise (49:16); he foretells total devastation for their land. The accusations have nothing to do with Israel, and the motifs in the announcement of judgment parallel what Jeremiah proclaimed to Judah in the same situation. Like Judah, Edom is warned not to revolt against Babylonia. To embody his message, Jeremiah adapts the familiar sapiential principle that "pride goes before a fall" (49:16).

---

148 On the meddling of Ammon, see Jer 40:14 and 41:10; on Edom's territorial claims, see Ezek 35:10, 12 and 36:5; on the expansion of the Phoenician sphere of influence, see Hans-Peter Müller, "Phönikien und Juda in der exilischen-nachexilischen Zeit," WO 6 (1970): 189–204. There remains only the question of how evident or at least foreseeable the economic competition already was in 587, the date of the oracle against Tyre (Ezek 26:1).

149 On their extent and date, see Huwyler, *Jeremia*, 207–233.

Remarkably, Jeremiah's oracles against Edom have been incorporated into Obad 1–14, 15b (vv. 1–5*) and expanded.[150] The expansion in verses 8–14 clearly includes new features. Not only is Edom charged categorically with the slaughter and violence done to its brother Jacob (vv. 9–10); it is also accused specifically of making common cause with the Babylonians on the day of Jerusalem's fall (vv. 11–12), gloating over the Judeans (v. 12), looting their goods (v. 13), and killing or handing over the fugitives (v. 14). These accusations point clearly to the early exilic period. Whether they are justified in this sweeping and general form is dubious, since no other text mentions any Edomite participation in the conquest of Jerusalem; Jer 40:11, furthermore, indicates that Judean refugees had found sanctuary in Edom.[151] However, these charges cannot come out of thin air; otherwise the hatred of Edom rampant since the exile would be inexplicable. These "brothers," with whom Judeans felt close ties despite the ups and downs of their common history, had changed sides in the hour of Judah's greatest need, collaborated with the Babylonians, and shamelessly exploited the weakness of Judah; this betrayal left the Judeans immensely embittered. In this new situation, the oracle against the nations became a medium of retaliation against a superior opponent, invulnerable in the political arena. Thus the judgment of God proclaimed by Jeremiah took on a new function: it avenged the wrong done the Judeans by the Edomites (Obad 15b). In the light of this new function of the oracle, it was only logical that later—probably postexilic—expansions should connect judgment on Edom with salvation for Jerusalem (vv. 15a, 16–18) and Judah (vv. 19–21).

Now there is some evidence to support Wolff's thesis that Obad 1–14, 15b represents the message of a cult prophet in the context of a liturgical lament memorializing the conquest of Jerusalem.[152] The beginning changes the Jeremiah text by substituting the first-person plural for the first-person singular, so that the speaker expresses solidarity with the congregation (Obad 1). Other features include the consistent treatment of the oracle as a divine utterance, the הֲלוֹא questions expecting assent ("would they not"/"will I not"; vv. 5, 8), and the repeated mention of the specific day on which Edom's transgressions took place (vv. 11–14). The expletives against Edom in verses 5, 6, 7bβ that interrupt the prophet's words

---

[150] Obad 15a, which extends the conflict with Edom to the "day of Yahweh against all nations," links the text to the subsequent expansions in vv. 16–18 and 20–21; cf. Wolff, *Dodekapropheton 3*, 19ff.

[151] As stressed (probably too strongly) by Bartlett, *Edom*, 156–57.

[152] *Dodekapropheton 3*.

addressed to Edom could be stylized interjections of the congregation. The introductory message formula, which might speak against a cultic *Sitz im Leben*, is clearly redactional.[153]

It is interesting that in this liturgical situation earlier unrealized oracles concerning Edom have been incorporated, albeit removed from their original setting and thus made anonymous. That it was Jeremiah who had uttered these oracles made no difference in a cultic context. In the Israelite cult, as in present-day Christian worship, there was no such thing as "intellectual property." The historical allusions in the concluding topical application suggest that the message of the cult prophet most likely dates from the early exilic period.[154]

Scholars have suggested repeatedly that the foreign nation oracles originated in cult prophecy or had as their *Sitz im Leben* a liturgical fast, where they served as a response to a communal lament.[155] However, the texts that can be cited for such a role are all exilic at the earliest (Pss 60; 137; Lam 4:21-22; 2 Kgs 19:21-28). Since the cultic use of a foreign nation oracle presupposes its function as an indirect message of salvation for Israel, which must be considered the real response to the lament of the community,[156] and since the foreign nation oracle probably did not acquire this function until the exilic period, all the evidence suggests that it did not become part of the cult (by way of liturgical lamentation) until that era.

The oracles against Edom may be used to illusrate this conclusion. Psalm 60, an exilic communal lament, cites an earlier war oracle, probably from the time of Josiah, in which Yahweh celebrates his victory over Judah's neighbors, including Edom (60:8-11 [6-9]). This oracle was originally set in the context of a royal prayer during a campaign against the Edomites; the prayer was also included in the psalm (60:11-13, 7 [9-11, 5]). By recollecting this earlier war oracle from Yahweh, which is closely

---

153 Cf. the unusual naming of the addressee ("to Edom") in the messenger formula, which turns it into a superscription, and the conflict with the first line of the oracle, which speaks of Yahweh in the third person.

154 Cf. Obad 11-14. Verse 7 poses a problem for an early exilic date. If we take into account Edom's complicity with the Babylonians in the conquest of Jerusalem (v. 11), the announcement that Edom will fall victim to the faithlessness of its allies would argue most strongly for a Babylonian assault on Edom. The most likely occasion would be Nebuchadnezzar's campaign in 582 against Moab and Ammon, recorded by Josephus (*Ant*. 10.181). However, there is some doubt about the historicity of this campaign (see p. 56 above). The only other possibility would by the campaign of Nabonidus in 553/552, which Bartlett (*Edom*, 159) now associates with Obad 7. Acceptance of this association would require dating Obad 1-4, 15b in the later exilic period.

155 Gunkel and Begrich, *Introduction* (III.1.1), 96-97; Hayes, "Usage," 87-89; etc.

156 See below.

related to the foreign nation oracle, the exilic community could shore up their confidence that, despite their political impotence, they were not helplessly exposed to the incursions of their neighbors, especially Edom. This example illustrates how, in the exilic context of liturgical lamentation, foreign nation oracles could serve to strengthen the Judeans' drive for self-preservation against their encroaching neighbors, even when they did not yet have the benefit of a clear oracle of salvation from Yahweh. That oracles against Edom played a particularly important role in exilic observances commemorating the conquest of Jerusalem is indicated by the imprecations in Lam 4:21–22 and Ps 137:7. It is quite possible that Obad 1–14, 15b originated as an oracle for such an occasion.[157] The extent to which other exilic oracles against Edom (Ezek 25:12–14; 35:1–15; Amos 1:11–12) or other neighboring peoples had or were given a cultic *Sitz im Leben* needs further study.[158]

If the reconstruction [... URU*A*]-*du-um-mu* in Chronicle 7, 1.17 is correct,[159] Nabonidus conducted a campaign against Edom in 553/552 in which Edom lost its political independence. This led to its economic and political decline, until it was eclipsed by the Arabs in the middle of the fifth century B.C.E. (cf. Geshem the Arab in Neh 2:19; 6:1, 2, 6). Malachi 1:2–5 paints a vivid picture of the destruction of Edom in the first half of the fourth century. Edom's slow decline was followed with rapt attention by the postexilic foreign nation oracles (Obad 16–18,[160] 19–21; Amos 9:12; Isa 34; 63:1–6). They tended to stylize Edom increasingly as the representative of all the Israel's enemies (Ezek 35:3–5; Obad 16–18), first placing it in parallel with Babylon (Jer 49:12–13, 17–18, 19–22) and then even substituting it for Babylon (Isa 34).

The oracles against Babylon are a third example. Far more than the Edom oracles, they play a special role among the foreign nation oracles. In Isa 13–14 and 21, they bracket the collection of foreign nation oracles in

---

157 Evidence for cultic use of oracles against Babylon appears in Jer 51:34–37, 51–53.

158 Höffken ("Untersuchungen," 180–205) sought to show that the oracles motivated by invective against Yahweh or Israel were most likely to have a cultic *Sitz im Leben*. It is probably true that the motif of abuse by the enemy is common in exilic communal laments (cf. Pss 44:14–15, 17 [13–14, 16]; 74:10, 22–23; 79:4, 12; 89:42, 51–52 [41, 50–51]; Lam 5:1), but the question whether specific foreign nation oracles originated in a cultic setting or are purely literary creations requires new study of specific texts.

159 Grayson, *Assyrian and Babylonian Chronicles* (II.1), 105.

160 Dicou (*Edom*, 69ff., 97–98) attempts to connect the later redactional stratum of the oracle against Edom in Obad 16–18 and Jer 49:12–13 with Nabonidus's campaign of 553/552. Both texts are dependent on the vision of the cup of wrath in Jer 25:15ff.; Jer 49:12–13 is also dependent on the secondary "refusal of the cup" scene in 25:27–29. Therefore, at least 49:12–13 must be postexilic. Cf. Huwyler, *Jeremia*, 328–29, 358–61.

the book of Isaiah; in Jer 50–51, they conclude the collection of foreign nation oracles in the book of Jeremiah and are almost as extensive as all the oracles concerning other nations put together. Finally, there is the lengthy poem in Isa 47. These oracles occupy this prominent position because Babylonia was the conquering power that had destroyed Jerusalem and had deported a portion of the Judean population. As such, in the postexilic period Babylon—far more than Edom—became the prototype of the hostile Gentile world. With some likelihood, we can assign Isa 13:17–22a;[161] 21:1–10; 46:1–4; 47:1–5*;[162] and most of Jer 50 and 51[163] to the exilic period, particularly the late years between 542 and 520. It is noteworthy that the book of Ezekiel contains no oracles against Babylon.

We must recall that the collapse of the Neo-Babylonian Empire was quite undramatic. After defeating the Babylonians at Opis at the beginning of October in 539, the Persians entered Babylonia on the twelfth of October without encountering major resistance. On the twenty-ninth of October, when Cyrus rode in triumph into the capital, a large fraction of the Babylonian establishment greeted him as a liberator. Therefore, there could be no talk of a fall or even a punishment of Babylon. Quite the contrary: Cyrus promoted the cult of Marduk and made Babylon one of the four capitals of his empire. Only during the reign of Cambyses (530–522) did the relationship between the Babylonians and the Persians sour. The fall of 522 and the summer of 521 saw two anti-Persian uprisings in Babylon that Darius had to quell by force. Around 482, new uprisings forced Xerxes to take harsher punitive actions against Babylon, to which a statue of Marduk in Esagila probably fell victim. However, the city and the temple of Marduk clearly remained intact during the following period. The importance of the city did not begin to diminish until the Hellenistic period, after the Seleucids founded their new capital of Seleucia, near modern Baghdad, around 300.

---

161 For the literary identification of the earliest portion of Isa 13, see Zapff, *Schriftgelehrte Prophetie*, 228–39.

162 See Oorschot, *Von Babel* (III.2.7), 152–59; Berges, *Buch Jesaja* (III.1.1), 154–59, 228–39.

163 See Hartberger, "An den Wassern," (III.1.1), 16–133. According to the account in Jer 51:59–64, a written copy of Jeremiah's oracles against Babylon was given to Seraiah ben Neriah when he accompanied King Zedekiah to Babylon in the year 594. Jeremiah ordered Seraiah to read them aloud in Babylon and, in a symbolic action, to tie a stone to them and drop them in the Euphrates. Historically, however, this episode is quite unlikely, since at the same time Jeremiah wrote a letter to the Babylonian golah telling them to prepare for a long stay (Jer 29:1–7). Such a public reading, which the Babylonians would have been unlikely to stand for, would have run counter to his own goal of dampening the hopes for return rampant among the exiles. We must therefore consider the account unhistorical. It is an attempt to ascribe to Jeremiah the oracles against Babylon, which are too late to be his, and to incorporate them into his book. See pp. 318–21 below.

There is only a single oracle against Babylon in the style of the preexilic foreign nation oracles, its perspective limited entirely to judgment on the foreign nation. In the immediate future—so Isa 13:17–22a proclaims in the form of an unmotivated announcement of disaster—Yahweh will stir up the fierce Medes (13:17–18); then Babylon, the "glory of kingdoms" (13:19), will suffer a fate as terrible as that suffered by the legendary cities of Sodom and Gomorrah. Only the insistence on total destruction of the proud metropolis, making it uninhabitable for all time, shows that the Babylonians are not some arbitrary foreign nation. Here we see the violent retribution of the helpless victims who had been forced to suffer the destructive power of the world empire. Since the prophecy totally ignores the actual course of historical events, it was probably uttered shortly before the end of the Neo-Babylonian Empire, when it was already evident that the chain of victories of Cyrus—who had already conquered the Median Empire in 500 and the Lydian Empire in 547/546—was unstoppable.[164]

Either by themselves or redactionally, all other oracles against Babylon refer to the deliverance of Israel from the Babylonian exile, thus constituting an important albeit frequently overlooked part of the late exilic message of salvation.

The oracle in Isa 21:1–10 bears the superscription מַשָּׂא, "utterance, burden," common in the collection of foreign nation oracles in the book of Isaiah. Formally, it is a complex account of a vision in which the description of what is seen in the vision (21:1*, 2*, 5, 8b) is interwoven skillfully with the account of the actual vision and audition (21:2*, 3, 6–8a, 9). The prophet describes in the first person how he saw a whirlwind advancing from the south (21:1), how he heard God's battle orders to Elam and Media (21:2) and then saw the Babylonian officers called to arms in the midst of a festive banquet (21:5), and finally how God involved him personally in these events: he was to post a lookout to observe troop movements (21:6–7). When the lookout had reported for duty and seen the advancing warriors (21:8), he proclaimed the crucial news to the prophet and all who might hear: Babylon has fallen, and all the images of its gods lie shattered (21:9). Only twice is this vivid account associated

---

[164] Zapff, *Schriftgelehrte Prophetie*, 169–71. Isa 13:17 as well as Isa 21:2 and Jer 51:11, 28 name the Medes rather than the Persians as the conquerors of the Neo-Babylonian Empire. This error does not betray ignorance of the historical situation. First, the two nations were closely related; second, the Medes, who had already established a mighty empire during the seventh century, were more ready to hand for formulating oracles from the perspective of Isaiah and Jeremiah. The foreign nation oracles mention the Persians only in Ezek 27:10 and 38:5, and then only as mercenaries in the armies of other nations, not as conquerors.

directly with the fate of Zion. There is a veiled allusion in 21:2: God motivates his command to Babylon's enemies by saying "her sighing" has come to an end. The identify of "her" is clear from the conclusion in 21:10, where the prophet turns to comfort Zion, tenderly calling the city "my threshed and winnowed one," in wordplay on the meaning of צִיּוֹן, "dry place." Yahweh will put an end to the sighing of threshed Jerusalem through the conquest of Babylon. Since the prophet addresses his listeners directly at the conclusion, we can say with certainty that this oracle was proclaimed publicly, probably on Mount Zion. Given its form, even an actual performance with dramatic voices or assigned roles is conceivable. As to its date, we may consider the final years of the Neo-Babylonian Empire, since "Media" and "Elam" can well refer obliquely to the Persian Empire. Hopes were rampant then among the Judeans for a possible regime change in far-off Mesopotamia. The function of this oracle was to reinforce these hopes through a "proleptic experience."

The extended oracle against Babylon in Deutero-Isaiah, Isa 47:1–15,[165] is more traditional in structure and again more focused on the fall of Babylon, but of course it is a part of Deutero-Isaiah's message of liberation; in the overall composition, it has a counterpart in the raising of Zion from the dust (52:1–2). In the first section (47:1–5), virgin Babylon, the "mistress of kingdoms" (47:5), who has hitherto enjoyed the luxurious position of a delicate and pampered queen, is ordered peremptorily by Yahweh to degrade herself to the status of a slave or a disgraced refugee. Here the foreign nation oracle clearly displays its ever-present magical overtones: the spell virtually conjures up the fall of Babylon. Then in 47:6–7 follows the accusation and in 8–11 the announcement of judgment together with additional accusations, as in prophetic judgment oracles: despite its wealth of sorceries and enchantments, Babylon faces ineluctable ruin. When 47:12–15 reiterate and amplify the accusation and announcement of judgment, challenging once again the helpless Babylonian sorcerers and omen experts, we have evidence of the conflict over God's governance of history, a conflict of deep concern to the Deutero-Isaiah group. Unlike the brief announcements in 13:19 and 21:9, the oracle in Isa 47 displays some knowledge of Babylonian civilization and a certain involvement with Babylon's fate. These features argue for an origin within the Babylonian golah.

In Isa 47, the connection with Israel appears in the accusation. It is not just Babylon's wisdom and magical expertise (47:10), her delusions of security (47:7, 8), and the hubris with which she claims absolute

---

[165] The earlier nucleus is found in 47:1–2, 5–8a, 10–15; see pp. 416–17 below.

uniqueness (47:8, 10), but also her merciless treatment of Israel (47:6) that now bring her downfall. The argument is nuanced: it is true that God was angry with Israel and therefore gave it into the hand of the Babylonians, but the Babylonian Empire showed the defeated no mercy and even imposed forced labor on the aged. Thus God's judgment on Babylon became a kind of vengeance (נָקָם: 47:3b) for the wrong done Israel, as the later expansion of the text explicitly states.

The motif of Yahweh's vengeance on Babylon, mentioned only once in the prophecy of Deutero-Isaiah, now becomes a kind of *cantus firmus* in the sweeping composite of oracles against Babylon in Jer 50–51 (נְקָמָה: Jer 50:15, 28, 34; 51:6, 11, 36), along with the motif of retribution (שׁלם *pi'el*, גְּמֻלוֹת: 50:29; 51:24, 56; cf. 51:35, 48). The kings of Media (5:11, 28) or the nations of the north (50:3, 9; 51:27, 48; echoing the language of Jeremiah's prophecy [cf. Jer 4–6; 46:6, 10]) will inflict Yahweh's revenge and retribution on Babylon, not only for the wrong it has committed (50:15), but above all for its violation of the Jerusalem temple (51:11), evidence of Babylon's arrogant defiance of Yahweh himself (50:29). For long years, Yahweh employed Babylon as his hammer to shatter nations and kingdoms; now Yahweh will repay Babylon for the wrong it did to Zion (51:20–24).

The extended collection contains some evidence that at least portions were recited publicly at everyday assemblies or on liturgical occasions. The conclusion of the "hammer poem" (Jer 51:20–24), for example, addresses an audience. Here, as in Isa 21:1–10, one might picture an actual staging. In Jer 51:34–37, a lament of Zion with a plea for retribution is followed by an oracle from Yahweh foretelling salvation for Zion and disaster for Babylon. In 51:51–53, a formally correct communal lament over the desecration of the temple is followed by an oracle against Babylon. Jeremiah 50:28 speaks of "the vengeance of Yahweh our God." Finally, we recall the shout of praise interjected by the congregation in 51:10. All this evidence points to a cultic setting. Even if the text is a literary imitation or stylization, it is quite likely that foreign nation oracles against Babylon were uttered in the context of the late exilic Judean cult.

However, we must ask how a single event, hardly imaginable more than a few years before, could spawn such an extensive tradition of Babylon oracles. The conclusion is inescapable: probably most of the oracles against Babylon came into being after 539 and were employed for years in secular or sacred convocations. Two considerations make this assumption plausible. First, Babylon was most certainly not destroyed in 539; the just vengeance that the Judeans had every right to expect from Yahweh was still to come. Second, the return of the exiles did not take place, as expected, immediately after 539. The first substantial group of returnees probably did not arrive in Jerusalem until 520 B.C.E. Many members of the

Babylonian golah clearly could not recognize the uneventful transfer of power from the Babylonians to the Persians as a sign from God that a new age had dawned. In this situation, the reuse and repeated recitation of oracles against Babylon after 539 were meant to provoke Yahweh's long-awaited retribution on Babylon, which would show to all the world that Yahweh was at work in world history as a just judge. As the many calls to flee from Babylon (Jer 50:8–10; 51:6, 45, 50) show, these oracles were also intended to persuade the Babylonian golah finally to return, since Yahweh's judgment on Babylon was imminent. When 50:33 says that those who had deported the people of Israel and Judah would refuse to let them go, and when 51:33 says that in "just a little while" (עוֹד מְעַט) the time of harvest would come for Babylon, we can hear a direct reference to the problems that arose after 539: the failure of the golah to return and the delay of God's judgment.

Gosse[166] and Berges[167] propose dating the Babylon oracles in Isa 13–14 and Isa 47 in the years 522–520. Whether this dating is correct for Isa 47 is uncertain.[168] However, substantial evidence supports dating much of the Babylon composite Jer 50–51 in this period. These years are particularly likely because from 522 to 520, after the murder of Gaumata, an epidemic of revolts against Darius convulsed the entire central and eastern region of the Persian Empire.[169] Babylon played a leading role in these revolts. Two revolts immediately broke out in Babylon: in the fall of 522 and the summer of 521; Darius was finally able to put them down, but only by large-scale military intervention.[170] It is likely, therefore, that the people in Judah saw the hoped-for judgment of Yahweh on Babylon actually taking place in this period and accompanied it with public recitation of foreign

---

[166] *Isaïe 13,1–14,23*, 271–72.

[167] *Buch Jesaja* (III.1.1), 363–64.

[168] It depends on how one understands the genesis of the book of Deutero-Isaiah, over which opinions differ (see pp. 391–93, 416–17 below). It is more likely that Isa 47 derives from outsiders associated with the Deutero-Isaiah group, since important elements of that group's theology are absent, such as Yahweh's governance of history. But that does not demand a diachronic explanation. The fact that the judgment announced in the text did not take place when Cyrus conquered Babylon does not necessarily argue for a pre-539 date, although it may. The text does not treat God's delayed judgment as a problem.

[169] See pp. 116–18 above.

[170] The concluding oracle, Jer 51:58, announces the destruction of Babylon's walls and gates (cf. Hab 2:13). According to Herodotus (*Hist.* 3.159), that is what Darius actually did when he put down these revolts. This would give us a date around 521 as a *terminus ante quem* for the completion of the composite. However, since the inscriptions of Darius do not confirm this destruction, there may be confusion with the punitive campaigns of Xerxes around 482. If so, the composite Jer 50–51 would not have been completed until some forty years later.

nation oracles. Now the long-awaited epoch had come; now it was finally time to return![171]

The retribution theology of the oracles against Babylon, offensive to modern ears, is eminently comprehensible from this perspective. The Judean theologians took up a prominent theme of their age: we may recall that Babylonian court theologians had taken the theologoumenon "Marduk's vengeance for Babylon" (i.e., divine wrath over the appalling devastation of the city and its temple wrought by the Assyrian king Sennacherib in the year 689) and made it the foundation myth of the Neo-Babylonian Empire.[172] They also persisted in their belief that there must be equitable compensation in history if Yahweh does in fact govern the history of the world. The destruction and plunder that Babylon, "the hammer of the whole earth" (Jer 50:23), had inflicted not only on Judah but also on other nations (51:25, 44) simply could not go unexpiated. Without such a caesura, the dawn of a new era in world history was simply inconceivable. Finally, we must remember that the Judeans, unlike the Babylonians, had no military forces ready to lend substance to their retribution theology. It was and always would be Yahweh's vengeance that the impotent people called for in their foreign nation oracles. However, this harsh theology of retribution certainly did have political consequences: the clear theological dissociation of the Judeans from the rebellious Babylonians helped make the Judeans trustworthy in Darius's eyes and reinforced the loyalty of the Judeans to the Persians.[173] The opportunity for long and productive cooperation lay open, with the result that there are no oracles against the Persians in the Old Testament.

---

171 Finally, the oracles in Jer 50–51 support in their own way the negotiations with the Persians in 521 that led to the return and the rebuilding of the temple (see pp. 125–26 above), as the Deutero-Isaiah group did in a different way with the composition and recitation of their prophecy in the same period.

172 See p. 51 above.

173 This is also the reason why the most extensive collection of oracles against Babylon appears in the book of Jeremiah, even though large sections of it are pro-Babylonian (Jer 25:1–11; 27–29; 39–43). With their reservations about a restoration on the preexilic model, the Deuteronomistic tradents of the book of Jeremiah or their successors urged loyal cooperation with the Persians (see pp. 325–27, 331–32 below). This about-face from the pro-Babylonian option to the anti-Babylonian option was supported theologically by the idea that Yahweh had given world dominion to "his servant" Nebuchadnezzar for only three generations (Jer 27:7) or seventy years (25:11–12; 29:10), after which the Babylonians likewise would reap the reward of their deeds and lose their political independence (25:12–14). If, as Jer 25:1 suggests, this period began with the fourth year of Jehoiakim (605), the year of Nebuchadnezzar's accession, then Babylonian hegemony ended in 535, four years before its actual historical end. In that year at the latest the tradents saw the possibility of a political reorientation (see p. 343 below).

III.1.5. "Sermons"

Gerstenberger, Erhard. "Predigt II. Altes Testament," *TRE* 27:231–35. **Jeremias,** Jörg. *The Book of Amos: A Commentary* (trans. D. W. Stott; OTL; Louisville: Westminster John Knox, 1998). **Köhler,** Ludwig. *Hebrew Man: With an Appendix on Justice in the Gate* (trans. P. R. Ackroyd; London: SCM, 1956). **Mathias,** Dietmar. "'Levitische Predigt' und Deuteronomismus," *ZAW* 94 (1984): 23–49. **Nicholson,** Ernest W. *Preaching to the Exiles: A Study in the Prose Tradition in the Book of Jeremiah* (Oxford: Blackwell, 1970). **Rad,** Gerhard von. "Die levitische Predigt in den Büchern der Chronik," in idem, *Gesammelte Studien zum Alten Testament* (2 vols.; TB 8, 48; Munich: Kaiser, 1958–73), 1:248–61. **Rad.** *Studies in Deuteronomy* (trans. D. Stalker; London: SCM, 1953). **Raitt,** Thomas M. "The Prophetic Summons to Repentance," *ZAW* 83 (1971): 30–49. **Tångberg,** K. Arvid. *Die prophetische Mahnrede* (FRLANT 143; Göttingen: Vandenhoeck & Ruprecht, 1987). **Thiel,** Winfried. *Die deuteronomistische Redaktion von Jeremia 1–25* (WMANT 41; Neukirchen-Vluyn: Neukirchener Verlag, 1973). **Weinfeld,** Moshe. *Deuteronomy and the Deuteronomic School* (Oxford: Clarendon, 1972). **Weippert,** Helga. *Die Prosareden des Jeremiabuches* (BZAW 132; Berlin: de Gruyter, 1973).

Besides the poetic genres already discussed, prose discourses came to play an increasingly important role during the exilic period; they are often parenetic in content and sometimes in style. They regularly address a group in the second-person plural. Typically they include appeals to hear, admonitions and warnings, and accusations (sometimes referring to past history), as well as conditional announcements of salvation and disaster (Jer 7:1–15; 17:19–27; 22:1–5; 42:10–17; 1 Kgs 9:1–7; Amos 4:4–13). Closer to pastoral instruction are Ezek 14:1–11; 18; 33:10–20, sometimes impersonal in style and related to the casuistry of sacral law. Whether to assign these and other discourses (such as Deut 4 and 30:15–20) to a "sermon" genre distinct from the prophetic oracle of judgment is a matter of scholarly debate.

Köhler introduced the term "sermon" to describe Deut 4:1, 6–8 in the year 1930/1931.[174] He understood it as denoting a particular textual style developed by the Jerusalem priesthood during the seventh century, following on eighth-century prophecy; this style is particularly common in the prose discourses of Deuteronomy. Von Rad used the term "sermon" in 1934, but not at that time to denote a genre. In his opinion, these discourses were the work of the Levites. Since Neh 8:7–8 assigns the duty of instructing the people in the law in a liturgical setting to the Levites, who also served as itinerant preachers, they were responsible not only for the

---

[174] *Hebrew Man*, 168–70.

many sermons in Chronicles (1 Chr 28:2–10; 2 Chr 15:2–7; 29:5–11; 30:6–9; etc.) but also for the discourses introducing and concluding Deuteronomy (Deut 6–11 and 28–31);[175] he therefore called this genre the "Levitical sermon."[176] Von Rad's theory won general acceptance but has recently encountered substantial resistance. Mathias has shown that Levitical "preaching" dates to the period of the Chronicler's History at the earliest (fourth or third century)[177] and that the parenetic discourses in question are not "real sermons, reproduced here."[178] Above all, the Deuteronom(ist)ic style "is not the style of a genre but of a period or an era, and can also be the style of a particular group."[179] Against attempts to interpret the prose discourses in the book of Jeremiah as sermonic, either in general[180] or in particular (Jer 7:1–15; 17:19–27; 22:1–5),[181] Weippert has pointed out that, like the poetic oracles, they also claim to be the word of Yahweh.[182]

However, these criticisms may themselves be criticized. In response to Weippert, it must be said that every sermon preached claims to be the word of God. In addition, her argument depends on the questionable assumption that the prose discourses are not the work of later redactors, as is generally held, but of Jeremiah. Mathias is correct in claiming that nowhere in Chronicles or elsewhere in the Old Testament do we find sermons that were actually delivered. It is nevertheless quite possible and, in the light of the evidence, not unlikely that the Deuteronomic and "prophetic" discourses reflect a rhetorical style actually used in Judah during the seventh and sixth centuries.[183] But the term "sermon" should not be understood too narrowly after the Protestant model. For example, the prose discourses mentioned above are for the most part not liturgical in nature. If, however, we take the term in the broader sense of a religious address to a community, then it is certainly appropriate. Gerstenberger argues for retaining it, since it is also sociohistorically useful: "the 'sermon' is a new genre that reflects the new structure of the 'religious community.'"[184] The whole area deserves a new study.

---

175 *Studies*, 66–69.
176 "Levitische Predigt," 258.
177 Mathias, "Levitische Predigt," 29–34.
178 Ibid., 43.
179 Ibid., 49.
180 Nicholson, *Preaching*, 116.
181 Thiel, *Deuteronomistische Redaktion*, 190–95.
182 *Prosareden*, 230–33.
183 Cf. the public recitations of the Deuteronomic law presupposed in 2 Kgs 23:2–3 and Deut 31:9–13.
184 "Predigt II," 234.

In view of the form-critical uncertainty, here we shall take as examples just two texts that can be considered "sermons" in the broader sense of the word and can be dated with some assurance in the exilic period. The first example is the "either/or sermon" identified by Thiel[185] in Jer 7:1–5; 17:19–27; 22:1–5 (cf. also Jer 42:10–17 and 1 Kgs 9:1–7). Apart from the messenger instructions ("Go and say") and the messenger formula that identify the situation, the sermon consists of an appeal to hear the word of Yahweh (Jer 7:2; 17:20; 22:2), a plural salutation, and admonitions or warnings (7:3–4; 17:21; 22:3), leading up to a conditional announcement of salvation (אם + consecutive perfect) in the event of obedience (7:3b, 5–7; 17:24–26; 22:4; 42:10–12) and a conditional announcement of disaster (אם לא + consecutive perfect) in the event of disobedience (17:27; 22:5; 42:13–16; cf. 7:8–12. 14–15). Like "real" sermons, all three addresses are based on "texts": 7:1–15 on Jeremiah's temple oracle (7:4, 9–12, 14*; cf. 26:4–5); 17:19–27 on exilic commandments governing the Sabbath (17:22; cf. Deut 5:12, 14); and 22:1–5 on Jeremiah's admonition to the house of David (21:12; cf. 23:3aβ). The oracle of Jeremiah on which 42:10–17 is based appears in 42:17. In addition to these formal parallels, all three addresses are delivered in the gate—whether of the temple (7:2), the city (17:19), or the palace (22:2)—the typical place for the legal assembly or the populace to gather; there is thus some reason to believe that they reflect an actual mode of preaching in the exilic period. It is important to note, though, that these "sermons" are not liturgical discourses: Jer 17 and 22 are delivered in totally secular settings; although Jer 7 takes place at the temple gate, it addresses people just arriving to participate in the cult.

According to Thiel, all the either/or sermons belong to the Deuteronomistic redaction of the book of Jeremiah, dating from about 550 B.C.E.[186] Formally, the Deuteronomistic disciples of Jeremiah borrowed the style of Deuteronomic parenesis, which likewise presented admonitions to obey Yahweh's commandments and warnings against disobedience and apostasy as alternatives, associated with conditional promises of salvation or disaster (cf. Deut 8:11–20; 11:8–17; 28; 30:15–20).[187] However,

---

185 *Deuteronomistische Redaktion*, 290–95.

186 This conclusion is modified on pp. 312ff. below: Jer 7:1–15 and 22:1–5 belong to the first Deuteronomistic redaction (ca. 550) and 42:10–17 to the second (ca. 540); 17:19–27 belongs to a late Deuteronomistic redaction and therefore dates from the postexilic period (fifth century). All these redactions, however, move within the same literary tradition.

187 The presentation of conditional announcements of salvation and disaster as alternatives ultimately derives from ancient Near Eastern international treaties, whose rhetoric the Deuteronomic reformers often borrowed (Weinfeld, *Deuteronomy*, 59–157). We also note prophetic admonitions (Amos 5:4, 6; Isa 8:12; Hos 14:2–9 [1–8]; Jer 3:22; 4:3; etc.; cf. Raitt, "Prophetic Summons," 34–35; Tångberg, *Prophetische Mahnrede*, 140ff.) and sapiential

they turned this style into a compact parenetic form, pithily contrasting right and wrong behavior. What is new is that for them the criterion of what was required and what was to be eschewed was no longer just the Mosaic torah but also and above all the proclamation of Jeremiah, which they cited, interpreted, and applied to the present. Thus the either/or sermon can be considered a noncultic rhetorical form in which Jeremiah's prophecy of judgment was received and interpreted during the exilic period.

The example of Jer 7:1–5 may illustrate briefly how this took place. At the beginning of their "sermon," the Deuteronomistic promoters of Jeremiah's prophecy placed an admonition of deep concern to them, here and elsewhere: all those addressed must fundamentally amend their ways and their doings (7:3a; cf. 18:11; 26:13; 35:15). They immediately linked this admonition with a conditional promise: Yahweh would then allow them to dwell "in this place" (7:3).[188] This meant concretely that he would protect them from further deportations. We may recall that those left behind had to suffer another such deportation in 582. The Deuteronomistic disciples of Jeremiah derived this positive alternative from the message of their master: since Jeremiah had proclaimed that the destruction of the temple and the land had been brought about by the social and religious misconduct of the people (7:9, 14), it followed that God's judgment would come to an end only if the whole nation was open to social and religious renewal.

The preachers believed that Jeremiah had also stated the negative alternative. Thus they finally came to their "text": they cited Jeremiah's blunt warning against misplaced trust in the temple (7:4). Thus they were in a position to cut the ground from under an attitude among the exiles that expected rebuilding the temple to provide the critical opportunity for a new beginning. If trusting in the temple was an illusion in Jeremiah's time, it could not be correct in the preachers' day. Zion theology had proved false; the only possible alternative—the preachers reiterated in a lengthy conditional promise (7:5–7)—must be a profound religious and ethical renewal of the people, meaning proper conduct within the community, protection of the weak, and rejection of all kinds of syncretism.

---

admonitions (Prov 1:8–19; 2:8–19; 3:1–12; etc.), which likewise are often motivated by conditional promises.

[188] The reading of the MT is correct; cf. the use of "in the land that I gave to your ancestors forever and ever" to interpret בַּמָּקוֹם הַזֶּה "in this place," in the promise presented by 7:7. The Deuteronomistic interpreters extended "this place," by which Jeremiah had meant the temple (cf. 12), to the land of Judah; the reading of Aquila and the Vulgate ("then I will dwell with you in this place") shows that they did not understand this extension.

In contrast to Jer 17 and 22, the Deuteronomistic preachers in Jer 7 did not proclaim the negative alternative in the form of a conditional announcement of disaster; instead, they paraphrased Jeremiah's famous oracle of judgment on the Jerusalem temple (7:9–12, 14*), which had provoked such furor at the beginning of Jehoiakim's reign (609 B.C.E.; cf. Jer 26). By means of the transitional 7:8, they created a timely connection: insofar as their listeners still based their hopes on the temple, they were acting just like their ancestors, who thought that they could cover up their social and religious misconduct in everyday life by devout participation in the temple cult. Thus these ancestors had already turned the Jerusalem temple into a den of robbers (7:9–11). It was therefore only logical that Yahweh should proclaim through Jeremiah the destruction of his sanctuary (7:12–14). The Deuteronomistic preachers continued to proclaim the already-realized message of Jeremiah concerning the Jerusalem temple but gave it a future orientation and expanded it to proclaim Yahweh's even more comprehensive rejection of those addressed (7:15). Thus they vividly confronted their listeners with the threat that Jeremiah's prophecy of judgment was by no means a thing of the past; worse could come if they still refused to respond to his message. They had even less reason than their ancestors to claim ignorance: they had been warned (7:13). In religious discourses before everyday assemblies, they tried not only to warn the people by recalling Jeremiah's message of judgment but also, on the basis of that message, to find a clear orientation for the future of the Judeans.

Amos 4:6–13*[189] provides a second example of the concern to gain a hearing for the prophetic message of judgment among the survivors of the catastrophe. The text begins with a long indictment in the second-person plural, in elevated prose. In it Yahweh describes how he brought upon the listeners a series of increasingly devastating plagues but was forced to discover each time that they did not return to him (4:6, 8, 9, 10, 11). Then follows Yahweh's declaration to Israel that he will continue to treat them the same way in the future[190] and a command to be ready for an encounter with their God (4:12). The text concludes with a brief participial hymn praising the overwhelming power of Yahweh as Creator of the world (4:13).

The litany-like structure of the indictment, the command to be ready to encounter God (cf. Exod 19:11, 15, 17), and the hymn all point to a

---

[189] Verses 7aβb and 8 represent an expansion related to the late exilic continuation in Amos 8:11–12; see pp. 224–27 below.

[190] Following the perfect tenses in 4: 4–11, the imperfect אֶעֱשֶׂה in 4:12 clearly refers to the future; the reference to the preceding plagues gives it an iterative sense: "I will again do so to you, O Israel."

cultic *Sitz im Leben*. The comparison of the worst plague, from which the listeners escaped by the skin of their teeth, to the destruction of Sodom and Gomorrah (Amos 4:11) suggests an exilic date (cf. Isa 1:9–10; with reference to Babylon: Isa 13: 9; Jer 50:40).[191] Thus we are probably dealing with a religious address composed for and set in exilic worship.

The motifs in the indictment recall catalogs of curses such as Deut 28:16ff. and Lev 26:14ff., which are related in turn to the punitive clauses of Neo-Assyrian treaties.[192] In the catastrophes Israel has experienced, the exilic community is told, Yahweh merely brought to pass the curses threatened in Deuteronomy should the covenant be broken. But since the accusation follows Amos 4:4–5 directly and thus presupposes that these words of Amos (and probably others) were read aloud in the context of worship, the covenant curses are identified with Amos's message of judgment: 4:12 deliberately uses the generalizing deictic particles כֹּה, "thus," and זֹאת, "this," to refer to both.

Amos's prophecies of judgment, so the preacher declares in his accusation, have already been realized in part in the disasters Israel has suffered. However, as he makes clear in 4:12a, they continue to stand as a threat over the exilic community. The purpose of the blows Yahweh inflicted, the community is instructed, was to incite Israel to return to him. Because Israel's past apostasy continued unabated, Yahweh had no choice but to intensify his punishments to the point of destroying Israel almost totally. This must be accepted. Now, however, everything depends on the decision of the survivors. Therefore the preacher demands that the community prepare itself for a cultic encounter with the God who punishes (4:12b). By responding with a doxology (4:13) that praises not only God's earth-shattering power but also God's plan in history, the community explicitly acknowledges the majesty and justice of this God who punishes. Thus the return to Yahweh that did not take place in the past is accomplished now in worship; at the same time, the prophetic word of Amos, largely rejected in the past, is clothed with all the dignity of a cultic oracle of God. The cultic address in Amos 4:6–13*, which like the other doxologies (5:8–9; 9:5–6; cf. 8:8) probably belongs to an early exilic redactional stratum of the book of Amos, thus demonstrates that during the exile worship came to play an important tutelary role.

There is further evidence that oracles of the prophets of judgment were read in the context of exilic worship and were collected for that purpose. For example, Jer 8:4–10:25* (omitting 9:11–15, 22–25; 10:1–16) represents a composite of oracles of Jeremiah that not only comprises

---

[191] See the discussion in Jeremias, *Book of Amos*, 73–74.
[192] Weinfeld, *Deuteronomy*, 116–38.

many lamentations but also culminates in an actual communal lament (10:23–25; cf. Ps 79:6–7). It was probably compiled for use in liturgical lamentation during the exile. If we take into account liturgical units such as Amos 4:6–13* as well as such prophetic composites for liturgical use, we observe that in exilic worship the liturgy of the word was clearly becoming more important than the performance of cultic actions. Thus we see in the exilic period the beginnings of a development that much later resulted in synagogue worship, in which the liturgy of the word (reading and exposition of scripture, confession of faith, prayer) takes center stage.[193]

III.2. EXILIC LITERARY WORKS

Besides minor collections and composites, the exilic period produced a great number of more extensive literary works. First is the prophetic literature. Since the prophets of judgment had foretold the catastrophe of the exile, the reappraisal of that crisis took place in large measure through the reception and interpretation of the literary heritage of the preexilic prophets of judgment (Hosea, Amos, Micah, Zephaniah, Jeremiah). This was the genesis of the prophetic books and collections of prophetic books. In addition, the exilic prophecy of salvation created its own literature, partially in additions to the writings of the prophets of judgment, partially in more or less independent works (Ezekiel, Deutero-Isaiah). Second, narrative and historical literature clearly continued to develop during the exilic period. In the face of threatened loss of identity, the foundational traditions were reinterpreted and combined into larger literary units (the exilic history of the patriarchs, the exodus, and Sinai). To counter the threat of an interrupted tradition, the first continuous historical work was written, embracing the history of Israel from the entrance into Canaan to the exile (the Deuteronomistic History).

---

[193] Nevertheless, the lack of sources leaves obscure the precise connection between exilic worship and synagogue worship. Between the two stretches a gap of at least three hundred years. The first epigraphic mention of a synagogue dates from the third century B.C.E.; the first building that can be identified as a synagogue is located on the island of Delos and dates from the first century B.C.E. The earliest synagogue excavated in Palestine is no earlier than the first century C.E. The same period also sees the first literary evidence of synagogue worship (Philo, Josephus, New Testament), which unfortunately provides only rudimentary information about its nature. For a treatment of the whole topic, see Lee I. Levine, "Synagogues," *NEAEHL* 4:1421–24, esp. 1422; Lester L. Grabbe, "Synagogues in Pre-70 Palestine: A Re-Assessment," *JTS* 39 (1988): 401–10; Grabbe, *Judaism from Cyrus to Hadrian* (2 vols.; Minneapolis: Fortress, 1992), 2:541–42.

Important and fruitful as the literary activity of the exilic period was on many fronts, there is no justification for trying to assign as much Old Testament literature as possible to this era. There is a tendency in current scholarship to describe many texts simply as "exilic-postexilic." Such a chronological term is much too imprecise: it covers half a millennium! Furthermore, the exilic period, even if defined (as in this book) as extending from 587 to 520, includes only the short span of sixty-seven years at most. If we also consider the difficult political and economic circumstances of the period, under which both the exiles and those left at home had to struggle, especially during the first years, the amount of time left for relatively undisturbed literary creation is reduced even more.

Questions of literary history cannot be discussed here. The salient points: contrary to the opinion of some scholars, I assume that the first coherent edition of the Pentateuch as a whole is not a product of the exilic period[194] but dates from the postexilic period (fifth century).[195] This means that the Priestly Document or the Priestly recension of the Pentateuch (P) should be dated in the fifth century, not as early as the sixth century.[196] At best the beginnings of the Priestly tradition (Sabbath, circumcision) go back to the late exilic period, which was not clearly differentiated from the tradition of the book of Ezekiel until the early postexilic period. It follows that the Priestly legislation, especially the so-called Holiness Code (Lev 17–26), likewise dates from the Persian era. The Deuteronomic legislation or at least its basic nucleus I date in the late preexilic period.[197]

III.2.1. The Book of the Four Prophets (Hosea, Amos, Micah, Zephaniah)

Ben Zvi, Ehud. *A Historical-Critical Study in the Book of Zephaniah* (BZAW 198; Berlin: de Gruyter, 1991). **Ben Zvi.** "Twelve Prophetic Books or 'The Twelve': A Few Preliminary Considerations," in *Forming Prophetic Literature: Essays on Isaiah*

---

194 See especially John van Seters, *Prologue to History: The Yahwist As Historian in Genesis* (Louisville: Westminster John Knox, 1992); Van Seters, *The Life of Moses: The Yahwist As Historian in Exodus–Numbers* (Louisville: Westminster John Knox, 1994).

195 Here I follow Erhard Blum, *Studien zur Komposition des Pentateuch* (BZAW 189; Berlin: de Gruyter, 1990).

196 For discussion of this dating, see Thomas Pola, *Die ursprüngliche Priesterschrift: Beobachtungen zur Literarkritik und Traditionsgeschichte von Pg* (WMANT 70; Neukirchen-Vluyn: Neukirchener Verlag, 1995), 31–40; Erich Zenger et al., *Einleitung in das Alte Testament* (3d ed.; Stuttgart: Kohlhammer, 1998), 112, 152ff. Whether it makes sense to reconstruct a "torso" for P extending only through Exod 40, as Pola proposes, may remain an open question.

197 For the evidence, see Albertz, *History* (II.4), 1:199–201.

and the Twelve in Honor of John D. W. Watts (ed. J. W. Watts and P. R. House; JSOTSup 235; Sheffield: Sheffield Academic Press, 1996), 125–57. **Blum,** Erhard. "'Amos' in Jerusalem: Beobachtungen zu Am 6,1–7," *Henoch* 16 (1994): 23–47. **Bosshard,** Erich. "Beobachtungen zum Zwölfprophetenbuch," *BN* 40 (1987): 30–62. **Bosshard-Nepustil,** Erich. *Rezeptionen von Jesaja 1–39 im Zwölfprophetenbuch: Untersuchungen zur literarischen Verbindung von Prophetenbüchern in babylonischer und persicher Zeit* (OBO 154; Fribourg: Universitätsverlag, 1997). **House,** Paul R. *The Unity of the Twelve* (JSOTSup 97; BibLit 27; Sheffield: Almond, 1990). **Jepsen,** Alfred. "Kleine Beiträge zum Zwölfprophetenbuch," *ZAW* 56 (1938): 85–100. **Jeremias,** Jörg. "Die Anfänge des Dodekapropheton: Hosea und Amos," in idem, *Hosea und Amos: Studien zu den Anfängen des Dodekapropheton* (FAT 13; Tübingen: Mohr Siebeck, 1996), 34–54. **Jeremias.** *The Book of Amos: A Commentary* (trans. D. W. Stott; OTL; Louisville: Westminster John Knox, 1998). **Jeremias.** "Die Deutung der Gerichtsworte Michas in der Exilszeit," *ZAW* 83 (1971): 330–54. **Jeremias.** "Hosea/Hoseabuch," *TRE* 15:586–98. **Jeremias.** *Der Prophet Hosea* (ATD 24/1; Göttingen: Vandenhoeck & Ruprecht, 1983). **Jones,** Barry Allan. *The Formation of the Book of the Twelve: A Study in Text and Canon* (SBLDS 149; Atlanta: Scholars Press, 1995). **Kessler,** Rainer. *Micha* (HThK.AT; Freiburg: Herder, 1999). **Metzner,** Gabriele. *Kompositionsgeschichte des Michabuches* (EHS.T 635; Frankfurt: Lang, 1998). **Nissinen,** Marti. *Prophetie, Redaktion und Fortschreibung im Hoseabuch: Studien zum Werdegang eines Prophetenbuches im Lichte von Hos 4 und 11* (AOAT 231; Kevelaer: Butzon & Bercker, 1991). **Nogalski,** James. *Literary Precursors of the Book of the Twelve* (BZAW 217; Berlin: de Gruyter, 1993). **Nogalski.** *Redactional Processes in the Book of the Twelve* (BZAW 218; Berlin: de Gruyter, 1993). **Rottzoll,** Dirk U. *Studien zur Redaktion und Komposition des Amosbuchs* (BZAW 243; Berlin: de Gruyter, 1996). **Schart,** Aaron. *Die Entstehung des Zwölfprophenbuchs: Neubearbeitungen von Amos im Rahmen schriftenübergreifender Redaktionsprozesse* (BZAW 260; Berlin: de Gruyter, 1998). **Schart.** "Zur Redaktionsgeschichte des Zwölfprophetenbuchs," *VF* 43 (1998): 13–33. **Schmidt,** Werner H. "Die deuteronomistische Redaktion des Amosbuches: Zu den theologischen Unterschieden zwischen dem Propheten und seinem Sammler," *ZAW* 77 (1965): 168–93. **Seybold,** Klaus. *Nahum, Habakuk, Zephanja* (ZBK.AT 24/2; Zurich: Theologischer Verlag, 1991). **Seybold.** *Satirsiche Prophetie: Studien zum Buch Zephanja* (SBS 120; Stuttgart: Katholisches Bibelwerk, 1985). **Striek,** Marco. *Das vordeuteronomistische Zephanjabuch* (BBET 29; Frankfurt: Lang, 1999). **Waschke,** Ernst-Joachim. "Die fünfte Vision des Amosbuches (9:1–4): Eine Nachinterpretation," *ZAW* 106 (1994): 434–45. **Weigl,** Michael. *Zefanja und das 'Israel der Armen': Eine Untersuchung zur Theologie des Buches Zefanja* (ÖBS 13; Klosterneuburg: Österreichisches Katholisches Bibelwerk, 1994). **Wolff,** Hans Walter. *Joel and Amos: A Commentary on the Books of the Prophets Joel and Amos* (trans. W. Janzen et al.; Hermeneia; Philadelphia: Fortress, 1977). **Wolff.** *Micah: A Commentary* (trans. G. Stansell; Minneapolis: Augsburg, 1990). **Zapff,** Burkard M. *Redaktionsgeschichtliche Studien zum Michabuch im Kontext des Dodekapropheton* (BZAW 256; Berlin: de Gruyter, 1997).

In the preexilic period, the radical prophets of judgment of the eighth century (Hosea, Amos, Isaiah, Micah) and the seventh/sixth century

(Jeremiah, Ezekiel) had generally met rejection; their words and writings were preserved only by small resistance groups. In the exilic period, however, they garnered broad social respect. Only a few had believed their claim to be divinely commissioned to deliver oracles from Yahweh (cf. the messenger formula כה אמר יהוה, "thus says Yahweh"). When their message turned out to be, for the most part, bitterly true, most of the exilic groups accepted their claim in principle, even though some had reservations on this or that point (e.g., criticism of the monarchy and the temple). This change of mind did not happen of itself: it was promoted by people who felt a special obligation to the message of the prophets of judgment; they engaged in an intensive labor of education and enlightenment in daily life and in the cult.[198] Thus the exilic period was marked by intense scrutiny of the oral and written heritage of the prophets of judgment.

For this reason, the preaching of all the preexilic prophets of judgment underwent more or less extensive exilic redaction. The exilic period marks the genesis of the prophetic books. Since the oracles of the various prophets were now considered the word of God, they came to be read increasingly in mutual relationship; there also arose the theological problem of their unity in God's mind and their significance as a body in Israel's history. As a consequence, the prophetic books were edited as a group. In other words, *topoi* and expressions characteristic of one prophet found their way into the books of others, and books of different prophets were even combined to form a single composite. One such composite originating in the exilic period is probably the book of the Four Prophets, comprising most of the present books of Hosea, Amos, Micah, and Zephaniah—a precursor of the book of the Twelve Prophets.

After the rise of form criticism, the study of the prophets concentrated for many years on the small and medium-size units, often in the interests of identifying the authentic voice of an individual prophet. In the last decade, however, with the rise of redaction criticism, interest has focused once more on the book of the Twelve Prophets as a whole.[199] That the book of the Twelve is meant to be more than a haphazard collection of documents assembled on a single scroll to save space is shown both by its generally chronological organization and by the use of catchwords to link the books, as demonstrated above all by Nogalski. This new approach based on redaction criticism can also appeal to Jesus Sirach's Hymn Honoring the Ancestors (second century B.C.E.), which

---

[198] See pp. 140ff. above.

[199] Bosshard, *Beobachtungen*; Bosshard-Nepustil, *Rezeption*; Nogalski, *Literary Precursors*; Nogalski, *Redactional Processes*; Jones, *Formation*; Schart, *Entstehung*; cf. the survey in Schart, "Zur Redaktionsgeschichte."

treats the "Twelve Prophets" as a unit (Sir 49:10). The textual tradition, however, has never assigned them a common title, as Ben Zvi rightly notes.[200] It is easy and understandable to exaggerate the new perspective, but we must remember that the book of the Twelve Prophets wants to be read not only as a unit (definitely polyphonic!) but also as a collection of individual documents.

The theory of a Four Prophets book comprising Hosea, Amos, Micah, and Zephaniah was proposed by Nogalski as a byproduct of his study of the Twelve Prophets.[201] For his starting point, he took the structural similarity of the superscriptions that set these prophets in historical sequence. He also noted the systematic arrangement of two northern-kingdom prophets paralleling two southern-kingdom prophets, the explicit linkage of northern and southern prophecy at the beginning of the book of Micah, and other evidence such as the use of catchwords. Nogalski identified this Four Prophets book as comprising Hos 1–14; Amos 1:1–9:6; Mic 1–3 + 6; and Zeph 1:1–3:8*. He called it the "Deuteronomistic corpus" on account of the Deuteronomistic flavor of certain compositional elements. Here he was able to utilize the observations of Schmidt[202] on the Deuteronomistic redaction of the book of Amos and those of Jeremias[203] on the exilic redaction of the book of Micah. Nogalski acknowledges the uncertainty of his hypothesis, since he was not able to carry out all the necessary textual studies.[204]

The first scholar to exploit Nogalski's theory was Schart,[205] who calls the Four Prophets the "D corpus" on account of certain stylistic features that differ from Deuteronomistic writings in general.[206] Unlike Nogalski, he assumes that there was already a preexilic fusion of the Amos and Hosea traditions, in order to explain certain linguistic and structural features (such as calls to hear) shared by these two prophetic books, which exhibit no Deuteronomistic features. It is questionable, however, whether these features are similar enough to establish literary dependence. It is quite sufficient to assume, with Jeremias,[207] that the disciples associated with each of the prophets were familiar with the work of the other group. Schart comes up with a detailed description of the intention of the Four Prophets book, which he delimits somewhat differently from Nogalski:

---

200 "Twelve Prophetic Books," 137.
201 *Literary Precursors*, 278–80; *Redactional Processes*, 274–75.
202 "Deuteronomistische Redaktion."
203 "Deutung."
204 *Literary Precursors*, 278.
205 *Entstehung*, 156–223.
206 Ibid., 46.
207 *Hosea*.

Hosea*; Amos 1:1–9:10*; Mic 1:1–3:12*; 6:1–16*; and Zeph 1:1–3:8*, (11–13?). According to Schart, the inclusion of Micah and Zephaniah took place in two stages. He assigns the following texts to the D corpus: Hos 1:1, 2b*; 2:6 (4); 3:1*; 4:1*; 5:1–2*; 8:1b; 14:2–4 (1–3); Amos 1:1, 2, 9–12; 2:4–5, 10–12; 3:1b, 7; 4:6–11*; 5:11, 25–26*; 8:4–7, 11–12; 9:7–10; Mic 1:1, 2b, 5a, 6–7, 13b; 2:3*; 6:2–16*; Zeph 1:1, 6, 13b, 17aβ.[208]

Although Schart's work clearly lays a more solid foundation for the hypothesis of an exilic Prophets book, certain methodological and factual difficulties remain.[209] Some have to do with the state of redaction criticism as such. There is still no scholarly consensus, for example, as to the criteria that must be met before we can speak of a deliberate compositional linkage (e.g., the use of catchwords) in contrast to random verbal echoes.[210] In my opinion, there must be specific conceptual or verbal linkages; in addition, at least one feature cited must be a redactional addition to its context. Furthermore, it is not clear how to identify the intention of such large-scale polyphonic composites; the linked texts always have their own messages, but redaction lends them different weight and hence sometimes a new meaning. I try to use the redactional linking texts as my starting point and then go on to identify the corresponding thematic threads in the earlier texts.

Other difficulties relate to the Four Prophets in particular. In contrast to the situation in the book of Jeremiah, the linking texts do not speak with a distinctly Deuteronomistic voice. Occasional points of contact with the Deuteronomistic History or JerD (Deuteronomistic Jeremiah) are observable, but there are others with Hosea, Amos, Jeremiah, and even Isaiah. Clearly the redactors did not speak the language of a school but preferred to draw on the prophetic writings with which they were familiar. Since the identity of the redactor(s) is still uncertain, I employ the shorthand siglum FPR (Four Prophets Redactor[s]). Actually, establishment of the Four Prophets hypothesis requires a precise analysis of all four books with the tools of both literary and redaction criticism. Schart has subjected only the book of Amos to detailed literary criticism. This is not the place for detailed exegesis of individual texts, but it will be necessary in the future to judge hypotheses generated by literary criticism of

---

208 *Entstehung*, 316.

209 Bosshard-Nepustil (*Rezeption*) shows how shaky the ground still is: despite his basic agreement with Nogalski's theory, he challenges once more the inclusion of Zephaniah. He does so on the grounds of his theory of parallelism between Isa 1–39 and the book of the Twelve. Perhaps it would be best to clarify the history of the book of the Twelve itself before embarking on such complex comparisons.

210 See the criticism (in part justified) of Ben Zvi, "Twelve Prophetic Books."

individual books by the criterion of whether they fit meaningfully into a history of the growth of the book of the Twelve. I note in passing that redactional hypotheses dating the genesis of substantial portions of the book of Hosea or Amos in the postexilic period[211] are incompatible with the theory of an exilic book of the Four Prophets.

A secure starting point for the theory that the writings of Hosea, Amos, Micah, and Zephaniah were joined in the exilic period to form a Four Prophets book is provided by the structure of their superscriptions:

Hos 1:1	The word of Yahweh (דבר יהוה)	that came to (היה אל) Hosea, son of Beeri,		in the days of Uzziah, Jotham, Ahaz, and Hezekiah, kings of Judah, and in the days of Jeroboam, son of Joash, king of Israel.
Amos 1:1	The words of Amos, who was among the shepherds, from Tekoa,	that he saw	concerning Israel	in the days of Uzziah, king of Judah, and in the days of Jeroboam, son of Joash, king of Israel, two years before the earthquake.
Mic 1:1	The word of Yahweh (דבר יהוה)	that came to (היה אל) Micah, from Moresheth,	that he saw concerning Samaria and Jerusalem	in the days of Jotham, Ahaz, and Hezekiah, kings of Judah.
Zeph 1:1	The word of Yahweh (דבר יהוה)	that came to (היה אל) Zephaniah, son of Cushi, son of Gedaliah, son of Amariah, son of Hezekiah,		in the days of Josiah, son of Amon, king of Judah.

---

211 Nissinen, *Prophetie*; Rottzoll, *Studien*; etc.

In the entire book of the Twelve, only these four books have superscriptions that include a date.[212] In each case, the dating is approximate: "in the days of" the kings of Judah from Uzziah to Hezekiah and Josiah; in the case of the prophets Hosea and Amos, who preached in the northern kingdom, the king of Israel (Jeroboam II, 787–747 B.C.E.) is also mentioned in a synchronistic style reminiscent of the Deuteronomistic History. It is noteworthy that the chronology based on the kings of Israel is even more vague than that based on the kings of Judah: in the case of Hosea, it ignores the numerous kings of Israel who appeared in quick succession down to the beginning of the reign of Hezekiah (725?–697). We may conclude that the redaction of the four books reflects a Judean perspective, but it is also noteworthy that a northern-kingdom prophet is assigned a special position: not only is he placed first, contrary to the historical chronology of the prophets, but he is given a ministry so lengthy that it overlaps both the second prophet of the northern kingdom, Amos (Uzziah), and the first prophet of the southern kingdom, Micah (Jotham, Ahaz, Hezekiah). At the same time—now in agreement with historical chronology—the superscriptions show that prophecy began somewhat later in Judah but lasted longer and, as Zephaniah attests, continued on in the seventh century under King Josiah.

Three of the four superscriptions begin with the same words: "The word of Yahweh that came to Hosea/Micah/Zephaniah." The singular is striking! The superscription of the book of Amos begins very differently, describing the book's content as "The words of Amos," probably because this book already had an earlier superscription of a different type (cf. Jer 1:1 and Isa 1:1), which FPR could not alter.[213] Nevertheless, FPR put forward the theologically sophisticated view that all the many and various words proclaimed over a long period of time represented the one word of Yahweh spoken at various times to various persons. All the words spoken by the prophets not only had a single direct divine origin but also were ultimately identical, because they were grounded in the one word of God. Since the same "word of Yahweh" theology and a similar style of dating appear in the superscription of the Deuteronomistic Jeremiah

---

[212] The superscription of the book of Joel imitates that of Hosea, Micah, and Zephaniah but does not contain a date. Obadiah, Jonah, Nahum, Habakkuk, and Malachi are also undated. Haggai and Zechariah are dated but not in a superscription; their dating is based on a different system, the regnal year of the Persian king, with month and day.

[213] Unlike the superscription in Jer 1:1, to which a relative clause could be added in 1:2, equating the "words of Jeremiah" with the word of Yahweh ("words of Jeremiah ... to whom the word of Yahweh came"), the superscription of the book of Amos already had a relative clause, so that adding a similar qualification would have been very difficult syntactically.

book (Jer 1:1–3), the superscriptions alone indicate a certain affinity between FPR and JerD.

In the preexisting superscription to the book of Amos, the question of whom the prophetic message was addressed to was important to FPR: "that he saw concerning Israel." This gave the redactor an opportunity for a transition in the superscription to the book of Micah to prophecy in the southern kingdom, which began with this prophet: "that he saw concerning Samaria and Jerusalem" (Mic 1:1). Here we already see an important goal of the Four Prophets book: it seeks to recount how the word of Yahweh, which began with Hosea, was addressed initially to the northern kingdom and then with Micah and Zephaniah came to Judah and Jerusalem.[214]

III.2.1.1. Micah

FPR further developed this concept of the word of God, already recognizable in the superscriptions, by reshaping the beginning of the book of Micah. He made the theophany in Mic 1:3–5a culminate in Yahweh's oracle of judgment against Samaria (1:6–7), to be followed by a prophetic lament that the "incurable wound"[215] previously inflicted on Samaria had now come to Judah and Jerusalem (1:8–9). The oracle against Samaria, which has created so many problems when the book of Micah is interpreted in isolation,[216] turns out to be a redactional construct: first, by borrowing motifs from 3:12 (1:6: עִי, "heap of ruins"; שָׂדֶה, "field"), it identifies the fates of the capitals of both kingdoms; second, by using several central terms from the book of Hosea,[217] it incorporates Hosea's preaching against Samaria (Hos 7:1; 8:5–6; 10:5, 7; 14:1 [13:16]) into the book of Micah; third, it introduces the religious accusation, which had not been part of Micah's preaching, into the book of Micah, thus standardizing the prophetical word of God. In addition, when Mic 1:7b uses the Hoseanic motif of playing the whore and a whore's fee in the sense of foreign

---

214 A comparable theology of the word of God in history appears already in Isa 5:25–29; 9:7–20 (8–21).

215 The MT, which reads the plural, despite the singular form of the adjective and verb, suggests a literary problem; see p. 213 below.

216 Scholars who considered the oracle against Samaria authentic had assumed that Micah's ministry began prior to 722, although the continuation in Mic 1:10ff. points to the time after 701 B.C.E.; cf. Wolff, *Micah*, 2–3. At the same time, they were forced to treat Mic 1:2–16 not as a rhetorical unit but as a redactional unit (Wolff, *Micah*, 50–51).

217 For example גלה, "lay bare": Hos 2:12 (10); 7:1; פְּסִילִים, idols": 11:2; אֶתְנַן, "fee of a whore": 2:14 (12); 9:1; עֲצַבִּים, "idols": 4:17; 8:4; 13:2; 14:9 (8); זנה, "play the whore": 1:2; 2:6–7 (4–5); 3:3; 4:10–15, 18; 5:3–4; 6:10; 9:1.

political "entanglements" (as it is used occasionally by Jeremiah [2:14–25] and Ezekiel [16:26–34]), Hosea's condemnation of foreign alliances (5:12–14; 7:8–9; etc.) is also incorporated into the book of Micah.

The identification of the compositional role played by the beginning of the book of Micah by Nogalski,[218] Schart,[219] and Kessler,[220] is correct in principle but needs to be confirmed by more detailed redaction criticism before it can be cited in support of an exilic Four Prophets book. If one follows Nogalski and Kessler in treating Mic 1:2–9 as a homogeneous literary unit,[221] then the compositional brackets of 1:2 and 5:14 (15); 6:1 mean that this unit presupposes the theme of the nations in Mic 4–5 as well as the criticism of the restored cult in 6:2–8; if so, as Kessler concludes, it cannot antedate the Persian period. There could not have been an exilic Four Prophets book. A further consequence of such a view would be that the whole of Mic 1–6 is a late redactional construct and that the earlier Micah tradition (1:10–3:12*) lacked a sensible introduction until some time in the Persian period.

However, Mic 1:2–9 is not homogeneous. The summons to the peoples to hear, coupled with the threat that Yahweh is about to appear as a witness "against them" (1:2), originally had nothing to do with a theophany of Yahweh against Israel. The transition to the latter at the beginning of 1:3 with the expression כי הנה, "For lo," is clearly artificial. Jepsen[222] had already pointed out that the theophany of Yahweh (1:3*, 4) was originally aimed directly at Judah, since the motivation in 1:5 speaks of the "transgression of Jacob" and the "sins of the house of Israel," expressions that refer unambiguously to the southern kingdom in the usage of Mic 1–3* (3:1, 9; cf. 1:14–15; 2:7). Only the questions in 1:5b with their assumption of the reader's assent ("What is the transgression of Jacob? Is it not Samaria? What are the high places of Judah? Is it not Jerusalem?) introduce a distinction between the northern and southern kingdoms, preparing for a transition to the theophany against Samaria. There is much evidence to indicate that FPR interpolated 1:1, 5b–7 into a preexisting earlier introduction to the book of Micah. The same hand was also responsible for the concentration of verbs in 1:3b: to the earlier theophanic description "and he came down upon the high places of the earth," FPR added the verb ודרך, "and trod," to establish a connection

---

[218] *Literary Precursors*, 129–37.

[219] *Entstehung*, 177–81.

[220] *Micha*, 80–94.

[221] Kessler, *Micha*, 87 singles out only 1:5b as a gloss but is unable to provide a good reason for its addition.

[222] "Kleine Beiträge," 97–99.

with the hymn in the book of Amos (4:3).²²³ Thus the compositional work of FPR left clearly demonstrable redactional traces.

There is just one difficulty with this clear redactional solution. Since the prophetic lament in Mic 1:8–9 is a reaction to the preceding theophany (cf. עַל־זֹאת, "therefore"), it must belong to the earlier introduction to the book of Micah (1:3–5a*, 8–9). In the present text, however, 1:9a ("for her wounds are incurable") refers back to God's judgment on the city of Samaria and hence to the Four Prophets redaction. However, it is quite likely that even here FPR modified the text. The meaning conveyed by the objective genitive modifying the subject of the verbless clause is not immediately clear but requires interpretive paraphrase.²²⁴ In addition, the plural noun joined with an adjective and verbs in the singular is conspicuous. The text may represent a copyist's error, but the incongruence could also be due to FPR's attempt to make clear, despite the syntax, that the prophet laments both the wound of Samaria and the wound of Jerusalem. The feminine suffix could also refer proleptically to Judah and Jerusalem. If so, as in 1:5b, FPR would be making his redactional work visible to all. It has often been suggested that the original text read "the wound of [= inflicted by] Yahweh."²²⁵ If at one time 1:8–9 originally followed 1:3–5a directly, "his wound" would also be possible.

When the redactor took the introduction to the existing book of Micah (Mic 1:3*–5a, 8, 9*) and wrote into it his conception of a divine judgment striking first the northern and then the southern kingdom (1:5b–7, 9*), at the same time adding a variety of references to the books of Amos (1:3b; Amos 4:13) and Hosea (1:6–7), he created a first, important pillar of the exilic Four Prophets books. At an appropriate point (1:13b, a text long viewed as a secondary addition²²⁶), he explained his view as to why Jerusalem had been included in the disaster: misplaced trust in arms, especially the chariots stationed in Lachish, represented

---

²²³ Schart (*Entstehung*, 177–78, 238–39) strangely assigns the theophany and the appeal to hear (Mic 1:2a, 3–4) to a stage of tradition subsequent to the Four Prophets book, which integrated Nahum and Habakkuk into the book of the Prophets. He calls this stage the "hymn stratum" because he also assigns to it the hymns in the book of Amos (Amos 4:12–13; 5:8–9; 9:5–6). As evidence of this association, he sites the linkage between Mic 1:3b and Amos 4:13. However, Schart overlooks the fact that this reference is clearly redactional. Furthermore, his theory that the hymns in the book of Amos were added after its Deuteronomistic redaction rests on shaky ground (see pp. 224–25 below).

²²⁴ In the other instances of מַכּוֹתֶיהָ, "its wounds," the antecedent always functions as an object (Isa 19:8; 49:17; 50:13).

²²⁵ Most recently Wolff, *Micah*, 40, 43.

²²⁶ Wolff, *Micah*, 50; Kessler, *Micha*, 108. Schart (*Entstehung*, 182) also assigns the verse to his D complex; cf. the reference back to 1:5.

"the beginning of sin to daughter Zion." Thus he included a charge already leveled by Isaiah (Isa 30:1–5, 15–17; 31:1–3) and also mentioned peripherally in Hosea (Hos 10:13b;[227] 14:4 [3]). Besides the social injustice that Micah had exposed, FPR, from his exilic perspective, believed that misplaced trust in arms had been primarily responsible for Jerusalem's fall. If one recalls the nationalists' risky policy of rebellion during the last years of Jerusalem, this verdict is absolutely accurate.

The redactor erected the second pillar of the Four Prophets book at the conclusion of the exilic book of Micah in Mic 5:8 (?), 9–13[228] and at the beginning of the book of Zephaniah in Zeph 1:4–6. These two texts, closely related in both style (וְהִכְרַתִּי, "I will cut off") and content, link the third and fourth books of the complex. That the book of Zephaniah seeks to reveal the consequences of the word of Yahweh for the southern kingdom is shown by the identification of "Judah and the inhabitants of Jerusalem" as addressees in the introductory section (1:4). In 1:3 (omitting the gloss in 1:3aβ), FPR probably established a further link with the first book of the complex (Hos 4:3).

In contrast to Mic 1:5b–7, the compositional function of Mic 5:9–13 in the structure of the Four Prophets book has not been noticed previously. This is because both Nogalski[229] and Schart[230] wanted to include Mic 6 in the exilic book of Micah. Now it is undoubtedly true that 6:2–8, 16 in particular exhibits linguistic and conceptual features that are Deuteronom(ist)ic. Since, however, the nucleus of the chapter, 6:2–8, presupposes an active sacrificial cult (cf. 6:6–7) and with the sequence "Moses, Aaron, and Miriam" (6:4; elsewhere only in 1 Chr 5:29 [6:3]) combines Deuteronomic and Priestly elements in a manner reminiscent of the Pentateuch in its final form, the whole chapter is probably postexilic.[231] That it is a late appendix to 1:1–5:14 is also indicated by 6:1, which marks a shift from the international perspective.

It is relatively certain that the book of Micah available to FPR included the sections 1:3*–5a, 9–13a, 14–16; 2:1–3, 6–11; 3:1–12. Here we probably have an edition of Micah oracles (still preserved, as far as we can tell, in 1:10–13a, 14–16; 2:1–3, 8–10; 3:2b–3, 5b–7, 9–12) from the time of the Babylonian threat to Judah, making the oracles topical and

---

227 Reading בְּרִכְבְּךָ (with the LXX): "Because you trusted 'in your chariots,' and in the multitude of your warriors."

228 The assignment of this text to FPR is assured by the reference back to Mic 1:7 in 5:12 and to 1:13 in 5:9. In addition, as in 1:6–7, there are many echoes of the book of Hosea.

229 *Literary Precursors*, 141–44.

230 *Entstehung*, 191–204.

231 Cf. also Kessler, *Micha*, 260–61.

commenting on them. In any case, the perceived relevance of Micah in this period is attested by Jer 26:17–29. It is more difficult to decide whether this edition already included some of the salvation oracles in Mic 4–5. Following Wolff, Kessler has once again proposed treating 4:8–5:3 (4) as an early exilic continuation.[232] Now it is certainly true that the salvation oracle in 4:9–10 and the lament in 4:14 date from the early exilic period. Whether this dating also includes the belligerent oracle against the nations (4:11–13) and the promise of a saving king (4:8; 5:3 [4]) is the question. Even if the short complex 4:8–5:3 (4) was in existence in the middle to late exilic period, this does not settle the question of when it was integrated into the book of Micah. Most likely the initial linkage combined 2:12–13 + 4:6–7 + 4:8–5:3 (4), to which 4:1–4 and 5:6–7 (7–8) were added in the Persian period. Finally, the bracketing verses 1:2 and 5:14 (15) were added. No other text in the exilic Four Prophets book voices hope for a restored Davidic monarchy (cf. Zeph 3:9–13; Amos 9:11–12 is later; in Hos 3:5, the words "and David their king" are secondary); I therefore assume that the book of Micah used by FPR did not contain any salvation oracles but ended with Mic 3:12.

Micah 5:9–13 (10–14) is related to 3:9–12 in that—as the catchword "in your midst" (3:11; 5:9, 13 [10, 14]) shows—both oracles are addressed to Jerusalem, even though the second-person suffixes have been repointed as masculines rather than feminines and now refer to the "remnant of Jacob" in 5:6–7 (7–8), a later addition. Therefore it is quite possible that 5:9–13 (10–14) originally followed 3:12. Only the introduction, now reminiscent of 4:6, is probably secondary. It is also possible that FPR, borrowing from the liturgical lamentations of the exilic period, employed 5:8 (9) as a transition: God responds to the community's petition to cut off (כרת, nip'al) the enemy by announcing a purifying judgment on Jerusalem. Dating 5:9–13 (10–14) earlier than the other salvation oracles of the chapter could explain why this oracle still limits itself to an exclusionary view of a new beginning.

Even though later expansions prevent us from reconstructing the literary context with certainty, we can see that FPR followed Micah's harsh oracle foretelling the total devastation of the temple mount (Mic 3:12)—which described the present situation of the exilic community—with Yahweh's announcement that he would continue his work of destruction, which had already devastated Israel and Jerusalem,[233] in an equally drastic but now limited manner: he would cut off (four times: וְהִכְרַתִּי, "I will cut off") everything that had given occasion for apostasy. The text speaks

---

232 *Micha*, 46.
233 See above.

first of horses and chariots (5:9b [10b]), showing that FPR continues to condemn those who trust in arms (cf. 1:13b; Hos 10:13; 14:14 [13]). The condemnation of arms is closely related to the destruction of cities (עָרִים) and strongholds (מִבְצָרִים) in 5:10a (9a), also criticized in Hos 10:14; 13:10; Amos 5:9. The fortified cities (הֶעָרִים הַבְּצֻרוֹת) are also the target of divine judgment in Zeph 1:16. Hosea 8:14, a secondary verse also from the hand of FPR, emphasizes fortified cities and strongholds as the characteristic sin of the southern kingdom, in contrast to the northern kingdom. The destruction of sorcerers and soothsayers in Mic 5:11 (12) addresses magical practices that were the focus of criticism in Deuteronom(ist)ic theology (Deut 18:10; Jer 27:9; cf. Hos 3:4). Their destruction leads to the removal of idols and pillars (masseboth; Mic 5:12a [13a]); here FPR returns to religious condemnation of Samaria (Mic 1:7) and recalls the similar censure of Hosea (Hos 11:2 and 3:4; 10:1–2). Both were already forbidden by Deuteronomy (Deut 5:8; 16:22). As a result of God's purifying judgment, Israel will no longer bow down to the work of human hands (Mic 5:12b [13b]) or worship idols, either religious (Asherim) or political (fortified cities), as 5:13 (14) finally insists once more. FPR probably borrowed the expression "work of your hands" from Hos 14:4b (3b) but extended it in the context of this post-Hoseanic verse ("we will not ride upon horses") in the spirit of Isaiah's political indictment to include political and military as well as religious self-reliance (cf. Isa 2:7–8; 30:15–17).

By placing this announcement of Yahweh's universal purifying judgment at the end of his Four Prophets book of Micah, FPR also marked out the salient points of a new beginning for Judah in exile. As the criterion for everything on which a future Israel must not build—assuming that it had not already been eliminated by the catastrophe of the exile—FPR focused primarily on the religious and political indictments of Hosea and Isaiah. As long as Israel refused to abjure religious and political idols, as it had been called upon to do in Hos 14:2–4 (1–3), Yahweh himself—as the redactor sets forth within the Four Prophets book—would purge his people by his judgment from all worthless and offensive dross.

It is surprising that FPR did not consider the social indictments of the prophets Amos and Micah in Mic 5:9–13 (10–14), even though he incorporated them into his overall work. Here we see a certain reassessment of the prophetic message. However, the book of Zephaniah shows that he definitely did not ignore them.

III.2.1.2. Zephaniah

The redactor linked the last book of his composite to the book of Micah by beginning it with an announcement of God's new purifying judgment

(Zeph 1:4–6). Here he drew consciously on the language and content of Mic 5:9–13 (10–14). Yahweh will cut off (וְהִכְרַתִּי: Zeph 1:4b, like Mic 5:9–12 [10–13]) from Judah and Jerusalem "the remnant of Baal" and all traces of foreign religious influence: the foreign priests, those who bow down (הִשְׁתַּחֲוָה: Zeph 1:5, like Mic 5:12b [13b]) to the astral gods on their roofs, the people who bow down to both Yahweh and "their king" (Zeph 1:5b), and all those who have turned away from Yahweh (1:6). This passage refers primarily to the alien cults that had invaded Judah in the seventh century, during the long period of Assyrian occupation, including worship of the god Adad-milki (King Adad).[234] This text has always been seen to exhibit certain ties to the account of Josiah's cultic reforms in 2 Kgs 23, especially 23:4–5, 12.[235] Josiah purified the Jerusalem temple of just those Assyrian cults mentioned in Zeph 1:4–6. It was clearly FPR's intent to locate Josiah's cultic reformation in the chain of God's acts of judgment on Israel:[236] what the prophet Zephaniah, who prophesied during the reign of Josiah (Zeph 1:1), proclaimed as Yahweh's purifying judgment was largely carried out by King Josiah.

Here the expression "remnant of Baal" in 1:4b is striking and has occasioned much puzzlement.[237] Its meaning becomes clear only in the context of the Four Prophets book, as Schart was able to demonstrate.[238] It refers to elements of Baal worship that still survived in Judah even after Hosea's condemnation (Hos 2:10, 15 [8, 13]; 7:15; 11:2, 7; 13:1) and God's punishment of the northern kingdom. With the purifying judgment carried out by Josiah at God's behest, in the eyes of FPR all the indigenous non-Yahwistic cults and all foreign syncretism remaining in the southern kingdom were removed. Hosea's indictment had achieved success.

Nevertheless, as FPR makes clear at the end of the text, Josiah's cultic reform did not solve the problem of apostasy from Yahweh and judgment on Judah. Besides those who worshiped foreign gods, there were still people who turned back from following Yahweh "by not seeking [בִּקֵּשׁ] Yahweh or inquiring [דרשׁ] of him" (Zeph 1:6; cf. 2:3a). For the formulation of this criterion, FPR draws on Hosea (Hos 3:5; 5:6; 7:10) and Amos (Amos 5:4, 6). Here was the point at which Zephaniah's prophecy of judgment had to be taken up and the social indictment of the prophets heard.

---

234 Albertz, *History* (II.4), 1:189–95.
235 See the discussion by Striek, *Vordeuteronomistische Zephanjabuch*, 95ff.
236 Similarly also Seybold, *Satirische Prophetie*, 85; and *Nahum*, 95.
237 Cf. the interpretative attempts of the Septuagint and Syriac; see also Striek, *Vordeuteronomistische Zephanjabuch*, 95–96.
238 *Entstehung*, 209.

Because these verses are in prose and recall 2 Kgs 23, scholars have often suspected them of being Deuteronomistic in origin. Seybold ascribes them to the redactor of the book of Zephaniah, which he considers a "Deuteronomistic document" in toto.[239] Strangely, Nogalski does not utilize this text in defining his "Deuteronomistic corpus."[240] Schart ascribes only 1:6 to the redactor of the "D corpus," although he recognizes the Deuteronomistic character of the whole.[241] It is characteristic of FPR to employ Deuteronomistic and prophetic conceptualities side by side. The use of rhythmic prose instead of poetry here may be due to a desire to assimilate the prophetic message stylistically to the account of Josiah's reform. Hosea 3:4 contains another extensive list of things that Israel will have to do without after the purifying judgment.

Unlike Seybold, I do not believe that the book of Zephaniah first came into being in the exilic period. The "day of Yahweh" composite in Zeph 1:7–18 and the associated appeal in 2:1–3 differ totally from 1:4–6 in ductus and content. This difference supports the thesis of Striek that there was a pre-Deuteronomistic book of Zephaniah, which he identifies as encompassing 1:3b–3:8*.[242] This estimate is probably too generous. The theory is true for 1:7–2:4*[243] but dubious for 2:5–3:8*. As Striek's analysis correctly shows, 3:6–8* is a redactional text[244] that relates the fate of Jerusalem to Yahweh's judgment on the nations. Thus the entire complex of foreign nation oracles and the cry of woe over Jerusalem (2:5–3:4) come from the author of 3:6–8. For cogent reasons, however, Striek assigns 3:2 and 3:7 to the Deuteronomistic redaction of the book of Zephaniah (on 3:2, cf. Jer 7:28 and 35:13, both JerD). Verse 7 at least cannot be removed from its context without robbing the whole argument of its point.[245] Therefore the whole composite 2:5–3:8* must come from the exilic

---

[239] *Satirische Prophetie*, 85.
[240] *Literary Precursors*, 176–77; 189–90.
[241] *Entstehung*, 107–9.
[242] *Das vordeuteronomistische Zephanjabuch*, 221–33.
[243] Contrary to the opinion of many scholars, the pre-Deuteronomistic book includes the first foreign nation oracle against the cities of Philistia in Zeph 2:4, since it provides the motivation for the exhortation in 2:1–3. A new section begins with the woe cry in 2:5 (cf. 3:1). The literary seam is also visible in the partial thematic overlap of 2:4 with the first of the oracles against foreign nations (2:5), since the coastlands addressed in the latter include Philistia. This delimitation of textual units is also supported by the scroll containing the book of the Twelve found at Wadi Muraba'at (Pierre Benoit, J. T. Milik, and Roland de Vaux, *Les grottes de Muraba'ât* [DJD 2; Oxford: Clarendon, 1961], 202, line 16).
[244] *Das vordeuteronomistische Zephanjabuch*, 181–93.
[245] God's account of having laid waste nations (3:6) serves no purpose if it is not meant as a cautionary example to Jerusalem (3:7). It cannot serve to motivate an appeal to hope for judgment on the nations, as Striek (ibid., 189) interprets 3:8.

redactor. The same redactor also used earlier material that does not necessarily go back to Zephaniah: Zeph 2:15 is more reminiscent of Isa 47:8, 10, and Zeph 3:3–4, 8 has parallels in Ezekiel's sermon on the sins of the various classes (Ezek 22:23–31). In the course of the exilic expansion of the book of Zephaniah, the universalizing epigraph in Zeph 1:2 was added together with its interpretation in 1:3aα, b, which recalls Hos 4:3.[246] Whether the universalistic bracketing verses 1:18aβ, b and 3:8bβ formed part of the exilic book or are the product of an "apocalyptic" redaction[247] is uncertain. The exilic book did not include the additions to the foreign nation oracles in 2:7, 9b; they are probably early postexilic expansions. Even later are the prose additions in 2:10–11 and 3:9–10 that speak of a conversion of the nations.

Of great importance for understanding the Four Prophets book as a whole is the question of where the exilic book of Zephaniah ended. It certainly did not include the salvation oracles in Zeph 3:14–20. The first, 3:14–15, is written in the (late) prophetic style of the Deutero-Isaiah group (cf. Isa. 52:7–10); it dates from the late exilic period at the earliest. On the other hand, 3:8 would be a very skimpy ending to the book, the more so since the end of the book of Micah already formulates at least negative criteria for a new beginning. It is thus quite likely that the somewhat tentative oracle of salvation in 3:11–13 constituted the conclusion of the exilic Four Prophets book. Several observations support this conclusion: (1) This oracle is the last of those that can be dated with confidence in the late exilic period. (2) Unlike the salvation oracles in 3:14ff., its terminology is closely related to 3:1–8.[248] (3) Like Mic 5:9–13 and Zeph 1:4–6, the text promises a purifying judgment, although its positive perspective advances cautiously beyond these texts. Schart also suggests that Zeph 3:11–13 may belong to the "D corpus."[249] He points out the use of the verb פשע, "sin," used only here in Zephaniah but common in Hosea, Amos, and Micah. The expression לא תוספי ... עוד, "you shall no longer," recalls Hos 1:6 and Amos 7:8, 13; 8:2. Schart nevertheless remains uncertain because the promise of a "people poor and lowly" on Mount Zion is usually associated with the postexilic religion of the poor. Zephaniah 2:3a, which tells the "poor/humble of the land" to seek Yahweh, is

---

[246] The references to the account of the deluge in Zeph 1:3* are by no means so detailed that the verse has to be ascribed to an "apocalyptic" redaction (contra Seybold, *Satirische Prophetie*, 99).

[247] Seybold, *Satirische Prophetie*, 100.

[248] Although not mentioned by name, Jerusalem, the subject of 3:1–5, 7, is addressed here. On מ/בקרבך, "from/in your midst" (3:11–12), cf. 3:3, 5. The expression עלילותך, "your deeds," refers back to 3:7. On עשה עולה, "do wrong" (3:13), cf. 3:5.

[249] *Entstehung*, 213–14.

commonly also assigned to this movement.²⁵⁰ However, since the expression עֲנִוֵי הָאָרֶץ appears already in Amos 8:4 (and Isa 11:4)—albeit without the article—and the exhortation to seek (בַּקְּשׁוּ) Yahweh refers back to Zeph 1:6, which was formulated by FPR, it is quite likely that both Zeph 2:3a and 3:11-13 are from FPR. Since FPR echoes Isaianic texts elsewhere, it is not surprising that the closest parallel to Zeph 3:12 is Isa 14:32. It is striking how tentative the notions of salvation still are in Zeph 3:11-13. At the conclusion of the Four Prophets book, we probably have one of the fundamental exilic texts from which the religion of the poor developed in the Persian period.

Summing up, we conclude that FPR drew on a small collection of Zephaniah's prophecies (1:7-2:4*); as its final verse shows, this document most likely dates from the time of the incipient Neo-Babylonian conquest of Palestine—compare Nebuchadnezzar's campaign against the Philistine cities, especially Ashkelon, in 604 B.C.E.²⁵¹ FPR made only minor changes in this material, probably being responsible only for 1:13b (cf. Amos 5:11; Deut 28:30, 39), 1:17aβ (cf. 2 Kgs 17:7), and 2:3a. By contrast, FPR composed 2:5-3:8, 11-13* himself, albeit making use of earlier material; his hand is especially evident in 3:2, 7, 11-13. Also from the hand of FPR is the introduction to the book in 1:1-6*; it uses an existing oracle as an epigraph in 1:2 and interprets it in 1:3 (cf. Hos 4:3) and 1:4-6 (see above).

In Zeph 1:7-18*, FPR had before him a gloomy textual composite that vividly proclaimed the imminent coming of the day of Yahweh to the upper classes of Jerusalem, from the officials and king's sons who dressed themselves in foreign attire (1:8) and performed strange magical rites (1:9) through the traders and money changers (1:11) to the wealthy who, grown fat on the lees of their wine, expected that Yahweh would do nothing (1:12) and thought that if worst came to worst their wealth would save them (1:18). This terrible announcement of judgment, itself reminiscent of Amos's prophecy concerning the day of Yahweh (Amos 5:18-20), FPR linked explicitly with the message of Amos by recalling in Zeph 1:13b Amos's announcement of judgment on cruel slave drivers (Amos 5:11). This is his message to the people of his own day: the social indictments of Amos—and probably also of Micah—are meant to be heard alongside

---

250 Seybold, *Nahum*, 115; Ben Zvi, *Historical-Critical Study*, 356-57; Striek, *Das vordeuteronomistische Zephanjabuch*, 244-45. Weigel (*Zephanja*, 110-19, 206-16) correctly rejects this assignment but ascribes all of Zeph 1:1-3:16, apart from a few glosses, to the prophet and totally ignores questions of redaction criticism.

251 Elements of Zephaniah's oracles can still be identified in 1:8aβ, 9, 10-11*, 12*, 14-16, 18aα; 2:1-2a, 4. The composite may also go back to him. Jeremiah, too, put together a new summary of his message in the year of crisis 605/604 (cf. Jer 36).

Zephaniah's delineation of the misconduct of Jerusalem's upper classes. The cynical self-assurance of these people, at ease with their wealth and caring not a whit about God (Zeph 1:12), was itself—as FPR makes clear in a commentary on 1:17—a sin against Yahweh. When Zephaniah saw Yahweh's judgment on the fortified cities and battlements (1:16), he was expressing his own view: despite the cultic and religious purification accomplished by Josiah, Jerusalem had perished through the social indifference and military delusions of its upper classes.

However, Zephaniah ended his ominous announcement of judgment with an ultimatum to the lower classes:[252] they must not let themselves be infected by the injustice and arrogance exhibited by the upper classes but must instead seek "righteousness and humility"—then they might have a chance of being hidden on the day of Yahweh's wrath (Zeph 2:1–2, 3b). The cautious promise of protection in Amos 5:14–15, couched in similar language, is here restricted to one social group. At the same time, Zephaniah cited the devastation threatening the Philistine cities as a cautionary example (Zeph 2:4).

In Zeph 2:5–3:13*, FPR turned these warnings into a large-scale historical reflection on Yahweh's judgment against the nations and Jerusalem, again drawing in part on Amos, this time the complex of foreign nation oracles in Amos 1:3–2:16. In an initial oracle of woe (Zeph 2:5), God had addressed the "word of Yahweh"[253] to the four points of the compass: the Phoenicians and Philistines to the west, the Moabites and Ammonites to the east, the Egyptians to the south, and the Assyrian capital of Nineveh to the north.[254] Thus Yahweh had threatened the nations with wholesale judgment. The only identifiable grounds was their arrogance, whether displayed in their treatment of Israel, as in the case of Moab and Ammon (2:5), or in their own hubris, as in the case of Nineveh, "the exultant city" (2:15). The second woe was addressed to Jerusalem, "the oppressing city" (3:1). Thus Jerusalem—like Israel in Amos 2:6ff.—was included in Yahweh's judgment. However, the city remained impenitent, refused to

---

[252] Following Seybold's interpretation of the difficult verses Zeph 2:1–2 (*Satirische Prophetie*, 110): "Stoop and gather! You people who mint no silver! Before the meadow is trampled! The day flies by like chaff!"

[253] Scholars have repeatedly proposed deleting this expression, found in the superscriptions of four books, but here FPR uses it deliberately to underscore the parallel between Yahweh's treatment of the nations and his treatment of Judah and Jerusalem.

[254] The text probably refers to earlier campaigns and conquests of the Neo-Babylonian Empire, from 612 (Nineveh) to 568/567 (Egypt). At the same time, we hear echoes of the threats posed by Judah's neighbors and the occupying forces of the Babylonians during the exilic period; cf. particularly the taunts of the neighbors in Zeph 2:8, mocking the severely reduced territory of Judah.

listen to the prophets, and placed its trust in wealth and arms rather than in Yahweh (3:2), as Zephaniah and the other prophets had foretold. Not all, however, shared this refusal to listen; it was most prevalent among the upper classes: the officials, judges, prophets, and priests (3:3–4). When Yahweh brought to pass his threatened judgment on the nations, destroying their fortified cities and battlements, the basis of their arrogance (3:6; cf. 1:16), he thought that Jerusalem, impressed by these events, would finally accept correction, so that he would not have to bring to pass his threatened judgment on the city. Instead "they," that is, the upper classes (3:4), were even more eager to make all their deeds corrupt (3:7). Therefore Yahweh, as ruler over the Gentile world, finally determined to assemble the nations against Jerusalem, to pour out his indignation "upon them"[255]—once more the upper classes of Jerusalem (3:8).

Up to this point in his historical reflections, FPR has followed the principles of prophetic and Deuteronomistic theology: after the example of Amos 1:3–2:16; 3:1–2; 9:7, he has criticized all arrogant claims to special status: Jerusalem was punished in the exactly the same way as the nations. Just as in Amos 2:11–13 (cf. also Amos 7:12–17; Mic 2:6–11; 3:5–8), he points out that it was refusal to listen to the prophetic word of God that made God's judgment on Israel and Jerusalem inevitable. The only original element is his claim that God's judgment on the nations had a pedagogical purpose for Israel, thus once more establishing a general theological justification for the catastrophe of the exile: Jerusalem was guilty and had been warned; Yahweh had proven himself to be a righteous judge (Zeph 3:5).[256]

What is new, however, is the effort of FPR to work out what he believes to be the salvific aspect of the catastrophe: he links Yahweh's decision to carry out his judgment with an appeal to a group to wait for him until the day when he will arise as a witness (Zeph 3:8a).[257] This

---

[255] The interpretation of עליהם has caused repeated problems. The nations and kingdoms just mentioned cannot be the object of God's indignation: if so, the whole argument would be nonsense. According to 3:6, the nations have already been judged. The popular emendation עליכם, "upon you," arises from the absolutely correct feeling that the logic must point to Jerusalem, but it overlooks the desire of the author, clearly expressed in the continuation (3:11–13), to distinguish various groups within Jerusalem.

[256] In Zeph 3:5, instead of the expected announcement of judgment, FPR clearly quotes from a hymn praising Yahweh's righteousness, new every morning. It is not by accident that the ancient dogma of Zion theology that Yahweh is present in the midst of Jerusalem (cf. Ps 46:6 [5]), blasphemously misapplied in Mic 3:11, is here given an ethical twist. In the text that follows, therefore, Yahweh can distance himself from the unjust actions of the Jerusalem upper classes.

[257] The reading of the Septuagint (לְעֵד), but the two possible meanings of the MT (לְעַד), "as booty" or "forever," also make sense and may hover in the background.

appeal is not addressed to all the inhabitants of Jerusalem, as is usually assumed, but only to the "poor/humble of the land, who do what is right," whom FPR also addressed in the second-person plural in 2:3. This devout underclass is to wait patiently for the day of judgment because Yahweh will then put an end to the tormentors who have made them despair of God's righteousness.

What this new and final purifying judgment of Yahweh on Jerusalem would mean is hinted at by FPR in the concluding oracle of salvation (Zeph 3:11–13). Yahweh will remove from Jerusalem the arrogant braggarts, leaving in its midst only a "people lowly and humble" (עם עני ודל). When the catastrophe eliminated the unrighteous, cynical, self-confident upper classes, Jerusalem received the opportunity for a new beginning. It need no longer be ashamed of its sinful past, because the last barrier separating it from God had been removed. The new beginning would be in the hands of the lower classes, the former victims of the unjust upper classes (on עני and דל, cf. Amos 2:7; 4:1; 5:11; 8:4, 6); therefore they would be immune to any kind of arrogance. They, the remnant of Israel, would "seek refuge in the name of Yahweh" (cf. Isa 14:32) instead of trusting in wealth and arms. Protected by God, they would be able to renounce wrong, lies, and deceit, which had formerly poisoned Judean society.[258] A peaceful and untroubled life in community would finally be possible. Therefore FPR, building on Zephaniah's exhortation (Zeph 2:1–2, 3b), called on the lower classes, who had been faithful to Yahweh, to continue even now to be true to themselves and not follow the errant ways of the upper classes (2:3a).

The utopian picture of Jerusalem society in the future sketched by FPR at the end of his composite includes none of the governmental institutions that characterized preexilic Israel. There is no monarchy; there are no state officials. There is no political, military, or economic elite.[259] FPR has followed to its logical end the indictment of Israel's domestic politics and social structure by the prophets whose message he summarized. A more radical conclusion is hardly conceivable, but he has taken the social conceptuality of an Amos or Micah and shifted it to the religious plane, following the lead of Isaiah. The "people humble and lowly" (Zeph 3:12) left after God's purifying judgment are no longer simply the economically vulnerable but also those who trust in God rather than wealth and power (cf. Isa 14:32). And the "poor/humble of the land" (Zeph 2:3) are

---

258 On עַוְלָה, "wickedness," cf. Hos 10:13; Mic 3:10; on כָּזָב, "lie," cf. Amos 2:4 (also from the hand of FPR); Hos 7:13; 12:2; on תַּרְמִית "deceit," cf. the synonymous מִרְמָה in Hos 12:1, 8; Amos 8:5; Zeph 1:9.

259 Ben Zvi, *Historical-Critical Study*, 353–56.

no longer simply exploited peasant farmers but also those who do what Yahweh decrees, who seek righteousness and humility. Isaiah's expectation that Zion would be rebuilt on a foundation of faith, justice, and righteousness (Isa 28:16–17a) represents much the same hope. Once again we see the concern of FPR to unify the voices of the prophets, with a striking emphasis on Isaiah.

III.2.1.3. Amos

Our analysis of this concluding section of the Four Prophets book allows us also to reconstruct its first section with some assurance. The book of Amos poses certain problems.

A Deuteronomistic stratum has long been recognized in the book of Amos; it can be ascribed to FPR, who also employs some Deuteronomistic language and ideas. The problem is simply that scholars vary in identifying the verses in question solely on the basis of literary and stylistic features, and there are no reliable criteria for determining the extent of the Deuteronomistic book of Amos. The thematic profile of the recension remains ambiguous. Only compositional criteria can assist analysis.

Schmidt, who identified the Deuteronomistic redaction, assigned to it the following verses: Amos 1:1*; 3:1*; 1:9–12; 2:4–5; 2:10–12; 3:7; 5:25–26.[260] Wolff generally followed Schmidt but proposed including 8:11–12.[261] Jeremias included the related texts 2:7b, 9; 3:13–14; 5:6.[262] Bossard-Nepustil added 4:6–13 to the list and, to be consistent, the other hymns in the book of Amos: 5:8–9 and 9:5–6.[263] The most extensive list is that of Schart, who also employed the criteria of redaction criticism: 1:1, 2, 9–12; 2:4–5, 10–12; 3:1b, 7; 4:6–11*; 5:11, 25–26*; 8:4–7, 11–12; 9:7–10.[264] Rottzoll reduced the list substantially: 1:1*; 2:10–11, 12b; 3:1b; 5:25–26.[265]

Bossard-Nepustil's theory that the hymns of the book of Amos along with Amos 4:6–11 should be assigned to the Deuteronomistic redaction of Amos and hence to the redaction of the Four Prophets book is untenable. As is clear from 4:6–13, these hymns point to liturgical use of the texts. If the formation of the Four Prophets book was intended to serve such a purpose—a theory contradicted by the very length of the composite text—one would expect a similar liturgical orientation in the other

---

260 "Deuteronomistische Redaktion."
261 *Joel and Amos*, 136–37.
262 *Book of Amos*, 8.
263 *Rezeption*, 348.
264 *Entstehung*, 317.
265 *Studien*, 287.

sections. However, the number of other passages that might be cited (Hos 12:6 [5]; Mic 5:8; Zeph 3:5) is simply too small. Also unpersuasive is Schart's assignment of Amos 4:6–11 to the Deuteronomistic redaction and the hymns (4:12–13; 5:8–9; 8:8; 9:5–6) to a post-Deuteronomistic redactional stratum that also added the books of Nahum and Habakkuk to the Four Prophets book: this theory gives up the long-recognized literary unity of 4:6–13.[266] Schart points out the affinities of Amos 4:6–11 with the Deuteronomistic language of Solomon's prayer at the dedication of the temple (1 Kgs 8),[267] but these affinities are by no means strong enough to demonstrate a Deuteronomistic origin of the passage in Amos: as the even stronger affinities with Lev 26 and Deut 28 show, both texts reflect the style of common catalogs of curses. Even more dubious is Schart's assignment of Amos 8:4–7 to the Deuteronomistic redaction.[268] This text is clearly compositional, but it has none of the features that might be called Deuteronomistic. Schart believes that the mention of the Sabbath in 8:5 indicates an exilic date, but he overlooks the fact that the text speaks of the Sabbath in parallel with the new moon; as the parallels in 2 Kgs 4:23; Isa 1:13; Hos 2:13 (11); Lam 2:6 show, the verse still represents the preexilic stage of development, when the Sabbath was probably a festival of the full moon, celebrated at the temple. During the exilic period, the Sabbath was separated from the lunar cycle and became a weekly observance, during which families honored Yahweh by refraining from work.[269] Therefore, 8:5 actually supports the preexilic origin of 8:4–7. Schart's theory that the hymns in the book of Amos, related to 8:4–7 through 8:8, presuppose the Deuteronomistic redaction loses its most important support if 8:4–7 does not belong to the Deuteronomistic redaction. On the contrary, there is some reason to assign 8:11–12 to the Deuteronomistic redaction or the "D corpus," as first proposed by Wolff[270] and argued by Schart.[271] The evidence includes the central importance attached to the word (singular!) of Yahweh, which recalls the superscriptions in Hos 1:1, Mic 1:1, and Zeph 1:1 (cf. Hos 4:1; Zeph 2:5); the use of the *topos* of seeking (בָּקֵשׁ) God (here uniquely changed to seeking the word of God), found also in Hos 5:6, 15; 7:10; Zeph 1:6; 2:3; and finally the metaphoric structure, which recalls Deut 8:2.[272]

---

266 Wolff, *Joel and Amos*, 214; Jeremias, *Book of Amos*, 69–76.
267 *Entstehung*, 70–72.
268 Ibid., 89–91.
269 See Albertz, *History* (II.4), 2:408–9.
270 *Joel and Amos*, 326.
271 *Entstehung*, 91–92.
272 At the same time, these verses also interrupt the language of 8:9–10 and 13–14, which are closely linked to the dirge in 5:2ff.

It is even more important to identify the end of the Deuteronomistic book of Amos. Noting that all the Deuteronomistic passages are integrated into the cyclic structure of the book that runs from Amos 1:1 to 9:5, Nogalski concluded that the Deuteronomistic book extended to 9:6.[273] This hymn does in fact make a good conclusion. In that case, however, the book of Amos would be the only one of the Four Prophets not to conclude with a statement of total, ineluctable judgment. Now Schart has proposed assigning 9:7–10 to the "D corpus."[274] The similarity of 9:7 to the Deuteronomistic redaction in 3:1b and especially the Deuteronomistic exodus formula included in both has long been noted. But 9:8, too, recalls the Deuteronomistic expression השמיד מעל פני האדמה (cf. 1 Kgs 13:34), and 9:10b takes up once again one of FPR's favorite themes: rejection of the prophets' message (cf. Amos 2:11–12; Zeph 3:2; etc.). These observations are further supported by the compositional observation that, like the conclusions of the exilic books of Micah and Zephaniah (Mic 5:9–13 [10–14]; Zeph 3:11–13; cf. Zeph 1:4–6), Amos 9:8–10 culminates in a purifying judgment. Here we can identify a unifying purpose at work. For FPR, the *topos* of purifying judgment is clearly the hermeneutical key for dealing in his own time with the prophets' message of universal judgment.

Although I am unable here to cite the evidence in detail, I assume the following stages in the growth of the book of Amos.

(1) A first book of Amos, from the end of the eighth century, in Judah (Assyrian crisis, 711–701 B.C.E.),[275] included Amos 1:1–8:3* and comprised the superscription "Words of Amos of Tekoa, two years before the earthquake," the composite of foreign nation oracles (1:3–8, 13–2:3, 6–9, 13–16), two collections of oracles (3:1–2*, 3–6, 8, 9–12, 15–4:3 and 5:1–7, 10–12, 14–17, 18–6:14), and a vision composite including the account of Amos's expulsion (7:1–8:2). It may have concluded with 8:3, with the shattered lament bewailing the end of Israel (8:2). With some assurance, we can ascribe the following to the prophet himself: the oracles in 2:6–9 + 13–16*; 3:3–6, 8, 9–11, 12 + 15; 4:1–3, 4–5; the fragments in 5:7, 10–12, 18–19, 21–24 + 27; 6:1–7*, 8–9 (?), 11, 12, 13–14; the vision cycle in 7:1–8 + 8:1–2; and possibly a few foreign nation oracles.

(2) A second book of Amos, from the late preexilic period (end of the seventh or beginning of the sixth century), comprised Amos 1:1–9:4*. Here the prophecy of Amos was stylized as a theophany of judgment

---

[273] *Literary Precursors*, 78–82.

[274] *Entstehung*, 94–96.

[275] Note the application to Judah in Amos 6:1 and the conquest of the Philistine city of Gath in 6:2, which took place in 711; see Blum, "Amos," 25–36. Blum posits an even earlier book of Amos, dating between 732 and 722 (39).

from Zion (1:2); isolated timely passages were added, such as 3:13–14 and 5:26; a continuation was appended interpreting earlier oracles of Amos: 8:4–7 (cf. 2:6–8); 8:9–10 (cf. 5:2–9); 8:13–14 (cf. 5:2ff.), as well as the clearly compositional fifth vision in 9:1–4, with 9:1 echoing 1:1* and 9:3 echoing 1:2 to form a framework.[276] To counter false hopes of salvation, the book proclaimed the end of the cult (9:1) and the ineluctable approach of judgment (9:2–4). Even deportation would give no chance for survival (9:4).

(3) A third book of Amos, from the early exilic period (sixth century), documents how Amos's prophecy was received and incorporated into exilic worship: 4:6–13; 5:8–9; 8:8; 9:5–6 (doxologies).

(4) The book of Amos as part of the Four Prophets book, from well on in the exilic period, comprised 1:1–9:10. The following verses are from the hand of FPR: 1:1b, 9–10, 11–12; 2:4–5, 10–12; 3:1b*, 7; 5:25 (?); 8:11–12; 9:7–10.

(5) Early postexilic continuations are found in 9:11, 12b, 13aα, 14–15; there are also later links to the book of the Twelve: 9:12a (cf. Obad 7–21) and 9:13aβ, b (cf. Joel 4:18 [3:18]). Compare also the bracketing of Joel 4:16 (3:16) with Amos 1:2.[277]

The book of Amos confronted FPR with a particularly difficult task. No other prophet had so radically proclaimed the end of the people of Israel (Amos 8:2). The radical nature of this prophecy was further emphasized in the late preexilic continuation, which countered burgeoning hopes for salvation with the message that God's universal judgment was imminent and inescapable (9:1–4). Was there any possibility of survival for the exilic generation in the face of God's rejection?

It would have been easy to limit Amos's message of radical judgment to the northern kingdom, to which it had originally been addressed, but the Judean reception of Amos's prophecy (Amos 6:1–7), which began with the first book of Amos immediately after the fall of the northern kingdom, stood in the way, as did the desire of FPR to demonstrate the unity of the prophetic word of God, which the exilic generation must take to heart, by bringing together the prophets of the northern and southern kingdoms. Thus he chose a different way of dealing with the prophecy of Amos: he provided a detailed motivation for the harsh message of judgment and differentiated it for his own generation. That the book of Amos includes more secondary motivations than the other three books is due to the radical nature of its message.

---

[276] Waschke ("Fünfte Vision") has demonstrated convincingly that the fifth vision represents a secondary interpretation.

[277] Nogalski, *Literary Precursors*, 104–22.

After adding to the oracles against foreign nations prophecies against Phoenicia and Edom, the two nations that oppressed the Judeans most severely during the exilic period (Amos 1:9–10, 11–12), FPR inserted into the introductory composite a special oracle of judgment against Judah (2:4–5) so that every reader would see immediately that everything Amos had said about the northern kingdom applied to Judah as well. No Judean of the exilic period would be able to ignore the word of God as being irrelevant. In particular, he accused the Judeans of rejecting the *tôrâ* of Yahweh and being led astray by their lies, which their ancestors had already followed after. Concretely, these charges probably refer to the failure of the Josianic reform (cf. Hos 8:1b, 12) and idolatry. But when FPR departed from Deuteronomistic usage by substituting "lies" (כזב) for the idols that led the people astray (cf. the catchword תעה: Hos 4:12; Mic 3:5), he probably wanted this term to include false reliance on the Jerusalem temple (Mic 3:11), Israel's elect status (Amos 3:1–2; 9:7), and military might (Mic 1:13).

The primary reason for the unbelievably harsh message of judgment that God had proclaimed through Amos was, in the opinion of FPR, not simply the social injustice that the prophet had exposed but also and above all the fate that he and his message had to suffer. As FPR could read in Amos 7:10–16, the priest of the temple in Bethel had forbidden Amos to prophesy and ordered him to leave the city. For the Judean redactor(s), this attack on the ministry of the prophets was the reason for Yahweh's irreversible decision to bring judgment on his people; therefore, the redactor(s) set this episode within the account of the vision in which Amos stated the grounds for his terrible message of judgment (8:1–2). FPR accepted this understanding and generalized it in a theological interpretation of history. In his opinion, calling the prophets—like bringing the Israelites out of Egypt, leading them in the desert, and giving them the land—was among the saving acts by which Yahweh sought to set his people apart and give them special protection (2:10–11). By seeing to it that nothing came to pass without revealing his decision to the prophets (3:7), Yahweh prevented his people from stumbling unwittingly into catastrophe. Prophecy of judgment, so FPR declares—enlisting the assent of his hearers (cf. 2:11b)[278]—had been an instrument of God's special care for his people. All the worse, therefore, was their disdain for the prophets of judgment in the preexilic period; it was not simply stupidity but ingratitude toward God, sin in the strict sense of the word. By forbidding the prophets of judgment to speak and thus silencing the word of God, previous generations had brusquely rejected God, leaving

---

[278] The tendency of FPR to ask rhetorical questions when he wants his hearers to accept a difficult reinterpretation is also illustrated by Amos 9:7 and Mic 1:5b.

God no other choice than to execute harshest judgment on them. Not even an appeal to Yahweh's election of Israel, in the past (3:1b, 2) or in the present (9:7), could alter the outcome.

In Amos 8:11–12, FPR depicts the consequences of this "sin against the Holy Spirit" for his own exilic generation: the prophetic word of Yahweh, formerly rejected so contemptuously, was no longer available, although it would have been as vital to survival as bread and water. The withdrawal of the word of God, which we now lament so bitterly (Ps 74:9)—so says FPR—was a direct consequence of this earlier contempt. Now, therefore, it was vitally important finally to give ear to it!

However, if the hour demanded new respect for the prophetic word of judgment, it became even more pressing to decide how the exilic period was to deal with the inexorable prophetic word of Amos, which seemed to rule out any future for Israel. Therefore FPR decided to append an interpretive appendix (Amos 9:7–10) to the existing book (1:1–9:6*).

First, he rejected any attempt to evade the message of judgment by an appeal to Israel's election (Amos 9:7). Even though Yahweh had brought Israel out of Egypt, Israel had no special claim on Yahweh. Israel meant no more to Yahweh—as FPR so provocatively puts it—than the Cushites in far-off Nubia; Yahweh, the lord of history, had also brought the Philistines and Arameans to Palestine from their original homelands— and who else? According to everything there was to read in the book of Amos (1:3–2:16; 3:1–2), the path of cheap grace was closed to the generation of the exile.

Nevertheless, the book's message of universal judgment had to be moderated if it was not to drive the exilic generation to despair. FPR achieved this moderation by reinterpreting the fifth vision (Amos 9:1–4) in 9:8: Yahweh's baneful eye—so he interprets 9:4—is no longer upon Israel as a whole but only "upon the sinful kingdom." Only this kingdom would he utterly destroy, causing it to vanish from the earth, since it had been directly responsible for expelling Amos (7:13). FPR based this interpretation on the prophet Hosea, who had often prophesied the end (Hos 1:4) or the rejection (13:9–11) of the northern monarchy. Several texts in the book of Hosea promised a future for God's people Israel after judgment (2:17ff. [15ff.]; 11:8ff.; 14:5ff. [4ff.]), but never for its royal house. FPR could therefore argue with some justification that Amos's message of universal judgment, the end of Israel, referred only to the political state of Israel (בית יעקב, "house of Jacob": 9:8b), not the people of God as such (cf. עַמִּי, "my people": 9:10a).

This condemnation was certainly addressed to the monarchy of the northern kingdom, which fell in 722. There seems to have been a widespread consensus concerning its disappearance not only in Judah but also in Samaria. In any case, so far as we can tell, the idea of reconstituting it never came under discussion, either during or after the exile. Instead, the Sanballat family was established in Samaria as a powerful dynasty of governors. It is not so clear to what extent FPR wanted to include the monarchy of the southern kingdom in this verdict. Schart prefers to restrict the criticism of monarchy in the Four Prophets book entirely to the northern kingdom.[279] He can cite the absence of any explicit criticism of the Davidides. Nevertheless, Zephaniah does include the king's sons in his criticism of the upper classes in Jerusalem (Zeph 1:8). The promises of a new Judean monarchy in Hos 3:5, Amos 9:11–12, and Mic 5:1–2 were not yet included in the Four Prophets book, and the concluding salvation oracle envisions a society without a king or governmental institutions (Zeph 3:11–13); it is therefore probable that FPR, like the Deutero-Isaiah group (Isa 55:5) and JerD (Jer 22:24–30), was against restoring the Davidic monarchy. If so, he understood his condemnation of the sinful kingdom as including both the northern and the southern kingdoms.

The end of the monarchy would free Israel from an institution that had repeatedly led it to sin against God and was decisively responsible for the catastrophe.

In the opinion of FPR, however, the people themselves had to undergo a purifying judgment: Yahweh would shake the house of Israel through a coarse sieve to remove all gross impurities, which would be caught in the sieve. This means that the prophecies of judgment in the book of Amos would henceforth apply only to the sinners contaminating the people of God; they would inevitably die by the sword (Amos 9:10a; cf. 9:1, 4; 7:11). It is not by accident that FPR describes these sinners as people who still refused to accept the message of the prophets of judgment. According to the words placed in their mouths, they still denied that any harm (רעה; cf. 9:4) could come from their transgressions (9:10b). In the view of FPR, those who had learned nothing from the prophets even after the catastrophe had no part in the Israel of the future.

III.2.1.4. Hosea

At the beginning of his work, finally, FPR placed the book of Hosea. This was by no means a foregone conclusion: as FPR well knew, Amos had preceded Hosea as a prophet and actually should have come first in the chronological schema of the Four Prophets book. He probably accepted this minor inconsistency because for him this prophetic book, as had become clear in many different ways, constituted the theological basis on

---

279 *Entstehung*, 227–29.

which he repeatedly interpreted the other three. We shall see evidence confirming this hypothesis, but there is still a problem: it has been almost impossible to identify a Deuteronomistic redaction of the book of Hosea.

Actually, since Perlitt, the single text Hos 8:1b has been accepted almost unanimously as a Deuteronomistic interpolation.[280] Schart believes that the D redaction also took the programmatic expression דבר יהוה, "word of Yahweh," used in the superscriptions and inserted it in Hos 4:1 to introduce the collection of oracles, instead of the demonstrative pronoun זאת (cf. the call to hear in 5:1) or the expression "this word," as in Amos 3:1; 4:1; 5:1. This theory is quite possible. Also acceptable is his proposed assignment of the explanatory "and they turn to other gods" in Hos 3:1bβ to the same hand (cf. Deut 31:18, 20). However, his inclusion of Hos 14:2–4 (1–3) in this group is questionable. It is a text that would be thoroughly appropriate to FPR, since it parallels misplaced trust in arms (cf. Isa 30:16) with idolatry and is also used compositionally (cf. Mic 5:12). However, Jer 3:22a cites both Hos 14:2aα (1aα) and 14:5aα (4aα); therefore the whole passage 14:2–9 (1–8) represents a supplement to the book of Hosea, which must have been added before Jeremiah's early ministry (627–609 B.C.E.).[281] On the basis of diction that echoes Deuteronomistic usage, only Hos 3:1bβ; 4:1*; and 8:1b can be assigned to FPR.

This leaves open the question whether FPR was also responsible for other secondary verses (Jeremias[282] cites Hos 4:5aβ, 10, 15; 5:5bβ; 6:10–11a; 7:10; 8:6a, 14; 9:4b; 10:15a; 11:5b, 6b, 10; 12:1b, 2aγ, 3a*, 5a*, 6 [11:12b; 12:1aγ, 2a*, 4a*, 5]; 13:2aβ, bα, 3), which scholars have long ascribed to various Judean redactors or have simply been unable to categorize. In my opinion, this assignment is reasonably certain in the case of 8:14, a verse that describes the typical sin of Judah as the multiplication of fortified cities, in contrast to the sin of the northern kingdom, which consisted in building sanctuaries while notoriously forgetting God. This accusation looks ahead to Zeph 1:16, where the catchword עָרִים בְּצֻרוֹת is firmly established; it also sets out within the Four Prophets book further links with Amos 2:5; 3:9; and Mic 5:10, 13 (11, 14). The designation of God as Israel's "Maker" recalls Deutero-Isaiah (Isa 44:2 and 51:13, likewise with שׁכח, "forget"), making an exilic dating of this verse likely.[283] Since the

---

[280] Lothar Perlitt, *Bundestheologie im Alten Testament* (WMANT 36; Neukirchen-Vluyn: Neukrichener Verlag, 1969), 146–52. Cf. Jeremias, *Prophet Hosea*, 104; Schart, *Entstehung*, 173.

[281] The changes in Hos 1:2b and 2:6 that Schart also assigns to the D redaction (*Entstehung*, 170–71) can come from that source only on the questionable assumption that the D redaction was responsible for the composite Hos 1–2 (or 1–3).

[282] "Hosea/Hoseabuch," 592.

[283] Contra Rainer Albertz, *Weltschöpfung und Menschenschöpfung: Untersucht bei Deuterojesaja, Hiob und in den Psalmen* (CThM.A 3; Stuttgart: Calwer, 1974), 39, 151–52. This

hand of FPR is visible both at the beginning (8:1b) and at the end of the chapter, it is quite possible that the polemic against idols in 8:6a derives from the same source; the interrogative style (text emended) could also support this conclusion (cf. Amos 2:11b; 9:7; Mic 1:5b). Next in order of probability is Hos 4:15, a text that likewise takes aim at the multiplication of cultic sites in the northern kingdom, warning Judah not to do the same and citing Amos 4:4; 5:5; 8:14. Since Amos 8:13–14 probably belongs to a late preexilic version of the book of Amos, the most likely date for Hos 4:15 is in the exilic period. Because Hos 1:5 and 1:7, like 8:14, thematize military power, these verses may also go back to FPR, since he adopts this theme repeatedly into his work (Mic 1:13b; 5:9–10 [10–11]), although it was sometimes already present in his material (Hos 14:4 [3]; Zeph 1:6). Finally, we come to the interpolated comment on Israel's refusal to return to Yahweh in Hos 11:5b, which draws on Jer 5:3 and 8:5 and also recalls Zeph 3:2. Since Hos 3:5 is still unfamiliar with the notion of the remnant found in Zeph 3:13, this expectation of a future return cannot go back to FPR,[284] but it probably did lay the groundwork for his thoughts (cf. Zeph 2:3).

In the book of Hosea, the hand of FPR is quite likely visible in Hos 1:5, 7; 3:1bβ; 4:1*, 15; 8:1b, 6a, 14; 11:5b. Possibly it is so little in evidence "because the D redaction found its theological conception already expressed in this document without the need for major intrusion."[285] I start by assuming that most of the book of Hosea (comprising both sections, 1–3 and 4–14) was already available to FPR in its present form. The composite of oracles in Hos 4–14, which Hosea's disciples probably assembled from the teachings of their master shortly after the fall of Samaria in 722 B.C.E. and then extended in 14:2–9 (1–8), must have existed in Judah by the last third of the seventh century at the latest, since Jeremiah cites its latest section (Hos 14:2, 5 [1, 4]) in Jer 3:22. The composite containing both narrative and oracles, Hos 1–3*, held together redactionally by 1:2, 2:6 (4), and 3:1, may date from the early years of Jeremiah, when the former northern kingdom appeared to have a chance for a new beginning after the retreat of the Assyrians. It did not yet include the salvation oracles 2:1–3, 20, 23–25 (1:10–2:1, 18, 21–23), which are probably postexilic. The inclusion of David in the expectations voiced in 3:5 also derives from postexilic discussion.

---

observation also argues against ascribing the verse to a preexilic assimilation of the book of Hosea to the book of Amos (Jeremias, "Anfänge," 39–41). Schart (*Entstehung*, 154–55) does not assign the verse to his tradent recension; he also rejects assigning it to the D stratum, in part because he does not assign Mic 5:9–13 (10–14) to the redaction of the Four Prophets book.

[284] Jeremias (*Prophet Hosea*, 57–58) assigns Hos 3:5 to an early editor, since Jer 2:19 (in its earliest version, found in the Syriac and Vetus Latina) already alludes to this verse.

[285] Schart, *Entstehung*, 169.

The book of Hosea was one of the sources on which Deuteronomic theology had already drawn; in it FPR found virtually all the themes he considered important, since he was influenced by, among other things, Deuteronomistic theology. The first of these themes was the fundamental sin of idolatry, which had driven not only the northern kingdom (Hos 2:4–17 [2–15]; 4:4–14; etc.; cf. Mic 1:6–7; 5:12–13) but also the southern kingdom (Zeph 1:4–6) to apostasy from Yahweh. Then there was misplaced trust in arms and alliances (Hos 5:11–14; 7:8–9, 11–12; 8:9; 10:13–14; 14:4 [3]), to which Judah was especially prone (Mic 5:9–10, 13 [10–11, 14]; Zeph 1:16). Finally, there was criticism of the monarchy (Hos 1:4; 3:4; 7:7; 10:7, 15; 13:10–11; cf. Amos 9:8) and the upper classes (Hos 5:1–2; 7:3–7, 16; cf. Zeph 3:3–4). Social misconduct (Hos 4:1–2) and rejection of the prophets (Hos 9:7–9, 17; cf. Amos 2:10–11; Zeph 3:2, 7) are also not absent.

There was little that FPR needed to add; he simply extended the argument here and there. At the very beginning of the book, following Hosea's prophecy of the end of the northern kingdom (Hos 1:4), he introduced the theme of "misplaced trust in arms," which appeared only peripherally in the book of Hosea (10:14; 14:4 [3]) but was important to him from his reading of Isaiah: the "bow of Israel" would be broken (1:5), and God's intervention to deliver Judah would therefore no longer be accomplished by force of arms but—as he only hints at here—in a manner unique to God (1:7). This theme is entirely appropriate to the proemium of a book focused on a purifying judgment on the fortresses (Hos 8:14; Mic 5:10, 13; Zeph 1:16) and arms (Mic 5:9) of Judah and where, with all arrogance purged away, only the humble and lowly will be left in Jerusalem (Zeph 3:11–13).

However, it was also important to warn the exilic generation once more of the danger of apostasy, which Hosea had exposed so dramatically in the northern kingdom. In Hos 4:15, citing the whoredom of Israel, FPR orders Judah not to visit Gilgal, Bethel, and Beer-sheba, already attacked in the book of Amos (4:4; 5:5; 8:14). There was obviously some danger that, with the destruction of the Jerusalem temple, the Judeans would be tempted to participate in the cult of these northern-kingdom sanctuaries or pilgrimage sites. This was particularly true of Bethel, which had become a close neighbor with the shift of Judean territory northward (to the region of Mizpah). FPR was concerned to counter any attempt born of exigency to undermine the cultic centralization achieved under Josiah.

The theology of Hosea seemed deficient to FPR only in that he introduced into Hos 8 a particularly terse summary of this theology, the Deuteronom(ist)ic theologoumenon of the covenant (8:1b), which is post-Hoseanic. Everything that Hosea castigates in chapter 8—the incessant change of rulers (8:4a), the manufacture of costly idols (8:4b), the state cult with its calf statue (8:5, 6b), the multiplication of sacrifices (8:11–13), the unrestrained forging of alliances and the ruinous attempts to curry favor with foreign powers (8:7–10)—all this FPR describes as breaking the covenant between Yahweh and Israel and transgressing its obligations (תּוֹרָה) as defined in the Deuteronomic law (cf. Deut 17:14–17; 5:8–9; 12:13–15; 23:22–24 [21–23]; 7:1–3). Thus he generalized Hosea's isolated reproach that the Israelites would disregard God's instruction (תּוֹרָה: Hos 8:12) even if it were written and grounded his accusations on the widely disseminated Deuteronomic reform theology. How important FPR felt this perspective to be is shown by his repetition of the charge of rejecting the law of Yahweh (תּוֹרַת יהוה), singling out the southern kingdom (Amos 2:4; cf. Zeph 3:4).

However, there was something even more important to FPR than underscoring the accusations of the book of Hosea and giving them a theological foundation. More than any other prophet of judgment, Hosea and his disciples had thought about the relationship between judgment and salvation and the possibility of a new beginning after the catastrophe. Here were oracles of salvation from the preexilic period, some integrated into judgment composites (Hos 2:4–17 [2–25]), others appended later (2:18, 21–22 [16, 19–20];[286] 14:2–9). All of this was enormously important to FPR, who sought after the catastrophe to develop a future perspective for the exilic generation based on the prophetic documents. It can be shown that he developed the central theological concept of his composite of prophetic books from the book of Hosea.

The entire book of Hosea is permeated with a repeated movement from judgment to salvation (Hos 2:4–18, 21–22 [2–16, 19–20]; 3:1–5; 4–11; 12–14); the salvation oracles always come at the end. Following this model, FPR placed at the end of the other three prophetic documents his oracles that set limits to judgment and looked forward to a salvific future (Amos 9:7–10; Mic 5:9–13 [10–14]; Zeph 3:11–13). Thus the entire Four Prophets book continued the trajectory of the book of Hosea. What this meant theologically for the exilic generation was that there would be no salvation for them without judgment or bypassing judgment, but only through judgment, with total acceptance of the prophets' accusations and God's punishments.

In the book of Hosea, the proclamation of both judgment and salvation involves a legal contest between Yahweh and his faithless people (cf. רִיב at the beginning in 2:4 [2]; 4:1, 4; 12:3 [2]). Yahweh contends dramatically

---

[286] I assume, with Jeremias (*Prophet Hosea*, 48–49), that these two salvation oracles were appended to 2:16–17 (14–15) at an early date by Hosea's disciples, while other salvation oracles in the second chapter were added in the postexilic period.

with his people. From the outset, however, the objective of his accusations and indictments, harsh and cruel as they seem, is Israel's return (2:9b [7b]; 5:15; 11:11; 14:2ff. [1ff.]) and a salvific new beginning of his relationship with his people (2:16–17 [14–15]; 14:5ff. [4ff.]), since despite every disappointment God cannot forswear his passionate love for them (11:1–4, 8–9). From this message, FPR was able to gain the crucial insight that even the catastrophe of the exile, in which God seemed so far off, could not mean the end of Yahweh's dealings with his people. This time, too, Yahweh's act of judgment must aim at a new beginning. It was the task of the exilic generation to discover the salvific elements of God's judgment. For this very reason, FPR conceived his notion of salvation in the form of a purifying judgment (Amos 9:7–10; Mic 5:9–13; Zeph 1:4–6; 3:9–11).

Hosea and his disciples recognized that God's judgment has a pedagogical function (Hos 5:1, 9). It is intended to teach Israel to whom it owes all that it has and all that it is (2:10 [8]; 11:3). Therefore, they often described God's judgment as revoking all God's beneficent gifts to Israel (Hos 2:11, 14 [9, 12]; 9:2), even the gift of the land itself (8:13; 11:5; 12:10 [9]), or as removing everything that had tempted Israel to turn faithless, from the Baalized cult to the calf at Bethel (2:13, 15, 19 [11, 13, 17]; 9:4–5; 10:5). Israel was confined to prevent her from going after her lovers, whether religious (2:8 [6]) or political (7:2; 8:12). Behind all these punitive acts stood God's purpose: to bring Israel back (2:9b [7b]).

All the elements of this privative judgment come together in the symbolic act described in Hos 3:1–5*. Just as Hosea is to love and marry an adulterous woman, then confine her to prevent further adulteries, so God will deprive faithless Israel of everything it enjoyed and everything that led it astray: king and court, sacrifice and sanctuaries, oracles of all kinds. All this was done with the intent that, after a certain length of time, the Israelites would return to seek their God.

It is quite apparent that FPR used this notion of pedagogical judgment from the book of Hosea to develop his concept of Yahweh's ongoing purifying judgment, a notion that he expounded in his Four Prophets book (Amos 9:7–10; Mic 5:9 –13 [10–14]; Zeph 1:4–6; 3:9–11). He appears to have taken Hos 3:1–5* as a kind of foundational text, since he constructed actual lists, such as that in Hos 3:4, of what Yahweh would take away. Of the six terms in Hos 3:4, he used the first four almost literally and the last two more generically.[287] Drawing on Hos 3:1–4, FPR used

---

[287] For מֶלֶךְ, "king," cf. מַמְלָכָה, "kingship," in Amos 9:8; for שַׂר, "government official," cf. Zeph 3:3, 11; for זֶבַח, "sacrifice," cf. Amos 5:25; for מַצֵּבָה, "massebah," cf. Mic 5:12 (13); for the oracular ephod and teraphim, cf. "sorcerers" and "soothsayers" in Mic 5:11 (12).

his work to challenge the exilic generation to understand the loss of the monarchy, the elite, military power, festal worship, and professional oracles, superficially a bitter experience, as an ultimately wise and loving pedagogical lesson of their God, by means of which everything that disrupted the relationship between Yahweh and his people was purged to make possible a new beginning, in righteousness and humility.

It is noteworthy that FPR emphasized the purifying nature of this privation more than Hosea had. This shift of emphasis also follows from the book of Hosea, which could say quite clearly that return was difficult (Hos 6:1–6; 7:10, 16), indeed that Israel was incapable of return (11:7). Since Israel's refusal to return was notorious, as FPR—stressing Israel's guilt—points out in 11:5b, Yahweh had to use extremely harsh discipline to heal Israel's disloyalty (14:5 [4]). He had to remove totally everything in which Israel had mistakenly put its trust (Amos 9:8; Mic 5:9–13 [10–14]; Zeph 1:4–5). Since Israel would not willingly give up its idols, God had to deliver Israel from them once for all through his purifying judgment. Therefore the new salvation that Yahweh enabled by this drastic step could not mean simple restoration of the preexilic status quo; neither could it embrace all Israel without distinction. It would encompass primarily the humble and lowly, who were immune to arrogance and injustice (Zeph 3:12). Besides these, it would include only those willing to accept God's pedagogy, as recorded in the Four Prophets book, and to be taught to seek righteousness and humility (Zeph 2:3).

More than the other three prophetic books, the book of Hosea revealed God's purpose in sending his prophets of judgment to Israel and Judah; therefore, it belonged at the head of the Four Prophets book, which sought to trace for the exilic generation the history of this prophetic word of God, often so harsh and for long periods so hard to bear, through more than two hundred years and to unlock its meaning to them.

At present, the place of origin and the sociohistorical setting of the Four Prophets redaction must remain conjectural, since the hypothesis is still too new and is burdened by many uncertainties. Since FPR appears to be familiar with both the Deuteronomistic History (cf. Zeph 1:4–6 and 2 Kgs 23) and JerD (cf. Zeph 3:2 and Jer 7:28), most likely it was drafted sometime after 550. The references in Zeph 2:15 to Isa 47:8, 10 and in Zeph 3:3–4, 8 to Ezek 22:25–31 might suggest a Babylonian origin, but Hos 4:15 argues against this localization, since it clearly deals with a problem in Palestine. Since the Four Prophets book as a whole gravitates toward Jerusalem (Micah, Zephaniah) and the purifying judgments in Mic 5:9–13 (10–14); Zeph 1:4–6; 3:1–13* focus on that city, it probably originated in Judah. It has both theological and political affinities with JerD, which also originated in Judah: theologically, for example, it places the prophetic word and the Deuteronomic *tôrâ* in parallel (Hos 8:1b, 13;

Amos 2:4); politically, it is hostile to the monarchy (Amos 9:8). However, unlike JerD, which distinguishes among the various officials, the Four Prophets book is critical of the whole elite upper class and more supportive of the underclass. Theologically, it is influenced not just by Deuteronomistic theology but especially by the writings of the four prophets and also, strikingly, by Isaiah. Elsewhere, relationships between Isaianic and Deuteronomistic texts are few and far between; the only instance of a redaction of Isaianic texts exhibiting Deuteronomistic influence is Isa 1:2–20. Whereas the Deuteronomistic History presents an Isaiah reinterpreted as a religious nationalist (2 Kgs 18–20), FPR adopts the early Isaianic traditions that were critical of the military and the government (Isa 14:32; 30:1–5, 16; 31:1–3). FPR is even further removed from the authors of the Deuteronomistic History, who famously ignore the prophets in question, than are the redactors of JerD. Since the latter, as descendants of the Shaphanides, probably represent the collective leadership of those who remained behind, FPR more likely belongs to a more radical group of theologians, in solidarity with the lower classes.

III.2.2. The Book of Habakkuk

Dietrich, Walter. "Habakuk, ein Jesajaschüler," in *Nachdenken über Israel, Bibel und Theologie: Festschrift für Klaus-Dietrich Schunck* (ed. H. M. Niemann, M. Augustin, and W. H. Schmidt; BEATAJ 37; Frankfurt: Lang, 1994), 197–214. **Haak,** Robert D. *Habakkuk* (VTSup 44; Leiden: Brill, 1992). **Jeremias,** Jörg. *Kultprophetie und Gerichtsverkündigung in der späten Königszeit* (WMANT 35; Neukirchen-Vluyn: Neukirchener Verlag, 1970). **Jöcken,** Peter. *Das Buch Habakuk: Darstellung der Geschichte seiner kritischen Erforschung mit einer eigenen Beurteilung* (BBB 48; Cologne: Hanstein, 1977). **Jöcken.** "War Habakuk ein Kultprophet?" in *Bausteine biblischer Theologie: Festgabe für G. Johannes Botterweck* (ed. H.-J. Fabry; Cologne: Hanstein, 1977), 319–32. **Koenen,** Klaus. *Heil den Gerechten, Unheil den Sündern! Ein Beitrag zur Theologie der Prophetenbücher* (BZAW 229; Berlin: de Gruyter, 1994). **Lescow,** Theodor. "Die Komposition der Bücher Nahum und Habakuk," *BN* 77 (1995): 59–85. **Nogalski,** James. *Redactional Processes in the Book of the Twelve* (BZAW 218; Berlin: de Gruyter, 1993), 129–81. **Otto,** Eckard. "Habakuk/Habakukbuch," *TRE* 14:300–306. **Otto.** "Die Stellung der Weheworte in der Verkündigung des Propheten Habakuk," *ZAW* 89 (1977), 73–107. **Otto.** "Die Theologie des Buches Habakuk," *VT* 35 (1985), 274–95. **Schmidt,** Hans. "Ein Psalm im Buche Habakuk," *ZAW* 62 (1950): 52–63. **Seybold,** Klaus. *Nahum, Habakuk, Zephanja* (ZBK.AT 24/2; Zurich: Theologischer Verlag, 1991). **Sweeney,** Marvin A. "Structure, Genre, and Intent in the Book of Habakkuk," *VT* 41 (1991): 63–83.

The book of Habakkuk was not included in the exilic book of the Four Prophets; it attained its initial, clearly identifiable literary form in the late exilic period. The difference is already apparent in the superscription:

"The oracle [הַמַּשָּׂא] that the prophet Habakkuk saw." It uses a term that appears also in the superscription of the book of Nahum;[288] the closest parallel is Isa 13:1, the superscription to the foreign nation oracles of the book of Isaiah (Isa 13ff.). The parallel is not accidental: the exilic book of Habakkuk also designs to be poetic work on the subject of a foreign nation. Just as the book of Nahum dealt with the destruction of the Neo-Assyrian Empire, so the exilic book of Habakkuk deals primarily with Yahweh's judgment on the Neo-Babylonian Empire. Despite this thematic parallelism, however, it displays an individuality that is connected with the particular history of the book itself. The references to the book of Nahum are a secondary addition of the postexilic period.[289]

The unique character of the book of Habakkuk lies in its mixture of psalmic and prophetic genres. The first section of the book (Hab 1–2) contains portions of a lament psalm in 1:2–4, 12–13, 14 (?), alternating strangely with prophetic descriptions of disaster (1:5–11, 14[?]–17). There is also a series of woe texts in 2:6b–19, following an oracle in 2:1–5, which both refers back to the laments and leads up to the woe texts. A new superscription introduces the second section of the book explicitly as "A prayer of the prophet Habakkuk." It comprises portions of two theophanic hymns (3:3–7, with Yahweh in the third person; 3:8–15, with Yahweh in the second person), bracketed by two short prayers of thanksgiving and petition (3:2, 16). There follows a first-person plural lament in 3:17 and an individual confession of trust in 3:18–19. The second superscription, notes on musical performance in 3:1 and 3:19, and the interpolated selah in 3:3, 9, 13 indicate that the third chapter was used liturgically. Such use is also suggested by the transitional cultic acclamation in 2:20, which is probably also intended to link with Zeph 1:7 and hence the Four Prophets book.

Besides the mixture of genres, there is a confusing juxtaposition of different themes. The lament psalm (Hab 1:2–4, 12–13) deals with the abuse of the righteous by the wicked and God's silence in the face of their suffering. Yahweh responds in 2:4, 5* that only the righteous individual has a promise of life, not the wicked, "whose soul is puffed up and is not right [text?]." Judgment on the wicked is also the theme of 3:13b–14, a

---

[288] The word derives from the expression נשׂא קוֹל, "lift one's voice, cry aloud" (cf. Judg 9:7; Isa 24:14; etc.), but there are also overtones of "burden."

[289] Especially by means of the hymn interpolated at the beginning the book of Nahum (Nah 1:2–10); this hymn and the hymn in Hab 3:3–15 bracket the two books. Apart from these hymns, there are actually rather few verbal echoes (Schart, *Entstehung* [III.2.1], 142–50). The points of contact are far too general to support Nogalski's theory (*Redactional Processes* [III.2.1], 146–54) that the exilic redaction of the book of Habakkuk employed Nahum as a model.

fragmentary passage clearly at odds with the rest of the hymn, which praises the coming of Yahweh to save (all) his people and his anointed (3:13a). The descriptions of disaster in 1:5–11, 15–17 portray the enormous military superiority of the Babylonians over all other nations. On the one hand, the text says that Yahweh has given them this power (1:6); on the other, it criticizes their self-aggrandizement (1:11, 16) and their excesses. The woe texts oddly castigate both social injustice (e.g., 2:6, 7a) and attacks on foreign nations (e.g., 2:7b, 8) in quick succession.

Fundamental to an understanding of the book is Jeremias's insight that the various indictments of the woe texts are to be understood diachronically as a late exilic reinterpretation of social indictments uttered by the prophet Habakkuk against the Judean upper classes (2:6b, 7, 9, 10a, 10bβ, 12, 15–16, 19aα), turning them into political indictments against the Babylonians (2:6a, 8, 10bα, 13–14, 17, 19b, 18).[290] This interpretation is almost universally accepted today, although some scholars divide up the verses somewhat differently.[291] For the most part I follow Seybold, but I agree with Jeremias that the woe texts begin in 2:6b rather than 2:5, since the redactor uses 2:5bβ, 6a to place them in the mouth of the nations. The exilic redaction of the woes thus appears in 2:5bβ, 6a, 7b, 8, 10bα, 13–14, 16–17, 18, 19b.

However, Jeremias's proposal to interpret the combination of lament and prophetic oracle against the background of cult prophecy has not stood the test.[292] The words spoken by God in Hab 1:5–11 are not a response to the prophet's lament; they are addressed to a group in the second-person plural. In addition, they speak of the nations rather than the wicked, who are the subject of the lament.[293] The same is true of 1:14ff. There is thus no evidence for the theory of Habakkuk the cult prophet. Jeremias is correct in observing that 1:14 actually belongs to the description of disaster; it has been assimilated secondarily to the prayer by being changed to the second-person singular, leaving the impression that the second prayer extends through 1:17.[294]

For the rest of the book, two primary explanations are currently offered. The first starts from the assumption that the laments and the

---

[290] *Kultprophetie*, 57–67.

[291] Otto, *Stellung*, 106; Otto, "Habakuk/Habakukbuch," 302; Koenen, *Heil*, 147; Seybold, *Nahum*, 67–69.

[292] *Kultprophetie*, 75–110; see also Jöcken, "War Habakuk ein Kultprophet?"

[293] The Septuagint and Syriac attempt to gloss over this inconsistency by making God the speaker and reading "Look at the faithless" instead of "Look at the nations." Jeremias (*Kultprophetie*, 75) is inclined to accept this reading, but it clearly is an attempt to avoid the problem.

[294] *Kultprophetie*, 79–80; contra Otto.

oracle in 2:1–5 together with the original woes constitute the core of the book. Habakkuk 1:12b was then used to link the descriptions of disaster with the laments. Otto is among those who accept this model: (1) core: 1:2–4, 12a, 13–14; 2:1–5aα, 6b–16*; (2) late preexilic redaction: 1:5–11, 12b; (3) exilic redaction: 1:15–17; 2:5bβ, 6a, 8, 10bα, 13–14, 17; (4) postexilic redaction: 1:1; 2:18–20; 3:2–16; (5) adaptation for liturgical use: 3:1, 17–19 and selah in 3:3, 9, 13.[295] Koenen generally follows Otto but includes 2:18, 19b, 20 in the exilic redaction.[296] Seybold, on the other hand, following Schmidt,[297] supports the theory that the laments and therefore the theme of the wicked versus the righteous in the book of Habakkuk derive from the postexilic incorporation of a lament concerning the deliverance of an innocent victim.[298] According to Seybold, the core comprises 1:6–11; 2:1–3, 5–19*; the exilic redaction adds 1:5, 14–17; 2:5b, 6a, 7b, 8, 10, 13–14, 16–17, 18, 19b; 3:1–13a, 15–16. The postexilic incorporation of the lament psalm adds 1:2–4, 12–13; 2:4; 3:13b, 14, 17–19.

Seybold's solution has one great advantage: it makes it possible to date the confrontation between the wicked and the righteous in a time where many other texts suggest that it belongs, namely, the social crisis of the Persian period (Pss 37; 73; Isa 57; Job 21; etc.).[299] Jeremiah 5:26 is the only other text clearly dating from the end of the seventh century that uses the term רָשָׁע, "wicked," which originally denoted a person found legally guilty, as a collective polemic term for the antisocial upper classes. It would therefore be remarkable for the prophet Habakkuk, who appeared before or contemporaneously with Jeremiah (ca. 630[300] or, more likely, ca. 605 B.C.E.), to use in its fully developed sense the terminology of socioreligious confrontation belonging to the later period. Seybold's theory also explains why the words of God in Hab 1:5–11 and 14–17 do not reply to the laments. Their reference is clear only if the wicked are identified with a foreign power. Demonstrably, however, this did not take place until the Persian period, when the prosperous aristocracy collaborated with the Persians (Pss 9–10, etc.). However, Seybold's hypothesis also has a weakness: he wants to keep 2:1–3, or at least 2:2–3, as part of the original core. But 2:1 refers back to the laments and cannot be separated from 2:2–3; these verses are obviously dependent on the

---

[295] "Habakuk/Habakukbuch," 301–2.
[296] *Heil*, 147.
[297] "Psalm."
[298] Seybold, *Nahum*.
[299] Cf. Albertz, *History* (II.4), 2:499–501. Nogalski (*Redactional Processes*, 137ff.) recognizes these traditio-historical associations when he speaks of a "wisdom-oriented layer" in the laments (150), but he does not draw any conclusions as to dating the material.
[300] On this early date, see Seybold, *Nahum*, 46; on the later date, see below.

oracle against Babylon in Isa 21:6, 8–9. Furthermore, the incorporation of the psalm should not be treated as mechanically as Schmidt and also Seybold do. What we are dealing with here is actually a postexilic revision of the book of Habakkuk in the interests of the conflict between the faithful and the antisocial upper class (cf. Isa 56–66), which connects with the elements of prayer and revelation in Hab 3:2, 16.

Thus my hypothesis concerning the history of the book's growth is a modification of Seybold's. The only verses that can be assigned with certainty to the original core are the woes in Hab 2:6b, 7, 9, 10a, 10bβ, 12, 11, 15, 19a and possibly the original form of the descriptions of disaster in 1:6–11*, 14–17* (cf. Jer 4–6); at least in 1:11 and 16–17, however, the latter have been modified so as to be anti-Babylonian. Not until the exilic period were these materials incorporated into an initial book of Habakkuk, comprising 1:1, 5–11, 14–17; 2:5bβ–19; 3:1*–13a, 15–16. The postexilic recension finally added 1:2–4, 12–13; 2:1–5abα, 20; 3:1*, 13b–14, 17–19.

The late exilic Habakkuk redactor (HR) addresses his audience at the beginning of his book (Hab 1:5), commanding them to look at the astonishing and unbelievable work done "in their days" by Yahweh.[301] What this refers to, as the following text makes clear, is the rise and fall of the Neo-Babylonian Empire, which convulsed the world in less than two generations! To portray its rise, HR drew on descriptions of disaster (1:6ff., 14ff.) with which the prophet Habakkuk had graphically warned the Judeans of the vast military superiority of the Neo-Babylonians, probably at the time of the battle of Carchemish (605 B.C.E.). The forces that Yahweh had summoned to execute judgment (1:7) would be swift, fearsome, and merciless. They would laugh as they laid siege to fortresses (1:10), seize dwellings not their own (1:6), gather captives like sand (1:10), and joyfully drag off hordes of prisoners like fish in a net (1:14–15).[302] The dramatic imagery used to describe the process of conquest recalls Jeremiah's descriptions of the enemy from the north (Jer 4:5–31; 5:15–17; 6:1–8, 22–26). A special feature is the emphasis on deportations; HR may possibly have chosen these particular descriptions because they reflected very directly the fate of his exilic audience. However, these references remain only allusions. His purpose was to represent the worldwide conquests of the Babylonians, which affected not just the Judeans but all

---

301 The MT reads פֹּעַל פֹּעֵל, "he was doing a work"; but when 1:2–4 are removed, there has been no mention of Yahweh, so that it is better to point the second word as a passive participle: פֹּעַל פָּעֵל, "a work was done" (passive with a divine agent).

302 In 1:14, the third person should be read; the second person of the MT is due to the secondary interpolation of the prayer in 1:12–13.

humankind. If Habakkuk's descriptions used by the redactor once had a Judean focus, the redactor left it out. The important thing was to demonstrate to his audience that their God Yahweh was at work in the sudden rise of the Babylonians to world dominion.

However, HR could look back on years of experience with Babylonian dominion; he retained very little of its positive aspect as the instrument of Yahweh's judgment, a theme still important to Jeremiah (Jer 27–28).[303] Instead, he revised the descriptions of disaster so that the rise of Babylon already held the seeds of its fall. In their arrogance, the Babylonians divinized their own power (1:11); indeed, they even offered sacrifice to the nets in which they captured vast quantities of people and property from the nations (1:16). Behind this description may stand the experience of the Babylonian golah: they and the tribute from Judah contributed directly to the construction of the splendid temples of Babylon and the glory of the cultic celebrations. But of course we are dealing with a polemic, written to denounce the narrow egotism and rapacious greed of the Babylonian policy of conquest.[304] In light of this military and economic self-aggrandizement, HR asks his audience—and naturally God as well—the decisive question: Had the "Babylonian fisher of men" not far exceeded and long since forfeited his divine commission? "Is he then to keep on[305] emptying his net, destroying nations without mercy?" (1:17). In the eyes of HR, it was the predatory policies of the Babylonians that destroyed their subject peoples.

Without any difficulty, after this intense criticism, HR could now borrow a series of woe oracles from the prophecy of Habakkuk, which had been aimed at the economic, social, and religious transgressions of the Judean upper class, and apply them to the foreign Babylonians. He did so by putting them in the mouth of people from the conquered nations that had been brought to Babylon.[306] Exiles from everywhere in the world raised their voices to indict the empire (Hab 2:5bβ, 6a). Two woes addressed to the prosperous, who multiplied their wealth by unfair lending practices (2:6b, 7a, 9), HR transformed into a general indictment of the Babylonians for their pillaging and bloody decimation of the nations (2:7b, 8). An indictment of unjust forced labor in the construction of cities and fortresses (2:12, 11) he reshaped in such a

---

[303] The only positive allusions are in Hab 1:7b and 9a, if indeed these verses are not secondary adaptations to chime with the prayer added later in 1:2–4.

[304] See pp. 58ff. above.

[305] With the Qere, dropping the copula before תמיד but retaining the interrogative particle, contra the Qere, the Septuagint, the Syriac, and one Hebrew manuscript.

[306] Hab 2:5bβ can easily have followed 1:17 directly before the interpolation of 2:1–5abα.

way³⁰⁷ that he could brand the brutal employment of deportees in the construction of "your house," probably Nebuchadnezzar's new palace,³⁰⁸ as a policy of extermination directed against the nations (2:16) and at the same time underscore the futility of their labor, because the Babylonian edifices were soon to be destroyed (2:13). Since HR here asks his audience directly whether they cannot see the hand of Yahweh at work here, the imminent fall of the Babylonian Empire must already be clearly visible. Because Babylon was actually taken in 539 without a struggle, the background of this passage is probably the sieges Darius felt compelled to conduct against the city to quell the revolts of 522/521.³⁰⁹ Since Yahweh was about to demonstrate his power through the fall of the Babylonian metropolis, HR expected that this power would soon enjoy universal recognition (2:14; cf. Isa 11:9).

However, the final fall of Babylon was still in the future, for HR reinterpreted the next woe oracle, in which Habakkuk had inveighed against the drinking bouts of the Judean upper class (Hab 2:15), turning it into a foreign nation oracle declaring that Babylonia, sated in contempt, would finally have to drink the cup in the hand of Yahweh (cf. Jer 25:15ff.; Isa 51:22–23), which hitherto had apparently passed it by (Hab 2:16). Even its finest and most precious idols—here, finally, HR adapts a religious indictment from Habakkuk (2:19aα)—would be unable to save it (2:18, 19b). HR supports this final verdict with an even more fundamental motivation: in his view, it was not only the Babylonians' violence against the people, cities, and lands of conquered nations but also their reckless violation of nature that would finally bring about their end (2:17). This charge probably refers to Nebuchadnezzar's partial deforestation of Lebanon to supply his long siege of Tyre (ca. 585–572 B.C.E.) and to provide material for his many construction projects.³¹⁰

The application of Habakkuk's social woe oracles to Babylonia, a foreign power, shows that during the exile there developed in Israel something like a sense of justice transcending one's own national borders. Habakkuk had castigated the unjust and antisocial conduct of the Judean upper class. Acceptance of this criticism as just was one of the great feats demanded of the exilic generation, especially on the part of the

---

307 HR probably shifted 2:11, which once followed 2:12, so as to treat the exploitation and building policies of the Babylonians in a single text.

308 See pp. 59–60 above.

309 This association is also supported by the inclusion of a slogan that had been used in Jer 51:58b with regard to the destruction of the walls of Babylon, probably around the same time; see pp. 194–96 above.

310 Cf. the Wadi Brisa inscription (*TUAT* 1/4:405).

upper class itself, on whom the punishment of deportation had fallen with particular severity. It also meant accepting the conquests and deportations of the Babylonian Empire as Yahweh's punishment. Now, toward the end of the exilic period, came the next step: the norms of justice laid down by the prophets in Israel were applied to Babylonia. Judged by this standard, the rapacious policies of the Neo-Babylonian Empire, though well within the bounds of normal practice, were no longer acceptable in the forum of the nations. This empire had been incapable of exerting its power justly, so it would soon perish.

Up to this point, the exilic book of Habakkuk had not mentioned Israel or Judah. The fall of the Babylonian Empire had universal causes, having to do with justice in the world of nations. Not until the third chapter do we find the application to Israel. The shift from historical interpretation and prophecy to the language of prayer, a change that later produced a new superscription (Hab 3:1), is due to the liturgical form of the assurance of salvation and must not be treated as a cue for literary dissection. Since almost all foreign nation oracles of the exilic period conclude with salvation for Israel,[311] Hab 3:2–13a, 15–16 almost certainly was part of the exilic book.

To pray that Yahweh would soon bring about the final fall of Babylon, with beneficial consequences for the Judean population, HR slipped into the role of mediator between Yahweh and the community (cf. Hab 3:2, 16). Responding on behalf of his audience to God's message in 1:6ff., he affirmed that he had noted Yahweh's "work" (פֹּעַל, as in 1:5) in history. He prayed for Yahweh to act quickly, and especially for Yahweh's mercy amid the wrath (רֹגֶז, literally "raging") manifested in the tumult of the nations. Then he or another person recited two ancient theophanic hymns (3:3–7, 8–13a, 15) celebrating Yahweh's earth-shaking coming to save his people. As a consequence of God's mighty intervention, both hymns spoke of disruption of the nations (3:6, 12), probably like what the community lived through during the revolts against Darius. However, the second hymn finally bore witness that all this tumult was for the benefit of Israel, as at the Sea of Reeds long before (3:13a, 15). In conclusion, HR understood this crucial knowledge imparted by the hymns as an overwhelming divine revelation (3:16a) and hoped that he and the community would be spared when the day of calamity finally overtook their Babylonian tormentors (3:16b).

The exilic book of Habakkuk thus aims to interpret history and foster hope. It seeks to impart to the exilic generation the knowledge that the

---

311 See pp. 176ff. above.

Neo-Babylonian Empire, though formerly empowered by Yahweh to rule the world, must soon perish—and why. The community must understand that in this tumultuous event Yahweh was at work to save his people. On the one hand, therefore, the book recalls the foreign nation oracles, on the other Deutero-Isaiah. It is—along with a few salvation oracles and foreign nation oracles—another example of liturgical assurance of salvation.

The book dates from the late exilic period, most likely the time of the revolts against Darius I (522/521), in which Babylon played a leading role (Hab 2:13; cf. Jer 51:58b). It emphasizes deportations (Hab 1:9, 14–15; 2:5bβ); it also displays truly impressive insights into Babylonian military and economic policies (1:16–17; 2:8, 17). Therefore, it could well have originated in Babylonia.[312] This origin is also suggested by 3:16, which describes the Babylonians as "the people who torment/encircle us."[313] If so, the Habakkuk redactor was striving to make the Babylonian golah realize that finally—after the disappointment of the year 539—the time of Babylon's punishment had come and the turning point of Israel's salvation was imminent. If this date and location are correct, HR was active in the period just before a large group of people in the golah—negotiating with Darius—decided to return.[314] The work of HR undoubtedly encouraged this decision. As the explicit mention of Yahweh's anointed in 3:13a shows, HR himself even hoped for a restoration of the monarchy. Here he was at one with the leaders of the golah, from whom the Deuteronomistic History emerged.[315]

---

312 A remarkable tradition in the story of Bel and the Dragon records that the prophet Habakkuk was transported to Babylon by an angel to feed Daniel in the den of lions (vv. 33–39; see pp. 29–30 above). This story may enshrine a memory that the tradition of this prophet, who had prophesied in Judah, was effectually helpful among the Babylonian golah. The fact that the Septuagint characterizes this Diaspora narrative as a Habakkuk prophecy (v. 1) is more understandable if the MT book of Habakkuk also came into being in the Babylonian golah.

313 The verb comes from the root גוד or גדד II, which is related to the noun גְּדוּד, "marauding band." Jeremias (Kultprophetie, 87) took the verb, which seems inappropriate to describe the actions of an empire, as evidence for his thesis that the text referred originally to the wicked. However, nothing is said of any purifying judgment on the wicked, who appear only in the postscript Hab 3:13b–14. This verb does fit, however, if the threat is seen from the perspective of a group that actually lived among the Babylonians. Specifically, it could mean that they were required to participate in the anti-Persian revolts.

314 See pp. 124–26 above. We shall see that the first edition of the book of Deutero-Isaiah came into being in the same period, albeit in Palestine (see pp. 397–404 below).

315 See pp. 284–85 below.

III.2.3. The Exilic Patriarchal History

Berge, Kare. *Die Zeit des Jahwisten: Ein Beitrag zur Datierung jahwistischer Vätertexte* (BZAW 186; Berlin: de Gruyter, 1990). **Blum,** Erhard. *Die Komposition der Vätergeschichte* (WMANT 57; Neukirchen-Vluyn: Neukirchener Verlag, 1984). **Blum.** *Studien zur Komposition des Pentateuch* (BZAW 189; Berlin: de Gruyter, 1990). **Carr,** David Mcclain. *Reading the Fractures of Genesis: Historical and Literary Approaches* (Louisville: Westminster John Knox, 1996). **Fischer,** Irmtraud. *Die Erzeltern Israels: Feministisch-theologische Studien zu Genesis 12–36* (BZAW 222; Berlin: de Gruyter, 1994). **Kessler,** Rainer. "Die Querverweise im Pentateuch: Überlieferungsgeschichtliche Untersuchung der expliziten Querverbindungen innerhalb des vorpriesterlichen Pentateuchs" (Diss. theol., Heidelberg, 1972). **Köckert,** Matthias. *Vätergott und Väterverheissungen: Eine Ausseinandersetzung mit Albrecht Alt und seinen Erben* (FRLANT 157; Göttingen: Vandenhoeck & Ruprecht, 1993). **Levin,** Christoph. *Der Jahwist* (FRLANT 157; Göttingen: Vandenhoeck & Ruprecht, 1993). **Römer,** Thomas. *Israels Väter: Untersuchungen zur Väterthematik im Deuteronomium und in der deuteronomistischen Tradition* (OBO 99; Fribourg: Universitätsverlag, 1990). **Schmid,** Hans Heinrich. *Der sogenannte Jahwist: Beobachtungen und Fragen zur Pentateuchforschung* (Zurich: Theologischer Verlag, 1976). **Schmidt,** Ludwig. *Literarische Studien zur Josephsgeschichte* (with A. Aemelaeus, *The Traditional Prayer in the Psalms*; BZAW 167; Berlin: de Gruyter, 1986), 181–297. **Schmitt,** Hans-Christoph. *Die nichtpriesterliche Josephsgeschichte: Ein Beitrag zur neuesten Penateuchkritik* (BZAW 154; Berlin: de Gruyter, 1980). **Seebass,** Horst. *Genesis* (3 vols. in 4; Neukirchen-Vluyn: Neukirchener Verlag, 1996–2000). **Van Seters,** John. *Abraham in History and Tradition* (New Haven: Yale University Press, 1975). **Van Seters.** *Prologue to History: The Yahwist As Historian in Genesis* (Louisville: Westminster John Knox, 1992). **Veijola,** Timo. "Das Opfer des Abraham, Paradigma des Glaubens aus dem nachexilischen Zeitalter," *ZThK* 85 (1988): 129–64. **Westermann,** Claus. *Genesis 12–36: A Commentary* (trans. J. J. Scullion: Minneapolis: Augsburg, 1985). **Westermann.** *Genesis 37–50: A Commentary* (trans. J. J. Scullion; Minneapolis: Augsburg, 1986).

Not just the prophetic traditions but also the historical traditions took on new meaning in the exilic crisis. This was especially true of the traditions surrounding the patriarchs and matriarchs. The reasons are complex. Stripped of the organizational structure of the state, Israel was largely reduced to the family as a basis for its common life. The traditions of the ancestors, using the fiction of a genealogical model to sketch the early history of Israel as a family history, provided a welcome means of maintaining Israelite identity. In the ancestors of the distant past, the now stateless Judean families of the exilic period had no difficulty rediscovering themselves. Besides this sociohistorical reason, there were theological reasons. God's saving gifts of the land, the temple, and the monarchy had proved fragile; Yahweh's dealings with the ancestors provided a final historical foundation, still intact, on which hope for overcoming the crisis could build. As has already been pointed out, we may assume that the exilic families, deported or remaining behind, could still experience Yahweh's protection, support, and protective intervention in their daily lives. Thus it is also likely that all the positive experiences of personal piety that over the centuries had entered the patriarchal narratives— whether the promise of a child to Sarah (Gen 18:1–15) or God's assistance to Jacob during his extended journeys (Gen 28:20; 31:5, 42)—spoke directly to the exilic families in their perilous situation and comforted them. Moreover, since these were the families of Israel's ancestors, their personal experiences of God took on meaning for all Israel, for all generations to come.

The great importance of the ancestors in the exilic period is illustrated by the frequent references to them in prophetic literature, now appearing for the first time (Isa 41:8–9; 51:1–2; 63:16; Ezek 33:24; 28:25; 37:25). This is especially true of Abraham, who does not appear outside the Pentateuch until after the exile.[316]

References back to the ancestors appear in various contexts and serve various functions. We know from Ezek 33:24 that even in the early exilic period those who had stayed behind defended or asserted their property claims vis-à-vis the deportees by appealing to Abraham, who had possessed the land even though he was just one man.[317] In the late exilic salvation oracles Ezek 28:25 and 37:25, the right of the exiles to return to Palestine and live there is grounded in Yahweh's gift of the land to "[his] servant Jacob." Isaiah 63:16 shows that exilic communal laments could appeal to the fatherhood of Abraham and Jacob to move Yahweh to have pity on their present descendants, even though the actual prayer finds God's fatherhood far more important.[318] This motif of confidence is also taken up by the exilic prophets of salvation. In the salvation oracle Isa 41:8–9, Yahweh addresses the Israel of the exilic period as "offspring of Abraham," whom he expressly calls "my friend." God's renewed pity on his afflicted people, the Deutero-Isaiah group emphasizes, is thus grounded in God's particularly close relationship with the patriarch, "taken and called from the ends of the earth." Thus the election of Israel is traced back to Abraham, before the failed history of the exodus and the

---

[316] The ancestors of the northern kingdom appear earlier: for example, Jacob in Hos 12:3–7, Joseph in Amos 5:6; cf. 2 Sam 19:21 (20); 1 Kgs 11:28. Especially striking is the relatively early appearance of Isaac in Amos 7:9, 16.

[317] The exiled prophet Ezekiel vehemently opposed this claim; cf. Ezek 11:14–21.

[318] The antithesis "Abraham does not know us and Israel does not acknowledge us; you, Yahweh, are our father" presupposes that others clearly believed that an appeal to the fathers could help in time of need. This will clarify my view stated in *History* (II.4), 2:405, which has been challenged by Aejmelaeus ("Prophet" [III.1.1], 42 n. 52).

occupation of the land, and the call of Abraham is made the prototype of the expected call for the exiles dispersed throughout the world to return. Finally, another aspect appears in the disputation Isa 51:1–2: the fact that a single couple chosen by Yahweh, Abraham and Sarah—in agreement with the genealogical model—multiplied and became the people Israel reveals to the shrunken community rebuilding Jerusalem[319] the enormous power inherent in God's blessing, giving them hope that they, too, will survive and multiply once more.

A grasp of the importance of the ancestors for the will to survive during the exilic crisis, for Israel's claim to the land, and for reestablishing Israel's relationship with God would lead one to expect that the patriarchal narratives, too, went through an important redactional stage in the exilic period. However, this expectation is not met by the traditional Documentary Hypothesis, still accepted by many exegetes: it dates the sources or redactions of Genesis in either the preexilic period (J usually tenth century, E usually eighth century, JE seventh century) or the postexilic period (P).[320] Only very recently have scholars put forward the theory of an exilic Patriarchal History (PH), either within the framework of the source model by dating a more or less abbreviated Yahwist in the exilic period[321] or in a new traditio-historical model by recognizing the exilic period as an important stage in the development of the patriarchal traditions.[322] Probably these new approaches are still a good distance from consensus, but they open the possibility of setting a substantial portion of the patriarchal tradition in Gen 12–50 within the framework we have been developing.

This is not the place for an extended treatment of the new discussion concerning the Pentateuch.[323] All we can do is cite the evidence for an exilic dating and attempt to determine the scope of the exilic Patriarchal History. Of course, the two questions are closely related.

---

319 Isa 51:1–2 probably belongs to the second edition of Deutero-Isaiah, dating from the end of the sixth century or the beginning of the fifth; see pp. 427–29 below.

320 Some attempts have been made to resolve this paradox by dating P in the late exilic period (538–520 B.C.E.; for example, Seebass, *Genesis*, 1:36), but this approach creates problems of dating with respect to the book of Ezekiel; see pp. 185–86 above and 352–54 below.

321 Van Seters, *Abraham and Prologue*; Schmid, *Der sogenannte Jahwist*; Köckert, *Vätergott*; Levin, *Jahwist*.

322 Blum, *Komposition*, 297–316; Carr, *Reading*, 143–232 (Carr dates his Proto-Genesis Composition cautiously between 722 and 560 [227] but leans toward the early exilic period [232]); Fischer, *Erzeltern*, 357–66.

323 For more details, see Seebass, *Genesis*, 1:14–36; Erich Zenger et al., eds., *Einleitung in das Alte Testament* (3d ed.; KST 1/1; Stuttgart: Kohlhammer, 1998), 84–124.

Blum has shown that the profile of PH is made up of commands to go coupled with promises (Gen 12:1–3; 26:21*; 31:13; 46:3–4).[324] The first two texts clearly belong to the same redactional stratum, since 26:1aβ, 2b refers back explicitly to 12:1, 10. The first evidence for an exilic date appears in 26:2b. Yahweh's strange command to Isaac not to go down to Egypt despite the famine but to stay in Palestine instead makes sense only against the background of a time when there were large-scale migrations to Egypt that presented a survival problem for the Judeans in Palestine. The first time this situation obtained was during the exile (Jer 41:16–43:7).[325] Similarly, Yahweh's command to Abraham to leave his kindred in Mesopotamia and to go to the land that God would show him was highly timely in the situation of the exilic period, when part of the population resided in Mesopotamia. Proponents of the classical Documentary Hypothesis repeatedly have interpreted the great promise in Gen 12:1–3, typical of the "Yahwist," as referring to the Davidic empire, but certain arguments stand in the way. Archaeological evidence shows that the political status of tenth-century Israel was much more modest than was hitherto assumed, so that the promise of a "great nation" and a "great name" are not nearly as appropriate as had been thought.[326] In addition, Gen 12:1–3 does not explicitly envision an Israelite state; this fact sets it apart from promises with political substance (Gen 25:23; 27:28–29, 39–40), which really do date from the early monarchy (tenth or ninth century). Furthermore, as Schmid[327] and Van Seters[328] in particular have pointed out, elements of the promise derive from royal theology, for example, the "great name" (cf. 2 Sam 7:9; 1 Kgs 1:47) and the "mediation of blessings" (cf. Pss 21:4 [3]; 72:6–7, 16, 17). Such a borrowing is hardly conceivable in a period when the monarchy was just becoming established; more likely it dates from a time when the monarchy had ceased to exist (cf. Isa 55:5 and in part Ps 89). Finally, Israel as mediator of God's blessings in Gen 12:3b is most reminiscent of the universalism of Deutero-Isaiah; similar formulas date from the late preexilic period (Jer 4:2) or the postexilic period (Zech 8:13), where they contrast with the lowly status of Israel among the nations after its political demise (cf. Pss 44:14–15 [13–14]; 79:4; Lam 2:15; Deut 28:37; Jer 24:9; etc.).[329] Against this array of

---

[324] *Komposition*, 297–301.
[325] Ibid., 345–46.
[326] Carr, *Reading*, 221.
[327] *Der sogenannte Jahwist*, 133–35.
[328] *Prologue*, 252–56.
[329] The parallels also belong either to the same redactional stratum (Gen 28:14) or even later strata (Gen 18:18; 22:18; 26:4 PD).

arguments, the recent attempt of Berge[330] has tried to establish a dating of the central promise text in the early period of monarchy on the basis of the expression מִשְׁפְּחֹת הָאֲדָמָה, "families of the earth," in Gen 12:3b, which he understands as meaning groups "either within or on the fringe of the settled territory of Palestine."[331] However, the evidence just cited contradicts his position, especially since the same expression occurs in the eighth century (Amos 3:2).[332]

Apart from Gen 26:2–3* and 12:1–3, the promises of land and increase that might be considered candidates for PH (13:15–16; 28:14) can be understood equally well if not better against the background of an age when Israel was no longer a "great nation" and no longer dwelt within secure borders. That the potential extinction of scattered groups of Judeans was a central problem of the exilic period is easily conceivable; it is attested explicitly in Jeremiah's exhortation to the golah to have their children marry "so as to multiply and not decrease" (Jer 29:6). Isaiah 5:1–2 shows that there were attempts to counter these fears even in the early postexilic period by reference to the ancestors. Furthermore, comparable promises of increase appear in other exilic texts (Jer 31:27; Ezek 36:10–11, 37–38; 37:26). There is a similar direct relationship between the promise of the land and the threat of losing the land through deportation and emigration. The earliest promises of the land outside Genesis are in Deuteronomy (Deut 6:10, 18, 23; 7:12–13; 8:1; 9:5; 10:11; etc.); here, too, they are not associated with the ancestors in general but specifically with the three successive patriarchs (Deut 1:8; 6:10; 9:5, 27; 29:12 [13]; 30:20; 34:4).[333] These promises are probably a reaction to the traumatic experience of the fall of the northern kingdom in 722, which made clear at a stroke that Israel could never be sure of its land. It is quite understandable that the even more traumatic experience of the fall of the southern kingdom should elicit additional promises of the land, comparable to the

---

330 *Zeit*, 51–76.

331 Ibid., 72.

332 The response by Seebass (*Genesis*, 2:16) also relies too heavily on the Documentary Hypothesis, which is the point at issue, to be persuasive.

333 Römer, *Israels Väter*. However, Römer seems to me to place too much weight on the sporadic differences between the ancestors of the exodus and the patriarchs. Of course, the tradition of the patriarchs and the tradition of the exodus were two distinct foundation traditions from the very outset; Hosea—here I agree with Römer—can still play off one against the other (Hos 12). In my view, however, the shapers of the Deuteronom(ist)ic tradition sought a synthesis of the various foundation traditions (Albertz, *History* [II.4], 1:224–30). That the evidence points to a fusion of the patriarchal and exodus traditions no later than the exilic period is shown by Deutero-Isaiah (Isa 41:8–9; 51:9–10) and not least by the exilic Patriarchal History.

exilic promises of a new occupation (Jer 23:3, 7–8; 29:10; 30:3; 32:36ff.; Ezek 11:17; 20:42; 34:13–14; 37:25). That conflicts over possession of the land during the exile could involve appeal to the ancestors is shown by Ezek 33:24; 20:42; 28:25; 37:25. As Carr has convincingly shown,[334] Hos 12:5–7 cannot be used to prove that in Hosea's time the promise of land and increase in Gen 28:14 was already part of the Bethel narrative (28:10–22).

Traditio-historical analysis raises a further objection to dating a first edition of the patriarchal narrative in the time of the early monarchy, as in the classical Documentary Hypothesis. Ever since Gunkel, it has become increasingly apparent that the traditions of the individual patriarchs had been subject to a process of growth and development, sometimes quite complex, before the "Yahwist" brought them together in a continuous narrative complex. But dating "J" in the early period of the monarchy allows no time for the individual traditions to come into being. If J is reassigned to the historically rather vague premonarchic period, as Westermann does most consistently, the result is that all references to the monarchic period even in early individual narratives (Gen 27:27–29, 39–40) must be treated as secondary additions. The only alternative is to assign the complex as a whole to a later period. If the first smaller narrative units—the Abraham-Lot narrative (Gen 13*; 18–19*), the Jacob narrative (Gen 25*; 27–33*), the Joseph novella (Gen 37–50*)—date from the early or middle period of the monarchy, as Blum and others have convincingly shown, then the redactor who put all these parts together cannot be assigned to the same period, not to speak of an earlier date. If we note that before this complex was formed, individual Judean traditions had been integrated into the story of Jacob and Joseph, which originated in the northern kingdom (Gen 34*; 38; 49), then the first edition of the patriarchal narrative can hardly antedate the fall of the northern kingdom in 722, in the wake of which many northern traditions came south with the refugees.

Originally, therefore, Blum dated the first patriarchal narrative ("Patriarchal History 1"), which combined the Abraham-Lot and the Jacob-Joseph stories for the first time, in this period.[335] He identified the linking element as the similarly formulated promises in Gen 13:14–17 and 28:13b, 14. But after Köckert[336] was able to show that the promise in 13:14–18 stands in clear narrative correspondence with 12:1–3,[337]

---

[334] *Reading*, 222–23.
[335] *Komposition*, 273–97.
[336] *Vätergott*, 250–55.
[337] The predictive formula "the land that I will show [ראה *hipʿil*] you" in Gen 12:1b corresponds to the imperative "raise you eyes and see [ראה *qal*] the land" in 13:14.

Blum gave up his "Patriarchal History 1."[338] Now the first continuous history was not put together until the exilic period, and then all at once (originally "Patriarchal History 2"). Thus Blum's position converges with the hypotheses of Carr and Van Seters, albeit with many differences in detail.[339]

Thus the existence of an exilic Patriarchal History has been gaining scholarly support and seems increasingly likely. The task is now to determine its scope. I take Blum's revised position as my starting point but supplement it with insights from Carr; finally, I discuss several critical questions raised by proponents of the Documentary Hypothesis.

Basically, the scope of the exilic Patriarchal History potentially includes all texts not belonging to either the Priestly redaction (PP) or the late Deuteronomistic redaction (PD) of the Pentateuch.

There is extensive consensus as to the extent of PP. In it I include Gen 11:28–32; 12:4b–5; 16:3, 15–16; 17:1–24; 19:29; 21:3–5; 23:1–20; 25:7–18, 19–20; 26:34–35; 27:46–28:9; 31:17–18; 35:9–15, 27–29; 36:1–43; 37:1–2; 41:45b, 46a; 46:6*, 7, 8–27; 47:11*, 27b–28; 48:3–7; 49:29–33; 50:12–13. Genesis 14 is even later.

In PD I include Gen 12:7; 15:1–12, 17–21*; 16:10; [18:17–19]; 22:15–18; [24:1–67]; 26:3bβ–5, 24; 28:15; [32:10–13]; 34:30–31; 35:1–7; 50:22b, 23a, 24, 26a. Parting company with Blum, I assign 48:15–16, 21a not to PD but to a second edition of PH.[340]

The remaining textual corpus, however, cannot be assigned without further ado to a single exilic Patriarchal History. Berge has called attention to the remarkable fact that Gen 46:1–5a, the fourth of the commands to go that according to Blum define the structure of PH, differs from 12:1–3 in one small stylistic point: it formulates the promise that God will make the patriarch "a great nation" (לְגוֹי גָּדוֹל) not with the verb עשׂה, "make, do," like 12:1b, but with the verb שׂים, "place, make."[341] Semantically, there is no difference, but Berge is right to ask whether the texts come from the same hand. That we are not dealing with a random variation in the choice of words is shown by the promises in Gen 21:13, 18,

---

[338] *Studien*, 214 n. 35.

[339] While Blum forgoes the "Yahwist" entirely, for Van Seters the Yahwist is the crucial historian. While Blum views the exilic Patriarchal History as a redactional stage in the assemblage of the entire Pentateuch (PD), for Van Seters J is responsible for the first inclusive conception of the Pentateuch. According to Carr, the "Proto-Genesis Composition" included at least the Primal History as well. Even though these scholars differ in their overall conceptions as well as in their treatment of individual texts, their positions are compatible, being based on a hypothesis of traditio-historical or literary augmentation.

[340] See below.

[341] *Zeit*, 34.

where God promises Hagar with reference to Ishmael that "I will make a (great) nation of him"; here the verb שׂים is used in both cases. Furthermore, both texts—unlike 12:1 and 26:2—use the designation Elohim, "God," rather than the divine name; they are therefore undeniably related. However, in our reconstruction of the exilic PH, we here confront once more the problem of the "Elohist."

Blum assigned the "Elohistic" Abraham narratives, Gen 20–22, more or less to PH, on the grounds that the formulation of God's command in Gen 22:2, "Go to the land ... one of the mountains that I will tell you," recalls the command to depart in Gen 12:1: "Go from your land ... to the land that I will show you," thus bracketing PH. However, since the divine command is an integral part of the individual narrative, he assumed that in formulating the compositional introduction in Gen 12 the redactor of PH had been inspired by Gen 22.[342] He also accepted the cult foundation note in 21:33, the beginning of which recalls 12:8, as evidence that the redactor of PH did in fact link a major portion of Gen 20–22 with 12–18*.[343] However, this apparently obvious solution presents a problem. The beginning of Gen 26, verses 1–3* of which were clearly revised by the redactor of PH, reflects only the story of the matriarch in 12:10–20; Blum therefore felt compelled to separate Gen 20 from PH, believing that the postexilic narrative, which also included the Beer-sheba episode in 21:22, 24, 27, 34, had been linked to PH by means of 21:25–26, 28–32 in order to create a kind of equalizer (26:13ff.).[344] Quite apart from the fact that the literary dissection of 21:22–34 is not convincing,[345] Blum, contrary to his own aim elsewhere, fragments the narrative composite Gen 20–22, even though its unity had been demonstrated (especially by Kessler[346]) on the basis of shared stylistic features, motifs, and geographical references. These common features include a curious use of the names for God that cannot simply be ignored.[347] Kessler coined the expression "Negev

---

342 *Komposition*, 330–31.
343 Ibid., 335.
344 Ibid., 405–16.
345 See the criticisms of Van Seters, *Prologue*, 247–48.
346 "Querverweise," 80–92.
347 I agree with Blum (*Komposition*, 471–75) that the so-called "names for God" in and of themselves do not constitute a criterion for literary analysis, since the generic term אֱלֹהִים, "Elohim, God," stands on a different semantic plane than the divine name יהוה, "Yahweh." But there are so many other stylistic features and motifs common to Gen 20–22 that there is not space to list them here. Furthermore, we are very likely dealing here with a stylistic choice as to whether an author deliberately distinguishes the general term from the divine name, like the author of 20–22, or uses the divine name throughout, like the author of Gen 12ff. It was one of the mistakes of the Documentary Hypothesis to employ the "names for God" criterion mechanically, without inquiring into the significance of the choice. See pp. 267–68 below.

group" for these narratives,[348] since they no longer have Abraham dwelling in Hebron (13:18; 18:1) but throughout the south (Negev, Gerar, Beer-sheba). We must also recall that both Gen 20 (cf. 20:11) and Gen 22 (cf. 22:12) focus on the theme of fear of God (יִרְאַת אֱלֹהִים)—especially in comparison to the Gentiles, who appear in a surprisingly positive light.

Genesis 20:13 obviously recalls the context of Gen 12:1–20; Gen 21:1–2, 6–7 describes the birth of Isaac, promised in Gen 18:1–15; and Gen 21:8ff. reintroduces the conflict between Sarah and Hagar of Gen 16. While all the texts speak a very different language, the simplest explanation is to assume that Gen 20–22 represents a variant recension of the Abraham narratives in Gen 12–19*, framed as a continuation.[349] The subject matter also suggests that Gen 20–22 is later than Gen 12–19*, since the Diaspora theme is central to Gen 20–21 and Gen 22 presses the problem of theodicy to its limit. The theory that a second redactor supplemented the exilic Patriarchal History also provides a simpler explanation for why the account of Isaac's birth (Gen 21:1–2, 6–7) does not chime with the conceptual framework and motifs of Gen 18:1–15.[350] The original account was removed because the second redactor wanted to replace it with his own composition, which wished to describe Isaac's birth only after Sarah was in jeopardy for a second time. Since several compositional texts in the second part of PH (Gen 46:1–5a; 48:13–15, 21b) are related stylistically and thematically to Gen 20–22, I assign them to this redaction. It probably also includes 16:9; 26:15, 18, which harmonize the double traditions.

Analyzing these observations regarding the so-called "Elohistic fragments" or the "Negev group" (Gen 20–22), I distinguish two exilic editions of the Patriarchal History: (1) an earlier edition (PH¹), whose redactor (RPH¹) was the first to combine the narrative complexes involving Abraham, Isaac, and Jacob-Joseph; he organized the resulting complex under the themes of a command to go to the land (Gen 12:1) and a command not to leave the land (26:2), associated with promises of the land, increase, and blessings (12:1–3; 13:14–17; 26:2–3*; 28:13b, 14); and (2) a later edition (PH²), whose redactor (RPH²) wanted to include the Diaspora theme (20–22), in

---

[348] "Querverweise," 91.

[349] There is one small problem with this approach: it requires us to assume that the continuator echoed the original in Gen 12:8 when formulating the "cult foundation note" in 21:33. On the other hand, he saw no contradiction between 21:33 and 34: despite the preexisting Beer-sheba tradition, the focus of this recension was on presenting Abraham's life as that of an alien (cf. 20:1; 21:23, 24). For him, Beer-sheba was in the land of the Philistines, whereas for the first edition of PH that city had become Judean territory by virtue of Isaac's treaty with Abimelech (26:23, 25–33).

[350] The three men do not return, as promised in Gen 18:10, 14; Sarah's disbelieving laughter in 18:12–13, 15 is not mentioned in 21:6.

the process adding a temporary permission to leave the land (46:1–5a), associated with a promise of increase (46:3) and several additional assurances of God's accompanying presence (46:4; 48:13–15, 21b). The following table outlines the textual organization of the exilic Patriarchal History.

Exilic Patriarchal History (Gen 12:1–50:22a)			
PH¹; *PH²*	Additions	Earlier Material	Derivation/Content
(11:28–30)			(Abraham's family in Mesopotamia)
12:1–3			God's command to go to the promised land
12:4a			Abraham goes
12:6–8			journey through the land (Shechem, Bethel-Ai), altar building, invocation
12:9			journey to the Negev; transition
	12:10–20		separate narrative: Sarah endangered in Egypt
13:1–4*			return to Bethel-Ai
		13:5–13	Abraham-Lot complex: separation from Lot
13:14–17			Overview of the land; promise of the land and increase
		13:18a	settlement at Hebron
13:18b			altar building at Hebron
	16:1–2, 4–14		separate narrative: expulsion of Hagar (16:9 *PH²*; 16:10 PD)
		18:1–15	Abraham-Lot complex: promise of Isaac
		18:16, 20–22a, 33b	Abraham-Lot complex: transition to Sodom narrative
		19:1–28	Abraham-Lot complex: destruction of Sodom
		19:30–38	Abraham-Lot complex: children of Lot: Moab and Ammon
20			Sarah endangered at Gerar
21:1–2, 6–7			birth of Isaac
21:8–21			expulsion of Hagar and Ishmael
21:22–32			Abraham's treaty with Abimelech
21:33–34			cultic tree at Beer-sheba, invocation, life as an alien
22:1–14, 19			sacrifice of Isaac

		25:21–34*	exposition of the Jacob complex
26:1–3abα*			prohibition against leaving, with promise
	26:1*, 6–27*		Isaac complex (26:25aα PH¹; 26:15, 18 PH²; 26:3bβ–5, 14 PD
26:25aα			Isaac builds an altar at Beer-sheba, invocation
		27:1–45	Jacob complex: Jacob deceives Esau and flees
		28:10–13aα, 16–21	Jacob complex: theophany at Bethel
28:13aβb, 14			promise of the land and increase
		29:1–33:20*	Jacob complex: Jacob and Laban, reconciliation with Esau
		34*	Judean addition: Levi's offense avenging Dinah
		35:6–8, 16–20	extended Jacob complex: Bethel cult, death of Rachel
		35:21–26	Judean addition: Reuben's offense
		37:3–35*	Joseph novella: Joseph sold to Egyptians
		38	Judean addition: Judah and Tamar (+ 37:28a, 32–33*, 36)
39:1*, 2–22			exilic addition: Potiphar's wife (+ 40:1, 3aβb, 5, 15)
		40–45	Joseph novella: testing of the brothers and reconciliation
46:1–5a			*permission to leave and assurance of God's presence for Jacob*
		46:5b, 6, 28–34	Joseph novella: Jacob resettles in Egypt
		47*	Joseph novella with extension: settlement in Egypt
		48*	linkage of Jacob and Joseph; blessing of Joseph's sons
48:13–15, 21b			*prayer for God's blessing and help for Joseph's sons*
		49	Judean extension: Jacob's blessing on his sons
		50:1–22a	end of the extended Joseph novella: burial of Jacob in Canaan and final reconciliation of the brothers

The sections following this literary reconstruction will interpret the two editions of the exilic Patriarchal History against their historical background. Such an analysis has hardly been attempted with such rigor previously. Our conclusions must therefore be considered preliminary.[351]

III.2.3.1. The First Edition of the Exilic Patriarchal History

It is no longer possible to reconstruct the beginning of PH^1 with confidence, since it was lost in the redaction of PP. Genesis 11:28–30 preserves fragments. It is not certain whether it had the patriarchs come from Haran in Syria, as in the Jacob tradition (cf. Gen 29–31), or whether RPH^1 had already shifted their home to Ur of the Chaldeans in southern Mesopotamia,[352] nearer the homes of the Babylonian golah. In any case, RPH^1 presented Abraham to the exiles as a shining example of return to their ancient homeland by taking the ancient memory that Israel's ancestors had entered Palestine from the northeast and stylizing it as an explicit command by Yahweh to the patriarch to leave his family in Mesopotamia to go to a land that God would show him (12:1). However comfortably the Judeans were settled in Babylonia, it was now time to sever all family ties to follow God's call, as Abraham had.

To ameliorate the risk of setting forth to a distant unknown, RPH^1 had Yahweh shower a veritable cornucopia of blessings on Abraham (Gen 12:2–3). God would make him (once again) a great nation (cf. 46:3; 21:[13], 18 PH^2; 18:18 PD; 17:20 PP)—that is, eliminate all the fears for survival arising from the decimation of the Judeans consequent on the deportations and the chaos of war. God would make his name great (like the king's name in former days: 2 Sam 7:9; 8:13; 1 Kgs 1:47; Ps 72:17), that is, give him recognition in the international world and thus overcome the political marginalization imposed on Israel since it had ceased to exist as a state. However, this international renown would not be achieved by war and conquest, as in the days of the kingdoms of Israel and Judah, but by God's making Abraham—and with him the new Israel—the recipient of blessings par excellence (12:2b) and the mediator of blessings "for all the families of the earth." These extraordinary promises of blessing were the response of RPH^1 to all the contempt poured on the Judeans by their neighbors during the exilic period (Jer 24:9; Zech 8:13; etc.). In these blessings, RPH^1 drew on the old royal theology (Pss 21:4 [3]; 72:6–7, 16, 17),

---

[351] Blum's *Komposition* is still the most ambitious attempt at historical interpretation. By contrast, the exilic period plays almost no part in the interpretations of Van Seters (*Prologue*) and Levin (*Jahwist*). Literary criticism is still preeminent.

[352] Gen 11:28 in its present form; then certainly in PP (11:31) and PD (15:7).

stripped of any imperial agenda by a "democratizing" translation. Of course Yahweh would not hand Abraham over to his enemies; anyone who sought to injure him with curses would be cursed in turn by Yahweh (12:3a). However, all who welcomed him with blessings (12:3a) and blessed each other in his name would share in the blessing of Abraham (12:3b). It is clear that RPH^1 here sketches the outline of a postpolitical relationship between Israel and its neighbors, to be realized in the milieu of the family. Here we find echoes of the notion of a positive universal role for Israel, actually made possible by the dissolution of its political structures and nurtured not least by the fundamental universal experience of personal piety.

In contrast to the contemporary dispute between those who were willing to return and those who were not, RPH^1 has Abraham obey without a word Yahweh's command to set out (Gen 12:4a). The patriarch—as the redactor pictures him to the audience—accepted God's great promises without any ifs, ands, or buts. Without mentioning any stopping places along the way, RPH^1 has Abraham traverse Palestine from north to south (12:6, 8), following the route of Jacob when he returned from Mesopotamia (33:17–18; 35:6–7). First he came to Shechem, then Bethel. By having Abraham, the ancestor of the southern tribes, visit these important cultic centers of the northern kingdom, RPH^1 wanted to demonstrate at the very outset the conciliatory objective of his Patriarchal History, embracing southern and northern traditions equally.[353] However, he does avoid bringing Abraham into direct contact with the sanctuary at Bethel, which had been problematic at least since the time of Josiah. Instead, he has him set up his tent and build an altar in the hill country between Bethel and Ai (12:8). By stating that at this altar Abraham called on the name of Yahweh for the first time in the promised land, he foregrounds the element of the word (cf. 13:4; 21:33; 26:25) that had become characteristic of exilic worship. However vague the location and however intangible the nature of this first act of worship, it established an initial relationship between Palestine and the patriarch.

However, RPH^1 deliberately depicts the rest of Abraham's journey in such a way that Abraham still does not know whether he is already in the land God has allotted to him. He has the patriarch travel farther south

---

[353] Here RPH^1 allied himself with the group of exilic theologians who saw the exile as an opportunity for a rapprochement between the inhabitants of the former northern and southern kingdoms (cf. Ezek 37:15–22; Jer 31:31–34 [JerD^3]; etc.). A similar thought appears already in Jer 31:10–14. The Deuteronomists of the Deuteronomistic History opposed hopes for reunification. For them, their brothers and sisters to north were incorrigible syncretists (2 Kgs 17:24–34a).

(Gen 12:9) and eventually, driven by a famine, enter Egypt. The old story of the matriarch (12:10–20) that RPH¹ incorporated into his narrative gave him a welcome opportunity to demonstrate dramatically to his exilic contemporaries, not a few of whom had preferred to emigrate to Egypt on account of the uncertain situation in Judah, that this other ancient riverine civilization, like Mesopotamia, was anything but the land allotted to Israel by Yahweh. Only at the cost of his wife's disgrace had the patriarch been able to save his life in Egypt by a devious ploy. Only through Yahweh's intervention had Sarah and he been able to survive this adventure. He is expelled from Egypt, wealthy but morally humiliated. When RPH¹ concludes the old story by having Abraham return directly to where RPH¹ had him build his altar between Bethel and Ai (13:1–4), it is to show the Egyptian golah that Abraham—unlike them—had learned his lesson: Egypt was not a place where Judeans could live without danger and compromise. They belonged back in Palestine!

At this point, RPH¹ was able to fashion a transition to the existing Abraham-Lot complex (Gen 13:5–13, 18a; 18–19*), which had been used in Judah during the early monarchy to reflect on why the Israelites had settled west of the Jordan and what their relationship was to the nations of Moab and Ammon east of the Jordan: since the land could not support the flocks of both Lot and Abraham, they agreed to separate. By choosing the plain of the Jordan, Lot seemed initially to have made the better choice, but after Yahweh's judgment on sinful Sodom, creating the hostile environment of the rift valley, he ended up in the remote region of Transjordania.

However, before all this takes place, as soon as Abraham acquires the land west of the Jordan and Lot separates from him, RPH¹ brings the opening scene of his narrative to its climax (Gen 13:14–17). Yahweh commands Abraham to stand near his altar between Bethel and Ai, clearly envisioned as being atop a high mountain,[354] and to look in all directions. All the land that he sees, Yahweh assures him, he will give to him and his offspring forever (13:14–15). With this solemn promise of the land, RPH¹ asserts, Abraham's arduous search for land has come to a happy conclusion: the land that Yahweh would show him (12:1) has finally been

---

[354] The *Genesis Apocryphon* (1QapGen XXI, 8–15) identifies the site, probably correctly, with the heights of *ḥṣwr*, i.e., Jebel el-ʿAṣur, probably the same as Baal-hazor (2 Sam 13:23) (see Florentino García Martínez and Eibert J. C. Tigchelaar, *The Dead Sea Scrolls: Study Edition* [2 vols.; Leiden: Brill, 1997–98], 1:44–45). This mountain is located about 4.5 miles north of Beitin, the modern equivalent of ancient Bethel, and reaches an altitude of 3,333 feet above sea level. Noth reports that it commands a wonderful view over all western Palestine, from Hermon in the north to Kadesh-barnea in the south and from the mountains of Hauran in the east to the Mediterranean in the west (*ZDPV* 82 [1966]: 264–70).

found! Because the land is so vast, Yahweh promises Abraham countless offspring (13:16) and commands him to take possession of it symbolically (13:17). RPH¹ has Abraham respond to this great affirmative promise by building another altar at Hebron (13:18b), Abraham's home in the Abraham-Lot complex (13:18a; 18:1).

Much of this introductory scene was actually composed by RPH¹; now he lets the older Abraham tradition speak for itself, largely unaltered. Having shown that Yahweh had allotted Israel a specific place on the map of the Near East, he borrows from Gen 18:1–15 the motif that Israel owed its very existence, profoundly threatened by Sarah's infertility, to God's promise. To the extent that RPH¹ is responsible for interpolating the separate older narrative of Gen 16* into the Abraham-Lot complex, he uses it to enhance this motif through contrast: the son of Gen 18, promised most improbably to childless Sarah by God, is finally born, whereas Sarah's attempt to get herself a child with the help of her maid is an almost total failure: Hagar is driven away pregnant. Through Yahweh's intervention the child does come into the world, but only to found a collateral line (the Ishmaelites).

How the Abraham narrative ended in PH¹ cannot be determined. Probably following Gen 19 the birth of Isaac was reported as foretold in 18:10, 14, but RPH² removed this scene and replaced it with 21:1–2, 6–7. Then there was probably a brief notice of Isaac's marriage and the death of Abraham and Sarah, episodes expanded extensively by later redactors (Gen 24 closely related to PD, Gen 23 and 25:7–11 PP).

The beginning of the Jacob complex (Gen 25:21–34*; 27:1–35:20*) was also replaced by PP (25:19–20). RPH¹ linked this complex to the Abraham narrative by inserting when God first speaks, during the theophany at Bethel, an inclusive promise of land, increase, and blessing (28:13aβb, 14), borrowing motifs from the theological climax of his own opening scene, 13:14–17 and 12:3. RPH¹ emphasizes that the promises to displaced Israel, marginalized and facing extinction, were repeated for each generation; through Jacob, the progenitor of the twelve tribes, they belong to all his contemporary descendants. In the case of this last of the patriarchs, therefore, he particularly emphasizes Jacob's "seed" (זַרְעֶ֫ךָ) by placing it at the end of 28:13b and 14.

Nevertheless, the narrative material RPH¹ had to work with posed a problem in presenting the patriarchs in unbroken genealogical succession: it did not provide an appropriate tradition for Isaac. The Abraham-Lot complex merely recorded his birth; the Jacob complex mentioned him as a young man at the birth of his children (Gen 25:24, 28) and then had a lengthy story of him as an old man shortly before his death (27:1–40). Since RPH¹ had at his disposal only a short and formalized Isaac complex (Gen 26:1–33*), describing Isaac in the prime of life, he had no recourse but to insert the latter into the opening of the Jacob complex, although it did not mention his children.

The Isaac complex[355] recorded how the second patriarch, an alien in Philistia, rose with God's help and blessing (Gen 26:12, 28, 29) from an endangered fugitive to a respected covenant partner of the Philistines. It suited admirably the conception of RPH[1], who therefore elaborated it to make it the second pillar of his work.

First, RPH[1] used the variant of the matriarch story (Gen 12:10-20) from the Isaac complex as an occasion to address once more the theme of the land allotted by God. In addition, he interpreted Isaac's finding refuge during a famine not in Egypt, like Abraham, but with Abimelech, the Philistine king of Gerar, by saying that Yahweh had expressly forbidden him to go down to Egypt and had commanded him instead to dwell in the land that he had appointed (Palestine; 26:2), thus recalling explicitly the scene he had framed to introduce his work (26:1aβ, 2b; cf. 12:1-20*). The point he was making to his audience was this: since Abraham did not yet know just what land was meant, Yahweh had put up with his detour to Egypt. There he had to learn his lesson. Meanwhile, however, the promised land had been identified: Yahweh had shown it to Abraham (13:13-14). It was Palestine, especially the territory west of the Jordan. Therefore, Yahweh now insisted that Isaac, as his father's son, do nothing to cast doubt on this clear identification. Thus RPH[1] claimed God's own authority to demonstrate to his contemporaries, by the example of the second patriarch, that emigration to Egypt such as had been common at the beginning of the exilic period (Jer 41:16-43:7) contravened God's will, even if it seemed justifiable on grounds of economic or other necessity.

Second, RPH[1] associated promises with this prohibition. Yahweh, he wished to make clear, had promised explicitly to stand by Isaac during his life as an alien in Palestine, to protect him, to bless him, and even "to give all these lands" to him and his descendants (Gen 26:3abα). These promises were deliberately formulated to fit the context of the existing Isaac tradition. Thus their narrative material provided a wonderful opportunity to demonstrate the first consequence of God's promises in the lives of the patriarchs: Yahweh's protection was demonstrated when Isaac's wife Rebekah—unlike Sarah before her—was not really threatened in Gerar. The Philistine king himself intervened effectually to keep the patriarch and matriarch inviolate (26:7-11). Isaac, an economic

---

[355] This complex may date from the end of the eighth century, when Hezekiah claimed hegemony over the Philistine cities; cf. 2 Kgs 18:8 and 1 Chr 4:39-40. See also Blum, *Komposition*, 304-3.

fugitive, became a rich man in Gerar (26:12–13) as a result of Yahweh's blessing. At first his wealth aroused the jealousy of the Philistines; having fewer rights, Isaac had to leave Gerar and was driven away from his well several times by the local shepherds (26:14–21). Thanks to God's assistance, however, he kept discovering new wells, until he finally discovered the well at Beer-sheba with its abundant water (26:20–23, 26–27).

At this point, RPH[1] modified the traditional text to tell how Isaac built an altar at Beer-sheba and called on the name of Yahweh (Gen 26:25aα). Thus Isaac, like Abraham before him (12:8), symbolically proclaimed his claim to this region on the Philistine border—an act not without danger after the earlier conflicts! As if by a miracle, everything ended happily. Impressed by such massive divine assistance and blessing, King Abimelech personally offered him a political alliance, agreeing that the pastures previously under Philistine control, including Beer-sheba, would henceforth belong indisputably to Isaac. God thus rewarded Isaac's obedient decision to remain in Palestine with territory in the southwest that had not been part of the land originally allotted to Israel (26:26–31). Now the peculiar plural in the promise of "lands" in 26:3bα[356] makes immediate sense: it was meant to encourage those left in Palestine, who had lost large regions of the land to their neighbors during the exile. Their faithful continuance in the land, RPH[1] was saying to them, would ultimately be rewarded by new land, as in the case of the patriarch Isaac.

RPH[1] was able to use the Jacob complex, which had originated in the northern kingdom during the ninth century, pretty much as it stood, because in one essential point it coincided perfectly with his conception of the promised land. After defrauding Esau of his blessing and fearing Esau's revenge, Jacob sought refuge with his Mesopotamian relatives in Haran. RPH[1] could not alter Jacob's flight: it was a central element of the story. He could only have Yahweh remind the third patriarch before he left Palestine, in a promise given during a nocturnal dream at Bethel, that the land on which he was lying—not northern Syria—was his homeland (Gen 28:13–16). RPH[1] was able to find God's intent that Jacob not remain in Mesopotamia expressed in God's explicit command to return, already part of the narrative tradition: "Return to the land of your kin" (Gen

---

[356] Apart from PD's inclusion of this verse in Gen 26:4, this is the only place where the ancestors are promised "these lands." Blum (*Komposition*, 299), followed by Seebass (*Genesis*, 3:280), has suggested that the plural is used because the promise of land was made in a foreign territory and was formulated specifically to exclude the land of the Philistines. If so, it is unclear why there should be any promise of land here at all.

31:13). By describing how Jacob obeyed this divine command and found his way back to Palestine despite many obstacles, RPH¹ was able to present this patriarch likewise to his audience as a model for return from the golah. Since Hosea had already made Jacob's return a model for the repentant return of Israel after the catastrophe (Hos 12:7 [6]), RPH¹ probably formulated his whole conception of return on the basis of the Jacob tradition.[357]

By the exilic period, the eighth-century Joseph novella (Gen 37–50*) had long been circulated in its expanded form combined with the Jacob complex. RPH¹ probably modified it at only one point: he added the episode of Potiphar's wife (Gen 39*) to rectify somewhat the uniformly positive picture that the novella painted of Egypt, which conflicted with his conception.[358] By incorporating an old Egyptian story, he created a typical Diaspora narrative, which used the fate of Joseph to illustrate both the opportunities and the dangers facing Israelites in a foreign land. On the one hand, Joseph's career gave RPH¹ an opportunity to represent Israel's effectual mediation of God's blessing, as Yahweh had promised to the patriarchs Abraham and Jacob (Gen 12:3; 28:14). Yahweh's assistance and blessing not only enabled Joseph to rise to the top within Potiphar's household but also benefited his Egyptian hosts (39:2–6a). From the time Potiphar appointed Joseph overseer of his house, his estate was virtually inundated with Yahweh's copious blessings—but this was only the one side. On the other, RPH¹ vividly illustrates the extreme dangers to which Joseph was exposed as a foreigner. Because he was handsome (39:6b), he aroused the sexual desire of Potiphar's wife. Loyal to his master, he resolutely resisted her advances. The native Egyptians then mercilessly brought him down, a "Hebrew slave" with no rights. Simply on the basis

---

[357] In the background, of course, there is also the Deuteronomic conception that the land is a gift given by Yahweh (Deut 6:10–19, etc.). To give it up would be tantamount to scorning God.

[358] Gen 39 has always stood out: unlike the rest of the Joseph novella, it uses the name "Yahweh" up to 39:9; furthermore, only here does Yahweh intervene directly in the course of events. It represents a kind of doublet to chapters 40–41. This situation has been difficult for the traditional Documentary Hypothesis to explain, because it would seem to suggest that in the novella, unlike elsewhere, "J" is later than "E." This problem led Schmitt (*Nichtpriesterliche Josephsgeschichte*, 81ff.) to modify the model and posit a late "Yahwistic" editing, which he dated in the exilic or postexilic period. This theory converges with the traditiohistorical view proposed here. While Blum does not discuss Gen 39, Carr (*Reading*, 209–10) assigns the theological framework of the chapter (39:2, 3, 5–6aα, 21–23) to his "Proto-Genesis Composition." However, the chapter constitutes a single literary unit: the peculiar character of the central section is due to the use of earlier Egyptian material here by RPH¹. The addition of Gen 39 also required some retouching of 40:1, 3aβb, 5b, 15; 41:12* ("a Hebrew youth") and 41:14* ("out of the dungeon").

of a false accusation by a slighted woman, he was thrown into prison without a chance to defend himself and without a trial (39:7–20). Finally, however, RPH[1] makes it clear that Joseph's sudden fall was not the end of the story: thanks to Yahweh's steadfast love, his new rise began even while he was still in prison (39:21–23). This profound vulnerability in a foreign land, which for RPH[1] probably echoed agonizing incidents experienced by the exilic generation, would not be lost on his audience when they read the Joseph novella.

If this redaction-historical reconstruction is correct, RPH[1] did not comment on Jacob's journey to see Joseph in Egypt. It did not really square with his conception, but the return of Jacob's family to the promised land was conceptually communicable through the exodus tradition, even though PH[1] had probably not yet made that literary connection. For RPH[1], it was undoubtedly an important element of the Joseph novella that the patriarch Jacob at least should return to Palestine and be buried there (Gen 50:1–11). The Israelites of the exilic period were scattered throughout the world of the Near East, but the lives of all three patriarchs had demonstrated impressively where Israel really belonged and where it would be offered an opportunity to live securely once more.

III.2.3.2. The Second Edition of the Exilic Patriarchal History

RPH[1] focused totally on the theme of return to Palestine. A second theologian working with the tradition of the ancestors was unwilling to let matters rest there. He was concerned, much more than RPH[1] in Gen 39 would have thought proper, to find an appropriate precedent in the history of the ancestors for the life of Judean families in the Diaspora. Therefore he undertook a further redaction of PH[1]. First RPH[2] composed a group of Abraham narratives (Gen 20–22) dealing with the life of the patriarch in southern Palestine (20:1), near the Philistine border. Although Abraham dwelt in Palestine, in the view of RPH[2] his life there was primarily that of an alien (20:1; 21:23, 24). The commentary of RPH[2] on the command to leave Mesopotamia in 12:1 appears in 20:13: "When God caused me to wander from my father's house ... in every land to which we come." In contrast to the conception of RPH[1], for RPH[2] God called Abraham not to a journey with a goal but to life as a perpetual alien.

In his variant of the matriarch narrative (Gen 20), his purpose was therefore to correct 12:10–20 by showing that it was by no means always the wicked "Gentiles" but often their own religious prejudices that caused trouble for the Israelites in foreign lands. Abraham had supposed that there was no fear of God (יִרְאַת אֱלֹהִים) in Gerar (20:11). Therefore, he had played the degrading game of concealing the fact that Sarah was his wife, provoking God's intervention against King Abimelech. To his shame, Abraham had to learn from Abimelech that a "Gentile nation" could also be righteous (צַדִּיק: 20:4). Abimelech generously made good the unintentional wrong he had committed (20:14, 16) and even—contrary to 12:12—invited Abraham and Sarah to settle wherever they pleased in his land. RPH² wanted to tell the Judeans in the Diaspora: your life could often be comfortable in a foreign land if you could get over your religious arrogance and realize that there is also morality and piety among your hosts. Indeed, by making Abraham a prophet (20:7), able to save his hosts from disaster by interceding effectually for Abimelech (20:17), he made it clear how he understood Israel's "mediation of blessings" to the nations: prayer on behalf of their alien neighbors (cf. already Jer 29:7). Thus RPH² had important and entirely positive experiences in the Diaspora suffuse his edition of the exilic Patriarchal History.

Oddly, RPH² delayed the account of Isaac's birth (Gen 21:1–2, 6–7) until after the story of Sarah and Abimelech. In his telling, Yahweh did not deal with the barren Sarah until after he had also lifted the curse of barrenness from the house of Abimelech. The statement that Yahweh's healing intervention for Abraham and Sarah went hand in hand with his healing of their alien hosts was so important to RPH² that he substituted his own account of Isaac's birth for the account in PH¹, which had followed chapters 18–19 directly. He also deliberately shifted Isaac's birth from Hebron to Philistia: in his view, the second patriarch was a child of the Diaspora!

Thus RPH² turned to the second theme of his narrative composite: the promise of a son and many offspring, and hence the question of survival. His new version of the Hagar story (Gen 21:8–21), which he placed immediately after the account of Isaac's birth, raised the stakes in the conflict between the two women, focusing it on the question of which child was to be the legitimate heir (21:10) and hence continue the line of Israel (21:12): Ishmael, the son of Sarah's maid Hagar, both conceived and—with the emendation introduced by RPH² in 16:9—born in the Judean heartland, or Isaac, the son of Abraham's primary wife Sarah, born in the land of the Philistines? RPH² framed the conflict in such a way that Abraham really did not want to part with either of his sons: they were both dear to him (21:11). It was not just Sarah but God who demanded that he make the sacrifice of giving up his son Ishmael (21:12–13). Thus both he and the exilic audience were instructed that now, when the borders of Israel were fragmented, it was not geographical location that determined legitimacy: everything depended on being born to a Jewish mother. Thus RPH² set a limit to the position of RPH¹: however important the land might be, it did nothing to define who was an Israelite and who was not. Legitimate offspring of Abraham could be born in a foreign land! There was also a further element: when the scattered Judean groups in the golah began increasingly to define themselves genealogically, mixed marriages with foreign women were tantamount to the dissolution of Israel. When God commanded Abraham to exclude Ishmael and Hagar from his family, the patriarch had to learn the painful lesson that assimilation was no longer the road to survival. However, this ethnic separation—and RPH² went on to emphasize this point in the rest of his narrative—by no means meant abandonment, human or religious. God gave to Hagar and Ishmael the same promise of becoming a great nation (21:13, 18) that Abraham and his descendants received (12:2). To assure that this promise would be realized, God also intervened to rescue Hagar and Ishmael just like Sarah and Isaac.

After describing how Abraham had made his life as an alien even more secure by a treaty with Abimelech, through which he acquired cultic and water rights at Beer-sheba (Gen 21:22–34), RPH² addressed the real threat to Israel's survival: it was not so much the lack of a homeland as the loss of children that profoundly threatened Israel's ongoing existence (22:1–19). Abraham had already been required to give up his firstborn son, whom Sarah and God had declared illegitimate. He had accepted this decision, however unwillingly (21:12–14). But what did it mean that God now required him to give back his only remaining legitimate son? RPH² played out this ultimately cruel possibility in the story of the sacrifice of Isaac. This time, too, Abraham acceded to God's inhuman command (22:2); he was prepared, hoping in God (22:8), to sacrifice his beloved son. When RPH² made God's command echo the command to leave Mesopotamia (12:1), he sought to make clear that the unreasonable demand to leave home and family was as nothing compared to the test Abraham was put to here: the sacrifice of his only legitimate son and therefore of his future. Superficially, this episode may reflect the bitter experience of high infant mortality that exposed the exilic families, already fighting for their lives, to the danger of extinction. How could Israel ever again become a great nation if God caused the death of so many young children? On a deeper level, RPH² was touching on the central doubt that assailed the exilic period: God seemed to have abrogated maliciously all the promises made to Israel. Did the most profound threat to Israel come not from the other nations but from none other than God?

Aware of these terrible questions, RPH² let his readers know at the outset that in making this ultimate demand God was testing Abraham (22:1a), and by showing them how the patriarch passed this test (22:12b), he made clear to them how their fear of God must differ from the respectable piety of the nations among whom they lived. Following the example of Abraham, they must steadfastly trust in God even when God seemed to be destroying their very life and future. Finally, he sought to assure them, Yahweh would not disappoint such absolute trust; even in alien lands, he would preserve Israel from extinction.

This profound reflection on Israel's situation in the Diaspora accounts for the deliberate differentiation between the word "God" and the name of God employed by RPH² in Gen 20–22. Normally, for him, the God whom Israel worshiped was simply God, who also governed with equity the fates of other nations (20:3, 17; 21:12, 17, 20) and thus linked Israel with the nations among whom the Israelites were living (Gen 20:11, 17; 22:12). Therefore RPH² usually called God Elohim. He chose the same term when God treated Israel neutrally (21:2) or even seemed alien and remote (22:1, 3, 8, 9). He used the name Yahweh only when God intervened on behalf of Israel's ancestors (20:18) or showed them mercy in some special way (21:1; 22:11, 14). Thus RPH² tried to combine both the particular and the universal aspect of relationship with God, while at the same time differentiating them conceptually.

Apart from the extensive addition in Gen 20–22, so far as we can tell, RPH² made few changes in PH¹. In the text as it stood, it was primarily the Joseph novella that reflected his positive assessment of the Diaspora; it is therefore no accident that he used it to expound and legitimate his theological position. In the fact that Jacob and his family had no trouble journeying to Egypt and even settling there (45:28; 46:5b, 28–47:12), he saw theological confirmation that the harsh command not to go down to Egypt formulated by RPH¹ in 26:2 could not embody God's absolute will. As a contrast, therefore, he framed a short episode of divine revelation (46:1–5a)[359] in which Jacob, after offering sacrifice at Beer-sheba, on Israel's southern border, is expressly encouraged by God to go down to Egypt, in spite of any fears he may have been harboring (46:1–3). God promises not to abandon him in a foreign land, as he might have feared, but to go down to Egypt with him (46:4a).[360] Thus God personally makes it clear that the relationship between God and Israel is by no means tied to the land; it could be as intense in the Diaspora as in Judah. A position

---

[359] The secondary character of the scene in its context is evident, since 46:5b directly continues 45:28. This text is usually assigned to "E," but Westermann (*Genesis 37–50*, 155) already recognized that the use of the term מראות in 46:2, found elsewhere only in Ezek 1:1; 8:3; 40:2; 43:3; Job 4:13, indicates "late language, at least that of the exile." The attempt by Schmidt (*Literarische Studien*, 185–88) to maintain Elohistic authorship is not convincing.

[360] Elsewhere the Hebrew verb ירד with God as subject refers to a demonstration of God's lovingkindess in a theophany (Exod 19:11, 20; 34:5) or historical intervention (3:8); it therefore has a double meaning here. Along with the offering of sacrifice—unusual in PH—in 46:1, the use of the term by RPH² is probably meant emphasize that Yahweh's lovingkindness toward Jacob was not at all dependent on the cult and the cultic purity of the land but was independent of both.

like that of many who stayed in Palestine during the exilic period, who held that the exiles were far distant from Yahweh (Ezek 11:15), was therefore theologically untenable. To underpin his belief to the contrary, RPH² appealed to two different conceptions of God. On the one hand, he had Yahweh present himself as הָאֵל, "the (only) God," in an absolute sense like that found in Deutero-Isaiah (Isa 40:18; 42:5; 43:10, 12; 45:22; 46:9). In other words, the domain of God's activity cannot be limited: it is universal. On the other hand, he had Yahweh foreground his function as family God ("the God of your father"). In other words: God is bound not to a geographical location but to a human group.³⁶¹ God could always be present with the group, wherever it might be. The patriarch Jacob and with him the Judeans in the Diaspora could be confident that Yahweh was with them, even in a foreign land. When RPH² placed yet another blessing in the mouth of the aged Jacob in Gen 48:15–16, where shortly before his death he recapitulates how the God before whom his ancestors Abraham and Isaac had walked had protected him throughout his life from the day of his birth, RPH² was painting for his readers a captivating picture of such familial piety, a way of life that could be lived by Judeans anywhere in the world. What he found essential was not geographical stability but a continuity of a personal relationship with God throughout the course of one's life and for generations to come. For RPH², not only Israel but also Israel's relationship with God was defined primarily genealogically. More important than returning—so we may summarize the perspective of RPH²—was care, wherever one might be, that the religion of the ancestors not lapse, that it be passed on from parents to children and grandchildren. Fundamentally, RPH² was convinced, the promise in Gen 12:2 that God would once again make of the families a great nation could also be realized in a foreign land (46:3bβ). To this end, he called to mind the exodus tradition.

It was not the intent of RPH² totally to negate the significance of the land, which RPH¹ had stressed as an indispensable element of Israel's relationship with God. As the end of the revelation scene shows, he too believed that Jacob's permission to go down to Egypt was coupled with the declaration that God would also bring him back again (Gen 46:4). As the reference to Jacob's death scene shows (cf. 50:1ff.), this meant primarily that he was to be buried in Palestine, as already recorded in the text of the expanded Joseph novella. In addition, however, the language undoubtedly alludes to the subsequent return home of the people brought out of Egypt (cf. 48:21b). In other words, even for RPH²

---

361 The "God of the fathers" is not a nomadic deity but a familial deity; see Albertz, *History*, 1:26–32.

permission to emigrate was temporary; life in the Diaspora was only a transitional stage that must end some time in the future, whether an individual took pains to be buried in Palestine or God would some day bring back the descendants of all those who had emigrated or been deported. When RPH² partially rewrote the Patriarchal History to illustrate and justify Israel's life in the Diaspora, the tradition of the exodus and occupation became its indispensable horizon for the future.[362]

Thus two distinct, well-defined positions engaged in theological debate in the two editions of the exilic Patriarchal History. The one, PH¹, basically defined Israel geographically, through the land that Yahweh had assigned to the ancestors. Logically, therefore, it urged all the groups in the Diaspora to return as soon as possible. The other, PH², defined Israel more genealogically, through legitimate descent from the families of the ancestors. It therefore provided theological justification for various groups to enjoy a temporary (albeit lengthy) period of life in the Diaspora. It is reasonable to assume that both positions were actually advocated and debated during the exilic period—at the earliest, when it became clear that the deportation policy of the Neo-Babylonian Empire was on the verge of changing (562 B.C.E.),[363] at the latest, when return became a realistic possibility (539–520). Of course, this was particularly true in the Babylonian golah, where families had to made a concrete decision, but such debates undoubtedly also took place among those left in Palestine and possibly, to a lesser extent, within the Egyptian golah. In any case, we know that the vast majority of the Egyptian golah remained in Egypt and that only a small fraction of the Babylonian golah were actually prepared to return. Thus the exilic Patriarchal History opened the theological debate over aliyah, return to the promised land, which has continued within Judaism to this day.[364]

Nothing definitive can yet be said about the date, geographical location, and sociohistorical setting of RPH¹ and RPH². The literature reveals

---

[362] Whether RPH² already knew a literary continuation in the story of the exodus and occupation or simply pointed the way to it conceptually is uncertain. According to Blum (Komposition, 396–99), the literary bridge between these two blocks of the Pentateuch was first constructed by PD (cf. Exod 1:6, 8 with Judg 2:8, 10). If so, RPH² laid the groundwork with his conception of such a continuation.

[363] See pp. 60ff. above.

[364] Within the Patriarchal History itself, the controversy continued in the postexilic period. PD—even more than RPH¹—stressed the duty to return, as shown by the forceful promises of the land included in this redaction (Gen 12:7; 15:7–21; 26:4–5; cf. 24:7). For PP, by contrast, the ancestors tended to personify life in the Diaspora. Therefore PP underlined the importance of circumcision (Gen 17); Palestine in the patriarchal period was still "the land where they were aliens" (Gen 17:8; 28:4; 37:1; Exod 6:4).

substantial differences of opinion. Carr prefers to date his "Proto-Genesis Composition" prior to the Deuteronomistic History (560 B.C.E.); according to him, its author was a Judean belonging to the erstwhile nonpriestly ruling elite.[365] Levin's "Yahwist" is also pre-Deuteronomistic; Levin sees in him a member of the court who was deported to Babylonia.[366] Van Seters assigns his "Yahwist" a post-Deuteronomistic date.[367] Veijola, finally, dates Gen 22 in the fifth century.[368] The analysis above places RPH^1 in the initial phase of the debate, when the possibility of return was first perceived and was still thought of overwhelmingly positively as a great God-given opportunity. The most likely date would be the first years of the Deutero-Isaiah group's preaching (ca. 550–539 B.C.E.; cf. Isa 48:20–21). The RPH^2 redaction belongs to a phase of disillusionment. The initial enthusiasm had died down; the Judean families had grown aware of the difficulties and risks involved in giving up everything they had labored for in Babylonia. During the long waiting period (539–521) before the first return actually began, RPH^2 provided theological fodder for all who had decided they would rather stay a while longer in Babylonia.[369] Since RPH^1 (Gen 39) and to an even greater extent RPH^2 (20–22) introduce the experience of life in the Diaspora into the Patriarchal History, both probably originated outside Palestine, most likely in the Babylonian golah.[370] With his vote for a speedy return, RPH^1 supported the group of leaders around Zerubbabel and the priest Joshua, who led the return in 520. However, he was clearly at odds with their political goals for the restoration: they had their eye on restoration of the Davidic monarchy and separation from Samaria (cf. Hag 2), goals also supported by the Deuteronomistic History (2 Kgs 17; 22–24; 25:27–20). With his transfer of royal functions to the people (Gen 12:2–3), RPH^1 was closer to the Deutero-Isaiah group and supported a consistent "all Israel" option that recalls the school of Ezekiel (Ezek 37:15ff.). He probably belonged to the

---

365 *Reading*, 227.
366 *Jahwist*, 434.
367 *Prologue*, 242.
368 "Opfer," 155.

369 The arguments assembled by Veijola ("Opfer," 149–57) for a late dating of Gen 22:1–19 suffice to refute assignment of the chapter to the eighth-century "Elohist" but are not persuasive in support of a fifth-century date, especially since Veijola limits his discussion to the chapter in question, even though he notes correctly that it cannot be separated literarily from its context (150).

370 The material from the Egyptian Tale of Two Brothers incorporated into Gen 39 makes it reasonable to ask whether RPH^1 might have originated in the Egyptian golah, but the negative assessment of Egypt in Gen 12:10–20; 26:2; 39 argues against such a provenance. Since many Egyptians lived in Babylonia, RPH^1 could easily have heard the story there.

Judean upper class but—influenced by prophetic thought—stood at some distance from its inner circle. By contrast, RPH² was forthrightly hostile to the ruling class and their religious nationalism; he, too, was influenced by the theology of the Deutero-Isaiah group (Gen 46:3) but radicalized its universalistic perspective. This picture of Abraham as a prophet interceding for the people among whom he dwells as an alien (20:7, 17) associates RPH² with a prophetically influenced Diaspora elite of whom we know little else.

III.2.4. The Deuteronomistic History

Albertz, Rainer. "Die Intentionen und die Träger des Deuteronomistischen Geschichtswerks," in *Schöpfung und Befreiung: Für Claus Westermann zum 80. Geburtstag* (ed. R. Albertz, R. W. Golka, and J. Kegler; Stuttgart: Calwer, 1989), 37–53. **Albertz.** "In Search of the Deuteronomists: A First Solution to a 'Historical Riddle,'" in *The Future of the Deuteronomistic History* (ed. T. C. Römer; BETL 147; Leuven: Peeters, 2000), 1–17. **Becking,** Bob. "From Exodus to Exile: 2 Kgs 17,7–20 in the Context of its Co-Text," in *Studies in Historical Geography and Biblical Historiography: Presented to Zechariah Kallai* (ed. G. Galil and M. Weinfeld; VTSup 91; Leiden: Brill, 2000), 215–31. **Blum,** Erhard. "Ein Anfang der Geschichtsschreibung? Anmerkungen zur sog. Thronfolgegeschichte und zum Umgang mit Geschichte im alten Israel," *Trumah* 5 (1996): 9–46. **Blum.** "Der kompositionelle Knoten am Übergang von Josua zu Richter: Ein Entflechtungs-vorschlag," in *Deuteronomy and Deuteronomic Literature: Festschrift C. H. W. Brekelmans* (ed. M. Vervenne and J. Lust; BETL 133; Leuven: Leuven University Press, 1997), 181–212. **Cross,** Frank Moore. "The Themes of the Book of Kings and the Structure of the Deuteronomistic History," in idem, *Canaanite Myth and Hebrew Epic: Essays in the History of the Religion of Israel* (Cambridge: Harvard University Press, 1973), 274–89. **Dietrich,** Walter. "Martin Noth and the Future of the Deuteronomistic History," in *The History of Israel's Traditions: The Heritage of Martin Noth* (ed. S. L. McKenzie and M. P. Graham; JSOTSup 182; Sheffield: Sheffield Academic Press, 1994), 153–75. **Dietrich.** "Niedergang und Neuanfang: Die Haltung der Schlussredaktion des deuteronomistichen Geschichtswerk zu den wichtigsten Fragen ihrer Zeit," *OtSt* 42 (1999): 45–70. **Dietrich.** *Prophetie und Geschichte: Eine redaktionsgeschichtliche Untersuchung zum deuteronomistischen Geschichtswerk* (FRLANT 108; Göttingen: Vandenhoeck & Ruprecht, 1972). **Dutcher-Walls,** Patricia. "The Social Location of the Deuteronomists: A Sociological Study of Factional Politics in Late Pre-exilic Judah," *JSOT* 52 (1991): 77–94. **Eynikel,** Erik. *The Reform of King Josiah and the Composition of the Deuteronomistic History* (OTS 33; Leiden: Brill, 1996). **Herodotus.** *The Histories* (trans. Robin Waterfield; Oxford: Oxford University Press, 1998). **Hoffman,** Yair. "The Deuteronomist and the Exile," in *Pomegranates and Golden Bells: Studies in Biblical, Jewish and Near Eastern Ritual, Law, and Literature in Honor of Jacob Milgrom* (ed. D. P. Wright, D. N. Freedman, and A. Hurvitz; Winona Lake, Ind.: Eisenbrauns, 1995), 659–75. **Hoffmann,** Hans Detlef. *Reform und Reformen: Untersuchungen zu* *einem Grundthema der deuteronomistischen Geschichtsschreibung* (ATANT 66; Zurich: Theologischer Verlag, 1980). **Knoppers,** Gary N. *Two Nations under God: The Deuteronomistic History of Solomon and the Dual Monarchies* (2 vols.; HSM 52–53; Atlanta: Scholars Press, 1993–94). **Koch,** Klaus. "Profetenschweigen des deuteronomistischen Geschichtswerks," in *Die Botschaft und die Boten: Festschrift für Hans Walter Wolff* (ed. J. Jeremias and L. Perlitt; Neukirchen-Vluyn: Neukirchener Verlag, 1981), 115–28. **Lohfink,** Norbert. "Gab es eine deuteronomistische Bewegung?" in *Jeremia und die Deuteronomistische Bewegung* (ed. W. Gross; BBB 98; Weinheim: Beltz Athenäum, 1995), 313–82. **Lohfink.** "Welches Orakel gab den Davididen Dauer? Ein Textproblem in 2. Kön 8,19 und das Funktionieren der dynastischen Orakel im deuteronomistischen Geschichtswerk," in *Studien zum Messiasbild im Alten Testament* (ed. U. Struppe; SBAB 6; Stuttgart: Katholisches Bibelwerk, 1989), 127–54. **Lohfink.** "Der Zorn Gottes und das Exil: Beobachtungen am deuteronomistischen Geschichtswerk," in *Liebe und Gebot: Studien zum Deuteronomium: Festschrift zum 70. Geburtstag von Lothar Perlitt* (ed. R. G. Kratz and H. Spieckermann; FRLANT 190; Göttingen: Vandenhoeck & Ruprecht, 2000), 137–55. **McConville,** J. G. "Narrative and Meaning in the Book of Kings," *Bib* 70 (1989): 31–49. **McKenzie,** Steven L. *The Trouble with Kings: The Composition of the Book of Kings in the Deuteronomistic History* (VTSup 42; Leiden: Brill, 1991). **McKenzie,** and M. Patrick Graham, eds. *The History of Israel's Traditions: The Heritage of Martin Noth* (JSOTSup 182; Sheffield: Sheffield Academic Press, 1994). **Na'aman,** Nadav. "The Deuteronomist and Voluntary Servitude to Foreign Powers," *JSOT* 65 (1995): 37–53. **Nelson,** Richard D. *The Double Redaction of the Deuteronomistic History* (JSOTSup 18; Sheffield: Department of Biblical Studies, University of Sheffield, 1981). **Noth,** Martin. *The Deuteronomistic History* (2d ed.; JSOTSup 15; Sheffield: JSOT Press, 1991). **Otto,** Susanne. *Jehu, Elia und Elisa: Die Erzählung von der Jehu-Revolution in die Komposition der Elia-Elisa-Erzählungen* (BWANT 152; Stuttgart: Kohlhammer, 2001). **Peckham,** Brian. *The Composition of the Deuteronomistic History* (HSM 35; Atlanta: Scholars Press, 1985). **Rad,** Gerhard von. "The Deuteronomic Theology of History in I and II Kings," in idem, *The Problem of the Hexateuch and Other Essays* (trans. E. W. T. Dicken; London: SCM, 1984), 205–21. **Römer,** Thomas C. "Transformations in Deuteronomistic and Biblical Historiography: On 'Book Finding' and Other Literary Strategies," *ZAW* 109 (1997): 1–11. **Rösel,** Hartmut N. *Von Josua bis Jojachin: Untersuchungen zu den deuteronomistischen Geschichtsbüchern im Alten Testament* (VTSup 75; Leiden: Brill, 1999). **Smend,** Rudolf. *Die Entstehung des Alten Testaments* (2d ed.; ThW 1; Stuttgart: Kohlhammer, 1981), 110–25. **Soggin,** J. Alberto. "Der Entstehungsort des deuteronomistischen Geschichtswerkes," *TLZ* 100 (1975): 3–8. **Van Seters,** John. *In Search of History: Historiography in the Ancient World and the Origins of Biblical History* (New Haven: Yale University Press, 1983), 209–353. **Veijola,** Timo. *Die ewige Dynastie: David und die Entstehung seiner Dynastie nach der deuteronomistischen Darstellung* (AASF.B 193; Helsinki: Suomalainen Tiedeakatemia, 1975). **Weippert,** Helga. "Das deuteronomistische Geschichtswerk," *TRu* 50 (1985): 213–49; **Weippert.** "Die 'deuteronomistischen' Beurteilungen der Könige von Israel und Juda und das Problem der Redaktion der Königsbücher," *Bib* 53 (1972): 301–39. **Westermann,** Claus. *Die Geschichtsbücher des Alten Testaments: Gab es ein deuteronomistisches Geschichtswerk?* (TB 87; Gütersloh: Kaiser Gütersloher Verlagshaus, 1994). **Wolff,**

Hans Walter. "Das Kerygma des deuteronomistischen Geschichtswerks," in idem, *Gesammelte Studien zum Alten Testament* (TB 22; Munich: Kaiser, 1964), 308–24. **Würthwein,** Ernst. "Erwägungen zum sog. deuteronomistischen Geschichtswerk: Eine Skizze," in idem, *Studien zum deuteronomischen Geschichtswerk* (BZAW 227; Berlin: de Gruyter, 1994), 1–11. **Zenger,** Erich. "Die Deuteronomistische Interpretation der Rehabilitierung Jojachins," *BZ* NS 12 (1968): 16–30.

Besides the "familial" foundation history, which dealt with Israel's ancestors, the history of Israel as a nation and a state paradoxically attracted renewed attention in the exilic period. After the states of Israel and Judah collapsed and their population was scattered to the four winds, the first "official" history of the nation of Israel was composed, the so-called Deuteronomistic History. To the best of our knowledge, it is the oldest historical work in the world.[371] Not until a century later did Herodotus, who has been called the "father of history," write his more comprehensive *Histories*.

Despite all the similarities in detail shared by the Deuteronomistic History and Herodotus's *Histories*,[372] an essential difference must not be overlooked:[373] unlike Herodotus, the Deuteronomistic History does not present the actual figure of the historian, taking a critical stance toward the subject matter and addressing commentary to the readers. Instead, its historical presentation keeps to the "paradigm of a traditional narrative, with no distance between communicator and text, between representation and reality."[374] This difference is due to the immediacy of the relationship between the Israelite historians and the audience they were addressing.

It is common knowledge that times of crisis and radical historical change have often led writers to record the history of the preceding period to prevent its being forgotten.[375] However, Israel's extraordinary will to survive is evidenced by its refusal to turn its back on its history even under circumstances so extreme that most nations would have disintegrated, even though that history seemed to be a dead end: instead, they wrote it down. This will finds expression above all in the intensive theological labor expended on this massive undertaking.

---

371 Van Seters, *In Search of History*, 362.
372 See Van Seters.
373 As pointed out by Blum, "Anfang," 11–20.
374 Ibid., 16.
375 In the fifth century B.C.E., Herodotus wrote his *Histories* in response to the turbulence of the Persian wars, the causes of which he sought to elucidate in his work. In the third century, Berossus and Manetho wrote their Babylonian and Egyptian histories in Greek in the light of the threat to their cultures presented by Hellenism.

This assessment assumes that a continuous presentation of Israel's beginnings (the Pentateuch) did not exist before the exile.[376] It is quite likely that during this period various individual narratives besides the exilic Patriarchal History were written down or reedited, such as a "Moses–plagues–exodus" account (Exod 1–15*) or a Sinai complex (Exod 19–24*; cf. Exod 32),[377] but there is too little evidence to warrant discussing these here.

Unlike the "exilic Patriarchal History," the hypothesis of a Deuteronomistic History has a long history and is generally accepted by scholars. Noth demonstrated in 1943 that the manifold Deuteronomistic passages that had been identified in the historical books—sometimes as a byproduct of source analysis—marked a continuous historical work extending from Deuteronomy through 2 Kings.[378] According to Noth, the Deuteronomist (Dtr), who should be thought of as both author and redactor, used a variety of existing materials (legal corpuses, lists, tales, historical narratives, chronicles, prophetic narratives, etc.) to create a substantially homogeneous work. Primarily by means of newly composed discourses (Josh 1; 23; 1 Sam 12; 1 Kgs 8:14ff.; 9:1–9) and reflective passages (Judg 2:6ff.; 2 Kgs 17:7ff.), he framed a historical account from the conquest to the loss of the land, interpreting and assessing it theologically. According to Noth, his purpose was to teach people to understand the disintegration of the nation, which he clearly considered "final and definitive,"[379] as "a divine judgment."[380] He composed his history in Palestine in the years following the last recorded event (2 Kgs 25:27: 562 B.C.E.), in the vicinity of Mizpah and Bethel.[381]

Subsequent scholarship has modified Noth's hypothesis at several points, but despite the flood of publications, apart from a few details there is no better solution in view. Nevertheless, the trend is toward increasing fragmentation of the historical work. The extensive scholarly discussion can only be summarized here, but detailed surveys are available.[382]

The debate began in 1961 when von Rad questioned Noth's interpretation of the purpose of the Deuteronomistic History.[383] He disputed

---

[376] Blum, *Studien* (III.2.3).

[377] See my remarks in Albertz, *History*, 1:71–72, 88–89.

[378] Noth, *Deuteronomistic History*.

[379] Ibid., 143.

[380] Ibid., 144.

[381] Ibid., 130, 145. This location, which Noth proposes with some hesitation, he bases on access to sources, the relatively prominent role that the local traditions of Mizpah and Bethel play in the work, and the absence of "any expectation for the future" (145 n. 1).

[382] Weippert, "Das deuteronomistische Geschichtswerk"; Knoppers, *Two Nations*, 1:1–54.

[383] "Deuteronomic Theology."

Noth's pessimistic reading; citing the dynastic promise to the Davidides in such texts as 2 Sam 7 and the characterization of David as the prototypical anointed king, he drew attention to a "messianic ideology" together with the Deuteronomic "homeland," which, as the pardon of Jehoiachin at the end of the Deuteronomistic History shows, gives the work an optimistic perspective on the future.[384] By contrast, Wolff associated the Deuteronomistic History closely with the prophecy of Jeremiah;[385] citing such texts as Judg 2:11–12; 1 Sam 7:3; 12:19; 1 Kgs 8:46–53, he concluded that "the call to repentance and return was the real concern of the work."[386] He also noted that this perspective found its fullest expression only in later additions such as Deut 4:29–31 and 30:1–10.

These insights paved the way for the use of literary analysis to explain the apparently divergent objectives. Since the 1970s, two primary models have been proposed. In Göttingen, Smend and his students (Veijola, Dietrich, et al.) have developed the so-called "strata model," which distinguishes three different Deuteronomistic strata: the Deuteronomistic historian (DtrH) framed the basic conception of the historical work; the prophetic redactor (DtrP) expanded it, primarily by inclusion of prophetic traditions; finally, the "nomistic" redactors (DtrN), whose interest focused on the law, added several more redactional strata.[387]

This hypothesis, which has gained many adherents in Germany, has still not been worked out fully and tested against the entire text. Furthermore, its supporters differ substantially regarding the delineation, dating, and aims of the strata. Dietrich dates all the strata in the relatively brief period between 580 and 560,[388] whereas Smend dates them all after 560.[389] Würthwein dates DtrP and DtrN "well into the postexilic period."[390] Veijola considers DtrH supportive of the monarchy, with a central role assigned to the promise of an eternal Davidic dynasty, whereas DtrP is hostile to the monarchy and DtrN seeks a compromise.[391] According to Dietrich, however, it is DtrN who in the books of Kings "insists most strongly on the uniqueness of the house of David, its special favor in the eyes of Yahweh, indeed its everlasting character."[392]

---

[384] "Deuteronomic Theology," 218–21.
[385] "Kerygma."
[386] Ibid., 321.
[387] Smend, *Entstehung*, 123–24.
[388] *Prophetie*, 143–44.
[389] *Entstehung*, 124.
[390] "Erwägungen," 11.
[391] *Ewige Dynastie*, 127ff.
[392] *Prophetie*, 142; but cf. his "Niedergang," 66ff.

These have been commendable attempts to sort out in precise detail the divergent aims represented in the Deuteronomistic History, many of which Noth overlooked, and to explain them by means of a theory of diachronic accretion. Still, after thirty years of hypotheses, it seems reasonable to doubt whether use of the imprecise methods of literary criticism to distinguish several continuous Deuteronomistic redactional strata that are terminologically and theologically closely related will ever lead to reasonably assured conclusions. Certain passages in the Deuteronomistic History do exhibit clear traces of literary revision, which can result in perceptible conceptual tensions. But such revisions often appear limited in scope, and they are usually integrated intelligently into the Deuteronomistic conception of history. For example, the notion of the "remaining land" is developed in Josh 23; Judg 2:6–10, 20–21; 3:1–6; it does not comport totally with the idea that all the land west of the Jordan was conquered, as related in Josh 2–12 (cf. the accommodation in Josh 13:1bβ–6). But this notion is then forgotten, and we find only a variation on the constant theme of why Israel went after foreign gods: it could not be led astray from without, only from within. Furthermore, the unconquered territory is given an explicit theological explanation (Judg 2:21–22).[393] I therefore find it more appropriate to ascribe such revisions to ongoing debate within the larger Deuteronomistic circle rather than attempt to identify clearly distinct Deuteronomistic authors and circles.

The second approach, the so-called "block model," was developed by Cross, who distinguishes two editions of the Deuteronomistic History.[394] A first edition (Dtr¹) ended with 2 Kgs 23:25a; it was written "as a propaganda work of the Josianic reformation and imperial program."[395] A second, exilic edition (Dtr²) extended the work down to the fall of Judah (2 Kgs 23:15b–25:30). To account for the catastrophe, it elaborated on the sins of Manasseh (2 Kgs 21:2–15) and inserted several references to the exile into Dtr¹ (Deut 4:27–31; 28:36–37, 63–68 [29:1]; 29:27 [28]) 30:1–10; Josh 21:11–13, 15–16; 1 Sam 12:25; 1 Kgs 2:4; 6:11–13; 8:25b, 46–53; 9:4–9; 2 Kgs 17:19; 20:17–18). The block model, with several variations, has found wide acceptance among English-speaking scholars. Nelson[396] expands it, assigning so many texts to Dtr² that the block model virtually

---

[393] For a discussion of this whole complex textual unit, see Blum, "Der kompositionelle Knoten."

[394] English scholarship often uses "DtrH" as an abbreviation for the Deuteronomistic History—not to be confused with the earliest stratum (the Deuteronomistic historian) of the Göttingen model!

[395] "Themes," 284.

[396] *Double Redaction.*

becomes a two-strata model. Strangely, he finds the literary seam between the two editions only in 2 Kgs 23:25//23:26.[397] Peckham[398] prefers to have Dtr[1] end with King Hezekiah (2 Kgs 19) and expands Dtr[2] into an extensive redactional stratum found not only in the historical books but also throughout the Pentateuch.[399] In Europe, some scholars have added a third stage to the block model. Drawing on Weippert's analysis of the formulaic language in the Deuteronomistic assessments of the kings,[400] Eynikel distinguishes a redactor of the books of Kings, whose work comprised 1 Kgs 3–2 Kgs 20, and two Deuteronomistic redactors.[401] The first expanded the work shortly after the death of Josiah by adding 2 Kgs 21:1–23:25; during the exilic period, the second not only continued it to the fall of Judah (2 Kgs 23:26–25:30) but also added Deut 1–1 Kgs 2 at the beginning and made the whole complex fundamentally dependent on Deuteronomy. Knoppers, however, returns to the original theory of Cross.[402] Among German scholars, the block model has found particular approval among Catholic exegetes (e.g., Lohfink). Today it may be considered the most widely accepted theory internationally.

However, this model also has clear weaknesses. It is true that the reign of Josiah constitutes the high point of the Deuteronomistic History, and at first glance it seems tempting to separate the solidly pro-Davidic royal theology of the Deuteronomistic History literarily from the emphasis on God's judgment, an interpretation of history that is often highly critical of the monarchy. There is nevertheless no clear literary seam to distinguish a Josianic edition of the Deuteronomistic History from an exilic edition. This difficulty is evident in the uncertainty involved in identifying such a seam: Cross finds it between 2 Kgs 23:25a and 23:25b, Nelson between 23:25 and 23:26. Weippert even shies away from precise identification, suspecting that it lies somewhere between 22:2 and 23:30.[403] Of course, the praise of Josiah's extraordinary devotion (23:25) contradicts the statement that Yahweh did not turn from his great anger against Judah (23:26), but this contradiction is marked grammatically (אַךְ, "still") and resolved semantically (the use of שׁוּב twice, in the sense of "turn to" and then "turn from").[404] In this deliberately formulated paradox, the Deuteronomistic authors addressed what was probably the most difficult

---

397 Ibid., 84.
398 *Composition.*
399 See the tables in *Composition*, 96–140.
400 "Die 'deuteronomistischen' Beurteilungen."
401 *Reform.*
402 *Two Nations.*
403 "Die 'deuteronomistischen' Beurteilungen," 332–33.
404 Noted most recently by Rösel, *Von Josua*, 102–5, reversing his earlier opinion.

theological problem they had to struggle with while composing their historical work: Why did Judah perish despite the Josianic reformation? Even though many a modern exegete finds their explanation—that the terrible sins of Manasseh were to blame—unpersuasive,[405] we have here a genuine theological problem that cannot be resolved by the techniques of literary criticism. The same is true of the purportedly sketchy and stereotyped style of the historical narrative after Josiah (23:31–25:30): after Yahweh determines to destroy Judah (21:12–15), theologically there is little more to say.

Strictly speaking, the fall of Jerusalem was at odds with Deuteronom(ist)ic theology; for the authors of the Deuteronomistic History, it took on the character of an inexplicable fate (cf. 24:3, 20). The block model also raises a methodological problem: its theoretical presuppositions all too often require assigning the texts of the Deuteronomistic History that allude to the exile to Dtr^2 without clear literary-critical evidence.

A further step is taken by those exegetes who so emphasize the distinctive features of Joshua, Judges, Samuel, and Kings, which Noth ascribed to their use of different sources, that doubt is cast on the very existence of a unified historical work. Würthwein, for example, questions whether there was ever a single continuous basic historical account (DtrH).[406] For Rösel, the stylistic and thematic differences within the ongoing motifs are so weighty that they cast doubt on the very existence of the Deuteronomistic History.[407] According to Westermann, who distinguishes schematically between narrative and interpretive texts, there never was a Deuteronomistic History but only a wide variety of Deuteronomistic commentaries.[408] This view would restore the scholarly status quo prior to Noth.

In the light of these methodological problems and the tendency toward fragmentation, it is good to recall that there have always been exegetes who maintained the unity of the Deuteronomistic History.[409] Hoffmann in particular has worked out a tightly woven network of cultic transgressions and cultic reforms in the books of Kings, not only demonstrating the presence of a continuous and coherent historical conception,

---

[405] E.g., Knoppers, *Two Nations*, 52; Knoppers assigns 23:26 the role of a *deus ex machina*, since Josiah had long since redressed the sins of Manasseh.
[406] "Erwägungen," 3.
[407] *Von Josua*, 36, etc.
[408] *Geschichtsbücher*.
[409] Hoffmann, *Reform*; Van Seters, *In Search of History*; McConville, "Narrative"; Albertz, "Intentionen"; with respect to Dtr^1, McKenzie, *Trouble*.

but also recalling a forgotten theme of the Deuteronomistic History. Van Seters has compared the Deuteronomistic History with the historiography of the surrounding ancient civilizations, showing clearly that particularly in the use of sources, which makes ancient historical works appear quite disparate to modern readers, there are clear similarities to Herodotus's *Histories*. McConville has called attention to the deeper meaning behind many seemingly contradictory texts. I myself have urged that the thematic tensions within the overall conception of the Deuteronomistic History—for example, between Deuteronomic theology and Jerusalem theology—should be understood as reflecting the particular origins of the Deuteronomistic authors and that stylistic and conceptual variations should be explained as emerging from controversy and debate within the Deuteronomistic group as a whole. In short, Noth's theory that the Deuteronomistic History was written by a single individual is probably no longer tenable, but its authors were so close ideologically and worked within so short a period of time that it makes little sense to try to distinguish them by literary analysis.

In conclusion, it should be noted that the textual complex Deut 1–2 Kgs 25 includes substantial post-Deuteronomistic additions, many more than those identified by Noth (Josh 13–22; Judg 17–21; 2 Sam 21–24; etc.), such as Josh 24; Judg 1; 2:1–5;[410] and many portions of the Elijah-Elisha narratives (1 Kgs 17–19; 2 Kgs 2–8; also 1 Kgs 20; 22:1–38).[411] Another clear addendum is 2 Kgs 17:34b–41. Bracketing out these passages increases the rigor of the historical work, but the term "post-Deuteronomistic," still used rather loosely by McKenzie, needs more precise definition.

It is reasonable, therefore, to follow Noth in maintaining the substantial unity of the Deuteronomistic History, though his sociohistorical placement of the author and his statement of the work's objective are unsatisfactory. Noth thought it necessary to set his Deuteronomist apart from all parties and institutions, with a critical stance toward the monarchy and priesthood as well as the prophets of salvation and judgment.[412] Such social isolation would leave the enormous influence of the Deuteronomist on the development of the Old Testament totally unaccountable. Von Rad, Cross, Hoffmann, and others maintain that the Deuteronomistic History—apart from its undisputed theological basis in Deuteronomy—displays great interest in the Davidic monarchy and the Jerusalem temple. If we take their observation seriously, within the

---

410 Blum, "Der kompositionelle Knoten."
411 Otto, *Jehu*.
412 *Deuteronomistic History*, 145.

spectrum of late preexilic groups known to us, the authors are most likely to be found among the successors to the party of religious nationalism, as I have argued in detail elsewhere.[413]

Noth downplayed the importance of Nathan's promise (2 Sam 7), since he believed that "the strong emphasis on the positive significance of the institution of the monarchy" was not "consonant with the mind of the Deuteronomist."[414] In addition, since 1 Kgs 8 focuses on the temple as a place of prayer rather than a place of sacrifice, he concluded that "the Deuteronomist was not interested in the actual practice of the cult."[415] Nevertheless, despite critical reservations about kingship as such (1 Sam 8:5–11; 10:19) and especially the kingship of Saul, the verdict of the Deuteronomists on the Davidic monarchy is overwhelmingly positive: not only do they frequently cite Nathan's promise (1 Kgs 2:4; 8:25; 9:5), but they also indicate that over the course of history this promise was able to mitigate God's judgment on Judah (1 Kgs 11:12–13; 15:4; 2 Kgs 8:19; 19:34). The Deuteronomists also devote so much attention to the Solomonic temple—its construction (1 Kgs 5–8), its cultic furnishings (1 Kgs 7:13–50), its cultic innovations (2 Kgs 16:10–18; 21:4 –8), and its restoration (2 Kgs 23), as well as its pillaging and destruction (2 Kgs 24:13–14; 25:13–17)—that Noth's assessment, which is still current, must be recognized as inappropriate Protestant prejudice and revised.[416] The emphasis on the temple's function as a place of prayer in 1 Kgs 8 is clearly a simplification due to the author's historical context, when the temple lay in ruins. Neither 1 Kgs 8 nor any other passage in the Deuteronomistic History plays off prayer and sacrifice against each other (cf. 1 Kgs 8:62ff.).[417] Furthermore, in the view of the Deuteronomists, Yahweh's choice of Jerusalem

---

[413] Albertz, "Intentionen," 40–49; *History* (II.4), 2:388–90; "In Search," 13–16. After the death of Josiah, I believe, the broad coalition that had supported the Deuteronomic reform split into two parties, one supporting religious nationalism, the other reform. The former was dominated by the leading priestly family, the Hilkiads, the latter by the leading administrative family, the Shaphanides (Albertz, *History*, 1:201–3, 231–42). This analyis, which also incorporates the observations of Crüsemann and Hardmeier, is corroborated by Lohfink ("Gab es," 352–57). Dutcher-Walls ("Social Location") comes to a similar conclusion, although she associates it with Dtr[1] in Cross's block model.

[414] *Deuteronomistic History*, 89.

[415] Ibid., 138.

[416] The insight of Na'aman ("Deuteronomist," 46–47), formulated in terms of the block model, holds true generally: "It seems to me that a third major theme—the continuity of the original cult in the temple of Jerusalem—must be added to the two grand themes of the Deuteronomistic History identified by Cross, the sins of Jeroboam and the promise of David."

[417] The same holds true for the "temple versus book" antithesis proposed by Römer ("Transformations," 5–6); the Deuteronomists clearly sought to subordinate the cult of the Jerusalem temple to the book of the Mosaic law, but not to replace the former with the latter.

as the only legitimate site for his cult repeatedly mitigated his judgment on Judah (1 Kgs 11:32, 36; 14:21; 15:4).

That the Deuteronomists actually viewed the Davidic monarchy and the Jerusalem temple as God-given benefits is also apparent from their treatment of the early monarchy: they described it as a second age of salvation, parallel to the age of salvation under Moses and Joshua (Deut 1–Josh 21), when God gave Israel the law and the land. No hint of apostasy darkened this period (cf. the return in 1 Sam 7:3–4 and the faithful obedience described in 1 Kgs 8:61; also the parallel statements in Josh 21:44–45 and 1 Kgs 8:56). Their nationalistic policies are illustrated by their approval of Hezekiah's rebellion against the Assyrians as an expression of trust in God (2 Kgs 18:5–8); they clearly disapproved of submission to the Assyrians, especially when voluntary (e.g., Menahem [2 Kgs 15:17–30] and Ahaz [16:5–8]).[418] As Hardmeier has shown,[419] the roots of the Deuteronomists in religious nationalism are even clearer in their inclusion of 2 Kgs 18:9–19:7, 32aβ–34, 8, 9a, 36aβ–37, a propagandistic narrative of the nationalistic party: during the Babylonian siege of Jerusalem in 588, the Deuteronomists' ancestors used the example of Sennacherib's campaign to demonstrate the theological validity of their desire to resist while denouncing the contrary prophecy of judgment by Jeremiah and Ezekiel as enemy propaganda. Finally, their attitude is clear in 2 Kgs 24–25, where they describe not only the loss of the land but also the destruction of the monarchy and temple in grim detail,[420] deliberately concealing the reasons why the probable ringleaders of the nationalistic party were condemned by the Babylonians (25:18–21a). The most prominent victim the Deuteronomists could think of was the high priest Seraiah, whose son furthermore was deported to Babylon (1 Chr 5:41 [6:15]). The striking lack of interest in social transgressions of the Mosaic torah on the part of the authors of the Deuteronomistic History rounds out the picture.

Under the pressure of events, however, the authors of the Deuteronomistic History had advanced beyond their preexilic posture of religious nationalism. They had learned from Deuteronomic theology to subordinate king and temple to the Mosaic torah and therefore to qualify the unconditional assurances of salvation based on them. They had learned from the prophets of judgment to understand and accept their national catastrophe as Yahweh's judgment on Israel's apostasy. However, they still sought to preserve for the future the religious institutions on which

---

[418] On the whole subject, see Na'aman, "Deuteronomist."
[419] *Prophetie* (II.2.2.2), 287ff.
[420] See pp. 8–12 above.

their ancestors had set their hopes, contrary to the all-embracing criticism of the prophets of judgment (Hos 13:9–1; Mic 3:11–12; Jer 7:4, 12, 14; 22:24–28*), whom they deliberately ignored in their history. The proposed sociohistorical setting of the Deuteronomists may plausibly explain what Koch called "the silence of the prophets in the Deuteronomistic History."[421]

Here we see already a need to revise Noth's statement of the purpose of the Deuteronomistic History. He was right to claim that it focuses on trying to explain the terrible catastrophe as Yahweh's righteous judgment. The Deuteronomistic History is a great confession of Israel's sin and a justification of God: Israel, not Yahweh, had been to blame for the downfall of Israel as a state; in the downfall of his people, Yahweh had demonstrated not his impotence but his power and righteousness in the governance of history. However, Noth's view that, for the Deuteronomistic History, God's judgment is final and definitive requires revision. As we have shown, the Deuteronomistic historians did indeed consider the exile an end of history, but definitely not a final end.[422] Otherwise they would hardly have taken the trouble to compose so extensive a history.[423] As a legacy from their ancestors, they possessed a potential for hope that one day the history of their nation would be able to continue. As they indicate with their concluding note about the release of Jehoiachin, the first prerequisite for such a continuation was a Davidic king, despite the collapse of the monarchy. The second, as exemplified by the cultic reform of Josiah, was the official Jerusalem cult purified of all syncretism.

Finally, we must try to identify the geographical origin and the date of the Deuteronomistic History. We may assume that the Babylonians—if only for reasons of internal security—gave high priority to deporting supporters of religious nationalism, while leaving sympathizers such as Gedaliah, Baruch, and Jeremiah in Judah. There is explicit evidence of such a policy for the golah of 597: in 594, hopes blazed up among the deportees for a quick return, hopes that were still being fanned by prophets (Jer 29:21–23; cf. 28:2–4; Ezek 13:16). From the time when Jerusalem was under siege, Ezek 24:21, 25 bears witness to highly emotional ties to the temple. Such feelings of religious nationalism long continued to survive in the golah: toward the end of the exilic period, the deportees collected donations of silver and gold to subvent the

---

[421] "Profetenschweigen."

[422] See pp. 11–12 above.

[423] Probably no historiography is entirely archival; even if it seeks only to recount what took place, it creates meaning and therefore expresses a will to live.

coronation of the Davidide Zerubbabel and the Hilkiad Joshua (Zech 6:9–15). Since a whole series of observations within the Deuteronomistic History itself also point to the Babylonian golah, there is much to suggest and nothing to contradict a Babylonian origin, instead of the Palestinian origin proposed by Noth.

This theory was already put forward by Ackroyd[424] and supported by Nicholson,[425] Soggin,[426] and Pohlmann;[427] I reintroduced it in 1997.[428] Noth's argument that sufficient sources were available only in Palestine is not persuasive, since it would clearly have been possible to rescue scrolls from the temple archives and bring them to Babylon "in their saddlebags," to use Lohfink's graphic expression.[429] Noth's observation that the Deuteronomistic History includes a wealth of local traditions from Mizpah (1 Sam 7:5–8:22; 10:17–27) and Bethel (1 Kgs 12:31–13:22; 2 Kgs 17:24–28) by no means indicates that its authors must have written there. Dietrich states that the Deuteronomistic redaction of the Jeremiah tradition probably also took place in this part of Palestine,[430] but this is irrelevant to the Deuteronomistic History, because (as we shall see), the two groups of Deuteronomistic authors are so different in perspective and origin that they could easily have written in different locales.[431]

The mention of prayer toward (דֶּרֶךְ) Jerusalem in 1 Kgs 8:48 (cf. 8:44) is clear evidence that the Deuteronomistic History was written in Babylonia rather than Palestine. The associated prayer (8:50) that Yahweh will grant the captives "compassion in the sight of their captors, so that they may have compassion on them," clearly refers to the sufferings of the exiles. Most scholars acknowledge this connection but, assuming a Palestinian locale, consider 1 Kgs 8:46–53 a late (even postexilic) addition to the Deuteronomistic History.[432] That this opinion is unjustified is apparent from the language of the verses in question, which continues the Deuteronomistic style of the passage preceding the petitions in 8:31ff. (note, for example, the expression בנה בית לשם יהוה, "build a house for the name of

---

[424] *Exile* (I), 65–68.
[425] *Preaching* (III.2.5), 116–22.
[426] "Entstehungsort," 6.
[427] *Studien* (III.2.5), 107–8.
[428] Albertz, "In Search," 14–16.
[429] "Gab es," 358.
[430] "History," 169–70.
[431] See pp. 322–27 below.
[432] Ernst Würthwein, *Die Bücher der Könige* (2 vols.; ATD 11; Göttingen: Vandenhoeck & Ruprecht, 1977–84), 1:100; Volkmar Fritz, *Das erste Buch der Könige* (ZBK.AT 10/1; Zurich: Theologischer Verlag, 1996), 96.

Yahweh," in 8:17, 18, 20, 44, 48; cf. v. 16).[433] In other words, the oft-noted stylistic differences between 8:46–53 and the preceding petitions (8:31–43) are due to the Deuteronomists' use in the petitions of an earlier tradition, which they expanded in 8:44–53. If this analysis is correct, the conclusion that the Deuteronomistic History originated in Babylonia is inescapable.

Further evidence of Babylonian origin is the concluding notice reporting the pardon of Jehoiachin (2 Kgs 25:27–30); it is probably not by chance that this passage provides a classic example of the fulfillment of the prayer in 1 Kgs 8:50. This short scene, with its intimate knowledge of events and language that echoes features of Neo-Babylonian,[434] most likely originated in close proximity to the Babylonian court. A golah perspective also best explains the notion of the Deuteronomistic History that the entire population of Israel and Judah, apart from an insignificant remnant, was sent into exile (2 Kgs 17:6, 23; 25:21). Finally, Deut 30:1–10 addresses the exiles directly, promising that Yahweh will bring them back if they return to him. The promise that they will once more "take possession of" (ירשׁ: 30:5) the land, as though by force as in the days of Joshua, once more provides a vivid insight into the perspective of the golah.

If we take into account the "official" nature of the Deuteronomistic History, its authors are most likely to be found among the two leading families of the Babylonian golah, the royal Davidides (Jehoiachin, Zerubbabel) and the priestly Hilkiads (Jozadak, Joshua), who also represented the symbolic figures or leaders of the nationalistic faction, which had moderated its views. The *terminus a quo* is the accession year of Amēl-Marduk, 562 B.C.E. Only the *terminus ad quem* is disputed. Exegetes today date the Deuteronomistic History in large part[435] or even entirely[436] in the Persian period; most of its texts still envision a period of exile with no clear end (Deut 4:25–28; 28:36, 63–68; 29:23–27 [24–28]; 1 Kgs 14:15; 8:46–50; 2 Kgs 17:6; 25:27–30), and only a few hint at a new demonstration of God's favor (Deut 4:29–31) or even foretell a return (Deut 30:1–10).[437] This is clearly a more modest notion of salvation than appears, for example, in the third edition of the Deuteronomistic book of Jeremiah (Jer 31–32 and 50–51). This evidence suggests that the conception and a large part of the text of the Deuteronomistic History must antedate 547/546,

---

[433] The parallels to the unusual expression "iron-smelter" used for Egypt in Deut 4:10 and Jer 11:4 also point unambiguously to the exilic period, at least in the case of the second.

[434] Zenger, "Deuteronomistische Interpretation," 16–17.

[435] Würthwein, "Erwägungen."

[436] Römer, "Transformations," 10–11.

[437] Hoffman ("Deuteronomist") makes a similar point, but dates Deut 30:1–10 as early as the time of Nabonidus (556–539 B.C.E.).

when Cyrus's brilliant Lydian campaign first made it possible to detect a change in the political climate. By contrast, texts such as Deut 4 and 30:1–10 probably date from the period after 539, the latter probably from a time when the advent of Darius (522/521) offered a realistic opportunity for return.

It is reasonable to assume that the release of Jehoiachin from two decades of detention, probably on account of the murder of Gedaliah, was the signal for the leadership of the Babylonian golah to prepare a history of Israel that both dealt with the catastrophe they had gone through and provided orientation for the future. It was finally clear that Yahweh had heard the exiles' prayers and had pitied their representative, delivering him from Babylonian despotism (1 Kgs 8:50; cf. Ps 89:47–52 [46–51]). After the death of Nebuchadnezzar, furthermore, there appeared to be a change in the policies of the Babylonian Empire, which could also mean a change for the better for the Judean minority.[438] It was therefore urgent to learn the correct lessons from Israel's disastrous history and to secure the options of religious nationalism.

The history conceived and gradually worked out by the Judean intellectuals associated with these leaders attempts in its very structure to do justice to both these tasks. It is held together by two thematic bonds: the land and the law. Because it seeks to deal constructively with the catastrophe of the exile, it sketches a great arc from the occupation to the loss of the land (Josh 1–2 Kgs 25).[439] Because of this forced parallelism, the history of Israel's beginnings could only be treated retrospectively (Deut 1–3). Because orientation toward the future was at issue, the fundamental norm, the torah of Moses (Deuteronomy), is placed at the beginning of the history and thus established implicitly or explicitly as the norm for the entire historical account; toward the end of the work, under Josiah, it is rediscovered in a book (2 Kgs 22:8–11; 23:25). King, temple, and nation are solemnly and officially made subject to it in a formal covenant ceremony (23:1–3), and the cult is purified according to its norms (23:4–24). All this does not prevent the loss of the land, but it provides an option for the future.

The Deuteronomistic History as a whole can be divided into four periods:

---

438 See pp. 60ff. above.

439 The theme of driving out nations already makes its appearance in Moses' historical retrospect, which speaks of the nations dispossessed by the Edomites (Deut 2:12, 22), the Ammonites (2:21), and the Philistines (2:23). From the Deuteronomistic perspective, Israel suffered a fate similar to that of other nations in Palestine; cf. the parallel between such dispossessions and Israel's deportation in 2 Kgs 17:8, 11.

Era	Dtr Material	God's Gifts
First foundation: Moses and Joshua (Deut 1–Josh 23)		
Moses' farewell discourse	Deut 1–31	the law
Command to occupy the land		
Acceptance of the law	Josh 1	
Occupation of the land	Josh 1–12	the land
Joshua's farewell address		
Conditional salvation or disaster	Josh 23	
The judges (Judg 2–1 Sam 12)		
Historical reflection: apostasy, punishment, repentance, deliverance (Deuteronomistic historical schema)	Judg 2:6ff.	
Samuel's farewell address; admonition to obey Yahweh despite the monarchy	1 Sam 12	
Second foundation: the united monarchy (1 Sam 13–1 Kgs 11)		
[Return to Yahweh]	1 Sam 7]	
Nathan's promise	2 Sam 7	Davidic monarchy
David's farewell address; Solomon's acceptance of the law	1 Kgs 2:1–9	
Solomon's prayer of dedication of the temple	1 Kgs 8	Jerusalem temple
Theophany: conditional salvation or disaster for the kings	1 Kgs 9:1–9	
The divided monarchy (1 Kgs 12–2 Kgs 25)		
Unconditional judgment → on the northern kingdom	1 Kgs 14:7–16	
Fall of northern kingdom	2 Kgs 17	first loss of the land
Historical reflection on the reasons		
Unconditional judgment → on the southern kingdom	2 Kgs 21:10–14	
Josiah's reform of the cult	2 Kgs 22–23	discovery of the law; purification of the temple
Fall of the southern kingdom	2 Kgs 24–25	second loss of the land; loss of king and temple
Pardon of Jehoiachin	2 Kgs 25:27–30	?

The Deuteronomistic History opens with a great farewell discourse delivered by Moses just before Israel's entry into the promised land, in which—with a retrospective summary of Israel's beginnings—he proclaims the Deuteronomic law to the people.[440] From the outset, the Deuteronomists make clear their conviction as to the essential theological foundations of Israel's existence: the wondrous acts of deliverance marking its earliest history and the concomitant demands of God laid down in the law of Moses. For the Deuteronomists, this Mosaic torah represents the first of Yahweh's salvific gifts to Israel; it also represents Yahweh's saving and sustaining presence, which gives Israel its life and orientation. Thus the Deuteronomists also saw to it that God's presence would continue to accompany the people through the future ages of their history. The Deuteronomic law was written down by Moses and entrusted to the Levitical priests and the elders, who were to proclaim it repeatedly (Deut 31:9ff.). Summarized on the stone tablets of the Decalogue, it was brought to Canaan by Joshua amidst signs and wonders recalling the passage through the Sea of Reeds (Josh 3). There a copy was written on Mount Ebal (Josh 8:30–35); it finally found its permanent home in the ark in the Jerusalem temple (1 Kgs 8:1, 4, 9). There, however, it lay forgotten—inexplicably[441]—until Josiah rediscovered it (2 Kgs 22). Nevertheless, the law of Moses was the norm by which the Deuteronomistic historians judged the entire history of Israel; the law determined for them its future course and outcome. According to the Deuteronomists, the alternative futures presented by the Deuteronomic law in blessings and curses, depending on whether the law was obeyed or disobeyed (Deut 28), governed the entire history of Israel from the beginning. Here, therefore, extrapolating from the Deuteronomic curses, they already alluded to the outcome (Deut 4:25–28; 11:17; 28:36, 63–68; 29:21–27 [22–28]).[442]

---

440 The following pages represent a revised and expanded version of my discussion in *History* (II.4), 2:387–99.

441 Between the report of the finding of the book of the law, intended to establish the law's ancient authority (2 Kgs 22–23), and the Deuteronomistic view that refusal to obey the Mosaic Torah (presupposing that it was known; cf. 2 Kgs 21:8–9) was the cause of the exile there is a conceptual contradiction that the Deuteronomistic History does not resolve. However, Josh 5:10–11 is a kind of counterpart to the statement in the account of the book's discovery that the Israelites had not celebrated a central Passover festival since the days of the judges (2 Kgs 23:22).

442 Lohfink ("Zorn," 148–55) has shown convincingly that the Deuteronomists mitigated the curses of Deuteronomy, which threatened the destruction of Israel (e.g., Deut 28:63), in the direction of Yahweh's rejection of Israel or the withdrawal of his presence (Deut 29:27 [28]; cf. 2 Kgs 17:18, 20, 23; 23:27; 24:3, 20).

Closer examination, however, shows that the Deuteronomists took only a portion of the Deuteronomic law as the criterion for their account of Israel's subsequent history: first the Decalogue's prohibition of other gods and images (Deut 5:6–10; cf. 4:15–24),[443] then the centralization of worship (Deut 12)[444] and the prohibition of pagan practices such as certain forms of divination (Deut 18:10, 14),[445] "Moloch offerings" (Deut 18:10; 12:31),[446] and cult prostitution (Deut 23:18–19).[447] Also included were the ban enjoined by the Deuteronomic law of war (Deut 20:15–17; cf. 7:2)[448] and the associated prohibition of covenants with Gentiles and intermarriage (Deut 7:2–3).[449] In short, the Deuteronomists were concerned only with the laws and commandments intended to secure the exclusive worship of Yahweh in sharp distinction from the surrounding world; in their view, the future of Israel depended on these laws. The Deuteronomistic historians simply ignored the social legislation of Deuteronomy, which was meant to secure the internal solidarity of the people of God

This selectivity was due to the demands of the exilic situation. Living as a minority surrounded by adherents of other religions, the exiles constantly faced the danger of syncretism, especially since in their public lives they could hardly avoid the Babylonian rituals, religious processions, and conceptions of the gods entirely (Deut 4:28; 28:26, 64; 29:16 [17]). In particular, the Deuteronomists addressed the danger of idolatry and astral worship (Deut 4:15–25, 28). In their environment, the question of social solidarity may well have taken a back seat to the burning problem of how to protect the religious and ethnic identity of the exiles, but we note also that that the Deuteronomists did not use a theological yardstick to measure some earlier internal social conflicts recorded in their history (1 Kgs 12; 21), reinterpreting them instead in religious terms (1 Kgs 11:1–13, 29–39; 12:15; 21:20–24); thus their one-sided approach appears to have been fundamental in character. It was probably due to their religious nationalism. Even just after the death of Josiah, it was typical of this movement to affirm the cultic aspect of the Deuteronomic reform but to deny its social aspect.[450] Thus the urgent demands of life in exile coupled with an instinctive partisan interest induced the Deuteronomists to write a history of Israel filled almost entirely with religious aberrations and

---

[443] Josh 23:7; Judg 2:11ff.; 1 Kgs 9:6, 9; 11:7–8; 14:8–9; 16:30–31; 2 Kgs 2:3–7; etc.
[444] 1 Kgs 11:7; 12:31–32; 14:23; 15:14; 22:44; 2 Kgs 12:4 (3); 15:4, 35; 16:4; 18:4; 21:3; 23:8.
[445] 1 Sam 15:23; 28:3ff.; 2 Kgs 9:22; 17:17; 21:6; 23:24.
[446] 2 Kgs 16:3; 17:17, 31; 21:6; 23:10.
[447] 1 Kgs 14:24; 15:12; 22:47; 2 Kgs 23:7.
[448] Josh 6:17ff.; 7:10ff.; 8:26–27; 9:3ff.; 10:28ff.; cf. 1 Sam 15:9ff.
[449] Josh 9:6ff.; 23:7, 12; Judg 2:2; 3:6; cf. 1 Kgs 11:3–4; 16:31; 2 Kgs 8:18.
[450] Albertz, *History* (II.4), 1:232–36.

struggles while omitting almost totally the social conflicts that most of the prophets thought were primarily responsible for the catastrophe.[451] The reception of Deuteronomy in the Deuteronomistic History was selective.

Besides the gift of the law, this first foundational phase included God's gift of the land. In a discourse couched in Deuteronomistic language, Yahweh explicitly encourages Joshua to enter the promised land; the success of the invasion depends on obedience to the law (Josh 1). Joshua thereupon conquers all the land west of the Jordan, following the requirements of the Deuteronomic law of war (Josh 2–12). Obedience toward Yahweh is demonstrated primarily by ruthless enforcement of the ban (Deut 20:1, 5–17; Josh 6:18–19, 21; 8:26; 10:33–40; etc.); only once is it not carried out (Josh 7) or cunningly evaded (Josh 9). The military annihilation of the former inhabitants of the land—fortunately only theoretical—that the Deuteronomists project onto the early history of Israel is once again born of the fear of being overwhelmed by foreign cultural and religious influences during the exilic period. At the same time, the vulnerability of the people led the Deuteronomists to paint a powerful picture of Yahweh's mighty presence in the Gentile world (3:11, 13; 4:24). It was important to them to maintain that the gift of the conquered land represented the total fulfillment of all God's promises, especially the promise of land to the patriarchs (21:45; cf. 23:14). Despite minor indiscretions (Josh 7 ; 9), they saw this premonarchic foundational period in a positive light. Yahweh was true to his promises, just as Israel was true to Yahweh (23:1–11). Not until the farewell address that the Deuteronomists put in the mouth of Joshua is there another warning of possible apostasy, which would be answered with the immediate loss of the land (23:6–7, 12–16). The Deuteronomists sought to make clear to their exiled compatriots that God's gift of the land was conditional from the outset on the worship of Yahweh alone.

In contrast to the radical historical perspective of their prophetic colleagues, who occasionally dated Israel's disobedience from the very day of the exodus (Jer 7:25–26; 11:7–8; Ezek 20; etc.), the Deuteronomists saw Israel's apostasy as beginning only after the death of Joshua. As to how it came about, there were differing views in this group of authors. Some thought it was because the people forgot the mighty acts of Yahweh (Judg 2:10, 12, 19; 8:34–35; cf. Deut 6:12–13), others that the former inhabitants of the land led them astray (Josh 23:7, 12; cf. Judg 2:2; 3:1–6; also Deut 7:1ff.). To explain the latter, some of the Deuteronomistic redactors

---

[451] The only ethical transgression condemned theologically in the Deuteronomistic History is David's adultery (2 Sam 11:27b–12:15a), but in the eyes of the Deuteronomists this was a pardonable sin (cf. 1 Kgs 15:5).

developed a rather complex theory that Joshua failed to complete the conquest of the land (Josh 13:1b–6; 23:4; Judg 3:3) because Yahweh was angered by Israel's apostasy (Josh 23:13; Judg 2:20–21).[452] Israel was thus confronted in its own land with the gods of the nations. Strictly speaking, this theory contradicts the account of the complete conquest of the land in Josh 2–12; it may have been confected to make conditions in ancient Israel resemble more closely the situation of the exile. Like the generation of the exile, the ancient Israelites lived in direct contact with adherents of other religions. Even then, intermarriage and covenants with Gentiles created a substantial danger of apostasy and had to be warned against (Josh 23:7, 12; cf. Judg 2:2; 3:6). In the eyes of these Deuteronomists, the danger that Israel's neighbors might tempt Israel into apostasy loomed over Israel's entire history (Josh 23:12ff.). Once again, the exilic fears of being overwhelmed by foreign influences are palpable.

Despite this danger, however, the period of the judges (Judg 2–1 Sam 12), which followed this foundational phase, was not a time of total apostasy. From the traditions of charismatic wars of liberation during the premonarchic period, the Deuteronomistic historians concluded that Yahweh must have demonstrated his favor repeatedly during these years; on this basis, they developed the theory of a continual cycle of apostasy, enemy threat, return to Yahweh, and deliverance during the period of the judges (Judg 2:10–16, 18–19). What they wanted to teach their exilic addressees was that there were phases in their own history when repentance—explicit rejection of syncretism (Judg 6:25–31), confession of sins and return to Yahweh (10:10, 16), and worship of Yahweh alone (1 Sam 7:3–4)—was still possible. Yahweh would respond with favor and deliverance (Judg 7; 11–12; 1 Sam 7:7ff.). Even during phases of Israel's apostasy, therefore, the situation was far from hopeless. Yahweh in his mercy could still vouchsafe the opportunity for a new beginning. For the Deuteronomists, such opportunities were concentrated in the period of the judges but did occur occasionally later, during the monarchy (2 Kgs 13:4; 14:25–27).[453]

Now we note with astonishment that the Deuteronomistic historians exempt the following era, the period of the united monarchy (1 Sam 13–

---

[452] Blum, "Der kompositionelle Knoten," 184–87.

[453] To challenge the unity of the Deuteronomistic History, exegetes have argued repeatedly that the book of Judges represents a cyclical view of history, clearly different from the linear view of the books of Kings (Rösel, *Von Josua*, 70ff.). In the first place, however, the movement is not cyclical but wavelike, reaching a clear peak in the forty years of Philistine oppression (Judg 13:1). Second, these elements are not limited to the book of Judges (cf. 2 Kgs 13:4–5; 14:25–27). Furthermore, 2 Sam 7:11 and 2 Kings 23:22 explicitly recall the period of the judges.

1 Kgs 10), from the general trend toward apostasy, treating it as a new period of pure, unadulterated faith in Yahweh. Toward the end of the period of judges, in their view, Israel returned to exclusive worship of Yahweh (1 Sam 7: 3–4) until the dedication of the temple (1 Kgs 8:61). It was Solomon in his old age—again seduced by foreign women—who once more went astray (1 Kgs 11:1–13). During the entire interim period, syncretism was not a topic of concern to the Deuteronomists— surprisingly, because the tradition they inherited provided several pretexts for raising the issue.[454] The most likely explanation for this remarkable situation is that the Deuteronomistic historians had a vital interest in keeping God's gifts of the Davidic monarchy and the Jerusalem temple, as well as the law and the land, free from any taint of syncretism. For them, the time from David and Solomon until the completion of the temple was, like the time of Moses and Joshua, a new age of salvation.

That the Deuteronomistic historians wanted to present the period of the united monarchy as a second foundational period for Israel is shown by the parallels and links they established between it and the premonarchic foundation period. At its conclusion, parallel to Josh 21:45 (cf. 23:14), Solomon once more expressly confirms the complete fulfillment of Yahweh's promises (1 Kgs 8:56). They established another parallel by including the theme of intermarriage at the end of the period of Joshua (Josh 23, etc.), parallel to 1 Kgs 11. The Deuteronomists established the theological connection between the two foundational periods by introducing a distinction into the Deuteronomic promise of the land: the promise was not fulfilled when Israel conquered the land under Joshua; Yahweh had also promised Israel a place of rest (מְנוּחָה), where the people could dwell in safety, secure against all the surrounding nations (Deut 12:9–10; 25:19). Yahweh had provided this place of rest during the time of Joshua (Josh 1:13, 15; 21:44; 23:1); in the period of the judges, however, Israel was threatened repeatedly by enemies on account of its notorious apostasy. Thus it was only David's glorious victories that finally enabled Israel to enjoy the promised place of rest (2 Sam 7:1, 10–11), as Solomon thankfully declares (1 Kgs 5:18 [4]; 8:56). The Deuteronomistic historians, following the principles of religious nationalism, were thus able to bring the early monarchy into alignment with the salutary beginnings of Israel's history, making monarchy and temple an indispensable element of their

---

[454] Michal's teraphim (1 Sam 19:13, 16; also mentioned with disapproval in 2 Kgs 23:24), Saul's visit to a medium (1 Sam 28:3–25), and Solomon's "high places" at Gibeon (1 Kgs 3:2ff.). Saul is rejected for failing to carry out the ban (1 Sam 15:23–26; 28:18), not for idolatry; 15:23 compares his failure to idolatry, without equating the two. On the contrary, Saul had forbidden necromancy and magic (28:3, 9).

nation's history and indissolubly linking the exodus theology of Deuteronomy with the king and temple theology of Jerusalem (1 Kgs 8:16–21).

At first glance, the Deuteronomistic account of how the monarchy came into being (1 Sam 8–12) appears at odds with this assessment, since it presents Israel's desire for a king in a very negative light, as an incomprehensible acceptance of the ways of other nations (1 Sam 8:5, 19–20). Worse still, to have a king means to reject Yahweh (8:7; 10:19) and to dismiss his saving power as the true king of Israel (10:19; 12:12, 17). This desire for a king is even equated with the apostasy of Israel's past (8:8). However, closer examination of the account reveals that the Deuteronomistic historians accepted these common arguments against monarchy only with reservations. The complex argumentation also suggests that the need for the institution of kingship was a subject of debate and controversy within the group of authors. Surprisingly, Yahweh reacts much more mildly to this "political apostasy" of the people than to syncretism: he has Samuel warn the people but finally grants their desire (8:9) and then personally sees to the choice (10:24) and appointment of Saul as Israel's first king (12:13). At the end, Samuel's prayer of intercession removes the last discordant note (12:20ff.).

This ambivalence serves three purposes. First, it is intended to subject the monarchy to the Deuteronomic law and to make the subsequent promises conditional upon observance of the law (1 Sam 12:10ff.; 1 Kgs 2:1–4; 9:4–5). Second, it lays the groundwork for the turbulence that afflicted the institution from the very beginning, with Saul's disobedience and Yahweh's rejection of his kingship (1 Sam 15). Third, it warns in advance that the monarchy will be of no avail if Israel sins (1 Sam 12:20–21, 24–25) and can even occasionally lead Israel into sin (1 Kgs 12:30; 14:16; 2 Kgs 21:9; etc.). However, none of this ruled out the enormous potential of the monarchy for salutary influence on the course of Israel's history.

In the eyes of the Deuteronomistic historians, the kingship of David was one of Yahweh's authentic gifts. David was chosen by Yahweh (1 Kgs 8:16), as the existing tradition already described in detail in the story of David's rise to power (1 Sam 16–2 Sam 5). He was totally obedient to Yahweh and his law (1 Kgs 11:38; 14:8; 15:5).[455] In the course of

---

[455] The view of David in the tradition made use of by the Deuteronomists, especially in the so-called "court history of David" (2 Sam 9–1 Kgs 2*), is distinctly more critical. Van Seters (*In Search of History*, 249–91) therefore eliminates it from the Deuteronomistic History as a secondary addition (comprising 2 Sam 2:8–4:12; 5:3; 6:16, 20–23; 9:1–20:22; 1 Kgs 1–2). This proposal goes much too far, since it sunders the web of allusions that links the pre-Deuteronomistic stories of David's rise with the court history. In addition, if we accept the MT, 1 Kgs 15:5 explicitly presupposes the Bathsheba episode.

Israel's history, his merits and the promise bestowed on him (2 Sam 7:14–16; 1 Kgs 2:4; 8:25; 9:5) were repeatedly able to mitigate (1 Kgs 11:12–13) or hold in check (1 Kgs 15:4; 2 Kgs 8:19) God's impending judgment. Despite all the dangers that the monarchy posed for Israel, it made a major contribution not only to the realization of God's promise of the land but also on many occasions to averting the imminent loss of the land. In addition, Davidic kings who fulfilled their responsibilities, such as David, Solomon, Hezekiah, and Josiah, played a major role in the realization of pure Yahwism in the sense of Deuteronomy. It is therefore no accident that the Deuteronomistic historians ended their history with a brief account of Jehoiachin's reprieve (2 Kgs 25:27–30). Many exegetes have wracked their brains over the significance of this scene, since the authors refrained from theological commentary, but if we note that none other than the last surviving Davidic king receives from the Babylonian authorities the compassion Solomon prays for 1 Kgs 8:50, it would appear that the authors sought to suggest that the divine choice of this royal house was beginning once more to extend a positive influence, as it had during Israel's earlier history.[456]

The positive assessment of the monarchy (with certain reservations), in the opinion of the Deuteronomistic historians, applied even more to the Jerusalem temple. Its construction was approved explicitly by Yahweh (1 Kgs 8:18–19) and was understood from the outset as fulfilling the Deuteronomic call for cultic centralization (8:16; cf. Deut 12:8ff.).[457] The construction and furnishing of the temple are described in detail (1 Kgs 6–7). In actuality, an existing Jebusite temple was probably just rebuilt,[458] but this fact is systematically suppressed. Throughout their history, the Deuteronomistic authors exhibit a striking interest in the temple treasure.[459] The installation of the Zadokites as a priesthood acceptable to God is reported and interpreted theologically (1 Sam 2:27–36; 1 Kgs 2:35), a clear sign that the interests of the Jerusalem priesthood are behind the

---

[456] The tentative character of this conclusion is probably due to Jehoiachin's death shortly after his release and the murder of Amēl-Marduk after just two and a half years on the throne. At a stroke, these events once more confused the situation for the leadership of the golah.

[457] This clearly positive assessment supports the view that the fundamental disapproval of the temple in 2 Sam 7:4b–7 represents a post-Deuteronomistic interpolation, as already suggested by its language, which is reminiscent of P (מִשְׁכָּן, "tabernacle," in 7:6; cf. Exod 25:9ff.) (Albertz, *History* (II.4), 1:118, 250 n. 32; for a different view, see Dietrich, "Niedergang," 65–66).

[458] Albertz, *History*, 1:128–32.

[459] See Josh 6:19, 24; 2 Sam 8:11–12; 1 Kgs 7:13–47, 48–50, 51; 14:25–28; 15:15; 2 Kgs 12:18–19 (17–18); 16:8; 18:15–16; 24:13–14; 25:13–17.

Deuteronomistic History. The leading priestly family of the Hilkiads—the high priests of the later monarchy—receive due mention (2 Kgs 18:19; 22:4; 25:19; etc.). The route taken by the ark until it was finally lodged in the most holy place of the temple is traced in detail (Josh 3–4; 1 Sam 4–6; 2 Sam 6). It is true that in 1 Kgs 8 the Deuteronomists have Solomon single out the function of the temple as a place of prayer, but in doing so they are merely reflecting their own period, when the only worship possible amid its ruins was ritual lamentation. Nevertheless, the Jerusalem temple was still for them the center of liturgical life; even the Babylonian golah remained in contact with it by facing in its direction to pray (8:48).

The Deuteronomistic historians explicitly drew on the notion of Jerusalem's election (1 Kgs 8:16 [cf. 2 Chr 6:5–6], 44, 48), which the Deuteronomic theologians had already used to interpret the ancient theologoumenon of Zion theology that called Jerusalem the city of God (Deut 12:14, 18, 26; 14:25; etc.; cf. Pss 46:5 [4]; 48:2–3 [1–2]).[460] During the subsequent course of history, this choice of Jerusalem, along with the choice of David, was for them an essential element in mitigating and delaying Yahweh's judgment on Judah (1 Kgs 11:32, 36; 14:21). Nevertheless, following the lead of Deuteronomic theology, the authors of the Deuteronomistic History modified Zion theology substantially. The election of Zion no longer embodied an unconditional guarantee of salvation. In their view, Yahweh's salvific presence was mediated by the tablets of the Decalogue in the ark (1 Kgs 8:6ff.) and was associated with observance of the torah of Moses (9:3–5). When Manasseh massively desecrated this temple with alien cults (2 Kgs 21:3–7), even its elect status could not save it from Yahweh's wrath (23:27). Thus the possibility that Yahweh might destroy his own sanctuary was made theologically credible (1 Kgs 9:7–8).

To prevent the destruction of the temple from affecting Yahweh himself, the Deuteronomists made every effort to spiritualize the earlier highly concrete notions of Yahweh's cultic presence in the temple. No longer did Yahweh dwell on Mount Zion (Pss 46:5 [4]; 76:3 [2]; 84:2 [1]; 132:7; 1 Kgs 8:12), as the exponents of ancient Zion theology asserted; neither did he cause his name to dwell there (Deut 12:11; 14:23; 16:2, 6, 11; 26:2), as the Deuteronomic theologians taught. Instead, he actually dwelt in heaven (1 Kgs 8:27). In the view of the Deuteronomistic historians, the temple was no longer built for Yahweh himself but "for his name" (בנה בית לשם יהוה: 2 Sam 7:13; 1 Kgs 5:17, 19; 8:17–20, 44, 48) or "for his name to be there" (היה שמי שם: 1 Kgs 8:16, 29; 2 Kgs 23:17) or "to put his

---

460 See also Ps 76:3 (2); the use of the verb בחר, "choose," in Pss 78:68 (67) and 132:13 is probably already due to Deuteronomistic influence.

name there" (שִׂים שְׁמִי שָׁם: 1 Kgs 9:3; 2 Kgs 21:7; cf. Deut 12:5, 21; 14:24). In other words, he was not present there but was merely accessible in a special way through prayer (1 Kgs 8:29–30). The temple continued to be a special locus of prayer even after its destruction made observance of the complete cult impossible (8:46ff.). By means of these theological modifications, the Deuteronomistic historians took into account both the failure of Zion theology and its claim that God had chosen the Jerusalem temple for all eternity (1 Kgs 9:3; 2 Kgs 21:7). The destruction of the temple did not mean that it was no longer chosen by God. That claim was indispensable; it embodied the fundamental potential for hope that Israel's history would continue.

After the salutary period of the united monarchy, the period of the divided monarchy (1 Kgs 11–2 Kgs 25) was, in the eyes of the Deuteronomistic historians, another period of apostasy. Like Joshua's farewell address (Josh 23), Yahweh's response to Solomon's prayer of dedication makes it unmistakably clear that the new divine institutions of the monarchy and the temple were contingent on obedience to the law (1 Kgs 9:1–9), already contemplating the possibility that they might be abrogated. In the opinion of the Deuteronomistic historians, however, the history of Israel during this era by no means declined inevitably toward this bad end. They were concerned instead to identify specifically various kinds of apostasy, to gauge the gravity of each, and to distinguish between better and worse historical phases. They used the detailed course of history to show how, even before the great catastrophe, minor and major crises were associated with apostasy from Yahweh and could be reversed at least in part by resolute repentance and return, as well as by Yahweh's patient forbearance.

To the Deuteronomists, the first great crisis, the break-off of the northern kingdom from the Davidic crown, was a direct consequence of the alien cults that the aging Solomon introduced for his foreign wives (1 Kgs 11:1–13). This development resulted immediately in a restriction on Nathan's promise for all Israel, so that the rebel Jeroboam received a similarly worded dynastic promise (11:29–39). Only in the diminished form that David would always have a lamp (נִיר) before Yahweh in Jerusalem (the so-called *nîr* promise: 11:36; 15:4; 2 Kgs 8:19) did Nathan's promise live on in the southern kingdom,[461] sustaining a reduced sovereignty for the Davidides. Even though the Deuteronomistic historians clearly conceived their history from a southern perspective, they believed that the northern kingdom, too, had a real chance at the outset.

---

[461] Lohfink, "Welches Orakel," 150–51, although he connects this promise with Dtr[1] of the block model.

Despite the dynastic promise and God's initial protection (1 Kgs 12:24), the Deuteronomists believed that the northern kingdom under Jeroboam, its first king, committed the crucial act of apostasy that was to cast its shadow over the rest of the kingdom's history: Jeroboam built national sanctuaries at Bethel and Dan, cutting the northern kingdom off from the Jerusalem cult (1 Kgs 12:26–32). In the eyes of the Deuteronomistic historians, this was an offense against the Deuteronomic centralization of the cult (Deut 12); it also involved worship at "high places" and, because of the golden calves, transgression of the prohibition of images (Deut 5:8–9)—in short, idolatry. It should be noted that for the Deuteronomists the "sin of Jeroboam" was not political but cultic apostasy.[462] It hung as a dark shadow over the entire history of the northern kingdom, occasioned the turbulence of civil wars, frequent usurpations, and shifting dynasties, and finally brought about the early demise of the state of Israel (722 B.C.E.). Here we see concrete evidence of the monopoly claimed by the Jerusalem priesthood within the group that produced the Deuteronomistic History, on the basis of which they not only legitimated Josiah's destruction of the northern shines, especially Bethel (1 Kgs 13:2, 32; 2 Kgs 23:15), but also continued to their own day to reject totally the cultic legitimacy of the Samarians (2 Kgs 17:24–32a).

The apostasy of the northern kingdom was aggravated, in the view of the Deuteronomists, when to idolatrous worship of Yahweh there was added public observance of the Baal cult, which Ahab introduced under the influence of his foreign wife (1 Kgs 16:31–33; 22:54). Under Ahab's son Joram, the northern kingdom appeared to have survived this absolute nadir, but a terrible judgment befell the Omrides: the usurper Jehu wiped out the entire royal house and eradicated the Baal cult of Samaria root and branch (2 Kgs 9–10). The Deuteronomists interpreted this massacre as the fulfillment of an oracle already spoken by Elijah during the reign of Ahab (1 Kgs 21:19–26); its fulfillment had been postponed (2 Kgs 9:7–10a, 36; 10:10, 17) because of the king's repentance (1 Kgs 21:27–29).[463]

---

[462] Cf. 1 Kgs 13:34; 14:9, 16; 15:30; 16:2, 26, 31; etc. This assessment is also true for the summary indictment in 2 Kgs 17:21, which says: "When he had torn Israel from the house of David and made Jeroboam king, Jeroboam drove Israel from following Yahweh and made them commit great sin." It was Yahweh, not Jeroboam, who brought about the political separation—as a punishment for Solomon's idolatry, exactly as described from the Deuteronomistic perspective in 1 Kgs 11:11–13, 29–39; 12:15. Jeroboam's sin was not that he tore Israel from the house of David but that he drove Israel from following Yahweh.

[463] Otto's study (*Jehu*, 253–57) has largely identified the original text of the Deuteronomistic History in the complex block between 1 Kgs 16 and 2 Kgs 10. It comprised 1 Kgs 16:29–33; 21:1–24, 27–29; 22:39–52; 2 Kgs 1:1–2, 5–8, 17–18*; 3:1–3; 8:16–10:36*, i.e., just two stories of Elijah and one of Elisha.

The Deuteronomists interpreted this outbreak of religious intolerance in a totally positive light. For his "zeal of Yahweh" (2 Kgs 10:16), Jehu received a limited dynastic promise, which restored a certain stability to the northern kingdom. However, the ongoing cultic break with Jerusalem prevented any real change for the better (2 Kgs 10:28–31). The northern kingdom suffered terribly under Aramean attack. The Deuteronomistic historians ascribed the retreat of the Arameans under Jehoahaz and Jeroboam II not to the kings' repentance but to Yahweh's compassion, as in the period of the judges (2 Kgs 13:4–5; 14:25–27). Still, the punishment for the sin of Jeroboam foretold by Ahijah of Shiloh in 1 Kgs 14:8–16 was only postponed, not revoked. It overtook the northern kingdom in 722 B.C.E., when Samaria was taken (2 Kgs 17:1–6), even though the Deuteronomists judged Hoshea, its last king, more kindly than his predecessors on account of his nationalistic policies (17:2).

The extended historical reflection inserted by the Deuteronomistic historians after this event (2 Kgs 17:7–23) once more tallies up all the transgressions of the northern kingdom that led to its demise. The primary blame rested on King Jeroboam, whose cultic policies, hostile to Jerusalem, had led Israel into sin (17:21–23). However, Israel itself had also gone astray. It should have known better, since Yahweh had called on it unceasingly to return to him and to obey his law (17:13–15, 23). The Deuteronomists had numerous prophets come forward, especially in the northern kingdom. Their primary function was to validate the justice of God's judgment by foretelling punishment, which inevitably came to pass. At the same time, it was their task to provide repeated opportunities for repentance through their indictments, admonitions, and warnings.[464] From the Deuteronomistic perspective, the demise of the northern kingdom was not inevitable but was rather due to refusal to heed the prophets' admonitions to repent and return to Yahweh.

It speaks well of the Deuteronomistic historians that, despite their repugnance at the cultic offenses in the north, they sought to prevent the fate of Israel from prompting any premature self-righteousness on the part of their primarily Judean audience.[465] Therefore, they included Judah in the indictments of the prophets (2 Kgs 17:13) and spoke of the sins that the southern kingdom had already committed or would commit in days to come (17:16–17; cf. 16:3–4; 21:3–6); they looked ahead to the demise of

---

[464] Cf. the prophetic indictments that could either lead to repentance (2 Sam 12; 1 Kgs 21) or be cast to the winds (1 Kgs 13).

[465] It is quite possible that descendants of exiles from the northern kingdom were also present in the Babylonian golah; see pp. 100 and 106 above.

Judah,[466] in which the rejection of "all the descendants of Israel" would be realized (17:19–20). Thus the Deuteronomists cannot be accused of evading their responsibility toward all Israel; finally, 2 Kgs 17:7–23 represents a general accounting for the sins of both kingdoms.[467]

Precisely because the Deuteronomistic historians felt a general responsibility toward all Israel, they could not be indifferent to the subsequent fate of their northern brothers and sisters. Thus they appended to their historical reflection a polemic vision of the later history of the former northern kingdom (2 Kgs 17:24–34a).[468] In gently mocking the flourishing syncretism of Yahwism with the religions of the people resettled in the north by the Assyrians, they were declaring a harsh theological verdict on the Samarians of their own exilic day. Among them apostasy from Yahweh continued unabated even after God's judgment had been imposed. The prophets' call to repent and to return to exclusive worship of Yahweh still went unheeded. This hybrid cult led the Deuteronomists to disavow the sanctuaries of the former northern kingdom totally. In their view, no new beginning of Israel's history could be expected from this quarter. If one of the northern compatriots, either in the Babylonian golah or in Palestine, wished to make a new beginning, the only choice was orientation toward Jerusalem.

From the Deuteronomistic perspective, the history of the northern kingdom, ending with this bleak prognosis, was defined entirely by apostasy, with only minor differences as to its extent. For the southern kingdom, the Deuteronomistic History paints a very different picture. The course of its history was marked by a cyclic alternation: waves of apostasy followed by waves of repentance and return. This history recalls the Deuteronomistic picture of the period of the judges, except that, in the history of the rump state of Judah, apostasy consisted in cultic and ritual transgressions and return involved more or less substantial cultic reforms.

After Solomon's reversion to syncretism, the first wave of apostasy reached its apogee under Rehoboam and Abijah, when high places were

---

[466] If the words "and he gave them into the hand of plunderers" in 2 Kgs 17:20 allude to the occupations of Judah, we have another parallel to the period of the judges (cf. Judg 2:14).

[467] As observed correctly by Becking, "From Exodus." Becking argues cogently for the unity of 2 Kgs 17:7–20, although he assigns 17:21–23 to an earlier Josianic stage. The final verdict on Judah, then, which many exegetes have thought to be lacking, is in fact present in 2 Kgs 17, albeit somewhat concealed.

[468] As the resumptive repetition in 17:40 and the balancing 17:41 show, 2 Kgs 17:34b–41 is a early post-Deuteronomistic expansion from the period following the restoration of the temple, pressing once more for the return of the northern Israelites (Albertz, *History* [II.4], 2:523–29).

built and temple prostitution was permitted (1 Kgs 14:22ff.),[469] in flagrant disobedience to the torah of Moses (Deut 12; 23:18–19). While such provincial sanctuaries ("high places") were tolerated before the building of the Jerusalem temple (1 Kgs 3:2–3), after Jerusalem was chosen to be the sole site where Yahweh was to be worshiped (1 Kgs 8:16), they represented for the Deuteronomists the primary transgression of the southern kingdom, done away with temporarily by the cultic reform of Hezekiah (2 Kgs 18:4) and permanently by the reform of Josiah (23:8). Yahweh did not respond immediately to this terrible offense against the Deuteronomic law of cultic centralization, quite comparable to the sin of Jeroboam, by determining to destroy Judah. For the Deuteronomistic historians, his compassion demonstrated the power of the promises bestowed on David and the Jerusalem temple (2 Kgs 14:21; 15:4–5). Yahweh limited his punishment to an invasion by Pharaoh Shishak (1 Kgs 14:25ff.). Judah enjoyed a longer and on the whole less turbulent history than the northern kingdom because, in the view of the Deuteronomists, Yahweh's promises associated with the monarchy and the temple mitigated and limited his judgment on Judah's apostasy.

The Deuteronomists judged the situation somewhat improved under Asa and Jehoshaphat, who did away with idols and abolished cult prostitution (1 Kgs 15:12–13; 22:47 [46]). They were therefore able to rebuild the military might of Judah. Soon afterward, however, there was another deep decline, when Joram and Athaliah imported the worship of Baal into Judah from the northern kingdom (2 Kgs 8:18; cf. 2 Kgs 11:18). Nevertheless, the result was only the loss of Edom (8:20ff.), not total judgment upon the royal house and the southern kingdom. Once again, Yahweh's compassion was due only to the *nîr* promise made to the Davidides and the courageous intervention of a Jerusalem priest, who restored the exclusive worship of Yahweh and saved the Davidic monarchy (2 Kgs 11:17–18).

The next four kings kept to this middle road. They maintained the exclusive worship of Yahweh but failed to abolish the cult of the high places (2 Kgs 12:4 [3]; 14:4; 15:4, 35); in consequence, three of them suffered personal disaster: Jehoash and Amaziah were assassinated, and Azariah was afflicted with leprosy. Then the situation worsened once more under Ahaz. Not only did he himself worship at high places, but he also introduced in Judah the so-called Moloch offering, the "abominable practice of the nations" (16:3–4). Therefore, he had to suffer a Syro-Ephraimite invasion and the loss of Elath to the Edomites (16:5–6). Ahaz

---

[469] According to the MT, Judah as a whole was responsible for this apostasy; the Septuagint blames Rehoboam.

completed the measure of his sin by calling in aid from the Assyrians at the cost of the temple treasure and subserviently erecting for them an altar of foreign design in the temple (16:10–18). In the eyes of the nationalistic Deuteronomistic historians, voluntary submission to a great power was a political and religious sellout, which they accordingly condemned.

In both respects, the reign of Hezekiah reprented a shining antithesis to that of his father. Hezekiah, the first king since Asa assessed as positively as David by the Deuteronomistic historians, did away for the first time with the fundamental evil of the high places; he also removed the last remnants of the image cult from the temple (Nehushtan: 2 Kgs 18:4). Furthermore, with unparalleled trust in God and obedience to the torah of Moses (18:5–6), he withstood the insolent and blasphemous attempts of the Assyrians to intimidate him. Therefore, he experienced a miraculous deliverance of Jerusalem from the superior forces of the Assyrians (19:9ff.) and an equally miraculous cure of his illness (20:1–11). For the Deuteronomistic historians, Hezekiah was a model of how cultic and religious adherence to Yahweh and resolute political resistance could assure survival and preserve national identity even against a superior world power. In their view, however, he would bitterly regret his naive trust in his Babylonian ally when this ally in turn became a world power (20:12–19; cf. 24:13).

To this point, the Deuteronomists' history of the southern kingdom is quite hopeful. It teaches that the kingdom's crises were brought about by apostasy from Yahweh, specifically the failure to complete the centralization of Yahweh worship at the Jerusalem sanctuary. However, it also teaches that ever and again in the past it had been possible to overcome these crises by reforming the cult on the basis of the Deuteronomic law—not least because the promises bestowed on the Davidic monarchy and the Jerusalem temple restrained Yahweh from giving free rein to his anger over Judah's apostasy. Thus history demonstrated the correctness of the religio-cultic side of Deuteronomic reform theology, augmented by elements of royal and temple theology.

The great problem facing the Deuteronomistic historians was that this optimistic theological theory was hard to reconcile with the actual course of history. In spite of everything, the final outcome had been a political demise of Judah comparable to the downfall of the northern kingdom, even though Josiah had undertaken an even more far-reaching reform of the cult. It would have been much easier to conclude that history had refuted Josiah's reform; during the exilic period, people undoubtedly reached this conclusion much more frequently and fundamentally than is recorded in Jer 44:15ff. To cut the ground from under this argument and to rescue the correctness of their theory, the Deuteronomists took a double approach at the end of their history. First, they confected an extremely negative turn of events under Manasseh, Hezekiah's successor: as an Assyrian vassal, they claimed, he voluntarily opened himself to the influence of foreign religions, introducing astral worship, images, "Moloch offering," and all manner of foreign divination in the Jerusalem temple (2 Kgs 21:2–7). Thus he brought the history of the southern kingdom to a nadir comparable to that of the northern kingdom under Ahab of Israel (21:3). These abominations—so the Deuteromists sought to explain the subsequent course of history—provoked Yahweh's judgment on the southern kingdom (21:10–16). Josiah was able to defer its imposition (22:18–20), but it could no longer be annulled (23:26–27). Second, they shaped the account of Josiah's cultic reform (2 Kgs 22:1–23:24) so as to make it the actual objective and climax of the entire history of the southern kingdom. It not only set right all the aberrations of Manasseh but also once for all did away with the cultic and ritual abuses that had occurred throughout the history of Judah. According to this Deuteronomistic conception, all the imperfect attempts at reform (Asa, Hezekiah, etc.) achieved their objective in the cultic reform of Josiah.[470]

The purpose of this presentation is clear when we look once more at the end of the history of the northern kingdom (2 Kgs 17:7–23). There the Deuteronomistic historians summarized all the sins of the northern kingdom and, in a spirit of self-criticism, included the sins of the southern kingdom. Looked at from the opposite perspective, this summary explained why Yahweh had rejected both kingdoms. Contrarwise, when shortly before the end of the southern kingdom's history these same historians summarized all the cultic and religious initiatives undertaken in Judah to return to Yahweh, they were attempting, with their eyes on the future, to maintain that under Josiah, and only then, the correct course had been set, which—as was clear from the previous course of history—offered a positive prognosis for the future. The Deuteronomistic historians could not deny that the history of the southern kingdom had also come to an ill end, recorded with striking brevity after the extended account of Josiah's reform (2 Kgs 23:31–25:26). For them, however, this end was only the consequence of a terrible but nevertheless very limited wrong turn. More important was the demonstration that

---

[470] The paraphernalia of Baal, Asherah, and the host of heaven were burned (2 Kgs 23:4; cf. 21:3–4); all the foreign methods of divination, including the astral cult, were eliminated (23:5, 24; cf. 21:6); the image of Asherah was removed (23:6; cf. 21:3, 7); cult prostitution was ended (23:7; cf. 1 Kgs 22:47 [46]; 15:12; 14:24); the high places were defiled and broken down (23:8–9; cf. 21:3, etc.); the "Moloch offering" at Topheth was eliminated (23:10; cf. 21:6; 16:3); the roof altars were torn down (23:11–12; cf. 21:4–5); the foreign cults introduced by Solomon were eradicated (23:13–14; cf. 1 Kgs 11:5–7).

only the way shown by Josiah in his reform offered a chance for Israel's history to continue beyond the national catastrophe. In their great historical work, the Deuteronomistic historians were by no means concerned simply to provide a theological explanation for the national disaster of 587. It was also their central purpose to show their exiled contemporaries the only way out of the crisis, namely, resisting the temptations of the foreign religion all around them and the pre-Deuteronomic practice exemplified by the Samarians and instead worshiping Yahweh alone in a religion centered on the Jerusalem temple. In their eyes, this meant that restoration of the state cult of Jerusalem[471] according to the norms of the Mosaic torah, as exemplified by King Josiah, and thus by implication restoration of the Davidic monarchy were crucial for a new beginning.

III. 2. 5. THE BOOK OF JEREMIAH

Albertz, Rainer. "Jer 2–6 und die Frühverkündigung Jeremias," *ZAW* 94 (1982): 20–47. **Biddle,** Mark E. *A Redaction History of Jeremiah 2:1–4:2* (ATANT 77; Zurich: Theologischer Verlag, 1990). **Brueggemann,** Walter. *A Commentary on Jeremiah: Exile and Homecoming* (Grand Rapids: Eerdmans, 1998). **Carroll,** Robert P. *Jeremiah: A Commentary* (OTL; London: SCM, 1986). **Duhm,** Bernhard. *Das Buch Jeremia* (KHC 11; Tübingen: Mohr Siebeck, 1901). **Goldman,** Yohanan. *Prophétie et royauté au retour de l'exil: Les origins littéraires de la forme massorétique du livre de Jérémie* (OBO 118; Fribourg: Universitätsverlag, 1992). **Gosse,** Bernard. "Trois étapes de la redaction du livre de Jérémie: La venue du malheur contre ce lieu (Jérusalem), puis contre toute chair (Juda et les nations), et enfin de nouveau contre ce lieu, mais identifié cette fois à Babylone," *ZAW* 111 (1999), 508–29. **Graupner,** Axel. *Auftrag und Geschick des Propheten Jeremia: Literarische Eigenart, Herkunft und Intention vordeuteronomistischer Prosa im Jeremiabuch* (BThSt 15; Neukirchen-Vluyn: Neukirchener Verlag, 1991). **Herrmann,** Siegfried. *Jeremia: Der Prophet und das Buch* (EdF 217; Darmstadt: Wissenschaftliche Buchgesellschaft, 1990). **Holladay,** William. *Jeremiah: A Commentary on the Book of the Prophet Jeremiah* (2 vols.; Hermeneia; Philadelphia: Fortress, 1986–89). **Hyatt,** J. Philip. "The Deuteronomic Edition of Jeremiah (1951)," in *A Prophet to the Nations: Essays in Jeremiah Studies* (ed. L. G. Perdue and B. W. Kovacs; Winona Lake, Ind.: Eisenbrauns, 1984), 247–68. **Levin,** Christoph. *Die Verheissung des neuen Bundes in*

---

[471] Knoppers (*Two Nations,* 249–50) righly emphasizes the ties linking the Deuteronomistic History with the state cult, which are quite consonant with the royal theology of the ancient Near East. It makes sense not only in the context of a preexilic Dtr[1] but also as an option during the exile. It was, after all, the Davidide Zerubbabel who directed the rebuilding of the temple very much in this spirit (Hag 2:4; Zech 4:9–10).

ihrem theologiegeschichtlichen Zusammenhang ausgelegt (FRLANT 137; Göttingen: Vandenhoeck & Ruprecht, 1985). **Lohfink,** Norbert. "Die Gattung der 'Historischen Kurzgeschichte' in den letzten Jahren von Juda und in der Zeit des babylonischen Exils," *ZAW* 90 (1978): 319–47. **McKane,** William. *A Critical and Exegetical Commentary on Jeremiah* (2 vols.; ICC; Edinburgh: T&T Clark, 1986–96). **Mowinckel,** Sigmund. *Zur Komposition des Buches Jeremia* (Kristiana: Dybwad, 1914). **Nicholson,** Ernest W. *Preaching to the Exiles: A Study in the Prose Tradition in the Book of Jeremiah* (Oxford: Blackwell, 1970). **Odashima,** Taro. *Heilsworte im Jeremiabuch: Untersuchung zu ihrer vordeuteronomistischen Bearbeitung* (BWANT 125; Stuttgart: Kohlhammer, 1989). **Pohlmann,** Karl-Friedrich. *Die Ferne Gottes: Studien zum Jeremiabuch: Beiträge zu den "Konfessionen" im Jeremiabuch und ein Versuch zur Frage nach den Anfängen der Jeremiatradition* (BZAW 179; Berlin: de Gruyter, 1989). **Pohlmann.** *Studien zum Jeremiabuch: Ein Beitrag zur Frage nach der Entstehung des Jeremiabuches* (FRLANT 118; Göttingen: Vandenhoeck & Ruprecht, 1978). **Römer,** Thomas. "How Did Jeremiah Become a Convert to Deuteronomistic Ideology?" in *Those Elusive Deuteronomists: The Phenomenon of Pan-Deuteronomism* (ed. L. S. Shearing and S. L. McKenzie; JSOTSup 268; Sheffield: Sheffield Academic Press, 1999), 189–99. **Rudolph,** Wilhelm. *Jeremia* (3d ed.; HAT 1/12; Tübingen: Mohr Siebeck, 1968). **Schmid,** Konrad. *Buchgestalten des Jeremiabuches: Untersuchungen zur Redaktions- und Rezeptionsgeschichte von Jer 30–33 im Kontext des Buches* (WMANT 72: Neukirchen-Vluyn: Neukirchener Verlag, 1996). **Seitz,** Christopher R. *Theology in Conflict: Reactions to the Exile in the Book of Jeremiah* (BZAW 176: Berlin: de Gruyter, 1989). **Seybold,** Klaus. *Der Prophet Jeremia: Leben und Werk* (Kohlhammer Urban-Taschenbücher 416; Stuttgart: Kohlhammer, 1993). **Stipp,** Hermann-Josef. *Jeremia im Parteienstreit: Studien zur Textentwicklung von Jer 26, 36–43 und 45 als Beitrag zur Geschichte Jeremias, seines Buches und judäischer Parteien im 6. Jahrhundert* (BBB 82; Frankfurt am Main: Hain, 1992). **Stipp.** *Das masoretische und alexandrinische Sondergut des Jeremiabuches: Textgeschichtlicher Rang, Eigenarten, Triebkräfte* (OBO 136; Fribourg: Universitätsverlag, 1994). **Stipp.** "Probleme des redaktionsgeschichtlichen Modells der Entstehung des Jeremiabuches," in *Jeremia und die "Deuteronomistische Bewegung"* (ed. W. Gross; BBB 98; Weinheim: Beltz Athenäum, 1995), 225–62. **Stulman,** Louis. *The Prose Sermons of the Book of Jeremiah: A Redescription of the Correspondences with Deuteronomistic Literature in the Light of Recent Text-Critical Research* (SBLDS 83; Atlanta: Scholars Press, 1986). **Thiel,** Winfried. *Die deuteronomistische Redaktion von Jeremia 1–25* (WMANT 41; Neukirchen-Vluyn, Neukirchener Verlag, 1973). **Thiel.** *Die deuteronomistische Redaktion von Jeremia 26–45* (WMANT 52; Neukirchen-Vluyn: Neukirchener Verlag, 1981). **Wanke,** Günther. *Jeremia*, vol. 1 (ZBK.AT 20/1; Zurich: Theologischer Verlag Zürich, 1995). **Wanke.** *Untersuchungen zur sogenannten Baruchschrift* (BZAW 122; Berlin: de Gruyter, 1971). **Weippert,** Helga. *Die Prosareden des Jeremia-buches* (BZAW 132; Berlin: de Gruyter, 1973).

Besides the Deuteronomistic History, no other exilic textual unit of the Old Testament underwent as extensive and thorough a Deuteronomistic editing as the book of Jeremiah. The existence of a Deuteronomistic book of

Jeremiah (JerD) was demonstrated by Hyatt[472] and Thiel[473] with strikingly similar results.[474] Thiel's primary aim was to identify the Deuteronomistic passages and distinguish them from their contexts; he envisioned a single Deuteronomistic redaction, which he dated in the period around 550 B.C.E.[475] In his view, it comprised Jer 1–45*, that is, most of the book, minus the foreign nation oracles in Jer 46–51 and post-Deuteronomistic additions. This hypothesis, which drew on earlier models based on the techniques of literary criticism,[476] was widely accepted. Since the 1970s, however, several studies have challenged more or less fundamentally the theory of a Deuteronomistic book of Jeremiah,[477] postulating instead supplementative[478] or alternative redaction-historical[479] models. Present-day scholarship, therefore, presents us with two more or less irreconcilable hypotheses: the model of a large-scale Deuteronomistic redaction and a variety of models based on small-scale accretions.

This controversy among present-day scholars is related to the bewildering variety of texts within the book of Jeremiah. First, we find a multiplicity of quite different genres: (1) poetic oracles of judgment and salvation, descriptions of disaster, and laments; (2) first-person prose accounts and prophetic narratives; and (3) prose discourses and reflections. Redaction history can find these different genres relevant to the growth and development of the book, whereas tradition history can treat them simply as different embodiments of the same material. Second, we frequently come upon formulas or idioms that appear in similar or identical form elsewhere in the book. In principle, these can be interpreted as stylistic features of a single author, but they can also be treated as deliberate allusions, references, or interpretations involving texts of different authors. Third, the book of Jeremiah, more than the other prophetic books, includes double traditions of the same text (6:12–15 = 8:10–12; 10:12–16 = 51:15–19; 15:13–14 = 17:1–4; 16:14–15 = 23:7–8; 23:19–20 = 30:23–24; 30:10–11; 46:27–28). This phenomenon does not suggest systematic redaction so much as uncontrolled textual augmentation, but it may be due at least in part to the inclusion of a particular oracle in different collections.

---

472 *Deuteronomic Edition.*

473 *Deuteronomistische Redaktion* (1973 and 1981).

474 See the synopsis in Herrmann, *Jeremia,* 80–81, which does, however, contain a few minor inaccuracies.

475 *Deuteronomistische Redaktion* (1981), 114.

476 Duhm, *Buch Jeremia;* Mowinckel, *Zur Komposition;* Rudolph, *Jeremia.*

477 Weippert, *Prosareden;* Holladay, *Jeremiah;* Stipp, "Probleme."

478 Pohlmann, *Studien;* Seitz, *Theology;* Stipp, *Jeremia.*

479 Levin, *Verheissung;* Carroll, *Jeremiah;* McKane, *Critical and Exegetical Commentary;* Schmid, *Buchgestalten* .

If we look back over the history of modern scholarship, we see that Duhm, who may be considered the first proponent of the Deuteronomistic book of Jeremiah hypothesis, also detected a process of accretion through which the book originally took shape. He distinguished (1) the poetry of Jeremiah (some 280 verses), (2) the book of Baruch (some 220 verses), and (3) a multiplicity of secondary additions (some 850 verses!), of which only a fraction were "Deuteronomistic."[480] Particularly with reference to the additions, he could say: "Thus the book grew slowly, almost as an unsupervised forest grows and spreads...; it is impossible to speak of a systematic composition, a homogeneous diction."[481] Duhm dates the various additions from the sixth century B.C.E. to the first. It is not surprising that adherents of accretion models, from Levin[482] to Schmid,[483] continue to cite this side of Duhm's analysis.

Early in his career, Mowinckel turned Duhm's supplement hypothesis into a source theory (which today must be considered a blind alley), probably under the influence of pentateuchal criticism.[484] He distinguished four sources: source A (JerA), the oracles and autobiographical narratives in Jer 1–25;[485] source B (JerB), third-party accounts (Jer 19:1–20:6*; 26; 28; 29*; 36; 37–43; 44*); and source C (JerC), lengthy discourses (Jer 7:1–8:3; 11:1–5, 9–14; 18:1–12; 21:1–10; 25:1–11a; 32:1–2, 6–16, 24–34; 34:1–7, 8–22; 35:1–19; 44:1–14; there is also a source D, postexilic oracles of salvation in Jer 30–31*. Mowinckel was ahead his time in recognizing the linguistic, stylistic, thematic cohesion and structural similarity of the texts assigned to source C; he thus worked out for the first time a consistent profile of the Deuteronomistic stratum in the book of Jeremiah.[486] But his source document hypothesis resulted in a relatively rigid picture of this stratum, which hardly did justice to its compositional function. Furthermore, short passages "in the style of C" could be understood only as the work of the redactors who compiled the sources, not as expressions of the Deuteronomistic redaction itself.[487] There was a long scholarly detour before Rudolph[488]

---

480 *Buch Jeremia*, x.
481 Ibid., xx.
482 *Verheissung*, 63.
483 *Buchgestalten*, 27.
484 *Zur Komposition*.
485 See the list in ibid, 20–21.
486 Ibid., 30–40.

487 That Mowinckel himself ran up against the limitations of his source hypothesis is shown by the fact that he found himself compelled for linguistic reasons to assign such texts as Jer 3:6–13; 22:1–5; 27*; 29:1–23*; 39:15–18; 45 to JerC, even though they were not "lengthy discourses" and contained allusions to JerA and JerB.

488 *Jeremia*.

recognized from the stereotyped introductions to such Deuteronomistic discourses in Jer 7:1; 11:1; (14:1); 18:1; (21:1); 25:1 that "source C furnished the basic stucture for the redactor" of the book of Jeremiah, "into which he inserted the rest of his material as appropriately as possible."[489] Following the lead of Hyatt,[490] he even suggested "that the author of the C sections was also the primary redactor of the book of Jeremiah."[491] Thus began the transformation of the source hypothesis into a redaction-historical hypothesis. Substantially, Rudolph made two changes. First, in an effort to reclaim as many passages as possible for Jeremiah, Rudolph assigned a majority of the salvation oracles (Jer 30–31) and the foreign nation oracles (46:1–49:33) to JerA. Second, while Mowinckel still dated JerC around 400 B.C.E., once Noth had established the exilic origin of the Deuteronomistic History,[492] Rudolph shifted the Deuteronomistic redaction of the book of Jeremiah to the exilic period.[493]

It was at this point that Thiel for the first time developed in detail the redaction-historical hypothesis that chapters 1–45 of the book of Jeremiah—still excluding the foreign nation oracles, but including the salvation oracles in Jer 30:1–31:34—owe their basic form to a Deuteronomistic redaction. The major burden of proof was borne by a painstaking linguistic analysis through which Thiel identified as Deuteronomistic many texts with parallels in the Deuteronomistic History or in accepted JerC texts, far more than the body of texts recognized as Deuteronomistic by Mowinckel and Rudolph. Thiel was also able to demonstrate that there was often a close linguistic and thematic affinity between JerD and the Deuteronomistic History, although JerD has its own distinctive profile, growing out of conflict with the prophecy of Jeremiah.[494] Thiel's

---

489 Ibid., xix.
490 "Deuteronomic Edition."
491 *Jeremia*, xx.
492 See p. 274 above.
493 *Jeremia*, xxi.
494 *Deuteronomistische Redaktion* (1981), 93–99. The contrary attempt of Weippert (*Prosareden*, 299) to demonstrate Jeremiah's authorship of the C texts on the basis of their "linguisitic independence" and "Jeremiaisms" leads nowhere, since she is unable to account adequately for their clearly Deuteronomistic sections. Schmid has also objected (*Buchgestalten*, 33) that "'Deuteronomistic' language is sometimes even a misleading criterion for identifying 'Deuteronomistic' texts, since there are sections in the book of Jeremiah that make use of Deuteronomistic language but are conceptually at odds with fundamental notions of Deuteronomy" (citing Jer 18:7–9 as an example). But this argument does not really impugn Thiel's methodology and conclusions, since it only makes it clear that we must expect to find differences between the Deuteronomistic History and JerD—and perhaps even within JerD. That the various Deuteronomistic parties also have their differences with Deuteronomy is no reason to doubt their fundamental acceptance of it as their standard. As

comparison of the language of JerD with that of the Deuteronomistic History has been criticized occasionally as methodological restriction.[495] Of course, we must remember that we do not know the extent of the Deuteronomistic History at the time of the Deuteronomistic redaction of the book of Jeremiah and that the latter may also have influenced the former.[496] It is also quite true that later redactors may have imitated the Deuteronomistic idiom.[497] In all fairness however, it must be said that Thiel has gone about his work with great care, while at the same time drawing judiciously on other observations from literary criticism, form criticism, and content analysis. Even if his results need correction here and there, they still constitute a relatively assured basis for further work.

In my opinion, further study is indicated in three areas. First, Thiel simply assumes that the Deuteronomistic redaction of the book of Jeremiah took place all at once; this assumption may reflect the ongoing influence of the earlier source theory, but this perspective does not allow enough scope for change and development of the expectations for salvation within the book. As Thiel himself has admitted, it is worth asking whether the Deuteronomistic redaction of the book of Jeremiah did not take place in several stages, which must in turn be distinguished more precisely from post-Deuteronomistic revisions.[498] Second, probably still influenced by the hypothesis of distinct sources, Thiel devotes relatively little discussion to the nature and method of the Deuteronomistic redaction.[499] Even now, too little attention has been paid to characterizing the composition and conception of the Deuteronomistic book of Jeremiah. Third, Thiel concentrates primarily on the JerC passages. The tradition history of the JerA and JerB texts, which enjoyed their own more or less extended history before being incorporated into the Deuteronomistic book of Jeremiah, should likewise be included in the redaction history of the book.

Strangely, however, scholars have devoted almost no further attention to the questions Thiel left open. Perhaps influenced by the relative inflexibility of his thesis, they have instead developed supplementary and alternative redaction-historical models. Pohlmann,[500] for example,

---

far as I know, the fact that the "Deuteronomistic" texts from Joshua through 2 Kings simply ignore the social legislation of Deuteronomy has not led anyone to dispute their Deuteronomistic character.

[495] Levin, *Verheissung*, 65; Stipp, *Jeremia*, 233–58.
[496] Levin, *Verheissung*, 64.
[497] Pohlmann, *Studien*, 16; Stipp, "Probleme," 245–46.
[498] *Deuteronomistische Redaktion* (1981), 122.
[499] *Deuteronomistische Redaktion* (1973), 283–289; *Deuteronomistische Redaktion* (1981), 100–106.
[500] *Studien*.

seeks to demonstrate the existence of a golah-centered redaction of the book of Jeremiah, comprising Jer 21:1–10; 24, a redactional stratum in Jer 37–44*, and possibly also 32:16–44. Its purpose, he believes, was to establish the special status of the first Babylonian golah in God's plan of salvation, over against the Judeans who remained behind and those who emigrated to Egypt.[501] He dates this redaction in the fourth century at the earliest.[502] Textually, this redaction coincides in part with the Deuteronomistic redaction of Thiel's reconstruction (Jer 21:1–10; 24). The major problem with Pohlmann's theory, I believe, lies in the supposed revision of Jer 43:1–7, which quite surprisingly describes the departure from Judah of all previously named segments of the population: linguisticially, it lies on a totally different plane from the programmatic chapter 24.[503] Here the absence of any linguistic evidence for the redactional stratum is distressingly apparent. Furthermore, the two parts of the supposed framework are far from congruent in their aim: Jer 24:5–7 does indeed focus on the first golah and its salvation, but chapters 37–44 do not mention this theme, being concerned only with the rejection of the Egyptian golah, which Jer 24 mentions only in passing (24:8bβ). Therefore, I agree with Pohlmann as to Jer 24, but I believe that this chapter is an isolated late Deuteronomistic supplement from a time when it had become normal for the Judean community to trace all its members back to the golah (mid-fifth century).

A further attempt to postulate a new redactional stratum in the book of Jeremiah was made by Stipp in 1992.[504] Within Jer 26, 36, and 37–45, he isolated a Shaphanide redaction (26:7, 8b*, 10–16, 24; 36:1–4, 6b–8*, 13, 17–19, 27*, 31–32; 39:14aα*; 40:1–3, 4b–6; 43:3, 6; 45:1–5), a partisan revision intended to support the claims of the Judean aristocracy in the power struggles of the early postexilic period. Stipp assigns this redaction to the post-Deuteronomistic period, but it coincides with JerD in 45:1–5, its compositionally important conclusion. Stipp does not reflect on whether this means that the Shaphanide recension rather than the Deuteronomistic recension was responsible for the section Jer 26–45.

---

[501] Ibid., 184–85.

[502] Ibid., 191. Apart from this dating, Seitz (*Theology*) largely follows Pohlmann. He believes that the redaction emerged from conflicts toward the close of the exilic period (295–96). However, this dating would poach on the preserve of the Deuteronomistic redaction, not only textually by also chronologically.

[503] Graupner (*Auftrag*, 190) tries to isolate the golah-centered additions in 41:10a*; 42:2aγb; 43:5aβb, 6a* in order lessen somewhat the disconcerting comprehensiveness of the departure for Egypt. His attempt is well intentioned but cannot cite any compelling literary-critical evidence.

[504] *Jeremia*.

Stipp's use of literary criticism to isolate the passages in question is hardly persuasive, and he cannot identify a social situation in the early postexilic period in which such a recension might have had a meaningful function;[505] the discussion that follows will ignore this theory.

These responses to the theory of a Deuteronomistic redaction of the book of Jeremiah are in unresolved competition with it. The accretion models more or less dissolve it or eliminate it entirely. McKane's two-volume commentary develops "the idea of a rolling corpus,"[506] that is, the notion that the book of Jeremiah came into being through a lengthy process of enrichment and reinterpretation of the textual material found in certain "kernels" or "reservoirs." Poetic verses can generate prose texts; poetic texts can trigger poetic compositions. Prose texts can influence or generate other prose texts.[507] In part, this approach addresses phenomena that Thiel had described as the interpretative work of the Deuteronomistic redactor. In the first volume, McKane gives the impression of wanting to dissolve the Deuteronomistic redactional stratum in a multifaceted process of accretion. In the second volume, however, he speaks once more in quite traditional terms of a "combination of a Baruch core and Deuteronomistic redaction."[508] Thus McKane does not develop the accretion model consistently.

Carroll's commentary[509] also posits a comprehensive Deuteronomistic shaping of the book of Jeremiah. The whole book is a collection of interpretations of the catastrophe of exile.[510] This exilic perspective so predominates that the person of the prophet disappears entirely. In addition, Carroll transforms the Deuteronomistic redaction into work carried out by many different groups: depending on the themes addressed, they represent very diverse interests.[511] Unfortunately, however, the textual and sociohistorical analyses both remain quite vague: Carroll thinks in very general terms of conflicts during the sixth and fifth centuries.[512]

Following on the work of Levin,[513] Schmid[514] undertook to reconstruct the redactional stages of the book of Jeremiah on a large scale on the basis of a more limited study of the expansion of the salvation oracles in Jer

---

505 Ibid., 297–98.
506 *Critical and Exegetical Commentary*, 1:l–lxii.
507 Ibid., 1:lxii–lxxxiii.
508 Ibid., 2:cxxxiv.
509 *Jeremiah*.
510 Ibid., 73–74.
511 Ibid., 69–71.
512 Ibid., 69.
513 *Verheissung*.
514 *Buchgestalten*.

30–31. Unlike McKane and Carroll, he believes that he can do without a stage of Deuteronomistic redaction. Here we can sketch his complex model only in broad outline.[515] By the late preexilic and early exilic period, the book of Jeremiah had grown in three stages to encompass roughly Jer 2–6*, 8–10*, 11–23*, and 46–51*; in the late exilic period (before 539), there was added the core of the collection of salvation oracles (30:4, 5–7, 12–17, 18–21*; 31:4–5, 15–22, 26), linked by the catchword אין שלום in 23:17 and 30:5. Between 539 and 520, inclusion of 31:6, 10–14 (parallel to Isa 49–54*) gave the book a Zion-theology facet. In the same period, the addition of Jer 32* gave it for the first time a narrative text having to do with possession of the land, establishing a correspondence between word and history that now made it possible to incorporate the prophetic narratives in Jer 26–45*. Finally, toward the end of the sixth century, the middle section of the book was restructured by including the notion of a Babylonian hegemony limited to seventy years (25:11–12; 29:10). This was followed by a redaction centered on the golah and another centered on the Diaspora. Surprisingly, Schmid eclectically assigns to a redaction that did not take place until the middle of the fourth century several important texts that help hold the book together, formerly ascribed to the Deuteronomistic redaction (1:10–11; 7:1–8:2; 18 (?); 11:1–14; 31:27–28, 31–33). The five or six stages of development that Schmid describes for the exilic period alone appear to open the way for a differentiated analysis of the nascent book of Jeremiah during this period. Despite many interesting observations, however, Schmid's reconstruction remains so vague and uncertain that it is ill suited to detailed interpretation of the text. It turns out that a redaction-historical reconstruction based primarily on subject matter and not checked whenever possible against linguistic evidence leads to extensive combinations that are almost beyond control. It is also disappointing that the hypotheses concerning the origin of the book based on one short section (Jer 30–31) are not evaluated by a redaction-historical study of the entire book. Schmid demonstrates convincingly that late texts such as Jer 33:14–26 and 29:16–20, which do not appear in the Septuagint, are intentional continuations of other texts (23:5–6; 24), as the explicit references show.[516] However, these texts must be kept distinct from phenomena that help define the large-scale structure of the book (superscriptions) or link texts to form new units (19:14–15; 21:1–10; 37:1–2), and if such redactional linkages speak a Deuteronomistic language, the hypothesis of a comprehensive Deuteronomistic redaction during the middle phase of the book's development is more probable.

---

[515] Ibid., 201–304.
[516] Ibid., 323–27.

Only recently has the theory of a Deuteronomistic redaction of the book of Jeremiah been restudied, with an attempt to distinguish multiple stages. Wanke, for example, distinguishes an early exilic edition of the book, comprising Jer 1–20* (without the confessions!); 25*; 26; 36; 45, which still focused entirely on interpreting God's judgment, and a late exilic or early postexilic edition, which—still influenced by Deuteronomistic ideas—added more narrative material in several stages (Jer 27–29; 32–35; 37–43).[517] Here the focus was on possibilities for future salvation, the restoration of Israel, and the renewal of Israel's relationship with God. Chapters 21–24, 30–31, and 46–51 were added even later. Römer, on the contrary, supports the view that the first Deuteronomistic book of Jeremiah comprised chapters 7–35, expanded in a second stage by the additon of 1–6 and 36–45.[518] His theory has been elaborated by Gosse, who believes that the book of Jeremiah underwent three stages of redaction.[519] The first stage, comprising Jer 7–35* (minus the confessions and the salvation oracles in 30–31), focused on prophecy of disaster against Jerusalem. The second, comprising Jer 1–45* (including 46–49* where they appear in the Septuagint), expanded the perspective of judgment to include Judah and Israel's neighbors. In the third stage, the book finally attained its full compass (Jer 1–51, in the order of the MT) and focused on revenge against Babylon (Jer 50–51) and salvation for Jerusalem and Judah (Jer 30–31). All three models have the merit of extending the clear theological development within the book over a longer period of time, but they have not been worked out fully, and their differences make it clear that identification of different Deuteronomistic redactions still awaits further study.

At most, these alternative models can modify the theory of a Deuteronomistic redaction of the book of Jeremiah as established finally by Thiel; they cannot replace it. The discussion that follows thus presents a modification of Thiel's hypothesis based on compositional analysis, with two aims: to differentiate diachronically several distinct Deuteronomistic redactions in the course of the exilic period (587–520 B.C.E.); and to distinguish these redactions more clearly from late Deuteronomistic and post-Deuteronomistic material added in the postexilic period. In the present state of our knowledge, such an attempt is obviously burdened with several uncertainties. In this restricted setting, unfortunately, I cannot lay out the evidence for my approach in every detail.

Every redaction-historical hypothesis must deal with the problem that the book of Jeremiah is extant in two recensions: the Masoretic Text

---

[517] *Jeremia*, 16–17.
[518] "How Did Jeremiah Become a Convert?" 192–93, 197–98.
[519] "Trois étapes."

and the Septuagint. As the Qumran fragments 4QJer[b.c.d] show, the latter also goes back to a Hebrew original. The LXX of Jeremiah is about one-seventh shorter than the Hebrew text; 93.8 percent of the pluses in the MT involve from one to five words; only 6.2 percent involve longer passages.[520] The existence of these two recensions does not impugn the theory of a Deuteronomistic redaction; as Stulman has shown, the shorter LXX text exhibits the most traces of Deuteronomistic redaction.[521] Nowadays an increasing number of scholars are generally inclined to give priority to the LXX text,[522] but the differences vary widely in nature, and each case must be decided on its own merits.[523] For example, it seems certain to me that the text of Jer 25:1–13a and Jer 33 in the LXX represents a more ancient tradition, but the placement of the foreign nation oracles after Jer 25:1–13, as in the LXX, appears not to represent the original order, even though the present MT in this area is later.[524] In doubtful cases, I do not base my interpretation on verses absent from the LXX (e.g., 27:7). Since the two textual traditions did not diverge until the fourth or third century, the LXX does not lead us directly to the "original" text in any case. A comparative redaction-historical study of the two versions is an urgent desideratum.

III.2.5.1. The Deuteronomistic Books of Jeremiah

The starting point for my redaction-historical analysis is the fact that the book of Jeremiah contains two conclusions, both bearing a clearly Deuteronomistic stamp (Jer 25:1–13abα*; 45:1–5). This double ending argues for more than one Deuteronomistic redaction of the book. Since we also find three editorial comments that refer explicitly to the book (סֵפֶר) or portions of it (25:13bα; 30:2; 45:1), all of which use Deuteronomistic language, I reckon with three Deuteronomistic editions of the book of Jeremiah during the exilic period.[525]

The first edition (JerD¹), clearly framed by an introductory chapter (Jer 1*)[526] and a concluding chapter (25:1–13abα*),[527] comprised the textual

---

520 Schmid, *Buchgestalten*, 323–24; for the details, see Stipp, *Das masoretische und alexandrinische Sondergut*.

521 *Prose Sermons*.

522 For example, Stipp, *Jeremia*; Huwyler, *Jeremia* (III.1.4).

523 As noted also by Schmid, *Buchgestalten*.

524 See below.

525 My analysis is a bit similar to that of Gosse, "Trois étapes."

526 Unlike Thiel, I believe that the entire chapter describing Jeremiah's call is Deuteronomistic, although probably only its second section (1:11–19) belongs to JerD¹ (see pp. 315–16 below). Elements of earlier traditions are present only in 1:11–14, 15.

527 I believe that the LXX preserves the earlier form of the text. Probably omission of the words "from Yahweh" in 25:1 led to the reshaping of divine discourse as prophetic

corpus Jer 1–25*. This is the book (הַסֵּפֶר הַזֶּה) referred to in the original concluding verse (25:13abα).[528] According to the superscription (1:1), it contains the "words of Jeremiah," more specifically, the words entrusted to him by Yahweh after his call in the thirteenth year of Josiah (627 B.C.E.; 1:2; 25:3). The date in the concluding discourse (25:1)—based on the tradition in Jer 36 concerning the public reading of the scroll—assigns the book to the fourth year of Jehoiakim (605). According to the superscription in 1:3, however, it contains the entire message of the prophet down to the fall of Jerusalem in 587. This minor inconsistency is clearly accepted deliberately[529] in order to lend the book the appearance of absolute authenticity: JerD¹ claims to be nothing less than an edition—silently expanded—of the original scroll personally dictated by Jeremiah to his companion Baruch. Since the emphatic oracle against Jehoiachin and his descendants (22:29–30) probably presupposes his release from prison (2 Kgs 25:27–30) in the year 562, a critical assessment would date this first Deuteronomistic edition of the book of Jeremiah around 550—that is, the period to which Thiel assigns the entire Deuteronomistic book of Jeremiah.

Of course JerD¹ did not include all of Jer 1–25*. Without going into detailed analysis, I identify the following material as secondary: Jer 1:4–11; 18[530] belong, I believe, to the second Deuteronomistic edition of the book. To the third Deuteronomistic edition belong the introductory salvation oracle Jer 2:2aβ, 3 and the expansion of the otherwise scanty salvation material by the addition of 3:14–15 and 23:1–4 (cf. Ezek 34); probably also the appended rhetorical material in 7:30–8:3; 19:6–9, 12–13 (cf. 32:16ff.), which expands on the indictment and announcement of judgment; also the conditional oracle of disaster or salvation addressed to Israel's neighbors in 12:14–17 (interpreting 18:7–10) and the appended prose section concerning false prophets in 23:23–32. Late Deuteronomistic expansions whose content places them in the postexilic period include the sermon concerning the Sabbath in 17:19–27 and the vision of

---

discourse in the MT. With Thiel (*Deuteronomistische Redaktion* [1973], 269ff.), I consider 1:9aβ and 11b–12 post-Deuteronomistic interpolations, occasioned by the later transfer of the foreign nation oracles to this position (see pp. 320–21 below).

528 Only the interpolation of 25:11b–12 shifts the focus of the book secondarily to the foreign nation oracles, especially the oracles against Babylon (Jer 50–51). This change contradicts the theme stated in 25:1 of the concluding discourse ("concerning all the people of Judah") and is not at all congruent with the content of Jer 1–25*.

529 Thiel (*Deuteronomistische Redaktion* [1973], 268–71) therefore considers Jer 25:1aβ–3a a post-Deuteronomistic addition. However, there is nothing incoherent about vv. 1–4 in their LXX form if one is prepared to supply the words "from Yahweh" in v. 1. The same chronological incongruity occurs in 45:1b, a text that Thiel is quite ready to assign to JerD.

530 See below.

the two baskets of figs in Jer 24. The latter chapter clearly does not belong to the first Deuteronomistic book of Jeremiah: its differentiated prophecy of judgment and salvation for specific groups is not mentioned in the concluding sermon appealing for return to Yahweh (25:5–13abα*); furthermore, what is probably the final verse of the oracle collection (23:22), with the catchwords is שׁוּב, "turn," דרך רע, "evil way," and רע מעללים, "the evil of their doings," points ahead directly to the concluding sermon (25:5). Other generally recognized additions that are even later (post-Deuteronomistic) include 3:16–18; 9:22–23, 24, 25 (23–24, 25, 26); 10:1–16; 12:12aβb; 15:21; 16:14–15, 19–21; 17:5–8, 9–10, 11, 12–13; 23:5–6, 7–8, 18, 19–20, 23–40; 25:9aβ, 11b –12, 13bβ.

Probably collections of Jeremiah's oracles existed even before the Deuteronomistic book of Jeremiah. Such collections are attested explicitly by the tradition of the so-called "original scroll" (Jer 36), according to which in the fourth year of Jehoiakim (605) Jeremiah is said to have dictated all the words he had previously spoken for Baruch to write on a scroll. After the first scroll was destroyed, he produced a second to replace it, adding "many similar words" (36:32). This is not the place to discuss the oft-debated question as to what this "original scroll" contained, but there was probably a written tradition of Jeremiah's words from this time forward. The existence of such a written record is also supported by the fact that in 1:1–3 the redactors of JerD[1] had to employ some awkward syntax to change an earlier superscription "words of Jeremiah" to accord with their principles by adding "to whom the word of Yahweh came" (1:2). The collection originally introduced by this earlier superscription cannot be identified with certainty, but it probably comprised at least the original core of Jer 2–6* (2:4–3:5; 3:19–4:2; 4:3, 5–6, 30).[531] Jeremiah 8:4–9:10; 10:17–25 represent a collection produced in the early exilic period, probably for liturgical use.[532] Other minor collections were assembled to reflect the interests of particular groups of addressees—for example, 21:11–22:30* concerning the royal house of Judah (possible from the time of the anti-Babylonian conspiracy in 594) and 23:9–22* concerning false prophets. As Thiel has shown convincingly,[533] the textual corpus of Jer 10–20* was assembled initially by the Deuteronomistic redactors, in

---

[531] Jer 2:4–4:2* probably goes back to the early period of Jeremiah's ministry, when the prophet addressed the inhabitants of the former northern kingdom ("Israel"), whereas 4:3–6:30 dates from the first years of the Babylonian threat (609–605 B.C.E.); see Albertz, "Jer 2–6." This analysis is rejected by Pohlmann (*Ferne Gottes*, 115ff.) and Biddle (*Redaction History*) but supported by Seybold (*Prophet Jeremiah*, 68ff.).

[532] See p. 203 above.

[533] *Deuteronomistische Redaktion* (1973), 139–229.

part from material already extant (oracles, narratives, and laments), to produce a well thought out composition. Jeremiah 13 represents a minor early composition on the destruction of the proud city of Jerusalem, dating from the time around 598/597.

Not long after this first edition, it was probably the same group of Deuteronomistic redactors who set out to assemble and edit the narrative tradition about Jeremiah (Jer 26–45*). Since this portion of the Jeremiah narratives does not have a separate superscription but does probably contain a concluding passage in Jer 45, it was probably edited from the very outset to supplement the first edition (JerD¹ + Jer 26–45* = JerD²). This is also clear from the fact that the redactors of JerD² maintained the fiction of JerD¹ that the book was written in the fourth year of Jehoiakim (25:1; cf. 45:1), even though the narrative tradition they used was set primarily in the time of Zedekiah or later (cf. Jer 27–29; 37–43). By deliberately recalling in their new conclusion the situation when Baruch "wrote all these words [meaning all the preceding material!] in a book [סֵפֶר] at the dictation of Jeremiah" (45:1), they identified their edition also, including the narratives, with the "original scroll."

As far as we can determine, the JerD² redactors used two means to link their new section with JerD¹. First, in Jer 35 they created a counterpart to the "repent and return" sermon in Jer 7 and 25 (cf. 35:15–16 with 7:3, 5, 7; 25:5). Second, they set their historico-theological reflection on Yahweh's worldwide ability to destroy and to build up at the very beginning (1:4–10) and approximately in the middle (18) of their new work.

Since JerD² was conceived somewhat later than JerD¹, the second section of the book was able to enshrine incipient hopes for salvation to come (29:10–14aα; 42:10–12). A foundation was laid for these hopes in an account of Jeremiah's call embodying new accents (1:4–10) and a reflection on God's salvific and baneful actions in history (18:1–12). By contrast, the collections of salvation oracles (30–31) and foreign nation oracles (46–51) display a salvation perspective so highly developed that they were probably not incorporated until the late exilic third edition; the same holds true, therefore, of the linking chapters 32 and 34.

The conclusions reached here deserve some explanation. With regard to the compositional function of Jer 35, its close linguistic and thematic affinities with chapters 7 and 25 have often been noted.[534] Its significance is further emphasized by a superscription (35:1) that also links with the Deuteronomistic structure of the first book (cf. 7:1; 11:1; 21:1). By shifting

---

[534] Most recently by Römer, "How Did Jeremiah Become a Convert?" 191–95. From this observation he derives a first book of Jeremiah extending from Jer 7 to 35, but this conclusion does not do justice to the terminal character of 25:1–13a*.

back to the time of Jehoiakim the symbolic action with the Rechabites following the events that took place under Zedekiah (27–29), the chapter also provides an antitypical transition to Jer 36.

A special superscription also singles out Jer 18; unlike the system of superscriptions in JerD¹ (Jer 7:1; 11:1; 21:1), it introduces only a chapter, not a section (8–10*; 11–20*; 21–23*). The Deuteronomistic reflection on history that grows out of the symbolic episode of the potter is unique (apart from 1:10) in including catchwords that recur only to the second, narrative portion of the book (26:3, 13, 19; 29:10–11; 36:3; 42:10).[535] Since all these passages are integral to JerD², it is a reasonable hypothesis that it was their authors who inserted Jer 18 into JerD¹, adapting its structure to the context (Jer 1–20, etc.). If we ignore the texts not belonging to JerD², Jer 18 stands about halfway between Jer 1 and 45. A word count shows that Jer 1–18* comprises about 45 percent of the text, 19–45* about 55 percent.

The same is true of the first section of the call chapter, Jer 1:4–10, which reaches its climax in Jeremiah's commission to destroy and to build nations and kingdoms (1:10). This text is referred to in 45:4 of the salvation oracle addressed to Baruch (45:1–5) that concludes JerD². The commission is also supported by the historical reflection in 18:7–10[536] and, rewritten from a positive perspective, in the great conditional oracle of salvation to those who stayed behind in the land (Jer 42:10–12) toward the end of JerD².[537] Since Jer 1 actually juxtaposes two calls, one to be a prophet of judgment and salvation to the nations (1:4–10), the other to be a prophet of judgment on Judah and Jerusalem (1:11–19), it is reasonable to assume that the authors of JerD² inserted their expanded vision of Jeremiah's commission before the call narrative of JerD¹ (1:11–19).

The oracle declaring that Yahweh would restore the fortunes of the Babylonian golah after seventy years (Jer 29:10–14aα) probably belongs to JerD²: first, it is presupposed by the undisputed verse 29:32; second, 29:10–11 refer to the historical reflection in 18:7–10; and third, the statement that Yahweh will set his word upright (הָקִים דָּבָר; NRSV: "fulfill his

---

[535] Cf. the characteristic expression "regret the disaster" (נחם על/אל־הרעה *nipʿal*) in 18:8, (10); 26:3, 13, 19; 42:10 and the expressions "intend to do something to someone" or "have plans for someone" (with חשב and מחשבה) in 18:8, 11; 26:3; 36:3; 29:11 (cf. 29:10). The latter appear in the same or similar form in 50:45 and 51:29, but these texts are not compositionally conspicuous enough to require assigning the foreign nation oracles to JerD².

[536] Of the six verbs in the series in Jer 1:10, five appear in 18:7, 9. There is also the expression "over nations and kingdoms," which reappears in the contextually appropriate singular in 18:7, 9.

[537] Of the six verbs in 1:10, four appear in 42:10, including the one that does not appear in 18:7, 9. The other texts that incorporate the verbs of destroying and building belong either to the third Deuteronomistic redaction (12:14–17; 31:27–28) or to later supplements (24:6).

promise") reappears in the concluding discourse of JerD², where it constitutes the rhetorical climax (44:28). It is noteworthy how abstract this promise of God's coming favor still is. The concrete promise that the Diaspora will be gathered (29:14aαb) is not found in the LXX and therefore probably represents a very late post-Deuteronomistic addition.

It would therefore be wrong to ascribe all the salvation oracles in the book of Jeremiah to JerD². The collection in Jer 30–31 contains oracles that clearly recall Deutero-Isaiah (31:7–9, 10–14; cf. 30:10–11 [not in the LXX]). This similarity presupposes that the tradents of Jeremiah came into contact with the Deutero-Isaiah circle, a connection that was probably impossible before 539. Jeremiah 30:18–22, too, speaks very concretely of rebuilding the land, a possibility only in the aftermath of Cambyses' invasion of Egypt. The final oracle against Babylon (51:58) probably dates from the period of the revolts against Darius in 522/521 (see 194–95 above). If we want to avoid the assumption that earlier precursors of these collections had already been incorporated into the book of Jeremiah, for which there is no evidence,[538] they must have been incorporated between 525 and 520. The promises in chapter 32, which is heavily Deuteronomistic, are also quite concrete. Since this chapter probably always served to link the collection of salvation oracles with the Jeremiah narratives, it too cannot have belonged to JerD². Jeremiah 33:1–13, 14–26 have long been recognized as post-Deuteronomistic continuations of the promises.[539] The concentration of superscriptions in 34:1, 8; 35:1 also indicates an unusual amount of redactional work in this section. Since 34:1–7 begins surprisingly with a salvation oracle for Zedekiah, only to follow it with an oracle of judgment on him and the aristocracy (34:8–22), the chapter probably has the function of reverting from the theme of salvation to the judgment theme of the narratives and must likewise belong to

---

[538] It is worth considering whether the collection of foreign nation oracles, minus the late oracles against Babylon, might have formed part of the book of Jeremiah at an earlier date, but without these oracles such a collection would lack a rhetorical conclusion. Apart from the oracles against Babylon, Israel appears as the beneficiary of Yahweh's acts against the nations only in Jer 46:27–28. To turn that passage into a conclusion, it would be necessary to separate the two oracles against Egypt (46:2–12, 13–25) and place the second at the end of the collection. There is no evidence in either the MT or the LXX that this was its original place. Huwyler (*Jeremia* [III.1.4], 346) believes that the Deuteronomistic book—as usually dated—"very probably contained the texts of Jeremiah and also (at least) some oracles against Babylon" (n. 61). However, this is a desperate expedient, since, on the one hand, he senses that without the oracles against Babylon the foreign nation oracles have no function in the book of Jeremiah and, on the other, he is well aware that the great majority of the Babylon oracles cannot possibly have come into being so early. But chapters 50–51 exhibit no redactional stages that would make it possible to distinguish between late and early Babylon oracles.

[539] Thiel, *Deuteronomistische Redaktion* (1981), 37.

the late exilic edition. The same is true of 43:8–13, which paves the way for the oracles against Egypt in chapter 46.

Thus we arrive at the probable content of JerD²: Jer 1:4–10 + JerD¹ (including Jer 18) + Jer 26; 27* (LXX); 28; 29:1–14aα, 15, 21–32; 35; 36; 37:1–43:7; 44; 45. I do not share Thiel's optimism about reconstructing the narrative material available to JerD². I would not go so far as Nicholson in identifying the Deuteronomistic redactors generally with the authors of the narratives,⁵⁴⁰ but it does seem to me that they left a much deeper impression on the narrative material than the few linguisitically identifiable Deuteronomistic formulas indicate. This holds true wherever the Deuteronomistic discourses appear in an uninterrupted literary context (e.g., 26:3–5, 13, 19aβ; 36:3, 7, 31). Here the Deuteronomistic redactors have reedited narratives or whole narrative sections to conform to their viewpoint. It holds true even more in texts where these redactors were largely responsible for shaping the entire setting (e.g., chapters 27 and 35). I find recognizable earlier narratives or episodes only in 26:20–23, 24; 28*; 36:9–26 and in the account of Jeremiah's imprisonment and release (37:11–40:6*), which is framed in turn by the account of Gedaliah's frustrated reform (37:3–10 + 40:7–43:7*). Baruch may have composed the latter two narratives.

The last event mentioned in JerD², Amasis's usurpation of the Egyptian throne from Pharaoh Hophra (Jer 44:29–30), took place between the years 571 and 567 B.C.E.; it is clearly mentioned as past history. The seventy years of world dominion given to Nebuchadnezzar (27:5; 29:10)—reckoning from the most probable date, his accession in 605—would not have ended until 535. Since this calculation has not been adjusted to the actual course of history, with the fall of the Babylonian Empire in 539,⁵⁴¹ JerD² must have been composed before the latter year. Thus the second edition of the Deuteronomistic book of Jeremiah probably dates from the years between 545 and 540 B.C.E.

The third edition of the book of Jeremiah (JerD³) represents a large-scale revision and extension of both parts of JerD². It was probably completed between 525 and 520, but still in the Deuteronomistic milieu.

---

540 *Preaching.*

541 Since the Babylon inscription of Esarhaddon (Riekele Borger, *Die Inschriften Asarhaddons Königs von Assyrien* [AfOB 9; Graz: self-published, 1956], 15) already mentions seventy years as a typical period of judgment, it is unlikely that this number was invented in Judah *post festum* (contra Schmid, *Buchgestalten*, 250ff.). It is too far off. However, it is worth considering whether the erroneous date given in 27:1 (cf. 28:1), which conflicts with the context and is not found in the LXX, was provided to make the seventy years agree with the real course of history.

The most important change was the inclusion of the collection of salvation oracles in Jer 30–31* and probably also the collection of foreign nation oracles in 46–51. The redactors made the supplementary nature of the salvation oracles clear in the new proem they formulated (30:1–3), in which Jeremiah receives a new commision to write in a "book [סֵפֶר] all the words" spoken to him by God (30:2)—that is, all the words after the fourth year of Jehoiakim (36:2; 25:1–3), which theoretically constituted the content of the previous book (25:13). Thus it was expressly claimed that Jeremiah had received more words from God than those hitherto considered his message, namely, having to do with the restoration of Israel's fortunes in the distant future (30:3). These were now to be published as a new section of the book. In this remarkable notion, the redactors of JerD³ indicated that in their time, besides the book of Jeremiah, there was a collection of oracles deriving in part from Jeremiah,[542] possibly used by the exiles in their worship; now, legitimated by God, this collection was recorded "officially" and included with the recognized message of the prophet. At the same time, by reshaping the conclusion of the collection (31:27–34) to reflect their own views, they gave it the stamp of theological "authenticity."

This left the Deuteronomistic redactors with the problem of where to insert the salvation oracles in the existing book of Jeremiah. They were appropriate neither to the end of the first section with its call to repentance nor to the end of the second with its message of judgment on the Egyptian golah. Only in two places did the book already suggest a turn from judgment to salvation: Jer 3:6–12, 19–4:1 with reference to the former northern kingdom, and 29:5–14aα with reference to the Babylonian golah. An interpolation in chapter 3 would have broken up the book, and so at the beginning of their new edition the redactors limited themselves to a brief hint of salvation to come (2:2aβ, 3; 3:14–15). The only place that made any sense at all was after Jer 29, even though this meant splitting up the narratives and leaving the final judgment to come later in the book. In any case, the interpolation of Jer 32 and 34, providing a transition to the narratives, restored the historical perspective.

The inclusion of the foreign nation oracles (Jer 46–51) is less easy to explain, because they have been subject to less Deuteronomistic editing and have been inserted in different places in the two recensions of the book of Jeremiah: at the end of JerD¹ (25:13a) in the Septuagint and at the end of JerD² (45:5) in the Masoretic Text. In the latter, the compositional

---

542 Jeremiah was probably responsible only for the oracles addressed to the former northern kingdom (Jer 31:2–6, 15–17, 18–20), uttered in the early days of his ministry, when the collapse of the Assyrian Empire after 640 B.C.E. appeared to set the northern kingdom free once more; cf. 3:12–13, 19–4:2. See also Albertz, "Jer 2–6."

inclusion of the extensive oracles against Babylon (50:1–51:58) and with them probably the entire collection is achieved by means of a story telling how Baruch's brother Seraiah, at Jeremiah's command, dropped a "book" (סֵפֶר) written by Jeremiah containing all these oracles into the Euphrates (51:59–64). This story links with the "book" theme of the previous redactions (25:13a; 45:1–2) and explains how another section came to be added to the book; thus it functions like the introduction to the collection of salvation oracles (30:1–3) and might well have been added by JerD³.

Thiel was unable to identify any Deuteronomistic editing of the foreign nation oracles and therefore assigned their inclusion to a post-Deuteronomistic redaction.[543] Huwyler, however, found a few traces of Deuteronomistic editing (Jer 46:25 with the interpolation of the salvation oracle 46:27–28; 48:13, 29–38a; 49:1, 2b), thus demonstrating the likelihood that the foreign nation oracles were also added under the aegis of a Deuteronomistic redaction.[544] He argued forcefully that they were positioned originally in Jer 25.[545] The assumption of multiple Deuteronomistic redactions lends even more support to this view. In this case, the clear reinterpretation of 25:1–13a by the addition of 25:9aβ, 11b–12, making it a transition to the foreign nation oracles instead of an oracle "concerning all the people of Judah" (25:1!), would be the work of JerD³. However, this explanation involves one great difficulty. The critical oracle against Babylon (50–51), which exceeds in length all the other foreign nation oracles and, unlike them, announces a turn to salvation for Israel, most probably came originally (as in the Masoretic recension) at the end, and the narrative of Seraiah's symbolic act (51:59–64 MT = 28:59–64 LXX) legitimated this concluding oracle and linked it with the narrative tradition. Originally, therefore, the foreign nation oracles probably concluded the second part of the book, containing narratives of Jeremiah. This location is also supported by the fact that otherwise two competing conclusions would have stood side by side, since at the end of the first part of the book it was further amplified by the symbolic description of the cup of wrath (25:15–38 MT; cf. 32 LXX). In addition, Schmid[546] has rightly pointed out that the end of the Jeremiah narrative (43–44) constitutes a thematic bridge to the first oracle against Egypt (46). The account of Jeremiah's symbolic action against Egypt (43:8–13), which in parallel with 51:59–64 establishes a narrative link with his proclamation of judgment on the Egyptian temples, probably also originated with JerD³.

---

[543] *Deuteronomistische Redaktion* (1973), 325–32.
[544] *Jeremia* (III.1.4), 325–32.
[545] Ibid., 332–81.
[546] *Buchgestalten*, 311–16.

If we accept the theory that the location of the foreign nation oracles in the Masoretic text is original, then at the end of their third edition the redactors were seeking to show how in their day, after so many missed opportunities for salvation, with the fall of Babylon, following the judgment on Judah and the nations Yahweh wished to offer his people Israel yet another possibility for a great future.

The shift of the oracles to judgment against the nations to precede the oracles of salvation for Israel and Judah documented in the LXX probably took place in the postexilic period (fifth or fourth century), under the influence of eschatological prophecy. It represents an attempt to make the structure of the book of Jeremiah conform at least partially to the tripartite structure of the books of Ezekiel and Isaiah: judgment on Israel, judgment on the nations, salvation for Israel. Because of the peculiar way in which the book of Jeremiah came into being, and especially the assignment of the narratives to a second section, this attempt could not produce an entirely satisfactory result. Therefore, the textual tradition represented by the MT—after it split off from the tradition represented by the LXX around the beginning of the third century—shifted the foreign nation oracles back to the end of the book, while leaving in place their bracketing texts in Jer 25:9aβ, 11b–12, 15–29, 30–38 (and adding 25:14). The result in the MT is a compromise: even before Yahweh's decision to restore the fortunes of Israel (Jer 30–31)—more precisely, as early as Nebuchadnezzar's great victory at Carchemish in the year 605 (25:1)—he had used Jeremiah to introduce the fall of the Babylonian Empire; however, this did not come to pass until long after the destruction of Jerusalem (Jer 39–40), after seventy years had passed (25:11).

The result of this redaction-historical analysis can be outlined thus:

Redactions	Date	Texts
JerD¹	ca. 550	core of 1:1–3, 1:11–25:13a* (minus 18; 24)
JerD²	545–540	1:4–10 + JerD¹ (with 18) + 26; 27* (LXX); 28; 29:1–14aα, 15, 21–32; 35; 36; 37:1–43:7; 44; 45
JerD³	525–520	1–51*; specifically 2:2aβ, 3; 3:14–15; 7:30–8:3; 12:14–17; 19:6–9, 12–13; 23:1–4, 23–32; 30:1–31:34*; 32; 34; 43:8–13; 46:2–51:64
Late Dtr additions	5th cent.	17:19–27; 24; 52?
Post-Dtr additions	4th–3d cent.	3:16–18; 9:22–23, 24–25 (23–24, 25–26); 10:1–16; 12:12aβb; 15:21; 16:14–15, 19–21; 17:5–8, 9–10, 11, 12–13; 23:5–6, 7–8, 18, 19–20, 33–40; 25:9aβ, 11b–12, 13b, 14, 15–29, 30–38; 27* MT; 29:14aβ, 16–20; 30:8–9; 33:1–13, 14–26; 46:1; 51:46

It still remains to identify the geographical and social milieu of the Deuteronomistic redactors. Thiel had demonstrated convincingly that the home of the Deuteronomistic book of Jeremiah was "undoubtedly the land of Judah."[547] This conclusion also holds for all three Deuteronomistic redactions distinguished here. They all share the deictic structure of the book, which refers repeatedly to "the land before you (Palestine)" ("in this place"), such as 7:7 (JerD^1), 29:10 (JerD^2), 32:37 (JerD^3). In addition, the conditional promises of being allowed to remain in the land (7:5–7; 25:5 JerD^1) and the emphatic warning not to emigrate to Egypt (42:7–22 JerD^2) betray the earnest desires and concerns of those who stayed behind. Even the late Babylon oracles added by JerD^3 display a clearly Palestinian perspective (51:50). Furthermore, conflicts with Canaanite cultic practices, which Stipp finds especially eloquent,[548] appear in all three redactional strata (JerD^1: 7:17–19; JerD^2: 44:15–28; JerD^3: 7:31–32; 19:6; 32:35). There are thus strong arguments for localizing the Deuteronomistic redactions of the book of Jeremiah in Palestine rather than in Babylonia, like the Deuteronomistic History.[549]

There are only two things that induce a few scholars to part company with the majority opinion and postulate a Babylonian origin, in whole[550] or in part,[551] for the Deuteronomistic book of Jeremiah. First is the assumption that, given the Babylonian origin of the Deuteronomistic History, JerD must also come from Babylon, since otherwise the many affinities between these two Deuteronomistic works would be hard to explain.[552] The other is the presence of a few texts in the book of Jeremiah that seem more or less clearly to represent the interests of the Babylonian golah (Jer 24; 40:7–44:20).[553]

The first assumption can be dealt with relatively easily. First, there were contacts by messenger and by letter—probably more often than Jer 29; 51 and Ezek 11; 18; 24 attest—between the Babylonian golah and those left behind. It is quite likely that people continued to be informed about major literary projects in both places. Second, it is important to remember that "Deuteronomism" should not be pictured as a well-defined group of disciples but as a "theological movement"[554] to which quite diverse groups with different interests could adhere. This will be confirmed with

---

547 *Deuteronomistische Redaktion* (1981), 113.
548 "Probleme," 244–45.
549 See pp. 282–84 above.
550 Nicholson, *Preaching*, 110–11; Lohfink, "Gab es" (III.2.4), 359.
551 Seitz, *Theology*, 213; Stipp, "Probleme," 250.
552 Lohfink, "Gab es," 359.
553 Nicholson, "Preaching," 110–11.
554 Albertz, *History* (II.4), 2:382.

respect to the Deuteronomistic History and the Jeremiah Deuteronomists; in fact, the assumption of different places of origin even helps explain their different emphases.

The assessment of the "golah-oriented" texts is somewhat more complex. Jeremiah 24 does in fact restrict the promises of salvation in the book of Jeremiah to the golah of 597 (14:5–7) by expanding the judgment on Zedekiah and those left behind beyond the year 587, in parallel with the judgment on the Egyptian golah—and contrary to Jeremiah's own words (cf. 32:15). However, even this text is clearly formulated from a Palestinian perspective: 14:5 describes the exiles as "those I have sent away from this place." Since the text also diverges from the Deuteronomistic redactions (especially JerD²) in substance[555] and diction, it can be understood as laying the groundwork for the idea (fully developed in the fourth century) that the entire postexilic community in Judah was descended from the golah (cf. Ezra and Nehemiah). The text was probably composed in fifth-century Judah some time after the exiles' return, but it still speaks a Deuteronomistic language. In any case, separating Jer 24 from the Deuteronomistic redaction makes its Palestinian interest more coherent.

Following Pohlmann and Seitz, Stipp labels Jer 37:3–43:7 "an account of the end of the Judeans in Palestine."[556] Relying especially on 42:12, he concludes that it originated in Babylonia.[557] Among other things, Pohlmann had ascribed this verse and the concluding section 43:1–7 to his golah-oriented redaction.[558] Now according to Thiel, 42:12 belongs to a large-scale Deuteronomistic reworking of the chapter, which includes 42:6, 9b–16, 18, 19–22.[559] Stipp's arguments to the contrary are not persuasive;[560] the either/or sermon in 42:7–18 is too clearly bound to JerD² formally (cf. 7; 22:1–5), compositionally (cf. the references in 42:10 to 1:10; 18:8; 26:3, 13), and linguistically. If 42:12 really indicated "the author's Mesopotamian perspective," as Stipp claims,[561] we should have to posit a Mesopotamian location for JerD² as well. Is it possible that the Deuteronomistic redaction of the book of Jeremiah migrated from Palestine to Babylonia with its second edition?[562]

---

[555] See below.
[556] *Jeremia*, 239ff.
[557] Ibid., 278.
[558] *Studien*, 132ff.
[559] *Deuteronomistische Redaktion* (1981), 62–66.
[560] "Probleme," 248–51.
[561] Ibid., 250.
[562] Seitz (*Theology*, 213 and passim) posits a migration of the Jeremiah tradition to Babylonia in connection with the third deportation in 582 B.C.E.

The MT of Jer 42:12 reads: "I will grant you mercy, and he will have mercy on you and restore you to your native soil."[563] The text refers to Nebuchadnezzar's returning of the Judeans addressed in the oracle at the behest of Yahweh. If this does refer to a return from exile, we would truly be dealing with a Babylonian perspective, but such a perspective would make no sense in the context, since those addressed are still in Palestine and are only considering migrating to Egypt because they fear Babylonian vengeance. It would presuppose deportation as an inexorable fate; such a deportation may have taken place in response to the murder of Gedaliah in 582 (cf. 52:30), but the narrative says nothing about it. On the contrary, the command to continue dwelling in the land and the promise in 42:10 presuppose that under the Babylonians life in Palestine had something to offer. If 42:12 were talking about exile or deportation, the context would require reversing the apodosis: "lest he deport you from your native soil." In other words, either the text refers to a restoration of ownership rights threatened by the incipient flight,[564] or—more likely—the reading of the MT is in error: the word והשיב should be interpreted not as a *hipʿil* of the root שוב, "return," but (with Aquila, the Syriac, and the Vulgate) as a form of the root ישב, "dwell."[565] The fact that the context speaks repeatedly of "dwelling in the land" (42:10, 12, albeit with ארץ) makes this interpretation all the more likely. If so, the original reading of the apodosis in 42:12 would have been: "that he may let you dwell on your own native soil."[566] Most likely, then, this verse is also consonant with the general Palestinian perspective of the Deuteronomistic redaction.

As the final argument for locating the redaction in Babylonia, we must examine Jer 43:5, which speaks of the departure for Egypt of "all the remnant of Judah." According to 43:6, this remnant included all the population elements mentioned previously: those left behind, the futigives who had returned, and those who had taken up with Gedaliah.[567] However comprehensive this emigration appears to be, the conclusions that these exegetes draw are simply not supported by the text, which neither

---

563 The LXX text, "I will grant you mercy and have mercy on you," is certainly the easier reading.

564 Rudolph (*Jeremia*, 255) suggests resettlement.

565 Thus the word should be vocalized as וְהֹשִׁיב and the preposition אל changed to על, "upon," or ב "in." The erroneous reading came about through the tendency in the late period of the formation of the book of Jeremiah to interpret the settlement of fugitive Judeans who originally had no connection with any deportation as a return from the Diaspora. The same tendency can be seen in the MT of Jer 40:12 and 43:5 (cf. LXX).

566 Duhm, *Buch Jeremia*, 322; Carroll, *Jeremiah*, 716; McKane, *Critical and Exegetical Commentary*, 2:1034–35.

567 Nicholson, *Preaching*, 110–11; Pohlmann, *Studien*, 158–59; Stipp, *Jeremia*, 267–71.

states that Judah lost all its population or that the Babylonian golah now represented the true people of God. The Babylonian golah is simply not within the purview of Jer 40–44. Quite the contrary: the emphatic condemnation of emigration to Egypt—even in JerD², toward the end of Babylonian rule—and the demand that the people continue to dwell in the land presuppose that the text was addressed to the Judeans left behind in the land, who were still tempted to emigrate to Egypt on account of the political uncertainty and economic hardship in Judah. In any case, emigration to Egypt was a Judean problem; it was irrelevant to the Babylonian golah. Only because emigration to Egypt threatened to bleed war-weary Judah to death during the exilic period did the Deuteronomistic book of Jeremiah condemn the Egyptian golah so bitterly. The description of the first emigration, after the murder of Gedaliah (41:1–7), can therefore be understood as a sweeping exaggeration on the part of the author (Baruch). His intent was to describe not "the end of the Judeans in Palestine"[568] but the total failure of Gedaliah's reform, for which he had had such high hopes.[569]

If we ask for a more precise location of the Deuteronomistic redactors in Judah, the most likely answer is the region of Mizpah and Bethel, which archaeology shows to have been largely spared the destruction of 588/587.[570] As the location of Gedaliah's capital shows, this region became the administrative center of Judah during the exilic period.

In contrast to other biblical authors, it is comparatively simple to identify the Deuteronomistic redactors of the book of Jeremiah and their social milieu, since they have given us in their book a literary memorial of the political faction to which they belonged.[571] Many of the deuteronomistically presented episodes and all the Jeremiah narratives take aim at the coalition of religious nationalists who, appealing to Zion theology (Jer 7:4), espoused the inviolability of Jerusalem and expected an imminent reversal of the capitulation of 597 (28:2–4) and, to the bitter end, miraculous deliverance from God (21:2; 37:3–11). Several such texts document the role of the Shaphanides and the reform coalition supporting them in protecting Jeremiah (26:24; 36:19), providing him with an opportunity to preach in public (36:10) and trying to have the king give his message a hearing (36:16, 25). If all three groups of Deuteronomistic redactors not only fully supported the antinationalistic and pro-Shaphanide program

---

568 Stipp.
569 The positive description of Gedaliah's reform (cf. Jer 40:12) itself argues against the Mesopotamian origin of Jer 40:7–43:7* espoused by Stipp.
570 See p. 73 above.
571 For a more detailed discussion, see Albertz, "In Searvh" [III.2.4], 11–13.

of the Jeremiah tradition but gave it their own added emphasis (cf. 21:1–10 JerD^1; 36:1–8, 27–32 JerD^2; 34 JerD^3), they at least stood close to the Shaphanide reform coalition in their theological and political attitudes. In placing a salvation oracle for Baruch at the end of the book (45:1–5), the redactors of JerD^2 obviously considered themselves the successors of that first faithful tradent of the Jeremiah tradition, who had enjoyed cordial relationships with the Shaphanides (36:10ff.) and was well known for his strongly antinationalistic attitude (43:3). Therefore, it is very likely that the Deuteronomistic redactors of the book of Jeremiah are to be found among the successors to the reforming Shaphanide officials who gained political influence in Judah under Babylonian auspices.[572] Unlike the authors of the Deuteronomistic History, who were recruited from exiled families of religious nationalists, they represented the opposition party in the late preexilic political spectrum.[573]

It seems likely that the reform coalition gained political influence under the Shaphanide Gedaliah, whom the Babylonians appointed governor. When Gedaliah was assassinated (probably in 582), some of those who had supported the reform project left for Egypt, taking Baruch and Jeremiah with them (Jer 43:6–7). However, some of the prophet's supporters returned to Judah (44:28), a turn of events that in fact contradicted Jeremiah's all-embracing prophecy of judgment on the Egyptian golah (42:17; cf. 44:12, 27). The occasion may have been Amasis's usurpation of the Egyptian throne (571–567 B.C.E.; cf. 44:29–30) and Nebuchadnezzar's concomitant attack on Eygpt,[574] which appeared to unsettle world history once more and confirm the prophecy of Jeremiah. Since the redactors of JerD^2 ascribed symbolic significance to these returnees as evidence that the prophetic word of Jeremiah had come to pass (44:28), they—bringing with them new elements of the Jeremiah tradition—may have spurred the successors of the reform coalition of Judah to begin examining and editing the Jeremiah tradition. Despite the failure of Gedaliah's reform, this later circle of Shaphanide supporters was probably of some influence on account of its pro-Babylonian stance during the whole period of Babylonian occupation. By introducing the notion that Yahweh had limited the period of Babylonian dominion to seventy years, JerD^2 gave the

---

[572] Lohfink ("Gattung," 342) had already advanced the theory that the Shaphanides had a hand in the work of the Deuteronomists. However, this is true only of the Jeremiah Deuteronomists, not the authors of the Deuteronomistic History.

[573] See Albertz, *History* (II.4), 1:231–42.

[574] See pp. 56–57 above. The deportation of Jews from Egypt to Babylon reported by Josephus (*Ant.* 10.182) in this context is historically improbable and is probably extrapolated from Jer 46:26.

reform coalition a means to interpret the collapse of the Babylonian Empire within the framework of Jeremiah's prophecy, so that they could collaborate with the Persians with equal loyalty. At the latest, JerD³ completed the turnabout to an anti-Babylonian and hence pro-Persian stance (cf. the Babylon oracles) by the time of the revolts against Darius (522/521), in which the city of Babylon played a leading role.[575] Only then did the hopes of these Judean leaders also become more focused on the golah.[576]

III.2.5.2. The First Deuteronomistic Book of Jeremiah

The structure of the first edition of the book of Jeremiah (Jer 1–25*) is relatively simple and straightforward. Following the superscription (1:1–3) and the account of Jeremiah's call to prophesy judgment on Judah and Jerusalem (1:11–19), the book is organized into four sections by four identical superscriptions: "The word that came to Jeremiah from Yahweh" (7:1;[577] 11:1; 21:1; 25:1;[578] cf. 1:2). The entire book, including its redactional sections, clearly presents itself as "the word of Yahweh" that came to Jeremiah; the concluding discourse expressly places Jeremiah in the sequence of the prophets sent repeatedly by Yahweh (25:3–4; cf. 15:1).

Structure of JerD¹								
Commission	Collection	Discourse	Collection	Discourse	Composite	Discourse	Collection	Final discourse
1:1–3	2–6	7:1–29	8–10	11:1–14	11–20*	21:1–10	21:11–22:29	25:1–13a*
1:11–19							23:9–22	

The redactors of JerD¹ worked by constructing prose discourses by God both to constitute the framework (Jer 1:11–19 and 25:1–13a*) and to subdivide the textual corpus (7:2–8:4*; 11:2–14; 21:2–10), sometimes

---

[575] See pp. 116–18 above.

[576] In JerD², the hope for return from the golah had still been expressed with great restraint (cf. Jer 29:10).

[577] The Septuagint does not contain the superscription in Jer 7:1; the chapter begins simply with the words "Hear the word of the Lord, all Judah." Here, I believe, we have a delibrate abridgement in favor of Jer 26.

[578] It is highly likely that the words מאת יהוה have dropped out in this last superscription, causing the MT to reformulate the passage as the words of the prophet. The LXX text in Jer 25 is clearly earlier.

drawing on earlier spoken words (7:4, 9–14*, 29) or narratives in the first or third person (1:11–14; 21:2–10*). Between these superscriptions and divine discourses they inserted existing oracle collections (2:4–6:30; 8:4–10:25*; 21:11–22:29; 23:9–22), some with intensive commentary; in addition, as Thiel has shown, in Jer 11–20* they created a composite of discourses, prophetic oracles, accounts of persecution, and lamentations uttered by Jeremiah, by means of which they sought to demonstrate how the attacks on the prophet made disaster inevitable.[579]

Structure of the Composite Jer 11–20					
Schema	I	II	III	[IV JerD²]	V
1. Occasion	11:1–5	14:1–9, 19–22	16:1–9	[18:1–4]	19:1–2
2. Judgment	11:6–17	14:10–18 + 15:1–9	16:10–13, 16–18	[18:5–17]	19:2–13
3. Persecution	11:18–25			[18:18]	19:14–20:6
4. Lament	12:1–6	15:10–20	17:14–18	[18:19–23]	20:7–13, 14–18
Remainder	12:7–17; 13				

In presenting the material, the redactors generally tried to follow a roughly chronological schema. At the beginning, they placed Jeremiah's early preaching to the former northern kingdom (Jer 2:4–4:2) and the announcement of the foe from the north who would bring devastation and disaster upon Judah (4:3–6:30). As far as we can determine, the former dates from the period between 627 and 609; the latter probably falls in the time between the death of Josiah (609) and the battle of Carchemish (605). Next the redactors included Jeremiah's temple sermon (7:1–29), which they dated (probably correctly) in the year of Jehoiakim's accession (609), probably because they already had before them the collection 2:4–6:30 and did want to interrupt it. Then they added a collection of Jeremiah oracles (8:4–10:25*) already much imbued with lamentation over the imminent disaster; these may represent Jeremiah's preaching during the years from 605 to 597. The redactors were well aware that real disaster was approaching: beginning in 9:15 (16), wherever the existing material gave an opportunity (10:17, 20–21) they spoke of exile as one element of the imminent catastrophe.[580] It is clear that they deliberately

---

579 *Deuteronomistische Redaktion* (1973), 287.
580 Jer 13:17, 19; 15:2; 16:13; 17:4; 20:4–6; 22:26, 28.

inserted the small collection dealing with fall of the proud city of Jerualem (Jer 13), which leads directly to the situation of the first deportation in 598/597, in their composite devoted to the persecution of Jeremiah (11–20). At its conclusion, they placed an explicit prediction of deportation to Babylon, aimed specifically at the prophet's opponents (20:1–6); here they mention the king of Babylon for the first time. In their introduction to the concluding section of the book (21:1–10), the redactors went directly to the time of the siege of the Jerusalem in 588. For this purpose, they incorporated two collections, one concerning the kings (21:11–22:29) and the other the prophets (23:9–22), first because the former extended into the period following the first deporation,[581] second because they finally wanted to make clear who, in their opinion, bore primary blame for the final downfall of Judah: the kings and the false prophets.[582]

In terms of content, the redactors of JerD[1] were primarily concerned with the reasons for God's judgment. They wanted to show their exilic contemporaries in excruciating detail why disaster had befallen Judah. To this end, they inserted question-and-answer catechisms in all four sections of their book (Jer 5:18–19; 9:11–15; [16:10–13]; 22:8–9) so as to teach even the most dense the reasons for their present misery. They agreed with the Deuteronomistic historians in seeing the primary cause to be apostasy from Yahweh and the worship of foreign gods (1:16; 5:19; 7:9, 18–19; 9:13–14 [14–15]; 11:13; 16:11; 19:4–5; 22:9; 25:6; etc.), but they differed from the latter in giving full weight to social transgressions, heeding the social indictment of Jeremiah (7:5–6, 9; 22:1–15, 17b; cf. 34:8–21 JerD[3]). Because they equated *tôrâ* with the prophetic word (11:1–14, 17 and 9:12 [13]; 16:11), reduction of the Deuteronomic law to its religious and cultic aspects was out of the question for them. Refusal to obey Yahweh's voice, Israel's fundamental sin from the day of the exodus (7:23–24; 11:4, 6–8) to the present (9:12 [13]), in the opinion of the JerD[1] redactors, involved relationship with God and relationship with neighbors in equal measure.

It was a major concern of the JerD[1] redactors to demonstrate to their contemporaries that the terrible catastrophe that had befallen them and their ancestors was not a sudden, blind stroke of fate. On the contrary,

---

581 The two oracles concerning Jehoiachin (Jer 22:24–27, 28–30), which the redactors edited extensively, probably date originally from the years 597 and 594.

582 Possibly the JerD[1] redactors did not have access to any collection of oracles from the time after 597. This lack might explain why in Jer 21:1–10 they had recourse to narrative material, which was extensively available for this period. The only oracle preserved in poetic form that clearly dates from this period is 38:22b, which is preserved within the account of Jeremiah's sufferings.

Yahweh had warned them repeatedly through his word (Jer 7:13; 11:7; 25:3; cf. 35:14 JerD²; 32:33 JerD³) and had constantly sent "his servants the prophets" to them (7:25; 25:4; cf. 26:5, 19; 44:4 JerD²) to call them to turn from evil (25:5; cf. 18:11; 35:14 JerD²) and amend their ways (7:3). They should have known better! Following the example of Jeremiah, who in his early ministry had offered the possibility of salvation to the inhabitants of the northern kingdom if they would return to Yahweh (3:12–13; 3:22–4:2) and had still hoped that a sincere new beginning could avert disaster when he first began preaching judgment on Judah (4:3, 14), the redactors even became convinced that, throughout the course of history leading up to the final catastrophe, Yahweh had offered the people of Judah and their kings real opportunities for salvation on several occasions (7:3–7; 11:6; 21:9; 22:1–5), which they could have seized if they had been willing. However, they wasted these opportunities. The road to ruin became inescapable when the Judeans conspired against Jeremiah (11:9), planned to kill him (11:19; 12:7; cf. 18:18 JerD²), and tried to divert him from his message by torture (20:1–6). In their opinion, this conduct not only reinforced God's refusal to allow Jeremiah to pray for the people (7:16–17; 11:4; 14:11–12) and turned his intercession on its head (15:10; 17:16, 18; cf. 18:20–21 JerD²) but finally even broke the covenant that Yahweh had made with Israel at the exodus (11:10). Therefore, there was a long period when God was beyond the reach of the Judeans' plaints (14:1–15:4). Only to those who fled Jerusalem during the final siege did the JerD¹ redactors, following the lead of Jeremiah, concede a chance for survival (21:9; cf. 38:2 JerD²).

However, absolving Yahweh of all blame for the disaster was not the only reason the redactors of JerD¹ stylized the catastrophe as criminal rejection of a chance for salvation. This explanation also gave them the chance to derive initial lessons for the future. If rejection of the word of God, as presented in the Torah and most recently in the prophecy of Jeremiah, had brought disaster (Jer 25:8–9), then the survivors of the catastrophe had a chance for the future only if they would finally hearken to this word. Therefore, the Deuteronomistic redactors, probably echoing their own preaching,[583] urged those who had been left behind to turn from their evil ways (25:5) and totally to amend their religious and social conduct (7:3, 5–7). Then, as Yahweh had promised in the time of Jeremiah, they would be allowed to dwell in the land that God had given their ancestors "forever and ever" (7:7; 25:5), as the redactors solemnly declared. These last words were probably spoken to counter the fear of

---

[583] See pp. 199–201 above.

further deportations and incursions by neighboring peoples, as well as the temptation to emigrate to places that offered a better chance for survival.

Unlike the Deuteronomistic historians, the Deuteronomistic redactors of Jeremiah did not base any hopes on the Jerusalem temple. On the contrary, after Jeremiah had rebuked reliance on the temple, nurtured by Zion theology, as a deception (Jer 7:4), his Deuteronomistic tradents in their temple sermon vehemently attacked the illusion that rebuilding the temple would lead to better times. In their view, better times would come only through amendment of life (7:3, 5–7). The temple cult was still in danger of concealing and legitimizing social injustice and religious abuses (7:11). Therefore, it had rightly been destroyed by Yahweh, a drastic measure to teach the Judeans a better way. In a departure from the Deuteronomistic historians, the Deuteronomistic interpreters of Jeremiah used a formula that no longer implied in any way Yahweh's presence in the Jerusalem temple, but only his right of possession.[584] Thus they virtually eliminated the sacral character of the sanctuary. Furthermore, their use of the Deuteronomic formula that described Yahweh's name as dwelling in his chosen temple to characterize the long-destroyed sanctuary at Shiloh (7:12) was a deliberate provocation directed at all those who still yearned for the Jerusalem temple.

The JerD[1] redactors reserved even harsher polemic for the Davidic monarchy. They agreed with the Deuteronomistic historians that God had rightfully visited his judgment on Josiah's son Zedekiah, the last vassal king (Jer 21:4–7; cf. 2 Kgs 25:1–7). Since his sons had been slain by Nebuchadnezzar and he himself had died in a Babylonian prison with his eyes put out, there was no future in his branch of the Davidic line. However, the two Deuteronomistic groups had totally opposite views of Jehoiachin. The Deuteronomistic historians took the release of Jehoiachin from prison as an occasion to believe (cautiously) that he might once again reign in Judah (2 Kgs 25:27–30), but the Deuteronomistic disciples of Jeremiah—once again following their master—most emphatically continued to maintain Yahweh's rejection of Jehoiachin and his family for all time to come (Jer 22:24–30). The whole land should hear: never again would one of his descendants have the chance to sit on the throne of David and reign over Judah! In the opinion of the Jeremiah tradents, this other Davidic line, descended from Josiah's son Jehoiakim, had reached a

---

[584] The formula reads הבית ... אשר נקרא־שמי עלי, "(the house) that is called by my name" (Jer 7:10, 11, 14; cf. 7:30; 32:34; 34:15 JerD[3]). It is by no means restricted to the temple itself; it can also be used of Israel (14:9) or Jeremiah (15:16); cf. Deut 28:10; Isa 63:19; Jer 25:29; Dan 9:18. Once in the Deuteronomistic History it refers to the temple (1 Kgs 8:43); see p. 294 above.

dead end (cf. 10:21; 13:18; 22:13–19). No salutary new beginning could be expected from that quarter. The new beginning for which the Deuteronomistic disciples of Jeremiah yearned must go much deeper: only an all-embracing religious and ethical renewal from below, affecting the entire population, not a limited royal reform from above, could offer a new future to stricken Judah. Thus the JerD¹ redactors in Judah clearly drew more radical conclusions from the historical catastrophe than did their historian colleagues in Babylon.

The great significance that the repudiation of Jehoiachin's line by JerD¹ must have had for the Judeans who remained behind is apparent: in the year 520, the prophet Haggai had to rescind in Yahweh's name the words of Jer 22:24–30 in order to proclaim Jehoiachin's grandson Zerubbabel pretender to the throne and focus of messianic hopes (Hag 2:20–23).

The de facto rejection of the whole Davidic royal house had a shattering effect on the book of Jeremiah, since it implied the abrogation of Nathan's promise in 2 Sam 7. JerD³ gave this change concrete form in the notion of a collective leadership ("shepherds": Jer 3:15; 23:1–4; cf. 30:21), displaying some affinities with the school of Ezekiel (Ezek 34). Alongside officials, the late Deuteronomistic addition in Jer 17:19–27 reintroduces kings into the picture of salvation (17:25), but without asserting their Davidic lineage. The introduction into the book of Jeremiah of hopes for a saving Davidic king is probably a post-Deuteronomistic development of the fourth and third centuries (22:5–6;[585] 30:8–9 [?]; 33:14–26[586]). When 23:5 goes on to say that God will raise up "for David" a "branch," the text is still careful to leave open the lineage of this new saving king. How offensive this reserve on the part of the book of Jeremiah with regard to expectations of a Davidic king was felt to be is clear from one of the latest texts in the book of Jeremiah, not found in the Septuagint, which finds it necessary to emphasize that Nathan's promise has not been revoked (33:14–26).

III.2.5.3. The Second Deuteronomistic Book of Jeremiah

The structure of the second edition of the book of Jeremiah (JerD²) is significantly more complex than that of the first:

---

[585] That the messianic promise in Jer 23:5–6 does not belong with 23:1–4 (JerD³) is clear from the fact that, although it links terminologically with 23:4 (הקמתי), the expectation of a new collective leadership ("shepherds") is transferred to an individual "branch."

[586] It is therefore unlikely that these verses refer to the conflict over Zerubbabel, as Goldmann argues (*Prophétie*, 225–26).

Structure of JerD²										
Call			Narr.	Narr.	Disc.	Narr.	Narr.	Disc.	Narr.	Disc.	Prom.
1:4–10		18	26	27–29	35	36	37–39	40:1–6	40:7–43:7	44	45
	JerD¹									
	1:1–25:13*									

Narr. = Narrative; Disc. = Discourse; Prom. = Promise

The appended narrative section is structured by a series of superscriptions ("The word that came to Jeremiah from Yahweh") followed by discourses (Jer 35:1; 40:1; 44:1). The first superscription, in 35:1, introduces a narrative that moves from events during the reign of Jehoiakim (35: Rechabites; 36: scroll) through a brief redactional bridge (37:1–2) directly to the time of the siege under Zedekiah and then the capture of Jerualem, which signaled the end of Jeremiah's sufferings (37:3–39:18). The fall of Jerusalem is followed by a second superscription, which introduces an account of the regime of Gedaliah, which had begun amidst high hopes (40:7–43:7). The third superscription (44:1) introduces an extended address to the rebellious Egyptian golah, which serves also as a final summary description of God's accomplished judgment (44:1–6, 9–10, 21–23). The first narrative sequence, which covers Jeremiah's temple sermon in the first year of Jehoiakim (26) and his conflicts with the false prophets of salvation in the time of Zedekiah, lacks a superscription. Possibly the superscription of the concluding discourse of JerD¹ (25:1) is meant to play this role. If so, then the second section of the book is also organized by superscriptions and discourses, except that a discourse and narrative sequence (25–29*; 35–39; 40–43) replaces the sequence of discourse and oracle collection. As the context would lead us to expect, the discourses are integrated more closely with the narrative: Jer 35 probably derives from what was originally a first-person narrative,[587] 40:1–6 from the end of the account of Jeremiah's sufferings. But Jer 44 is fully comparable in length and ductus to the discourses of the first section of the book.[588] The

---

[587] Cf. 35:3; 35:12, which the MT presents as a third-person report, is also presented by the LXX as a first-person account.

[588] Especially Jeremiah's temple sermon in chapter 7, with which it also has thematic affinities; cf. 7:18–19 and 44:15–25.

similarity of organizational principles—visible only when chapters 30–34 are omitted—confirms once more the assumption that the redactors of JerD² are more or less identical with the redactors of JerD¹.

In addition to the Deuteronomistic superscriptions and discourses, the introductions to the narratives, some with dates (Jer 26:1; 27:1;[589] 28:1; 36:1), further subdivide the material. They show that by and large the redactors of JerD² also followed a chronological arrangement. At the beginning, they placed the earliest account of Jeremiah's temple sermon (26), set in the year 609, and at the end, the latest accounts of events before and after the fall of Jerusalem (37–39; 40–43). However, exegetes have repeatedly noted what appears to be a disrupted chronology, which jumps back and forth between the time of Jehoiakim (26; 35–36) and the time of Zedekiah (27–29; 37ff.).[590] This observation has led some to suggest a different original sequence[591] or to eliminate certain chapters,[592] but when we recognize that the redactors deliberately used the transitional passage 37:1–2 to link the fall of Jerusalem directly with Jehoiakim's blasphemous destruction of the prophetic word of God, it is clear that they were guided by thematic and well as chronological principles, if need be at the expense of chronological continuity. Because they attached great importance to their theologically weighty explanation of God's judgment, they could not place chapters 27–29 after chapter 36, where they belong chronologically. Less explicitly but still clearly, chapter 26 and chapters 27–29, although separated by a period of fifteen years, are linked by a thematic antithesis: the true prophets Jeremiah and Uriah are contrasted with the false prophets Hananiah, Ahab, and Zedekiah in Jerusalem and Babylonia. This antithesis gives the JerD² redactors an opportunity to distinguish their true prophecy, based on the preaching of Jeremiah, from false promises of deliverance (contrast 29:5–7, 8–14aα and 29:21–23, 28). Then, in 35:1, the redactors returned explicitly to the time of Jehoiakim, clearly intending to use the first ([25]; 26–29) and second (35–39) narrative sections to traverse the period between Jehoiakim and Zedekiah twice, the second time contrasting positive and negative protagonists as antitypes (Rechabites–Jehoiakim). If we recognize that the redactors of JerD² were concerned to distinguish the prophecy of Jeremiah from false prophecy of

---

[589] The clearly erroneous dating of Jer 27 in the year of Jehoiakim's accession (cf. 28:1) was probably occasioned by a scribal emendation that sought to reconcile the seventy years of Babylonian rule predicted in Jer 29:10 with historical reality (609–539 B.C.E.); see Schmid, *Buchgestalten*, 224–25. The total absence of an introduction in the LXX can hardly represent the original form of the text.

[590] Duhm, *Buch Jeremia*, xv, 219–20.

[591] Rudolph, *Jeremia*, xvi.

[592] Wanke, *Jeremia*, 17.

salvation, to describe right and wrong responses to this prophecy, and thus to display the critical cause of the catastrophe, the temporal sequence of the narratives, which seems so strange at first glance, makes good sense.

We have already discussed how the JerD² readactors used Jer 1:4–10 and 18 to link their work with their earlier edition of the book of Jeremiah.[593] By placing the account of Jeremiah's call at the beginning of their new edition, they introduced the theme that Jeremiah had been a true prophet who fulfilled the criteria laid down by the Deuteronomic law concerning prophets (cf. the inclusion of Deut 18:18b in Jer 1:7bβ, 10). Thus they created a counterpart to Jer 26, the initial text of the narrative section, which had the same purpose (cf. the allusion to Deut 18:20 in Jer 26:9, 16). At the same time, they constructed a new framework for their book: the call of Jeremiah at the beginning, with its promise of God's presence and support, corresponds to the promise given to Jeremiah's faithful companion Baruch at the end (45:1–5).[594] Thus they introduced a new perspective on Jeremiah as the agent of God's universal work of judgment and salvation; with the help of this perspective, they introduced a new structure undergirding the entire book, with the newly included chapter 18 as a centerpost (1:10; 18:7–11; 42:10; 45:4; cf. 29:11; 26:3, 13, 19; 36:3, 7).

Thematically, the JerD² redactors followed JerD¹ but continued to develop the options laid out there. They emphasized once more that the catastrophe of the exile had been brought about by refusal to obey the prophetic or directive word of Yahweh (Jer 35:15–16; 44:4–5) and especially by idolatry (44:3, 5, 21, 23). They used an original arrangement of the narrative tradition to demonstrate "historically" that Judah had some chance for survival (26:3; 27:11; 35:15; 36:3, 7) only as long as Jeremiah was allowed to preach his message of repentance and judgment freely (26; 27–28; 29:24–32), safe from attacks of the people and their spiritual leaders. However, when their notorious refusal to obey God's word (35:15–16) reached the point that King Jehoiakim did not shrink from frivolously burning the scroll embodying the prophetic word of God (36:21–31), the road to ruin was inescapable (37–39). Afterwards Jeremiah, even if left alone, could point out only slim possibilities for limiting the catastrophe a bit (38:2, 17, 20), but even these were thwarted by disbelieving disregard of his words and cold-blooded violence to his person.

---

[593] See pp. 315–16 above.
[594] They also added another piece to the framework: with the catchword שקד, "watch," in Jer 44:27, the concluding judgment discourse refers back to Jeremiah's call vision in 1:11–12.

The redactors of JerD¹ had still been primarily concerned to follow the lead of Jeremiah (Jer 5:1–6; 6:13, 27–30) in pointing out the collective guilt of all the people (7:29) and the danger confronting the prophet at the hands of all the leadership (1:18b; 11:9). The JerD² redactors found themselves induced by the narrative tradition they incorporated to distinguish those individuals and groups whose guilt was greater from those whose guilt was less. Not all had been equally to blame for the fall of Jerusalem! There had been individual officials such as Ahikam ben Shaphan and Ebed-melech the Cushite who had protected Jeremiah when his life was in danger (26:24; 38:7–13); there had been groups of officials (26:10–16), especially the Shaphanides (36:10–20), who defended Jeremiah against attacks, supported his message, and opened themselves to hear the word of God he proclaimed. The scribe Baruch ben Neiriah had even placed himself in the service of the prophetic message, at the risk of his own life (Jer 36). Those who bore the most guilt for the disaster were the kings Jehoiakim and Zedekiah, the officials (36:24–26) and military officers (38:1–6) in the thrall of religious nationalism, and high-ranking priests and prophets of salvation such as Pashhur, Zephaniah, and Hananiah (20:1–6; 29:24–29; 38; cf. 26:8, 11, 16). By formulating new words of judgment on those who rejected the prophetic word of God (29:32; 36:31) and words of salvation for Jeremiah's supporters (39:15–28; 45:1–5), they were clearly taking a partisan position in the exilic conflict over who had been to blame. In their opinion, the position of religious nationalism had been totally compromised. For the incipient new beginning, the only people who could legitimately claim political and intellectual leadership were those whose ancestors had been on the side of Jeremiah, such as Baruch and the Shaphanides, or those who were now prepared to obey the prophet word of God. In JerD², the attempt of JerD¹ to come to overcome the past became a struggle for legitimate leadership in the future.

The JerD² redactors also adopted the theology of missed opportunities for salvation (Jer 26:3; 35:14–16; 36:3, 7) but extended it explicitly into the exilic present: in 35:15, they took up the conditional promise of JerD¹ that the people might continue to dwell in the land (7:3, 7; 25:5) and in 42:10–12 expanded it into a solemn assurance of God's favor to those left behind. Once Yahweh had imposed judgment on Judah and Jerusalem—they had Jeremiah declare—he stood ready to turn completely around and bring salvation (42:10); he would see that they received mercy from the Babylonian king and live in their native land (42:11–12). This promise depended upon a single condition: they must continue to dwell in the land and not let some kind of fear persuade them to emigrate to Egypt. The specific situation to which the Deuteronomistic redactors addressed this promise was, as the narrative context indicates, fear of Babylonian vengeance for the murder of Gedaliah. However, there were other aspects to the problem, as we see from the mention of war and starvation as motives for emigration (42:14). For the redactors, the promise went beyond the immediate situation and was intended to counter an ongoing depopulation of the land. However, even this great opportunity that Yahweh had offered those who remained behind largely went begging, since a substantial group, even if not all, of those who had been relatively close to Jeremiah and Baruch and had supported the reforms of Gedaliah nevertheless decided to emigrate. This group not only disregarded God's offer of salvation but believed that in Egypt they could simply continue the old preexilic syncretism (44:15–18). Therefore, as the JerD² redactors emphatically declared, they fell victim once for all to God's judgment. The Egyptian golah could have nothing to do with a new beginning in Judah; it served as a horrible example of obduracy, from which the Deuteronomistic reformers sought to distance themselves as much as possible.

The Babylonian golah was another matter entirely. These exiles had not left the land of their own free will but had been driven out before Yahweh. Jeremiah's letter to them had already suggested the prospect of a possible turn for the better, albeit only in the distant future (Jer 29:5–7). Thus the JerD² redactors, possibly because of disappointing experiences with their own clientele in Judah, no longer set their hopes exclusively on a new beginning in the land but included the return of the Babylonian exiles. In the light of the political developments that appeared to be taking place in distant Persia, they expanded Jeremiah's letter to the exiles, formulating for them a new albeit still very abstract promise (29:10–14aα): after seventy years of Babylonian rule, Yahweh would visit the exiles, fulfill his promise to them, bring them back home, and allow them to find him if they would seek him with all their heart. This promise, too, was conditional; just like those who had been left behind, the exiles were called upon to grasp the great opportunity God was offering them. In the context of the letter, the demand that they turn to Yahweh, formulated by the Deuteronomistic redactors of Jeremiah as an echo of the Shema (Deut 6:5), naturally implied rejection of the false expectations associated with religious nationalism (Jer 29:7–8, 21ff.), against which Jeremiah had contended earlier.[595]

Roughly in the middle of their book, following Jeremiah's parable of the potter (Jer 18:1–6), the JerD² redactors reflected the profound change from a time of judgment to a time of salvation, which they foretold for those left behind as well as for the Babylonian exile:

---

[595] There is explicit evidence for this demand: a clearly Deuteronomistic text (Jer 29:32b) excludes Shemaiah of Nehelam, a spokesman for the nationalistic party within the Babylonian golah, along with his descendants from the coming salvation of the people.

Jer 18:7 At one moment I may declare concerning a nation or kingdom, that I will pluck up and break down and destroy it,
8 but if that nation, concerning which I have spoken, turns from its evil, I will change my mind about the disaster that I intended to bring on it.
9 And at another moment I may declare concerning a nation or a kingdom that I will build and plant it,
10 but if it does evil in my sight, not listening to my voice, then I will change my mind about the good that I had intended to do it.

In their first edition of the book of Jeremiah, the Deuteronomistic redactors had still believed on the basis of their Deuteronomistic theology that, just as Yahweh had reacted to Israel's apostasy with judgment, so he would respond to Israel's return with salvation (Jer 7:3, 7; 25:5; cf. 35:15). Now the drastic change in the political world order that was becoming apparent, coupled with many past disappointments, caused the redactors of the second edition to expand their idea of how Yahweh acted in history. There were different periods in the history of a nation or empire; sometimes God envisioned disaster for it, sometimes salvation; sometimes God wished to break it down, sometimes to plant it. Why this was so ultimately lay hidden in God's freedom. The intended disaster was often provoked by human wickedness, whereas salvation remained totally unfathomable. However, Yahweh was not simply blind fate; he announced his intentions in advance, for good or ill, and was prepared to revise them on the basis of human response. If the message of judgment caused people to turn from their wickedness, he would change his mind (נחם nip^cal) about the intended disaster; if they reacted to the message of salvation with heedless disobedience, then he would change his mind about the foretold salvation (18:8, 10). In other words, Yahweh's actions in history were determined by a tacit pedagogical purpose; in both good and ill, he intended people to turn from their wickedness. Therefore the response of a people to God's message of judgment or salvation was crucial: the actual aim of Jeremiah's message of judgment had been the return of the Judeans to Yahweh so that he could change his mind about the prospective disaster (26:3, 13, 19; 36:3). But this opportunity for salvation, always present even in periods of judgment, was repeatedly lost. Nevertheless—the JerD^2 redactors now realized—this failure did not spell the end to Yahweh's pedagogy. Even after the imposition of judgment, of his own free will he could regret the disaster and, for example, announce salvation for the Judeans left behind (42:10), but he could also announce for the more distant future his now fully realized salvific purpose, for example, for the Babylonian golah (29:10–11). Thus for both groups the end of the era of judgment and the coming of an era of salvation was rung in. It was appalling that one important group among those left behind in Judah had basely rejected the new offer of salvation. It was therefore all the more important that the rest of those in Judah and the Babylonian golah should seize the offer.

All that could be descried from the history of Israel still held true, the JerD² redactors realized, and on a universal scale. They had learned from Jeremiah that Yahweh also governs the fates of the other nations. Even though they probably did not include the foreign nation oracles in their book, they must have been familiar with them, at least in part. Moreover, the Jeremiah tradition that they incorporated involved the surrounding nations repeatedly in the prophet's preaching and ministry (1:14–15; 4:2, 7; 10:25; 27–28).

Finally, their thought was shaped by the startling realization that even for the Babylonian Empire, to which Yahweh had given world dominion (27:5–6), the era of tearing down was coming within the foreseeable future (29:10). Thus the JerD² redactors grounded their new theology of history in the call of Jeremiah (1:4–10). In their view, Yahweh had destined Jeremiah to be a "prophet to the nations" even in his mother's womb (1:5), to play a decisive role in realizing God's governance of the world. He was to proclaim to the nations God's intentions toward them, for good or ill, to give them a chance to avert the ill and not to forfeit the good. Not only was he deeply involved in God's destruction and building of kingdoms (1:10), but he also shared in making known the pedagogical and moral purpose of Yahweh's actions in history. In the eyes of the Deuteronomistic redactors, this was the crucial role Jeremiah played in the turbulent phase of Near Eastern history that they and their ancestors had just experienced.

III.2.5.4. The Third Deuteronomistic Book of Jeremiah

The third Deuteronomistic redaction of the book of Jeremiah (JerD³), finally, was largely responsible for the complex structure of the book as we have it today:

Structure of JerD³					
	Salvation oracles	Narrative salvation discourse	Narrative transition		Foreign nation oracles
JerD²	30–31*	32	34	JerD²	46–51*
Jer 1–45					

We have already pointed out that the second edition of the book of Jeremiah, comprising oracles of judgment (Jer 1–25*) and narratives

(26–45), had no really appropriate place for an extensive collection of salvation oracles or for a collection of foreign nation oracles. Therefore the JerD³ redactors decided to interpolate their collection of salvation oracles immediately following to the passage where their predecessors had referred most clearly to a future reversal of fortunes, 29:10–14aα, albeit at the cost of interrupting the narrative sequence. Since inserting the extensive salvation oracles into the letter itself would have separated the narrative from the sending of the letter and its consequences, the only alternative was to insert the collection after Jer 29. However, since the redactors wanted place their new book of salvation oracles as close as possible to the letter on the same theme and present them in parallel, they had to dispense with the "discourse–collection" schema established in JerD¹. Instead, they placed their discourse commenting on the oracles after the collection (Jer 32) by expanding the account of Jeremiah's optimistic purchase of a field, a symbolic act he had performed in the year before Jerusalem's fall, appending to it an extensive reflection on why there could be be a change from God's judgment to God's salvation (32:15–44).[596] By means of a lengthy episode from the same period describing a withdrawn emancipation of slaves (Jer 34), the JerD³ redactors returned to the narrative sequence and its historical perspective.[597] This organizational schema, which departs from the normal structure of the book, was imposed by the context; it probably led the redactors to produce the unusual concentration of superscriptions within this section (30:1; 32:1; 34:1, 8). Finally, they added an interpretive framework to the collection of salvation oracles (30:1–3; 31:1, 27–34).

To link the greatly expanded message of salvation with the first section of the book, the redactors drew on the language of Jeremiah's call (Jer 1:10, 11–12), promising that soon Yahweh's work of building would replace his work of destruction in history (31:27–28). Thus they explicitly continued the theology of history of JerD². At the same time, they also added a brief promise for Zion (3:14–15) where the text already spoke of salvation for the former northern kingdom.

Despite the complexity of these operations, the JerD³ redactors' placement of the oracles of salvation in the middle of the book was more than

---

[596] Besides many thematic ties (cf. Jer 31:31, 33 with 32:39–40), the JerD³ redactors established a compositional linkage (שׁוּב שְׁבוּת, "restore the fortunes") between the concluding words of the discourse (32:44) and the introduction to the collection (30:3). Jer 33 is a post-Deuteronomistic expansion, the second part of which (33:14–26) is not even present in the Septuagint.

[597] The theme of covenant (Jer 34:4ff.) and covenant transgression (34:18) also establishes a thematic linkage with 31:31–33 and 32:40.

a makeshift. The theme of the missed opportunity for salvation already permeated the earlier editions (7:1–15; 25:3–7; 42:7–22) and was underscored by the redactors through their insertion of chapter 34. If we take this aspect into account, the placement of the salvation oracles makes very good sense within their Deuteronomistic theology: the ominous historical perspective of the rest of the book was intended as a serious warning this time not to squander the geat opportunity for salvation being offered by God.

By adding the collection of foreign nation oracles at the end of the book, culminating in the final dethronement and destruction of Babylon (Jer 50–51), the JerD³ redactors presumably created another favorable prospect for the deliverance of Israel and Jerusalem (46:27–28; 50:4–5, 17–20, 33–34; 51:34–37), to take place after Yahweh's judgment on his people and their neighbors. They used Seraiah's symbolic act against Babylon (51:59–64) to link the collection with the narratives of the second part of the book, thus giving their edition a conclusion somewhat analogous to that of JerD² (Jer 45). They also used Jeremiah's symbolic act against the gods of Egypt (43:8–13) to introduce the oracles against Egypt at the beginning of the foreign nation oracles (46:2–12, 13–24). Then, before all the oracles of judgment, they inserted in 2:2aβ, 3 an oracle of salvation to Israel; with its promise of punishment for all who self-righteously exploited her (2:3), they marked at the beginning of the book the trajectory that would lead to the judgment on Babylon at its end (50:7; 51:64).[598] In the first part of the book (12:14–17), finally, they included Judah's neighbors in the Deuteronomistic theology of history of their predecessors.[599] The extent to which the redactors edited the collection of foreign nation oracles itself awaits further study.

Within Jer 46–49, Huwyler assigns Jer 46:25, 27–28; 48:13, 29–38a; 49:1, 2b to a Deuteronomistic redaction.[600] A similar study of 50–51 has yet to be made (cf., for example, 50:2, 4–7, 44–46; 51:24, 27–29, 44, 47, 52). It is still unclear how to assess the peculiar superscription in 46:1; 47:1; and 49:34: "What came to Jeremiah as a Yahweh word concerning...," found in similar form in 14:1. Is it a mark of Deuteronomistic redaction,

---

[598] The two verbs of Jer 2:3, אכל, "eat," and אשם, "be guilty," occur also in 50:7, the latter only in these two places in the book of Jeremiah. For אכל, see 50:17; 51:34; also 5:17; 8:16; 10:25; 12:9; 30:16. The expression רעה תבא עליהם, "disaster comes upon them," in 2:3 reappears in 51:60, 64. These previously overlooked compositional links make the assignment of 2:2aβ, 3 to a pre-Deuteronomistic redaction, as proposed by Odashima (*Heilsworte*, 139ff.), very unlikely.

[599] The remarkable notion in Jer 34:1, 17 that "all the kingdoms of the earth" took part in the siege of Jerusalem is connected with the universal perspective of the JerD³ redactors.

[600] *Jeremia* (III.1.4), 325–32.

since it recalls the usual Deuteronomistic superscription "The word that came to Jeremiah from Yahweh," or is it a result of the (second) shift of the foreign nation oracles mentioned in 25:13 to the end of the book, so that the relative clause in 25:13bβ came to stand independently?[601]

Thus the third Deuteronomistic edition of the book of Jeremiah sketches a mighty drama involving Yahweh and his people over a period of some one hundred years, including not only Israel's neighbors but also the great powers Assyria, Egypt, and Babylonia. This drama proceeded in several cycles of judgment and salvation. It began, at the time of Jeremiah's call in 627, with the fall of the Assyrian Empire, which appeared to mean the end of judgment and the beginning of a new era of salvation for the former northern kingdom (Jer 2:4–4:2). However, this opportunity was squandered (4:10). The drama continued with the rise of the Babylonian Empire (4:3–28:17), to which not only Judah—despite Yahweh's continual warnings—but also Egypt and the surrounding nations fell vicitim (46–49). Yahweh entrusted Nebuchadnezzar with world dominion (27:5–6) and appointed him as his instrument of judgment. The drama took a crucial turn when Jeremiah announced that the rule of Babylon would be limited to seventy years (29:10–11). Again there was a great opportunity for salvation, this time for all groups, Israelites as well as Judeans, both the exiles and those left behind (29–32)—but again this opportunity was squandered (34–36). Transgression of the Torah and base contempt for the prophetic word of God would lead of necessity to total destruction (37–39). After this dramatic climax of judgment, the Judeans left behind were granted a more limited possibility of salvation under Gedaliah and even after his assassination (40–42), but this opportunity, too, was largely squandered. A major portion of the population left for Egypt, remained obdurate, and thus vanished from the stage (43–44). However, this did not prevent Yahweh from demonstrating his power over history against the neighboring nations (46–49) and arousing the "kings of Media" to destroy the Babylonian Empire (50:2, 11–13), inflicting retribution for all its wickedness, violence, and greed. Thus he would soon usher in the great change of fortunes predicted for his entire people.

Down to this still-unrealized proclamation of salvation, JerD³ is primarly an ambitious theological interpretation of history. It is a lesson concerning Yahweh's faithful righteousness and Israel's notorious perfidy, demonstrating how Israel repeatedly squandered the opportunities for salvation given by God. Its object is to instruct Israel not to squander

---

[601] Huwyler, *Jeremia*, 371ff.

once more the great new opportunity announced by the victories of Darius over the Babylonian rebels (522/521).

Central as the new message of salvation was to the JerD³ redactors, they considered it equally important to identify clearly the causes of the disaster. In the discourse they composed (32:16–35), they reviewed once more the whole history of Israel's guilt, from exodus to exile. They listed in minute detail all the religious and cultic lapses of the nation, the astral cult (32:29), the worship of idols and images in the temple (32:34), and the Moloch offerings in Topheth (32:35). If it is true that they reworked earlier discourses to frame a detailed indictment and threaten a new judgment (7:30–8:3; 19:6–9, 12–13), their concern was to name every possible sin that Israel must put away if the new beginning was to succeed.

However, precisely because the Deuteronomistic redactors were concerned to keep alive the history of Israel's guilt and the ensuing catastrophe, they had to explain to their disheartened addressees how, despite all their misery, Yahweh could bring about a change of fortunes. To this end, they staged a dialogue between Jeremiah and God, in which the disheartened prophet presented his complaint, asking how God had been able to speak of salvation in the midst of catastrophe, as had happened when Jeremiah bought the field in Anathoth (32:6–15). The answer given by the Deuteronomistic theologians was clear: the basis for the change of fortunes was neither Israel nor Jerusalem. Both had provoked Yahweh to anger from the very beginning (32:30, 31). The basis was solely Yahweh, the mighty Creator of the world (32:17) and the God of all flesh (32:27), for whom "nothing is too hard" (32:17, 27). True, his eyes are open to all the ways of mortals, and he rewards them according to their deeds, but he nevertheless shows mercy to the thousandth generation (32:18–19). In the end, therefore, it was only Yahweh's extravagant mercy, spoken of already in the Decalogue (Deut 5:9–10), that caused this God to turn and show Israel lovingkindess once more. It was not some promise associated with the monarchy or the temple, as the authors of the Deuteronomistic History believed. It is therefore no accident that those two institutions, considered indispensable for the future by the Deuteronomistic historians, in the eyes of the JerD³ redactors played practically no role in the new beginning for Israel.[602]

Even though the JerD³ redactors incorporated and affirmed in their work the late exilic promises of the return of the golah, population increase, resettlement of lost territories, rebuilding of cities, and a

---

[602] The temple is scarcely mentioned at all (50:28 [not in the LXX]); 51:11), the monarchy only in the context of replacing the Davidides (30:21) and pluralistic diversification (3:14–15; 23:1–4).

prosperous and secure life (Jer 31:27; 32:37–44), they focused their expectations on a radical renewal of Israel's relationship with God. Here, too, they emphasized the discontinuity on the human plane. Even after Israel had broken the covenant between Yahweh and his people (31:32), as the JerD¹ redactors had already noted (11:10; 22:9), Yahweh's forgiveness (31:34) would establish a new or everlasting covenant (31:31, 33; 32:40), which would finally bring to fruition the intimate relationship between Yahweh and his people envisioned at the time of the exodus from Egypt (31:33; 32:38; cf. 7:23; 11:4). The new covenant would establish Israel's relationship with God on a totally new footing: now Yahweh would no longer put his *tôrâ* before the Israelites (נתן לפני: 9:12 [13]; 26:4; 44:10) but put it within them (נתן ב) and write it on their hearts (31:33; cf. 32:39, 40). The commanding voice of God would no longer come to them from without; it would become so central to their very being that they could no longer turn away from Yahweh. In the eyes of Jeremiah's Deuteronomistic disciples, the aim of Yahweh's great historical pedagogy, as presented by Jeremiah, was to internalize the *tôrâ* for each individual Israelite. Their belief that their own work of theological instruction would soon be superfluous (31:34) reveals the utopian nature of their expectations: even the burden of issuing new editions of the book of Jeremiah, which they had borne through thirty long years, would finally be lifted from them.[603]

It is interesting that the JerD³ redactors could even involve the Gentile nations in the learning process that was the object of Yahweh's historical pedagogy. On the one hand, by punishing Babylon, God made it clear that all who believed they could exploit Israel with impunity on account of its sin (Jer 2:2aβ, 3; 30:16–17; 50:6–7) would not escape. On the other, Yahweh would grant to Israel's evil neighbors (12:14), who had misappropriated his heritage during his execution of judgment on Israel (12:7–10), a salutary future in the midst of his people, after plucking them up and bringing them back, if they would learn the ways of Israel's religion and be converted to him (12:16–17). The JerD³ redactors had made the breakthrough to the realization that Yahweh, as Creator of the universe and God of all flesh (32:17, 27), used ethical criteria to judge and treat all human beings equally (32:19). Unlike their colleagues the Deuteronomistic

---

[603] The theory that the book of Jeremiah went through three Deuteronomistic redactions makes it possible to posit an ongoing development of Deuteronomistic theology within the book. Thus it also presents a solution to the problem illustrated by Schmid's decision not to assign Jer 31:31–34 to a Deuteronomistic redaction despite its clearly Deuteronomistic language (*Buchgestalten*, 302–4), on the grounds that its conceptual departures from other Deuteronomistic sections of the book make it anti-Deuteronomistic.

historians, who opted for strict separation, they therefore espoused a cautious missionary opening of Israel's religion.

Building on the heritage of the prophets and the interests of Judah during the exile, in the course of three editions the Deuteronomistic Jeremiah book evolved a Deuteronomistic theology that—despite many similarities—exhibits a profile clearly distinct from the theology of the Deuteronomistic History.

III.2.6. THE BOOK OF EZEKIEL

Becker, Joachim. "Erwägungen zur ezechielischen Frage," in *Künder des Wortes: Beiträge zur Theologie des Wortes* (ed. L. Ruppert, P. Weimar, and E. Zenger; Würzburg: Echter, 1982), 137–49. **Collins,** Terence. *The Mantle of Elijah: The Redaction Criticism of the Prophetical Books* (BibSem 20; Sheffield: JSOT Press, 1993), 88–103. **Davis,** Ellen F. *Swallowing the Scroll: Textuality and the Dynamics of Discourse in Ezekiel's Prophecy* (JSOTSup 78; Sheffield: Almond, 1989). **Ebach,** Jürgen. "Kritik und Utopie: Unterschungen zum Verhältnis von Volk und Herrscher im Verfassungsregister des Ezechiel (Kap. 40–48)" (Diss., Hamburg, 1972). **Feist,** Udo. *Ezechiel: Das literarische Problem des Buches forschungsgeschichtlich betrachtet* (BWANT 138; Stuttgart: Kohlhammer, 1995). **Garscha,** Jörg. *Studien zum Ezechielbuch: Eine redaktionsgeschichtliche Untersuchung von 1–39* (EHS.T 23; Bern: Lang, 1974). **Greenberg,** Moshe. "The Design and Themes of Ezekiel's Program of Restoration," *Int* 38 (1984): 181–204. **Greenberg.** *Ezekiel 1–20: A New Translation with Introduction and Commentary* (AB 22; New York: Doubleday, 1983). **Hölscher,** Gustav. *Hezekiel: Der Dichter und das Buch* (BZAW 39; Giessen: Töpelmann, 1924). **Hossfeld,** Frank Lothar. "Ezechiel und die deuteronomisch-deuteronomistische Bewegung," in *Jeremia und die "deuteronomistische Bewegung"* (ed. W. Gross; BBB 98; Weinheim: Athenäum Beltz, 1995), 271–95. **Hossfeld.** *Untersuchungen zur Komposition des Ezechielbuches* (FB 20; Würzburg: Echter, 1977). **Krüger,** Thomas. *Geschichts-konzepte im Ezechielbuch* (BZAW 180; Berlin: de Gruyter, 1989). **Lang,** Bernhard. *Ezechiel: Der Prophet und sein Buch* (EdF 153; Darmstadt: Wissenschaftliche Buchgesellschaft, 1981). **Lang.** *Kein Aufstand in Jerusalem: Die Politik des Propheten Ezechiel* (SBB; Stuttgart: Katholisches Bibelwerk, 1978; 2d. ed., 1981). **Lust,** Johan, ed., *Ezekiel and His Book: Textual and Literary Criticism and Their Interrelation* (BETL 74; Leuven: Leuven University Press, 1986). **Macholz,** Georg Christian. "Noch einmal: Planungen für den Wiederaufbau nach der Katastrophe von 587: Erwägungen zum Schlussteil des sog. 'Verfassungsentwurfs' des Hesekiel," *VT* 19 (1969): 322–52. **Odell,** Margaret S. "You Are What You Eat: Ezekiel and the Scroll," *JBL* 117 (1998): 229–48. **Pohlmann,** Karl-Friedrich. *Das Buch des Propheten Hesekiel (Ezechiel)* (2 vols.; ATD 22; Göttingen: Vandenhoeck & Ruprecht, 1996–2001). **Pohlmann.** *Ezechielstudien: Zur Redaktionsgeschichte des Buches und zur Frage nach den ältesten Texten* (BZAW 202; Berlin: de Gruyter, 1992). **Schulz,** Hermann. *Das Todesrecht im Alten Testament: Studien zur Rechtsform der Mot-Jumat-Sätze* (BZAW 114; Berlin: Töpelmann, 1969). **Wilson,** Robert R. "An Interpretation of Ezekiel's Dumbness," *VT* 22 (1972): 91–104. **Zimmerli,** Walter.

Ezekiel: A Commentary on the Book of the Prophet Ezekiel (trans. R. E. Clements; 2 vols.; Hermeneia; Philadelphia: Fortress, 1979–83). **Zimmerli.** "Das Phänomen der 'Fortschreibung' im Buche Ezechiel," in *Prophecy: Essays Presented to Georg Fohrer on His Sixty-Fifth Birthday* (ed. J. A. Emerton; BZAW 150; Berlin: de Gruyter, 1980), 174–91. **Zimmerli.** "Planungen für den Wiederaufbau nach der Katastrophe von 587," *VT* 18 (1968): 229–55.

Although it came into being only slightly later than the Deuteronomistic Jeremiah books, the Ezekiel book has a very different literary appearance. True, this second great prophetic book of the exilic period begins with a call narrative (Ezek 1–3); true, here too we find—even more consistently realized—the same rough division into three sections: "oracles of judgment against Israel" (4–24), "oracles of judgment against the nations" (25–32), and "oracles of salvation for Israel" (33–48) that the book of Jeremiah also exhibited now and then in the course of its transmission (cf. the LXX). However, it gives the distinct impression of being a much more unified composition. Apart from a few poems (17:1–10) and songs (19:1–14; 24:3b–5; 31:1–9; etc.), the entire book is composed in elevated, slightly rhythmic prose. It does not represent a collection of prophetic oracles but a sequence of discourses, often lengthy, addressed to the prophet by God, often introduced by the stereotyped salutation בֶּן־אָדָם, "son of man, mortal." There is no riotous juxtaposition of first-person narratives, third-person narratives, and prophetic oracles as in the book of Jeremiah. The entire book of Ezekiel is stylized as a first-person account by the prophet, who describes his visions (1–3; 8–11; 37; 40ff.) as well as his messages and commissions from God. Even Ezekiel's symbolic actions are recounted only rarely (12:7; 24:18–19); usually they are presented as commissions from God (4–5; 12:3–6, 18–20; 21:23–32; 24:15–17; 37:15–17), thus maintaining the book's theocentric perspective. This literary form bespeaks a strong and consistent creative will. There is also a chronological system that embraces not just portions but the entire book, beginning with Ezekiel's inaugural vision in the year 594 (1:2), through the siege (589: 24:1) and conquest of Jerusalem (586: 33:21), and ending with the prophet's final vision (574: 40:1).[604] Finally, the book of Ezekiel speaks a

---

[604] The years are counted from King Jehoiachin's exile (Ezek 1:2) or "our exile" (33:21; 40:1) in the year 598/597; as Kutsch has shown (*Die chronologischen Daten* [II.2.2.2], 33–71), the year 598 is included in the count. The only exception is 24:1, which identifies the first year of the siege of Jerusalem by the regnal year of King Zedekiah, as in 2 Kgs 25:1. Only the emended oracle concerning Tyre (Ezek 29:17–21), which was not formulated until after the siege of the city was broken in 572, departs from the clear chronological sequence, for reasons of content. See the chronological statements in 1:1, (2); 3:16; 8:1; 20:1; 24:1; 26:1; 29:1, 17; 30:20; 31:1; 32:1, 17; 33:21; 40:1. On 1:1, see p. 354 below.

very different language than JerD; Deuteronomistic expressions appear here and there, but only in relatively late salvation oracles.[605] Instead, the book exhibits clear affinities with Priestly language (P, especially the Holiness Code in Lev 17–26), which are concentrated in a few texts (3:17–21; 14:1–11; 18; 22:1–16; 33:1–20; 40ff.)

All these observations argue that the Ezekiel book came into being in a different way and in a different milieu than the Jeremiah books. The evidence suggests written composition from the outset and a prophetic/priestly origin.

Until the beginning of the twentieth century, the stylistic features of the Ezekiel book led most exegetes to consider it a single whole and to ascribe it either to the prophet himself or to a later pseudepigraphist.[606] Critical analysis of its literary integrity began relatively late. Hölscher's 1924 study came as a thunderbolt: he drew a sharp distinction between the poetry and the book of Ezekiel.[607] Keeping only 170 verses, about one-eighth of the text, as the work of the prophet, Hölscher described the book as a fifth-century "polemic of the Zadokite priesthood in Jerusalem."[608] The redactor "deliberately assumed the mask of the earlier prophet Ezekiel."[609] In the 1950s and 1960s, it appeared that Zimmerli's model of an accretion to Ezekiel's oracles by the school of Ezekiel had succeeding in mediating between the prophet and the literary form of the book. More recent scholarship tends to two extremes, either treating the book as a single whole and ascribing it to the prophet[610] or dissecting it so extensively by literary analysis that the person of Ezekiel disappears altogether.[611] A generally convincing application of literary criticism still is not to be found.

In his massive commentary, Zimmerli was concerned not to deny the prophet "a genuine experience underlying his prophetic preaching."[612] At the same time, he sought to do justice to the book's literary character. His solution was to distinguish between the prophet Ezekiel and a school of Ezekiel, related by the model of accretion. By this he means "a process of successive supplementation of a kernel element, the ideas of which have been developed and expanded."[613] Zimmerli believes it important to

---

[605] Hossfeld, "Ezechiel," 293–94.
[606] See Feist, *Ezechiel*.
[607] *Hesekiel*, esp. 7–25 and 26–42
[608] Ibid., 40, 31.
[609] Ibid., 40.
[610] Greenberg, *Ezekiel 1–29*.
[611] Garscha, *Studien;* Pohlmann, *Ezechielstudien* and *Prophet Hesekiel*.
[612] *Ezekiel*, 1:19.
[613] Ibid., 1:334.

maintain that such later interpretations follow "the basic line drawn by the prophet himself."[614] For a long time, this model seemed to have the advantage of leaving the literary growth of the book relatively open while at the same time preserving access to the prophet. The former reflected the character of the book, in which there are no linguistic features distinctive of particular sections, despite suggestions of literary expansion. The latter was congruent with conservative interest in the *ipsissima vox* of the prophet. Only in retrospect has it become clear that Zimmerli's literary and form-critical analysis did not really arrive at the "authentic" situation of the prophet's preaching, nor did it do justice to the interests of his school.[615] The latter remained quite shadowy throughout his discussion.[616] If the disciples had nothing substantial to add to what their master had said, the heuristic advantage of distinguishing the two is slight.

Because Zimmerli's approach represented a compromise, it is not surprising that Ezekiel scholarship could develop in totally divergent directions after him. On the one hand, Lang made the prophet more accessible, but in contrast to the priestly and theological image that Zimmerli assigned to him, Lang uncovered the active political role that the prophet had played during the political rebellion of Zedekiah.[617] He interpreted Ezekiel's strange symbolic actions as street theater (Ezek 4–5; 12:1–15; 21:23–37), his similitudes (17:1–10) and fictive lamentations (19) as tools of direct political conflict. On the other hand, many have attempted to develop Zimmerli's fluid accretion model into a more precise theory of literary expansion. Hossfeld adopted this approach with a very conservative agenda, distinguishing six different redactional strata but dating them all in the sixth century. So far, however, he has not extended his hypothesis to the entire text of the book. Hossfeld's analysis, however, has made it clear that the work of Ezekiel himself must be distinguished from that of his preexilic precursors much more clearly than Zimmerli realized and must be explained on the basis of the particular needs of the exilic period.[618]

More radical are the hypotheses put forward in the literary criticism of several former Marburg scholars. In his study of the death penalty in the Old Testament, Schulz claimed that the texts in the book of Ezekiel characterized by the language and forms of sacral law (3:17–21; 14:1–11,

---

[614] Ibid., 1:25.
[615] See the critique of Davis, *Swallowing*, 15–19.
[616] Zimmerli, *Ezekiel*, 1:71*.
[617] *Kein Aufstand*.
[618] "Ezechiel," 510–18.

12–20; 18:1–20; 22:1–16; 33:1–20) should be assigned to an original Deutero-Ezekielian stratum, which was later reedited.[619] Garscha elaborated on this suggestions, distinguishing a total of eight stages in the growth of the book of Ezekiel, extending into the Hellenistic period.[620] In his opinion, a first edition of the prophetic book (VEz), which already comprised Ezek 1–39* in a somewhat different sequence, was produced in the fifth century. It was followed by a Deutero-Ezekielian revision (DEz) from the first half of the fourth century, characterized by polemic against those left behind in Judah. The stratum identified by Schulz reappears in Garscha's work as a sacral law stratum (SEz), dating from around 300. According to Garscha, only the core of 17:2–20* and 23:2–25* may possibly be assigned to the prophet Ezekiel. "Thus the prophet vanishes almost totally in the darkness of history."[621]

Pohlmann's literary criticism employs a model with the same basic approach but differing in detail.[622] The earliest part of the book, in his opinion, comprises poetic texts,[623] specifically a collection of lamentations (Ezek 19:2–9*; 31:2–6*, 12–13*; 19:10–14*; 15:2–4) from the period following the first or second deportation.[624] The allegory in 17:1–10 is related to this collection. These texts lament and explain the catastrophe that has just taken place; they have little to do with prophecy and nothing at all to do with any prophet named Ezekiel but were composed by members of the Jerusalem upper class, in part by its pro-Babylonian faction.[625] According to Pohlmann, the author of 17:1–10 merely "drapes the prophetic mantle over the imagined speaker" in 17:9–10.[626] An early prophetic book, he believes, took shape in Palestine during the exilic period; its purpose was to demonstrate the fulfillment of prophecy.[627] This book comprised the core of 4–7; 11:1–13; 12:21ff.; 14:1–20; 17:1–18; 18; 19/31; 15:1–6; 21:1–5; 24; 36:1–15; 37:11–14. It was left for a golah-oriented redaction at the end of the fifth century to produce the book of Ezekiel with its unmistakable theological profile.[628] In this book, which corresponds to Garscha's DEz, Pohlmann includes 1:1–3; 3:10–16; 8–11*; 14:21–23; 16:6–8; 17:19–24; 24:25–27*; 33:21–33; 37:1–10. However, the exclusive bias of this stratum in favor

---

[619] *Todesrecht*, 163–87.
[620] *Studien*.
[621] Ibid., 287.
[622] *Ezechielstudien* and *Prophet Hesekiel*.
[623] Cf. Hölscher, *Hesekiel*.
[624] *Prophet Hesekiel*, 1:36–38, 292–97.
[625] Ibid., 1:247.
[626] Ibid., 1:250.
[627] Ibid., 1:34–36.
[628] Ibid., 1:27–30.

of the golah of 597 was leveled by several Diaspora-oriented redactions produced during the fourth century (including 12:1–16; 20; 36:16ff.; 37:15ff.; 38–39). Finally, there was an apocalyptic redaction.

These more radical critical hypotheses, which attempt to trace the growth of the book of Ezekiel in specific detail, suffer from methodological and historical problems. The use of hypothetical biases to differentiate redactional strata in a book with many repetitions but no clear stylistic breaks is extremely difficult. As the divergent conclusions show, it demands too much of the crude methods of literary criticism, especially since some of the distinctive features, such as the appearance of poetry or the language of sacral law, can be explained as well if not better by traditio-historical analysis, as representing the inclusion of alien genres. It is quite true that several passages in the book of Ezekiel contain polemic against the claims of those left behind and bias in favor of the exiles,[629] but Pohlmann's inability to assign to the golah-oriented redaction the two texts that exhibit this bias most clearly, 11:14–21 and 33:21–33, since the former also exhibits Diaspora-oriented features,[630] demonstrates that this bias cannot be associated clearly with a particular redactional stratum. Here Pohlmann imports an explanatory model from his exegesis of Jeremiah, which I believe encumbers rather than facilitates an understanding of the book of Ezekiel.[631] Furthermore, neither Garscha nor Pohlmann can explain why in the fifth or fourth century—150 to 200 years after the end of the exile—it should be necessary to defend the claims of the golah against the claims of those left behind in Judah. This model of the book's origin also leaves unexplained why the book was associated with the name of the prophet Ezekiel (not only in 1:3, a redactional note, but also in 24:24, firmly anchored in the body of the book).

Since these accretion hypotheses do not produce convincing results, models with more emphasis on the unity of the book have taken on

---

[629] It does seem to me, however, that Pohlmann greatly exaggerates this tendency. The golah is included in the "rebellious house" (Ezek 2:7; 3:9, 26–27; 12:2–3, 9; 17:12), just as those left behind are included in the house of Israel (11:15; 12:23). The prophet criticizes the golah as well as those left behind, albeit sometimes more gently (12:21–25, 26–28; 33:23–29, 30–33). Ezek 14:22–23, a passage to which Pohlmann attaches great importance for the golah-oriented redaction (*Ezechielstudien*, 6–11), does not argue the exclusive claims of the first golah at the expense of the second; its point is rather that Yahweh had cause to destroy Jerusalem.

[630] His complex argument (*Hesekiel*, 1:166) that Ezek 11:14–21 originated with the golah-oriented redaction but that "its actual intent ... can only be guessed" because the Diaspora-oriented redaction has revised it only demonstrates the difficulty of assigning it to a literary stratum, the more so because Pohlmann cannot point to any stylistic or grammatical seam in the text.

[631] *Studien* (III.2.6).

increased importance. The most radical proposal in this direction is that of Greenberg.⁶³² Departing sharply in his commentary from Zimmerli's approach, he explicitly interprets the book as a single literary unit, while also understanding it as the work of the prophet. His "holistic method" turns up many literary and thematic interconnections that had not been recognized by the methods of literary criticism, but Greenberg's almost total rejection of a diachronic perspective prevents him from properly appreciating the process of interpretation internal to the book and forces him to compress the book's formation into the brief period between 593 and 571. The solution of Becker is equally radical.⁶³³ He rightly asks, "What would a linguistically homogeneous book actually have to look like if the book of Ezekiel cannot count as one?"⁶³⁴ He points out that it is mostly the postulate of a prophet who delivered his message orally that casts doubt on the apparent unity of the book. By characterizing the book of Ezekiel as a pseudepigraphic written composition of the fifth century, he believes that he can to do justice to its homogeneity and literary character without further problems. However, this amazing solution runs up against the difficulty that all other extant pseudepigraphical works are ascribed to imposing figures of the past (Moses, Daniel, Enoch); apart from his book, Ezekiel is totally unknown.

A middle course like that of Krüger therefore appears most attractive.⁶³⁵ Apart from a problematic apocalyptic redaction around the year 200, Krüger simply distinguishes between an "early book of Ezekiel" (EB)⁶³⁶ and later redactional material. Regarding the latter, Krüger cites Josephus's statement that Ezekiel was in Babylon when he prophesied the future fate of his people but wrote down his message and sent it to Jerusalem.⁶³⁷ This theory would explain the literary quality of many of the prophet's utterances; it would also account for their circulation in several versions and the frequent difficulty of distinguishing clearly between the prophet and his interpreters. It also provides a plausible explanation for a "school of Ezekiel": the prophet needed a "workplace" and was dependent on intermediary interpreters.⁶³⁸ Even more important than the concrete model is Krüger's decision to date the issuance of the prophetic book late in the exilic period, when it already included the bulk of the present text

---

632 *Ezekiel 1–20.*
633 "Erwägungen."
634 Ibid., 139.
635 *Geschichtskonzepte.*
636 Ibid., 306–94.
637 *Ant.* 10.106.
638 Krüger, *Geschichtskonzepte*, 396–98.

(Ezek 1–24; 33–37; 40–48).[639] This dating makes it possible to do full justice to the book's combination of judgment and salvation prophecy and the fact that the book frequently looks back retrospectively on the catastrophe, without casting doubt on the book's literary unity. According to Krüger, EB essentially contains a program for reconstruction[640] that favors—here his approach resembles that of Pohlmann—"the Babylonian golah as the foundation and starting point for the reconstitution of Israel."[641] Such a conception of the book of Ezekiel is quite congruent with the approach of Davis, who strongly emphasizes the literary character of Ezekiel's prophecy.[642]

The unique quality of the book of Ezekiel is connected not only with Ezekiel's location in exile, which forced him to commit much of his message to writing so that it could be published in Jerusalem, but also and above all with its date: it was not composed until late in the exilic period. The *terminus a quo* is 574, the year of the prophet's last vision, which in fact enabled the visionary conception of the entire book (Ezek 1–3; 8–11; 40–48). However, the promises of return and reconstruction (34; 36–37) require a later date. Even an announcement of judgment such as 13:9, which foretells that the false prophets of salvation "shall not remain in the council of my people, nor be enrolled in the register of the house of Israel, nor shall they enter the land of Israel," presupposes the possibility of a new beginning. But this turn of events was unimaginable before Cyrus's victorious campaign in Lydia in 547/546 B.C.E. The detailed plans for the new temple and the reorganization of the community in Palestine in chapters 40–48 make sense only at a time when people felt a new beginning to be imminent, following the fall of the Babylonian Empire in 539 at the earliest but probably not until Cambyses' Egyptian campaign in 525. Since the sometimes utopian conceptions of Ezek 40–48 agree only very slightly with the reality achieved after 520, it is highly unlikely that they were developed after the temple was finished in 515. Apart from chapters 38–39, which are clearly secondary, there is nothing to suggest a dating much after this *terminus ad quem*. In addition, the book's knowledge of many historical details from the period between 594 and 572 (17:13–14; 21:25–26 [20–21]; 28:17–21; etc.) argues for a sixth-century dating. For the origin of the book of Ezekiel, then, we arrive at the time between 545 and 515, a period of some thirty years.[643] Most of

---

[639] See the chart in the appendix to Krüger's study.
[640] Krüger, *Geschichtskonzepte*, 317ff.
[641] Ibid., 323.
[642] *Swallowing*.
[643] See Collins, *Mantle*, 94–96.

the process of composition occurred in Babylonia,[644] but the final phase may well have taken place in Palestine.[645]

This means that the book was probably written not by Ezekiel himself but by the first and second generations of his disciples. If we assume that he was thirty years old in the fifth year after the deportation of Jehoiachin (594; cf. Ezek 1:2), he would have had to attain the truly biblical age of 109 to have lived as late as 515.[646] Furthermore, the last date given in the book (572) is connected with an emendation that the prophet obviously felt compelled to make when the siege of Tyre was broken off (29:17–21), whereas there was no analogous emendation concerning the oft-foretold deportation of the Egyptians (29:12; 30:23, 26; 32:9), which never happened during Nebuchadnezzar's Egyptian campaign in 568/567. It is therefore highly probable that Ezekiel died between these two dates, sometime around 570.[647] However, this means that only after the temple vision in 574, toward the end of his life, could Ezekiel begin to conceive the book that was to contain his legacy for the future. This history also accounts for the book's use of autobiographical style. However, it was written down and updated, on the basis of the prophet's material, by Ezekiel's disciples. The differences between the expectations for the future in chapters 34–37 and those in 40–48[648] may be due to the work of a new generation of disciples in the latter.

Such a view of how the prophetic book took shape has significant methodological consequences for its exegesis. Large sections of the book are retrospective; it includes topical prophecy only in its visions of the future after the exile. It treats the catastrophe of 587 as an event of the distant past and asks what conclusions might be drawn about a possible new beginning in the future. It is therefore an exilic book in the literal sense. This means that we have only very limited access to the immediate

---

644 Most likely in the vicinity of Nippur, where most of the book is set—in other words, probably at some remove from the leaders of the golah in Babylon itself, where I believe that the Deuteronomistic History originated.

645 A Palestinian setting is suggested by the clear affinities of the book of Ezekiel to JerD³—for example, the relationship between Ezek 34:1–15 and Jer 23:1–4 as well as between Ezek 11:19; 36:26–27 and Jer 31:33.

646 One arrives at this estimate if the difficult date given in Ezek 1:1, "In the thirtieth year," equated by 1:2 with "the fifth year of the exile of King Jehoiachin" (= 594 B.C.E.), is interpreted as referring to Ezekiel's age at the time of his call. See Zimmerli, *Ezekiel*, 1:100–101; Pohlmann, *Prophet*, 47–49.

647 This assumption also explains why there are no oracles against Babylon in the book of Ezekiel, if in fact the cryptic oracle of the sword in Ezek 21:34–37 is not to be interpreted in this sense.

648 These differences have to do especially with the person and position of the future king; see pp. 364 and 371–72 below.

message of the prophet, especially his preaching in the years before 587. The retrospective process has long since amalgamated it into the overall concept of the book; in part, it can be reconstructed historically, but not textually. However, the very abandonment of the attempt to distill the original message of the prophet from the book of Ezekiel makes it possible to read the book for the most part as a single literary unit. The only clearly secondary material is the Gog/Magog section (Ezek 38–39);[649] there may also be some secondary additions to salvation oracles (e.g., 34:25–31; 36:33–36, 37–38). Contrary to Krüger,[650] however, the foreign nation oracles in Ezek 25–32[651] were already part of the late exilic book.

It is no accident that the prophet Ezekiel vanishes almost entirely behind his book. Since Ezek 1:1 presents the book as a personal legacy in the first person, originally there was no regular superscription introducing the author. Such a superscription was added redactionally in 1:3. Since the name יְחֶזְקֵאל (yəḥezqēʾl, "God has made strong" → Ezekiel) is well established in 24:24, there is no reason to doubt the accuracy of this identification, which states that he was a priest, the son of Buzi. The book frequently states that he conducted his ministry in Babylonia among the exiles, more specifically at Tel-abib, by the river or canal Chebar in the Nippur region (1:1; 3:11, 15; 10:15, 20; 11:24); he was transported to Jerusalem only in ecstatic visions (8–11; 40:1ff.). Since the chronology of the book speaks of the years of Jehoiachin's exile and occasionally includes the prophet among the exiles (33:21; 40:1: "year of our exile"), it is likely that Ezekiel was in the golah of 598/597.

Ezekiel received his call in the year 594; he withdrew to his house (Ezek 3:24; 12:1–7), and people had to come to him to seek or hear the word of God (8:1; 14:1; 33:30–33). Unlike the prophets of salvation, he obviously did not appear at the regular evening council (סוֹד) of the men (13:9) but kept at a distance (3:25). Even his symbolic actions probably were performed in or near his house (12:1–7; cf. 4:1–3, 9–11; 5:1–2). Although the people treated his "performances" more like entertainment (33:30–33) and complained that his message was incomprehensible (21:5 [20:49]), Ezekiel enjoyed some respect among the elders of the golah; we are told more than once that they sought him out (8:1; 14:1; 20:1). Before

---

[649] In these chapters, Yahweh finally displays his greatness and glory to the nations in Palestine (38:1, 6, 23; 39:21) at the end of days (39:8, 16). Here we are approaching the realm of late prophetic/apocalyptic concepts (cf. Zech 9 and 14). The addition is written in a different style; it also requires in Ezek 39:25–29 a new transition to chapter 40, after the one already given in 37:24–28.

[650] *Geschichtskonzepte*, 298–306.

[651] See pp. 185–86 above, where the collection of these oracles was dated in the late exilic period on the basis of internal evidence.

587, however, he denied their requests to intercede for them (14:1ff.; 20:30–31). It is in this sense that we should probably also understand his speechlessness (3:26; 24:27; 33:22): until God's judgment had been fulfilled, he could serve only as a mouthpiece for Yahweh's message of judgment (3:27), not as a "mediator" (אִישׁ מוֹכִיחַ) between God and God's people (3:26).[652] The book itself mentions only the prophet's oral preaching (14:1; 20:1; 21:5 [20:49]; 24:18–20; 33:30–33; 37:18); only the motif of eating the scroll (3:1–3) might be understood as suggesting written prophecy (cf. Jer 1:9–10).[653] Apart from that, however, it is likely that Ezekiel's physical and social isolation led him more than once to use written communication to spread his message in the golah and among those left in Judah.[654] Politically, like Jeremiah (Jer 27–29), Ezekiel attacked Zedekiah's policy of revolt against Babylon in 594 and 590 (Ezek 17; 19; 21:23–32; 12:1–15). As we learn from Jeremiah's letter, these uprisings also aroused the hopes of the religious nationalists in the golah (Jer 29). The prophetic messages probably went back and forth between Judah and Babylonia. Ezekiel was married; his wife died suddenly when the siege of Jerusalem began. He himself probably lived until around 570.

The unity of the book of Ezekiel is even more obvious when we examine its structure. More clearly than the other prophetic books, it is divided into three parts: oracles of judgment against Judah and Jerusalem (Ezek 1–24), oracles of judgment against the nations (25–32), and oracles of salvation for Israel and Jerusalem (33–48), the so-called "eschatological schema." The first section clearly culminates in the fall of Jerusalem. In 24:1–2, the prophet learns from God that the siege of Jerusalem has begun, and in 24:26 he is told that a fugitive will come bearing important news. The third section begins with the fall of Jerusalem: the fugitive arrives and reports the fall of the city (33:21). Then the book moves in stages (leadership [34], land [35–36], people [37]) to the rebuilding of the temple, the capital, and the entire social structure (40–48). The catastrophe of 587 is not described but only represented symbolically by the prophet's mourning after the death of his beloved wife (24:15–24), but it is nevertheless the conceptual and compositional center of the book of Ezekiel.[655] In contrast to the Deuteronomistic History, for instance, the

---

[652] This is the correct interpretation of this often misunderstood passage; cf. Amos 5:10; Job 9:33; also Wilson, "Interpretation," 97–101; similarly Greenberg, *Ezekiel 1–20*, 120–21; Davis, *Swallowing*, 52–56.

[653] Davis, *Swallowing*, 217–37; but see the criticism of Odell ("You Are," 241–44), who emphasizes that the eating internalizes Yahweh's irrevocable judgment on the people within the prophet.

[654] Josephus, *Ant.* 10.106.

[655] As observed similarly by Krüger, *Geschichtskonzepte*, 317.

Ezekiel book marks it not as the end of history but as both a conclusion and a new beginning of Israel's history. The gap between the siege and city's fall is deliberately filled by the oracles against the nations (25–32). It is not least their derision of the ravaged temple, city, and land and their contempt for Israel (25:3, 8; 26:2) that move Yahweh to intervene and deliver his people (36:2, 3, 16–21; etc.).[656] Since the entire drama of Yahweh and his people and his city, both judgment (5:5, 8, 15; 12:16; 20:9, 14, 22; 22:16) and salvation (34:5, 8; 35; 36:2–3, 20–23, 30), is played out before the eyes of the nations and with their involvement, the foreign nation oracles also belong to the exilic book of Ezekiel.

This historical drama is framed by events in heaven seen by Ezekiel in a vision. At the beginning of the book, in his great vision of the chariot throne (Ezek 1:4–28), Ezekiel sees the glory of Yahweh (כְּבוֹד־יהוה), actually enthroned in the temple, appear to him at the time of his call in the midst of the Babylonian golah (1:28ff.). Contrary to the Jerusalemites' belief that the exiles are far from Yahweh (cf. 11:15), Ezekiel and his fellow exiles are thus involved by God in the quarrel with rebellious Israel (2:2–5). The prophet learns the full significance of this theophany in a later vision (8–11). Transported in ecstasy to Jerusalem, Ezekiel sees the glory of Yahweh leave the desecrated temple and city (8:4; 9:3; 10:18–20; 11:22–23), dooming both to destruction. Finally, in his great temple vision at the end of the book, the prophet sees the glory of God return to the new temple (43:1–12), to reside among the Israelites forever (43:7). Thus God's presence is restored to godforsaken Jerusalem. However, the return of the כְּבוֹד־יהוה demands a total architectural, organizational, cultic, and political restructuring of the temple and society (43:7–12, etc.). This theological framework firmly joins the first and third sections of the book. It is therefore highly probable that there was never a book of Ezekiel without the temple vision (40–48), although extensive expansion has almost turned these chapters in a separate section of the book.

This summary already reveals in outline the theological program of the book of Ezekiel. The destruction of Jerusalem and its temple constitutes the midpoint to and from which everything moves. On the one hand, the book offers a theological explanation of why this destruction could take place. On the other, it works intensively to develop from the catastrophe criteria for the new beginning. For its theological basis, it draws primarily on priestly theology, specifically the priestly theology of the sanctuary.[657] As the departure of God's glory followed by its return

---

[656] For more details, see pp. 186–87 above.

[657] The כְּבוֹד־יהוה is also the focus of the later sanctuary theology of P; cf. Exod 24:16–17; 40:34–35; Lev 9:6, 23.

shows, the new beginning does not follow the catastrophe seamlessly, without a break; the continuity is established only by God. Therefore, the new beginning must meet God's demands.

Other structural features of the book therefore serve to signal the antithesis between the first section and the third. Two shorter visions, each set in "the valley" (הַבִּקְעָה), constitute an inner frame. In Ezek 3:22–27, the prophet is isolated from his people by being bound with cords and rendered speechless; until the fall of Jerusalem, he is prevented from serving as a mediator (אִישׁ מוֹכִחַ) between God and the people. In 37:1–11, however, the prophet employs his effectual word to the full for the benefit of Israel, in his vision breathing new life into the dead people. There are four corresponding complementary discourses: two concerning judgment and two concerning salvation. In Ezek 6, judgment and devastation are proclaimed to the mountains of Israel; in 36:1–15, salvation and resettlement. Drawing on the message of Amos 8:2, Ezek 7 announces the end to the land and its inhabitants;[658] in Ezek 37, Israel, now nothing but a heap of dry bones, is restored to life.

To distinguish the third section even more clearly from the first, Ezek 33 constitutes an introduction to the third section, in which motifs from the call chapters (Ezek 2–3) reappear. The office of sentinel to which Ezekiel was appointed in 3:16–21 is solemnly renewed in 33:1–9 (3:17 = 33:7), but with a new emphasis. In the period of judgment, the prophet's task was to warn the wicked and the righteous on God's behalf; in the period of salvation now dawning, he is especially responsible for seeing that the wicked turn from their ways (33:8–12). At the same time, the text refers back to Ezek 18, which expatiates on the question of individual responsibility among the exilic generation (cf. 33:12–20 with 18:20–31).[659] The prophet's speechlessness commanded by God in 3:26—that is, the restriction of his prophetic ministry to no more than conveying the message of God's judgment (3:27)—comes to an end with the news that this judgment has been carried out (33:21–22). From now on, Ezekiel can minister in solidarity with his people on their behalf. Finally, both the call (2:5–7) and the new commission (33:30–33) reflect the success or failure of Ezekiel's prophetic mission; in the latter, the criticism of those addressed is clearly more mild.[660] The fulfillment of Ezekiel's prophecy of judgment

---

[658] The MT of Ezek 7 is seriously corrupt, possibly because several versions of the text have been interwoven. A shorter, clearer version can be recovered from the LXX.

[659] It is probably not by chance that Ezek 18 is placed midway between the call chapters (1–3) and the prophet's new commission (33).

[660] The description of Israel as a rebellious house (בֵּית מְרִי) is restricted accordingly to Ezek 1–24 (2:5–8; 3:9, 26–27; 12:2–3, 9, 25; 17:17; 24:3). It reappears only once, in 44:6 (LXX; the

should lead them to recognize him as a prophet in their midst and put trust in his message (2:5; 33:33). As the table shows, the very structure of the book seeks to establish how the task and position of the prophet are transformed once God's judgment on Jerusalem has been fulfilled.

Section 1: Ezek 1–24 Judgment on Judah and Jerusalem		
1–3	Chariot throne vision and call	
	1:4–28	Appearance of the כבוד־יהוה in Babylonia
	2:1–3:15	Call
		2:1–7; 3:4–9 Obduracy of the people (2:5 par. 33:33)
		2:8–3:3 Authorization to speak (eating the scroll)
	3:16–21	Appointment as sentinel
	3:22–27	Visionary encounter with the כבוד־יהוה in the valley (cf. 37)
		3:25 Binding of the prophet; social isolation
		3:26 Speechlessness of the prophet; intercession impossible (cf. 24:27; 33:22)
4–5	Symbolic actions: siege of Jerusalem and deportation	
6	Judgment on the mountains of Israel (contrast 36)	
7	End for the land and its inhabitants	
8–11	Vision: departure of the כבוד־יהוה from the desecrated temple (cf. 43:1–12)	
12	Symbolic action: deportation; judgment on Zedekiah	
13–14	Judgment on false prophets; intercession forbidden	
15	Parable of the useless vine	
16	Parable of the nymphomaniac adulteress (historical retrospect; cf. 23)	
17	Allegory of the eagle and the treacherous vine; judgment on Zedekiah	
18	Didactic discourse on individual responsibility in the exilic generation (cf. 3:18–21; 33:10–20)	
19	Lament for the Judean royal house	
20	Intercession forbidden; didactic discourse on the history of Israel's apostasy	
21–22	Judgment on desecrated Jerusalem	
23	Parable of the unrestrained sisters (historical retrospect; cf. 16)	

MT reads just מְרִי), which criticizes the Israelites for having allowed foreigners to participate in the temple cult.

24	24:1–2	Beginning of the siege of Jerusalem
	24:3–14	Parable of the filthy pot (Jerusalem)
	24:15–24	Death of Ezekiel's wife; symbolic mourning of the prophet
	24:25–27	Arrival of fugitive and the end of Ezekiel's speechlessness foretold (33:22)

Section 2: Ezek 25–32 Judgment on the nations

25	Neighbors
26–28	Tyre
29–32	Egypt

Section 3: Ezek 33–48 Salvation for Israel and Jerusalem

33	33:1–9	Renewal of Ezekiel's appointment as sentinel (3:16–21)
	33:10–20	Possible return of the wicked (18:21–32)
	33:21–22	Arrival of the fugitive; news of the fall of Jerusalem (24:25) Speechlessness ends (cf. 3:26; 24:27)
	33: 23–29	Judgment on the incorrigible Judeans left in Jerusalem
	33:30–33	Recognition of Ezekiel's authority by the people (cf. 2:5)
34		Judgment on the shepherds; deliverance of the flock
35–36		Judgment on Edom; salvation for the mountains of Israel (cf. 6)
37		Vision in the valley: revival of dead Israel (cf. 7 and 3:22–27)
40–48		Vision of the new temple and reorganization of society
	40–42	Plan of the new temple
	43:1–12	Entrance of the כבוד־יהוה into the new temple
	44–46	Access; priests and Levites; role of the prince
	47–48	Water from the temple; distribution of the land; reordering of temple, city, and monarchy

Of course, the usual assignment of the message of judgment to section 1 and the message of salvation to section 2, followed here for simplicity's sake, does not reflect the full complexity of the text. Examination of the book in greater detail shows clearly that even in Ezek 1–24 oracles of judgment frequently lead into expression of hope (5:3–4, 13?; 6:8–10; 11:14–20; 12:16; 14:11, 22–23; 16:53–58, 59–62; 17:22–24; 20:32–44; cf. 28:25–26). Yet more striking, even in chapters 33–48 we find a wide range of oracles of judgment: against those left in Israel (33:23–29), the shepherds of Israel (34:1–10), the fat sheep of the flock (34:17–22). The prophecy of judgment against avaricious Edom (35) provides the background for the prophecy of salvation to the mountains of Israel (36:1–15).

The oracle of salvation in 36:16–28 evolves from a retrospective summary of earlier wrongs (36:17–19). Even the concluding temple vision includes harsh words against Israel (44:6–7) and its princes (45:9). Thus the book of Ezekiel contains not just one but a multiplicity of movements from judgment to salvation.

We find prophecies anticipating salvation following prophecies of judgment in many of the prophetic books, such as in the book of the Four Prophets.[661] The school of Ezekiel also seeks to assert that salvation can come only through judgment, that is, that Ezekiel's preexilic prophecy of judgment embodies a critical potential for a salvific future. Only in the book of Ezekiel, however, do we find at least some prophecies of salvation that cannot be set aside as redactional additions to prophecies of judgment, as exegetes have often tried to do in their search for the *ipsissima vox* of the prophet. Literarily, the two elements are often so closely entwined that one must assume that the prophecies of judgment were composed from the outset with an eye to their conclusion in salvation.[662] Clearly the book of Ezekiel is to be read from the very start from the perspective of the conditions needed for a new beginning.[663] The real uniqueness of the book consists in the strongly critical potential inherent in its message of salvation. The disciples of Ezekiel were clearly concerned to maintain that it was inappropriate simply to expect that the future would bring a restoration and continuation of the preexilic way of life. They believed that there was no such thing as automatic transition to salvation: there must be a caesura, a real new beginning.

The critical potential that the prophecy of judgment brings to the new beginning is extraordinarily diverse. It would appear that the disciples of Ezekiel wanted to summarize the whole spectrum of indictments voiced by that the prophets of the past, although it is impossible to miss a specifically priestly emphasis due to the origin of Ezekiel and his circle. At the center stood polemic against idols (Ezek 6:4, 6; 7:20; 8:10, 12; 11:21; 20:8, 20; 21:3–4; 36:18; etc.) and idolatry (6:9; 14:3ff.; 16:17–22; 20:16, 24, 31; 23:7, 30; etc.), high places (6:4, 6; 18:6, 11, 15; 20:28; 21:9), pagan rites

---

661 See pp. 222–24, 229–30, 234–36 above.

662 Krüger (*Geschichtskonzepte*, 207–14) has demonstrated this convincingly for Ezek 20, but it is also true for 11:14–20 and 14:11, 22–23. In 16:53–58 and 59–62, we appear to have two different conclusions to the parable of lewd Jerusalem.

663 By contrast, the attempt to come to terms with the past clearly plays a smaller role in the book of Ezekiel than in the book of Jeremiah. It is present to a degree in the historical parables Ezek 16 and 23 (cf. esp. 16:43 and 23:46–49). It is also manifest in the theological perspective of the exiles of 587, who testify to their own misdeeds in order to justify Yahweh's harsh judgment on Jerusalem to the nations (12:16) and the members of the first golah (14:22–23).

(cf. 8:14, 16, 17; 16:20–21; 23:37, 39), and divination (13:17–23); here the book concurs with the Deuteronomists. Profanation of the Sabbath was addressed as a transgression specific to the exilic period (20:13ff.; 21:7; 23:38); the inclusion of sexual abominations (18:6; 22:10; 33:36; 36:17; cf. 18:6) and contempt for holy things (22:8) reflected specifically priestly interests. Through all these transgressions, the Judeans had defiled the temple (5:11; 8:3, 6; 23:38–39), Jerusalem (9:9; 22:4; 24:11, 13), and the land (36:17).

However, Ezekiel's disciples were far from limiting themselves to these religious, cultic, and ritual transgressions. With great vigor and detail, they addressed social evils such as violence (7:10, 23; 8:17; 12:19), bribery (22:12), exploitation of the weak (18:7–8, 13; 22:7, 12, 25, 29; cf. 33:15), and contempt for elderly parents (22:7). From their priestly perspective, the shedding of innocent blood merited special condemnation (7:23; 9:9; 22:3–4, 6, 9, 13; 24:7–8; 33:25; cf. 35:6); they repeatedly branded Jerusalem "the bloody city" (22:2; 24:6, 9). Finally, they directed their critical attention to the perilous and ultimately ruinous policy of trust in alliances (11:16; 16:23–34; 17:7, 11–18; 21:28–30 [23–25]; 23:3–7, 40–45) and branded Zedekiah's abrogation of the vassal treaty a breach of faith with Yahweh (17:19–21). All areas of Israel's life, in their opinion, were permeated with faithlessness (מעל: 14:13; 15:8; 17:20; 18:24; 20:27), willfulness (מרה: 5:6; 20:8, 13, 21), and rebelliousness (מרד: 2:3; 17:15; 20:28) toward their God. In summarizing the wrongs committed by Jerusalem (22:1–16) and its political and religious leaders (22:23–31) in a veritable catalog of sins, drawing also on their casuistic description of the wicked and the righteous (18:1–20), they were seeking to define the criteria that had to apply to everyone for the reconstruction of society.

The same purpose was served by their frequent explicit reference to God's laws, the first time this theme appears in a prophetic book. When they castigated offenses against God's laws (5:6–7; 11:12; 20:13, 18–19, 21, 24), defining the content of these laws in prophetic indictments (18:9, 21; 33:15) and demanding their observance in the future (11:20; 36:27; 37:24), they were apparently striving to turn the prophetic indictments of the past into binding guidelines for the future.[664]

---

[664] That Ezekiel's disciples drew on an existing legal tradition is obvious. However, the affinities with the so-called Holiness Code (Lev 17–26), sometimes quite close, should be interpreted in the opposite direction, as evidence that prophetic elements from the Ezekiel circle later influenced the reforming legislation of the priests. That the Ezekiel circle borrowed certain existing structural and thematic elements of priestly sacral law (compare, for example, the law concerning sexual conduct in Lev 18:19 with Ezek 18:6, and note the formal correspondences between Ezek 14:3, 7 and Lev 17:3, 8) is beside the point.

Because the goal of Ezekiel's disciples was all-embracing renewal of their people, they had to strive to reinforce the sense of individual responsibility within the exilic generation. Therefore, they vehemently attacked the notion that the all members of exilic generation were doomed to bear the guilt of the preceding generation, especially since those left in Judah were self-righteously applying this notion to the golah (Ezek 18:1–20; cf. 18:2, 19). Using the casuistry of sacral law, they insisted that each individual member of the golah who met the criteria of prophetic ethics was set free from the intergenerational catena of guilt to receive God's assurance of an opportunity for life (18:14–20). At the same time, the disciples of Ezekiel had to deal with the danger that their unmitigated prophetic indictment would be so devastating that the people they were addressing would believe that they were doomed to perish (מקק, lit. "rot away") under the burden of their terrible sins (33:10; cf. 24:23; 4:17). To counter this plaint, they applied a casuistic principle of sacral law: individuals are not defined by their actions for all eternity (33:12).

The wicked have the opportunity to repent and mend their ways at any time (18:21–23; 33:14–16) because God has no pleasure in their death (18:23, 32); the righteous who commit iniquity while trusting in their own righteousness will die (18:24; 33:13). Having pointed out the sins of the past, Ezekiel's disciples therefore saw it as their task to motivate their fellow Israelites to turn back from them (14:6; 18:30–31; 33:11; cf. 20:18–19). They defined themselves as lookouts who, like sentinels, had to warn all the people of approaching danger and were therefore personally responsible to God (3:18, 20; 33:6, 8); here we see how seriously they took their task. The programmatic statement of this self-definition at the beginning of both parts of the book (3:16–21; 33:1–9) bespeaks an individualistic and pastoral perspective seemingly at odds with Ezekiel's collective and absolute prophecy of judgment prior to 587; it makes sense only from the transformed perspective of what was necessary during the late exilic period. Now the task was to make the prophetic indictments serviceable for the ethical instruction of the members of the golah. In fact, the entire book of Ezekiel was to serve this purpose.

At bottom, the critical potential of the prophecy of salvation probably also comes from the prophet himself. He countered the exiles' despairing plaint that their life force had dried up (Ezek 37:11b) with his vision of Yahweh's restoration of Israel to life, a restoration that he promoted through his powerful prophetic word (37:1–11a). However, this heartening vision had a profoundly critical implication: there could be no unbroken continuity between the Israel of the past and the Israel of the future. The old Israel was dead; it had come to an end, as Amos had foretold (Amos 8:2; Ezek 7). The future Israel was to be a new creation by God, no longer identical with the old—in other words, not all those whose families had survived the catastrophe should conclude that they would automatically belong to the new Israel, not to mention enjoy their old position. From this critical starting point, the disciples of Ezekiel evolved a variety of notions as to who would constitute Israel in the coming age of salvation.

In principle, the promise embraced the entire golah, initially the golah of 597 (Ezek 11:17–20) but then, after they also experienced God's judgment (11:21; cf. 9:10), the golah of 587 as well (6:8–10; cf. 12:16; 14:22–23). Yahweh would assemble once more from among the nations those who had met the full fury of his wrath and bring them back to the land of Israel (11:17; 34:12–14; 36:8, 24; 37:12–14). Many of those who had remained in Judah, however, were incorrigible; they had challenged the property rights of those in the golah and had continued to practice their abominations as though nothing had happened. For them, the school of Ezekiel foretold yet another judgment (33:23–29),[665] but this did not imply their total exclusion, as the oracles of salvation for Jerusalem show (16:53–58,[666] 59–63). The hopes for salvation even extended to Israelites dwelling in the former northern kingdom (16:61; 37:15–19; 47:15–48:29).

In principle, then, all Israel could share in the coming salvation—but not the religious and political leaders. The school of Ezekiel insisted vehemently that the false prophets of salvation who as early as 594 had inflamed the nationalistic hopes for Jerusalem's deliverance (Ezek 13:16) were definitively excluded from the house of Israel and were not to enter the land of Israel (13:9). Such irresponsible prophets, who had misled the people with their constant talk of šālôm (13:10) and thus prevented them from changing their ways, were useless for the new beginning. The female prophets who practiced private divination got off easier. Although they had also prevented the repentance of the wicked, they were only to lose their influence (13:17–23). Harsher treatment awaited the elders who outwardly had behaved devoutly and responsibly, coming to the prophets to seek a salutary response from God, but who in their private devotions had continued secretly to practice idolatry (14:1–11).[667] Speaking with the authority of sacral law, the Ezekiel school pronounced them excluded from the people of Yahweh (14:8). The same verdict was passed on any prophet who aided and abetted these elders with a word of God (14:9–10). The goal was to assure that in the future

---

[665] The expression גְּאוֹן עֻזָּהּ, "proud might," in Ezek 33:28 in fact presupposes that the temple was still standing (cf. 24:21), but this oracle was still placed after the news of Jerusalem's fall (33:21).

[666] That this promise addresses the previous inhabitants of Jerusalem, not the golah, is shown by the allusion to Zedekiah's treaty abrogation in Ezek 16:59 (cf. 17:16).

[667] This charge may refer to the use of amulets; cf. Ezek 14:3.

irresponsible local authorities would no longer prevent Israel from attaining an unsullied covenant relationship with its God.

Thus it is not surprising that the disciples of Ezekiel introduced the message of salvation in their book with an indictment of the shepherds of Israel (Ezek 34:1–6). They, the kings and officials who had borne the responsibility for Israel in its previous history, had selfishly exploited the flock entrusted to them instead of aiding its weak and infirm members and keeping it together. The present condition of Israel, decimated and scattered, was the consequence of their irresponsibility. Therefore God would call them to account and personally replace them as shepherds, to bring the flock together again and feed them with good pasturage on the mountains of Israel (34:7–15).[668] In the eyes of the Ezekiel school, there could also be no continuity at the pinnacle of political authority. In the light of their proven irresponsibility, the monarchy and the bureaucracy had to be deprived of power; Yahweh would rescue his sheep from their mouths (34:10). Only then, and only after God had personally established a just settlement by judging between the fat and the lean sheep of the flock (34:16, 17–22), could a restoration of the monarchy come to pass (34:23–24).

However, the disciples of Ezekiel were not of one mind as to who the king should be. The authors of Ezek 17:22–24 indicated that the new king would be a descendant of Jehoiachin; the authors of 34:23–24 and 37:24–25 resolutely awaited a new David.[669] The authors of 37:20–22, however, left the question open, merely stressing that there would be a single king for the two reunited kingdoms. Finally, the authors of the blueprint for the new society in chapters 45ff. bluntly restated their criticism of the monarchy in 45:9 and drew from it the conclusion that the prince (נָשִׂיא) had to be stripped of his political power (46:16–18) and sacral functions (45:16–17; 46:1 –10). Thus the critical potential that the disciples of Ezekiel put in play through their message of judgment and salvation concerning their religious and political leaders was considerable.

---

668 Both formally and materially, the combination of judgment oracle and salvation oracle for the shepherds strongly recalls Jer 23:1–4, which probably originated with the redactors of the third Jeremiah book around 520. It is impossible to demonstrate conclusively that the disciples of Ezekiel are dependent here on JerD³, but their hostility toward authority and other factors discussed below clearly bring them closer to JerD than to the Deuteronomistic History.

669 Jer 23:5–6, probably a late Deuteronomistic addition, also speaks of a new king under whom Judah would be saved, but this text avoids identifying the king with David or the Davidides; it says merely that Yahweh "will raise up for David a righteous branch," i.e., a new shoot (cf. Zech 3:8). On this point, the Jeremiah Deuteronomists were much more radical: they had definitively ruled out the enthronement of any descendant of Jehoiachin (Jer 22:24–29; see pp. 331–32 above).

The disciples of Ezekiel, however, went a step further. Starting with God's refusal to be consulted by the elders of Israel, in a great didactic discourse (Ezek 20) they developed a view of Israel's history so radically negative that they left their addressees bereft of any possible grounds for hope. In this view, Israel's apostasy made a farce of the exodus itself (20:5–10). True, Yahweh chose Israel and swore to bring the Israelites out of Egypt into the promised land (20:5–6), but when Israel refused to heed Yahweh's call and turn from idolatry (20:7–8a), he took the idols of Egypt from them by force. The exodus from Egypt was thus more a purgative judgment than a saving event (20:8b–10). Israel also made a farce of the gift of ordinances and statutes in the wilderness (20:11–17). Israel rejected the laws through which all were to receive life and profaned the Sabbaths intended as a sign between Israel and God. The generation of the exodus did indeed escape destruction, but Yahweh abrogated his promise of the land while they were still in the wilderness (20:15). The salvific gift of the land was lost even before it was given.

With the next generation, Yahweh made a second effort in the wilderness (Ezek 20:18–26). He called on them to turn their backs on the laws and idols of their parents and instead obey his statutes and ordinances (20:18–20). However, the children also rebelled against Yahweh and refused to turn from their evil ways (20:21). So even then Yahweh reached the decision to scatter them in exile (20:23). Indeed, he went so far as to give them statutes that were not good, that embodied no promise of life (20:25–26). Thus even the law itself was infected by their apostasy.

To this point, this retrospective vision of Israel's earliest history reads almost like a polemical counterpart to the Deuteronomistic History. If the authors of the Deuteronomistic History tried to restrict the history of Israel's apostasy, the disciples of Ezekiel intentionally made it all-embracing. There was no initial golden age, as the Deuteronomists maintained. Everything from the earliest years of Israel's history that they held so dear, on which Israel might ground its hope for the future—the exodus, the gift of the law, the promise of the land—fell into the maelstrom of Israel's apostasy and became severely compromised. In the Deuteronomistic History, the Torah of Moses had been the only gift of God left to Israel after the loss of the land. For these historians, therefore, it constituted the one secure basis and norm for the future.[670] The disciples of Ezekiel wrenched even this last shred of continuity from the hands of their audience. Since it was not clear which of the laws were not

---

[670] See pp. 286–87 and 301–2 above.

good, the Torah needed critical review—surely, in the eyes of these disciples, on the basis of prophetic preaching!

Skipping the following generations, the disciples of Ezekiel turned to the leaders of their own exilic generation, recounting the sins of their ancestors (Ezek 20:27–29) and accusing them, despite the catastrophe, of defiling themselves with similar idolatry (20:30–31aα).[671] God would refuse to be consulted by such people, who had learned nothing but believed that they could simply carry on in the ways of their ancestors (20:31aβb). But the disciples of Ezekiel could not maintain so blunt a refusal in the context of the late exilic period, when hopes for salvation were burgeoning everywhere. Their audience objected, half despondently and half defiantly, that if Yahweh continued to refuse deliverance, their only recourse was to assimilate to their neighbors and adopt their manner of worship (20:32). The disciples of Ezekiel were ready with an answer, but the return they promised the leaders of the golah (20:33–38) was totally different from what the latter had expected. Like the exodus from Egypt, the second exodus from Babylonia would be a judgment of purgation. Yahweh would indeed use all his power to bring the exiles out from among the nations, but he would enter once more into judgment with them "in the wilderness of the nations" (20:33–36); all the notorious sinners would be separated from the people and not permitted to enter the land of Israel (20:37–38).[672] Thus the disciples of Ezekiel erected a bar to participation in the coming salvation of Israel that affected not just the religious and political leaders of the people but all members of the golah.

---

[671] The specifics of the indictment are not clear. Since Ezek 20:40–41 strongly emphasizes the Jerusalem temple as the only legitimate cultic center, one might think that the offerings of the exiles mentioned in 20:31 were attacked because they transgressed the Deuteronomic centralization of the cult. However, since the same context mentions idols (20:31, 39) and the MT of 20:31 refers to the cult of Moloch, it seems more likely that the passage has to do with the adoption of a pagan rite, possibly the offering or, better, consecration of children to Yahweh. The "statute that is not good" (20:25) that Yahweh gave the Israelites in his wrath clearly refers to the law of the firstborn in Exod 34:19, which stipulates that everything that opens the womb belongs to God; in Israel, since time immemorial, this requirement had been fulfilled by a substitutionary offering in the case of human firstborn. It is reasonable to suppose, however, that it opened the door to adoption of a pagan rite. See Albertz, *History* [II.4], 1:190–94.

[672] The MT of Ezek 20:37 is the harder reading; Greenberg (*Ezekiel 1–20*, 372–73; followed by Krüger, *Geschichtskonzepte*, 268–69) has show that it is preferable to the LXX. The translation is: "Then I will make you pass under the staff and bring you within the obligation of the covenant." The *hapax legomenon* מָסֹרֶת stands for מַאֲסֹרֶת, literally "bond," but used like אִסָּר (Num 30:4) in the metaphorical sense of "obligation." The first action refers not simply to counting (the animals in a flock) but also to selection (cf. Lev 27:32); the second action refers to internalizing the laws, like the creation of a new heart and a new spirit (Ezek 11:19; 36:26–27).

The notion of a purgative judgment at the end of the exilic period appears only in the book of Ezekiel; with it, the authors vehemently opposed the view of the Deutero-Isaiah group that the exile had expunged the sin of Jerusalem and that a new age of salvation had already dawned (Isa 40:1–2). Their representation of this judgment as an expression of Yahweh's royal sovereignty was probably meant as a polemical reply to the message of the competing prophetic group (cf. Isa 40:9–11; 52:7–12). Clearly they saw in the unconditional message of salvation for all the exiles the nascent danger of cheap grace, which imperiled the new beginning they desired. In addition, Ezekiel's disciples were once more impugning the authors of the Deuteronomistic History, which explains why they alluded to Deuteronomistic ideas and terminology.[673] They could not share the Deuteronomists' assumption that there would be an all-embracing conversion of the golah during the exile (Deut 4:30; 30:2; cf. Ezek 6:8–10). They believed that the conservative hopes for a simple restoration of the preexilic status quo, especially the official cult of Jerusalem, did not do justice to Yahweh's demands (cf. Ezek 20:40ff.). For a real new beginning to be possible, there had to be a break with the past. Alongside the purgative judgment, therefore, the disciples of Ezekiel developed additional ideas of an all-embracing renewal. When the exiles returned, God would do away with their wanton hearts and eyes (6:9) and subject them to a thorough cultic purgation (36:25), so that they would discard their idols (11:18). Or God would plant within them a new will (11:19; 36:26–27),[674] so that they would naturally observe his laws (11:20; 36:27). After this salutary renewal, at the latest, those who returned would loathe (קוט *nipʿal*) their former abominations (6:9; 20:43; 36:31; cf. 16:53, 63) and thus distance themselves from their evil past.

In the light of Israel's notorious faithlessness, Ezekiel's disciples denied almost totally any continuity of sacred history with the past; they also restricted entrée to salvation in the future. Their view raised the question of where any hope might lie for a continuation and improvement of the history of Yahweh and Israel. The answer that Ezekiel's

---

[673] Clearly attempting to convince their Deuteronomistic colleagues, the disciples of Ezekiel grounded the new purgative judgment in the statement that Yahweh would act "with a mighty hand and an outstretched arm," a favorite expression of the Deuteronomists in the context of the exodus (Deut 4:34; 5:15; 11:2–3; 26:8; Jer 32:21) to demonstrate Yahweh's power over the Egyptians. The only other text that uses this language critically against Israel is Jer 21:5.

[674] Here the expectations of Ezekiel's disciples coincided with those of JerD³ (cf. Jer 31:33). The fact that Ezek 18:31 calls on the house of Israel to get themselves such a new will is not an inconsistency; it only illustrates the theologically necessary overlap of divine initiative and human willingness for repentance and salvation.

disciples found was strictly theological: the continuity of history could not be established by Israel, by Israel's conduct, or by any God-given benefit such as the land or the law, but only by God's own deity. Throughout the past, as Ezekiel's disciples had shown, it was only Yahweh's concern lest the destruction of Israel should profane his name in the sight of the nations that had prevented this history from ending long before (Ezek 20:9, 14, 22). Accordingly, they maintained, Yahweh would extend his saving history with Israel into the future solely for the sake of his name (20:44). As long as Israel lived in exile, its inferior way of life profaned the holy name of Yahweh in the eyes of the nations, since it was the people of Israel with whom Yahweh had linked his name (36:18–20). Therefore Yahweh had to end the dispersal of his people "out of concern for his holy name" (36:31), that is, for the sake of his own repute throughout the world, and see to it that his relationship with his people was restored.[675] Ultimately—as Ezekiel's disciples sought to drum into their addressees by constant repetition of the recognition formula—the goal of the entire drama of God and God's people, in both judgment and salvation, was that Yahweh's divinity be known and recognized by Israel (20:38; 36:11; etc.) and among the nations (36:23; etc.).

The innovative power inherent in the critical potential of the message of salvation in the book of Ezekiel is apparent in the vision of the new temple, which involves not just a thorough reform of the cult but a reordering of the whole social structure (Ezek 40–48). This section of the book has therefore been called a "draft constitution."[676] In its present fully developed form, it probably goes back no earlier than the second generation of Ezekiel's disciples, when the possibility of return and reconstruction was almost palpable (525–515 B.C.E.). The starting point, which can no longer be reconstructed textually, was a vision of Ezekiel himself in 574, in which he saw the Jerusalem temple "like the structure of a city" on a high mountain (40:2). Implicit in these words are probably both its isolated location and its fortress-like structure, embodying in a nutshell the whole design for reform: the architectural and organizational independence of the new Jerusalem temple (40:5–43:15). This meant nothing less than a radical break with the preexilic tradition of the state cult, still embraced, for example, by the authors of the Deuteronomistic History even in exile.

---

[675] Cf. the covenant formula as the objective of the promises in Ezek 11:20; 14:11; 34:20, 30; 36:28; 37:27.

[676] See, for example, Ebach, "Kritik"; also the more detailed discussion in Albertz, *History* (II.4), 2:427–36. That the program of reform, its gradual development notwithstanding, is generally cohesive has been shown above all by Greenberg, "Design."

The theological presuppositions of the proposed reform are actually quite traditional, being rooted in the Jerusalemite conception of the temple as the throne of Yahweh in his glory (Ezek 43:7; cf. Isa 6:1ff.) and the fundamental priestly distinction between sacred and profane (Ezek 42:20). Yahweh had forsaken the old Jerusalem temple and left it to be destroyed because it had been terribly profaned (8–11), not least because the priests had not been so punctilious in distinguishing between sacred and profane (22:26). From this circumstance, the disciples of Ezekiel concluded that in the future the norms governing the holiness of the temple had to be strengthened substantially and observed much more carefully if the temple was to do justice to Yahweh's demands. Thus they had the decisive portion of the vision in which the glory of Yahweh returns to the temple (43:1–13) go directly to the decisive point: Yahweh bitterly laments that the Judean kings had expected to live as his next-door neighbors, with only a wall between them (43:8), and had defiled his holy name by placing their sepulchral monuments within the temple precincts (43:7). In the future, therefore, he demands physical distance. In other words, Ezekiel's followers recognized that the intimate architectural and organizational integration of temple and palace characteristic of preexilic Jerusalem since Jebusite times had compromised Yahweh's divinity and sullied his holiness.

This insight had far-reaching consequences. The first was architectural: the new temple should be a fortress-like structure some 850 feet square, as shown to the prophet in a kind of visionary tour (Ezek 40:5–42:20).[677] Surrounded by a high outer wall and guarded by three gates of enormous dimension, it was to stand totally separate from the palace and other secular buildings; access to it was to be controlled by the priests themselves. A second wall between the outer and inner courts, again guarded by three mighty gates, provided additional protection, guarding the area where the sacrificial cult was performed from any possible profanation. The same purpose was served by a gigantic building (*binyān*) behind the temple, measuring about 170 feet by 130 feet, with no other function (41:12–15). The temple itself was divided in turn into three section of increasing holiness: vestibule, nave, and most holy place (40:48–41:1). With this total of six grades of increasing holiness, the school of Ezekiel sought by architectural means to contain the danger of profaning the temple. Should the structure nevertheless be contaminated by any sins of those taking part in worship, they provided for a semiannual atonement ritual to purify the temple (45:18–20).

---

[677] See the plan on page 370 below.

Plan of the Temple

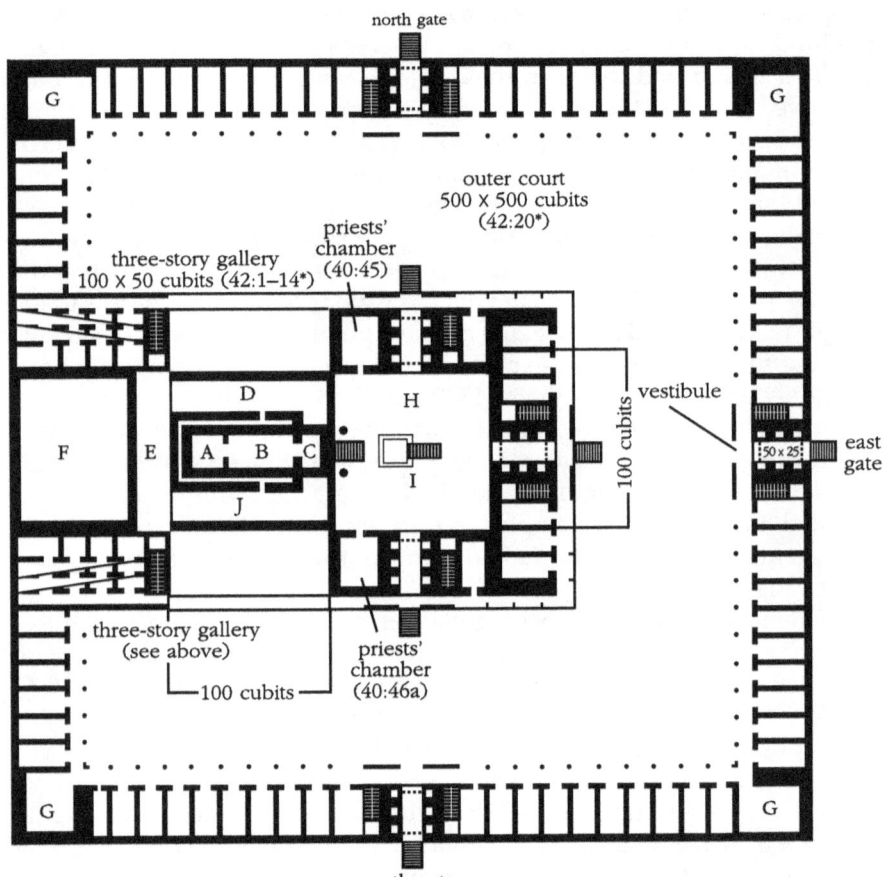

A	קדש הקדשים	most holy place
B	היכל	nave
C	אולם	vestibule
D	מנח	"free space"; 20 cubits wide (41:9b–11)
E	גזרה	restricted area; 20 cubits wide (41:13–15*; 42:10)
F	בנין	building; 100 × 80 cubits (41:12–15*)
G		kitchen (46:21–24)
H		inner court; 100 × 100 cubits
I		altar of burnt offering (43:13–17)
J		side chamber (41:5b–9a)

After Hans Ferdinand Fuhs, *Ezechiel II* (Die Neue Echter Bibel AT 22; Würzburg: Echter, 1988).

The second consequence affected the organization of the cultic personnel, treated in the second section of the "draft constitution" (Ezek 44–46), which deals with questions of access. First the disciples of Ezekiel rejected the preexilic practice of delegating to foreigners the mundane and dirty jobs associated with the temple (44:6–8),[678] since their presence had presented a constant danger of desecration. In the future, only Israelites would have access to the temple (44:9). However, since the sacrificial cult in the strictly separate inner court had to meet much higher standards of purity, the reformers had no choice but to introduce a distinction within the Israelite priesthood. Ministry at the altar and in the temple building itself was to be taken over exclusively by the old Zadokite priesthood of Jerusalem (44:15–16; cf. 40:6b; 43:19; 48:11). The routine jobs, however, such as guarding the gates and slaughtering the private sacrifices of the laity, were to be performed by the Levites (44:10–14). Important as their function was as mediators between the priests in the inner court and the laity in the outer, they had to be excluded from priestly ministry in the strict sense for reasons of holiness (44:13).

The second generation of Ezekiel's disciples, who emerge here as members of the Zadokite priestly lineage, explained this downgrading of other priestly families by claiming that the latter had led Israel into sin during the preexilic period (Ezek 44:10, 12). These "Levites" were probably descended from priests associated with the old provincial sanctuaries (cf. 2 Kgs 23:9).[679] As the vicious polemic shows, the private interests of the Zadokites were clearly an issue in this proposed reorganization, but it must be remembered that the concept of the Levites serving as minor clergy alongside the priests, which became the norm in the postexilic period, sprang from a serious concern to guarantee the holiness of the new Jerusalem temple.

The third consequence was the desacralization of the king. In the preexilic period, the kings had naturally claimed priestly office for themselves on the grounds of their divine sonship; the disciples of Ezekiel stripped the future king of virtually all cultic functions (Ezek 46:1–10). As their exaggerated notions of holiness dictated, only Zadokite priests who had previously undergone strict rites of purification were allowed to enter the inner court to perform the sacrificial cult (45:17–19). As a necessary consequence, the king was denied the right to offer sacrifice (46:2) and was even forbidden to enter the inner court (46:2, 8). The

---

[678] We may recall the Gibeonite hewers of wood and drawers of water (Josh 9:23), as well as the temple slaves (nətînîm) and "slaves of Solomon" (Ezra 2:43–58).

[679] As already suggested by Wellhausen; for further details, see Albertz, *History* (II.4), 2:430–31.

disciples of Ezekiel did concede the future prince certain liturgical privileges: he could consume his own private sacrificial meals in the walled-up east gate (44:3), through which the glory of Yahweh had entered; he was also permitted to observe the official sacrificial ceremonies from the threshold of the inner east gate (46:2). However, these privileges could not alter the fact that cultically he had the legal status of a layperson. The future king would no longer be a cultic mediator but simply the most distinguished representative of the lay community (46:10). This may be the reason why the authors of the "draft constitution," unlike the rest of the book of Ezekiel, always refer to the future king as נָשִׂיא, "prince," rather than מֶלֶךְ, "king."[680]

The fourth consequence was a reorganization the sanctuary's economic support. In the preexilic period, the Judean kings had supplied animals for the official sacrificial cult from the flocks belonging to their domain and paid the priests as crown employees. The temple could be freed from royal supervision and made self-governing under its priests and Levites only if the support of the sacrificial cult and its personnel could be reconstituted. The disciples of Ezekiel thought to finance the cult by imposing a relatively small tax on the entire population (Ezek 45:13–15).[681] They continued to assign to the prince the function of collecting this tax and forwarding it to the temple for the official sacrifices, thus recalling the earlier function of the king as provider for the sanctuary (45:16–17). However, the temple cult was now supported by the people, in accordance with the reformers' notion that Yahweh desired to reside in the temple "among the people of Israel" (Ezek 43:7, 9). Cultically, the prince would function only as *primus inter pares* within the lay community.

Finding a new way to support the priests was more complex because it required agrarian reform. The disciples of Ezekiel were realistic enough to realize that the tax supporting the cult, deliberately kept low, was insufficient to support the priests and Levites in addition to providing the sacrificial offerings, even if it were to be raised (Ezek 44:28–31). Therefore they conceived an entirely new kind of cultic tax (תְּרוּמָה, "lifting, contribution, portion"). A strip of land was to be set apart separate from the tribal territories; both the priests and the Levites would be assigned areas of 10,000 by 25,000 cubits, totaling fifty-two square miles (45:1–8;

---

[680] Ezek 44:3; 45:7–9, 16–17, 22; 46:2, 4, 8, 10, 12, 16–18; 48:21–22. In 43:7, 9, the title מֶלֶךְ refers to the former kings. By contrast, Ezek 1–39 uses both titles: cf. 37:22, 24 (מֶלֶךְ) and 34:24; 37:25 (נָשִׂיא).

[681] It amounted to an annual levy of just 1.7 percent of the wheat and barley, 1 percent of the oil, and 0.5 percent of the sheep and goats.

48:8–14). This land was called a "portion for Yahweh" (48:9) or a "holy portion" (48:10, 20–21). The priests were to reside within their allotted portion and were probably also allowed to keep cattle (45:4);[682] the Levites were even allowed to own private land (תְּרוּמַת הַקֹּדֶשׁ) within their portion and engage in agriculture (45:5).[683] This provision was so contrary to the ancient requirement that the Levitical priests own no property (Deut 18:1–2) that the text was later amended, but clearly the reformers found it more important to keep the burden on the general population as low as possible by having the priests be wholly or partially self-supporting than to honor ancient traditions grown obsolete.

The fifth consequence, finally, was a total reorganization of Israel's primary institutions within the framework of an ambitious program of land reform. This program is the subject of the constitution's third section (Ezek 47–48). The disciples of Ezekiel devised an ideal redistribution of the land west of the Jordan among the twelve tribes of Israel (47:13–48:29). Each tribe would receive an equal portion[684] as its inalienable inheritance (נַחֲלָה; 47:13–14). A river issuing from the temple would compensate miraculously for the disadvantages of the Judean desert and the Dead Sea in the south (47:1–12). Even aliens would be included in the allotment of the land (47:22). This vision clearly reflects an idealized picture of a pre-monarchic egalitarian society. The goal of this land reform was to use the new beginning after the exile as an opportunity to reverse the sharp economic and social divisions that had come to infect Israelite society during the monarchy.

This goal was attainable only if the dominant institutions that had come into being during the formation of the state—the monarchy, the temple, and the capital—which had been primarily responsible for the rise of social classes, could be better integrated into society. The disciples of Ezekiel attempted to achieve this goal by using geographical and organizational separation to limit the concentration of power enjoyed by these central institutions in the preexilic period. To this end, the reformers developed a relatively complex geographical model: as they envisioned

---

[682] Reading the generally accepted reconstruction וּמִגְרָשׁ לְמִקְנֶה, "and pasture for the cattle"; cf. the LXX and Josh 14:4; 21:2.

[683] Reading with the LXX עָרִים לָשֶׁבֶת, "cities to live in." This means of supporting the Levites later proved impracticable. Num 18:25–32 instead assigns them a portion of the general tithe.

[684] The words "Joseph 'two' portions" in Ezek 47:13b are clearly a gloss to reconcile the distribution of the land in this passage with Josh 17:14ff. (Zimmerli, *Ezekiel*, 2:518). The only distinction among the tribes is their proximity to the temple. On this basis—in a departure from preexilic reality—Judah is situated immediately north of the *tərûmâ*, Benjamin immediately south.

it, a strip 25,000 cubits wide would be set apart from the territory of the tribes as a holy portion (48:8–14). Within this portion, a square 25,000 cubits on a side would be further set apart. The northern portion of the square, 10,000 cubits wide, would be allocated to the priests, and the central portion, also 10,000 cubits wide, to the Levites. The southern portion, 5,000 cubits wide, would provide the land for the capital. The rest of the strip, east and west of the square, would belong to the prince.[685]

First, with this geographical model, Ezekiel's disciples separated the temple from the capital. As they imagined it, the temple was to be located in the midst of the land of the priests, with the capital some six miles to the south, separated from it by the land of the Levites. The capital thus became a purely secular administrative center. Second, they separated both the temple and the capital from the monarchy. While the former were set within the separate square, the crown lands were assigned to the portion of the strip outside the square. This geographical separation reflects a corresponding organizational separation. As already noted, the temple was no longer to be under the supervision of the prince; it was to be governed exclusively by the priests and Levites. The capital, furthermore, was no longer to be the property of the king, as it had been since the time of David; it was to belong to all the tribes of Israel collectively and to be administered collectively by all of them (Ezek 45:5; 48:15–18). The land belonging to the city (some ten square miles) was to provide an economic base for the civil service (48:18), so that it would no longer be necessary to levy taxes to support the administration. In addition, the prince was prevented from seizing the land belonging to the tribes and was forbidden to give any of his lands to his servants in perpetuity (46:16–18). This ruled out the most important mechanism that had led in the preexilic period to the development of a class of large landowners at the expense of small farmers. The disciples of Ezekiel were concerned to contain the power of the prince for all time by changing the structures of the state. Inspired by the lessons learned from the prophets of judgment, they used their priestly categories (sacred versus profane) to achieve a real division of power among the monarchy, the priests, and the local authorities unparalleled in clarity in the ancient world. Nowhere else in Israelite prophecy is the new beginning of Israel after the exile thought through with such radical logic.

Of course, only a small fraction of this radical reform program could be realized after 520. Much of it was so unrealistic—moving Jerusalem six

---

[685] Cf. the diagram in Zimmerli, *Ezekiel*, 2:535. Zimmerli's diagram needs to be emended by placing the land of the priests to the north and the land of the Levites in the middle. See the diagram on page 375.

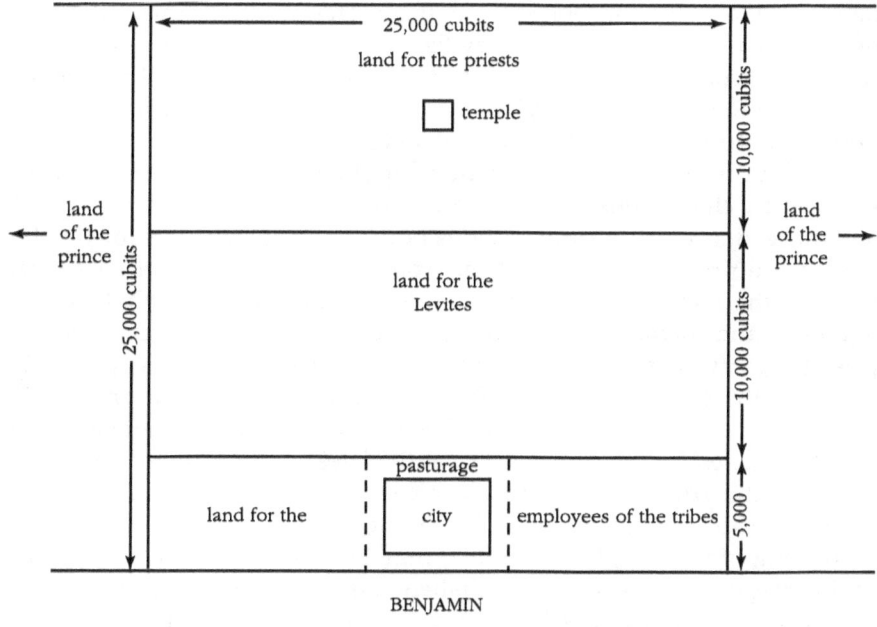

miles south, to give but one example!—that it was a nonstarter. The vision of an egalitarian society remained utopian. During the reconstruction of Judean society, the people hearkened back to tribal models of the premonarchic period (assembly of elders, popular assembly), but it proved impossible to eliminate social inequalities, and in the course of the fifth century these inequalities once again triggered a profound social crisis in Judah. Neither was it possible to impose the principle that priests, Levites, and civil servants had to be self-supporting. On the contrary, the tax burden increased enormously, not least because maintenance of the temple was very costly. At one crucial point, however, the initiative of Ezekiel's disciples met with success: independence of the priesthood and self-governance of the Jerusalem temple. This development included the division of the temple personnel into priests and Levites. The disappearance of Zerubbabel made priestly self-governance easier. At the same time, the desacralization of the king undertaken by Ezekiel's disciples meant that the old notion of a state cult had become otiose. The temple cult could go on without the king.

If we look for examples foreshadowing the separation of the temple from the monarchy, the most immediate is Babylonian. Since time immemorial, the temples in Mesopotamia held vast properties and represented real economic centers; they enjoyed greater independence from the palace than the temple in preexilic Judah, even though the Neo-Babylonian kings tried to exert more control over them. The enormous quadratic plan of the new temple as conceived by Ezekiel's disciples, clearly separated from its surroundings, could reflect Babylonian prototypes. It resembles the plan of the quadratic Babylonian ziggurat more closely than the traditional longitudinal plan of the Jerusalem temple.

Still unresolved is the relationship between the priestly party inspired by the prophetic tradition responsible for the book of Ezekiel and the leaders of the Jerusalem priesthood, the Hilkiads, presumed to be among the proponents of the Deuteronomistic History. Probably both were of the ancient Jerusalemite Zadokite lineage. Nevertheless, the language and theology of the former distinguish them clearly from the priestly party with Deuteronomistic leanings. The latter probably included the first high priest after the return, Joshua ben Jehozadak. Soon, however, there must have been a shift of power between the priestly parties: by the fifth century at the latest, the dominant representatives of the priesthood exhibit clear linguistic and theological affinities with the disciples of Ezekiel. The indictment of Joshua during the rebuilding of the temple (cf. Zech 3) may be associated with an attempt by the reforming priesthood to challenge his office. It would seem that Joshua's opponents accused him of not meeting their criteria of holiness, which were clearly much more strict (3:3).

III.2.7. The Book of Deutero-Isaiah

Abma, Richtsje. "Travelling from Babylon to Zion: Location and Its Function in Isaiah 49–55," *JSOT* 74 (1997): 3–28. **Albertz**, Rainer. "Das Deuterojesaja-Buch als Fortschreibung der Jesaja-Prophetie," in *Die Hebräische Bibel und ihre zweifache Nachgeschichte: Festschrift für Rolf Rendtorff* (ed. E. Blum et al.; Neukirchen-Vluyn: Neukirchener Verlag, 1990), 241–56. **Baltzer**, Klaus. *Deutero-Isaiah: A Commentary on Isaiah 40–55* (trans. M. Kohl; Hermeneia; Minneapolis: Fortress, 2001). **Barstad**, Hans M. *The Babylonian Captivity of the Book of Isaiah: "Exilic"Judah and the Provenance of Isaiah 40–55* (Serie B–Skrifter 103; Oslo: Novus, 1997). **Begrich**, Joachim. *Studien zu Deuterojesaja* (ed. W. Zimmerli; TB 20; Munich: Kaiser, 1963 [originally published 1938]). **Berges**, Ulrich. *Das Buch Jesaja: Komposition und Endgestalt* (HerBS 16; Freiburg: Herder, 1998). **Coggins**, Richard J. "Do We Still Need Deutero-Isaiah?" *JSOT* 80 (1998): 77–92. **Duhm**, Bernhard. *Das Buch Jesaja* (HK 3/1; Göttingen: Vandenhoeck & Ruprecht, 1892; repr. 5th ed., 1968). **Elliger**, Karl. *Deuterojesaja in seinem Verhältnis zu Tritojesaja* (BWANT 63; Stuttgart: Kohlhammer, 1933). **Elliger**. *Deuterojesaja. 1. Teilband, Jesaja 40:1–45:7* (BK 11/1; Neukirchen-Vluyn: Neukirchener Verlag, 1978). **Gitay**, Yehoshua. "Deutero-Isaiah: Oral or Written?" *JBL* 99 (1980): 185–97. **Haag**, Herbert. *Der Gottesknecht bei Deuterojesaja* (EdF 233; Darmstadt: Wissenschaftliche Buchgesellschaft, 1985). **Hardmeier**, Christof. "'Geschwiegen habe ich sein langem ... wie eine Gebärende schreie ich jetzt': Zur Komposition und Geschichtstheologie von Jes 42:14–44:23," *WuD* 20 (1989): 155–79. **Hermisson,** Hans-Jürgen. *Deuterojesaja* (BK 11/2; Neukirchen-Vluyn: Neukirchener Verlag, 1987). **Hermisson.** "Einheit und Komplexität Deuterojesajas: Probleme der Redaktionsgeschichte von Jes 40–55 (1989)," in idem, *Studien zu Prophetie und Weisheit: Gesammelte Aufsätze* (FAT 23; Tübingen: Mohr Siebeck, 1998), 132–57. **Hermisson.** "Neue Literatur zu Deuterojesaja," *TRu* 65 (2000): 267–84, 379–430. **Hermisson.** "Das vierte Gottesknechtlied im deuterojesajanischen Kontext," in idem, *Studien zu Prophetie und Weisheit,* 220–40. **Höffken,** Peter. *Das Buch Jesaja* (2 vols.; NSK.AT 18; Stuttgart: Katholisches Bibelwerk, 1993–98). **Kiesow,** Klaus. *Exodustexte im Jesajabuch: Literarkritische und motivgeschichtliche Analysen* (OBO 24; Fribourg: Éditions Universitaires, 1979). **Koole,** Jan L. *Isaiah: Part III* (trans. A. P. Runia; 2 vols.; Kampen: Kok Pharos, 1997–98). **Kratz,** Reinhard Gregor. *Kyros im Deuterojesaja-Buch* (FAT 1; Tübingen: Mohr Siebeck, 1991). **Leene,** Henrik. "Auf der Suche nach einem redaktionskritischen Modell für Jesaja 40–55," *TLZ* 121 (1996): 803–18. **Matheus,** Frank. *Singt dem Herrn ein neues Lied: Die Hymnen Deuterojesajas* (SBS 141: Stuttgart: Katholisches Bibelwerk, 1990). **Melugin,** Roy F. *The Formation of Isaiah 40–55* (BZAW 141; Berlin: de Gruyter, 1976). **Mettinger,** Tryggve N. D. *A Farewell to the Servant Songs: A Critical Examination of an Exegetical Axiom* (SMHVL 1982-83/3; Lund: Gleerup, 1983). **Michel,** Diethelm. "Deuterojesaja," *TRE* 8:510–30. **Michel.** "Das Rätsel Deuterojesaja," in idem, *Studien zur Überlieferungsgeschichte alttestamentlicher Texte* (TB 93; Gütersloh: Kaiser, 1997), 199–218. **Mowinckel,** Sigmund. "Die Komposition des deuterojesajanischen Buches," *ZAW* 49 (1931): 87–112, 242–60. **Oorschot,** Jürgen van. *Von Babel zum Zion: Eine literarkritische und redaktionsgeschichtliche Untersuchung* (BZAW 206; Berlin: de Gruyter, 1993). **Schmitt,** Hans-Christoph. "Prophetie und Schultheologie im Deuterojesajabuch: Beobachtungen zur Redaktionsgeschichte von Jes 40–55*," *ZAW* 91 (1979): 43–61. **Schoors,** Anton. *I Am God Your Saviour: A Form-Critical Study of the Main Genres in Isa. XL–LV* (VTSup 24; Leiden: Brill, 1973). **Steck,** Odil Hannes. *Bereitete Heimkehr: Jesaja 35 als redaktionelle Brücke zwischen dem ersten und dem zweiten Jesaja* (SBS 121; Stuttgart: Katholisches Bibelwerk, 1985). **Steck.** *Gottesknecht und Zion: Gesammelte Aufsätze zu Deuterojesaja* (FAT 4; Tübingen: Mohr Siebeck, 1992). **Weippert,** Manfred. "Die 'Konfessionen' Deuterojesajas," in *Schöpfung und Befreiung: Für Claus Westermann zum 80. Geburtstag* (ed. R. Albertz, R. W. Golka, and J. Kegler; Stuttgart: Calwer, 1989), 104–15. **Werlitz,** Jürgen. *Redaktion und Komposition: Zur Rückfrage hinter die Endgestalt von Jesaja 40–55* (BBB 122; Berlin: Philo, 1999). **Westermann,** Claus. *Isaiah 40–66: A Commentary* (trans. D. M. G. Stalker; OTL; Philadelphia: Westminster, 1969). **Westermann.** "Sprache und Struktur der Prophetie Deuterojesajas," in idem, *Forschung am Alten Testament: Gesammelte Studien* (2 vols.; TB 24, 55; Munich: Kaiser, 1964–74), 1:92–170; published separately with a bibliographical supplement by A. Richter (CThM.A 11; Stuttgart: Calwer, 1981). **Williamson,** H. G. M. *The Book Called Isaiah: Deutero-Isaiah's Role in Composition and Redaction* (Oxford: Clarendon, 1994).

Unlike the books of Jeremiah and Ezekiel, the "book of Deutero-Isaiah" is not a clearly distinct entity. It is simply one section of the traditional book of Isaiah. The identification of Isa 40–55 as an independent literary unit composed by an author other than the eighth-century prophet Isaiah is a hypothesis of historical criticism.[686] Döderlein (1775) and Eichhorn (1783) were the first to recognize the independence of Isa 40–66; Duhm then split off chapters 56–66.[687] Since Duhm, exegetes have distinguished three divisions: Proto-Isaiah (1–39), Deutero-Isaiah (40–55), and Trito-Isaiah (56–66). This hypothesis has been largely accepted, even outside the narrower circle of biblical scholarship, but recently critical voices have been heard.[688] The unresolved question of how the three sections are related traditio-historically or redactionally is still hotly debated.

Since the formation of the book of Isaiah as a whole extends into the postexilic era far beyond the period of the exile, the problem can only be touched on here. The primary issue is whether Deutero-Isaiah was conceived from the outset as a continuation of Proto-Isaiah (roughly Isa 1–32*)[689] or originated as an independent work that was linked subsequently with Proto-Isaiah, either earlier[690] or later.[691] The former possibility is suggested by the absence of any superscription in Isa 40 and many stylistic and material affinities, such as between Isa 40 and Isa 6;[692] the latter is suggested by the clear compositional linkage of 40:1–2 with 52:7–10 and 40: 6–8 with 55:10–11.[693] One possible solution is that the individual or group we call "Deutero-Isaiah," considering themselves late disciples of Isaiah (cf. the affinities between 50:4–9 and 8:1–4, 16–18; 30:8–10),[694] initially composed a separate document, which at a later redactional stage was linked to the extant Isaiah tradition of Isa 1–32*.[695]

---

[686] It rests primarily on the mention of the Persian king Cyrus, who reigned from 559 to 530 B.C.E., in Isa 44:28 and 45:1. He appears anonymously in 41:2, 25; 42:6 (?); 45:13 (?); 46:11; 48:14–15 (?).

[687] *Buch Jesaja*, 1892.

[688] Coggins, "Do We Still Need Deutero-Isaiah?" Coggins (78) criticizes the very use of the term "Deutero-Isaiah" by Old Testament scholars, including me. He believes that the identity of Isa 48:22 and 57:21 is sufficient argument against treating chapters 40–55 as a separate unit (79). He goes on to claim that the impossibility of assigning a date or geographical location to the author of the work means that the term "Deutero-Isaiah" should not be used. Unfortunately, Coggins makes no contribution to the question of how better to account for the clear stylistic, linguistic, and theological features characteristic at least of Isa 40–52 than by positing a distinct author or authorial group.

[689] Williamson, *Book*.

[690] Berges, *Buch Jesaja*: fifth/fourth century.

[691] Steck, *Gottesknecht*: third century.

[692] Williamson, *Book*, 30–40; Albertz, "Deutero-Jesaja Buch," 242ff.

[693] See below.

[694] See Williamson, *Book*, 94–115; Albertz, "Deutero-Jesaja Buch," 253–54.

[695] See the discussion of the second edition below; also Berges, *Buch Jesaja*, 541ff.

The relationship between Deutero-Isaiah and Trito-Isaiah is another problem. Elliger still assumed that Trito-Isaiah was a disciple of Deutero-Isaiah who not only composed Isa 56–66 but also edited 40–55;[696] the third section of the book of Isaiah, however, proves to be a loose compendium of texts by very different authors. Chapters 60–62 are most closely related to Deutero-Isaiah in language and subject matter; they probably represent the earliest core of Trito-Isaiah. Most scholars assume that Isa 60–62 should be dated after the bulk of Deutero-Isaiah, but it remains unsettled whether portions of 40–55 might be later than 60–62 or might have been influenced by texts in the third section of the book.[697]

Alongside the Four Prophets book, the Deuteronomistic books of Jeremiah, and the Ezekiel book, the book of Deutero-Isaiah represents the fourth great prophetic work that came into being during the exilic period. It differs from the others in speaking its own unique language: a prophetic language neither Deuteronomistic nor priestly, but strongly influenced by the Psalms. There are also clear material differences. The Four Prophets book was still deeply involved in coming to terms with the catastrophe (purgative judgment), and the Deuteronomistic books of Jeremiah developed in stages the vision of a salvific new beginning; the book of Ezekiel, drawing on the catastrophe, sought to define the criteria that a future society must meet in the eyes of God. From the very outset, however, the book of Deutero-Isaiah proclaims the dawn of a new age of salvation in radiant jubilation:

> Isa 40:1 Comfort, O comfort my people, says your God.
> 2 Speak tenderly to Jerusalem, and cry to her:
> Truly she has served her term, truly her guilt is removed,
> for she has received from the hand of Yahweh double for all her sins.

The theological difference is also apparent in the structure of the book. In the second Deuteronomistic book of Jeremiah (Jer 1–45), the fall of Jerusalem comes toward the end (Jer 39); in the Ezekiel book, it constitutes the midpoint toward which everything moves and from which everything evolves. However, the book of Deutero-Isaiah looks back on it from the very outset: God's judgment on Jerusalem lies in the past; a new era of God's mercy and favor has dawned. Therefore, the central focus and turning point of the book is the fall of Babylon (Isa 47);[698] it concludes

---

[696] *Deuterojesaja in seinem Verhältnis*.
[697] Steck, *Gottesknecht*, 123–25; Berges, *Buch Jesaja*, 545; Werlitz, *Redaktion*, 341–43.
[698] The third edition of the Deuteronomistic book of Jeremiah still places the fall of Babylon at its very end (Jer 50–51); the book of Ezekiel, strangely, does not even mention it.

with the miraculous resurrection of Zion (49–54). Thus the book of Deutero-Isaiah is the only prophetic book of the exilic period that contains nothing but prophecy of salvation. This is because it dates from the end of the exilic period and the beginning of the postexilic period. It has ties not only historically but also materially with the books of the two early postexilic prophets Haggai and Zechariah (1–8).

Like all exilic prophecy of salvation, the prophecy in Isa 40–55 is anonymous. To postulate a prophetic figure called "Deutero-Isaiah" who could appear on the same stage as Jeremiah or Ezekiel is a highly questionable makeshift; its ongoing popularity may be due to the desire to identify a concrete individual as the author of texts that are so significant to Christians.[699] However, we know next to nothing of such a person. The very notion that a single individual was responsible for Isa 40ff. is suggested only by the 1QIsaᵃ and LXX text of 40:6a: "A voice says, 'Cry!' And I said, 'What shall I cry?'" The MT has the third-person singular, leaving the subject of question undefined: "And someone says, 'What shall I cry?'" I consider the MT the harder reading. It is supported by 40:1–2, where the command to "comfort" is addressed to a group in the second-person plural (like the command to "proclaim" in 48:20). We find similarly ambivalent language in the third Servant Song, 50:4–9. Although this is the only one of the four Servant Songs that can be interpreted with some justification as referring to a single prophetic individual, we nevertheless find the peculiar statement "Adonai Yahweh gave me a tongue of those who are taught.... Morning by morning he wakened my ear, to listen as those who are taught" (both times לִמּוּדִים). As Williamson has rightly noted, this language recalls the "disciples" among whom Isaiah sealed up his teaching (8:16).[700] In other words, the speaker here clearly sees himself as belonging to a circle of disciples, the members of which in turn see themselves as successors to the group of disciples that the prophet gathered about him in the eighth century. There is thus some evidence to support Michel's theory that "Deutero-Isaiah" is a prophetic school.[701] This view does not rule out the possibility that there was a prophet of salvation (whom we may call Deutero-Isaiah) who shaped the uniquely poetic and powerful language of the book, but such a figure should be pictured as the leader of a group that took collective responsibility for the good news and continued to set it down in writing even into the postexilic period. The peculiar mixture of psalmic and prophetic language suggests

---

[699] As suggested (critically) by Coggins, "Do We Still," 91.
[700] *Book*, 107–8.
[701] Michel, "Deuterojesaja," 519–21, esp. 521; *Studien*, 216–17; also Albertz, *History* (II.4), 2:414–15.

that this group may have comprised descendants of nonpriestly cultic ministers, primarily temple singers[702] but also cult prophets. The prominence of Zion theology in the book (40:2, 9–11; 41:27; 44:26, 28; 45:13; 46:13; 49:14ff.; 51:17–19; 52:1–2; 54) points more specifically to the former personnel of the Jerusalem temple. Such an origin would naturally bring the Deutero-Isaiah group close to the descendants of the party of religious nationalism, which before the exile had been among the most bitter enemies of Jeremiah.[703] This identification also chimes with their orientation toward the Isaiah tradition, which—in an Assyria redaction designed to convey a message of salvation during the reign of Josiah[704]—in the late preexilic period grounded the rebels' hope that Yahweh would deliver Jerusalem from the Babylonians.[705] It is all the more astonishing how far the Deutero-Isaiah group, influenced by prophetic inspiration and the political circumstances of the early Persian period, distanced themselves, at least in part, from the nationalistic ideas of their earlier environment.

"Deutero-Isaiah" is thus an appropriate designation for a book containing prophecies of salvation and a group of prophets responsible for it. In this case, where the book itself is based on a historical-critical hypothesis, it is necessary to define critically the extent of this book, its literary integrity, and its structure. Strangely, however, redaction criticism approached Deutero-Isaiah much later and more slowly than the other prophetic books. This hesitation may be due on the one hand to the density of its poetic language (in contrast to Ezekiel) and the absence (for the most part) of clear features that aid literary criticism (e.g., poetry/prose, unlike Jeremiah), but also to the theological esteem many of its texts enjoy. Until the 1960s, most scholars considered the book of Deutero-Isaiah largely homogeneous.[706] For years, as a result, especially in Germany, they addressed only questions of form criticism and literary composition.[707] After an initial isolated assay by Elliger,[708] study of the redaction history of Deutero-Isaiah began only some thirty years ago.[709]

---

702 As proposed especially by Westermann, *Isaiah 40–66*, 8.

703 Albertz, *History* (II.4), 1:236–41.

704 Hermann Barth, *Die Jesaja-Worte in der Josiazeit: Israel und Assur als Thema einer produktiven Neuinterpretation der Jesajaüberlieferung* (WMANT, 48; Neukirchen-Vluyn: Neukirchener Verlag, 1977).

705 Albertz, *History* (II.4), 1:239–41.

706 Westermann, *Isaiah 40–66*.

707 Mowinckel, "Komposition"; Begrich, *Studien*; Westermann, "Sprache"; Schoors, *I Am God*; Melugin, *Formation*.

708 *Deuterojesaja* (1933; cf. 1978).

709 Schmitt, "Prophetie"; Kiesow, *Exodustexte*; Hermisson, "Einheit"; Steck, *Bereitete Heimkehr*.

The detailed redaction history models produced recently by Kratz,[710] Van Oorschot,[711] Berges,[712] and Werlitz[713] differ in detail but generally converge on a consensus. Surprisingly, however, the book of Deutero-Isaiah, itself a theoretical construct of historical criticism, continues to be the subject of serious compositional analysis that deliberately studies the "final text" synchronically.[714] Despite this methodological incongruity,[715] this approach has also yielded important insights.

Duhm considered the book of Deutero-Isaiah—in sharp contrast to the book of Jeremiah—to be basically unitary.[716] In his view, the only secondary interpolations are the Servant Songs (42:1–4; 49:1–6; 50:4–9; 52:13–53:12), which he assigned to a postexilic author, a few polemics against idols (44:9–20; 46:6–8; etc.), and a few additions in chapters 48–52, for which he held the redactor of chapters 40–66 responsible.

With some variations, this was the prevailing view through the time of Westermann's commentary.[717] He, too, believed that the Servant Songs were interpolated (42:1–4; 49:1–6; 50:4–9) or appended (52:13–52:12) secondarily; the addition of the first three led to later expansions (42:5–8 [9]; 49:7–12; 50:10–11). Unlike Duhm, however, Westermann assigned the first three to Deutero-Isaiah. Other intrusive additions included all the polemics against idols, which Westermann treated as constituting a cohesive stratum (49:19–20 + 41:6–7; 42:17; 44:9–20; 45:16–17, 20b; 46:5–8). There were also a few hortatory and criminative additions (44:21, 22b; 45:9–10; 48:1*, 4, 5b, 7b, 8–10, 18–19, 22; etc.) reminiscent of Trito-Isaiah (48:22 = 57:21). We shall see that compositional analysis and redaction criticism do not justify excluding the first two groups, the Servant Songs and the polemics against idols, primarily on account of their unique subject matter. Whereas Duhm read the book of Deutero-Isaiah as a sequence of shorter or longer poems, form-critical analysis (beginning in 1910) sought to differentiate and delimit the textual units more clearly on the basis of genre. After the initial investigations of Gressmann, Mowinckel, and Köhler, Begrich's 1938 study[718] was largely successful: he identified

---

710 *Kyros.*
711 *Von Babel.*
712 *Buch Jesaja.*
713 *Redaktion.*
714 Mettinger, *Farewell*; Matheus, *Singt*; Abma, "Travelling"; Koole, *Isaiah*; Baltzer, *Deutero-Isaiah.*
715 If there is such a thing as a "final text," it obviously embraces the entire book of Isaiah.
716 *Buch Jesaja,* 14–15.
717 *Isaiah 40–66,* 29–30.
718 *Studien.*

oracles of salvation and favor, judgment discourses, and disputations. Westermann elaborated on his results, identifying assurances of salvation, announcements of salvation, judgment discourses against the nations, judgment discourses against Israel, disputations, royal oracles, and (eschatological) hymns.[719] The proposed differentiation of salvation oracles was confirmed by Schoors.[720] Apart from certain minor differences in identification and delimitation, we have here a generally accepted conclusion of Deutero-Isaiah studies, on which both compositional analysis and redaction criticism can build.

The Genres in Deutero-Isaiah according to Westermann		
assurances of salvation	41:8–13, 14–16; 43:1–3a, 5–7; 44:2–4, (5)	cf. 54:4–6
announcements of salvation	41:17–20; 42:14–16; 43:14–15, 16–21; 49:14–21	
disputations	40:12–17, 21–31; 44:24–28; 46:9–11; 48:1–11*; 50:1–2	
judgment discourses against the nations	41:1–4, 21–29; 43:8–13; 44:6–8; 45:21, 21–25*	
judgment discourses against Israel	42:18–25*; 43:22–28*	
royal oracles	45:1–7	cf. 45:11–23*; 48:12–16a
eschatological hymns	42:10–13; 44:23; 45:8; 48:20–21; 49:13; 52:9–10	cf. 51:3

There is nevertheless some debate as to whether we are dealing here with authentic genres or literary imitations. While Westermann believed that a cultic *Sitz im Leben* (liturgical lament) was possible for at least the two genres of salvation oracle, scholars today are more inclined to the view that the genres have already been adapted extensively for the purposes of prophetic proclamation.

Even on the basis of genre analysis, Westermann was able to make several fundamental observations on the composition of the book of Deutero-Isaiah.[721] Following the work of Hessler, he recognized the concluding function of the so-called "eschatological hymns." He also saw that the genres of assurance of salvation, announcement of salvation,

---

719 "Sprache," 117–63.
720 *I Am God;* see also pp. 169–70 above.
721 "Sprache,"164–65.

and judgment discourse as distinct entities appeared almost exclusively in the portion of the book preceding the Cyrus oracle; after the caesura at Isa 48:21, we find composites with elements of different genres and free variations. This observation confirmed through structural analysis and form criticism the previously noted organization of the book into two portions with different subject matter (Jacob/Israel in 40–48 and Jerusalem/Zion in 49–55). Finally, Westermann emphasized the use of a prologue (40:1–11) and epilogue (55:6–13) to frame the book, with the strikingly extensive disputation in 40:12–31 likewise playing an introductory function.

However, Westermann was unable to recognize fully the revolutionary significance of his analysis, because he took the secondary status of the Servant Songs for granted. He therefore felt compelled to distinguish the eschatological hymns that concluded major portions of the book (Isa 44:23; 48:20–21; 52:9–10) from those that followed the Cyrus oracle (45:8) and the first two Servant Songs along with their expansions (42:10–13; 49:13).[722] Melugin, who examined strictly synchronically the significance of the "basic units" for the composition and structure of the book as a whole,[723] questioned this distinction[724] and was the first to observe that the intentional structure of the book—allowing for some modifications in detail—is based on the hymns.

The Structure of Deutero-Isaiah according to Melugin		
Prologue	40:1–11	
Introductory disputation	40:12–31	
Part 1	41:1–42:13	42:10–13
Part 2	42:14–44:23	44:23
Part 3	44:24–48:21	45:8 (?); 48:20–21
Part 4	49:1–13	49:13
Part 5	49:14–52:12	52:9–10
Part 6	52:13–55:5	
Epilogue	55:6–13	

He was able to show that part 1 comprises two parallel series of genres. The sequence judgment oracle against the nations (Isa 41:1–7), two

---

722 Ibid., 162–63.
723 *Formation*.
724 Ibid., 81–82.

assurances of salvation (41:8–13, 14–16), and announcement of salvation (41:17–20) parallels the sequence judgment oracle against the nations (41:21–29), Servant Song and call oracle (42:1–4, 5–9), and eschatological hymn (41:10–12). Hardmeier was able to identify similar parallel rhetorical sequences in part 2: announcement of salvation (42:10–16 par. 43:16–21), judgment discourse against Israel (42:18–25 par. 43:22–28), assurance of salvation (43:1–3a par. 44:1–5), and judgment discourse against the nations (43:8–13 par. 44:6–8), with a concrete announcement of deliverance in the middle (43:14–15) and an exhortation at the end (44:21–22).[725] Going beyond Melugin, Mettinger was able to point out structural relationships between the eschatological hymns, the Cyrus oracle (45:1–7), and the Servant Songs (49:1–6; 52:13–53:12).[726] Even if not all the relationships are equally convincing, he has shown that the Cyrus oracle is framed by hymns (43:23; 45:8), just like the second Servant Song (48:20–21; 49:13). This arrangement gives the second Servant Song, clearly placed intentionally between the Jacob/Israel portion (41–48) and the Zion/Jerusalem portion (49:14ff.), an emphatic compositional location. Matheus was able to confirm this insight.[727] Thus the perspectives of form criticism and composition criticism have made a substantial contribution to illuminating the structure of the book. In the process, they have produced weighty arguments for treating at least the first two Servant Songs as integral parts of the book, contrary to Duhm and his followers.

It argues for the clarity of the compositional features in Deutero-Isaiah that redaction criticism also took as its point of departure an eschatological hymn (Isa 52:9–10) that, together with the message of Yahweh's return to Zion (52:7–8) and the command to depart (52:11–12), marks a possible conclusion to the book. Elliger[728] believed that this passage marked the end of the Deutero-Isaiah collection assembled by Trito-Isaiah.[729] To the inner inclusio, formed by the parallel announcements of good news in 40:9–11 and 52:7–12, Trito-Isaiah added an outer inclusio, dealing with the prophet's call (40:1–8) and death (the appended fourth Servant Song, 52:13–53:12). Somewhat later, he added chapters 54–55 and created yet another inclusio, on the theme of the enduring

---

[725] "Geschwiegen," 167ff.
[726] *Farewell*; see the chart on 27.
[727] *Singt*.
[728] *Deuterojesaja in seinem Verhältnis*, 265–67.
[729] According to Elliger, Trito-Isaiah also lightly edited this collection, which consisted in part of existing smaller collections: Isa 42:6b, 19–23; 44:26bβ, 28b; 45:9–10, 13bβγ, 14aα; 46:12–13; 47:1–15; 48:1bγ2, 4, 5b, 8b–10, 16b, 17–19; 49:7aβ–8aα, 8baβ, 22–26; 50:1–3, 10; 51:4–5, 10b, 12–14; 52:3. See the table, 305–7.

power of God's word (40:7–8 and 55:10–11). There were also additions by other hands, such as the polemics against idols.⁷³⁰

Although literary analysis of the book of Trito-Isaiah has rendered obsolete the theory that Trito-Isaiah edited and augmented the book of Deutero-Isaiah, all recent redaction criticism has attempted to follow in the footsteps of Elliger. The first step was taken by Schmitt, who detected a "scholastic redaction" in Isa 48:1bβ, 2, 5b, 7b, 8b, 9–11aβ, 17–19 and Isa 55—in other words, where Elliger had seen the hand of Trito-Isaiah—as well as in 40:1–11 (see esp. 40:6–8).⁷³¹ A further important step beyond Elliger was taken by Kiesow.⁷³² Corresponding to the three hymns and commands to depart in 48:21–22; 52:7–12; and 55:12–13, he postulated three redactional stages of the book of Deutero-Isaiah, each with a matching counterpart in the prologue: the first stage was the core collection, 40:3–5* + 40:13–48:21*; the second was the first expansion, 40:1–2, 9–11 + core collection + 49:1–52:10. This was augmented by a second expansion, which bracketed the existing text by adding 40:6–7 and 52:13–55:13.⁷³³

The three redactional stages postulated by Kiesow were worked out in greater detail by Van Oorschot,⁷³⁴ although he concluded that the core stratum of Deutero-Isaiah (Dtjes G) included only texts from Isa 40:12–46:11*.⁷³⁵ Although the end of the Jacob/Israel portion appears to have been reached, redaction criticism clearly does not identify the conclusion of the earliest redactional stage with the command to depart in 48:20–21, which exhibits unmistakable linguistic affinities with the eschatological hymns, especially 44:23; 49:13; and 52:9–10. In Van Oorschot's analysis, the transition to the first conclusion of the book in 52:7–10 was a product of the "first Jerusalem redaction" (Dtjes Z),⁷³⁶ which added a prologue consisting of 40:1–5*, 9–11 at the beginning of the text. While the core originated in Babylonia in the period after 550, the first book of Deutero-Isaiah was composed in Palestine around 521/520. Shortly afterward, the Servant Songs 42:1–4; 49:1–6; and 52:13–53:12 were added. According to Van Oorschot, the book was expanded again around the turn of the fifth century by the addition of the "imminent expectation" stratum (R¹), which stresses the imminence of salvation to counter the challenge posed by the failure of salvation to arrive (42:5–9, 10–13;

---

730 Table, 305–7.

731 "Prophetie," 49–61.

732 *Exodustexte.*

733 See the schema at ibid., 165.

734 *Von Babel.*

735 About 40 percent of the total material, according to the calculations of Leene, "Auf der Suche," 812.

736 *Von Babel*, table, 345–47.

46:12–13; 48:12–16; 49:7–13; etc.). The second third of the fifth century saw a second edition of the book, including the "secondary Zion stratum" (R²), which extended the text to 55:11 (49:24–26; 51:1–2, 7–8, 12–15, 20–23; 54–55; etc.) and also added another bracket to the prologue (40:3aα, 6–8*, corresponding to 55:10). It was this addition that gave the prologue the character of an implicit call narrative. The retroactive legitimation of the prophetic message was also furthered by the addition of the third Servant Song (50:4–9). Finally, there were added a redactional stratum of "obedience and blessing" (R³: 42:24–25; 43:22–24, 26–29; 48:1–11*, 17–19) and the idol stratum. Van Oorschot's redactional hypothesis also offered a possible explanation for the fluctuation between universalistic and particularistic texts in the book of Deutero-Isaiah: universalistic stages of the tradition (Dtjes G, the Servant Songs) were followed by two particularistic redactions (R¹, R²).

The major problem presented by Van Oorschot's impressive hypothesis is identification of the core stratum, which is based on the thinnest evidence. Van Oorschot claims that it comprised four minor collections, but there are no structural elements to identify these collections, since Van Oorschot eliminates all the eschatological hymns except for 45:8, on the grounds that they point beyond the bounds of Isa 40:12–46:11. In his model, the hymns in 44:23 and 52:9–10 were not added until the stage of Dtjes Z. He is even forced to assign 42:10–13 and 49:13 to the "imminent expectation" stratum, since they presuppose redactionally the Servant Songs, which were not included until after Dtjes Z. The question is: Is it conceivable that the identical structural element originated in three different redactions?

This problem may have moved Berges, who otherwise closely follows Van Oorschot's model, to date the inclusion of the Servant Songs earlier in the redactional process.[737] He, too, takes the small core Isa 40:12–46:11* as his starting point. Then, however, he interpolates a new redactional stratum, the "golah redaction," which he claims was composed in 522/521 by a prophetic group of returning exiles. This redaction already included the first Servant Song (42:1–4) and three eschatological hymns (42:10–12; 44:23; 48:20–21) and therefore comprised the whole Jacob/Israel portion (40:12–48:21*). This was followed, according to Berges, by the "first Jerusalem redaction," which also came into being among the returnees after 515. It expanded the book by adding the prologue (40:1–5, 9–11) and an initial Zion portion (49:14–52:12*), which it linked by inserting the second Servant Song with its additions and hymn

---

[737] *Buch Jesaja*, 322–68.

(49:1–6, 8–12, 13).[738] The advantage of this solution is that it assigns the eschatological hymns to just two redactions, both originating in the same milieu, and accomplishes the textual linkage of the book's two portions much more elegantly. The problem is simply that it sunders the close affinities between the hymns in 44:23 and 49:13, on the one hand, and 48:20–21 and 52:9–10, on the other,[739] by assigning them to two different redactional strata. Also problematic is the theory that there is a conclusion to the book at the end of Isa 48, after Oorschot had already shown that this merely concludes one portion.[740]

It is noteworthy, however, that Berges—with good reason—disputes the existence of an "imminent expectation stratum," as proposed (on different grounds) by Van Oorschot[741] and before him by Hermisson,[742] because it lacks a distinctive profile and the problem of delayed salvation cannot be limited to a single stratum.[743] The existence of such a stratum has not been demonstrated.

Against Kiesow's attempt to separate Isa 40–48 and 49–55 on redactional grounds, Hermisson had objected as early as 1989 that it was inappropriate to limit the prophet to the all too modern concept of a "theology of the way": "If Deutero-Isaiah had simply sent his hearers into the desert without allowing them to arrive at their destination, he would have earned their displeasure."[744] From 40:5, 41:27, and 45:13, 14, he concludes that even the Jacob/Israel portion of the book set its sights from the outset on the return of the exiles and the glorification of Yahweh in Zion. The differing subjects of the two portions should be interpreted as a deliberate shift of perspective: "The patriarch Jacob represents God's chosen Israel from the perspective of departure and journey.... The figure of Zion, however, as the chosen mother city of all Israel, represents Israel from the perspective of arrival."[745] Whether this structure reflects the conception of the Deutero-Isaiah group from the outset or came into

---

[738] Like Van Oorschot, Berges (*Buch Jesaja*, 368ff.) identifies a "second Jerusalem redaction" around the middle of the fifth century. He differs with Van Oorschot in postulating a very late date for the composition and inclusion of the fourth Servant Song.

[739] See Mettinger, *Farewell*, 27.

[740] Such a conclusion is also postulated by Höffken, *Buch Jesaja*, 2:17. Höffken also posits only a single redactional stage, which included everything through chapter 55. This conclusion at the end of chapter 48 appears even more problematic in the light of the statement "Yahweh has redeemed his servant Jacob" in Isa 48:20, which anticipates the Servant Song in 49:1–6.

[741] Von *Babel*, 197ff.

[742] "Einheit," 140–41.

[743] Berges, *Buch Jesaja*, 338.

[744] "Einheit," 148.

[745] Ibid.

being only through successive stages need not concern us; I believe that Hermisson has correctly identified the first tangible conception of the book as a whole. The break after 48:21 simply marks the end of a chapter, not the end of a book.

The breadth of Hermisson's conception means that redaction criticism can ignore any truly compositional endings (Isa 52:7–12, with 52:13–53:12 added). He seeks and finds the basic core of Deutero-Isaiah in every chapter from 40 through 55 without distinction, even including the four Servant Songs.[746] However, Hermisson passes over too quickly the linguistic and form-critical features that distinguish the second portion, which scholars since Elliger have observed repeatedly.

Here the proposal of Steck appeared to offer a radical but better solution.[747] In his opinion, the departure and arrival perspectives both belonged to the core stratum, which he dated shortly after 539. This core, however, consisted primarily of material from the first portion of the book, Isa 40:1–5 through 48:21*; the only material from the second portion was the conclusion 52:7–10, (11–12?). The large intervening gap was filled relatively quickly (roughly by 521)[748] by three "Zion continuations" (first the imperative poem 51:10a, 19–23; 52:1–2; 54:1; next 49:14–16; 51:18; and last 50:1–3; 51:12–15; 52:3; 54:4–8).[749] Finally, around 520, the "supplementary Cyrus stratum" with its interpolated Servant Songs was added, a notion that Steck borrowed from his student R. G. Kratz. This addition established the present transition (49:1–6, 7–13) to the Zion portion.[750] Apart from the questionable hypothesis of such small-scale "Zion continuations," with which Steck appears quite comfortable even though 54:1, 4–8 goes beyond the recognized conclusion to the book in 52:7–10, this perplexing solution suffers from the defect that there is no way to link 52:7–12 directly with 48:20–21. The returnees mentioned in 48:21 never arrive in Jerusalem (their arrival now appears in 49:11–12, 17–21, 22–23). The shift from the departure perspective to the arrival perspective is abrupt, and the placement of two hymns in closest proximity does not chime with the regular compositional structure of the book.

---

[746] See the table in "Einheit," 155. According to the calculations of Leene ("Auf der Suche," 812), the core comprises 70 percent of the text. In Hermisson's model ("Einheit," 155), there are three subsequent stages of the tradition: inclusion of the Servant Songs with the addition of the eschatological hymn in 49:13 (stage 2); qārōb or "imminent expectation" stratum (stage 3, with the possibility of combining stages 2 and 3 [313 n. 87]); idols (stage 4); other texts (stage 5).

[747] *Gottesknecht*, 96–125.
[748] Ibid., 187–88.
[749] See the table at ibid., 125.
[750] Ibid., 188.

Building on Steck's study of Isa 49–55, Kratz produced a detailed redactional analysis of 40–49.[751] Unlike Van Oorschot, Kratz finds a cohesive core comprising Isa 40:1–5 to 48:20–21 + 52:7–10, some 56 percent of the text.[752] This core includes two eschatological hymns, 42:10–13 and 44:23. Next this core was augmented by Steck's "Zion continuations," to which Kratz assigns from 40–48 the references to Zion in 41:27; 44:26b, 27; 45:14*, which Hermisson had cited as evidence for the unity of the Deutero-Isaianic conception.[753] Kratz's real accomplishment, however, is to have recognized in Deutero-Isaiah a second redactional stratum deeply interested in the Persian king. He calls it the "supplementary Cyrus stratum" and associates it with the accession of Darius. Kratz assigns the following texts to it: 41:1aβ MT; 41:25aβ MT; 42:5–7; 44:28; 45:1*, 3*, 5*; 45:11a, 12–13bα; 45:18, 22–23; 48:12–15, (16b?); 51:4–5* (?); 52:11–12; 55:3–5 (?). From the observation that 42:5–7 interprets the first two Servant Songs, 42:1–4 and 49:1–6, Kratz argues consistently that it was the redactor of this stratum who inserted the Servant Songs into the book. Finally, Kratz identifies an idol stratum and a "Servant Israel" stratum, both originating in the fifth century.

It is dubious whether the supplementary Cyrus stratum really extended beyond the conclusion of the book in Isa 52:12.[754] It is also worth asking whether the addition to the second Servant Song in 49:8–13[755] should not also be assigned to this stratum (parallel to 42:5–7) and whether the argument that this stratum was responsible for including the Servant Songs does not apply, strictly speaking, only to the first two. Nevertheless, Kratz's identification of a "supplementary Cyrus stratum" has greatly strengthened the likelihood that the book of Deutero-Isaiah underwent a major redaction around 520 B.C.E., as claimed by Van Orschoot (Dtjes Z) and Berges (golah redaction, first Jerusalem redaction). Furthermore, the various models converge on the theory of another major edition of the book during the fifth century (Kratz: "Servant Israel" stratum; Van Oorschot: secondary Zion stratum; Berges: second Jerusalem redaction). Nevertheless, the fact that Kratz, too, has to assign

---

751 *Kyros*; see the table on 217.

752 Leene, "Auf der Suche," 812.

753 See above.

754 Here Kratz simply follows the constraints of Steck's accretion model, without asking whether it is really consonant with his redactional model.

755 Kratz (*Kyros*, 135–39) does not assign Isa 49:7, 8–13 to the supplementary Cyrus stratum, primarily because it reflects a Diaspora perspective that extends beyond the Babylonian golah. He assigns the text instead to the late "Servant Israel" stratum. However, it must be asked whether this thematic feature, which might even be intentional, outweighs the parallel structure of 42:1–13 and 49:1–13.

the structural element of the eschatological hymns to two different redactional stages (core: 42:10–13; 44:23; 52:9–10; "Servant Israel" stratum: 45:8; 49:13) shows clearly that the final answer has not yet been found.

We may now ask where a synthesis of these convergent new redactional theories might lie. Werlitz has devoted considerable thought to this question in a survey of the relevant research.[756] As the title of his book (*Redaktion und Komposition*) suggests, he proposes to combine insights gained by synchronic study of the book's composition[757] with the observations of redaction criticism to yield a useful model.[758] Methodologically, this approach means departing from the postulate formulated by Hermisson in 1989, which has hitherto dominated redaction criticism of the book of Deutero-Isaiah: "Redaction criticism must precede composition criticism."[759] Instead, composition criticism must provide a constant frame of reference and corrective for redaction criticism, and vice versa. Both methodological approaches must be employed recursively, as in a feedback loop. Or, in more practical terms, a satisfactory literary and redactional study of the book of Deutero-Isaiah must yield editions with a distinct beginning and end, a clear structure, and a meaningful sequence of texts. In addition, the redactional process must be demonstrated on the basis of the existing text.

Werlitz has sketched the results that a new methodological approach along these lines might achieve.[760] According to him, a major edition of the book, comprising Isa 40:1–52:10*, was produced in Jerusalem between 539 and 520 by the Deutero-Isaiah group upon their return from Babylonia. This "authorial collective"[761] made use of individual texts and minor collections (42:14*–44:8*) from Babylonia. These included not only the first three Servant Songs but also a collection of polemics against idols (40:19–20 + 41:6–7; 46:6–7; 44:12–13, 14–17, 20 [?]). However, the group was also able to include material from the Jerusalem tradition, such as the imperative poem (51:9–10a, 12b [?], 17–23*; 52:1–2*). From this truly heterogeneous material, the redactors shaped a book framed with a prologue (40:1–2, 3–5*) and an epilogue (52:7–10), structured by means of five eschatological hymns (42:10–13; 44:23; 45:8; 48:20–21; 49:13), and organized into a Jacob/Israel portion and a Zion/Jerusalem portion by

---

[756] *Redaktion*.
[757] Westermann, "Sprache"; Melugin, *Formation*; Mettinger, *Farewell*; Hardmeier, "Geschwiegen."
[758] *Redaktion*, 237–82.
[759] Hermisson, "Das vierte Gottesknechtlied," 135.
[760] *Redaktion*.
[761] Ibid., 289.

means of the command to depart in 48:20–21 together with the second Servant Song. The book was intended to unfold a revelatory chain of events "from Babylon to Jerusalem" and to persuade its readers to accept the coming of salvation it proclaimed.[762] Methodologically significant is Werlitz's conclusion that the redactor of the edition was actually responsible for the compositional elements recognized by compositional criticism as fundamental to Isa 40–52. According to Werlitz, the redactors' own contribution consisted of 40:1–2, 3–5*, 17 (?), 18; 41:5, 27; 42:5–9, 10–23; 44:10–11 (?), 21–22 (?), 23; 45:1*, 8; 46:3–4 (?), 5, 12–13 (?); 48:1–11*, 20–21; 49:7–12, 13, 14–21; 51:18; 52:7–10. It also included all the eschatological hymns, both commentaries on the first two Servant songs, and the earliest announcements of salvation for Zion. This list reveals interesting overlaps with the supplementary Cyrus stratum of Kratz and the first Jerusalem redaction of Van Oorschot. At present, therefore, we can see the outlines of a relatively economical redactional model, comprising only two stages for the initial phase and approximating once more Elliger's 1933 model: (1) existing traditional material, which represents neither a "core" in the sense of Kratz nor a set of "minor collections" in the sense of Van Oorschot, and (2) a book edition that clearly came into being after 539. Werlitz goes on to suggest how he sees the further development of the book, including a scholastic redaction, a Trito-Isaiah redaction, and a complete book of Isaiah redaction, but this part of the argument is less convincing. It should also be noted that, besides the early polemics against idols, which emerged from direct confrontation with the Babylonian cult, Werlitz believes that additional polemics were added later (40:16 [?]; 42:17; 44:9, 18–19; 45:16, 20b).

Drawing on this methodological trend and adopting the observations and suggestions of Werlitz, Kratz, Van Oorschot, and Berges, I attempt here to develop a vision of the origin and early redactional history of the book of Deutero-Isaiah that will find general acceptance. Once again, I must limit myself to essentials.

As the preceding discussion has shown, the book of Deutero-Isaiah possesses two conclusions: Isa 52:7–10, 11–12 and 55:6, 8–9, 10–11, 12–13. I therefore assume that—apart from a few minor additions—it went through two editions. In addition, the command to comfort (נחם pi^cel) Jerusalem (40:1–2) and to build a highway for Yahweh (40:3–5*) as well as the mandate to Jerusalem to herald the good news of Yahweh's arrival (מְבַשֶּׂרֶת, "messenger [fem.] of joy": 40:9–11), despite minor differerences, are fulfilled in 52:7–10 (נחם pi^cel in 52:9, מְבַשֵּׂר, "messenger [masc.] of joy,"

---

[762] Ibid., 322.

in 52:7);[763] the first edition (DtIE[1]) thus comprised Isa 40:1–5*, 9–52:12*. The second edition (DtIE[2]) used 40:6–8*and 55:10–11 as a new frame, emphasizing the power and endurance of God's word. Thus the book attained its full compass. When we note that the inclusion of a dialogue between voices crying out (40:6 and probably also 3aα) in the prologue establishes a link with Isa 6 (cf. 6:4, 8), it is possible that at this stage the book of Deutero-Isaiah was also incorporated into the book of Isaiah.

III.2.7.1. The First Edition of the Book of Deutero-Isaiah: Reconstruction

In determining which texts were included in DtIE[1], there are several important considerations. Since the texts bracketing the book at its beginning (Isa 40:1–5*, 9–11) refer to Jerusalem, there must have been a Zion/Jerusalem portion (49–52) from the start in addition to the Jacob/Israel portion (40–48). Both the repeated mention of Zion in texts belonging to the Jacob/Israel portion (44:26bαγ) or added redactionally (41:27; 44:28b; 45:13; 46:13) and the presence in both portions of the so-called eschatological hymns associated with the bracketing texts (42:10–13; 44:23; 45:8; 48:20–21; 49:13; 52:9–10)[764] further confirm this. The absence of hymns structuring the text in 53–55 makes it clear once more that these chapters belong to a different edition.

The second Servant Song (Isa 49:1–6*) together with its interpretation (49:8[765]–12) constitutes an indispensable link between the Jacob/Israel portion and the Zion/Jerusalem portion. That it was included in DtIE[1] is further emphasized by the fact that the expression "his servant Jacob" in the hymn associated with the command to depart (48:20–21) anticipates the Servant Song, and the bracketing eschatological hymn at the end of the commentary (49:13) ties the entire portion into the underlying structure of the book. Furthermore, the command to depart is carried out

---

[763] In Isa 52:7–8, Yahweh returns alone, in 40:10–11, the exiles are with him; in 52:7–8, the good news is addressed to Jerusalem, in 40:9, she proclaims the good news to the cities of Judah. In 52:11–12, the golah is addressed. These differences persuade Werlitz (*Redaktion*, 260–65, 344–45) to omit 40:9–11 and 52:11–12 from the book edition, but eliminating them leads to unconvincing conclusions. Isa 40:9–11 could be a fragment from the encouraging message of the group during their work in Jerusalem. The description of Yahweh returning alone while the golah is commanded to return makes very good sense when one realizes that the Deutero-Isaiah group composed their book to pave the way for return.

[764] Isa 51:3 might also be a fragment of a hymn, but since it does not have a clear compositional function, it is more likely to be a late addition.

[765] The oddly complex double introduction to God's words shows that 49:7 is a secondary addition, probably added by the redactor who appended the fourth Servant Song in 52:13–53:12 after E[1] was complete.

within the text: with 49:12, the perspective shifts to Zion. The people who were commanded to set out in 48:20 are now in Jerusalem. After the redemption of the people (48:20; 49:13), therefore, the comforting of Jerusalem can begin in 49:14, as commanded in 40:1. Against all attempts to delete 49:1–13 from the text, it must be pointed out that Zion's lament in 49:14, "Then Zion said, Yahweh has forsaken me...," cannot follow 48:21.[766] In addition, the Servant's command to listen in 49:1 clearly echoes God's command in 41:1. Isaiah 49:1–13 thus not only serves as an important bridge between the two portions of the book but also ties the first portion together.

Since Isa 49:1–13 is an important compositional element of the text, it was very likely created by the redactor of DtIE[1] (RE[1]), who took an existing Servant Song (49:1–6*) and furnished it with a commentary (49:8–12) linking it to its context and gave it special emphasis by bracketing it with hymns (48:20–21; 49:13). The only other text for which the redactor provided such bracketing hymns is the Cyrus oracle (44:23; 48:8). Against Duhm[767] and many who have followed him, we must therefore insist that at least the Servant Song in 49:1–6* was an indispensable part of the very first edition of the book of Deutero-Isaiah.

Now Isa 42:1–13, in the first portion of the book, comprises a sequence of texts parallel to 49:1–13: it begins with a Servant Song (42:1–4) followed by a commentary (42:5–9), and concludes with an eschatological hymn (42:10–13). In addition, with the functional qualifier לאור גוים, "a light to the nations" (42:6), the commentary picks up a catchword from the second Servant Song (cf. 49:6), recalling the commentary on the latter (cf. 49:8) by using in parallel the expression ברית עם, literally "covenant of the people" (42:6), probably in the sense of "self-commitment on behalf of humanity."[768] From the first Servant Song, it incorporates and emphasizes the word ארץ, "earth," in the sense of "universal human habitat" (42:4, 5), thus establishing a correspondence between the spirit (רוח) infused in the Servant (42:1) and the spirit or breath that gives life to all humankind (42:5). However, this means that the commentary already presupposes both Servant Songs.[769] Since the

---

[766] Isa 48:22, which corresponds to 57:21, is an addition by the redactors of the larger book of Isaiah, intended to exclude the wicked from the salvation described in Isa 49ff.

[767] *Buch Jesaja*, 14.

[768] The context ("who gives breath to the people upon [the earth]," Isa 42:5) clearly indicates that the word עם, usually used for the people of Israel, here refers to all humanity.

[769] Among more recent exegetes, only Berges (*Buch Jesaja*, 344) has questioned this conclusion, which is now widely accepted (Westermann, *Isaiah 40–66*, 98–99; Van Oorschot, *Von Babel*, 229ff.; Kratz, *Kyros*, 131–35; Werlitz, *Redaktion*, 279–80). Berges's argument is answered by the identification of the individual "called" in 42:5–9 with Darius I (see below).

catchwords כבוד, "glory," and תהלה, "praise," in 42:8 also link the commentary firmly to the "eschatological" hymn 42:10–13,[770] which belongs to the underlying structure of the book, it is highly likely that it too, like 49:8–13, comes from the hand of RE[1], who again took an existing Servant Song (42:1–4) and incorporated it into his book by formulating and adding 42:7–9 and 10–13. In the process, he arranged the introduction in chapter 41 so as to produce two almost parallel textual sequences:[771]

41:1–7	Judgment on the nations	41:21–28	Judgment on the nations
41:8–13	Assurance of salvation: Servant Israel	42:1–4	Servant Song
41:14–16	Assurance of salvation	42:5–9	Commentary on Servant Song
41:17–20	Announcement of salvation	42:10–13	"Eschatological" hymn

Thus the Servant Song and its commentary end up parallel to the two assurances of salvation for Jacob/Israel: Yahweh's lovingkindness toward Israel has its counterpart in the mercy he shows the nations. The compositional hand at work here confirms our earlier conclusion: DtIE[1] also included the first Servant Song. More important, because the commentary on the Servant Song is one of the central texts of the "supplementary Cyrus stratum" in Kratz's redactional model,[772] its author was clearly identical with RE[1]. If so, we may reclaim for RE[1] other texts that Kratz has assigned convincingly to the same stratum. In my opinion, these include the reworking of the Cyrus oracle in 44:28b; 45:1*, 3*, 5*; the secondary "Cyrus" oracles in 45:11a, 12–13bα and 48:12–16a; and the concluding command to depart in 52:11–12. There are also several disputation passages that either like 42:5 underscore the habitability of the world (45:18–19) or like 42:9 emphasize that the promised deliverance is imminent (46:12–13; 48:1–11*).

---

[770] In this case, the term "eschatological" is not entirely justified, since Isa 42:10–13 is the only hymn that does not anticipate deliverance as already accomplished (perfect tense) but exalts it as a new event in the future, now being foretold (imperfect).

[771] Cf. Melugin, *Formation*, 93–102.

[772] *Kyros*, 128–44. Kratz fails to recognize this insight (128–30) because he separates 42:8–9 from the commentary in 42:5–7 on literary grounds and assigns it to the late "Servant Israel" stratum, while assigning the hymn in 42:10–13 to the core stratum. However, not only do 42:8–9 flow absolutely seamlessly from 42:5–7; they are even metrically necessary: without them the hemistich 42:7bβ would be left dangling in the air. The shift to the second-person plural at the end of 42:9 does not indicate a different source but marks the transition to 42:10ff., since it addresses those who are to call for the nations' praise. The echo of judgment discourses in these verses is likewise intentional; it chimes with the free treatment of traditional genres generally characteristic of RE[1].

Within Isa 41:1–42:13, 41:5 has been used at the end of the first oracle of judgment against the nations (41:1–4) to introduce a polemic against idols (41:6–7), clearly a secondary addition. Without it, however, the adversative beginning of the salvation oracle in 41:8 ("But you, Israel, my servant"), contrasting Yahweh's openhanded words of comfort to his people with the frenzied activity of the pagan idol-makers (cf. the word play on the verb חזק, "grasp," in 41:6, 7, 9), would be syntactically meaningless—41:8 cannot possibly follow 41:4! The composition then returns twice to the theme of idols (41:29; 42:8), the second time in a passage composed by RE¹. Thus there is much evidence for Werlitz's belief that RE¹ was also responsible for including some of the polemics against idols.[773] An equally clear redactional integration is also recognizable in 40:18 + 19–20, 44:10–11 + 12–17[774] and 46:5 + 6–7. The Deutero-Isaianic tradition already included polemic against the chief Babylonian deities Bel and Nabu (Nebo) in 46:1–2, which—on the analogy of Isa 41—RE¹ used to contrast Yahweh's lovingkindness toward Israel (46:3–4).

The argument that these polemics are theologically inferior to the other texts of Deutero-Isaiah was persuasive only so long as people pictured Deutero-Isaiah as a distinctive prophetic personality who wrote the book himself. However, as our examination of the Servant Songs has shown from a different perspective, the book is better thought of as a composite.[775] The polemics against idols—which furthermore are limited to the Jacob/Israel portion, set in Babylonia—can very easily have originated in the environment of the prophetic group in controversy with Babylonian religion. RE¹ included them because—in their own earthy, satirical way—they could help promote the new monotheistic faith.

The textual corpus of the Zion/Jerusalem portion (Isa 49:14–52:12*) is harder to delimit, since it has undergone more subsequent revision. Clearly DtIE¹ includes the contentious comforting of Zion in 49:14–21, which echoes the command in 40:1–2 and represents a kind of counterpart to the introductory disputation in 40:12–31; it was probably formulated by RE¹.[776] With Van Oorschot and Werlitz, I believe that DtIE¹ also included the core of the so-called imperative poem in 51:9–10, 17, 19; 52:1–2, which might represent a Jerusalem tradition. The catchword זרוע יהוה, "arm of Yahweh" (51:9), links it with the concluding eschatological hymn (52:10) and thus with the fundamental structure of the book.

---

[773] *Redaktion*, 221–35.

[774] Isa 44:9, 18–19 and possibly also 20 represent secondary revisions.

[775] Werlitz, *Redaktion*, 232, calls it a *mixtum compositum*.

[776] Whether the appended announcements of salvation in 49:22–23, 24–26 already belonged to DtIE¹ at this stage is unclear, since they exhibit many affinities with Isa 60–62.

In addition, it is linked to its context redactionally (i.e., by RE¹) by 51:18 (cf. 49:21).⁷⁷⁷ With Werlitz and against Van Oorschot, I would also include the third Servant Song (50:4–9), which is linked in turn with the imperative poem by the catchword עור, "waken" (50:4; cf. 51:9, 17; 52:1). Unlike the first two songs, which dealt with the mission of the Servant, this Servant Song deals with the internal self-assurance of the prophetic group (a psalm of trust); therefore, RE¹ did not have to provide it with a topical commentary.⁷⁷⁸ The controversy in 50:1–2 is probably also a piece of borrowed tradition, but the short instruction addressed to Israel in 51:4–5 could well have been formulated by RE¹ to secure for the second portion of the book the broad perspective of salvation for the nations sketched in the first and second Servant Songs. Although from 49:8 on the "Servant" is concerned only with comforting and delivering Zion, this broader perspective remains Yahweh's option for the future.⁷⁷⁹ This passage, too, is linked with the imperative poem that follows and the concluding bracket by the mention of God's arm (זרוע; cf. 51:5, 9; 52:7).

Thus the text and structure of DtIE¹ can be presented in the following table.⁷⁸⁰ Passages composed by RE¹ are indicated by bold type, interpolations by italics.

First Edition of the Book of Deutero-Isaiah (DtIE¹): Isa 40:1–52:12*		
40:1–5, 9–11* Prologue	**40:1–2**	commission to comfort the people and Zion
	40:3aβ–5	commission to prepare a way for Yahweh
	40:9–11	herald's instructions: arrival of Yahweh in Zion (with the golah)

---

⁷⁷⁷ Whether Isa 51:20–23 likewise represents a topical expansion by RE¹ is unclear. The subject matter, vengeance on Babylon, would fit very well with the year 521, but stylistic features (the command to hear in 51:1, 7; 55:3 and the addressing of Jerusalem as "O afflicted one," as in 54:11; cf. also 51:20b with 54:9) suggest the later edition, as proposed (also tentatively) by Van Oorschot (*Von Babel*, 133–34, 255–56).

⁷⁷⁸ The commentary in 50:10–11, which now has the poem refer to the righteous and the wicked, belongs (with 48:22) to a redaction influenced by the Trito-Isaiah section.

⁷⁷⁹ The MT of this much-debated text makes perfect sense. In some manuscripts and in the Syriac version, the nations are addressed, which conflicts with the use of the third-person plural for the nations in 51:5b. The reason for the textual uncertainty is the use of the term לאום, "nation," for Israel, although elsewhere it is used only for the other nations. Here, however, the term is chosen deliberately to make it clear that God considers Israel only one nation among many to be set free by God's chosen agent (42:6–7). The shift of the terms "teaching," "justice" (cf. 42:2–4), and "light for the nations" (42:6; 49:6) from the Servant to God is not a fundamental change, but situational.

⁷⁸⁰ Diverging somewhat from Werlitz, *Redaktion*.

	Jacob/Israel Portion (40:12–49:13*)	
40:12–31 Introduction	40:12–1, 16, **17, 18,** 19–20, 21–31	disputations: Yahweh's omnipotence and goodness
41:1–42:13: Section 1	41:1–4, 5, 6–7, 8a, **8b, 9,** 10–13, 14–16, 17–20	exchange 1: JN, OS, OS, AS
	41:21–26, 27, 28–29; 42:1–4, **5–9**	exchange 2: JN, SS1, commentary
	42:10–13	eschatological hymn
42:14–44:23: Section 2	42:14–16, 18–25*; 43:1–3a, **3b–4** (?), **5–7,** 8–12	collection, exchange 1: AS, JI, OS, OS, JN
	43:14–15	middle of collection: AS: deliverance from Babylon
	43:16–21, 22–28*; 44:1–**4, 5,** 6–8, **10–11,** 12–17, (20), 21–22	collection, exchange 2: AS, JI, OS, JN + polemic against idols and exhortation
	44:23	eschatological hymn
44:24–48:21*: Section 3	44:24, 26bα¹, **ba²,** 26bβ–28a, **28b;** 45:1aα¹, **aα²βb,** 2–4, **5,** 6–7	exchange 1: Cyrus oracle, reworked
	45:8	eschatological hymn
	45:11a, 12–13bα, **14–15, 18–19,** 20a, **21–23, 24–25**	exchange 2: topical royal oracle; JN: invitation to the survivors of the nations
	46:1–2, **3–4, 5,** 6–7, 9–11, **12–13**	exchange 3: fall of the gods of Babylon
	47:1–2, 5–8a, 10–15	exchange 4: fall of Babylon
	48:1abα, 3, 6–7a, 8a, 11*, 12–16a	exchange 5: new salvation with a new king
	48:20–21	Command to depart, eschatological hymn, wandering
49:1–13*: Section 4	49:1–4, **5,** 6, **8–12**	SS2, commentary: commission to lead the return
Transition	**49:13**	eschatological hymn
	Zion/Jerusalem Portion (49:14–52:12*)	
49:14–50:2* Introduction	**49:14–21;** 50:1–2	contentious comforting of Zion

50–52*: Section 5	50:4–9; **51:4–5**	SS3, interpretation of SS1 and SS2
	51:9–10, 17, **18**, 19;	imperative poem: lament and
	52:1–2	awakening of Zion
52:7–12: Finale	**52:7–10**	return of Yahweh to Zion; Yahweh's sovereignty established; eschatological hymn
	52:11–12	call to return

Legend: AS = anouncement of salvation; JI = judgment on Israel; JN = judgment on the nations; OS = oracle/assurance of salvation; SS = Servant Song

III.2.7.2. The First Edition of the Book of Deutero-Isaiah: Place and Date

Kratz has made a convincing case for dating his "supplementary Cyrus stratum" around the time of the accession of Darius I:[781] the redaction is responding to the hope that the expectations of Deutero-Isaiah, which went unfulfilled when Cyrus entered Babylon in 539, might possibly be realized after 520 with the support of Darius "on the basis of an earlier decree of Cyrus: return and laying of the cornerstone of the temple under the leadership of Zerubbabel."[782] As we have seen, the "supplementary Cyrus stratum" coincides almost completely with the redactional work of RE¹; therefore, the first edition of the book of Deutero-Isaiah likewise falls within this period.

Nevertheless, I believe that one minor chronological correction is needed. Kratz assumed that the supplementary stratum made Cyrus, not Darius, responsible for the return of the exiles and the rebuilding of the temple (Isa 44:28; 45:13). He therefore identified the influence of a "(proto-)Chronistic theology" like that found later in the book of Ezra (chapters 1–6) and decided on a date "between 520 and 515 or shortly afterwards,"[783] since such a theology is detectable at the earliest in the prophet Haggai. This chronology would have seen Darius firmly in control, and DtIE¹ would already be looking back on the successful return of the Zerubbabel group.

Several arguments tell against this late chronology. First, the rebuilding of the temple is not the central theme of DtIE¹ as it is in Haggai. RE¹ mentions it only briefly in Isa 44:28. The command to bring back the temple vessels in 52:11, at the end of the book, shows that

---

[781] *Kyros*, 186.
[782] Ibid., 191.
[783] Ibid.

rebuilding the temple is more an option for the future. RE¹ is more interested in the general restoration of Jerusalem and the cities of Judah (44:26b; 45:13) along with the return and resettlement of the golah (40:10; 42:7; 45:13; 49:8).

Second, the royal oracles, which RE¹ reworks (42:5–9; 45:11–13*; 48:12–16a), deliberately do not mention the king by name. The redactor left the readers totally free to connect them with Darius, for whom—as we shall see—they were originally composed. The failure to name him explicitly has nothing to do with any (proto-)Chronistic theology, itself a questionable entity.[784] It reflects instead an intention to present the opportunity for salvation under Darius as the fulfillment of the Cyrus prophecy prior to 539, unfulfilled during subsequent history. In other words, RE¹ had to let Darius cloak himself in Cyrus's mantle to show the group that the prophecy of the group, despite all doubts, was still credible.

Third, the texts surrounding the "Darius oracles" still reveal that they are describing something totally new, just beginning in the redactor's day (42:9, 10; 48:6b–7a, 16a). This observation points to a time shortly after Darius usurped the throne from the magus Gaumata in September 522,[785] an event that produced a firestorm of uprisings throughout the central and eastern regions of the Persian Empire. The city of Babylon played a leading role: it rebelled against Persian rule in two uprisings, first in October of 522 and then again in August of 521. Both times Darius was compelled to use significant military force to put down the uprisings. We have proposed that the first half of 521 probably saw negotiations between Darius and the leaders of the Judean colony in Babylon, which led to the first large-scale return in the year 520.[786] Since DtIE¹ urges the readers to seize the chance to return without delay, now that return is finally possible (52:11–12), it must have been written before the arrival of the Zerubbabel group in 520 and probably before the successful conclusion of the negotiations. For the first book of Deutero-Isaiah, then, we arrive at a date in the dramatic year 521 B.C.E.,[787] when the throne of Darius was still far from secure and the possibility of return was by no means assured.

---

[784] The theory of a (proto-)Chronistic theology is based on a questionable statistical comparison of the language of the book of Haggai with that of the Chronicler's History; see Albertz, *History* (II.4), 2:455–56. But these two works are separated by 150 to 250 years!

[785] For detailed discussion, see pp. 124–26 above.

[786] See pp. 119–24 above.

[787] Van Orschoot (*Von Babel*, 166) dates his Dtjes Z "around the years 520/521 B.C.E., a turbulent period both in Judah and in the Persian Empire." Thus the various models also converge on a date.

Instead of the "supplementary Cyrus stratum" proposed by Kratz,[788] we should speak of a "Darius edition" of the book.

Traditionally, the vast majority of scholars have located the composition of the book of Deutero-Isaiah in Babylonia. Barstad has discussed the work of these scholars in detail.[789]

Beginning with De Wette (1833), general considerations led most scholars to accept a Babylonian origin; in the twentieth century, this position was argued particularly by Sellin (1920) and Kittel (1927), who pointed out stylistic affinities of Deutero-Isaiah with certain Babylonian texts.[790] However, occasional voices were always raised in support of other locations, such as Egypt or Palestine. Duhm, for example, situated Deutero-Isaiah in the Lebanon region on account of the סִינִים mentioned in Isa 49:12, whom he identified with the Sinites of Gen 10:17.[791] However, it has since been shown that 49:12 refers to exiles from Syene = Aswan (cf. the standard reading סְוֵנִים səwēnîm in 1QIsa^a). There is evidence of a Jewish military colony on the island of Elephantine there since 525 at the latest. In an earlier study, Barstad (along with others) had argued for a Palestinian origin on the basis of the command to depart in 52:11: "Depart, depart, go out from there [מִשָּׁם]!" Now, however, he does not find the deictic evidence persuasive, since Deutero-Isaiah is a fictive poetic work.[792]

Today it is relatively simple to deal with the problem that many passages in Deutero-Isaiah point to Babylonia while others point to Jerusalem. When we examine the text in detail, we see that the Jerusalem references are concentrated in the prologue and the second portion of the book (40:1–2, 9–11; 49:14–15; 51:17–19; 51:2–3; 52:7–10, 11–12), while the evidence for a Babylonian origin is limited to the Jacob/Israel portion.[793] Since the book itself presents the journey of the message of comfort from Babylon to Zion (48:20–49:14), redactional or traditio-historical criticism opens the door to the hypothesis that the Deutero-Isaiah group was originally active in Babylonia, where most of the material assembled in 41–48 originated, but then moved to Jerusalem, where they continued their work. The prophetic group probably composed DtIE[1] upon their

---

788 *Kyros*.
789 *Babylonian Captivity*.
790 Ibid., 43–46.
791 *Buch Jesaja*, 373.
792 *Babylonian Captivity*, 65 n. 10.
793 For example, the description of a procession of Babylonian idols in 46:1–2; also Yahweh's self-glorification in 44:24ff. and 45:7, 8, which appears only here in the Hebrew Bible but is a standard Babylonian hymnic form (cf. *SAHG*, 67–68; Westermann, "Sprache," 145–46). Parapola (*Assyrian Prophecies* [III.1.3], 4–5) even cites an example of such self-glorification in the context of a salvation oracle for a king (Esarhaddon).

return to Jerusalem. Here, too, there is a recognizable consensus among recent scholars.[794]

Werlitz assumes that the Deutero-Isaiah group returned shortly after 539,[795] but I prefer to think of a later return, associated directly with the first contacts between the leaders of the Babylonian golah and Darius in the winter of 522 or the spring of 521. This date is suggested by the command to the prophetic group to "flee" (ברח) Babylonia (48:20), more appropriate to a time when Babylon was in revolt and the province was at war with Darius (522/521). The book itself also presents the train of events in such a way that the Servant, who had long been unable to carry out his mission of "raising up the tribes of Jacob and restoring the survivors of Israel" (49:6a) and therefore had been entrusted with a mission to the nations (49:6b; cf. 42:1–4), after the call of Darius[796] received a new commission from God "to establish the land, to apportion the desolate heritages" (49:8). This mysterious figure, if connected in some way with the prophetic group (as will be established below), must have arrived in Jerusalem just a year or so before the arrival of the returnees led by Zerubbabel and Joshua (521 B.C.E.).

This identification of the date and location of DtIE[1] provides the key to its interpretation. It was written well after 539, Cyrus's conquest of Babylon, and the fall of the Neo-Babylonian Empire. The soaring hopes of the Deutero-Isaiah group some twenty to twenty-five years before, as the young Persian king advanced speedily from victory to victory—in 550, he conquered the Median capital of Ecbatana, in 547/546 all of Asia Minor—had not been realized. On the contrary, Cyrus had staked everything on the Babylonian card; when he entered Babylon without resistance on October 29, 539, he had himself welcomed by the priests of Marduk as "the chosen agent" of the god Marduk, "whose rule pleased Bel and Nabu and whose reign they desired to rejoice their hearts."[797] Whether and to what extent Cyrus intervened on behalf of the Judean golah is disputed; possibly he returned the temple vessels taken by Nebuchadnezzar.[798]

---

[794] Kratz, *Kyros*, 186, for his "supplementary Cyrus stratum"; Van Oorschot, *Von Babel*, 167, for "Dtjes Z"; Berges, *Buch Jesaja*, 368–69, for his "golah and first Jerusalem recension"; Werlitz, *Redaktion*, 287–89, 321–22, for his "book edition."

[795] *Redaktion*, 292–93.

[796] The association of this oracle with Darius eliminates the problem of why, after the defeat of Babylon (Isa 47), the text should return to the call of Cyrus. If connected with Darius, the text fits into the "chronological" sequence of Isa 45–48: call of Cyrus (45:1–7), fall of Babylon (47), call of Darius (48:12–16a), departure (48:20–21). The content of 48:14–15, too, is quite appropriate to Darius; see pp. 417–18 below.

[797] Cyrus Cylinder, lines 12, 22; *TUAT* 1/4:408–9.

[798] See pp. 122–24 above.

However, the course of events had disproved the message of the Deutero-Isaiah group—that Yahweh had called Cyrus for the sake of Israel (Isa 45:4) and granted him all his victories (45:2–3) so that he would promote the rebuilding of Jerusalem (44:26b*) and establish throughout the world that Yahweh alone is God (45:6). Contrary to expectations (47*), Babylon had not been taken and humbled; instead, the city became one of the four Persian capitals. Meanwhile, Jerusalem lay in ruins. Only with the Egyptian campaign of Cambyses in 525 did Judah, on the southwest flank of the enormous Persian Empire, appear on the political radar screen of the Persians. The Deutero-Isaiah group had been forced to suffer long years of disappointment, waiting, and failure. With the passage of time after 539, political developments had exposed their message to increasing doubt, rejection, and indifference.

They were all the more electrified in the fall of 522, when, after the chaos of Darius's uprising against Gaumata, a man ascended the throne who was prepared to establish peace within the empire, ground its policies on new legal principles, and grant more independence to the nations within his empire (Isa 42:6–7; 49:8–9). Did not this change offer the Judean population of the empire a new opportunity to return and rebuild their homeland? Was not Yahweh again at work to accomplish once for all the deliverance of his people? In the light of the political turnabout that now seemed possible, the prophetic group decided to come forward as heralds of Yahweh's good news (41:27) and to hasten to Jerusalem as the vanguard of the golah, to spread the news of Yahweh's miraculous intervention to deliver Israel. They needed to gain the support of those who had stayed in Judah for the great project of return. Once in Jerusalem, they decided to summarize their prophecy in a book in order to arouse and inspire the populace.

The book is clearly a literary unit but closely follows the dictates of oral communication in its language and diction (many imperatives and interrogatives, alternating voices, linguistically imaginative scenarios). With Gitay[799] and Hardmeier,[800] we shall categorize it as literature intended for public recitation. The most likely *Sitz im Leben* is the local assembly (סוֹד) that gathered every evening in the villages, for which the book of Lamentations and some of the foreign nation oracles were also written.[801] The organization and structure of the book make it quite likely

---

799 "Deutero-Isaiah," 190ff.
800 "Geschwiegen," 163.
801 See pp. 156 and 192–94 above. This does not rule out the possibility that the Deutero-Isaiah group first proclaimed their message orally. An original setting in the exilic cult cannot be ruled out for the assurances and announcements of salvation (see pp.

that it was recited by alternating voices and in part by a chorus (hymns). Some dramatization is also quite possible.[802]

Dramatic recitation of the book amid the cities and ruins of Judah was meant to help break down the resistance, mistrust, lethargy, and hopelessness of those who remained behind in order to pave the way for the great opportunity of salvation just emerging, sixty-six years after the catastrophe.

We must recognize clearly that the notion of several thousand returning exiles will hardly have been viewed with enthusiasm by most of those who had stayed in Judah, especially since many of these exiles were descendants of the former upper class. Would they not claim their old properties and positions of leadership? Quite practical problems also multiplied: Where could these people be accommodated in the poor, afflicted land, still suffering the ravages of war? How could they be fed? We do not know how the responsible authorities in Judah participated in the negotiations of the golah with Darius, but it is obvious that somehow they had to accept the return and that the majority of the population had to support the program of repatriation.

III.2.7.3. The First Edition of the Book of Deutero-Isaiah: Interpretation

To underline the credibility and purpose of their message in the face of doubt and resistance, the prophetic group presented their own long history in their book. As though only yesterday, they had received from their God the all-controlling message of comfort: "Comfort, comfort my people, speak tenderly to Jerusalem." The servitude of the city, still lying in ruins, was ended, her sins were forgiven, the exile was over (Isa 40:1–2). Like royal engineers, they had been commissioned to build for Yahweh a highway through the desert to prepare the way for his return to Zion and the revelation of his kingship to all the world (40:3–5*; 52:7, 10). Therefore, now they called on Jerusalem to proclaim to the cities of Judah the good news of Yahweh's return as well as the return of the exiles (40:9–11).

169–75 above). However, the individual texts and collections—insofar as they can be identified—were all fixed in writing before they were incorporated into the book. This development may be due both to the nature of the original public reading and to the long wait for salvation.

802 This possibility provides the justification for Baltzer's theory (*Deutero-Isaiah*, 22–23) that the book of Deutero-Isaiah is the libretto of a liturgical drama. However, his reconstruction of its organization into scenes is often highly speculative and goes too far. The drama is clearly a genre invented by the Greeks, not found in early Judaism before Ezekiel the Tragedian (second century B.C.E.).

However, before this goal, already anticipated in the prologue, could be achieved, their message had to overcome great obstacles. The first was the skepticism of their audience, initially in Babylon and now in Judah (Isa 40:12–31). Did Yahweh, the God of this tiny ethnic group, have the power to impose his will on nations as powerful as the Babylonians and the Persians (40:15–17)? Were not their gods much more powerful (40:18–20, 25–26)? Did Yahweh act at all in history on the basis of moral categories and rational principles (40:13–14)? Was he even still interested in his people; was he prepared to vindicate them (40:27–31)? At the very beginning of their work, the Deutero-Isaiah group addressed all these challenges raised by their audience; they had heard them already in Babylon. They attempted to picture the supreme greatness and power of their God by recalling what they remembered from the old hymns describing his work as Creator of the world and Lord of history (40:22–24, 28). Had Yahweh not always been a God who brought princes and rulers to naught (40:23)? They mocked the ridiculous idols (40:19–20) and sought to demystify the astral cult, having acquired ample knowledge of both in Babylonia (40:26). However, they also reminded their listeners that Yahweh had always been a God who gave power to the faint and strengthened the powerless (40:29) and would therefore help them now as well.

After this disputatious introduction, the prophetic disciples gave their audience an insight into how the message of salvation had first reached the Babylonian golah (Isa 41:1–20: section 1, first exchange). Yahweh himself had engaged the nations in a forensic debate concerning who controlled history. He revealed that he alone stood behind the breathtaking victories of Cyrus—he, who controlled all of history (41:1–4). While the nations in their terror knew nothing better than to work together manufacturing idols (41:5–6), the Lord of the universe demonstrated his lovingkindness toward his servant Jacob[803] and comforted him, promising his saving presence and help (41:8–10). He had promised to eliminate the countless enemies to whom Jacob saw himself exposed in an alien

---

[803] The remarkably lengthy introduction to the salvation oracle was probably expanded in Isa 41:8b, 9 by RE¹ (cf. the similar technique in 45:1* and 49:5), most likely to establish a parallel between Jacob and Abraham and thus include the Judean audience in the assurance of salvation addressed to the golah: during the exile, as we know from Ezek 33:24, they were fond of appealing to this "southern" patriarch (cf. 48:1). By moving the call of Abraham to the "ends of the earth," RE¹ made him the prototype of the exiles, so as to merge the two groups. The appeal to Jacob/Israel by the Deutero-Isaiah group during their Babylonian period was associated with their hope that salvation would come to all Israel (cf. 46:9). Perhaps they also specifically wanted their message to include the exiles from northern Israel deported by the Assyrians.

land (41:11–12). Indeed, he even had held out the prospect of making this helpless minority resemble Cyrus in his extraordinary chain of victories (41:14–16).[804] To the poor and needy thirsting in the desert, he had promised miraculously to transform the wilderness into an arboretum, to make them understand that Yahweh's creative power lay behind the political upheavals convulsing the world (41:17–20).

However, the promise of salvation had not been fulfilled quite so simply, so RE[1] added a second, parallel exchange (Isa 41:21–42:13: section 1, second exchange), in which he introduced to his audience a new version of his message that would help them understand the nature of the present moment. He began once more with a judgment discourse of Yahweh against the nations (41:21–29), continuing the debate begun in 41:1–4: Yahweh summons the gods of nations to the bar and declares to them that it was he who not only had stirred up Cyrus, who was even now trampling on the representatives of Babylonian power (41:25), but also had announced Cyrus's victorious progress from the beginning (41:26). Indeed—as the prophetic disciples introduced their argument from prophecy—it was Yahweh alone, in the past and in the present, who foretold what was to come (41:22–23). Ever since Isaiah and the other prophets of judgment had predicted the fall of Judah and Israel, Yahweh had demonstrated his predictable, purposeful governance of history down to the coming of Cyrus. The gods of the nations could produce nothing comparable and were unmasked in their impotence (41:24, 28–29). To meet the present situation, RE[1] added yet another argument (41:27): the fact that Yahweh had first sent a bearer of good news (מְבַשֵּׂר) to his own city, that is, had brought the prophetic group to Jerusalem so quickly, to convey the latest news of salvation through the public reading of their book, was a further demonstration that Yahweh alone controlled history.

Still, the military campaigns of Cyrus did not by themselves achieve the goal of Yahweh's historical plan. Therefore, RE[1] added from his sources a text in which the Deutero-Isaiah group had reflected on itself, its community in exile, and its role in Yahweh's historical plan after 539. If Israel, Yahweh's chosen servant (41:8–9), was still living in exile and would obviously continue to do so for some time, even after Cyrus came to power, then Yahweh must have some special purpose for Israel. The result of this reflection is recorded in the first so-called Servant Song (42:1–4), in which Yahweh presents his chosen servant (עֶבֶד, ʿebed) to the world and clothes him with his spirit (רוּחַ), to bring forth justice to the nations, particularly to strengthen the weak. The prophetic

---

[804] My interpretation of the rather bellicose motif of the threshing sledge, in parallel with the metaphor of enemies scattered by the wind like chaff (Isa 41:2, 15–16).

group had recognized that Yahweh sought to establish not just political sovereignty, exercised through Cyrus, but also another form of sovereignty manifested in protective justice. The agent of this new sovereignty, based on justice and morality, was to be his chosen one (בָּחִיר). The context (cf. 41:8–9: עֶבֶד, בחר) makes it clear that this figure represents the golah together with its spiritual leadership, the Deutero-Isaiah group itself.

The identity of the "Servant of Yahweh" is the most ancient and controversial problem in the interpretation of Deutero-Isaiah. For a long time, a vast range of irreconcilable individual and collective interpretations competed with each other; more recently, scholars have sought mediating answers. For details, the reader may consult Haag's survey of the relevant scholarship.[805] If we eschew Christian apologetics and recognize that at least the first two Servant Songs were integral to the earliest identifiable book of Deutero-Isaiah,[806] the answer is relatively simple. Up to Isa 42:1–4, the book does not mention any chosen figure other than Jacob/Israel (41:8–9); furthermore, oracles of salvation (41:8–13) exactly parallel the Servant Song (42:1–4) in the composition of this part of the book. The accepted rules of exegesis leave no choice but to identify the Servant with Israel. This at least was the view of RE[1], the redactor and author of this book, who was a member of the Deutero-Isaiah group. There is simply no more authentic interpretation. The theory that the text referred to some other figure before it was included in the book is pure speculation. Therefore, several more recent studies interpret the Servant of the first Servant Song as representing Israel, more specifically the golah, with only minor variations.[807]

The second Servant Song (49:1–6*) makes it clear that the Servant also has a mission to Israel, namely, to raise up the tribes of Israel once more by bringing back the golah (49:6). It is therefore necessary to extend the collective interpretation so that the Servant can also represent the Deutero-Isaiah group as the vanguard preparing the way for the returning golah. Since 49:6 also assigns this group a universal mission, it should probably be thought of as representing the golah in 42:1–4 as well. The third Song (50:4–9) clearly refers to a representative of the prophetic group, in conflict with his people; the fourth (52:13–53:12), as we shall see, refers to all Israel (golah and Zion) without any prophetic representatives. In short, the Servant of the Servant Songs is not a single figure, certainly not a single individual, but Israel under various guises (golah,

---

[805] *Gottesknecht.*
[806] Contra Duhm, *Buch Jesaja*, 14, and many others.
[807] Van Oorschot, *Von Babel*, 192–96; Berges, *Buch Jesaja*, 358ff.; Werlitz, *Redaktion*, 271–76.

Zion, prophetic group), seen from the common perspective of their function—different in different situations—in God's plan of salvation.

Our long sojourn in an alien land—the returning Deutero-Isaiah group declared to those who had remained in Judah—played an important role in God's historical plan. Yahweh used us to test a totally new form of sovereignty, based not on power but on justice.[808]

The exciting novelty now proclaimed by the prophetic group was that Yahweh, in his nature as the only God (הָאֵל) and Creator of the world, who bestows on all people (עַם) on earth his life-giving breath and inspiring spirit (רוּחַ), has summoned a new regent just as the Servant foretold, who would exercise this new form of sovereignty (Isa 42:5–9). God would make him a "commitment on behalf of humanity" (בְּרִית עָם, lit., "covenant of the people") and a "light to the nations" (42:6). In other words, this ruler would first submit to justice and thus promote the well-being and moral orientation of the nations. He would intervene on behalf of the powerless and those condemned unjustly by freeing the prisoners and those languishing in dungeons (42:7). Thus he would restore to all within his sway their freedom and the dwelling place for which they had been created. According to the ductus of the text, the new ruler would exercise a new style of sovereignty, liberating and humane, subservient to justice, and thus benefit all nations of the world. However, when the Deutero-Isaiah group recited their work, they naturally led all their listeners to hope that Israel would benefit (cf. 45:13). Concretely, their incredible new message was this: Darius, the Persian king, who had just seized the throne, would also deliver Israel from its Babylonian captivity.[809]

Westermann declared that "42:5–9 is among the pericopes of the book of Deutero-Isaiah that have so far eluded real explanation."[810] The main problem is identifying who is called. The interweaving of political and "spiritual" functions in Isa 42:5–7 left scholars uncertain whether the text referred to the Servant[811] or to Cyrus.[812] The proposed identification with Darius can resolve this question. Of course, the text presents an

---

[808] The book of Habakkuk shows that prophetic circles in exile judged the alien Babylonian authorities and hence the course of history by the standards of justice that grew out of the prophets' criticism of social injustice within Israel.

[809] It is probably no accident that only when the text wishes to represent the return from Babylonia as an act of liberation do we find the image of the Babylonian exile as captivity (= imprisonment); in addition to Isa 42:7b, see also 49:9; 61:1; also Isa 14:17 and Jer 50:33.

[810] *Isaiah 40–66*, 98.

[811] Duhm, *Buch Jesaja*, 313–14; Westermann, *Isaiah 40–66*, 98–100 (uncertain); Van Oorschot, *Von Babel*, 232.

[812] Elliger, *Deuterojesaja*, 228–29; Kratz, *Kyros*, 130–31; Berges, *Buch Jesaja*, 344–45.

idealized picture, for Darius undoubtedly used force of arms to put down the revolts that flared up following his usurpation. Nevertheless—possibly just because up these revolts—he was intent on basing the Persian Empire on a new legal order (Aram. דָּת *dāt*, "law, truth"), as his Behistun inscription already shows.[813] That members of the Judean minority in Babylon were aware of this new idea, probably not as a reality but as propaganda, is quite likely. The surprising thing is that the prophetic group assessed it so positively. Possibly it did converge with their own ideas. That the benefits of the political concept promoted by Darius were not generally recognized at the time the text was composed (521 B.C.E.) may explain the statement in Isa 42:7a that Darius's mission, besides liberation, included "opening eyes that were blind." The singular expression הָאֵל יהוה, "the God Yahweh," which identifies the God of Israel as a manifestation of "the one and only Creator God," might reflect the new religious policies of Darius.[814]

Finally, the prophetic group includes the call of Darius among Yahweh's glorious acts and cites the earlier prediction of his beneficent regime to the Judean public[815] as an example of proof from prophecy (Isa 42:8–9). That the group could foretell not just Cyrus but now also Darius (42:9) is another proof of Yahweh's unique governance of history.

At the end of the first portion, therefore, the people reciting the book called on their audience to praise God (42:10–13). All the inhabitants of the earth should join in their praise, from the farthest seas to the remotest deserts. The whole world should give glory to Yahweh in response to his mighty governance of history. However, since revolts against Darius continued and his rule was by no means established, Yahweh would come to his aid as a warrior and triumph over his enemies (42:13).

The martial language of the first hymn is also best explained if the text refers to Darius. The Judean minority so identified themselves with Darius that they declared his enemies to be the enemies of Yahweh. In the context of this reinterpretation, the martial image of Israel as a threshing sledge in the salvation oracle from the time of Cyrus (Isa 41:15–16) now means that Israel, firmly loyal to Darius, will help put down the uprisings and establish the new legal order (41:1–4).

---

813 *TUAT* 3/1:424, §8; cf. DNa §3 and DSe §3, 4 in Pierre Lecoque, *Les inscriptions de la Perse achéménide* (L'aube des peuples; Paris: Gallimard, 1997), 220, 233.

814 Cf. the similar expression "the God [הָאֵל], the God of your father" in Gen 46:3, a text belonging to the second edition of the exilic Patriarchal History (PH²), dating from the same period.

815 The shift to the second-person plural at the end of Isa 42:9, which has often led scholars to separate vv. 8–9 from 42:5–7, results from the author's desire to include the Judeans in the political upheaval just described.

Following this highly topical first section, in section 2 (42:14–44:23) the prophetic disciples turned their gaze once more to the past, making use of an earlier collection that originated in the period of their Babylonian ministry (42:14–44:8, 21–22*).[816] It describes a controversy between Yahweh and his people in two exchanges (42:14–43:15; 43:16–44:23). It all began when Yahweh broke his long silence to announce salvation (42:14), proclaiming his intent to overcome all obstacles and guide the golah on the road back to their homeland (42:15–16). However, the message of salvation encountered a further obstacle: the people of the golah were blind and did not know the way (42:16), they were deaf and could not hear the message (42:18). Therefore, Yahweh had to enter into controversy with his people (42:18–25*). They had learned nothing from their doleful history (42:20); Yahweh himself had to show them their wretched plight (42:22–23). They had repressed their sin; Yahweh had to remind them that it was not by accident but by his own decree that they had fallen victim to foreign powers (42:24a, 25). Like other exilic prophets and prophetic groups, the Deutero-Isaiah group had to reappraise Israel's sinful history before the message of salvation could be heard.

Yahweh alone, the Deutero-Isaiah group maintained, had brought about the turning point. In an oracle of salvation (Isa 43:1–3a), out of pure constancy he showed his lovingkindness to his people and promised them his help in any possible straits. This pure, unmerited love—as RE[1] interpreted the message to his audience—would soon lead Yahweh to bring scattered Israel back, not just from Babylonia, but from the ends of the earth (43:3b–4, 5–7).[817] The goal of Yahweh's saving work, the prophetic disciples concluded from the earlier collection, was not simply to restore Israel but to have his people, once blind and deaf, serve as a witness in his contention with the nations and their gods (43:8–13). Israel, Yahweh's chosen servant, had personally experienced in its own history Yahweh's power to judge and save; its mission was therefore to bear witness before all the nations that its God is God alone. This transformation

---

[816] On the interpretation of this section, see Hardmeier, "Geschwiegen," 167–78; he also recognizes the parallel structure centered on Isa 43:14–15. On the traditio-historical assignment of the material, see Werlitz, *Redaktion*, 239–50. RE[1] was probably responsible for 43:3b–4, 5–7; 44:10–11 and the inclusion of the polemic against idols in 44:12–17, 20. Isaiah 42:17, 19, 21, 24b; 43:28a; 44:9, 18–19 are later additions.

[817] The double salvation oracle is a single compositional unit; cf. the frame in Isa 43:1, 7. That RE[1] was already looking forward to a return of the entire Diaspora is shown clearly by 49:12. In welcoming even the Egyptian golah ("land of Sinim" = Syene/Aswan), RE[1] differs diametrically from JerD. The notion that Yahweh gave Egypt as Israel's ransom might reflect the campaign of Cambyses in 525–522, which led to the incorporation of Egypt into the Persian Empire.

of Israel from a blind people to a witness on behalf of monotheism was the real purpose of Israel's deliverance from Babylon, which the prophetic disciples had spoken of at the very heart of the collection (43:14–15), if only briefly.

The second exchange began with Yahweh's announcement of a new exodus (43:16–21), but he had to contend with the fact that the exiles so mourned their earlier history as Yahweh's people (43:18) that they could not even imagine a new act of salvation on his part (43:19). A further obstacle to the message of salvation, the prophetic disciples were sure, was Israel's extreme self-pity. Therefore, Yahweh had to engage his people once more in vigorous controversy (43:22–28*). While the exiles whined about going unrewarded for bearing the burdens of the preexilic cult, Yahweh pointed out to them that, to the contrary, it was they who had burdened him with their constant sins (43:24). With all their impressive sacrificial cult, they had not served him (עבד) but enslaved him (עבד hip'il)! With their long history of sin, it was not without reason that he had abandoned them, but he nevertheless declared himself ready to blot out all their transgressions for his own sake (43:25). Only this recognition of sin and clarification of responsibility could open the way to restoration of Israel's shattered relationship with God. Then Yahweh's lovingkindness toward his chosen servant Israel could appear once more in an oracle of salvation (44:1, 2–5). This time, even as the servant doubted his very survival, God promised miraculous increase—amplified by RE[1] with the notion that soon members of other nations, too, would be able to join Israel (44: 5). Now reassured, Israel could once again be appointed as a witness, to confess Yahweh's exclusive divinity and faithfulness (44:6–8).

RE[1] reinforced this monotheistic confession by inserting into the earlier collection two existing satirical polemics against idols (44:10–11 + 12–13, 14–17, 20). The idol-maker who cuts down a tree in the forest, throws part of it in his stove for heat, uses another to prepare a tasty meal, and carves the rest into an idol that he prays to save him—all that must have drawn a laugh every time it was recited. In addition, any of the Judean audience who joined in the laughter was half won over to the new-fangled monotheistic faith brought by the prophetic group from Babylonia: "How stupid! How could anyone hope to be saved by a piece of kindling wood (44:17), while Yahweh governs the history of the world to save his people!"

The prophetic disciples followed this satire with the concluding exhortation of the collection,[818] which appeals directly to the listeners to

---

818 Scholars have questioned repeatedly whether this exhortation really was part of the earlier collection; cf. Werlitz, *Redaktion*, 248–50. Its later inclusion, say by RE[1], could be

return to the God who alone can save (44:21–22); they sought to include those who had remained in Judah in the same restored and renewed relationship with God that they had preached to the Babylonian golah. All Israel was Yahweh's servant and should fully realize its role by returning (שׁוּב) to its deliverer. The return they preached was not a prerequisite for the message of salvation but a personal appropriation of the purified relationship between Yahweh and his people as described by the group, beginning with a recognition of sin and concluding with acceptance of the promised forgiveness (44:22) and the role of witness. Whoever entered into this renewed relationship with God could also affirm wholeheartedly the great opportunity for salvation spoken of by the prophetic group.

The redactor also concluded this second section of the book with a brief hymn (Isa 44:23) calling on all creation to praise Yahweh for intervening miraculously to shape and reshape history. He had not only done what was necessary to deliver Israel but had so reshaped Israel that, as his witness, it could contribute to his worldwide glorification (פּאר hitpaʿel; cf. 49:3). For the Deutero-Isaiah group, the renewal of Israel for the new beginning was not the focus of attention it was for the disciples of Ezekiel and the Jeremiah Deuteronomists, but without such a renewal, they, too, could not conceive such a new beginning.

Once God had removed the external obstacles confronting the message of salvation in section 2, in the lengthy section 3 (Isa 44:24–48:21*) the Deutero-Isaiah group set about presenting the message itself as it developed historically, in order to overcome any internal reservations standing in its way. After it had been shown that the group's message had largely come to pass already, from the time of Cyrus (44–45) through the fall of the gods of Babylon (46) and the city itself (47) to the call of Darius (48), the listeners should be convinced that the remaining portion, the return of the exiles and the rebuilding of Jerusalem, would soon be realized (49–52*). This section is therefore organized historically and reveals the hand of RE¹ more clearly than the previous sections. It is held together internally by the motif of Yahweh's claim to be God alone (44:5, 6, 14, 18, 21, 22; 46:9; 47:8, 10; 48:12b).[819]

---

supported by the argument that the clearly redactional verse Isa 44:1 and the exhortation constitute a bracket. Without the exhortation, however, the collection, which focuses on the relationship between Yahweh and Israel, would lack an appropriate conclusion, so the bracket probably belongs to the collection itself. The exhortation makes perfect sense if it dates from the early period of the Deutero-Isaiah group, when it was still busy coming to terms with the catastrophe. For RE¹, God's forgiveness already lies in the past.

[819] The last text, Isa 48:12b, varies the stereotyped formula "I, Yahweh, and no other" by linking back with the first section (41:4).

In the **first exchange,** the prophetic disciples presented the Cyrus oracle (Isa 45:1–6), which had constituted the heart of their preaching in Babylonia. The oracle had already been bracketed by Yahweh's contentious self-glorification (44:24–28*;[820] 45:7), intended to mitigate the offensiveness of calling the Persian king "Yahweh's anointed [מְשִׁיחוֹ]" (45:1): If there is no aspect of reality not created by Yahweh, the almighty Creator of the world (44:24), not even darkness and woe (45:7),[821] who would deny that Yahweh could also call the alien king of Persia, should he so desire? Just as he was able to command the waters of chaos, so he could appoint Cyrus as his own king to carry out his will (44:27, 28a), for example, to help carry out his wish to rebuild Jerusalem (44:26b*).

Meanwhile, however, this Cyrus oracle had become even more problematic. As was clear to everyone in the year 521, it had not come to pass. Babylon had not been captured and sacked, as the Deutero-Isaiah group had predicted prior to 539; neither had Cyrus done anything recognizable to rebuild Jerusalem. Therefore, RE[1] undertook some retouching of the oracle: with an extensive expansion of its introduction, he opened the possibility of a peaceful occupation of the city (45:1*, from the words "to Cyrus"); by means of small changes in the oracle itself (45:3*,[822] 5), he shifted the emphasis in such a way that, although the call of Cyrus was indeed for the benefit of Israel (45:4a), its primary purpose was to promote the effective recognition and implementation of Yahweh's sole divinity. This change introduced the theme that RE[1] wished to dominate all of section 3, which he used to interpret the long wait of eighteen years for salvation: Yahweh had a far greater religious objective (45:3b, 6).

However, this did not settle the political problem, so RE[1] inserted into the introduction to the Cyrus oracle two brief topical references that now, under Darius, entered the realm of the possible: since sizable groups of returnees could now be expected, the rebuilding was expanded to include the cities of Judah (Isa 44:26ba[2]; cf. 40:9); it was also implied that Cyrus had already issued the order to rebuild Jerusalem and its temple, even though he had not been able to carry it out (44:28b).[823]

---

[820] The verses Isa 44:25–26a probably belong to the second edition of the book of Deutero-Isaiah (cf. Van Oorschot, *Von Babel,* 277–78).

[821] This all-inclusive creation formula of the Deutero-Isaiah group goes beyond conventional language: in Gen 1:2–3, God creates only light, not darkness.

[822] By inserting the first two words למען תדע, "so that you may know," RE[1] turned the motivating predication "For I am Yahweh, who calls you" into a statement of what was to be known: "that I am Yahweh" (for a more detailed discussion, see Kratz, *Kyros,* 19–35).

[823] The interpolation in Isa 44:26b is apparent from the replacement of a bicolon by a tricolon whose first and third stichs belong together; 44:28b diverges from the participial construction and takes up the subject matter of 44:26b.

Earlier we proposed the theory that the edict of Cyrus in Ezra 1:2–4 is not historical and that its Aramaic version in Ezra 6:3–5 (up to 6:4) might represent a decree issued by Darius in 521. At most, the order to return the temple vessels in Ezra 6:5 (cf. 1:7–8) could go back to Cyrus.[824] Thus the suggestion of the Deutero-Isaiah group in Isa 44:28b is either a "pious fiction" born of the need to prove the continuity of their prophecy, in which case it would be the source of the later theory of the book of Ezra, or else the Jewish leaders, in their negotiations with Darius, really did appeal—rightly or wrongly—to promises made by Cyrus, and the usurper Darius might have thought it wise to follow explicitly in the footsteps of the founder of the empire. If the latter, the legend was born of political calculation, and the disciples of Deutero-Isaiah merely disseminated it.

Once again, RE[1] bracketed the reinterpreted Cyrus oracle with a short hymn, formulated (as the context required) as a self-glorification of Yahweh (Isa 45:8). Thus the prophetic group expressed once more the central role that this oracle played for them.

RE[1] forged an additional interpretative device by introducing into the **second exchange,** outside this framework, a royal oracle of his own authorship, in which he aligned Darius with Cyrus (Isa 45:11a, 12–13bα).[825] Yahweh insisted on arousing another king after Cyrus, according to RE[1], because, as Creator of the world, he had made the earth for human habitation[826] and was also the Creator of Israel. It was therefore important to complete the work of salvation already begun. While Cyrus had only spoken of rebuilding Jerusalem (44:28b), Darius would accomplish this himself (emphatic הוא) and also set Yahweh's own golah free (45:13). This was the new and topical message of the prophetic disciples! However, they presented it simply as the continuation of their earlier preaching.[827]

Here in the middle of their work the prophetic disciples already anticipated its end. From this point on, they could pursue the religious

---

[824] See pp. 121–23 above.

[825] The confrontational question in Isa 45:11b is inconsistent with the emphatic הוא, "he," in 45:13; it belongs with the introductory 45:9–10 (Kratz, *Kyros*, 94–97). Probably 45:9–10, 11b, 13bβ belong to the second edition of the book.

[826] Cf. Isa 42:5; therefore Isa 45:12 and 48:13 place the creation of the earth before the creation of the heavens, a sequence found elsewhere only in Gen 2:4.

[827] I would point out how circumspectly the group updates their earlier prophecy. The actual Cyrus oracle in Isa 45:1–6 is changed slightly in emphasis, but—as far as we can tell—it is not altered in substance. The new interpretation is provided only by the texts framing the oracle. Clearly RE[1] hesitated simply to manipulate earlier oracles recorded by the prophetic group.

consequences of the Cyrus oracle. The first was nothing less than a universal extension of the religion of Israel (45:20a, 21–23). The prediction of Cyrus's victorious advance had been fulfilled, so now, for one last time, Yahweh summoned to the bar the survivors of the nations who had escaped Cyrus and asked them whether they would not recognize him as the only God (45:21). What is more, Yahweh invited them to accept help from him, the only righteous God and savior (45:22), and he swore by his own self that all would one day worship him (45:23). This breathtaking conclusion, which the prophetic group came to from their discovery of consistent monotheism, meant nothing less than a redefinition of their own religion.[828] It was a change so radical that it must have appeared highly suspect to other groups in Israel (the authors of the Deuteronomistic History, the school of Ezekiel), although at the same time the redactors of JerD³ in Judah were very cautiously considering embracing members of the neighboring nations.[829] RE¹ therefore found it necessary to open the text with a long twofold introduction. On the one hand, he presented his audience with a little scene where some people from Nubia, subjugated by Cambyses, paid homage to the Persian king (45:14–15).[830] They acknowledged that the only God was at work in Cambyses' victories (45:14), as had been foretold in the Cyrus oracle (45:5–6), but complained that so far they had experienced only the hidden face of that God, not the savior as he had revealed himself to Israel (45:15). Thus the audience should learn to sympathize with the victims of the foreign nations. The Judeans should not want Yahweh all to themselves.

On the other hand, RE¹ confronted his audience with a divine disputation (45:18–19): since Yahweh had created the earth as a habitation, not a chaos (45:18, echoing and accentuating 45:12), the establishment of Yahweh's unique divinity could not result in the destruction of all

---

[828] Isa 45:20–25* is the most important passage from which developed the understanding of the exile as a great missionary opportunity; cf. Dan 4–6 LXX and Bel and the Dragon (see pp. 22–27 above). Paul still cites it to justify the mission to the Gentiles (Phil 2:10–11; cf. Rom 14:11).

[829] See pp. 344–45 above.

[830] The MT uses second-person singular suffixes, thinking of Zion or the golah (cf. Isa 45:13), but this understanding of the text makes no sense. Nowhere else does the Jacob/Israel section address Zion, and there is no reason why the Nubians from the far southwest of the Persian Empire should encounter the Babylonian golah in the east. Ibn Ezra and Luther already read masculine suffixes, referring to the Persian king in 45:13—Darius, in my understanding (see Baltzer, *Deutero-Isaiah*, 309–12). Verses 16–17 belong to the secondary polemics against idols (Werlitz, *Redaktion*, 231–32). For a detailed discussion of this difficult passage, see R. Albertz, "Loskauf umsonst? Die Befreiungsvorstellungen bei Deuterojesaja" in *Freiheit und Recht* (ed. C. Hardmeier, R. Kessler, and A. Ruwe; Gütersloh: Chr. Kaiser, 2003), 360–79.

nations except Israel. And since Yahweh had made his voice heard not in some remote region but rather at the heart of the civilized world, his words had to be deeply informed by the principles of public weal (צֶדֶק) and justice (מֵישָׁרִם; 45:19). Therefore Yahweh had no choice but to include the other nations in his saving work along with Israel. Because this was true—so RE[1] interpreted the earlier preaching of the group (41:11)—the elimination of Israel's enemies would come about differently than expected: they would come to Yahweh of their own free will and kneel in shame before him (45:24). However, this wondrous extension of Yahwism, RE[1] concluded to conciliate his audience, would not annul the special relationship between Israel and its God (45:25).

The second religious consequence, the prophetic disciples made clear in the **third exchange,** was the fall of the two main Babylonian gods, Bel (Marduk) and Nebo (Nabu), under whose burden the animals bearing their images in procession collapsed (Isa 46:1–2). They had not been exiled, as the group had once foretold. On the contrary, Cyrus had promoted the cult of Marduk and restored the images brought to the capital by Nabonidus to their ancestral cultic homes.[831] However, when Babylon revolted against Darius, the cards were reshuffled.

RE[1] used this earlier polemic text as an occasion to append a didactic exhortation, based in part on existing elements (Isa 46:6ff., polemic against idols; 46:9–11, disputation). Unlike the Babylonian gods, which had to be borne about, Yahweh would bear Israel as a mother does her child; he would save Israel in the end, no matter how long the coming of salvation was delayed (46:3–4). Yahweh simply could not be compared with the lifeless idols (46:5 + 6–7). Therefore he would accomplish his historical plan and bring to pass what he had foretold (46:9–11). Thus the prophetic disciples sought to comfort and reassure all who had grown disheartened[832] at the long-delayed coming of salvation and assure them that Zion's salvation was at hand (46:12–13). When they mentioned Cyrus here for the last time, shortly before the fall of Babylon, speaking of him as the "bird of prey" whom God would summon from the east (46:11) to carry out his historical purpose (עֵצָה; 46:10), they had in mind primarily the capture of Babylon, as they had foretold prior to 539. However, they also had in mind Darius's conquest of Babylon, which had aroused everyone's spirits in the fall of 522. Thus here the two sovereigns coalesced; with complete justification, Yahweh could call them both "the man of his purpose" (אִישׁ עֲצָתוֹ: 46:11).

---

831 See the Cyrus Cylinder, lines 30–32: *TUAT* 1/4:409.
832 Reading אִבְדֵי לֵב with the LXX. The reading of the MT, "you stubborn of heart," came into being when the accusatory verse Isa 46:8 was inserted by the scholastic redaction.

In the **fourth exchange,** therefore, moving on to the political consequences of the Cyrus oracle, the prophetic disciples spoke first of the fall of Babylon (Isa 47:1–2, 5–8a, 10–15).[833] This foreign nation oracle, probably composed even before 539 in the milieu of Deutero-Isaiah group,[834] had also not been fulfilled under Cyrus, who had entered Babylon without a struggle in 539 and been greeted as a liberator by elements of the Babylonian establishment. However, Darius's violent conquest of Babylon in December of 522, repeated in November of 521 after a new uprising in August, signaled the epochal turning point. It would be hard to overestimate the shock that these events triggered for both the golah and those who had remained in Judah. It can also be sensed in the oracles against Babylon in Jer 50–51;[835] in Judah, it evoked the third Deuteronomistic redaction of the book of Jeremiah (JerD³).[836] At last Yahweh seemed to have repaid the Neo-Babylonian Empire for all the suffering, devastation, and exploitation it had caused! For the Deutero-Isaiah group, too, the final fulfillment of the prophecy of Isa 47 in their day was the central piece of evidence that their prophecy had been credible; it encouraged them to record it in a book and recite it publicly. Here they could count on the total approval of their audience. That is why the text of Isa 47 was so indispensable for them. One characteristic of this oracle was that it had categorized the arrogance of Babylon as a claim to omnipotence (47:8, 10: "I and no one besides me"). This claim stood diametrically opposed to Yahweh's claim to be God alone (45:5–6, 18, 21–22; 46:9). Thus the disciples of Deutero-Isaiah demonstrated that it was their monotheistic faith that exposed Babylon's self-idolization and laid the theological basis for the downfall of the metropolis.

Following this event, so crucial for the credibility of their message, the prophetic disciples began the **fifth exchange** with an eloquent exhortation (Isa 48:1–11*, 12–16a) formulated by RE¹.[837] Here for the first time they explicitly addressed the Judeans, their immediate audience (48:1).[838]

---

[833] Isa 47:3–4, 8b–9 contrasts Babylon with the picture of Jerusalem sketched in Isa 54 and therefore probably belongs to the second edition of the book; cf. the more detailed analysis of Van Oorschot (*Von Babel,* 152–59).

[834] See pp. 193–94 above.

[835] See pp. 195–96 above.

[836] See pp. 318ff. above.

[837] Specifically, Isa 48:1abα, 3, 6–7a, 11*, 12–16a; verses 1bβ, 2, 4–5, 7b, 8b–10, 17–19 belong to the scholastic redaction, as already noted by Schmitt ("Prophetie," 52–53). Verse 16b is a secondary reinterpretation of the Darius oracle, making it refer to the Servant of Yahweh; cf. 61:1.

[838] "And those who came forth from the 'loins' of Judah," reading וּמִמְּעֵי; but the MT, "from the waters (sperm)," yields a similar sense. It is also possible that Judean society was already addressed in the expression "house of Jacob" (Isa 46:3; 48:1).

They were to hear "this," the announcement of the fall of Babylon, and observe that it really took place "suddenly" (48:3), just like other predictions of the Deutero-Isaiah group (the victory of Cyrus). Since they had heard and experienced all this, they should be so convinced of the trustworthiness of the message that they would spread it abroad themselves (48:6a). However, "from this moment" Yahweh would once more announce something "new" (48:7a), which he would now, after the fall of Babylon, bring about solely for his own sake (48:8a, 11*). After everything that had been foretold and come to pass, this would be equally trustworthy. Thus the prophetic disciples once more built tension in their audience. What was the new, urgent message after this epochal caesura? The audience will already have guessed the answer from the allusions to section 1 (cf. 48:5 with 42:9, 48:11b with 42:8b): the call of a new king, the call of Darius (48:12–16a)![839]

Much more enthusiastically than in the Cyrus oracle, the audience is called on to welcome this new call of a ruler as a crucial message of salvation (cf. the appeals to listen and hear in 48:12, 16a). Once more Yahweh emphasizes that he alone governs all history (cf. 41:4). Just as he had called Israel, created the earth, and continued to call on the stars of heaven, so he had now called Darius (קרא: 48:12–13, 15). He would prosper Darius's difficult road as usurper through all the uprisings, and "in Babylon" Darius would carry out Yahweh's will and command (literally "arm"; 48:14). The nature of his rule and the substance of Yahweh's will had already been described in 42:6–7 and 45:13: righteousness, justice, liberation, the return of the golah, and the rebuilding of Jerusalem. As a ruler crowned with so many blessings, Darius received a title of honor transcending even the messianic title of Cyrus: "Yahweh loves him" or "Yahweh's friend" (48:14),[840] a title given elsewhere only to Abraham (41:9, also RE¹). When, in conclusion, the prophetic disciples have God emphasize that he had not spoken in secret (cf. 45:19) but had been present "there," in Babylon, since the time when this critical event took place, they were perhaps trying to say that the negotiations about the return taking place even then between Darius and the golah were under his special protection.

---

839 Quite apart from its "chronological" position in the book, the substance of the royal oracle in Isa 48:12–16a is highly appropriate to Darius. Verse 15 can refer to the ongoing uprisings and verse 14 to his personal involvement in the pacification of Babylon, which lasted from the winter of 522 to the summer of 521 (see p. 125 above); this makes it possible to interpret בְּבָבֶל in its simplest locative sense, as proposed by Kratz (*Kyros*, 124–25). As Kratz has shown, the conventional translation of the preposition in a hostile sense ("he shall work my will on Babylon"), forced by the assumption that the oracle refers to Cyrus, is grammatically dubious.

840 The MT has a perfective form, the LXX and 1QIsaᵃ a participle.

Thus at the conclusion of the third section, the prophetic disciples sounded the call to go out from Babylon and flee from the Chaldeans (Isa 48:20). They felt that this call was addressed first and foremost to them, who had fled the civil war in Babylonia, to bring to the whole world but especially to the Judeans the joyful good news that Yahweh had delivered his servant Jacob. However, the call to go out and to proclaim Yahweh's praise was also addressed to the golah, of which the prophetic group understood itself to be the vanguard. Thus in a proleptic vision of the golah's return they described how the returnees would be led through the desert and miraculously supplied with water, just as in the exodus (v. 21; cf. Exod 17:6). Thus RE¹ also concluded this section with a hymn of praise, albeit adapted to reflect its contextual position in the book.

Having traced the course of their message of salvation down to the time of Darius and beyond the borders of Babylonia, the prophetic disciples found it important to describe how it finally came to Jerusalem. Therefore they followed the first portion of their book, set in Babylonia, with a second short section (**section 4,** Isa 49:1–6*, 8–12), which was also intended to serve as a transition to the second portion of their book, set in Jerusalem. In 41:27, they had indicated that they alone had understood the historical and theological significance of the preaching of their good news in Jerusalem. For them, it was nothing less than further proof that Yahweh alone was God. Thus it is not surprising that here RE¹ included in his book another reflective passage on the role played in God's historical plan by the prophetical group and the golah: the so-called second Servant Song (49:1–4, 6).

Here, in contrast the first Servant Song (42:1–4), the Servant himself appears before the forum of the nations. He recounts proudly how Yahweh called him from his mother's womb, making him a sharp sword in his hand and a polished arrow in his quiver (49:2). However, this martial image of Yahweh as a warrior who conquers the world with Israel as his "weapon,"[841] reminiscent of preexilic royal theology (Ps 2:8–12a), was shattered by the Deutero-Isaiah group: the sword has become the mouth of the Servant (Isa 49:2a); the glorification of Yahweh (פאר *hitpaʿel:* 49:3; cf. the group's use of the same verb in 44:23), the end for which Yahweh chose Israel to be his Servant, was henceforth to be accomplished by the witness of his Servant, exercising the office bestowed on him in exile (43:10, 12; 44:8). With the exile, the Deutero-Isaiah group concluded, Israel had been given a new function in Yahweh's historical plan: it was

---

841 If the text is not emended, 49:3 secures the interpretation of the Servant in Isa 49:1–3 as Israel. The context formulated by RE¹ (48:20) points in the same direction.

now to bear witness to Yahweh's exclusive power to save not by force of arms but by fragile words.

Still, what was the good of such a function if Israel itself was not saved? The prophetic disciples, who had led the vanguard of witness in the golah, had been sorely tested by salvation's long delay. They had to admit that their unceasing prophetic ministry of preaching and persuasion had been a meaningless failure (Isa 49:4a). Despite extraordinary efforts, return of the exiles and reconstruction in Judah had not been accomplished (49:6a). They could only leave to God the recognition of their work and the success ("reward") of their efforts (49:4b).

In response to their plaint, the prophetic disciples affirmed, Yahweh had given them—and through them the golah—a new mission in his historical plan (Isa 49:6). He found the task of return and reconstruction "too light a thing." Instead, he appointed them to be a "light to the nations," a universal mediator of salvation on behalf of the whole world. Despite the failure of their salvation to arrive, the golah, and above all the Deutero-Isaiah group, could thus contribute in a new way to the glorification of Yahweh in the Gentile world as long as they still lived in exile (cf. 42:1–4).

In the light of the nascent reversal of fortunes in 521, RE¹ created a twofold commentary on these existing reflections from the years following 539. First, with Isa 49:5, he created a new introduction to the words of God in 49:6;[842] second, he added a new response from God at the end (49:8–12).[843] In 49:5, he mitigated the failure of the prophetic group retrospectively by stating that the mission of the chosen Servant included the return of Israel to Yahweh. Despite the delayed arrival of salvation, the prophetic group had been quite able to accomplish this religious mission of restoring the relationship between Israel and God (44:22) and had thus received honor and strength from Yahweh (49:5b).[844] In 49:8–12, RE¹ was able to connect the Servant's new mission with the fact

---

[842] The device of expanding an introduction so extensively as almost to disrupt the grammar appears also in Isa 41:8b, 9 and 45:1*; it is connected with the hesitancy of RE¹ to alter existing oracles of Yahweh directly. The secondary nature if 49:5 is apparent from both the repetition of 49:1 and 6a and the fact that 49:5b fits so poorly into the ductus of the text that scholars have repeatedly proposed transposing it, usually to follow 49:3 (Duhm, *Buch Jesaja*, 358; and even recently Van Oorschot, *Von Babel*, 188 n. 47). However, the short introduction in 49:6 without mention of the subject is quite sufficient (cf. 49:3), especially since God is named at the end of 49:4.

[843] Isa 49:7 is a secondary addition intended to call attention here to the fourth Servant Song, appended to DtIE¹.

[844] This interpretation helps explain the difficult verse Isa 49:5b; the first verb can be pointed as a consecutive imperfect (following the Syriac).

that his universal mission had not canceled his internal mission; the latter had now—as salvation was dawning (cf. 48:6b, 7)—taken on increased importance.

Yahweh's new response to the Servant's lament was not guarded, like the first, but full of mercy and lovingkindness: now that the "time of favor" and the "day of salvation" had come, God gave the Servant the fullest support (Isa 49:8). Like Darius earlier (42:6), God would make him a בְּרִית עָם, a "commitment on behalf of the people," except that for the Servant, unlike the Persian king, עָם meant not the entire population of the empire but just the people of Israel. Specifically, his role included the authority to establish the land of Judah, to apportion the desolate heritages anew, and to give the prisoners in Babylon permission to return (49:8–9; cf. 42:7; 48:20). By deliberately paralleling the mission of the Servant with that of Darius, RE¹ was saying that he saw his own prophetic group or the leaders of the golah coming after as agents of the new Persian king, who was called by God to rule on the basis of law and justice. On Yahweh's initiative, Darius and the golah would work together to restore Israel.[845]

To suggest how successful this cooperation would be, RE¹ described how the exiles, miraculously led and shepherded by God, would come to Jerusalem from all corners of the earth (Isa 49:9b–12). Unlike the redactors of JerD² (cf. Jer 44), he expressly embraced the Judeans who had emigrated to Egypt.

At the conclusion of the fourth section, RE¹ placed another eschatological hymn, confirming that Yahweh had indeed comforted (נחם *pi'el*) Israel (Isa 49:13). The good news had finally come to Jerusalem. At the same time, the hymn strongly emphasizes this concluding section of the first portion of the book, which described the call and changing mission of the Servant. Only the Cyrus oracle receives similar emphasis. At the same time, it establishes compositional links with the second section, which deals with the renewal of the relationship between God and Israel (cf. 42:23), and the prologue (40:1).

At the beginning of the **second portion** of the book, which deals with the restitution of Jerusalem, the prophetic disciples placed a lengthy, contentious announcement of salvation for Zion (Isa 49:14–21), followed by a disputation (50:1–2). Both passages contend with the pusillanimity and doubts of the Judeans, which confronted the disciples upon their return to their homeland. At the beginning of the first portion of the book, they had

---

[845] Here I see yet another allusion to the negotiations I have postulated between Darius and the golah, which probably took place during the first half of the year 521, while Darius was resident in Babylon.

been forced to deal with comparable doubts among the golah (40:12–31). The book deliberately parallels both population groups; both had to learn.

In Isa 49:14ff., the Deutero-Isaiah group also began the task of comforting Zion, as God had called them to do (40:1–2). The prophetic disciples had to concede that the release of the golah (48:20) and the comforting of the people (49:13) had been far from successful in comforting Zion. The city, still in ruins and almost empty of inhabitants, was a symbol of godforsaken desolation that cried out to heaven. The disciples had to confront this plaint (49:14). Yahweh protested that he could no more forget Jerusalem than a mother could forget her children (49:15). The blueprint for rebuilding Jerusalem was already inscribed on the palms of his hands (49:16), and soon the builders would flood in and the Babylonian destroyers would be gone forever (49:17, 19). The city would soon bedeck herself like a bride with the returnees (49:18). The incredible would come to pass: there would be too little room in Jerusalem (49:20); the bereft and barren city would ask in consternation where all these children were coming from (49:21)! By contrasting the desolate ruins with such an image of deliberately exaggerated, exuberant vitality, the prophetic disciples sought to hearten their pusillanimous listeners so that they could at least imagine a new beginning.[846] These disciples also had to contend with doubts as to God's faithfulness, pointing out to those who had remained behind that they had brought about the destruction of the city and the long years of foreign rule through their own sins (50:1; cf. 43:27–22). Against doubts as to whether Yahweh was even in a position to carry out his work of salvation, they appealed to his power as Creator and victor over chaos (50:2; cf. 42:15; 51:9–10).

Following the contentious and comforting introduction to the second portion of the book, later revisions have made it difficult to identify the material of section 5 with the same confidence. If the reconstruction outlined above is correct, the prophetic disciples began it with a text in which they gave their listeners an insight into their own personal relationship with God, the so-called third Servant Song (Isa 50:4–9).[847] Here a spokesperson for the group affirmed his unshakable trust in God in the face of the hostility and mockery that came his way from the people. There was no denying it: not a few of those dwelling in Judah responded with hostility to the message that the repatriation of the

---

[846] The additional announcements of salvation in Isa 49:22–23 and 24–26 are probably later additions (Werlitz, *Redaktion*, 308–13). Werlitz assigns them to a redaction connected with "Trito-Isaiah" (341–42).

[847] Isa 50:10 and 11 are late additions from the "righteous versus wicked" perspective of the Trito-Isaiah section.

golah was imminent. The prophetic group nevertheless kept at their work, waiting every morning for God to inspire them with words to comfort and sustain the weary and indifferent even in this tense atmosphere (50:4). By thus witnessing publicly to their personal faith, the group sought to provide an encouraging example for all who were still fearful and hesitant.

How tenaciously the Deutero-Isaiah group went about their work is shown by the fact that during their time in Jerusalem, when they were engaged primarily in preaching their message of comfort to Jerusalem, they nevertheless continued to disseminate the universal message (Isa 51:4–5) entrusted to them during their exile in Babylonia (49:6).[848] The commission to concentrate on the return and resettlement of the golah (49:8–12) had not abrogated the Servant's universal function in God's historical plan but had merely particularized it. Therefore, the prophetic disciples instructed their listeners that, despite Yahweh's clear display of lovingkindness toward his people and city, it remained his will to orient the nations to his law and bring them his aid. If the Deutero-Isaiah disciples now left to God functions that they had previously assigned to the Servant (42:4; 49:6), this was probably just because they still assumed that the entire golah would return. Thus their mission would be fulfilled, and Yahweh himself would establish his salvific sovereignty over the world, though it was still the job of the prophetic group to keep the universal message alive.

Now, however, the most important thing was to bring to fruition the message of comfort for Jerusalem. In preparation for the grand finale, RE[1] incorporated the imperative poem Isa 51:9–10, 17, 19; 52:1–2, a text that had probably originated in Jerusalem, and inserted 51:18 to link this poem with the introduction to the second portion of the book (cf. 49:21).[849] In response to a communal lament designed to awaken the arm of Yahweh (51:9–10), which also appealed to the battle with chaos and the exodus, God answered Jerusalem, still desolate under the sign of God's wrath, with a call to rouse itself (51:17). Since as yet she had no children to lend her support, she was totally reliant on Yahweh's comfort (51:18–19). Then, finally, God called on Zion to awake, rise from the dust, and put on once more her beautiful garments (52:1–2). Decked in royal raiment, the holy city was to await the arrival of her divine king.

---

[848] Isa 51:1–2, 3 (?), and 7–8 belong to the second edition of the book; 51:6 is an apocalyptic revision.

[849] Cf. Van Oorschot's reconstruction (*Von Babel*, 128–41). It is not clear whether Isa 51:20–23 also belongs to DtIE[1]; I assign it to DtIE[2]. Isa 51:12–15 and 52:3 certainly belong to DtIE[2]; 51:11 = 35:10, 51:16, and 52:4–6 are even later.

With Zion thus made ready, the prophetic disciples came to the great finale of their book (Isa 52:7–10, 11–12), probably composed as a unit by RE¹. With rhapsodic joy, they extolled the bearer of good news (מְבַשֵּׂר), now arriving from Babylon (cf. 41:27), who proclaimed the news of salvation in Judah and to Zion the vital message: "Your God has now become king!" (52:7). They described the rejoicing of the sentinels that broke out at the sight of Yahweh's return to Zion (52:8). With this demonstrable and visible display of Yahweh's lovingkindness to his devastated city, as the book was recited, the long-awaited turning point, the end of the exile, had come. Therefore, for one last time, the prophetic disciples called for praise of God (52:9–10). They commanded the very ruins of Jerusalem to break forth into song, because now Yahweh had not only comforted (נחם *piᶜel* 52:9; cf. 49:13) his people but had also redeemed (גאל) Jerusalem. Now God's liberation embraced not only the golah (48:20; cf. 44:23) but also Jerusalem and Judah. However, that was not all: Yahweh had also demonstrated his power to save before the eyes of all the nations, laying the cornerstone for the universal extension of his worship (52:10; cf. 45:20a, 21–25). From Zion, Yahweh would visibly exercise his kingship over all creation throughout the world (cf. 40:5).

It is not entirely clear how the Deutero-Isaiah group actually pictured this establishment of Yahweh's kingship on Mount Zion. It would appear, however, that for them it did not include any reestablishment of the Judean monarchy as it had existed politically in the preexilic period (cf. Ps 2). The absence of any mention of the Davidic monarchy and the transfer of the royal titles "anointed of Yahweh" to Cyrus (Isa 45:1) and "beloved of Yahweh" to Darius (48:14; cf. Ps 47:5 [4]) suggest the contrary. To exercise Yahweh's political dominion, there was room only for the Persian Great King. For Israel, there was only the "office" of the Servant—but this office, according to our interpretation, embraced the entire nation or its religious leaders and was restricted to the legal and religious domain. It is not clear, however, whether the prophetic group had any intention of extending this constellation into the future. It may be that for them the establishment of Yahweh's unmediated kingship marked the beginning of a new age and a new reality, which they could not or would not describe. It remained for DtIE² to reach the logical conclusion of extending the Davidic promises to the people or Zion and to substitute the pilgrimage of the nations to Zion for universal political dominion (Isa 55:5).

The Deutero-Isaiah group had cast itself in the role of this laudable bearer of good news (Isa 41:27). With this finale, they had faithfully fulfilled their mission of comfort announced at the beginning of the book (40:1–2). Just one element was still missing for salvation to be realized: the actual return of the exiles. Here in the finale, in contrast to the anticipatory description in the prologue (40:9–11), the prophetic disciples separated this return from the return of Yahweh. This decision reflected the historical reality of the year 521. At the same time, here at the end of their book, they displayed once more their intent to do everything possible to further their deepest concern. The ringing call to the exiles to depart "from there" (מִשָּׁם: 52:11)—primarily from Babylon, but also from other places where they were living[850]—was not really meant to instigate the exiles to make their decision, since they were out of earshot. Its purpose was rather to enhance the readiness of those in Judah to receive with joy the multitudes that would soon arrive. The exiles and émigrés were to see that they were heartily welcomed in Jerusalem. Since this awakening (52:1) and the arrival of Yahweh had turned Jerusalem once more into a "holy city," the anticipation of the prophetic disciples transformed the return into a procession: the returnees were to avoid all occasions of impurity; their advance would be guarded before and behind by Yahweh (52:12). Since Yahweh's return made the temple necessary once more, the return of the temple vessels was also important (52:11). In contrast to the exodus from Egypt, which had to take place in great haste (Exod 12:11; Deut 16:3), the new exodus was to take place with all the solemnity due the king on Mount Zion.

Exegesis of DtIE[1] in such detail has been necessary, not only to demonstrate that it is a clearly definable unit stylistically, compositionally, and conceptually, but also to show that it can and should be read as a single book. We have seen that such a *lectio continua* yields a coherent narrative with a clear trajectory, in which every element has its historical, theological, and rhetorical place. Of course, identification of such a clearly organized book depends on my theory that some of the oracles previously associated with Cyrus must be interpreted as relating to Darius.

Since the subsequent redactional stages postdate the end of the exile as defined for purposes of this book (520 B.C.E.), we can discuss them only briefly.

III.2.7.4. Appendix: Fourth Servant Song (Isa 52:13–53:12)

After this powerful finale, no real continuation is possible. The so-called fourth Servant Song (Isa 52:13–53:12) clearly has the nature of an appendix that is no longer an integral part of the fundamental structure (hymns)

---

[850] This deixis was formerly a reason for questioning the Babylonian setting of Deutero-Isaiah (Bartstad, *Babylonian Captivity*, 64–65). The absence of a specific toponym here (in contrast to Isa 48:20) has often been noted; it is due to the expectation of DtIE[1] that the return would encompass more than the Babylonian golah (cf. 49:12 and possibly 43:3b–5).

and ductus of DtIE¹.⁸⁵¹ Since the catchword "arm of Yahweh" in this Servant Song (53:1) refers back to the finale (52:10) and the poem also contains echoes of the first and second Servant Songs (52:13, cf. 42:1–6; 53:4, cf. 49:4), it presupposes the existence of DtIE¹. The ties with Isa 54–55, however, are so minor that it probably was composed before DtIE².⁸⁵² As the finished structure of the long first-person plural account in 53:1–11aα and the framing speeches of God (52:13–15; 53:11aβb–12) show, it is a separate rhetorical unit that could be recited or staged independently of DtIE¹. It came into being only in loose association with DtIE¹ and was appended to the edition by means of 49:7, which constitutes a secondary introduction to the words spoken by God in 49:8–12. This introduction was framed to ensure that the fourth Servant Song would be understood as a further commentary on the second Song in 49:1–6*, even though the long text had to be appended at the very end, since it would otherwise have disrupted the structure of the edition. This redactional association with 49:6 in particular and the repetition of the catchword "arm" from 52:10 provide a reasonably reliable key to the purpose of the "Song": it reinterprets the universal function of the Servant vis-à-vis the nations.

The interpretation of the fourth Servant Song has been hotly debated; we will not go into the details here.⁸⁵³ At first glance, it seems reasonable to understand the Servant of the Song as an individual: in the middle section, a group describes the Servant's wretched life (Isa 53:2–3), suffering (53:5–6), death (53:7–9), and revitalization (53:10–11)—all entirely appropriate to an individual. Even today, many prefer to understand the text as a reflection on the death of Deutero-Isaiah and on his prophetic office.⁸⁵⁴ In this case, the "we" who are startled to discover that the one they had despised had vicariously borne their sins would be Israel.⁸⁵⁵ In this interpretation, however, it is hard to explain why the fate of a single individual—whose significance, furthermore, did not extend beyond the boundaries of Israel—should have startled kings and nations (52:14–15).

---

851 Werlitz, *Redaktion*, 282. Contra Mettinger (*Farewell*, 25–27), the call to Jerusalem to rejoice in Isa 54:1–3 is not an eschatological hymn, and 54:3 is only a secondary fragment. There is thus no evidence for a compositional contrast of the Cyrus oracle (44:24–45:7) with the fourth Servant Song (52:13–53:12).

852 They are limited to accidental echoes (cf. 52:14a and 54:1b) and insignificant uses of the same word (Berges, *Buch Jesaja*, 405–6). Berges's conclusion that the fourth Servant Song was inserted after the "second Jerusalem redaction" is therefore built on sand.

853 For a review of earlier scholarship, see Haag, *Gottesknecht*.

854 Steck, *Gottesknecht*, 22; Hermisson, "Das vierte Gottesknechtlied," 231.

855 Hermisson, "Das vierte Gottesknechtlied," 232. This interpretation appears to be supported by the MT in Isa 53:8, "for the transgression of my people" (עַמִּי), but the reading "his people" (עַמּוֹ) of 1QIsaᵃ is preferable.

In addition, the motif of the Servant's receiving a portion of the spoil along with the many and the strong is inappropriate to an individual. Since 53:11aβb says explicitly that the Servant makes "the many" righteous, and elsewhere in the Song the catchword רַבִּים, "many," clearly refers to the nations (52:14, 15; 53:12), the atoning function of the Servant is universal, as the allusions to 49:6 and 52:10 confirm. In this case, however, the "we" of the middle section refers to the nations and kings.[856] Despite the individualistic features, the object of their startled account can only be an entity such as the people of Israel. Recently, therefore, an increasing number of scholars have inclined toward a collective interpretation of the fourth Servant Song.[857]

In Isa 42:1–4, Yahweh presented exiled Israel to the nations as a mediator of justice; in 49:6, he commissioned Israel to be a universal mediator of salvation. Now in 53:1–11aα, the startled kings and nation see in retrospect how Israel had mediated on their behalf: through its very existence, unimposing from the start, through the unspeakable suffering it had been forced to undergo throughout its history, and through its scandalous downfall, Israel had vicariously borne all their sins (53:4–6).[858] Silently submissive, Israel had borne the sins of the whole world, concentrated upon it by Yahweh, thus bringing to the world the unmerited opportunity for authentic life. In this way, the author of the fourth Song sought retrospectively to give a profound meaning to the exile that Israel had suffered, a meaning that for the first time lent it positive significance within the framework of universal history.

However, the positive significance of Israel's suffering could be recognized only because Yahweh had clearly and unambiguously shown

---

[856] The argument that the kings could not be speaking in Isa 53:1ff. because 52:15 says that they have shut their mouths (most recently Hermisson, "Das vierte Gottesknechtlied," 230) does not hold water, since the context shows that 52:15 refers to a first reaction of awed astonishment (described in different words in 49:7). In fact, the shift from the third-person framework to the first-person account ("and that which they had never heard [שָׁמְעוּ] they now observed. Who would have believed what we have heard [שְׁמֻעָה]...?") supports the assumption that the kings just mentioned should be thought of as the speakers of the "we" section.

[857] Mettinger, *Farewell*, 38; Weippert, "Konfessionen," 110; Van Oorschot, *Von Babel*, 192–96; Berges, *Buch Jesaja*, 403–11 (Zion).

[858] The fact that elsewhere DtIE[1] makes the sins of Israel responsible for the suffering of the exile (Isa 40:2; 43:24–28*; 50:1) does not weigh against this interpretation, since the text speaks from a different situation: after forgiveness (40:2; 43:25) and a new beginning. In addition, the Song was probably composed not by RE[1] but by another member of the Deutero-Isaiah group. This notion might, however, be related to the motif that Israel or Zion had received "from Yahweh's hand double for all her sins," i.e., had suffered inordinately (40:2). Furthermore, the Song calls Israel "righteous" before God only because it has vicariously borne the iniquity of others (52:11aβ).

lovingkindness to his Servant, had raised him up from his "death" and restored him (Isa 53:10; cf. Ezek 37:1–15).[859] Only the revitalization of a nation apparently dead could evoke the astonishment and critical self-examination of the other nations. Thus the author of the Song expressed the conviction that, because Israel had sacrificed itself on behalf of the nations, Yahweh would once more exalt his people (52:13) and raise them up to be an equal and respected member of the world of nations (53:12).[860]

This interpretation allows us to assign a rough date to the fourth Servant Song. The Zerubbabel group must have returned and the first stages of reconstruction must have begun, but the establishment of a stable and respected society appears to be difficult. Consequently, I would propose the years following 515 B.C.E. The author probably belonged to the still-existing Deutero-Isaiah group but was not, as the linguistic and conceptual idiosyncrasies of the text show, identical with RE¹.

III.2.7.5. The Second Edition of the Book of Deutero-Isaiah

The second edition of the book of Deutero-Isaiah (DtIE²) brought the first edition with the addition of the fourth Servant Song to its present compass (Isa 40–55*). Its redactor (RE²) added the new chapters 54–55* and tied them to the material preceding the fourth Servant Song by means of bracketing exhortations with appeals to hear such as "Listen to me" (Isa 51:1–2, 7–8, [21]; 55:1–5). In addition, by inserting 40:6–8*, RE² created a new framework surrounding his entire book (with 55:10–11), intended to emphasize the enduring efficacy of God's word in the face of all obstacles (cf. 44:25, 26a). Finally, he assimilated the prologue to Isa 6 by introducing anonymous voices speaking as though from heaven (40:3aα, 6aα; cf. 6:4, 8), establishing a theological and possibly also literary link with the book of Proto-Isaiah (roughly Isa 1–32*). The judgment passed in the heavenly council that Isaiah had been compelled to experience and proclaim (6:9–11) had been explicitly annulled by the mandate to comfort given to the Deutero-Isaiah group (40:1–2, 3–5). Thus the prophecy of Deutero-Isaiah became part of the book of Isaiah, within which it rang in a new period of God's intentional action in history.[861]

---

[859] This interpretation also chimes with the observation that in late exilic times only the notion of a collective "resurrection" (cf. Ezek 37) is attested, never an individual resurrection; Isa 26:19–20; 1 En. 22:12–13; Dan 12:1–2 date from the third and second centuries.

[860] As the motif of "dividing the spoil" shows, Van Oorschot's notion (Von Babel, 193) that the Servant would be exalted to become ruler of the world clearly goes beyond the intent of the text.

[861] Cf. Isa 5:19; 8:10; 14:26; 29:23–39; 30:1; 40:13; 44:26a (RE¹); 46:11; see Albertz, "Deuterojesaja-Buch," 248–53.

My reconstruction of DtIE² largely coincides with the "secondary Zion stratum" (R²) of Van Oorschot,[862] which corresponds in large measure to the "second Jerusalem redaction" of Berges.[863]

The structure of DtIE² is strongly dependent on DtIE¹; the textual extent of the redaction can be outlined as follows:

Second Edition of the Book of Deutero-Isaiah (DtIE²): Isa 40:1–55:13		
40:1–11 Prologue	40:3aα, 6, 8	endurance of God's word; assimilation to Isa 6
40:12–49:13* Jacob/Israel portion	44:25, 26a	establishing the prophetic word
	45:9–10, 11a, 13bα	controversy with the nations
	47:3–4, 8b–9	Babylon the antitype of Zion
49:14–55:5* Zion/Jerusalem portion	51:1–2, 7–8, 20–23; 52:3	exhortations and controversies
	54:1–3, 4–6, 7–8, 9–10	blessing and eternal salvation for Zion
	54:11–12, 14–17a	miraculous restoration of Zion
	55:1–5	invitation to grasp salvation
55:6–13* Epilogue	55:6, 8–9	exhortation and controversy
	55:10–11	effectiveness of God's word
	55:12–13	joyous pilgrimages

Since the second edition of the book shifts the emphasis to Zion, it is likely that DtIE² was produced in Jerusalem. It is impossible to assign a precise date, since there are no unambiguous historical reference points. Clearly external enemies are threatening Judah once more (Isa 51:12, 13; 54:14–17), and there is an ongoing population deficit (51:1–2; 54:1–3). This description could fit any time between the completion of the temple in 515 B.C.E. and the rebuilding of Jerusalem's wall in 445. However, the dating of Trito-Isaiah cautions against assigning too late a date to DtIE². The earliest portions of Trito-Isaiah (Isa 60–62) date from the first half of the fifth century at the latest.[864] Since they presuppose Isa 54–55 (cf. 55:5

---

[862] *Von Babel*, 241–94.

[863] *Buch Jesaja*, 385–411. Van Oorschot also includes Isa 49:24–26 (*Von Babel*, 244–47) and 50:4–9 (279–83) but assigns 55:12–13 (275 n. 188) to a "greater Isaianic" recension.

[864] The presence of the temple is presupposed (Isa 60:13), but the wall has clearly not been rebuilt (60:12). Later texts in the book of Trito-Isaiah date from the middle of the fifth century: Isa 58 reflects a social conflict reminiscent of Neh 5, and 63:1–6 presupposes the

with 60), DtIE² must have been produced at the end of the sixth or the beginning of the fifth century.

Van Oorschot's dating of his "secondary Zion stratum" creates a problem, since he has to find a place preceding it for his "imminent expectation stratum" (sixth/fifth century).[865] Therefore, he prefers a date in the middle of the fifth century (after the assassination of Xerxes in 465?) and questions the generally accepted date of Isa 60–62. However, since the hypothesis of an "imminent expectation stratum" has not stood the test,[866] this is not a real problem. Berges dates the "second Jerusalem redaction" in the middle of the fifth century because he needs room for his "golah redaction" (539–521 B.C.E.), which is followed by the "first Jerusalem redaction" after 521.[867] He therefore has to accept a dating of Isa 60–62 before the completion of the Deutero-Isaiah book (Isa 54–55),[868] which creates substantial traditio-historical problems. Here, too, elimination of the "golah redaction" enables an earlier dating. If 51:20–23 does belong to DtIE², which is not entirely certain, the two Babylonian revolts against Xerxes in 484 and 482 may stand behind the wish for vengeance on Babylon.

Despite the enthusiasm that DtIE² tried to kindle, reality lagged far behind the message of the Deutero-Isaiah group. True, a sizable group of exiles had returned to Judah with the permission and logistical support of Darius (520 B.C.E.); true, the rebuilding of the temple had been tackled under difficult economic circumstances (Hag 1). However, political crises involving the Persian authorities (Ezra 5:3–17) and conflicts among the various groups and parties, which had developed quite divergent and in part utopian ideas about the new beginning, as well as conflicts with neighbors and with residents who had come from everywhere (Ezra 4) and the failure of other groups to return, prevented a rapid consolidation. The lofty expectations aroused by the prophetic disciples in 521 had not been fulfilled.

The second edition of the Deutero-Isaiah book is characterized by a renewed defense of the prophetic message against substantial obstacles and doubts. Even the new framework within which RE², a prophetic disciple of the third generation, set his book reveals the shift of battle lines. The message that the inquiring disciple had been commissioned to deliver at the outset was assurance that Yahweh's word would prevail

---

overrunning of Edom by the Arabs in this period. Therefore, Isa 60–62 cannot be assigned to the end of this period.

[865] *Von Babel*, 290–91.
[866] Berges, *Buch Jesaja*, 338.
[867] Ibid., 412.
[868] Ibid., 549–50.

against all earthly powers (Isa 40:6, 8;[869] cf. 51:7, 12). Yahweh would also fulfill the prophetic word, in contrast to the words of the pagan diviners and the local sages (44:25, 26a). At the conclusion, RE² expresses confidence that Yahweh himself will see to the confirmation of his word (55:10–11). Ultimately, it was neither Cyrus nor Darius who would accomplish Yahweh's plan for salvation (44:28a; 48:14) but rather the prophetic word of God itself (55:11). The abandonment of the political arena by the Deutero-Isaiah group and their retreat to the purely religious sphere are palpable here.

That the circle to which the prophetic group recited their texts had also narrowed is shown by the exhortations in 51:1–2 and 51:7–8 that frame the earlier text 51:4–5.[870] The hearers are addressed as people who pursue salvation (51:1) and bear the Torah in their hearts (51:7). This description fits the devout followers of the prophets: on the one hand, they have internalized the Torah quite as envisioned by the Jeremiah Deuteronomists (JerD³; cf. Jer 31:33); on the other, they are still awaiting the great turning point that will bring salvation and are unwilling resignedly to come to terms with reality. RE² used the example of their ancestors Abraham and Sarah to demonstrate that God's incalculable blessing had been able to effect miraculous increase since time immemorial and encouraged them not to retreat in the face of the scorn and mockery showered on them by the realists.

In a similar vein, toward the end of the new edition, RE² called on those thirsting for salvation to grasp the message of the book (Isa 55:1–3a) and never to flag in seeking Yahweh (55:6).[871] Thus he reinforced his belief that Yahweh was still near despite all disappointments. The prophetic disciples nevertheless felt compelled to allay the doubts of their dwindling circle of followers by declaring that Yahweh's plan for salvation far transcended all human thoughts and expectations (55:8–9), so no one should be too quick to be dissuaded from awaiting its realization.

More specifically, as RE² interpreted the earlier promises of the book, this plan envisioned a miraculous increase in the population of Jerusalem (54:1–3; cf. 49:18–21), total renewal of Yahweh's former love for Zion

---

[869] Isa 40:6b, 7a does not represent a lament of the prophetic disciple, answered by 40:8; there is no sign of any change of speakers. Instead, 40:6b and 8 constitute the response to the question in 40:6a. Verse 7 is not in the Septuagint; it represents a dittography and a gloss. The gloss in 40:7b interprets the grass that withers as the people, whereas actually it refers to the disciple's enemies (cf. 51:12).

[870] Isa 51:6 is a late apocalyptic interpolation (cf. 24:1–10) and 51:3 is a fragment of a hymn that might belong to a greater Isaianic redaction (cf. 51:11; 35:10).

[871] Isa 55:7 extends the exhortation to the wicked. Its secondary character is clear from its use of דֶּרֶךְ, "way," in the sense of "way of life" rather than "plan for salvation," as in 55:8.

(54:4–6; cf. 49:14–15; 50:1), and restoration of the city to its former splendor (54:11–12, 14, 17a).[872] To maintain in the face of all doubts that the degree of salvation already achieved could never be lost, RE[2] never tired of describing how this miraculous transformation would result in a permanent condition: "eternal deliverance" (צְדָקָה לְעוֹלָם: 51:8), "everlasting love" (חֶסֶד עוֹלָם: 54:8), and an eternal "covenant of peace" (בְּרִית שָׁלוֹם: 54:10; cf. בְּרִית עוֹלָם: 55:3b).

It must be acknowledged: the fears that the exilic period of judgment might still be in effect or that Yahweh wanted once again to put an end to the new beginning in Judah were not pure invention. For the most part, Jerusalem still lay in ruins; the inchoate new society was threatened on all sides by mistrustful neighbors.[873] Therefore, RE[2] proclaimed that in the future no attack on Jerusalem would be provoked by Yahweh. On the contrary, Yahweh's creative power enabled him to destroy the military might of the attackers, which was under his control (54:15–17a).

In an effort to downplay the theological significance of the ongoing threats, RE[2] also markedly relativized the exilic period. Yahweh had turned away from Jerusalem in anger only "for a moment," and his overflowing wrath would never again touch the city (Isa 54:8–9). To make clear that the time of catastrophe was irreversibly over and that the new salvation could never be lost, RE[2] even recalled the primal example of the deluge (54:9–10): just as Yahweh had sworn to Noah never again to cause the waters to go over the earth, so now he swore never again to overwhelm Jerusalem with his wrath.

To reinforce the credibility of the new eternal covenant that Yahweh wished to make with the postexilic generation, RE[2] cited his assurances of steadfast, sure love for David (55:3–5; cf. Ps 89:50 [49]; 2 Sam 7), which had always claimed to hold for all eternity, and transferred them to the people and to Jerusalem.[874] This was a risky move, for it was this very guarantee of permanence given by Yahweh that seemed to be confuted totally by the fall of the Davidic monarchy and its thwarted restoration

---

872 Isa 54:13 interrupts the building context and includes the prophetic disciples among the precious stones adorning the new Jerusalem; 54:17b, like the later Trito-Isaiah strata, limits the description of salvation to the servants of Yahweh (cf. 65:8–9, 13–15; 66:14).

873 The bitter controversy with the Gentiles over Yahweh's intervention on behalf of Israel with which RE[2] bracketed the Darius oracle in 45:9–10, 11a, 13bβ shows that foreigners living in or around Judah sneered at the notion that Yahweh had intervened in the course of history with such favoritism toward the returnees, for which they ultimately paid the price. Unlike RE[1] (43:3b–5), RE[2] therefore took pains to emphasize that the redemption of the golah was without money (52:3), i.e., came at no one's expense.

874 Cf. the masculine (Isa 55:5a) and feminine (55:5b; cf. 60:9) suffixes: the former refers to the people, the latter is meant to include the city.

in the person of Zerubbabel.[875] Therefore, RE² interpreted the promised universal dominion of the Davidic king (Ps 2:7–8) in terms of universal witness to the nations (Isa 55:4). This office had always been implicit in the political subjugation of the nations on behalf of Yahweh, but it had not achieved its true religious goal, which had to wait for the Deutero-Isaiah group to discover it as a function of Israel during the exilic period (43:10, 12; 44:8). That Yahweh's promise to David continued unbroken would henceforth be validated by the universal witness of Israel and Zion: Israel would call nations totally unknown, and people from foreign nations would come running to Zion to learn more about this wonderful God (55:5). The worldwide political dominion of the king would now be replaced by the worldwide witness of the people on behalf of Yahweh; the subjugation of the nations round about Zion (Ps 46:7–11 [6–10]) would be replaced by a continual pilgrimage to Zion, which the nations would freely undertake. Finally, this worldwide pilgrimage to Jerusalem—here RE² took up the concluding theme of the first edition (Isa 52:11–12)—would include the Diaspora that had not yet returned (55:12–13).

The "democratization" of the Davidic covenant by RE² has its parallel in the reservations of the Deuteronomistic Jeremiah book about the restoration of Jehoiachin's descendants (cf. Jer 22:24–20).[876] In this hot political debate, the Deutero-Isaiah group stood firmly in the corner of the successors to the Shaphanide reform faction, opposing the groups from the Diaspora (the authors of the Deuteronomistic History, the school of Ezekiel, Zechariah) and from Judah (Haggai) that wanted a restored Davidic monarchy. That the returned Deutero-Isaiah group enjoyed a rapprochement with the late tradents of the Jeremiah book in Palestine is suggested by the inclusion of salvation oracles in JerD³ that are reminiscent of "Deutero-Isaiah" (Jer 31:7–9, 10–14; 46:12–13; cf. 30:10–11) as well as by the inclusion in Isa 51:7 (DtIE²) of the notion of the Torah written on the heart from Jer 31:33. The diffidence toward the temple in both editions of the Deutero-Isaiah book is also paralleled in the book of Jeremiah, despite their disagreement about Zion theology.

The way in which the expectation of universal salvation of RE² blunted the imperial hopes of the preexilic theology of king and temple shows once more how far the events of the exile had led the Deutero-Isaiah group to move in three generations from the earlier religious nationalism of the Jerusalem cultic personnel. After the exile, nothing was what it had been before.

---

[875] See pp. 130–31 above.
[876] For details, see pp. 331–32 above.

IV. THEOLOGICAL CONTRIBUTION

Albani, Matthias. *Der eine Gott und die himmlischen Heerscharen: Zur Begründung des Monotheismus bei Deuterojesaja im Horizont der Astralisierung des Gottesverständnisses im Alten Orient* (Arbeiten zur Bibel und ihrer Geschichte 1; Leipzig: Evangelische Verlagsanstalt, 2000). **Albertz,** Rainer. "Hat die Theologie des Alten Testaments doch noch eine Chance? Abschliessende Stellungnahme in Leuven," in *Religionsgeschichte Israels oder Theologie des Alten Testaments?* (ed. B. Janowski and N. Lohfink; Jahrbuch für biblische Theologie 10; Neukirchen-Vluyn: Neukirchener Verlag, 1995), 177–87. **Albertz.** "Religionsgeschichte Israels statt Theologie des Alten Testament! Plädoyer für eine forschungsgeschichtliche Umortientierung," in *Religionsgeschichte Israels oder Theologie des Alten Testaments,* 3–24. **Albertz.** "Die Theologisierung des Rechts im Alten Israel," in *Religion und Gesellschaft: Studien zu ihrer Wechselbeziehung in den Kulturen des Antiken Vorderen Orients* (ed. R. Albertz and S. Otto; AOAT 248; Münster: Ugarit-Verlag, 1997), 115–32. **Bertholet,** Alfred. *Wörterbuch der Religionen* (2d ed.; Stuttgart: Kröner, 1962).

No era in Israel's history contributed more to theology than the exile. Vital elements that were to leave their mark on later Judaism and Christianity were reshaped or discovered in the exilic period: their heightened sense of sin and moral seriousness, their geographical spread and universality, and their sometimes utopian character. Never before had Israel experienced more profoundly the extraordinary range of action and depth of being of its God; never before had its God been the source of more painful suffering and enthusiastic joy than in the seventy-seven long years of the exilic period (597–520 B.C.E.): destructive in wrath and productive in mercy, upright judge, purposeful guide of history, Lord over all nations and their gods, Creator of the world—in short, the only God. I venture to claim that without the experience of the exile, Israel would never have made the discovery of monotheism in the strict sense;[1]

---

[1] As defined by Bertholet (*Wörterbuch,* 369), monotheism is "belief in a single God that fundamentally rules out any belief in the existence of other gods."

without it, Israel would never have transcended the limits of its national religion; without it, the idea of a worldwide mission would never have emerged within Israel. In short, without the exile of Israel, there would be no Judaism, Christianity, or even Islam in the distinctive form we know these three world religions.

The rich and varied theological discourse that went on during the exile has already been presented in detail in our survey of the biblical picture of the era (part I) and in our interpretation of the literature of the period (part III). To examine it once more here in the requisite detail would expand this book far beyond any reasonable compass. The reader is therefore referred to these chapters. A detailed account of the history of theology during the exilic period will be found in my history of Israel's religion;[2] chapter II.4 of the present book contains a short summary of social and religious changes.[3] Here we shall merely summarize selectively some theological points discussed during the exile that, in my opinion, have immediate significance for the present.[4]

IV.1. THEOLOGICAL APPROPRIATION OF A CALAMITOUS HISTORY

It is of lasting importance that the Israel of the exilic period did not run away from its catastrophic history but instead seized the political catastrophe as an opportunity to examine its past theologically. This was a painful process, extending over two or three generations. It began with laments and confessions of sin in worship (Pss 44; 74; 79; 89; Lam 5) and in public assemblies (Lam 1; 2; 4), went on to include the reception of preexilic prophets of judgment (Hosea, Amos, Isaiah, Micah, Habakkuk, Zephaniah, Jeremiah, Ezekiel), and concluded with the Deuteronomistic History and the retrospective prophetic books (the Four Prophets book, the Deuteronomistic Jeremiah books, the Ezekiel book). Amid the almost unrelieved darkness of the exilic period (after 562 B.C.E.), successors to the religious nationalists among the prominent families of the Babylonian golah set out to compose the first official history of Israel, from the entrance into Canaan to deportation from the land—in

---

2 *History* (II.4), 2:369–436.
3 See pp. 132–38 above.
4 This choice accords with my understanding of biblical theology, which has its interpretational context in the present; see Albertz, "Hat die Theologie," 182–84. The theological discussion itself, by contrast, belongs to the discipline of the history of Israel's religion; see Albertz, "Religionsgeschichte," 14–21.

itself an extraordinary development. That they also openly blamed the people and the kings and sought to demonstrate on the basis of past history how their sins against Yahweh had led to catastrophe borders on being a minor miracle when compared with the repression of the history of National Socialism in Germany after 1945. However, even the Deuteronomistic Historians could not jump over their own shadow. Belonging to the circles whose policies had led inevitably to catastrophe, they spread the blame equally but did not name the ones actually responsible. They emphasized the religious and cultic transgressions of Israel and its kings while omitting to mention social injustices. Indeed, they could not bring themselves to see that the disastrous policy of allying with Egypt, which had provoked the devastating invasions of the Assyrians and Babylonians, was to blame. True to their tradition, they continued to commend Hezekiah's policy of rebellion as an expression of trust in God (2 Kgs 18:5–6) and assessed Zedekiah's defection from Nebuchadnezzar more as a tragic turn of fate (2 Kgs 24:20). Moreover, they did not have the heart to include in their history the primary critics of their predecessors, the prophets of judgment. Despite their endeavor to look the question of guilt in the eye, they believed that there must be limits to self-indictment.

Again, it is astonishing that people in exilic Israel did not rest content with this guarded treatment of their own guilt, so natural in human terms. There were other groups that gainsaid the authors of the Deuteronomistic History. Although theological allies, the Deuteronomistic redactors of the Four Prophets book followed Hosea and Isaiah in castigating the policy of reliance on arms and alliances as one of the primary sins of Israel and Judah; Yahweh had undercut the material basis of this policy once for all through his great purgative judgment (Hos 5:11–14; 10:13–14; 14:4 [3]; Mic 5:9–10, 13 [10–11, 14]; Zeph 1:16). In addition, the Deuteronomistic editors of the Jeremiah book, also following the prophets, insisted that social injustices had led inevitably to the destruction of the temple (Jer 7:9–14) and the conquest of Jerusalem (34:8–22). They did not hesitate to name the ones actually responsible for the political catastrophe (21:1; 36:23–24, 26; 37:3, 13, 15; 38:1), reminding their readers that it had been the nationalistic officials and officers who had encouraged Zedekiah in his calamitous policies (37:17–18; 38:14–28). They also insisted on rehabilitating by name the adversaries of these nationalists, the Shaphanide reform party, who had intervened on behalf of Jeremiah and been forced into opposition (36:12, 14, 25). Here, too, personal interests were involved: the rehabilitation of their own ancestors was at risk, as well as their own claim to exercise leadership in place of the former establishment. However, there was even more at stake: all sins must be admitted honestly and those who had been primarily responsible must be named, lest the same mistakes be repeated after the new beginning and the same families take the helm once more without effective remorse. Therefore, it was important that the mocked and despised prophets of judgment finally receive the public respect due them. Therefore, it was important to study their legacy carefully, to determine where the point of no return had been, where the opportunities for salvation offered by God had finally been squandered and the catastrophe had become inevitable. Astonishingly, all the Deuteronomistic editors of the exilic prophetic books arrived at the same conclusion that the authors of the Deuteronomistic History had not wanted to hear: when the message of the prophets of judgment was silenced by intimidation and force, God's judgment was ineluctable (Amos 2:11–12; 7:12–8:2; Jer 11–20). The conclusion was clear: only if each was prepared to face unsparingly the radical indictment of prophets of judgment, only if each was prepared to break radically with former errors and transgressions, did Israel have a chance for a new beginning.

Thus the extended discussion over guilt and identifying the guilty carried on among the various Israelite intellectual groups during the exilic period is a fascinating example of the great seriousness and commitment with which Israel really attempted to learn the right lessons from a disastrous past. Such attempts are not always condemned to fail, as people often claim—out of resignation or cynicism. The exilic discussion is instead a successful example of how a nation can deal creatively with its own guilty past. Assimilation of this past contributed significantly to Israel's survival. It is an encouraging protest against the enduring desire to repress and the powerful inclination simply to continue as before. All the groups of exilic theologians were well aware that a new beginning could not be conjured up simply by admission of guilt and repentance. A new beginning could be vouchsafed only by God's merciful forgiveness of all guilt (Jer 29:10–14*; 31:31–33; Isa 40:1–2; 44:21–22). Without admission of guilt and repentance, however, the opportunity of the new beginning would not be recognized (Isa 44:21–22); it would not be grasped but squandered once more. An authentic new beginning, we can learn from the exilic theologians, cannot be had cheaply, since God's grace and mercy are precious.

It is a remarkable phenomenon that the major Christian churches, though they constantly preach God's forgiving grace in Jesus Christ, have a very difficult time admitting their mistakes—not to mention their sins— of the past. The Protestant churches in Germany have taken decades to concede—cautiously—their guilt vis-à-vis the Jews. Will there one day be an assimilation of the whole guilty Christian past that led to Auschwitz? Since Israel's assimilation of guilt took three generations, I am not yet ready to give up hope.

IV.2. THEOLOGICAL INTERPRETATION OF HISTORY

The exilic period was not only the era when the first official history of Israel (DtrH) was written; it was also the golden age of Israelite theology of history. Precisely because Yahweh's actions in history during this era long appeared impenetrable, prophetic circles paid close attention to the history of their period and interpreted it theologically. Moreover, because Israel was no longer the partner but now more often the victim of rising and declining world powers (Assyrians, Babylonians, Persians), these circles conceived history as never before in terms of world history. This vision is attested by the numerous foreign nation oracles produced during the exilic period and brought together in extensive composites (Isa 13–22*; Jer 46–51; Ezek 25–32). However, the exilic prophetic books in their totality—the second and third editions of the Deuteronomistic Jeremiah book (Jer 1–45* and 1–51*), the Ezekiel book, and the first edition of the Deutero-Isaiah book (Isa 40:1–52:12)—likewise represent ambitious reflections on history, in which the various prophetic groups delineated a mighty historical drama involving Yahweh and his people and embracing all of world history. It is not by chance that Jeremiah is called to be a prophet to the nations in JerD² (Jer 1:5).

Since the impenetrability of Yahweh's actions in history represented the central challenge during the first half of the exilic period (cf. Isa 40:13–14, 27), the historians and the disciples of the prophets labored in various ways to discover and explicate in their interpretations a divine rationality and morality in the course of history. The Deuteronomistic Historians, surveying Israel's past, worked out a precise correspondence between Yahweh's punishment and deliverance and Israel's apostasy and return (Judg 2:10ff.). By shaping their history in such a way that there was always ample warning of the consequences of apostasy (Josh 23; 1 Sam 12; 1 Kgs 9:1–9; etc.), they removed God's actions in history from the sphere of blind fate and lent them a perspicuous and moral character.

Along the same lines, the redactors of JerD² formulated an actual law governing Yahweh's actions in history, which governed all nations and kingdoms (Jer 18:7–10). At one moment Yahweh might declare disaster for a nation, at another salvation, but in each case he announced his intention, giving the nation a chance to act accordingly: if it turned from its evil, he was prepared to change his mind about the disaster; if it rejected the offer of salvation, he would withdraw it. Thus the disciples of Jeremiah gave Yahweh's actions in history an explicitly pedagogical quality. At the same time, they tried to avoid the danger of the determinism that emerged in the historiography of the Deuteronomistic Historians. There were indeed contingent events, specifically God's free and ultimately unaccountable decisions for salvation or judgment, but they did not descend blindly on humankind: God always offered an opportunity to respond positively or negatively.

However, the most substantial universal theology of history during the exilic period was put forward by the Deutero-Isaiah group. Quite in the manner of the Isaiah tradition, they emphasized the purposeful character of Yahweh's actions in history (Isa 46:9–11) and elevated the awareness that for two centuries Yahweh had used his prophets to proclaim his actions in history to the central proof that Yahweh alone was God.[5] Both the fall of Jerusalem and the rise of Cyrus were part of a divine plan and demonstrated Yahweh's sovereignty over history (41:22–23). Furthermore, the Deutero-Isaiah group did not hesitate to connect Yahweh's plan to deliver Israel and Zion with the Persian king Cyrus. This move made their prophecy highly vulnerable after 539 B.C.E., when Cyrus failed to do anything significant to deliver Israel. The prophetic group did not let this failure (cf. 49:46) disorient them but continued to ruminate on Yahweh's historical plan. They recognized that Yahweh must still have some purpose for exiled Israel and hit on the revolutionary idea of the golah as a mediator of justice and salvation (42:1–4; 49:6). They anxiously studied the course of history until they discovered that Darius, who had likewise intended to base his imperial policies on justice and law, must be the deliverer of Israel called by God (42:5–9; 45:11–13*; 48:12–16a), and they set the wheels in motion to assure that this God-given opportunity to return and rebuild Jerusalem would be seized and turned into political reality.

Such a theology of history has become alien to us twentieth-century Christians. After the disaster of World War I, when all the Christian nations of Europe claimed that God was on their side and demonized each

---

[5] Albani (*Der eine Gott*, 123–24) asserts once more that it was essentially belief in creation—that this concept does not appear in the Old Testament appears not to bother him—that was the foundation for Deutero-Isaiah's monotheism. In disagreeing with me, he cites Isa 45:7, 18, but a careful reading of these texts shows clearly that 45:6 presents worldwide recognition that Yahweh alone is God as one of the purposes for which Yahweh has called Cyrus, whereas Yahweh's self-predication as Creator of the world and Lord of history (!) in 45:7 belongs to the disputations framework for the call of Cyrus (cf. 44:24). In 45:18, the parallel predications of Yahweh as Creator of the world and as the only God undergird the statement that Yahweh created the world for human habitation and therefore wishes to call the nations to salvation, not destroy them. The fact remains that all the texts that seek to prove that Yahweh alone is God argue solely on the basis of his governance of history (41:1–7, 21–28; 43:8–12; 44:6–8, 10ff.; 45:20–25). Even in 40:12–26, which is concerned only with Yahweh greatness, not his uniqueness, Yahweh's power over history is not restored by means of creation, as Albani asserts (124 n. 486); instead—just as in the hymns—creation of the world and action in history stand in parallel (40:12–17*, 22–23).

other, after the horrors of bestial genocide and the murder of the Jews on an industrial scale that a hitherto mostly Christian Germany inflicted on all of Europe, German theologians in particular have largely abandoned any attempt to connect God with history. They prefer to restrict themselves to the individual, interpersonal sphere and to emphasize the religious and otherworldly nature of Christian redemption.[6] The problem with such an approach is that it leaves the whole domain of international politics and world history almost totally untouched by God. Thus every idol imaginable happily moves in to fill this vacuum, virtually ignored by theology, whether in the name of the cold war or globalization. Since the idolatrous Führer cult surrounding Adolf Hitler, of course, any identification of a political leader with God's plan of salvation is extraordinarily risky. However, we must be clear: without the identification with Cyrus and Darius proposed by the Deutero-Isaiah group, there would have been no return of the golah groups, no new beginning in Judah, and thus no Judaism and no Christianity. In situations of crisis, only theological interpretation can lend history the clarity that enables correct decisions and produce the consensus to carry them out. Only such an interpretation of history makes it possible to take a critical stance toward the supposedly predetermined course of history and discover history's hidden ethical dimension. I therefore believe it essential for Christian theology in the twenty-first century to recover God's action in history as an object of serious theological reflection and to develop criteria for protecting the theological interpretation of history from abuse and transformation into ideology. Here, I believe, the exilic theologies of history can make a contribution.

IV.3. FOILING IMPERIAL THEOLOGY

Politically insignificant as the tiny state of Judah had been in the preexilic period, nevertheless, like the great empires of the ancient Near East, it developed an imperial royal theology in which the Davidic king subdued the nations by force of arms for the God of Israel (Ps 2:6–12). Yahweh then made him ruler of the world (Pss 2:8; 72:10–11) and promised that the Davidic dynasty would endure forever (2 Sam 7:11b–16; Ps 89:27–38 [26–37]).[7] When the last Davidides had been deposed and imprisoned by

---

[6] The difficult question of whether and how after the Shoah Jews can speak of God's acting in history can be answered only by the Jews themselves. Our perspective here is that of the perpetrators, not the victims.

[7] See Albertz, *History* (II.4), 1:116–22.

Nebuchadnezzar in 597 and 587 B.C.E., this imperial theology was confuted (Lam 4:20; Ps 89:39–40, 50 [38–39, 49]). This turn of events posed a hotly debated question for the various exilic groups of theologians: What was the future of the monarchy and its theology? The Deuteronomistic Historians contented themselves with partial disarmament and making the king subservient to the Deuteronomic law (Deut 17:16, 19–20; 2 Kgs 23:1–3), while continuing to set their hopes in Jehoiachin and his family (2 Kgs 25:27–30). The school of Ezekiel expected God's purgative judgment on the monarchy and the upper classes (Ezek 34:1–22), after which a new David might be appointed (34:23–24; 37:24–25), with severely limited power (46:16–18) and an office totally shorn of the nimbus of sacrality (45:16–17; 46:1–10). The Jeremiah Deuteronomists flatly rejected any restoration of the Davidic monarchy.[8] For them, Jeremiah's damning verdict on Jehoiachin was final (Jer 22:24–30).

The disciples of Deutero-Isaiah were the most creative in their treatment of the ancient royal ideology: they transferred the titles "anointed of Yahweh" and "beloved of Yahweh" from the Davidic king to the Persian kings Cyrus and Darius (Isa 45:1; 48:14): in other words, Yahweh now exercised worldwide dominion over foreign rulers. Furthermore, exiled Israel itself was to take on the role of Servant of Yahweh, no longer to subjugate other nations to Yahweh but to establish justice for them (42:1–4) and to serve as mediator of their salvation (49:6). Yahweh's worldwide dominion was thus separated totally from the political dominion of Israel.

Qualitatively, too, the disciples of Deutero-Isaiah realized that the meaning of God's universal dominion had been transformed: its purpose was now to liberate the oppressed and strengthen the powerless—first captive Israel (Isa 40:29–31; 41:17; 42:22; 49:9) but then all the victims of political hegemony (42:6–7; 45:22). In the future, this would be achieved not by military might but by means of justice on behalf of the weak (42:3; 51:4–5). Yahweh's sole divinity made all absolute imperial claims to power contingent (47). Yahweh would achieve worldwide recognition that he alone was God by inviting the other nations to share in his salvation (45:20a, 21–25); Israel would play the role of Yahweh's witness before the world (43:10, 12; 44:8). Thus the brand new possibility of mission replaced the old claim to world dominion. It was therefore only logical that later disciples of Deutero-Isaiah should transfer to the people as a whole the promises given to the Davidic monarchy: Yahweh's eternal covenant with his people would now be realized in the pilgrimage of all nations to Zion (55:3b–5).

---

[8] See pp. 331–32 above.

What the exilic theologians accomplished here was nothing less than a consistent separation of divine sovereignty from royal sovereignty. They depotentiated or negated the royal office but derived from it a universal task for Israel: no longer world dominion but mission and mediation of justice. They recognized that Yahweh's esteem as lord and king over all the world would suffer profoundly if his power were to be confused with their own political interests. No one could be compelled to recognize his divinity by force, but only persuaded by words.

In light of these theological insights, we must ask in horror how it had been possible for Christianity, which harvested the fruits of early Judaism's flourishing mission, to corrupt its mission repeatedly well into the nineteenth century by employing force of arms and serving colonial interests. Does not the missionary imperative read: "Go therefore and make disciples of all nations ... and teach them to obey everything that I have commanded" (Matt 28:19–20)? Not a word about subjugation; on the contrary, Jesus Christ claims for himself all power in heaven and on earth (28:18). When Christian churches and nations thought they could usurp God's power and help their mission along by coercion, they relapsed not only from the New Testament but also from insights that Israelite theologians had already achieved in the exilic period. The church can bear credible witness to Jesus Christ only if it takes care to keep its own interests separate from its religious mission. In addition, in the political sphere, the vision of the disciples of Deutero-Isaiah remains yet to be discovered: that the church, following in the footsteps of God's Servant Israel, has a mission to promote the resolution of international conflicts through fair and impartial justice (Isa 42:1–4; cf. 2:1–5).

IV.4. GOD'S GLORY AND SEPARATION OF POWERS

In the preexilic period, temple and palace not only constituted an architectural unity but were linked by many institutional and familial bonds. The temple of Jerusalem was also the chapel of the Davidides and the royal state sanctuary. The king supported the sanctuary and the priesthood and personally performed high sacral functions. The priests were royal officials, their higher ranks related to the royal house by marriage. At core, even the capital was a royal freehold.[9] Especially during the seventh century, when Judah consisted of not much more than a rather large capital city and its hinterland, the extensive royal family, the royal

---

[9] Albertz, *History* (II.4), 1:128–32.

officials, the military, and the priesthood along with the urban aristocracy constituted a tightly connected power elite that held all the reins.

An initial attempt at separation of powers was undertaken by the Josianic reform. The king lost his legislative authority and was made subservient to the authority of the Mosaic law ("Proto-Deuteronomy"; Deut 17:14–20). The judges were made independent of the monarch (16:18–20) and came under the supervision of a superior court constituted of leading laity and priests (17:8–13). This development was a first step in the direction of a constitutional monarchy, but it was interrupted by Josiah's death and the failure of his reform.[10]

When Jehoiachin was released from a Babylonian prison in 562, the possibility of a restoration of the Davidides appeared on the horizon; the authors of the Deuteronomistic History, working among the leadership in exile, campaigned to continue the development reached under Josiah, which had been interrupted by his death and the failure of his reform. That would probably have meant a constitutional monarchy obedient to the Torah, but also a continuation of the traditional state-cult principle. Such a resumption of the tie linking the royal house with the temple and its priesthood was probably also the goal of the high priest Joshua, who, with Jehoiachin's grandson Zerubbabel, led the group returning in 520.

The reform-minded priesthood that gathered about the prophet Ezekiel had a much more radical solution. In their view, the fact that the glory of Yahweh had departed from the preexilic temple and thus abandoned it to destruction (Ezek 8–11) necessarily implied that a new temple to meet the requirements of Yahweh would have to be configured entirely differently, architecturally and organizationally. The physical amalgamation of temple and palace, they recognized, had infringed on Yahweh's majesty and holiness (43:1–13). Therefore, the temple had to be separated completely from the centers of political power. That meant its physical separation from the capital and, as a consequence, priestly autonomy (45:1–8). Only so could the requisite holiness of the temple be assured. The disciples of Ezekiel even planned that the temple should be largely independent economically and the priests self-sufficient. The only function of the prince would be to collect the small temple tax from the people (45:13–17). During worship, he was to have a place of honor among the laity, but he no longer had any claim to sacrality (46:1–10). Along with this separation of temple and palace, the reforming priests also campaigned for a division of political power. The king and his officials, subject to certain restrictions, would have free disposition only over

---

10 Albertz, *History* (II.4), 1:203–5, 225–26; Albertz, "Theologisierung," 124–130.

the crown lands (46:16–18); the capital, conceived as a kind of federal district, was to be administered by workers from all the tribes (45:5; 48:15–18). In this design for reform, the institutions of palace, temple, and capital, intimately entwined before the exile, were to be strictly separate in the future.

The design of the school of Ezekiel could not be realized as planned; it was too utopian. However, it led to the independence of the priesthood after the exile and the autonomy of the Jerusalem temple. The thwarted restoration of the Davidic monarchy helped prepare the ground for its success. Under the umbrella of the Persian provincial administration, the postexilic community was governed by a college of priests, a council of elders, and a popular assembly.[11] In short, a form of separation of powers materialized, which attempted to do more justice to the glory of Yahweh.

When we keep in mind this development, we are forced to ask how, until the most recent past, so many fusions of throne and altar can have appeared under Christian aegis. At the end of World War I, the German Protestant state churches considered the basically supportive separation of church and state written into the Weimar constitution a malicious imposition sponsored by socialists hostile to the church; if they had treated it instead as a theologically necessary and long overdue action befitting the majesty of their God, the subsequent course of church history in Germany would have been different. If the German pastors had realized that a true appreciation of the majesty of their God necessarily implied separation of political powers, their relationship to Weimar democracy as well as National Socialist dictatorship would have taken a different form.

For a modern society in which Christians and Jews exercise public responsibility, it is of great importance constantly to evoke the heritage of the biblical tradition. I hope that this book, devoted to one of the most exciting periods of the Old Testament era, may contribute to that end.

---

[11] See pp. 131–32 above.

PRIMARY SOURCES INDEX

HEBREW BIBLE (following the Masoretic Text)

Genesis		26:15	254
11:28–30	257	26:18	254
12:1–3	249–54	27–33*	251
12:1–9	257, 258–59	27:27–29	251
12:10–20	253, 259	27:39–40	251
13*	251	28:13–14	251, 254, 260
13:1–4	259	28:20	247
13:5–13	259	31:5	247
13:14–17	251, 254, 259–60	31:13	249, 262
13:15–16	250	31:42	247
13:18a	259–60	34*	251
13:18b	260	37–50*	251, 263
16*	260	38	251
16:9	254	39*	263, 270 n. 370
17:12	107	46:1–5a	252–54, 267–68
18–19*	251, 259	46:3–4	249
18:1–15	247, 254, 260	48:13–15	254–55
20	264	48:15–16	268
20–22	253–54, 264–67	48:21b	254–55
20:7	271	49	251
20:17	271	50:1–11	264
21:1–2	265		
21:6–7	265	**Leviticus**	
21:4	107	11	108
21:8–21	265–66	12:3	107
21:13	252	17–26	361 n. 664
21:18	252	25:1–7	13
21:22–34	266	26:34–35	13
22:1–19	266, 270	26:43	13
25*	251		
26:1–33*	260–62	**Deuteronomy**	
26:1–3	249, 253	4	284

4:15–28	288	7:3	275
5:6–10	288	7:7ff.	290
7:2–3	288	8–12	292
11:17	287	12:19	275
12	288		
12:9–10	291	**2 Samuel**	
14	108	6	294
18:10	288	7	275, 280
18:14	288	7:1	223
20:1	289	7:10–11	223
20:5–17	289	7:13	294
20:15–17	288	7:14–16	293
23:18–19	288	11:27b–12:15a	289 n. 451
25:19	291		
28:36	287	**1 Kings**	
28:63–68	287	2:1–4	292
29:21–27	287	2:4	280, 293
30:1–10	284	2:35	293
31:9ff.	287	5–8	280
		5:17	294
		5:19	294
Joshua		5:18	291
1–12	289	6–7	293
1:13–15	291	8	283–85
3	287	8:16–21	292
3–4	294	8:25	280, 293
8:30–35	287	8:46–53	275
13:1b–6	290	8:50	286
21:44	291	8:56	291
21:45	289	8:61	291
23	291	9:1–9	295
23:1	291	9:4–5	292
23:1–16	289–90	9:5	280, 293
		11	288
Judges		11:1–13	291, 295
2:10–19	290	11:12–13	280, 293
2:11–12	275	11:29–39	295
2:20–21	290	11:32	281, 294
3:3	290	11:36	281, 294
6:25–31	290	11:38	292
7	290	12	288
10:10	290	12:24–32	296
10:16	290	12:28–30	8
11–12	290	13:2	296
		13:32	296
1 Samuel		14:8	292
2:27–36	293	14:8–16	297
4–6	294		

14:15–16	8	21:2–15	276
14:16	292	21:4–8	280
14:21	281, 294	21:9	292
14:22ff.	299	21:10–16	301
15:4	280, 293, 295	22:1–23:24	301
15:4–5	299	22	287
15:5	292	22:4	294
15:12–13	299	22:8–11	286
16:31–33	296	23	217, 280
21	288	23:1–25	286
21:19–29	296	23:15	296
22:47	299	23:17	294
22:54	296	23:25–26	277
		23:27	11, 294
2 Kings		23:31–25:26	301
8:18ff.	299	23:36	79
8:19	280, 293, 295	24–25	5–13, 74, 81–82, 281
9–10	296	24:1	53
11:17–18	299	24:8	79
12:4	299	24:12	79–81, 85
13:4–5	297	24:13–14	280
14:4	299	24:14–16	83–85, 90
14:25–27	297	24:18	79
15:4	299	24:20	54
15:17–20	281	25:1ff.	54–55
15:29	8	25:1–26	91
15:35	299	25:8	78, 81
16:3–18	299–300	25:11	83–84, 88
16:5–8	281	25:12	82
16:10–18	280	25:13–17	280
17:1–23	297	25:18	107, 294
17:6	284	25:21	81, 284
17:7–23	301	25:27–30	61, 103–4, 109, 284, 293, 331
17:21–23	8		
17:21	296 n. 462	**Isaiah**	
17:23	11, 284	2:1–4	176
17:24–34a	296, 298	7:4–7	184
17:34b–41	298 n. 468	11:1–10	176
18:4ff.	300	13–14	138, 190, 195
18:5–8	281	13:17–22a	192
18:9–19	281	14:28–32	184
18:37*	281	15–20	138
18:19	294	17–19*	184
19:34	280	17:1–6	184
20:1–19	200	20:1–6	184
20:12–19	48 n. 6	21	138, 190–93
21:2–7	294–95, 301		

40:1–2	379	45:20–25	138
40:1–5	393, 404	46:1–2	105, 396
40:3aα	428	46:1–13	416
40:6–8	428, 431	46:5–7	396
40:6aα	380, 428	46:11	111
40:9–10	178	46:12–13	395
40:9–11	134, 393, 404	47	138, 182, 191, 193–94, 195, 417
40:12–31	105, 405, 440 n. 5	48:1–11	395
40:18–20	396	48:1–16a	311
40:27	105	48:6b–7a	400
41	395–96	48:8	394
41:1–20	405–6	48:12–16a	395, 400
41:2	111	48:14	424
41:5	396	48:20–21	178, 393, 419
41:8–9	247	49:1–6	407
41:8–13	169	49:1–13	393–94, 419–21
41:14–16	169, 406	49:6	402, 423
41:17	174	49:7	426
41:17–20	173	49:7–12	173, 423
41:21–42:13	406–9	49:8	174, 402
42:1–4	406	49:10	176
42:1–13	394–95	49:12	176, 401
42:5–9	400	49:13	178
42:9–10	395, 400	49:14	105, 394
42:10–13	178	49:14–21	396, 421–22
42:14–17	173	49:14–26	173
42:14–43:15	410–11	50:1–2	105, 398, 421
43:1–4	169	50:4–9	380, 398, 407, 422
43:5–7	169	51:1–2	247, 396, 428, 431
43:16–21	173	51:4–5	398, 423
43:16–44:23	411–12	51:7–8	428, 431
44:1–5	169	51:9–10	147, 150
44:5	138	51:9–19	174, 396
44:10–17	396	51:9–52:6	173, 423
44:23	178, 393	52:7–10	134, 424
44:24–45:8	413	52:9–10	178, 396
44:25	431	52:11–12	395, 400–401, 424
44:26a	431	52:13–53:12	407, 425–28
44:28	111, 395, 399	54–55*	428
45:1	424	54:1–3	178, 431
45:1–7	111, 395	54:4–17	432
45:6–7	440 n. 5	54:14–17	176, 432
45:8	178	55:1–5	428
45:11–13	395, 399, 400	55:1–9	431
45:11–25	414–15	55:3–5	432
45:14–17	173	55:4–5	134
45:18–19	395, 440 n. 5	55:4–8	169

PRIMARY SOURCES INDEX

55:5	138, 176	19:12–13	343
55:10–11	428, 431	20:1–6	330, 336
55:12–13	433	21:1–10	326–28
63:7–64:11	146, 151, 165	21:4–7	331
63:16	247	21:9	330
64:7	136	21:11–22:29	328
		22:1–5	199
Jeremiah		22:1–15	329
1–25*	312–15, 327–28	22:17b	329
1*	312–13	22:5–6	332
1:3	79	22:24–30	110, 131, 331–32
1:4–10	315–16, 335, 339	22:29–30	313
1:11–19	316, 327	23:9–22	328–29
1:16	329	24	323
2:2aβ	319, 341, 344	24:8	98
2:3	319, 341, 344	25–29	333–34
2:4–6:30	328	25:1–13a	312–13, 318–20, 327
3:14–15	319, 340	25:1–13a LXX	312
5:18–19	329	25:3–9	330
7:1–7	131	25:11–12	2, 14, 39, 41
7:1–15	199–201	26	335–36
7:1–8:4	327–28	26–45*	315–18
7:3–25	330–31	26:24	325
7:4	325	27–28	54, 335
7:30–8:3	343	27:5–6	339
8:4–10:25*	202, 328	28:2–3	175
9:11–15	329	28:2–4	98, 325
11–20*	328–29	28:4	103
11:1–19	329–30	29:1–7	99
11:2–14	327	29:7–8	337
11:4	329	29:10	2, 14, 39, 41
12:7	330	29:10–14aα	315–16, 337–38
12:7–17	344	29:21–32	99, 334, 337
12:14–17	341	30–31	317–20, 339–40
13	329	30:1	311
14:1–15:4	330	30:3b–6	175
14:7–14	174	30:8–9	332
15:1–4	174	30:10–11	169
15:10	330	30:12–15	175
16:10–13	329	30:16–17	176, 344
17:16	330	30:18–20	175
17:18	330	31:7	178
17:19–27	199, 332	31:8–9	175
18	315–16, 335	31:10–11	178
18:7–10	338	31:10–14	175
19:4–5	329	31:15–17	175
19:6–9	343	31:18–20	175

31:27	344	42:10–14	315–16
31:31–34	344	42:10–17	199
32	340	42:12	323–24
32–35	317–18	43–44	320
32:1	79, 81	43:1–7	308
32:6–35	343	43:3	326
32:15	177, 179	43:5–6	324
32:17	344	43:7–44:30	97
32:19	344	43:8–13	318, 341
32:27	344	44:1–23	333–35
32:37–44	344	44:15–18	337
33 LXX	312	45	316
33:14–26	332	45:1–5	312, 326, 335
34	326, 340	46–49	138
35	315	46–51	319–20, 341–42
35–39	333–35	46:1–12	185
35:14–16	335–36	46:2	80
36	314, 325–26, 336	46:3–12	184
36:3	335	46:14–24	184
36:7	335	46:27–28	169
36:21–31	335	47:1–7	325
37–39	335	47:2–6	184
37:3–11	325	48*	184–85
37:3–43:7	323	49*	184
37:5	55	49:3–5	182, 185
37:9–10	5	49:7–16	185, 187
38:2	5	49:21	136
38:17–18	5	50–51	138, 190, 194–96
38:19	88	50:6–7	344
38:28b	5	51:58	317
39–43	5–7	52:5	79
39:1ff.	56	52:12	78, 81
39:2	79	52:28–30	78, 84–89
39:3	62	52:29	80
39:9	88	52:30	2, 74, 94–95
39:13	62		
39:15–18	336	**Ezekiel**	
39:19–20	91 n. 173	1:4ff.	356
40	94	2:3–5	356
40–43	333	3:1–3	355
40:4	56	3:16–21	362
40:6–10	91–93	3:22–27	357
40:14	56	3:26–27	355
41:1–2	94–95	6	357
41:15	56	6:8–10	363, 367
41:16ff.	95	7	357, 362
42:10	338	8–11	356

8:1	100	36:18–23	368
11:14–21	92	36:24	363
11:16–21	105, 363, 367	36:25–27	367
12:1–15	355	37	357
13:9	106 n. 206, 352	37:1–11	177
13:9–23	363	37:1–19	362–63
14:1	100	37:11	136
14:1–11	363	37:25	247
14:6	362	38–39	354
16:53–63	363	40–48	130, 352–53, 368–76
17	355	40:1	81
17:11–21	99	41:8–16	136
17:22–24	364	43:1–12	134, 356
18	105	44:1–5	136
18:1–24	362	45:16–17	364
18:30–32	362	46:1–18	134, 364
19	355	47:15–48:29	363
20	365–68		
20:1	100	**Hosea**	
20:30–32	109	1–3	232
21:23–32	100, 355	1:1	209–10
24:15–24	100, 355	1:5–7	232
24:21	100	2:1–3	232
24:27	355	2:20	232
25–32	138, 354–55	2:23–25	232
25:1–5	182	3:1–5	235
25:1–28:24	183, 186	3:1bβ	232
28:25–26	186, 247	3:5	232
29:12	353	4–14	232
29:17–21	186, 353	4:1	231
30:23	353	4:15	232–33, 236
30:26	353	6:1–6	174
32:9	353	8:1b	232–33, 236
33	357–59	8:6a	231
33–48	359	8:13	236
33:1–16	362	8:14	231–32
33:21	80	11:5b	231–32, 236
33:22–23	168, 355	14:2–9	231
33:23–29	92, 363		
33:24	105, 166, 247	**Amos**	
34–37	185, 353	1:1	209–10
34–39	168	1:1–8:3*	226
34:1–25	364	1:1–9:4*	226
34:12–14	363	1:1–9:10	227
36:1–15	357	1:2	215
36:8	363	1:3–2:3	181, 184
36:11	368	1:9–12	228

2:4–5	227–28, 237	**Habakkuk**	
2:10–11	228	1–3	238–41
3:1–2	229	1:5–17	241–42
3:7	228	1:9–17	245
4:6–13	201–2, 225, 227	2:5bβ	245
5:8–9	202, 227	2:5bβ–19	243
8:1–2	228	2:8–17	245
8:4–7	225	3:1–16	244
8:8	202, 227	3:13a	245
8:11–12	225, 229	3:16	245
9:1–4	227		
9:5–6	202, 226–27	**Zephaniah**	
9:7–10	226, 228–29, 234	1:1	209–10, 217
9:8	236	1:1–6	220
9:11–15	227	1:4–6	214–17, 235–36
		1:7–18	220–21
Obadiah		1:7–2:4	218–20
1–14	188	2:1–4	221, 223
1–21	138	2:3	236
8–15	182	2:5–15	182 n. 131
15a	188	2:5–3:8	218–20
15b	188	2:5–3:13	221–22
16–21	188	2:15	236
		3:2	236
Micah		3:3–4	236
1:1	209–10	3:8	236
1:2	215	3:9–20	219
1:3–5a	214	3:11–13	175, 234–36
1:3–9	211–12	3:12	223
1:9–13a	214	3:14–15	178
1:13b	213		
1:14–16	214	**Haggai**	
2:1–3	214	1–2	124
2:6–11	214	1:1	120, 130
2:12–13	175, 215	1:4–12	128
3:1–12	214	1:12	130
4:1–4	215	1:14	130
4:6–7	175, 215	2:3–9	128
4:8	177	2:4	130
4:8–5:3	215	2:6–9	175
4:9–10	175, 179	2:21b–23	175
4:11–13	175	2:20–23	128, 131, 332
5:1–4a	177		
5:6–7	215	**Zechariah**	
5:8–13	214–16, 234–36	1:8–16	128
5:14	215	1:12	2
6	214	1:17	177

2:1–4	128	13–14 LXX	22–27
2:14–16	178	**Ezra**	
4:1–6aα	128	1:1	2
4:9	120	1:1–3	12
4:10aβ–14	128	1:1–11	14
4:11–14	130	1:2–4	121
6:1–8	128	1:7–11	121–23
6:9–14	126, 128	2	14, 120, 124, 127
6:10–11	102	2:3–20	106
6:11	130	2:36ff.	100
7:2ff.	141	2:39–62	106
7:5	2, 95	2:59	100, 137
8:4–5	177	3:1	14
8:18–19	141	3:2–3	120
8:19	95	3:8–10	120
		4:1–24	121
Psalms		4:3–4	14
22	169	5:2	130
44	142	5:3–17	129
60	142, 175, 189	5:3	118
74	142–44	5:5	120
74:9	174, 179	5:6	118
74:12–17	150	5:24	120
77	161	5:14–16	120–21, 123–24
79	143–44	5:16–21	14
85	144, 174	6:2–5	121–22
89	104, 144–45	6:3–4	129
89:10–13	150	6:5	14
137	104, 159	6:6–12	129
137:7	190	6:6	118
		6:13	118
Lamentations		6:21	132, 137
1	151–52, 154–56	7:20–26	132
2	152–58	8:1–30	127
3	136, 151, 158, 161–65	8:17	100
3:57	170, 173	10	106, 132
4	151, 153–58		
4:21–22	175, 189	**Nehemiah**	
5	93, 95, 145–46, 155, 158	5:1–13	132
		7	127
Daniel		7:5	137
1–6	16–23	7:5ff.	106
1:1	74	12:23–28	132
2–7	17, 41–44	13:23–27	106
4–6 LXX	27		
7:1–14	22		
9	39–40		

1 Chronicles
3:17–19   106–7
5:41   107

2 Chronicles
36   12–15, 81–82
36:6–7   75
36:10   79
36:22   2

APOCRYPHA AND PSEUDEPIGRAPHA

Tobit
1:3–3:6   31–32
3:11–15   33
13–14   33–34
14:4   30

6:2   35
7:23–29   35
8–12   35
8:18–33   37
16:3–5   35

Judith
1:11–12   35
2   34
3:8   35
4   35
5:5–21   36

1 Esdras
3:1–5:6   28–29, 125 n. 264

1 Enoch
85–90   40–41

EXTRABIBLICAL SOURCES

Herodotus
1.74   63 n. 63
1.183   27 n. 48
2.161–163   56 n. 32
3.61–67   117
3.89–97   118–19
3.159   195 n. 70

Josephus, *Against Apion*
1.128–160   47 n. 3
1.156   57 n. 36
1.158   65 n. 70
1.159   57 n. 38

Josephus, *Antiquities*
10.96ff.   75

10.106   351 n. 637, 355 n. 664
10.110   55
10.181   94 n. 73, 189 n. 154
10.181–182   56
10.182   326 n. 574
10.186–281   47 n. 3
10.228   57 n. 36
11.9   102 n. 197
11.13–14   120 n. 246

Dead Sea Scrolls
4QJer$^{b.c.d}$ 312
4Q242   21 n. 27, 110

GENERAL INDEX

acrostic 151, 156
Adad-milki 217
Amasis 56, 326
Amel-Marduk 3, 21, 61–62, 103–4
Amos (book) 201–2, 224–30
apocalyptic 38–44
assembly *See* assembly of the nations; sôd (assembly); popular assembly
assembly of the nations 424, 433
assimilation 102, 105–6, 266
assurance, confession of *See* confession of assurance
Assyrian deportations *See* deportations, Assyrian
Assyrian golah 32, 100, 105–6
Baal worship 217, 299
Babylon 17, 27, 48–49, 59–60, 65, 69–70, 113–14, 117, 190–96, 341, 379, 396, 402, 416
Babylonian Chronicle 47, 53–54, 73–74, 78
Babylonian conquests 50–58, 61–62, 67, 95, 138, 242–44
Babylonian deportations *See* deportations, Babylonian
Babylonian golah 3, 14, 22, 28, 72, 83, 86, 88–89, 98–111, 134–36, 193, 245, 257–58, 265–66, 269, 283, 308, 322, 337
Babylonian religion 26, 136, 172
Bel 15, 23–24, 411, 416
Belshazzar 3, 18–19, 21, 42, 63–64, 111
bēt ʾābôt 106, 131, 137
blessing, mediation of *See* mediation of blessing
Cambyses 21, 117, 124, 317, 352, 403
Carchemish 52, 75, 79, 141, 185, 241, 321, 328

chaos monster 25–26, 42, 150
circumcision 107, 136–37, 204
college of priests *See* priests, college of
confession of assurance 149, 165, 172
confessional badge 107, 136
council of elders *See* elders, council of
covenant 145, 234, 286, 330, 344, 408, 432–33, 442
cult 98, 132, 156, 163, 174–75, 189–90, 194, 199, 206, 233, 266, 280–81, 286, 294, 301, 322, 331, 371. *See also* Josiah
Cyrus 2, 12, 14, 21–22, 27, 29, 69–70, 111, 113–16, 159, 191, 284–85, 352, 399, 400, 402, 411–16, 441.
 edict 119–20, 414
 religious policy 113–16, 121–22
 See also Deutero-Isaiah (book)
Daniel (book) 16–22, 27, 39–40, 41–44, 75
Darius I 19, 21, 28, 39, 117–20, 178, 191, 195, 245, 285, 317, 390, 399, 400–402, 412, 418, 421, 424, 440
 religious policy 117–18, 122, 129, 409
Darius oracle *See* Deutero-Isaiah
Davidic monarchy 9, 126, 129, 131, 215, 230, 270, 179–81, 291, 331–32, 424, 432–33, 441–42, 445. *See also* Nathan's promise
deliverance *See* salvation
deportations 70–90
deportations, Assyrian 8, 30, 75–76, 82, 87–88, 100
deportations, Babylonian 9–11, 14–15, 31, 33, 76–90
Deutero-Isaiah (book) 376–433
 Cyrus oracle 384–85, 394–95, 413–16, 418

-457-

458　ISRAEL IN EXILE

Darius oracle　400, 408–9, 414–15, 418
date　399–400, 403, 428–30
Deutero-Isaiah (person)　380–81
　disputations　383–84, 395, 416, 421
　history of scholarship　382–92
　locale　401
　monotheism　134, 415, 440
　polemic against idols　382, 391–92, 396, 416
　Servant Songs　380, 384–85, 390, 393–96, 407–9, 419–23, 425–28
　structure　397–99, 429
　universalism　415, 423, 433
Deuteronomistic History　271–302
　date　275–76, 282–83
　history of scholarship　274–79
　kingship　275, 279–81, 291–92
　law　286–87, 288–89, 296, 301–2
　locale　282–87
　structure　286
　temple　280–81, 293–95, 300–301
Edom　96, 104, 153, 185–90, 359
Egyptian golah　7, 96–98, 134, 259, 269, 308, 319, 323, 333, 337
elders, council of　96, 100–101, 131, 135, 375
election, divine　126, 166, 187, 229, 247, 293–94, 365
Elephantine　74, 97–98, 121, 401
Enoch (book)　40–44
Esarhaddon　31, 49
exile, blame for　*See* guilt
exile, end of　2–3, 29, 42, 69–70, 119–29, 192–96, 338–39, 400
exile, new beginning after　103, 200, 216
exile, return from　*See* return
exile, understanding of　4–44
Ezekiel (book)　345–77
　date　352–54
　Ezekiel (person)　354–55
　draft constitution　356, 364, 368–76
　history of scholarship　347–52
　kingship　364, 371–72, 374
　renewal　356–57, 362, 367
　structure　346, 355–56, 358–59

　temple　352–57, 368–70
family piety　32, 135–36, 165–66, 173, 258
foreign nation oracles　179–96, 226–27, 319–20, 341
Four Prophets (book)　205–37
　date　236–37
　history of scholarship　206–9, 212–13, 218–20, 224–27, 231–32
　intention　206, 216, 222–23, 226, 229, 235–36
　locale　236–37
　superscriptions　209–10
Gaumata　117–19, 195, 400, 403
Gedaliah　2, 3, 5–7, 11, 56, 75, 82, 91, 94–95, 104, 130, 141, 282, 318, 324
God　*See* Yahweh
golah　362
　organization　100–101, 106–7, 131–32
　See also Assyrian golah; Babylonian golah; Egyptian golah
guilt　13, 105, 146, 329, 335, 361, 411, 436–38
Habakkuk (book)　237–45
Hezekiah　75, 184, 281, 299–300
history, theology of　14, 39, 221–22, 338–39, 367–68, 439–41
hope　99–100, 104, 126, 163, 193, 244, 295, 363
Hosea (book)　230–37
identity　101, 106–7, 109, 131, 135–37, 139, 203
idols, polemic against　*See* Deutero-Isaiah (book)
Jehoiachin　9, 53, 61, 72–73, 78–80, 98, 102–5, 110, 126, 130–31, 145, 275, 282, 284–85, 293, 313, 331–32, 353, 433, 442, 444
Jehoiakim　9, 14–15, 17, 20, 53, 74, 80, 91, 201, 313–14, 319, 328, 331–32
Jeremiah (book)　302–346
　date　304, 313, 315–18
　foreign nation oracles　187, 194–96, 306, 319–20, 341
　history of scholarship　304–12
　kingship　94, 329, 331

locale 322–25
  seventy years 310, 316–18, 321, 326, 337, 342
  structure 327–28, 333, 339
  temple 200–201, 331, 334
Jeroboam, sin of See sin
Jerusalem
  destruction 10, 15, 72, 90–91, 142, 191, 315, 321, 356
  fall 5–6, 34, 56, 78, 94, 143, 158, 188, 333, 346
  rebuilding 39, 119–32, 373–74, 413–14, 422
  siege 5, 10, 35, 55, 91, 141, 346, 355
  See also temple; Zion
Joseph novella 263–64, 267
Josiah 8, 142, 217, 258, 277–78, 285, 328, 444
  cultic reform 8, 92, 98, 109, 130, 157, 217, 228, 233, 277, 282, 300–301, 313
Judah, people left in 90–96, 105, 128, 134, 137, 166, 204, 247, 262, 268, 269, 322–23, 330, 336–37, 339–40, 349, 362, 417, 422, 425
judgment 4, 8, 11, 33, 40, 90
  announcement of 187, 193, 216, 220, 313, 323, 336, 352, 357
  pedagogical purpose 202, 222, 235–36, 338–39, 344, 439
  prophets of 143, 158, 168, 183, 203, 206, 216–17, 228, 238, 279, 281, 352, 357–60, 406, 436–38
  purifying 215–17, 223, 226, 230, 233–36, 365–67, 379
Judith (book) 34–38
justice 157, 224, 243, 297
kingship 40
  criticism of 133–34, 229, 280, 292, 329, 364
  sacral 134, 371, 374, 442
  See also monarchy
lament 140–66. See also Zion
lament, liturgical 141, 151, 158, 165–66, 169, 174–75, 179, 188–89, 202–3, 294, 383
Lamentations (book) 151–66

land 9, 246, 261, 264–65, 268–69, 276, 286, 322, 336, 365–66, 373–74
law See Deuteronomistic History
Marduk 26, 48–51, 58, 70, 114, 191, 196, 402, 416
mediation of blessing 249, 257, 263, 265
messenger formula 172, 174
Micah (book) 211–16
mission 345, 415, 420–21, 423
Moloch 288, 299, 301, 343, 366
monarchy 9–10, 126, 130, 133, 215, 229–30, 270, 279–81, 291–92, 331–32, 424, 432–33, 442, 444. See also Davidic monarchy
monotheism 18, 134, 411, 415, 417, 435, 440
Nabonidus 21, 47, 55, 64–70, 110–11, 113–15
  religious policy 65–66, 68–69, 110, 123
Nabopolassar 47, 50–51, 55, 64
Nathan's promise 145, 280, 295, 332
nationalists, religious See religious nationalists
Nebuchadnezzar 3, 5, 9–10, 17–18, 34–35, 42–43, 47, 52–60, 75, 78–80, 97, 99, 103, 186, 318, 321, 324, 342, 353, 442
Neco II 53, 142
Neriglissar 61–63
northern kingdom, sin of See sin
oracles See foreign nation oracles; salvation oracle; war oracle; see also Deutero-Isaiah (book)
parties See reform party; religious nationalists; Shaphanides
Patriarchal History 203, 246–71, 273
  history of scholarship 248–54
  land 247, 261–62, 264–65, 268
  life in the Diaspora 254, 264–66, 269
  names of God 253, 267
  structure 255–56
Persian Empire 113–19, 131–32
poor 219–20, 223
popular assembly 131, 136, 375

priests, college of 131, 135–36, 362–63, 371–76
promises 177, 230, 317, 322, 340, 363–654, 433
    blessing 254, 256, 260, 265
    David 145, 275, 281, 295, 332, 424, 432–33
    increase 250, 254–55, 260, 265
    land 9, 250, 254, 260, 262, 280, 293, 322, 365
    nîr 295, 299
    son 254, 265
prophecy of salvation *See* salvation
prophecy of judgment *See* judgment
rebellion 49, 66, 91, 94–95, 98, 117, 156, 184, 195, 214, 281, 355, 403, 417
reform party 6, 93, 95, 105, 130–31, 325–27, 332, 337
religious nationalists 93, 95, 98–100, 102, 104, 110–11, 126, 128–31, 142, 156–58, 179, 271, 280–82, 284, 288, 291, 325–26, 336–37, 355, 381, 433, 436
renewal *See* Ezekiel (book)
restoration 112, 119–32, 135, 270, 432–33, 445
retribution theology 37, 51–53, 64, 159, 190–96, 311
return 2, 12, 29, 36, 98, 102, 106–7, 115, 119–28, 146, 194, 262–63, 269, 368, 399–400
revolt *See* rebellion
Sabbath 13–14, 108, 135, 137, 199, 204, 225, 361
sacral kingship *See* kingship
salvation
    announcement of 168, 173–78, 383–85
    opportunity for 6, 321, 330, 337, 341, 400, 404, 412, 438
    prophecy of 128, 136, 157, 167, 173–74, 179, 203, 247, 279, 334–35, 352, 380
salvation oracle 136, 164, 166–73, 179, 281, 383
salvation, promise of *See* salvation oracle

Sennacherib 31, 48–49, 51, 55, 64, 75, 89, 93, 281
separation of powers 374, 443–45
sermons 197–203, 313–15, 323, 328, 331
Servant Songs *See* Deutero-Isaiah (book)
seventy years 2, 13–15, 39, 41, 128, 310, 316, 321, 326, 337, 342
Shaphanides 91, 110, 130, 133, 325–26, 336
Sheshbazzar 120–21, 123–24
siege of Jerusalem *See* Jerusalem
sin 366–67, 435–37
    of Jeroboam 8, 296–97
    of the northern kingdom 233, 296–97, 301
    of the southern kingdom 216, 233, 300–301
social indictment 133, 214, 216, 239, 243, 288, 329–31, 361
sôd (assembly) 156, 175, 194, 403
southern kingdom, sin of *See* sin
Story of the Three Youths 28–29
synagogue 109, 203
syncretism 135, 200, 217, 282, 288, 290, 298, 337
temple 100, 109, 139, 166, 217, 279–81, 293–95, 299, 368–76
    desecration 37, 158, 194, 371
    destruction 10, 34, 52, 65, 91, 100, 133, 141–43, 146, 200, 281, 294, 356, 437
    Elephantine 97
    rebuilding 12, 14, 28–29, 39–40, 68, 107, 115, 119–30, 134, 200, 331, 368, 376, 399
    theology 133, 144, 155, 292, 300, 302, 310, 325, 331, 381
    vessels 9–10, 14–15, 18, 28, 120–23, 399
    See also Jerusalem; Zion
Three Youths *See* Story of the Three Youths
Tobit (book) 30–34
Tyre 57, 61, 185–86, 353
universalism *See* Deutero-Isaiah (book)

vengeance theology *See* retribution theology
war oracle 175, 182–83, 189
worship, exilic 108–9, 158, 179, 197–99, 201–2, 225, 227, 258, 294, 319, 328
Xerxes 27, 120, 191, 430
Yahweh
  just judge 195, 222
  kingship 25, 42, 134, 367, 405, 423–24
Zedekiah 5, 11, 54–55, 79–80, 91–92, 99, 103–4, 317, 323, 331, 333–34, 336, 348, 355

Zephaniah (book) 216–24
Zerubbabel 28, 107, 120, 125–26, 128, 270, 283–84, 332, 399, 402, 433
Zion
  lament 152–57, 175, 194
  presence of God 55, 133, 152–57, 193, 294, 331, 369, 423
  theology 133, 157, 200, 294–95, 310, 325, 331, 381, 385, 389–90, 404, 422–23, 433
  See also Jerusalem; temple

www.ingramcontent.com/pod-product-compliance
Lightning Source LLC
Chambersburg PA
CBHW021350290426
44108CB00010B/176